MW01630502

Peter Paul Rubens
The Drawings

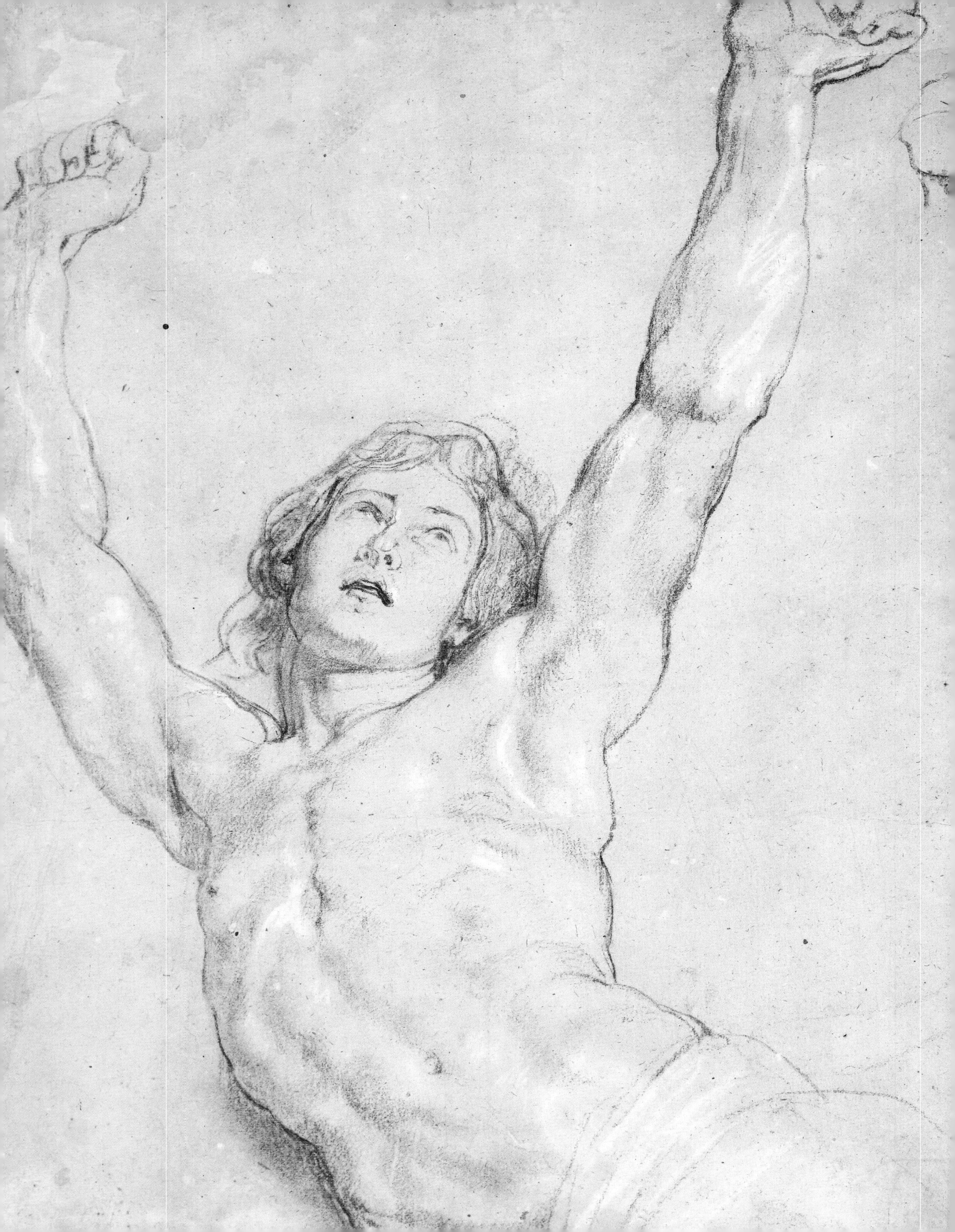

Peter Paul Rubens
The Drawings

Anne-Marie Logan in collaboration with Michiel C. Plomp

The Metropolitan Museum of Art, New York

Yale University Press, New Haven and London

This volume is published in conjunction with the exhibition "Peter Paul Rubens (1577–1640): The Drawings," held at The Metropolitan Museum of Art, New York, from January 15 to April 3, 2005.

The exhibition is made possible by
the Government of Flanders and FORTIS BANK

Additional support has been provided by The Schiff Foundation.

The exhibition catalogue is made possible by The Drue E. Heinz Fund and the Doris Duke Fund for Publications.

The exhibition was organized by The Metropolitan Museum of Art, New York, and the Albertina, Vienna.

An indemnity has been granted by the Federal Council on the Arts and the Humanities.

Published by The Metropolitan Museum of Art, New York

John P. O'Neill, Editor in Chief
Jane Bobko, Senior Editor
Bruce Campbell, Designer
Peter Antony, Chief Production Manager
Douglas Malicki, Production Manager
Minjee Cho, Desktop Publishing
Jayne Kuchna and Jean Wagner, Bibliographic Editors

Separations by Nissha Printing Co., Ltd., Kyoto, Japan
Printed and bound by Nissha Printing Co., Ltd., Kyoto, Japan

Jacket/cover illustration: Peter Paul Rubens, *Young Woman Looking Down (Study for the Head of Saint Apollonia),* early 1628. Gabinetto Disegni e Stampe degli Uffizi, Florence (cat. no. 68)

Frontispiece: Peter Paul Rubens, *Study for the Figure of Christ,* ca. 1610. Fogg Art Museum, Harvard University Art Museums, Cambridge, Massachusetts; Gift of Meta and Paul J. Sachs (cat. no. 37)

On page 60: Peter Paul Rubens, *Seated Male Youth* (detail), ca. 1613. The Pierpont Morgan Library, New York (cat. no. 45)

Cataloging-in-publication data is available from the Library of Congress.

ISBN 1-58839-139-6 (hc: The Metropolitan Museum of Art)
ISBN 1-58839-141-8 (pbk: The Metropolitan Museum of Art)
ISBN 0-300-10494-4 (Yale University Press)

Contents

Sponsor's Statement

The Government of Flanders is delighted to support The Metropolitan Museum of Art in bringing the drawings of Flanders' most famous son to the great city of New York.

Peter Paul Rubens lived and worked in Antwerp in a tumultuous time in our history, a time that was vital to the shaping of Europe as we know it today. In his life as well as in his legacy, Rubens was and is an esteemed representative of the proud city on the Scheldt River and, by extension, of contemporary Flanders and the cultural heritage of the Low Countries. As one of the most versatile and innovative artists of his time, he was known throughout Europe. By employing his skills as an artist, collector, architect, entrepreneur, and diplomat, he developed and used his extensive network to bring about better understanding on a harshly divided continent.

Rubens's drawings are literally master drawings. In them, more than in many of his other works, the hand of the master himself is undeniably present in the most direct way. His flamboyant person and his unique artistry have become a Flanders trademark. Art, creativity, innovation, and entrepreneurship, as eloquently embodied in Rubens's work, are among the pillars of Flanders' cultural identity. They serve as positive, optimistic signs of an open society that invites influences from around the world and proudly carries those influences in its cultural heritage.

Flanders today finds itself yet again at the center of a European unification process, with its capital, Brussels, as the de facto capital of the European Union. Rubens's hometown of Antwerp, the fourth-largest seaport in the world, has reclaimed its vital role as the engine of the Flemish economy. Flanders, a unique, autonomous region, thrives as a vibrant society that builds on many of the same traits that characterized the area in the sixteenth and seventeenth centuries—traits championed not only by Rubens but also by many of his fellow Flemish masters, in many of the Flemish art cities we still know and enjoy today.

The forces that were behind Rubens's genius are also behind the explosion of many of Flanders' contemporary artists onto the world scene. In areas from modern dance to visual arts, design, fashion, and architecture, Flemish artists are finding their own niche in which to experiment and to explore.

The Government of Flanders is convinced that artistic expression and cultural awareness are crucial elements in the vitality of a modern and open society. Peter Paul Rubens embodies these elements more than any other figure in our cultural heritage. Hence we are proud to share this legacy with the rest of the world through this partnership with The Metropolitan Museum of Art.

Geert Bourgeois
Minister of the Government of Flanders

Sponsor's Statement

Fortis Bank is pleased to partner with The Metropolitan Museum of Art as a sponsor of "Peter Paul Rubens (1577–1640): The Drawings."

Peter Paul Rubens is widely regarded as one of the world's greatest painters and draftsmen, and as the most prominent artist of the seventeenth-century Flemish school. A supreme master of the imagination, he was also a successful ambassador, scholar, classicist, architect, humanist, and teacher. As a painter, he transformed the myriad influences he absorbed from classical, Renaissance, and contemporary masters into his own individual and original style.

Fortis Bank chose to sponsor this exhibition to celebrate an artist who shares his roots with us in the Low Countries. Rubens broadened his horizon beyond those boundaries, as does Fortis today by operating in sixty-five countries. Fortis draws inspiration from such a multifaceted master by promoting diversity and innovation as key characteristics of its business.

Fortis honors its social commitment by supporting cultural events to make art more accessible to the general public. It is especially rewarding to collaborate with The Metropolitan Museum of Art in presenting Rubens's drawings, which are evidence of his genius. Unlike many of his monumental paintings, which were largely executed by his apprentices, the drawings are generally products of his own hand and are considered by connoisseurs as the real gems of this master's work.

Fortis is an integrated financial services provider headquartered in Belgium and the Netherlands and ranks among the top twenty European financial institutions.

Fortis is honored to be associated with The Metropolitan Museum of Art and is proud to present Peter Paul Rubens and his drawings.

Filip Dierckx
CEO Merchant Banking,
Fortis Bank
Member of the Executive
Committee of Fortis

Jacques Thys
U.S. Country Manager
Fortis Bank

Directors' Foreword

Not since 1977, when the quadricentennial of the birth of Peter Paul Rubens (1577–1640) was celebrated in numerous exhibitions throughout Europe, has there been as much interest in the artist's work as we are witnessing at this moment. In 2004 the career of the great Flemish painter, draftsman, and diplomat was the subject of special exhibitions in Antwerp, Braunschweig, Frankfurt, Genoa, Greenwich (Connecticut), Kassel, and Lille; in December of that year three concurrent exhibitions focusing on Rubens as a painter opened in Vienna. Rubens was a pan-European artist who was equally at home in the courts of the Southern Netherlands, France, Spain, and England. In the early seventeenth century he furnished paintings and tapestries to the royal families of Europe, as well as to such highly respected collectors as the Duke of Buckingham, the Earl of Arundel, the Duke of Lerma, and the Marquis of Leganés.

It is our great pleasure to celebrate Rubens with the present exhibition devoted to his drawings. The exhibition includes some of Rubens's finest studies, which have been selected from more than forty collections in some thirty cities worldwide and which attest to his astonishing talent and inventiveness in the medium of drawing. Indeed, the exhibition is the first comprehensive overview of Rubens as a draftsman. In Vienna the exhibition was augmented by thirty-eight oil sketches and paintings by Rubens, exemplifying the stages in his creative process that followed upon drawing. Organized by the Albertina, Vienna, and The Metropolitan Museum of Art, New York, the exhibition has been long in the planning, and it is appropriate that it concludes the wealth of recent events honoring Rubens.

More than thirty of Rubens's most admired drawings, from the world-renowned collection of the Albertina, are the centerpiece of the exhibition. Most of these sheets, including stunning portraits of the artist's family, are being shown for the first time to the American public. Complementing the selection from the Albertina are almost one hundred works from other collections of Rubens's drawings, some long established in Europe and Russia and others of more recent creation in the United States. Foremost among the latter are the holdings of Rubens's drawings at The Metropolitan Museum of Art and the J. Paul Getty Museum, Los Angeles. These collections were built largely through the efforts of George R. Goldner, Drue Heinz Chairman of the Department of Drawings and Prints at the Metropolitan since 1993, and Curator of Drawings and Curator of Paintings at the Getty from 1982 to 1993. In recent years he has found and acquired more Rubens drawings than any curator or private collector in the world, and he has enthusiastically supported this exhibition. Several recently discovered Rubens drawings acquired by him are being shown for the first time. The display of these works, together with little-known or newly found drawings from other collections, will expand our understanding of Rubens as a draftsman and stimulate new research.

We would like to acknowledge the invaluable scholarship of Anne-Marie Logan, Guest Research Curator, and Michiel C. Plomp, Associate Curator, in the Department of Drawings and Prints at the Metropolitan Museum. Thanks are due to them for the selection of works in the New York exhibition and for the insightful essays and entries in the New York catalogue. Heinz Widauer, curator of the exhibition at the Albertina, was an invaluable liaison between New York and Vienna during the past two years.

At the Metropolitan Museum, Mahrukh Tarapor, Associate Director for Exhibitions, Martha Deese, Senior Assistant for Exhibitions, and Rebecca Noonan, Assistant Counsel, assisted innumerable times in negotiating loans and answering lenders' questions. In the Department of Drawings and Prints, Rachel Stern oversaw the show's administration.

The Metropolitan Museum is extremely grateful to the Government of Flanders, whose invaluable support of the exhibition has greatly enriched this project. We are also deeply indebted to Fortis Bank for its crucial assistance toward the realization of this exhibition. Likewise, we remain grateful for the generosity of The Schiff Foundation. The Museum would also like to thank The Drue E. Heinz Fund and the Doris Duke Fund for Publications for their vital contribution toward the publication of this catalogue. Finally, we remain ever thankful to the Federal Council on the Arts and the Humanities.

Philippe de Montebello
Director
The Metropolitan Museum of Art

Klaus Albrecht Schröder
Director
Albertina, Vienna

Acknowledgments

This exhibition could not have come to fruition without the enthusiastic support of George R. Goldner, Drue Heinz Chairman of the Department of Drawings and Prints at The Metropolitan Museum of Art, New York, and Klaus Albrecht Schröder, Director of the Albertina, Vienna, who promised to lend the best Rubens drawings from the Albertina's world-famous collection. They recognized early on the great potential of a collaboration between New York and Vienna. We are grateful to Philippe de Montebello, Director of The Metropolitan Museum of Art, for supporting the exhibition and making the enormous resources of the Museum available to this project. Mahrukh Tarapor, Associate Director for Exhibitions, Martha Deese, Senior Assistant for Exhibitions, and Rebecca Noonan, Assistant Counsel, offered much-appreciated assistance in the negotiation of loans. At the Albertina we were helped enormously by Heinz Widauer, curator of the exhibition in Vienna, Cornelia Zöchling, Registrar, Marian Bisanz-Prakken, Ulrike Ertl, Hanna Singer, Elisabeth Thobois, and Ulrike and Brigitte Willinger.

We thank the many museums and private collectors who generously agreed to lend their drawings to the exhibition and did not tire of our many questions during its preparation. These include Ronald de Leeuw, Ger Luijten, and Marijn Schapelhouman, Rijksmuseum, Amsterdam; Pauline W. Kruseman and Norbert Middelkoop, Amsterdams Historisch Museum; J. F. van Regteren Altena, Amersfoort, and Mrs. A.W.L. van Regteren Altena-van Royen, Amsterdam; Francine de Nave, Museum Plantin-Moretus, Antwerp; Hein-Thomas Schulze Altcappenberg and Holm Bevers, Staatliche Museen zu Berlin, Kupferstichkabinett; Jochen Luckhardt and Thomas Döring, Herzog Anton Ulrich-Museum, Braunschweig; Pierre Cockshaw, Raphaël De Smedt, Alain Jacobs, and Nicole Walch, Bibliothèque Royale de Belgique, Brussels; Thomas W. Lentz and William W. Robinson, Harvard University Art Museums, Cambridge, Massachusetts; William P. Stoneman and Hope Mayo, Houghton Library, Harvard University, Cambridge, Massachusetts; Duncan Robinson, David E. Scrase, and Janie Munro, Fitzwilliam Museum, Cambridge; Peter Day and Charles Noble, The Devonshire Collection, Chatsworth, Bakewell; James Cuno, James N. Wood, and Suzanne Folds McCullagh, The Art Institute of Chicago; Katharine C. Lee Reid, Charles L. Venable, Henry Hawley, and Heather Lemonedes, Cleveland Museum of Art; Rainer Budde and Uwe Westfehling, Wallraf-Richartz-Museum–Fondation Corboud, Cologne; Sir Timothy Clifford, Christopher Baker, Emilie Gordenker, and Valerie Hunter, National Gallery of Scotland, Edinburgh; Annamaria Petrioli Tofani, Galleria degli Uffizi, Florence; Herbert Beck and Martin Sonnabend, Städelsches Kunstinstitut und Städtische Galerie, Frankfurt am Main; Julian Treuherz and Xanthe Brooke, Walker Art Gallery, Liverpool; Neil McGregor, Antony V. Griffiths, and Martin Royalton-Kisch, The British Museum, London; Mark Jones, Janet Skidmore, Susan Lambert, and Miranda Percival, Victoria and Albert Museum, London; Deborah Gribbon, William H. Griswold, and Lee Hendrix, The J. Paul Getty Museum, Los Angeles; Carter Foster, Los Angeles County Museum of Art; Hélène Lorblanchet, Bibliothèque, Musée Atger, Montpellier; Irina Antonova, Natalija Markova, and Vadim Sadkov, The State Pushkin Museum, Moscow; Michael Semff and Thea Vignau-Wilberg, Staatliche Graphische Sammlung, Munich; Mrs. Mon Muellerschoen, Munich; Mr. and Mrs. H. Rodes Hart, Nashville, Tennessee; Charles E. Pierce Jr., Rhoda Eitel Porter, Egbert Haverkamp-Begemann, Jennifer Tonkovich, and Kate Stewart, The Pierpont Morgan Library, New York; Christopher Brown, Timothy Wilson, Jon J. L. Whiteley, Geraldine Glynn, and Katia Pisvin, Ashmolean Museum, Oxford; Henri Loyrette, Françoise Viatte, Carel van Tuyll van Serooskerken, Varena Forcione, Catherine Loisel, and Bernadette Py, Musée du Louvre, Paris; Mària van Berge-Gerbaud, Hans Buijs, and Stijn Alsteens, Collection Frits Lugt, Institut Néerlandais, Paris; Wojciech Suchocki and Grażyna Hałasa, Muzeum Narodowe, Poznań; Hugo C. Bongers, Sjarel Ex, Bram W.F.M. Meij, and Albert Elen, Museum Boijmans Van Beuningen, Rotterdam; Mikhail Piotrovsky and Alexei Larionov, The State Hermitage Museum, Saint Petersburg; Görel Cavalli-Björkman, Solfried Söderlind, and Ulf Cederlöf, Nationalmuseum, Stockholm; Christiaan P. van Eeghen, The Hague; Ph. Maarschalkerweerd, Marten Loonstra, and B. Woelderdink, Koninklijk Huisarchief, The Hague; Earl A. Powell III, Alan Shestack, Andrew Robison, Margaret Morgan

Grasselli, and Greg Jecman, National Gallery of Art, Washington, D.C.; Michael Conforti, Brian Allen, and James Ganz, Sterling and Francine Clark Art Institute, Williamstown, Massachusetts; Lady Jane Roberts and Martin Clayton, Print Room and Royal Library, Windsor Castle.

For advice and practical assistance, we are also indebted to the following colleagues: Luca Baroni, Katrin Bellinger, Nancy Bialler, Piero Boccardo, Marian Burleigh-Motley, Vincent Ducourau, Georgina Duits, Charles Dumas, Nicole Garnier, Marvin Hayes, Urs Kram, Erik Löffler, Caroline Meckler, Jörg Martin Merz, E. James Mundy, William O'Reilly, Gregory Rubinstein, Nicolas Schwed, and Anne Varick Lauder. We owe special thanks to art historians involved in Rubens research who were often busy preparing their own exhibitions but still found time to answer questions: Arnout Balis, Kristin Belkin, Karen Bowen, Nils Büttner, Carl Depauw, Fiona Healy, Ulrich Heinen, Dirk Imhof, Justus Lange, Jeffrey M. Muller, Nora de Poorter, Konrad Renger, Nico van Hout, Ari Verburg, Alejandro Vergara, Hans Vlieghe, Jeremy Wood, and the staffs of the Rubenianum, Antwerp, and the Netherlandish Institute for Art History, The Hague.

Thanks are also due to The Honorable Renilde Loeckx-Drozdiak, Consul General of Belgium in New York, and her predecessor, Stéphane De Loecker; His Excellency Frans van Daele, Ambassador of Belgium to the United States; and our colleagues at the Representation of the Flemish Government in the U.S.

Many of our colleagues at The Metropolitan Museum of Art assisted in the organization of the exhibition and in the preparation of the accompanying catalogue. We thank, in particular, curators Joan R. Mertens and Christopher S. Lightfoot in the Department of Greek and Roman Art; Walter Liedtke, Keith Christiansen, Andrea Bayer, and Maryan Ainsworth in the Department of European Paintings; Linda Wolk-Simon; and Carmen C. Bambach, Nadine M. Orenstein, and Perrin V. Stein in the Department of Drawings and Prints. Marjorie Shelley, Sherman Fairchild Conservator in Charge for Works on Paper, answered many queries. In the conservation departments, we also thank Alison Gilchrest, Research Associate, for her examination of drawings by infrared reflectography; Silvia Centeno, Associate Research Chemist; and Rachel Mustalish, Associate Conservator.

Linda M. Sylling, Manager for Special Exhibitions and Gallery Installations, and Nina S. Maruca, Associate Registrar, guided many of the organizational aspects of the exhibition, for which we are grateful. Our thanks also go to Carol E. Lekarew and Deanna D. Cross of the Photograph and Slide Library. Kit Basquin, Molly Carrott, David del Gaizo, Ricky Luna, Constance McPhee, Elizabeth Zanis, and Mary Zuber in the Department of Drawings and Prints were always ready to offer us assistance when needed. Kenneth Soehner and the many kind staff members at the Thomas J. Watson Library facilitated our research on Rubens in manifold ways.

The tremendous organizational skills of Rachel Stern were invaluable. She was responsible for the complex administration of the exhibition, including everything from ordering and organizing photographs, preparing reports for the indemnity application and immunity from seizure, and reading proofs of the catalogue to communicating with lenders, especially the Albertina. Her competence and good humor were much appreciated. Toward the end of the project we received considerable help from Veronica White, a doctoral candidate at Columbia University and an intern in the Department of Drawings and Prints.

We are grateful to John P. O'Neill, Editor in Chief and General Manager of Publications, for the superb realization of this book. The efforts of Margaret Rennolds Chace, Managing Editor, were indispensable to its timely production. Jane Bobko, Senior Editor, cannot be praised enough for her patience, precision, and dedication. She and Elizabeth K. Allen, who shared in the book's editing, are thanked enormously for the improvements, large and small, that they have brought to the text. Heartfelt thanks are also owed to the bibliographic editor, Jayne Kuchna, who was assisted by Jean Wagner. Peter Antony's close attention to color and detail in the Museum's publications is well known; in this case he traveled specially to Vienna to view almost every drawing. We are also indebted to the book's designer, Bruce Campbell, and to Douglas Malicki, Production Manager, and Minjee Cho, Desktop Publishing Assistant.

Additional thanks are due to Michael Langley for the exhibition design, to Sophia Geronimus for the graphic design, and to Clint Coller and Rich Lichte for the lighting design.

Anne-Marie Logan
Guest Research Curator
Department of Drawings and Prints
The Metropolitan Museum of Art

Michiel C. Plomp
Associate Curator
Department of Drawings and Prints
The Metropolitan Museum of Art

Lenders to the Exhibition

The numbers in the following list refer to works in the catalogue.

Austria

Vienna, Albertina 11, 18, 40, 41, 43, 44, 50, 58, 59, 60, 62, 63, 64, 65, 66, 69, 70, 71, 72, 77, 78, 81, 83, 84, 85, 86, 87, 96, 97, 99, 102, 111

Belgium

Antwerp, Museum Plantin-Moretus / Stedelijk Prentenkabinet 54, 110

Brussels, Bibliothèque Royale Albert Ier, Cabinet des Estampes 15

France

Montpellier, Musée Atger 29

Paris, Collection Frits Lugt, Institut Néerlandais 113

Paris, Musée du Louvre, Département des Arts Graphiques 4, 14, 106, 109

Germany

Berlin, Staatliche Museen zu Berlin, Kupferstichkabinett 6, 24, 33, 90, 108

Braunschweig, Herzog Anton Ulrich-Museum, Kunstmuseum des Landes Niedersachsen 5

Cologne, Wallraf-Richartz-Museum–Fondation Corboud, The Collection of Drawings and Prints 20

Frankfurt am Main, Graphische Sammlung im Städelschen Kunstinstitut 2, 27

Munich, Staatliche Graphische Sammlung 13

Italy

Florence, Gabinetto Disegni e Stampe degli Uffizi 68

The Netherlands

Amsterdam, Amsterdams Historisch Museum 26, 91, 92

Amsterdam, Rijksmuseum 32

Rotterdam, Museum Boijmans Van Beuningen 35, 56, 88

The Hague, Koninklijk Huisarchief, Collection of Her Majesty The Queen of The Netherlands 39

Poland

Poznań, Fundacja im. Raczyńskich, Muzeum Narodowe 95

Russia

Moscow, The State Pushkin Museum of Fine Arts 21

Saint Petersburg, The State Hermitage Museum 9, 22

Sweden

Stockholm, Nationalmuseum 67, 74

United Kingdom

Cambridge, The Syndics of the Fitzwilliam Museum 61

Chatsworth, The Duke of Devonshire Collection and the Chatsworth Settlement Trustees 100, 117

Edinburgh, National Galleries of Scotland 10

Liverpool, National Museums (The Walker) 17, 115

London, The British Museum 12, 47, 48, 82, 101, 103, 104

London, Victoria and Albert Museum 76, 116

Oxford, The Ashmolean Museum 79, 105

Windsor Castle, Her Majesty Queen Elizabeth II, Royal Library 31, 36, 89

United States

Cambridge, Massachusetts, Houghton Library, Harvard

Peter Paul Rubens
THE DRAWINGS

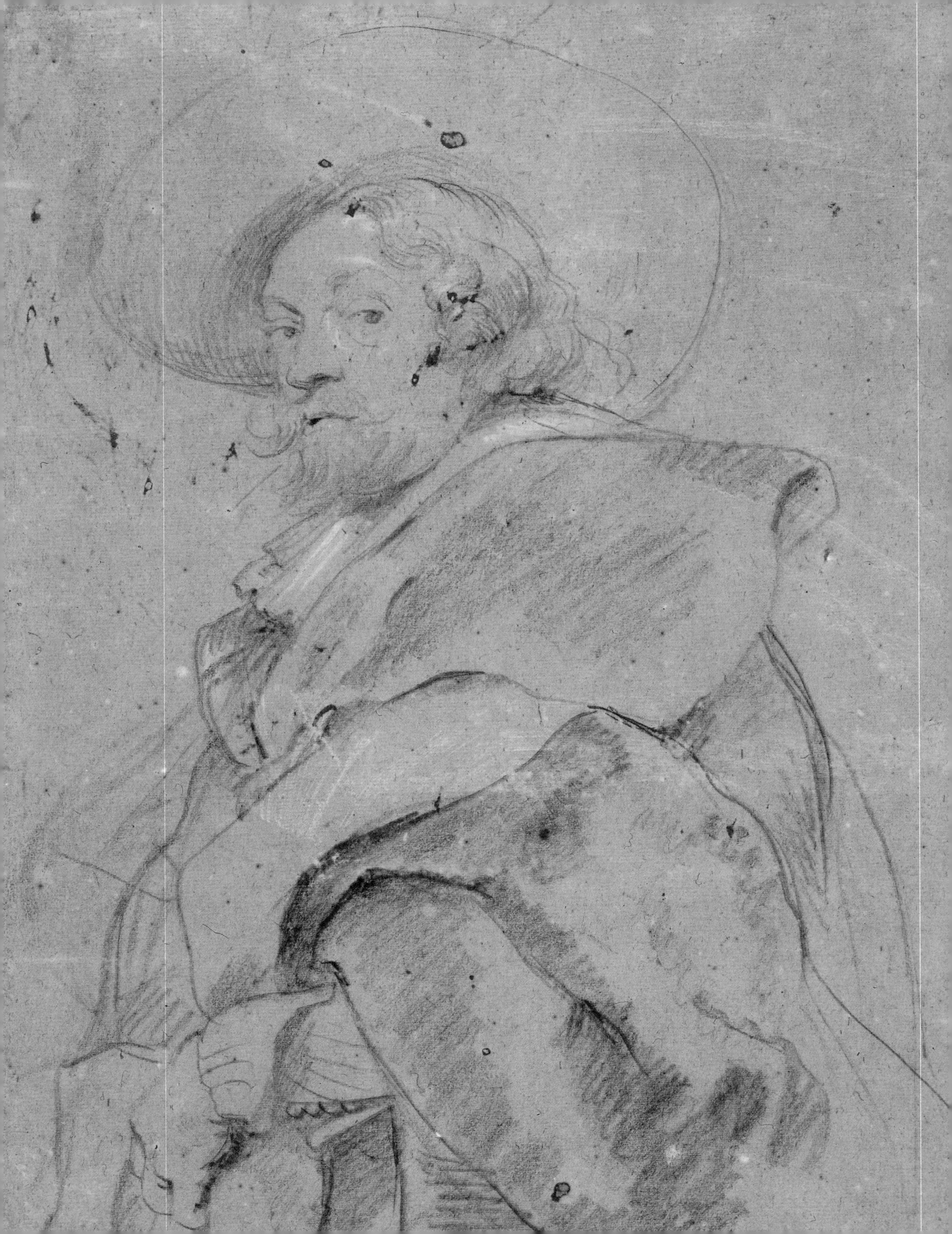

PETER PAUL RUBENS AS A DRAFTSMAN

Peter Paul Rubens (1577–1640) was extremely careful with his drawings and kept them together all his life. There are even indications that he did not want other people to look at his drawings and designs.[1] To a modern person this behavior may seem strange, but it really is not. For a seventeenth-century artist, drawings were indispensable in numerous ways, especially in a large studio. They were made for the creation of new paintings; collaborators used them to assist the master on these paintings; and they served as instructional material for pupils to copy. The drawings were guarded from the outside world because they were considered a kind of studio secret; the competition could well exploit designs for new compositions if they were released prematurely. How precious Rubens considered his drawings is evident from his testament, which stipulated that they should be passed on to any of his sons or sons-in-law who became a painter; only if it became clear, once all his children were grown, that none would become an artist or marry one could the drawings be dispersed.[2] (Rubens did not provide for the possibility that one of his daughters might become an artist.) For all these reasons it is almost certain that Rubens would never have allowed his drawings to be shown in an exhibition like the present one. Drawings were private, strictly for the studio, strictly an element in his working process. To display his drawings publicly, so that everybody could see his searching, his sweat and toil, would probably have felt entirely inappropriate.

Since Rubens made drawings only for himself or for use in the studio, there was no reason to sign them. Whenever his name appears on a drawing, it is a later addition, most likely written by a collector. For modern connoisseurs who wish to get a proper picture of which drawings are by the master and which are not, this is, of course, a serious setback. Inscriptions, however, can be useful; their graphological evidence, combined with stylistic analysis, can establish a drawing's authenticity. The inscriptions on Rubens's drawings are usually personal remarks about what impressed him in the subject he has just recorded, or they are records of necessary information he might otherwise forget. For example, in the costume study *Robin, The Dwarf of the Earl of Arundel* (fig. 9), Rubens added notes on color, interspersed with brief descriptions of the garment. In some of his landscape studies Rubens not only jotted down observations on color, as in the close-up nature study *Study of Blackthorn with Bramble and Other Plants* (fig. 20), but also made note of optical phenomena, as in the late study *Trees Reflected in Water at Sunset* in London (cat. no. 104). Most of these inscriptions are written in Rubens's native tongue, Flemish. On occasion he used Latin. Italian was used for inscriptions meant to be read by others, such as the humanist Nicolas-Claude Fabri de Peiresc with whom Rubens was collaborating on a book project (cat. no. 24), or the stucco worker who was to execute a relief according to Rubens's design (cat. no. 52).

Given their private character, there was no need for Rubens to date his drawings, either. If we want to get an idea when certain drawings were made, we have to resort to circumstantial evidence, such as letters, contracts, dated paintings, or dated prints. It is, for example, thanks to a number of letters of 1620 between Rubens, the agent of Wolfgang Wilhelm, Duke of Neuburg, Count Palatine (1576–1653), and the duke himself that we can connect Rubens's drawing of the *Birth of the Virgin*, now in the Hart Collection (cat. no. 52), to a relief in the duke's church in Neuburg and deduce when the drawing was made.[3] An association with paintings—the majority of

Fig. 1. Peter Paul Rubens, detail of *Self-Portrait*, ca. 1635–38. Black chalk and traces of heightening with white on yellowed paper; traces from verso of figures in pen and ink, 461 x 287 mm (18⅛ x 115⁄16 in.). Département des Arts Graphiques du Musée du Louvre, Paris (20.195)

Rubens's drawings are preparatory for paintings—is often helpful in finding the date for a drawing. Fortunately, many contracts or payment records for Rubens's more important commissions have survived and offer us a useful framework. Rubens signed the contract for the *Raising of the Cross* altarpiece now in Antwerp Cathedral in June 1610 and completed the painting within a year. This means that the individual figure studies for this work (cat. nos. 37–39) likely date from the second half of 1610. The character of a drawing related to a painting is critical, however, for while Rubens usually worked on a detailed study of a specific figure while his painting was in progress, he sometimes made a drawing of an exploratory nature before the contract was signed. Drawings related to printmaking, a distinct category within Rubens's drawn oeuvre, can generally be dated without much of a problem. Title-page designs tend to date from shortly before the time the related books were published, and the same is true of preliminary drawings for dated engravings or etchings.

The absence of a signature and a date at times makes it difficult to form a proper idea of Rubens's drawn oeuvre or of his development as an artist. Moreover, Rubens used drawings for many purposes, and their variation in type, technique, and style is often disconcerting and bewildering. The drawings he made in preparation for paintings, for instance, are very different from those made in preparation for prints. But even within the category "drawings for paintings," there are huge discrepancies in style and technique. Rubens's dialogue on the page with his distinguished artistic predecessors yielded not only more or less straightforward copies but also drawings to which he gave a "face-lift," that is, old master drawings that he sometimes extensively retouched. Rubens's drawings can vary so widely that one sometimes wonders whether the same artist made them. But indeed he did, and often at almost the same time.

Types and Techniques

Rubens's Copies

Throughout his life Rubens made copies after other artists' work. He made them in the form of drawings, oil sketches, and paintings. The inventory of his estate drawn up after his death in 1640 listed no fewer than thirty-two painted copies after Titian (ca. 1487/90–1576) and nine after Raphael (1483–1520). Artists represented by one copy included Leonardo da Vinci (1452–1519), Tintoretto (1518–1594), Pieter Bruegel the Elder (1525/30–1569), and Adam Elsheimer (1578–1610). In all likelihood Rubens made these copies for himself; we know, however, that he also painted copies on commission, for instance, for the Gonzaga in Mantua and for Rudolf II in Prague. Today copying is frowned on. That was definitely not the case in Rubens's time, when copying was a basic practice in art education. Leonardo, for example, advised as early as 1490–92 that "the artist should first exercise his hand by copying . . . a good master."[4] Copying was also the easiest way of acquiring a reproduction of another artist's work. Reproductions—in the seventeenth century, mostly copper engravings—were limited, sometimes expensive, not always very good, and often rendered in reverse from the original. For Rubens, who had so many interests in so many art forms, it was almost a necessity to make copies. Indeed, he continued copying throughout his life. Eventually all these copies added up to a rich collection of themes and motifs for future work.

The number of painted copies Rubens made was certainly impressive; the number of *drawn* copies, however, was many times higher. The earliest known works on paper by Rubens are also his earliest known drawn copies, after the forty-nine *Dance of Death* woodcuts designed by Hans Holbein the Younger (1497/98–1543) and published in 1562.[5] Probably aged twelve or thirteen, Rubens faithfully recorded the woodcuts in their entirety, although he enlarged them slightly. It is interesting that the drawings, by such a young artist, are not slavish copies. Rubens sometimes added more volume to the figures, animated people's faces, and simplified backgrounds. The people generally express more fear than in Holbein's originals, and Death is often more vehement in his actions. In his copy after Holbein's *Ploughman and Death* Rubens even gave Death a more explicit guise: instead of glimpsing only the back of Death's head, as in the sixteenth-century woodcut (fig. 2), we see his gruesome profile (fig. 3). We will notice such changes, in which Rubens often reveals his own drawing style, more often in his later copies.

Fairly quickly, probably only one or two years later, Rubens became more selective and copied only what interested him in a composition rather than the entire scene. In a drawing in New York (cat. no. 1) he combined details—an image of Job's wife and another of Judith and Holofernes—copied from separate woodcuts in the so-called Stimmer Bible (1576). On a sheet of *Four Studies of Female Nudes*, today in the Louvre,

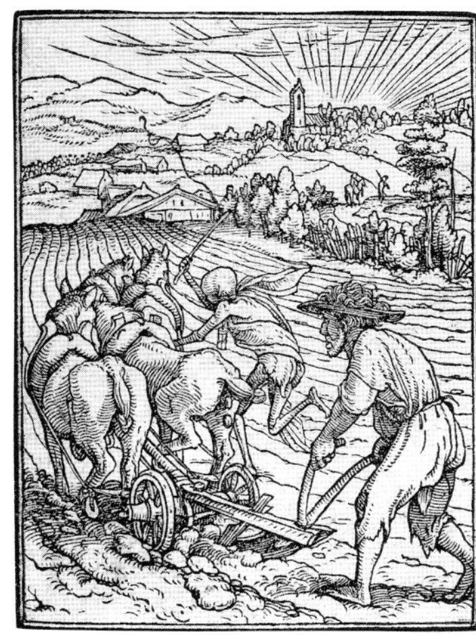

Fig. 2. Hans Holbein the Younger, *The Ploughman and Death.* Woodcut, 65 x 48 mm ($2\frac{1}{2} \times 1\frac{15}{16}$ in.). The Metropolitan Museum of Art, New York; Rogers Fund (1919.57.37)

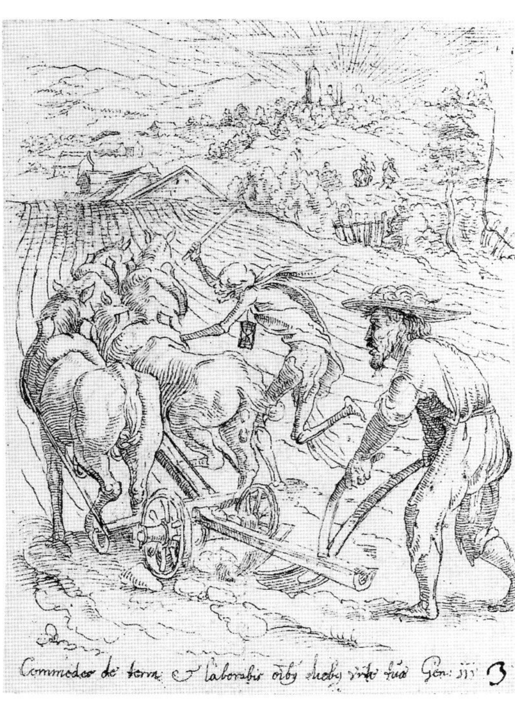

Fig. 3. Peter Paul Rubens after Hans Holbein the Younger, *The Ploughman and Death.* Pen and brown ink, 101 x 76 mm (4 x 3 in.). Museum Plantin-Moretus / Stedelijk Prentenkabinet, Antwerp (OS.192, folio 3)

Rubens copied three figures of Eve from three different woodcuts by Tobias Stimmer (1539–1584) and a fourth one from a woodcut by Jost Amman (1539–1591).[6] On another sheet (cat. no. 2) Rubens assembled into a new scene figures copied from two engravings by Hendrick Goltzius (1558–1617).

During his eight years in Italy (1600–1608), Rubens visited Rome twice, from late July 1601 to late January 1602 and from November 1605 to late October 1608. Copying played a big part in absorbing the art of classical antiquity. During his Roman sojourns the young Flemish artist drew (often more than once) the *Laocoön* group, the *Belvedere Torso* (cat. no. 34 verso), the *Centaur Tormented by Cupid* (cat. nos. 20, 21), the *Dying Seneca* (now known as the *Borghese* or *African Fisherman;* cat. nos. 22, 23), the *Hercules Farnese,* and the *Farnese Bull.*[7] We have evidence that Rubens drew still more classical statues, for example, the *Apollo Belvedere*, a *Seated Bacchus,* the *Hermes Belvedere,* and *Silenus Leaning against a Tree Trunk.*[8] The evidence comes from the so-called Rubens *cantoor* drawings, an assemblage of more than five hundred drawings after Rubens, largely made by his pupil Willem Panneels (ca. 1600–1634), who joined the Antwerp studio in the early 1620s and left in 1630. (The *cantoor* was the private room in Rubens's house where the artist kept his drawings, oil sketches, and other valuable objects.) Since the *cantoor* group, which is today in the Statens Museum for Kunst in Copenhagen, contains many copies after drawings by Rubens that are no longer known, it is obviously of great value, although artistically the sheets are not always of the highest quality.[9] Combined with the original drawings, this large body of copies makes clear that Rubens's drawings constituted a veritable inventory of the famous ancient statuary to be found in Rome in the first decade of the seventeenth century.

In his intense involvement with classical antiquity Rubens followed the example of earlier Netherlandish artists such as Jan Gossaert (1478–1532), Maarten van Heemskerck (1498–1574), Lambert Lombard (1505–1566), Frans Floris (1520–1570), and Hendrick Goltzius, who had all traveled to Italy and recorded what impressed them in drawings. Although it is unlikely that Rubens saw any of Goltzius's drawings in Rome,[10] a comparison of their copies is illuminating, since both focused on statues, apparently ignoring other types of antiquities. Each depicted a single sculpture on a single sheet, often drawing it from more than one angle and using black or red chalk. Goltzius, however, made his copies primarily with the intention of creating prints after them; therefore he drew with painstakingly accuracy and from a clear viewpoint (the front or the back). He made sure to include the base of the statue, sometimes even adding passersby to give an idea of the scale. Rubens made his drawings solely for himself, however, in order to practice drawing, to have depictions of

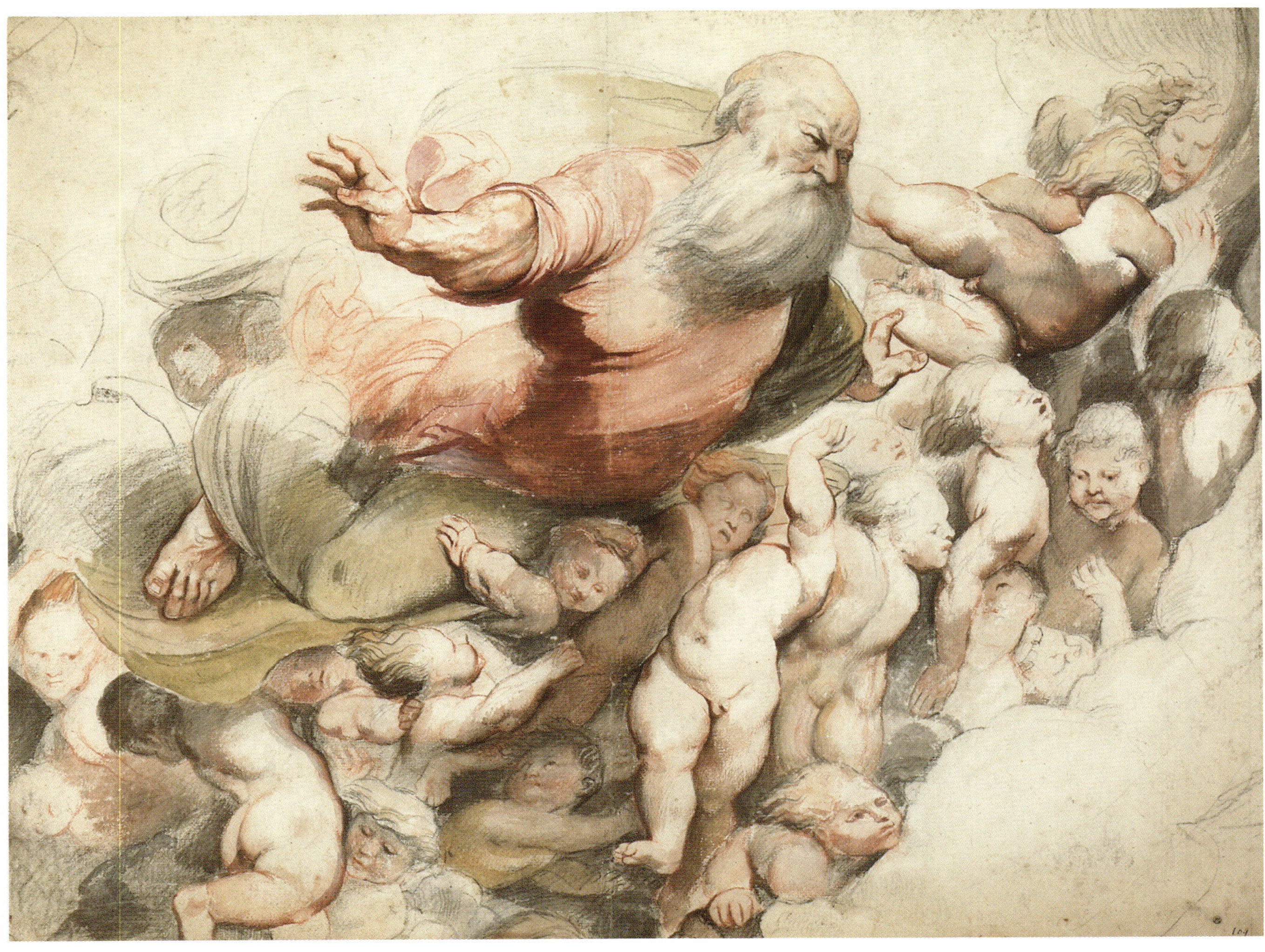

Fig. 4. Peter Paul Rubens after Giovanni Antonio da Pordenone, *God the Father Supported by Angels*. Black and red chalk and watercolor, 347 x 453 mm ($13^{11}/_{16}$ x $17^{13}/_{16}$ in.). The Samuel Courtauld Trust, Courtauld Institute of Art Gallery, London (D 1978.PG.50)

these outstanding works (to take home), and to study the anatomy of the sculpted figures. Thus Rubens's copies are not always very detailed, and sometimes they do not show the statue in its entirety. There was no need for him to depict the statue from the clearest vantage, and he produced unprecedented views of the ancient sculptures, such as his side views of Laocoön's torso now in Dresden and Milan.[11]

What is perhaps most interesting (and certainly uncharacteristic of his predecessors) is that in several cases Rubens appears deliberately to have avoided the impression that he was copying sculpture, leaving out the bases of statues, sometimes ignoring superficial damages, and even trying to disguise that the sculpted bodies were severely mutilated. By drawing the broken arms and legs imprecisely and leaving them vague, he sometimes suggested that the figure was not incomplete—the artist had simply decided not to draw it all (see, for example, the *Centaur Tormented by Cupid* in Moscow, cat. no. 21). This tampering recalls one of Rubens's well-known admonitions: "An artist must breathe life into those ancient works he depicts in his art, and if necessary 'adjust' the source to achieve the desired image."[12] We see this tendency already in some of his drawings after the antique. In his *Two Studies of a Boy* in the British Museum, London,[13] clearly based on the antique sculpture of the *Spinario* (Palazzo dei Conservatori, Rome), one boy looks up toward the spectator as he would in real life. In his copy after the *Belvedere Torso* (cat. no. 34 verso) Rubens gave the mutilated statue a head and strings of hair. The use of red chalk in both these drawings was probably also deliberate, to simulate living flesh.

Rubens's use of red chalk in the aforementioned two drawings is an example of how the artist chose a medium appropriate to the object he copied. For his earlier copies after prints, Rubens had used pen and brown ink and brown wash, a technique that allowed him to capture the precise details of engravings and etchings. For his copies after the antique, chalk was ideal for the suggestion of soft flesh; it also did much to diminish "the effect of stone" that the artist loathed.[14] In Italy Rubens continued using black and red chalk for his copies, usually reserving the red chalk, sometimes enhanced with brush and red ink, for naked body parts. As far as we know, only in his copies after Giovanni Antonio da Pordenone's colorful frescoes in the Chapel of the Annunciation in Treviso Cathedral was Rubens enticed to switch to watercolor (fig. 4).

Besides classical statues, Rubens carefully studied and copied the works of Italian Renaissance artists like Leonardo, Raphael, Giulio Romano (1499?–1546), and Michelangelo (1475–1564) during his years in Italy. A sketchbook that in all likelihood he used in Rome is said to have contained many "illustrations in pen after the best Masters, and principally after Raphael."[15] Unfortunately, this book, the so-called *Pocket Book,* was destroyed in the eighteenth century. With regard to Michelangelo we are luckier: eight impressive copy drawings in black and red chalk after the prophets and sibyls painted on the Sistine Chapel ceiling have survived (see cat. no. 4). Large and detailed, they are eloquent testimony to Rubens's enormous admiration for the great Italian artist. Rubens copied the prophets and sibyls accurately, but in a copy after one of the *ignudi* from the Sistine ceiling (fig. 11) Rubens considerably increased the musculature in the youth's body—as if he were enlivening an antique statue. On the whole, Rubens made few copies after Italian artists. Many, like the ones after Raphael, are probably lost. In addition, Rubens seems to have hired people to make copies for him.[16]

Shortly after Rubens returned to Antwerp at the end of 1608 he undertook another project that involved copying, recording fifteenth- and sixteenth-century portraits and costumes in the so-called *Costume Book* (see the "Sketchbooks" section below). A decade later, in 1622, Rubens collaborated on a project initiated by the French antiquarian Nicolas-Claude Fabri de Peiresc (1580–1637) and promised to provide drawings after antique gems and cameos in preparation for engravings to be published in book form. Although the project eventually was abandoned, Rubens produced at least nine careful drawings that faithfully reproduce antique gems, including the *Antique Cameo with Claudius and Agrippina* (cat. no. 24) and the drawing of the Gemma Tiberiana, in Antwerp.[17] The last time we encounter Rubens as a copyist is during his visit in 1628–29 to Madrid, where he was said to have painted copies of all the Titians in the Spanish royal collections. On a drawing from that sojourn (cat. no. 7), Rubens recorded selectively in chalks on paper some of the heads in, and partial figures from, three of Titian's paintings, including the *Diana and Callisto.*

Compositional Drawings

"Please be advised that the final work will be very different from these drawings, which are lightly and quickly put on paper to give merely an idea, but later we will make the sketches [*dissegni,* probably oil sketches] and also the painting with all possible care and diligence." With these words inscribed on a drawing representing *King David Playing the Harp* (fig. 5),[18] Rubens briefly explained how he approached a commission for a work of art. It is one of his rare statements about his working procedure. The inscribed drawing may have served as a reply to a patron who had inquired about commissioning a work with biblical scenes. Apparently nothing came of it.

Despite Rubens's words, *King David Playing the Harp* is far from a sketch dashed off on paper; it is, rather, a neat compositional drawing that seems to have been created after some deliberation. The artist's true initial compositional drawings, however, such as the *Studies for the Visitation* (fig. 6), really were rudimentary, quick ink sketches, mostly in mere outline. These early ideas were so hastily, almost chaotically, jotted down on paper that they were intelligible only to Rubens himself. He could not send them to patrons, but had to make a neater version, as he did with *King David Playing the Harp.* Relatively few of Rubens's first quick jottings have survived. As soon as the artist had arrived at the next stage in the preparation of the work (a clearer compositional drawing or an oil sketch), the *prima idea* could be discarded. Furthermore, drawings collectors in the seventeenth and eighteenth centuries usually had little regard for such quick sketches and therefore took no particular care to preserve them.

To begin a composition with rudimentary pen sketches is usually considered to be an Italian habit,[19] one that Rubens might have learned during his eight-year stay in Italy. Giorgio

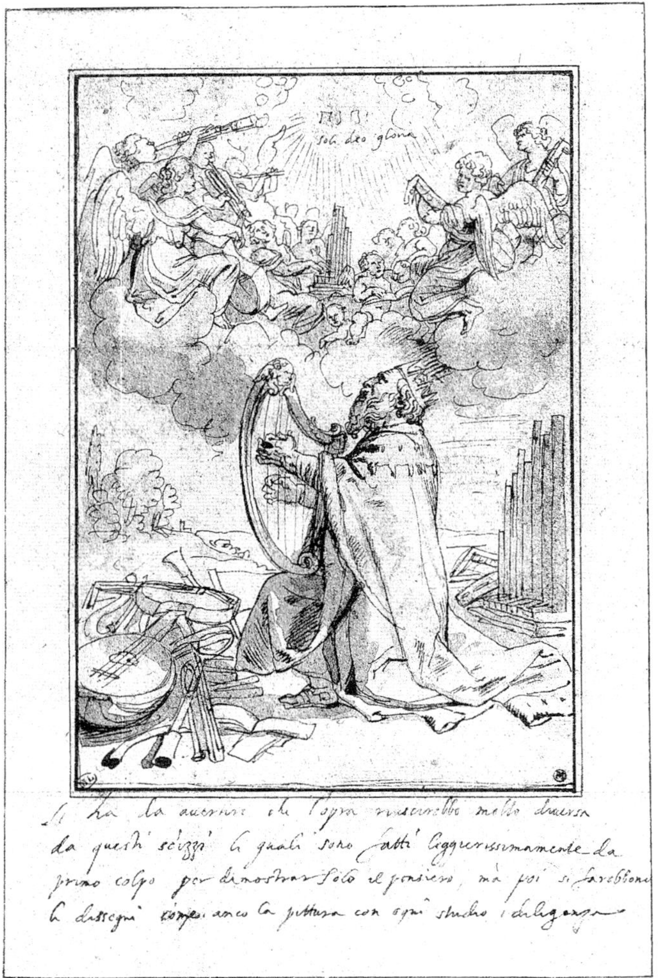

Fig. 5. Peter Paul Rubens, *King David Playing the Harp*, ca. 1612. Pen and brown ink and brown wash, 181 x 150 mm ($7\frac{1}{8}$ x $5\frac{7}{8}$ in.). Département des Arts Graphiques du Musée du Louvre, Paris (20.221)

Vasari (1511–1574), the Italian painter, draftsman, writer, and collector, called such a sketch "a rough draft of the whole" ("una sola bozza del tutto").[20] Rubens's teacher Otto van Veen (1556–1629), who himself spent several years in Italy, also seems to have used the rudimentary compositional sketch. Rubens therefore might have been introduced to the practice in Antwerp, even before he went to Italy. In seventeenth-century Flemish inventories such sketchy preliminary drawings are sometimes referred to as *crabbelingen*, "scribbles."[21]

Rubens's initial compositional drawings allow us a view into his creative process in general and into the "birth" of a number of particular works. We see how Rubens tries out certain possibilities by repeating figures or figural groups several times on the same sheet of paper, sometimes adjusting them slightly, sometimes dramatically. Given this process of searching, it comes as no surprise that some figures in Rubens's drawings seem to have more than two legs (see cat. no. 110) or multiple arms. Rubens did not hesitate to draw into or over a figure that he had already outlined. Some sections of an initial sketch can be clearly worked out, while others are barely indicated. Quick initial sketches, where one can follow the artist's mind and hand seemingly overflowing with ideas, include *Three Sketches for Medea and Her Children* (cat. no. 8 verso), *David and Goliath* (cat. no. 29 verso), *Studies for Silenus and Aegle* (cat. no. 31 recto), and *Seventeen Studies of Dancing Peasants for a Kermis* (cat. no. 103 recto). Prime examples of "neat" compositional drawings are the two studies of the *Continence of Scipio,* one in Berlin (cat. no. 33) and the other in Bayonne (fig. 75).[22]

For both his hasty and his finished compositional drawings Rubens used pen and ink, preferably the traditional brown or reddish brown bistre ink, which was made from oven soot. Compositional drawings executed in chalk are rare in Rubens's oeuvre. He used chalk in Italy for the *Baptism of Christ* of about 1604 (cat. no. 14) and the *Study for the Circumcision* of early 1605 (cat. no. 17). The former is carefully drawn in black chalk only; the latter, showing more forceful, freer strokes, is drawn in black and some red chalk. Squared for transfer, both drawings resulted in large altar paintings. To judge from surviving examples, Rubens employed chalk for compositional drawings even less frequently after his return to Flanders in 1608. In the 1620s he utilized black chalk in the two known compositional drawings for the ceiling decoration of the Jesuit church (today Saint Charles Borromeo) in Antwerp: *Saint Gregory Nazianzenus* (Fogg Art Museum, Cambridge) and *Saint Athanasius* (State Hermitage Museum, Saint Petersburg).[23] In the mid-1630s he executed *Hercules Strangling the Nemean Lion* (cat. no. 110) in black and red chalk. Rubens probably found chalk's softness and lack of clarity to be drawbacks in his compositional drawings. "Scribbles" in ink were better suited to quickly jotting down ideas.

From the 1620s, Rubens's urge to prepare a painting with one or more preliminary drawings seemed to diminish. This is especially evident in his large cycles of paintings dedicated to episodes from the lives of the Roman consul Decius Mus, the emperor Constantine the Great, Marie de Médicis of France, and Achilles. For all four series, just two double-sided compositional drawings are known, both of them for the Medici cycle (one of them, *The Majority of Louis XIII,* is now

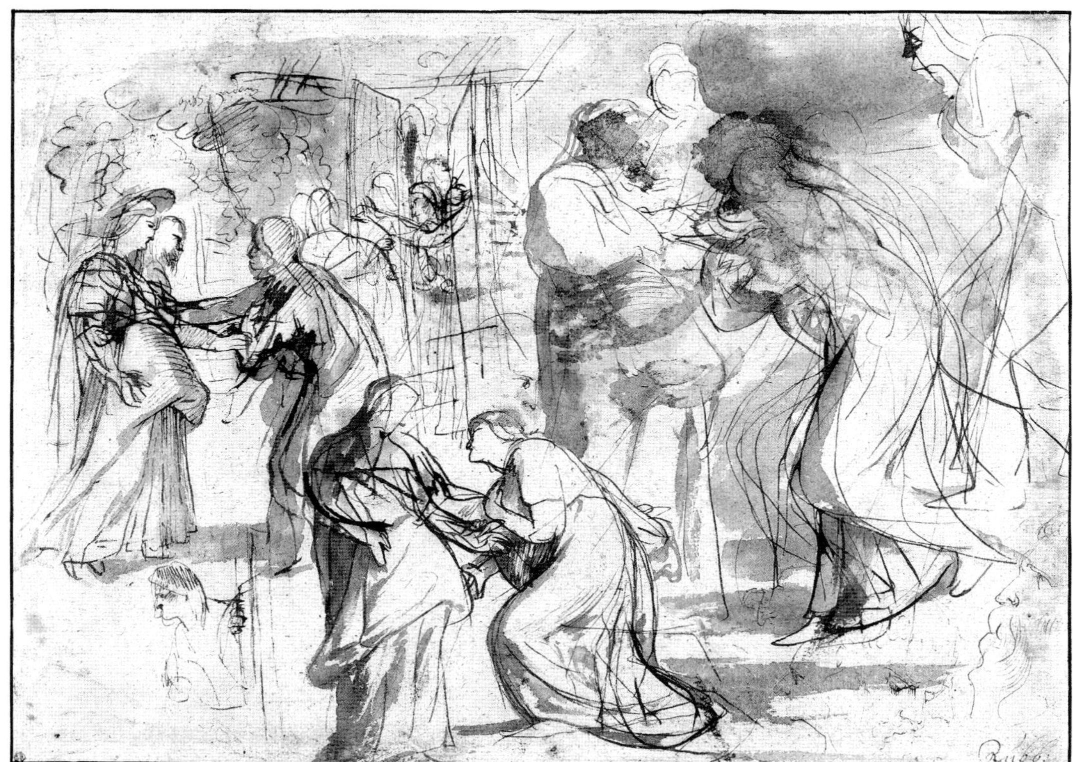

Fig. 6. Peter Paul Rubens, *Studies for the Visitation*, 1611. Pen and brown ink and brown wash, 265 x 360 mm ($10\frac{7}{16}$ x $14\frac{3}{16}$ in.). Musée Bonnat, Bayonne (1438 recto)

in the Louvre, Paris).[24] In preparation for these large cycles Rubens created oil sketches for each painting, sometimes two for one subject: an initial one in shades of brown, called a *bozzetto,* and a second, more elaborate one in color, called a *modello.* In these cases Rubens's working method did not really change, however: he switched from a compositional drawing to a painted *bozzetto* to fix his early ideas, but the colored oil sketch was still "step two" in the process. Indeed, at that time the distinction between a drawing and an oil sketch was not that clear. In the Flemish of the day, *teekening* could mean "drawing" as well as "oil sketch."[25]

Drawings from the Model

Once Rubens had thought out the composition of a certain work through his *crabbelingen* or compositional drawings and had put it down properly in an oil sketch, his next step was to make individual studies in black chalk of the most important figures in the work. For that purpose Rubens must have had at his disposal models whom he could ask to pose in the position already basically established in the oil sketch. In these drawings the artist refined the pose of the figure and studied and improved such details as facial expression, the musculature of a naked figure, or the intricate folds of a garment. It was not always necessary for Rubens to draw the entire figure; sometimes the upper body, clasped hands, or an outstretched arm was enough. He apparently used only male models, even when, as in his *Female Nude: Study for Psyche* (cat. no. 36), the figure studied was a woman.[26] In his oil sketches Rubens calculated the general lighting, but he determined the exact shading in the drawings after life.

Comparing a figure from one of Rubens's oil sketches with the drawing from the model that followed makes plain the function of these studies and the significant changes they sometimes brought about. In his oil sketch for the large altarpiece of the *Miracles of Saint Francis Xavier,* Rubens depicted a shortsighted, unpleasant old man groping his way forward with a staff in his right hand (fig. 109). In his drawing after a model for this particular figure (cat. no. 64), Rubens introduced only a few changes—which made a world of difference. A change in age—in the drawing the man is much younger—makes the figure more sympathetic. More important, in the drawing (and in the final painting) the man's groping arms are no longer widespread but straight and held close together, an easily read indication that the man is not shortsighted but blind. This circumstance now includes him among the sick gathered before Saint Francis

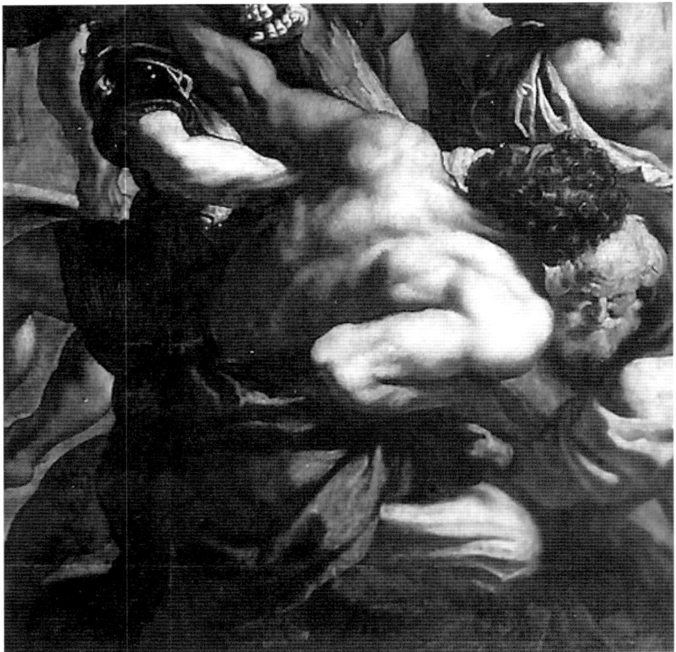

Fig. 7. Detail of central panel of Peter Paul Rubens, *The Raising of the Cross,* ca. 1610–11, Antwerp Cathedral (fig. 87)

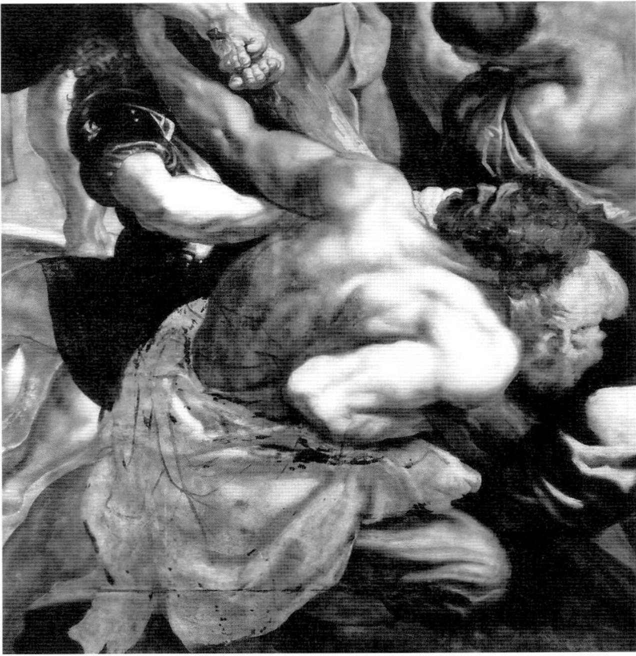

Fig. 8. Infrared reflectogram of detail of central panel of Peter Paul Rubens, *The Raising of the Cross,* ca. 1610–11, Antwerp Cathedral (fig. 87)

Xavier and amplifies the saint's miraculous healing power. Thus the alterations made in Rubens's drawing from the model enhance the message of the painting.

Rubens preferred black chalk, at times heightened with white chalk, for his drawings after the model. Chalk allowed for fine, soft gradations in modeling. Red chalk is rare and found only in the 1630s, for example, in the *Study of a Seated Woman, Turned to the Right* (cat. no. 109); this study, however, is associated with a painting by Rubens of his second wife, Helena Fourment, and may be a special case. For the most part Rubens used off-white paper; no drawings by him on colored paper are known. Although in general Rubens used large sheets of paper, he often ran out of room for the figure. Thus, as in his *Kneeling Male Nude Seen from Behind* (cat. no. 35) and *Study for the Figure of Christ* (cat. no. 37), he inserted hands, parts of the lower leg, or feet in separate sketches alongside the main figure.

Rubens's drawings after the model made in preparation for a painting should be distinguished from a drawing type that looks comparable but is not the same: the "academy" or academy study. In order to learn how to draw, and also to maintain the skill, (young) artists drew after the posed model, probably from the sixteenth century on. Since this teaching method was generally practiced at an academy—one privately organized in an artist's studio or a public institution established by the authorities—the studies produced became known colloquially as "academies." The "academies," however, were not drawn with a specific artwork in mind, as in Rubens's case; they were for study purposes only. Whether Rubens ever made academy studies is unknown. We do have a report, however, that at about age forty—the report dates from 1618—Rubens declared drawing from the model as taught in the academy to be of "little or noe purpose."[27]

Rubens was hardly the first to make drawings after the model for a specific goal, however. In Italy this practice was already well established—Raphael and Michelangelo had made large numbers of figure studies in preparation for their paintings—and it was also in Italy that Rubens started making such studies. Two such sheets from his Italian years are known: *Two Men Holding the Shaft of the Cross* (fig. 16), which he drew for his *Raising of the Cross* altarpiece for the church of Santa Croce in Gerusalemme, Rome (1601–2; destroyed), and *Man Holding a Staff* (Gabinetto Nazionale delle Stampe, Rome), a likely preliminary study for the *Adoration of the Shepherds* for the church of the Oratorians in Fermo (1608; Museo Civico, Fermo).[28]

Annibale Carracci (1560–1609)—one of the few contemporary Italian artists that Rubens seemed to have highly respected—may have served as Rubens's example in this matter. The Bolognese artist, together with his brother, Agostino (1557–1602), and his cousin Ludovico (1555–1619), greatly enhanced the role of drawing in the pursuit of a more naturalistic rendering of the subject, especially of the human figure. The Carracci stressed the study of nature and hence accorded much importance to drawing from life, and not only from the posed model.[29] Shortly before Rubens's first stay in Rome (1601–2), Annibale Carracci finished the decoration of the ceiling of the Palazzo Farnese's gallery. Rubens doubtless saw and admired this wonder of modern Rome. As it is almost certain that Rubens and Annibale met in Rome, one may surmise that Rubens saw some of the six hundred or so preliminary drawings Annibale had made for the ceiling decoration. The strongest argument for Annibale's influence, however, may be the close technical and stylistic resemblance of Annibale's and Rubens's black-chalk drawings after the model.[30]

After his return to Antwerp in 1608, Rubens further explored the possibilities of drawings after the model. They were an important stage in getting the figures in his paintings exactly as he wanted them, and they were essential as time-saving devices. From the 1610s Rubens was extremely popular and continuously received commissions for new work. To satisfy this great demand Rubens took on many pupils and assistants. A description of Rubens's studio in 1621 by Otto Sperling (1602–1673), the physician to the Danish court, makes clear that many paintings at that time were collaborations. In one room Sperling saw "many young painters who worked on different pieces on which Sr. Rubens had drawn with chalk and put a spot of color here and there; the young men had to execute these paintings which then were finished off with lines and colors added by Rubens himself."[31] Indeed, recent infrared reflectography shows that there are initial chalk drawings of the sort Sperling described on the ground layer of the prepared panel of Rubens's Antwerp altarpiece of the *Raising of the Cross* (see figs. 7, 8).[32] However, as these rudimentary sketches only outline the figures, it is inconceivable that they were adequate for the aspiring artists in Rubens's studio to continue their work. They must have needed more guidance, and it is generally assumed that the master provided this through drawings after the model.

There are telling differences between the initial rough sketch of the crouching man seen from the back who is trying to hold up the Cross, visible through infrared reflectography (fig. 8), and the drawing after the model for the same figure (cat. no. 38). Rubens outlined the figure on the central panel of the *Raising of the Cross* triptych only to place it within the composition; the extended left arm is visible, and a few additional chalk (?) strokes indicate the loincloth. There are no demarcations of the muscles on the man's back and arms. The anatomical details that the assistants were to follow were supplied, instead, by Rubens's drawing after the model. That he supervised his assistants is evident from the final touches he made to the figure: he bent the man's right arm more, making the muscles around his shoulder bulge; he lowered the figure's left arm slightly and turned it just enough that his hand could grip the side of the Cross; and he made the loincloth bulkier (fig. 7).

Drawings from the model are most numerous in the 1610s, when Rubens had his large studio. They grew rarer as Rubens—and some of his assistants—became more experienced. The artist resumed drawing from the model in the 1630s, in his many large chalk studies for the *Garden of Love* painting of about 1632–33 (see cat. nos. 90–92).

Drawings for Portraits

Rubens apparently was a reluctant portrait painter. Early on, during his service to Vincenzo Gonzaga, the Duke of Mantua, he wrote that he would make portraits only if this work led to "greater things."[33] Nevertheless, Rubens painted a number of portraits during his employment by the duke. These include the *Duke of Lerma on Horseback* (fig. 48), the *Mantuan Friendship Portrait* (Wallraf-Richartz-Museum, Cologne), *Vincenzo Gonzaga and His Family Adoring the Holy Trinity* (fig. 51), and several portraits of Genoese aristocrats. A few preparatory drawings for these portraits and some related sheets have survived. We have the *modello* for the equestrian portrait of Lerma, executed in great detail in pen and wash over traces of black chalk (cat. no. 13), as well as the rather precisely drawn portraits in black and red chalk of Francesco Gonzaga (Nationalmuseum, Stockholm) and Ferdinando Gonzaga (fig. 17), a portrait of an unknown bearded man (Albertina, Vienna), and the study for a portrait of Jan Woverius (cat. no. 11). Like his compositional drawings created in Italy, these portrait drawings show great variety, especially in technique but also in style, suggesting that the young artist was still searching for the best method of preparing them.

After returning to Antwerp from Italy in 1608, Rubens was able to avoid official portraiture for some time. From the 1620s, when his career as a diplomat took flight and he was often visiting foreign courts, the demand for painted portraits—which he, in his function as painter-diplomat, could not refuse—began to rise. Indeed, we have a firsthand report from 1620 about a portrait session with Rubens. Aletheia Talbot, the wife of the Earl of Arundel, passed through Antwerp in the summer of that year with her marshal, jester, dwarf, and large greyhound. Francesco Vercellini, one of the earl's secretaries, who traveled with Aletheia, wrote in a letter to Arundel: "It was arranged that her Excellency, my Lady should come the following day to sit, which she did; and he [Rubens], full of courtesy, completed her portrait, with Robin the dwarf, the fool, and the dog. A few small details that are yet lacking he will furnish tomorrow. . . . As the said Signor Ribins [Rubens] had not at hand a sufficiently large canvas he painted [or drew; *ha ritratto*] the heads as they are to be; drew on paper the postures and the dress; and took the whole portrait of the dog. So it will remain while he is arranging the canvas, when, with his own hand, he will copy what he has done."[34] This canvas is today in the Alte Pinakothek, Munich. It shows Aletheia Talbot sitting on a terrace and caressing her large dog, with Robin the dwarf at her right with a falcon on his right arm and the jester at her left.[35]

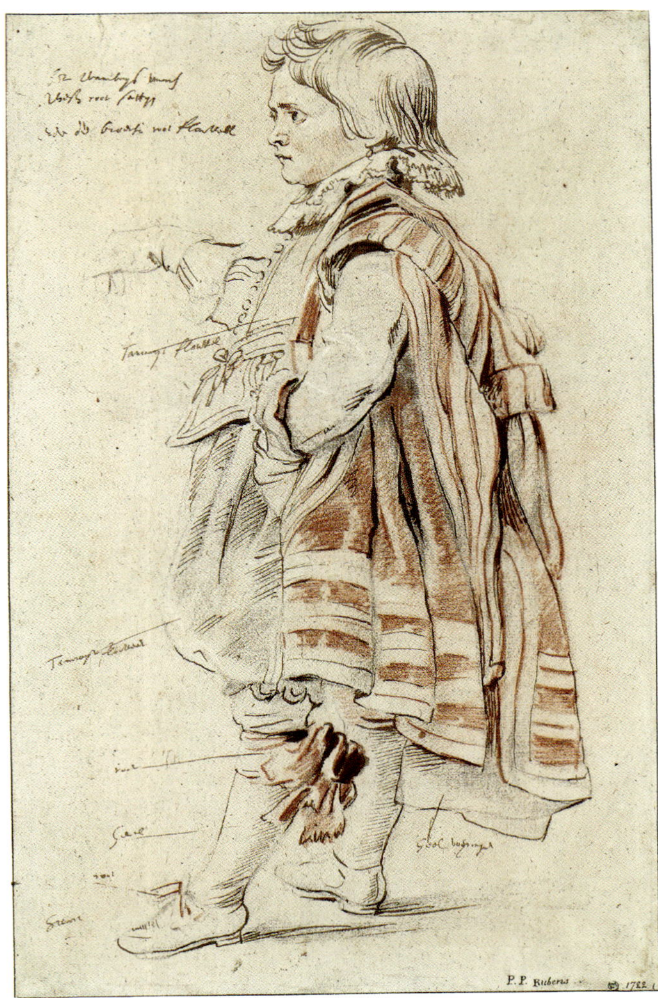

Fig. 9. Peter Paul Rubens, *Robin, the Dwarf of the Earl of Arundel,* 1620. Black and red chalk, heightened with white, accented with pen and brown ink, 408 x 258 mm (16 1/16 x 10 1/8 in.). Nationalmuseum, Stockholm (NM H 1913/1863)

The conditions described by Vercellini may have been exceptional, owing to Rubens's lack of a proper canvas. Enough preparatory drawings by Rubens survive, however, to support Vercellini's account of the artist's use of two distinct types of preliminary drawings for portraits: studies of the sitter's pose and costume (and on occasion, the setting)—such as the drawing *Robin, the Dwarf of the Earl of Arundel* (fig. 9),[36] preserved from Aletheia Talbot's 1620 sitting—and studies of the head. Rubens had already explored both types of drawings in Italy. However, an elaborate, painstakingly executed sheet like the 1603 study for Lerma's portrait (cat. no. 13) was out of the question in the 1620s, when Rubens was so busy. Indeed, in a drawing of 1629–30 for a portrait of the English collector Thomas Howard, 2nd Earl of Arundel (cat. no. 80), a helmet on a table and a curtain are only vaguely indicated behind the figure of the earl, outfitted in armor. Another preliminary drawing for Arundel's portrait, also from 1629–30 (cat. no. 79), is a head study. In his head studies of the later 1620s and early 1630s, such as his study of about 1631 for a portrait of Helena Fourment (cat. no. 88), Rubens refined his use of black, red, and white chalks. (This *trois crayons,* or three chalks, technique became very popular in France in the eighteenth century among artists like Antoine Watteau [1684–1721] and François Boucher [1703–1770], who may have been influenced by Rubens's drawings.)

The portrait drawings that Rubens made of members of his family—his two wives, his children, and other close relatives (cat. nos. 81–86, 88)—seem to have been created as private studies, probably meant largely for the artist's own enjoyment. Only occasionally were these personal documents translated into oil. A portrait drawing of about 1621 of Rubens's first wife, Isabella Brant (cat. no. 82), was used for a painting of

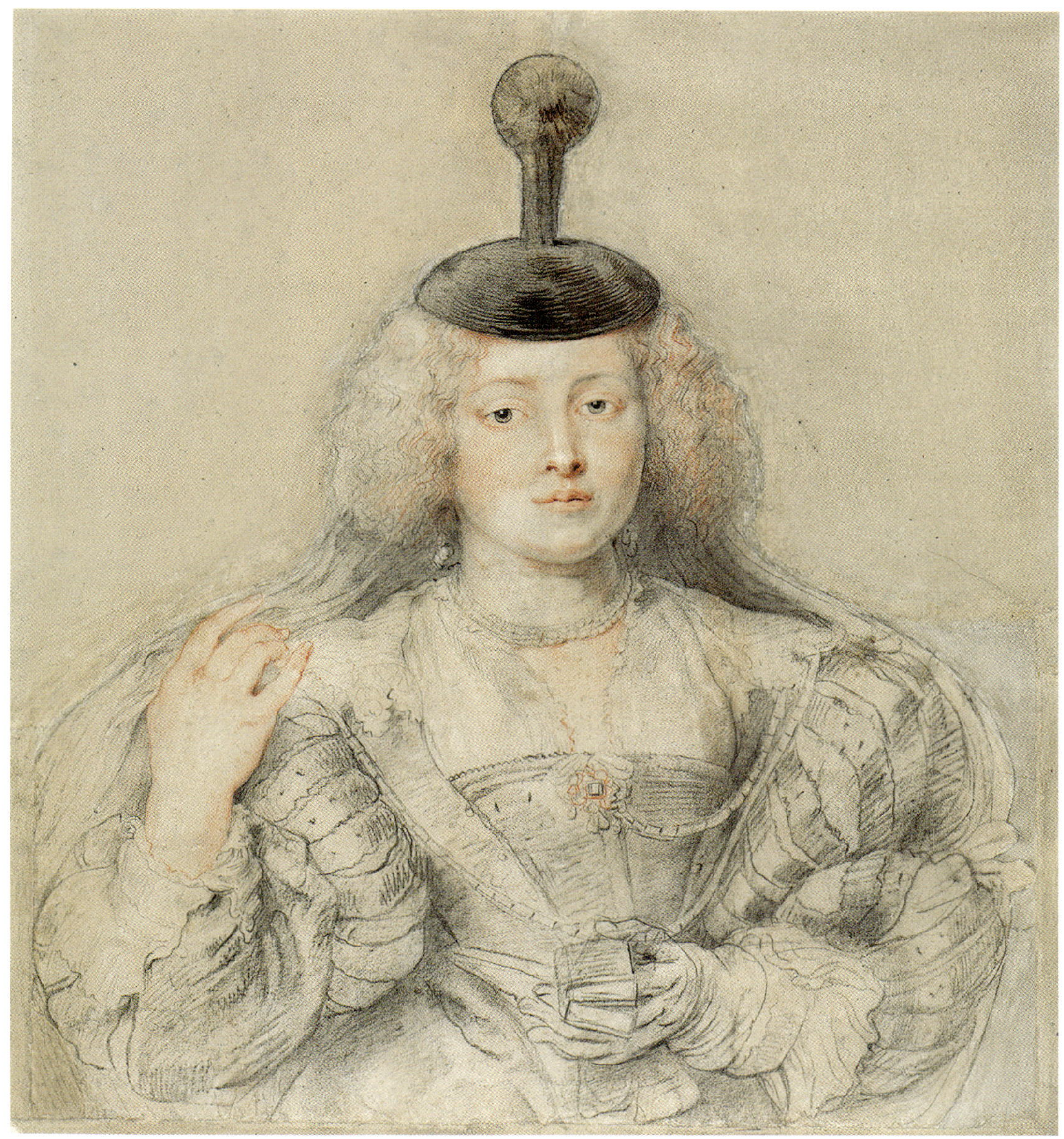

Fig. 10. Peter Paul Rubens, *Helena Fourment*, ca. 1630–32. Black and red chalk, heightened with white, partially reinforced with pen and ink, 612 x 550 mm (24 1/8 x 21 5/8 in.). Courtauld Institute of Art Gallery, London (D.1978.PG.64)

about the same time (fig. 128)—not by Rubens, however, but by his pupil Anthony van Dyck (1599–1641). It has been suggested that Van Dyck gave the painting, which shows Isabella in front of the family's Antwerp home, to Rubens as a gift. (Whatever Van Dyck's motivation, the incident shows that he had access to at least some of Rubens's private drawings.) Rubens based his well-known full-length portrait of his sons Albert and Nicolaas, now in the Liechtenstein Museum, Vienna (fig. 132),[37] on head studies of his sons, one now in the Albertina (cat. no. 86), the other lost and known only through a copy. He also seems to have utilized portraits of Albert and Nicolaas as infants for depictions of the Christ Child (see cat. nos. 59, 81).

Rubens's highly finished study of about 1630–32 of Helena Fourment (fig. 10)[38] is the most extraordinary and celebrated drawing among the artist's portraits of his family members. It is also by far his largest portrait drawing. Holding a small prayer book in one hand and moving her mantle (attached to a cap with a large pom-pom) over her shoulder with the other, Helena is captured just as she is leaving for, or returning from, church.

Her sumptuous clothing resembles the fashionable attire of the young women in Rubens's *Garden of Love* painting (see cat. nos. 90–92). Rubens may have made an initial brief sketch of Helena before creating this elaborate portrait, which in turn may have inspired his late canvas *Helena Fourment and Frans Rubens,* today in the Louvre, Paris.[39]

Drawings for Prints

Rubens's involvement in printmaking began in earnest when he was about thirty. Unlike Rembrandt (1606–1669), his counterpart in the Northern Netherlands, or Giovanni Benedetto Castiglione (1609–1664) in Italy, or Jacques Callot (1592–1635) in France—to name the three most prominent seventeenth-century printmakers in Europe—Rubens hardly touched the etching needle or the engraving burin.[40] Nevertheless, his participation in printmaking set new standards, especially for book illustrations and the reproductive print. He also helped to resurrect the woodcut technique and to bring it to new heights.

Rubens was one of the rare major artists who engaged in designing title pages and book illustrations (cat. nos. 49–51). Given that Antwerp at that time was one of the most active printing centers in Europe and profited handsomely from the export of books, maps, pamphlets, and almanacs, his involvement is not difficult to understand. Rubens was also a learned man—a *pictor doctus,* as his contemporaries sometimes called him—who was interested in books and had a large library. Finally, he had been a close friend, since Latin school, of Balthasar Moretus (1574–1641), the most important member of the distinguished Plantin Press in Antwerp. Rubens and Moretus collaborated for thirty years.

Rubens's first experience preparing drawings for publication was during his second visit to Rome (1605–8), when he furnished five designs after Roman statues and architectural fragments (all now lost) for engravings to illustrate his brother Philip's book *Philippo Rvbenii Electorum Libri II* (Two Books of Selections by Philip Rubens);[41] this book on ancient customs and costumes was published by Jan Moretus (1543–1610), Balthasar's father, at the Plantin Press in 1608. The engravings after Rubens's drawings were by Cornelis Galle the Elder (1576–1650), who was then living in Rome and knew the Rubens brothers.

Rubens created more than forty title pages for books published by the Plantin Press between 1609 and 1645 and in 1666. Twenty of them were for publications dealing with theology and church history.[42] In his title-page designs he maintained the layout in general use during the sixteenth and early-seventeenth centuries, in which architectural details were combined with tomb sculpture, forming a so-called sepulchral altar.[43] However, he increased the size and volume of the figures, reduced their number, and depicted them in a livelier manner. At times he eliminated the framing architecture altogether, substituting an open space with landscapes. In contrast to his predecessors, he also tried to relate his title page to the content of the book. Rubens found inspiration for his designs in written sources about the gods and religious customs of the ancients. His proficiency in Latin, the language of the majority of his sources, was invaluable.

Rubens's collaboration with Balthasar Moretus, who took over the Plantin Press in 1610, began about 1612 with drawings for two new illustrations for an edition of the *Missale Romanum* (Roman Missal) published in 1613. One of them, the *Adoration of the Magi* (cat. no. 49), was reused for the press's 1614 edition of the *Breviarium Romanum* (Roman Breviary), with additional illustrations after Rubens's drawings, including the *All Saints* (cat. no. 50). For Rubens, working on book illustrations and title pages seems to have been a form of relaxation, a fun job that tested his knowledge and that he performed on Sundays or holidays. In a letter of September 13, 1630, to Balthasar Cordier (1592–1650), a Jesuit born in Antwerp and living in Vienna who was inquiring about commissioning a drawing from Rubens, Balthasar Moretus explained that he usually gave the artist six months to reflect upon a title page and execute it at his leisure, and only on holidays, as he did not do this kind of work on regular workdays; otherwise, he would demand one hundred florins for a single design.[44] Rubens was paid according to the size of the drawing, and the sums were relatively small: twenty florins for a folio page, twelve for one in quarto, eight for one in octavo, and five for even smaller ones. (The artist often waived his payment and accepted books in exchange.)[45]

Rubens drew his preliminary designs for title pages and book illustrations in a fine pen and added light washes to indicate light and dark areas. There is often little or no visible underdrawing in black chalk. Short pen strokes to indicate the modeling were made in parallel lines only, to allow the engraver more freedom to add cross-hatching with the burin. If the book's author approved of Rubens's design, the drawing and the copperplate for the engraving were usually sent to

Cornelis Galle the Elder, the preferred engraver of Rubens and Moretus. Once the copperplate was engraved, proof impressions of the print were taken and sent to the publisher and to Rubens. If needed, the artist would make corrections with a fine pen and brown ink.[46] These were usually minor and included additional strands of hair or slight alterations in a figure's face or extremities. Rubens used brush and grayish body color to lighten or delete areas. These designs for title pages and book illustrations can be dated rather precisely since—until the late 1630s—Rubens prepared them shortly before their publication; at least five designs, however, were not published until after Rubens's death in 1640.

We can only guess why Rubens began the enterprise of having prints made after his paintings. He was familiar with the engravings Marcantonio Raimondi (ca. 1480–ca. 1527) had produced after Raphael's paintings and those Cornelis Cort (1533–1578) engraved after Titian's; he may simply have decided to do likewise. He may also have wished to use prints to satisfy the immense demand for his paintings, which he was unable to meet in spite of his large and well-organized workshop. In a 1635 letter to his friend Peiresc, Rubens said that through the prints he hoped to gain honor rather than any financial benefit.[47] However, we may wonder whether this was really the case and whether Rubens did not in fact receive a percentage of the profit from sales of the prints.

In preparation for the prints, assistants in Rubens's studio (not necessarily the engravers) produced careful, large drawings after the artist's paintings. These designs were all begun in black chalk and gone over in part with pen and brown ink; on some we find additional work in brush and gray and brown wash heightened with white. Rubens carefully supervised their making, sometimes adding corrections (see below). Today the draftsmen remain largely anonymous; their primary task was to copy the paintings carefully, avoiding any intrusion of personal style. However, the art theorist Giovanni Pietro Bellori (1613–1696) tells us that Anthony van Dyck was one of them.[48] On the basis of this statement and stylistic comparison, several sheets preparatory for engravings after Rubens have been attributed to him: *Lot and His Family Leaving Sodom*, *Saint Francis Receiving the Stigmata*, and the *Adoration of the Shepherds,* all now in the Louvre, Paris.[49] There are many more drawings for reproductive engravings preserved in the Louvre, the majority of them once owned by Everhard Jabach (1618–1695), one of the early collectors of Rubens's drawings. It therefore seems likely that these drawings have remained together from the time they left Rubens's studio, where the artist probably kept them as a group.

When the assistant had finished the drawing, Rubens would go over it, making changes with pen and brush and brown ink. With the pen he would place accents in faces, hair, arms, and legs; the different layers added with the brush were to introduce shadow. Sometimes Rubens made major alterations in the preliminary design for the engraving, as one can see in the drawings of *Queen Tomyris with the Head of Cyrus* (cat. no. 55) and the *Feast of Herod* (cat. no. 57). An intervention by Rubens in the *Assumption of the Virgin* drawing of about 1624 (cat. no. 53) changed the subject from a conventional Assumption scene into one in which Christ welcomes his mother into heaven. In general, however, such rigorous reworkings are the exception.

Interventions large and small in the preparatory drawings are a clear indication of the seriousness with which Rubens approached putting his paintings into print. He also watched closely over the production of the engravings. Meticulous corrections are found on proofs of his prints. Indeed, Rubens seemed to have been highly demanding. In the case of the engraver Lucas Vorsterman (1596–1675), the artist was perhaps too much so. Their collaboration ended abruptly in 1622 (and was resumed only briefly in the late 1630s), when, it seems, Rubens and Vorsterman were at loggerheads over a particularly complicated design.

Between 1633 and 1635, during the last decade of his life, Rubens became involved in the production of woodcuts. In the early 1630s the highly skilled Christoffel Jegher (1596–1652/53) was creating woodcuts for the Plantin Press in Antwerp, which may have caught Rubens's interest. Rubens and Jegher together prepared drawings for woodcuts after the *Garden of Love* (cat. nos. 93, 94) and the *Rest on the Flight into Egypt* (cat. no. 95), and in so doing they modified the compositions of the original paintings. Jegher's woodcuts after the two exceptionally large drawings based on the *Garden of Love* mark the high point in this endeavor.

Drawings Retouched by Rubens

Artists were among the very first to collect old master drawings, probably starting in the fifteenth century in Italy; they did it to learn and to enjoy. Soon this activity spread to the North. Famous early artist-collectors included Giorgio Vasari,

Ludovico, Agostino, and Annibale Carracci, and Bartolomeo Passarotti (1529–1592) in Italy, and Lucas de Heere (1534–1584), Joris Hoefnagel (1542–1601), and Cornelis van Haarlem (1562–1638) in the Netherlands. Rubens joined right in. He may have started collecting drawings in Italy because of his great admiration for Italian art. The drawings he collected there were also a wonderful remembrance of his years in the South.

Old master drawings nowadays are considered untouchable, almost holy. This was not the case in the sixteenth and seventeenth centuries. Vasari, for instance, usually cut the drawings he owned to what he considered the proper format and pasted them on mounts—sometimes in configurations of several sheets—on which he drew elaborate frames. Cornelis Dusart (1660–1704) heavily reworked the drawings he inherited from his teacher Adriaen van Ostade (1610–1685), probably in order to make them more salable. The collector Everhard Jabach hired an artist to work on several drawings in his collection that he considered unfinished. (Only recently has scholarly attention been paid to this phenomenon.)[50] Many of these "finishing-up" activities were later concealed, especially from the nineteenth century on, when drawings came to be seen as an artist's most intimate, private expressions. The retouches Rubens added to drawings, however, have always been acknowledged and generally admired.[51] This may have been owing to the large number of drawings he retouched, and probably also to his fame.

More than two hundred drawings retouched by Rubens are known. The majority are drawings by sixteenth- and early-seventeenth-century Italian artists.[52] About forty of them are by or after Giulio Romano; some twenty reflect compositions by Raphael; eighteen are after Polidoro da Caravaggio (1490/1500–?1543). Rubens also retouched drawings by Northern artists, but those are less numerous. One especially instructive example is the drawing of a *Hawking Party* by Bernaert van Orley (ca. 1488–1541) or a member of his workshop, today in the British Museum, London.[53] Rubens doubled the dimensions of the small Van Orley drawing, which is only a fragment of a larger sheet, by enlarging it on two sides. With black chalk and brush and dark brown ink and wash Rubens superbly "restored" the cut-off limbs of the hunters and their horses and carried his retouches into the sixteenth-century drawing, thus integrating the old with the new.

Rubens's interventions, however, were not always this drastic. Usually they consisted of light retouchings in media similar to those of the underlying original drawings. For instance, on drawings in red chalk he preferred to work with red ink, which he applied with the tip of the brush, as is visible in his retouched copy after Raphael, *The Prophets David and Daniel* (cat. no. 114). He retouched pen drawings with the tip of the brush and dark brown ink after he had cleared the specific area with cream or grayish white body color. Retouchings where body color is involved—Rubens did not restrict its use to pen drawings but also employed it on drawings in red or black chalk—are generally easier to detect, because they are often more extensive, as we see in *God the Father* (cat. no. 115) and *Fashionable Young Woman Holding a Shield* (cat. no. 117).

Rubens was not one of those artists or collectors who retouched old master drawings in order to make them look nicer, so that they either would be more salable or would more closely reflect the taste of the time. He never sold his drawings—on the contrary, he kept them until his death and even made a provision in his will that they stay together, within his family, for an allotted time. In addition, Rubens never shared his drawings with friends or like-minded connoisseurs but, rather, considered them material for his private use. What, then, was his reason for retouching so many drawings by other artists? Rubens himself never gave an answer. However, Roger de Piles (1635–1709), the early biographer of the artist, probably got it right when he wrote that Rubens retouched drawings in order to "stimulate his senses and to heat up his genius."[54] In other words, this work was a challenge to his creative spirit and inventiveness.

We do not know when Rubens began to retouch drawings. It is logical to assume that he acquired most of his Italian drawings during his eight years in Italy, but did he also start to retouch them there? And if so, how often and how many? One may wonder whether he spent much time on this in Italy when he could visit the original works of art. As a young artist from the North, he might at first have hesitated to interfere in works by (or attributed to) Leonardo, Raphael, and Giulio Romano. We will probably never know the exact course of events. However, it seems likely that the bolder the intervention, the later in life he did the reworking. A rare case where we can date the retouching reasonably well is the drawing of about 1633–35 after the right portion of Rubens's *Garden of Love* painting (cat. no. 94)—where Rubens intervened in *his own* work. On this sheet Rubens drew an initial design in black chalk; Christoffel Jegher went over it in pen and brown

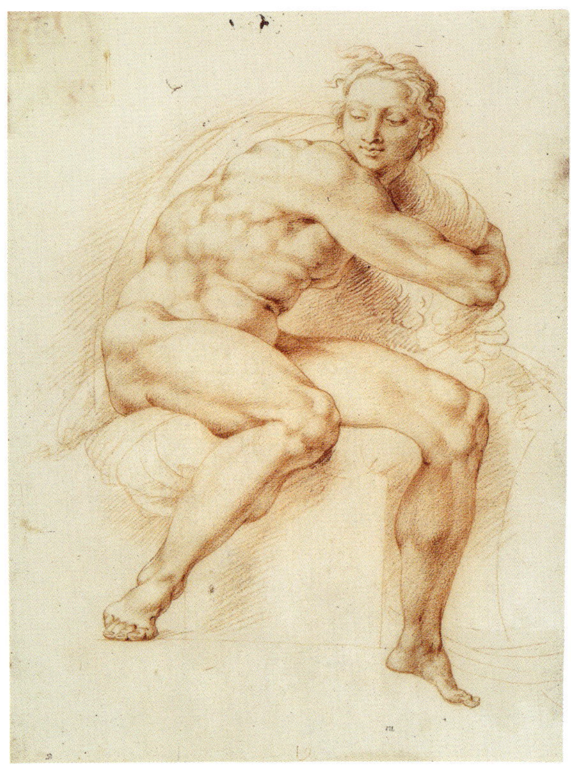

Fig. 11. Peter Paul Rubens after Michelangelo, *Nude Youth Turning to the Right*, ca. 1601–2. Red chalk with touches of brush and red wash, 388 x 278 mm (15¼ x 10¹⁵⁄₁₆ in.). The British Museum, London (1870 8 13 882)

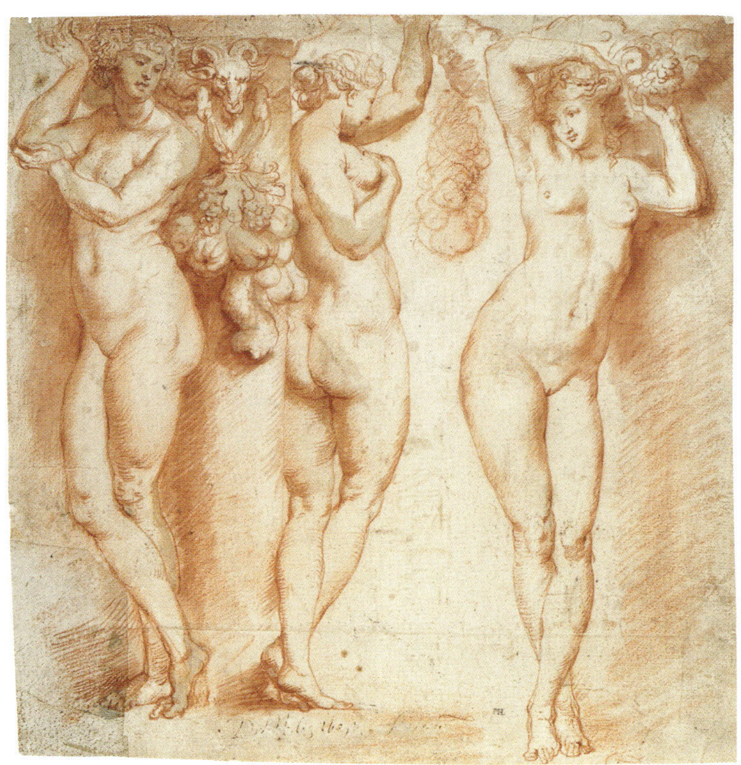

Fig. 12. Circle of Francesco Primaticcio, *Three Nude Women Holding Garlands*, 1600–1625. Red chalk, heightened with white, 264 x 253 mm (10⅜ x 9¹⁵⁄₁₆ in.). Museum Boijmans Van Beuningen, Rotterdam (V 6)

ink; and after the drawing had served its purpose as the design for Jegher's woodcut, Rubens retouched it with brush and ink and gouache *and* altered the initial composition, probably on the spur of the moment.

Since Rubens's retouchings are often difficult to discern, so cleverly did he apply them, there has been some discussion where the original drawings end and his retouchings begin. To show the difference between a copy entirely by Rubens and a drawing he only retouched, it may be fruitful to compare Rubens's *Nude Youth Turning to the Right* (fig. 11),[55] which he copied after an *ignudo* in Michelangelo's Sistine Chapel ceiling, with a drawing in red chalk that Rubens retouched, *Three Nude Women Holding Garlands* (fig. 12), by an artist from the circle of Francesco Primaticcio (1504/5–1570).[56] The *Nude Youth* is one of the rare drawings that everyone agrees is by Rubens's hand alone. For this sheet he used red chalk and did some work, likely at the same time,[57] with the tip of the brush and red wash to delineate leaves in the wreath around the youth's head. The fine hatching to indicate the modeling of the muscles corresponds to that in Rubens's copies after antique sculpture. The drawing of *Three Women* also shows retouches with the tip of the brush and red ink, especially in the women's faces, in the contours of the arms and legs, and in the restructuring of the ram's head. However, some of these areas—for example, in the face of the caryatid at the left and the fruit garland next to her—were first covered with beige body color. The work with the tip of the brush was added on top of it. First covering the section to be reworked was Rubens's customary procedure when retouching a drawing by someone else. Nothing needed to be covered with opaque body color in the *Nude Youth*, since Rubens drew it from the beginning to his satisfaction.

When Rubens retouched a drawing he characteristically inserted the original sheet into a larger piece of paper (rather than enlarging it on each side, as with the Van Orley fragment) and extended missing details into the added margins. One of the most famous such drawings is the exceptionally large *Fight for the Standard* (fig. 13), which is often published,

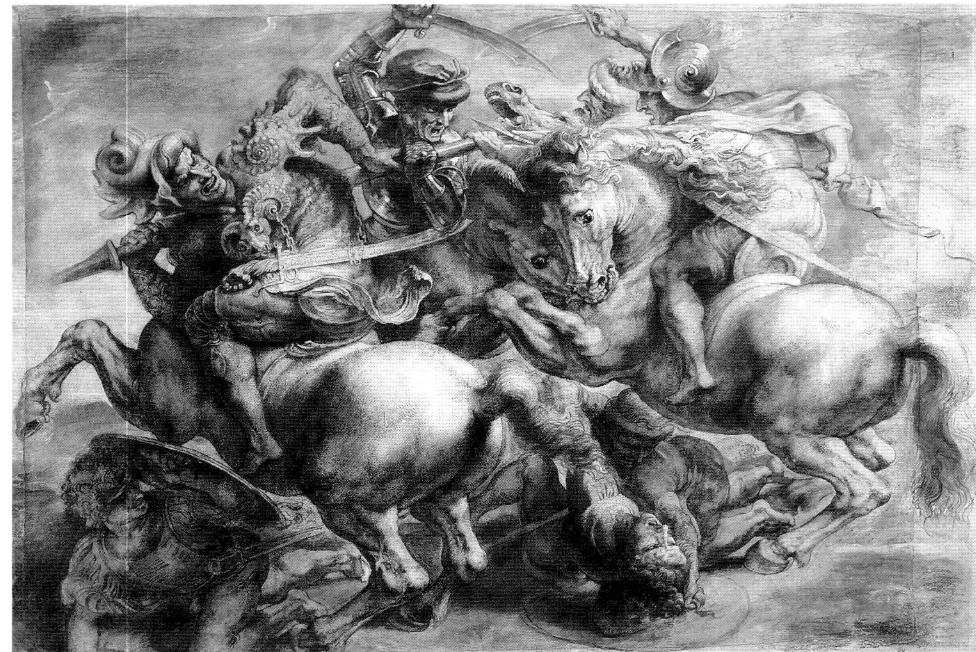

Fig. 13. Italian 16th-century copy after Leonardo da Vinci, restored and reworked by Peter Paul Rubens, *The Fight for the Standard*, ca. 1615–16. Black chalk, traces of white highlights, pen and brown ink, reworked by Rubens with brush and brown and gray-black ink, gray wash, and white and bluish gray gouache, over copy inserted into a larger piece of paper, 453 x 636 mm (17⅞ x 25$^{1}/_{16}$ in.). Département des Arts Graphiques du Musée du Louvre, Paris (20 271)

erroneously, as a copy by Rubens after Leonardo and which is usually dated between 1600 and 1608, when Rubens was in Italy.[58] In fact, however, Rubens worked on top of an anonymous sixteenth-century copy after the central section of Leonardo's lost fresco of the *Battle of Anghiari* (commissioned about 1503 for the Sala del Gran Consiglio of the Palazzo della Signoria, Florence). After inserting the earlier sheet into a larger one, Rubens proceeded to rework the entire drawing with a brush and bluish green body color that at times changes to white. He completed the horse's tail at the right, the horse's hoof at the left, the footman's knee at the bottom left, and the horseman's fingers at top center left. The soldier's right arm and hand brandishing a sword at top center right and extending into the margin are entirely Rubens's invention. The dramatic result is that the two swords of the battling horsemen cross more or less in the center of the composition.[59] Rubens reworked the drawing heavily, which suggests that it is the work not of a young but of a more mature artist. Rubens may have retouched the sheet only about 1615–16,[60] when he began a series of hunting pictures for members of the court of the Southern Netherlands and thus became interested in depictions of fierce battles.

The Sketchbooks

Almost every drawing by Rubens was made with another work of art in mind. In contrast to Rembrandt, who made many drawings of religious subjects just to train his mind and who drew countless landscapes and scenes of daily life for relaxation, Rubens was always thinking ahead and already busy with the next step. Even in his sketchbooks or the drawings related to architecture—the works discussed below—we encounter the same purposefulness.

Rubens drew most of his studies on single sheets.[61] Nevertheless, he also used sketchbooks—or bound together drawings in series—throughout his career. A sketchbook concerning costumes is today still essentially intact; others, on anatomy and an assortment of other topics, are known only through some loose sheets or copies. The 1678–79 inventory of Rubens's collaborator Erasmus II Quellinus (1607–1678) mentions two or three sketchbooks (or books with drawings) by the master. One of these was apparently devoted to architecture.[62]

Rubens's most discussed but least known sketchbook is the one that is now generally referred to as the *Pocket Book*. Unfortunately, it was lost in a fire in 1720.[63] We know about it only from descriptions, partial transcriptions, and at least two, and possibly a few more, loose sheets.[64] The first person to mention the *Pocket Book* was Giovanni Pietro Bellori, who wrote in 1672 in his *Vite* that he had seen "a book in his [Rubens's] hand, in which there were observations on optics, on symmetry, on proportions, on anatomy and on architecture, with an inquiry into the principal passions of the soul, and actions based on descriptions by Poets, with examples of the work of the painters. There are battles, shipwrecks, games, love scenes, and other passions and events, transcribed from some of the verses of Virgil and others, with images principally after Raphael and the Antique."[65] From this description and from a comparable one by Roger de Piles, who owned the *Pocket Book* at least by 1699, it is clear how seriously the young Rubens took his profession and how deeply absorbed he was by classical antiquity, not only through studying antique works of art but also through reading ancient sources. (He wrote many of the texts in the *Pocket Book* in Latin.) Rubens seems to have been interested in the theory of "ut pictura poesis" (as is painting so is poetry; the phrase is derived from Horace's *Ars poetica*), and it may have been at the heart of the *Pocket Book*.[66] During the sixteenth and seventeenth centuries the relationship between painting and poetry was emphasized; Horace's phrase became the motto of art theorists who wished to elevate the status of painting to that of poetry and the liberal arts. While Rubens may have begun the *Pocket Book* in Flanders, before he left for Italy in the spring of 1600, he wrote the largest part of it during his years in Italy.[67] A double-sided sheet with *Studies for Hero and Leander* on the recto and a *Battle Scene between the Greeks and Amazons and Studies for Samson* on the verso (cat. no. 10) may have survived from this fascinating, mysterious sketchbook.

Rubens's student Willem Panneels noted on several anatomical drawings he made that they were copies after Rubens's originals in the artist's "annotomibock" (anatomy book). The existence of a book by Rubens with anatomical drawings was confirmed in 1987 by the appearance on the London art market of eleven of Rubens's original drawings.[68] Thanks to these examples, we know that the sketchbook included écorchés and flayed torsos, arms, and legs; there was also one anatomical drawing of a horse. We do not know where Rubens studied anatomy, however. He may have become interested in beginning an anatomy book after having examined notebooks on anatomy by Leonardo, which he likely saw in 1603, when he traveled to Spain at the behest of the Duke of Mantua; de Piles reports that Rubens was very taken by these drawings.[69] Rubens may also have been familiar with a book by Andreas Vesalius (1514–1564) on human anatomy, *Opera Anatomica;* a copy published in Basel in 1555 apparently was in the artist's library.[70] Rubens probably used his *Anatomy Book* to instruct the pupils in his studio, possibly having them copy after his drawings as Panneels had done.[71] One of the Rubens drawings sold in 1987, *Anatomical Studies: A Left Forearm in Two Positions and a Right Forearm,* is today in the Metropolitan Museum (cat. no. 16).

The only Rubens sketchbook whose contents have largely survived is the so-called *Costume Book,* today in the British Museum, London.[72] The volume has not been preserved in its original makeup, however: it is in an eighteenth-century binding; some original sheets appear to have been lost, and some unrelated sheets appear to have been added. It contains approximately 250 studies of fifteenth- and sixteenth-century costumes and portraits of Flemish and Burgundian nobility, as well as depictions of hunting scenes, dancing couples, people with exotic hats, Turkish, Arabic, and Persian figures, and men in armor. Most of the folios are filled with numerous images, often tightly cramped on the page. Rubens copied the majority of these images from other artists' works, including the *Mémoriaux* of the Flemish artist Antonio de Succa (before 1567–1620), today in the Bibliothèque Royale Albert Ier, Brussels,[73] costume manuals, and model books. At times Rubens transformed the stiff figures of his sources into lifelike human beings. For this reason, the images in the *Costume Book* were long thought to be studies that Rubens drew from life or directly from the tomb sculptures and similar monuments catalogued by De Succa and others.[74]

Rubens worked on the drawings in the *Costume Book* from about 1609 through 1612.[75] He used a fine pen exclusively, sometimes adding a thin wash. The drawings are amazingly free of corrections. While the volume may have been used for instruction in his studio, its primary purpose was to serve as a visual repository of costumes that the artist could draw on for his paintings. The *Costume Book* was not compiled in preparation for a history of the counts of Flanders, as some were led to believe by an inscription in French on the first leaf of the book as it is currently bound.

Unfortunately, Rubens's sketchbook on architecture, mentioned in the 1678–79 inventory of Quellinus, has not been preserved. We know from several other sources, however, that Rubens had a serious interest in architecture. In Italy he purchased the plans and elevations of twelve Genoese villas and palaces built in the third quarter of the sixteenth century, which he later published (in 1622) under the title *Palazzi di Genova,* with seventy-two plates.[76] In 1615 he purchased two different editions of Vitruvius's *De architectura* and the five then-published volumes of Sebastiano Serlio's influential

Renaissance treatise on architecture.[77] At about the same time he had an Italian-style palazzo added next to his Antwerp house, to serve as his studio, and also became deeply involved in the design of the new Jesuit church in Antwerp (now Saint Charles Borromeo), for which construction began in April 1615 and which was dedicated in September 1621. Three designs by him for facade decorations have been preserved on two sheets, *Two Angels Blowing a Trumpet* (Pierpont Morgan Library, New York) and *Cartouche Supported by Cherubs* (British Museum, London).[78] In addition to his designs of 1620 for painted ceiling decorations, Rubens submitted a design for the high altar of the church and collaborated on a drawing for the stucco ceiling decoration of the Mary Chapel, added in 1625; both studies are now in the Albertina, Vienna.[79] Rubens emphasized the contours in these very finished drawings, to guide the craftsmen as they translated the designs into stone. In this feature the sheets resemble Rubens's 1620 drawing for a relief of the *Birth of the Virgin* (cat. no. 52).

Rubens's Development as a Draftsman

Early Training and Stay in Italy, 1591–1608

Rubens began his training as an artist in 1591, when he was fourteen years old. He studied first with the landscapist Tobias Verhaecht (1561–1631), from 1592 with Adam van Noort (1562–1641), a painter of religious scenes and portraits, and from about 1594 or 1595 with the learned Otto van Veen, the most authoritative of his three teachers and one of the most eminent artists in Antwerp at the time. The drawings by Rubens that have survived from this period are all copies, mostly after sixteenth-century book illustrations. As copying was part of an artist's training since the Middle Ages, this should not surprise us. Apprentices learned the trade by copying older masters.[80]

The earliest known drawings by Rubens—the copies he made after one of the most popular illustrated books of the sixteenth century, Hans Holbein the Younger's *Dance of Death*—probably date from a year or two before his apprenticeship with Verhaecht. The drawings are on the whole more or less standard exercises in the copying of prints (see figs. 2, 3). Within a few years, in Rubens's copies from about 1596–99 after Tobias Stimmer (see cat. no. 1), Jost Amman, the Petrarch Master (Hans Weiditz? [1500–1536]), Hendrick Goltzius, and again Hans Holbein, we encounter an artist who extracts individual figures and motifs from various sources and combines them in pattern-book style, selecting only motifs that he liked or wanted to add to his repertory. Later still, about 1598–99, in drawings after Goltzius (see cat. no. 2) and Johannes Stradanus (1523–1605),[81] Rubens experimented with yet another method of copying: he took figures from different sources and combined them in new compositions. Most of these copies are done in pen and ink, in a style that stresses the outlines. Shading can be accomplished with washes, as in the *Dance of Death* drawings, but is usually achieved through hatchings, plain parallel hatchings, and elaborate layers of cross-hatching. Not surprisingly, one can trace most of these characteristics back to the prints Rubens copied. However, by adding a few lines here or leaving out a few there—not to mention his corrections in perspective—Rubens usually improved the composition and with it the impact of the image.

The earliest paintings attributed to Rubens reflect quite closely those of his teacher Van Veen. The same cannot be readily said of Rubens's earliest known drawings.[82] At first glance Van Veen's elaborate oil sketches—the only drawings we know by him—seem to have nothing in common with Rubens's early drawings. However, the apprentice may have picked up more than is generally acknowledged. It is interesting to note that the complex layers of oil and gouache in Van Veen's grisailles hide pen-and-brown-ink outlines and hatchings that are not unlike those by the young Rubens.[83] Rubens may also have become aware of the possible benefits of oil sketches in the working process during his time with Van Veen, though, admittedly, Rubens's oil sketches later in his career were usually done on panel.[84] Another habit or technique Rubens may have taken up in Van Veen's studio is the rough initial composition sketch in pen and brown ink. As has been mentioned above (see the discussion under "Compositional Drawings"), Rubens usually began work on a complicated composition by hastily jotting down with pen and ink his very first ideas. Such "scribbles," often hardly legible, form a distinct category in his drawn oeuvre. Grisailles by Van Veen in the Musée des Beaux-Arts, Rouen, and recently in the art trade indicate clearly that Rubens's teacher began his compositions with comparable illegible pen-and-ink scribbles. Finally, Van Veen and Rubens shared the habit of writing on their drawings.[85]

Why no initial studies by the young Rubens have survived is unknown. Like many beginners, he may have drawn on erasable drawing boards or small tablets *(tafeletten)*.[86] One can also speculate that, after his eight-year stay in Italy, which had a deep impact on his attitude toward art and, implicitly, on his drawing style, the artist was no longer interested in his first efforts and discarded them. It was logical for him to have kept his copies after Holbein, Stimmer, Goltzius, and others, as these were instructive; more important, these representations could prove useful later on, as inspiration and as visual documentation. Drawings after Amman or Stradanus, for instance, were worth keeping out of archaeological and antiquarian interest, while copies after Holbein and the Petrarch Master contained invaluable information about life in the sixteenth century. That Rubens indeed later used these sixteenth-century examples in his own works is clear from several borrowings.[87] The total lack of early originals, however, remains somewhat discomforting, especially given the pivotal role his own drawings played in his studio in later years. Time and again, sometimes decades later, the artist returned to his earlier work.

In May 1600 Rubens traveled to Italy, where he stayed for eight years. He was in the service of Vincenzo Gonzaga, Duke of Mantua (r. 1587–1612), a cousin of Archduke Albert, governor of the Southern Netherlands. Rubens's position as court painter in Mantua afforded him many opportunities to travel—to Rome, Florence, Madrid, and Genoa, among other places. In some of these cities he painted large altarpieces for important churches. In Genoa Rubens created a new type of portrait: splendid depictions of aristocratic ladies in fashionable dresses against an open background. Especially after the consistent and rather uniform works of his early Antwerp years, the drawings from his Italian period show a bewildering array of subjects, techniques, and styles. This diversity can be explained by several factors. As a young, ambitious Northern artist transplanted in Italy, the cradle of the arts, Rubens must have been like a sponge absorbing new and different art treasures every day. Paper, of course, was the easiest material with which to take in this new world properly and document it. Pen and brown ink, however, might not always be the right medium for these wonders, and in Italy he encountered many more possibilities, including chalk, which was not commonly used in the Netherlands at the end of the sixteenth century. Finally, from 1598 Rubens was no longer a pupil but a proper master, whose horizon, naturally, was not limited to copies.

Of course Rubens did not forget everything he had learned in Antwerp, and certain "Italian" drawings, such as the *Anointing of Christ* (fig. 14)[88] and the *Descent from the Cross* (cat. no. 9), have features in common with his early copies after prints. In these two drawings we encounter, just as in his copies after Holbein and Stimmer, pen and brown ink enlivened with hatchings and washes; the emphasis remains on the outlines. The greater freedom of line, particularly in the *Descent from the Cross,* and the strong chiaroscuro imparted by the brushwork are nonetheless remarkable. Especially in the *Anointing,* Rubens seems to have been concerned with the effect of light, exploring all variations from white (he left parts of the paper untouched) to almost unthinned dark brown. Many quotations from Italian art have been identified in the *Anointing.* The general composition, for example, is based on a print by the Venetian artist Giovanni Battista Franco (ca. 1498–1561).

During his stay in Italy Rubens tried color in his drawings, apparently for the first time. The most vibrant examples are two copies he made after frescoes by Giovanni Antonio da Pordenone (1482/83–1539) in the Chapel of the Annunciation in Treviso Cathedral: *The Emperor Augustus and the Tibertine Sibyl* (Musée du Louvre, Paris)[89] and *God the Father Supported by Angels* (fig. 4).[90] Both large sheets are executed with the brush and watercolor over an initial sketch in black chalk, with some red chalk reserved for areas of flesh. These painterly copies are far removed from the careful pen work after Goltzius that Rubens had done only a few years earlier, although the emphasis on the outline is still evident. Despite their energy, these sheets have some raw and awkward qualities and therefore should be dated shortly after Rubens's arrival in Italy.[91]

Red and black chalk also seem to have had great appeal for Rubens while he was in Italy. His eight large copies, in these two chalks, after Michelangelo's prophets and sibyls from the Sistine Chapel ceiling were probably made in 1601–2, during his first visit to Rome.[92] Rubens drew the first sheets in the series entirely in black chalk and added the red chalk only as an afterthought.[93] In the drawings we witness the growing confidence of the young Flemish artist and the increasing quality of his draftsmanship. The young draftsman, full of admiration for the great Italian master, wanted to have a grip on these venerable figures from one of Rome's most influential masterpieces. From the volume of the bodies to the pleats in the garments and to the musculature of arms and shoulders, nothing escapes his attention.

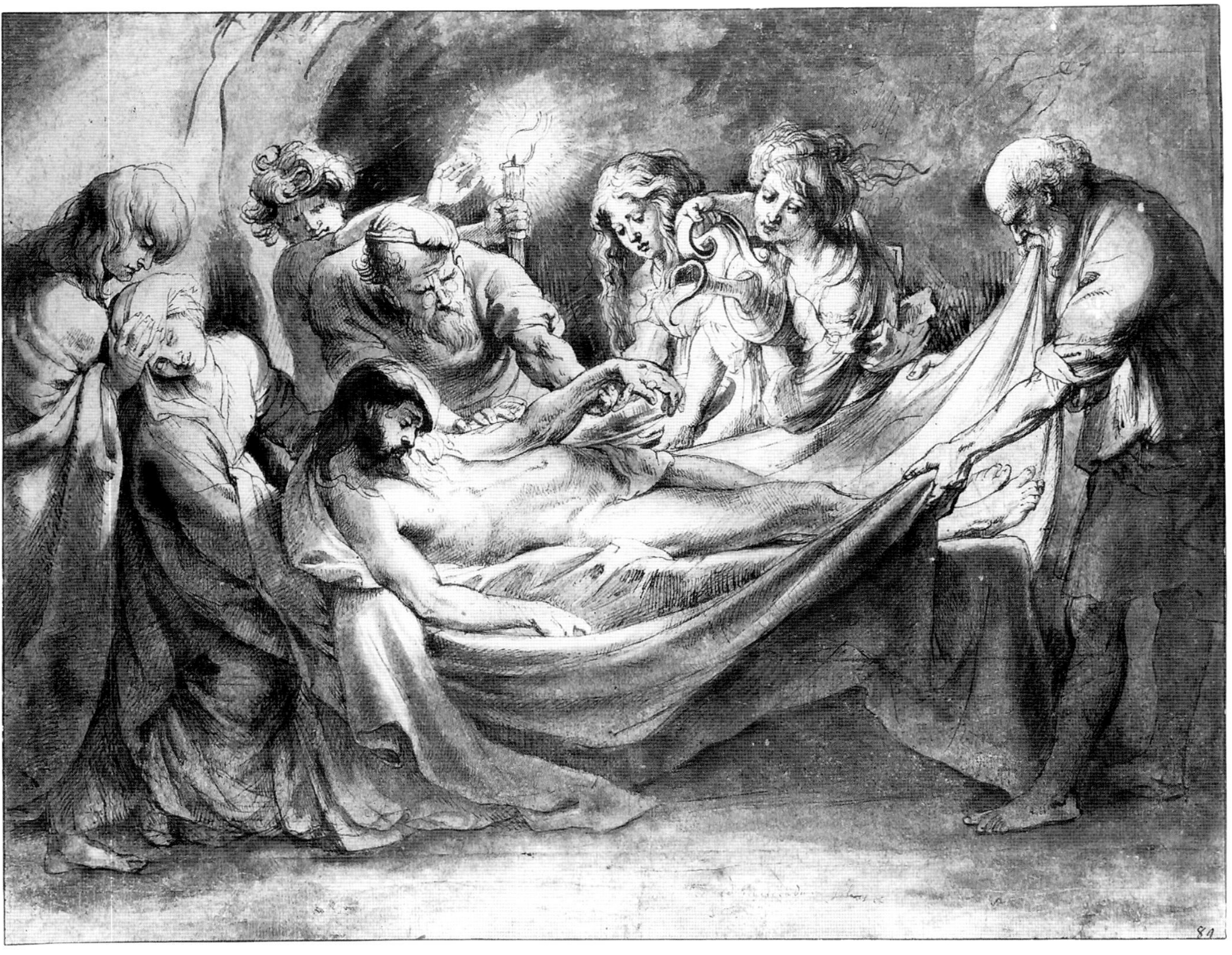

Fig. 14. Peter Paul Rubens, *Anointing of Christ*, ca. 1600–1602. Pen and brown ink, gray and brown wash, 324 x 408 mm ($12\frac{3}{4}$ x $16\frac{1}{16}$ in.). Museum Boijmans Van Beuningen, Rotterdam (MB 340)

Rubens's red-chalk drawing *A Nude Youth Turning to the Right*, after one of Michelangelo's so-called *ignudi*, also from the Sistine Chapel ceiling (fig. 11), is a telling departure from the accurate copies of the prophets and sibyls. It probably dates from 1606, during the artist's second visit to Rome.[94] Rubens considerably increased the musculature of the body, changing Michelangelo's languid figure into a tense and active bodybuilder. Was this alteration deliberate, and should we therefore interpret it as an example of Rubens's trying to surpass his admired predecessor?

All the copies after antique sculpture that Rubens made while he was in Italy (see cat. nos. 20–23) were done in chalk, usually black chalk. (He used red chalk occasionally, as in his copy after the *Belvedere Torso* [cat. no. 34 verso].) He apparently also used black chalk for drawings after the model (as he continued to do after he returned to Antwerp). Unfortunately, however, we know of only two drawings after the model from Rubens's years in Italy: the *Man Holding a Staff* in the Gabinetto Nazionale delle Stampe, Rome,[95] and *Two Men Holding the Shaft of the Cross* (fig. 16; see also cat. no. 30 verso), cut into three pieces at a later date but still readable. In Italy about 1600, chalk—black and red—was used throughout the peninsula, so Rubens could have picked up this *nouveauté* anywhere. However, the use of black chalk for large drawings of single figures from life, in poses needed for future works of art, was a particular practice in the school of the

Carracci in Bologna and Rome. It is therefore logical to assume that Rubens adopted this method, unheard of in the Netherlands at the time, during his Italian travels. Moreover, Annibale Carracci was one of the few contemporary Italian artists Rubens seems to have admired.[96]

The lack of more drawings by Rubens from the human figure during this period—in preparation for his *Baptism of Christ* altarpiece for the church of Santissima Trinità in Mantua (see cat. no. 14) and for altarpieces in Rome and Genoa—is a reminder that we are dealing with an oeuvre that has come down to us in fragmentary form. Compositional drawings from these years are also lacking. For several important paintings that Rubens made in Italy—for instance, the altarpieces of the *Transfiguration* and *Vincenzo Gonzaga and His Family Adoring the Holy Trinity* (fig. 51), both for the church of Santissima Trinità in Mantua, or his Genoese *Portrait of Giovan Carlo Doria on Horseback* (Galleria Nazionale della Liguria a Palazzo Spinola, Genoa)—we have no compositional drawings. In addition, those that have survived—the Michelangelesque *Baptism of Christ* (cat. no. 14), the sketchy, Zuccaro-like *Study for the Circumcision* (cat. no. 17), and the *Adoration of the Image of the Virgin and Child* (cat. no. 18), for altarpieces in Mantua, Genoa, and Rome, respectively—exhibit significant differences in technique and state of execution. Some surviving compositional drawings from Rubens's Italian sojourn, such as the *Battle of the Greeks and Amazons* (cat. no. 12), do not relate to any known paintings by Rubens and were perhaps preliminary drawings for works that were never realized.

Antwerp, 1608–20

Rubens returned from Italy to Antwerp in early November 1608, and his fellow countrymen quickly recognized his talent. Before a year had passed, Archduke Albert and Archduchess Isabella, the rulers of the Southern Netherlands, appointed him court painter. He had already received many prestigious commissions from private patrons and various groups in the city—for a painting for the Antwerp city hall and for two important altarpieces for the two largest churches in Antwerp—as well as offers to paint altarpieces for churches in nearby Mechelen (Malines), Brussels, and Ghent. From now on his workflow only increased, and from the early 1620s it also included many foreign commissions. To produce the commissioned canvases, which were often very large, and to engage in a range of other activities—designing title pages for books, commissioning engravers, publishing a book on architecture—Rubens created a large, well-organized studio, with pupils, assistants, and collaborators. The studio was in his own house in Antwerp, since his generous employers, Albert and Isabella, allowed him to live and work there instead of at the court in Brussels.

Although Rubens was never bound by fixed rules of procedure, in the first years after his return to Antwerp he developed a relatively strict approach to his paintings and, consequently, to some of his drawings, relying heavily on his studio. His method—largely an Italian one, which in all likelihood he learned in Italy—was basically as follows: he started by making quick compositional drawings, outlines jotted down in pen and brown ink, to visualize his initial ideas. These helped him to figure out the basic composition, which, in the next step, he put down in an oil sketch. This Rubens showed to his patrons, and if they approved, he started the actual painting. (From the 1620s on, he gave the oil sketch to his collaborators so that they could begin work on the painting.) The oil sketches, however, were not blueprints that needed only to be enlarged. Rather, in the next step—making specific drawings from life for the most important figures in the painting—Rubens generally came up with many adjustments, large and small. These drawings, for which models posed in the posture required in the painting, enabled Rubens not only to determine the exact bearing of the protagonists, along with the appropriate musculature, hairstyle, and lighting, but also to find the most telling facial expression. With these drawings after the model in hand, a collaborator, or Rubens himself, was able to finish the painting properly.

In his early years in Antwerp Rubens created a group of compositional drawings that stand out stylistically and technically. The artist first made a sketch with a fine pen and then added washes with a broad brush in a boisterous, almost wild way. Among this group are several sheets with subjects of particular physical or emotional violence, almost complementing the frenzied drawing style: *Salome with the Head of John the Baptist* (cat. no. 26 recto), *Judith Killing Holofernes* (cat. no. 27), and two images of *Susanna* (cat. nos. 25, 29 recto). Eventually, this way of drawing proved very influential for Rubens's younger assistant and collaborator Anthony van Dyck, practically becoming his hallmark. (Consequently, over the years a number of these sketches, including *Salome* and *Judith Killing Holofernes,* have been attributed, erroneously, to

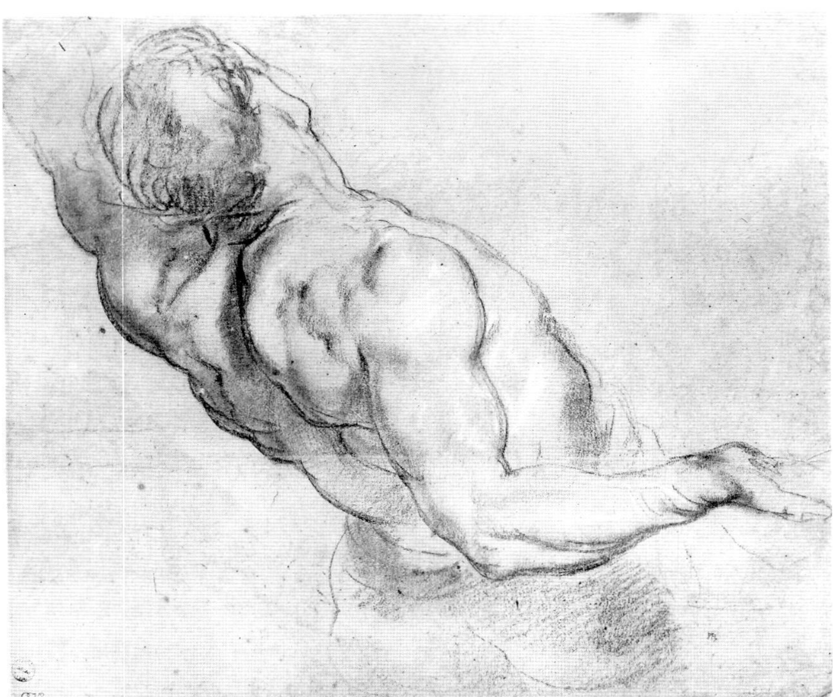

Fig. 15. Peter Paul Rubens, *Nude Man Seen Partly from Behind.* Black chalk, heightened with white, 315 x 367 mm (12⅜ x 14⁷⁄₁₆ in.). The Ashmolean Museum, Oxford (WA 1855.179)

Fig. 16. Peter Paul Rubens, *Two Men Holding the Shaft of the Cross,* 1601–2 (reconstruction). Top left: black chalk, 242 x 238 mm (9½ x 9⅜ in.). Courtauld Institute of Art Gallery, London; bequeathed by Count Seilern as part of the Princes Gate Collection (D 1978. PG.56 verso). Bottom left: black chalk and touches of brush and grayish brown wash, 142 x 214 mm (5⁹⁄₁₆ x 8⁷⁄₁₆ in.). The Metropolitan Museum of Art, New York; Gift of Mr. and Mrs. Janos Scholz (52.214.3 verso). Right: black chalk, 360 x 265 mm (14³⁄₁₆ x 10⁷⁄₁₆ in.). Musée Bonnat, Bayonne (1438 verso)

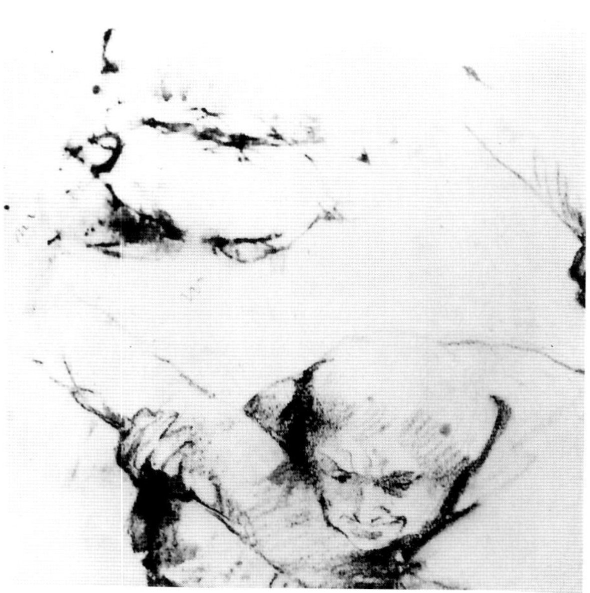

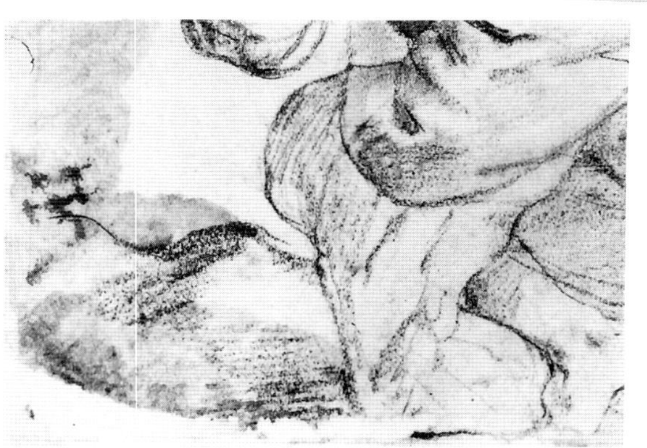

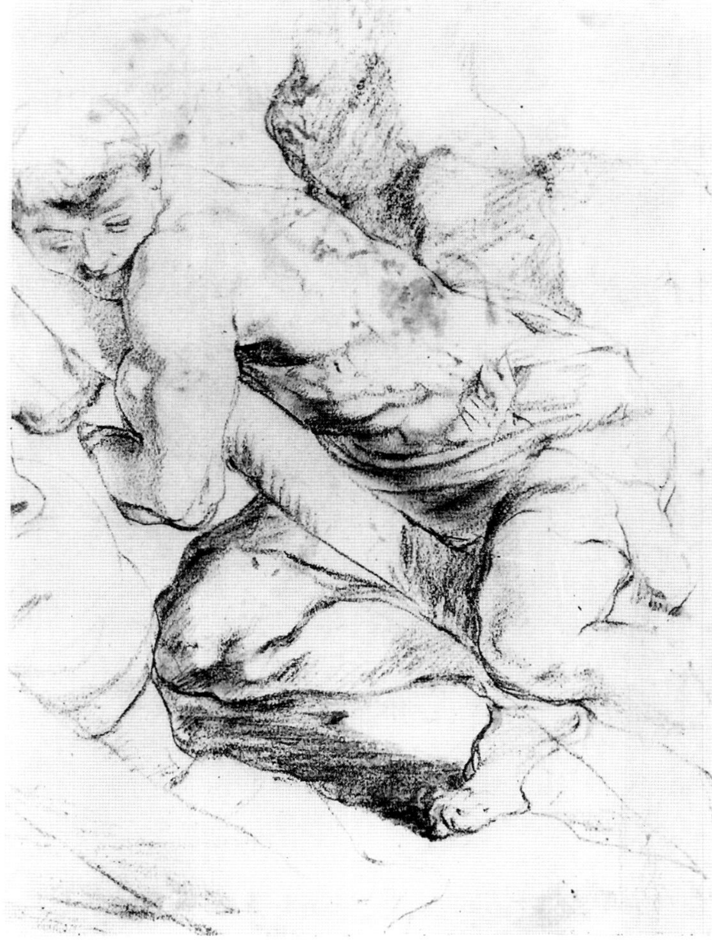

Van Dyck.) In time Rubens moved on to a slightly different style for his *primo pensiero* compositional drawings. The *Studies for the Visitation* (fig. 6) and the *Presentation in the Temple* (cat. no. 30 recto), both from 1611, are good examples. They seem to be drawn with even more haste, the lines are simpler, the forms are blocklike, and the washes are decreasing in importance. Among the characteristic "scribbles," or sketchy preliminary drawings, in which Rubens ceased to use the brush completely, are *Diana with Nymphs Unloading Deer from a Donkey* (cat. no. 32 recto) and the *Virgin and Child Adored by Saints* (cat. no. 34 recto).

Of Rubens's studies after the model from this period, the most impressive group is probably the four surviving sheets relating to the central panel of his enormous 1610–11 triptych, the *Raising of the Cross* (fig. 87), today in Antwerp Cathedral. The studies—one for the figure of Christ (cat. no. 37) and three for his executioners (fig. 15; cat. nos. 38, 39)[97]—show how well Rubens had studied Michelangelo and antique sculpture. Muscles are rendered with the utmost precision, and the three executioners exude an utterly convincing strength. Comparing these drawings to a drawing of male figures from Rubens's years in Italy, *Two Men Holding the Shaft of the Cross* (fig. 16; see also cat. no. 30 verso), we can see that the artist's style has changed significantly. While the earlier drawing shows insecurity in several repetitions of general, wavy outlines, as well as a lack of depth and little knowledge of anatomy, the *Raising of the Cross* drawings demonstrate a complete mastery of line (despite an obvious pentimento in cat. no. 31) and correct modeling of the figure. The clarity and sureness of line of these and comparable drawings, such as the *Seated Male Youth* (cat. no. 45) and the studies of a *Tartar Huntsman* (cat. no. 61) and a *Blind Man with Outstretched Arms* (cat. no. 64), were probably not solely the result of Rubens's looking at Italian examples and improving his skills, however. They were in all likelihood also a consequence of the secondary purpose of these sheets: Rubens's pupils used them while working on the final paintings, so the more legible the figure studies, the better.

1621–40

In the early 1620s Rubens apparently altered his working method drastically. Certain drawing types, including compositional drawings and figure studies, almost disappeared, while other types, and even other techniques, came to the fore. The compositional drawing was largely replaced by the oil sketch, whose numbers rose steeply.[98] For the large cycle devoted to the life of Marie de Médicis (altogether, twenty-one lifesize paintings with complicated compositions full of figures), for instance, only two double-sided compositional drawings are known—and twenty-eight oil sketches.[99] The most likely explanation for this change is that as an older, more experienced artist, Rubens no longer needed compositional drawings all the time, whereas oil sketches, which included color, became more and more vital: patrons had to see them for approval, of course, and perhaps more important, they were needed to get his assistants started. At this stage of Rubens's career, saving time was essential.

A good example of a compositional drawing from the 1620s is the study for *The Majority of Louis XIII* (Louvre, Paris), one of the rare works on paper in preparation for the Medici cycle.[100] The composition is jotted down in quick, summary lines of pen and brown ink. For the lower part of the ship the artist needed only three lines; for the royal couple, the allegorical figures, and all the rigging, just a few more. The same economy can be observed in earlier drawings, such as the *Martyrdom of Two Saints* (Museum Boijmans Van Beuningen, Rotterdam)[101] and the *Continence of Scipio* (cat. no. 33). From the 1620s on, however, we have *only* such hasty compositional drawings. The *Virgin and Child Adored by Saints* (cat. no. 34 recto), preparatory to Rubens's 1628 altarpiece in the Antwerp church of Saint Augustine (fig. 77), also displays this cursoriness, and its seemingly haphazard arrangement of apparently unrelated groups of figures illustrates beautifully how Rubens's thinking and sketching went together. Comparable sketches in which we can observe the evolution of Rubens's thinking are the *Centaurs Embracing* (Courtauld Institute of Art Gallery, London)[102] and *Seventeen Studies of Dancing Peasants for a Kermis* (cat. no. 103). Again, such thinking on the page can be seen earlier, in *Three Sketches for Medea and Her Children* of 1600–1604 (cat. no. 8 verso) and *Studies for the Death of Dido* (fig. 47), for example, but the style of the later examples is freer, the scale is larger, the lines are thinner, and the mind that is drawing seems as if in a trance.

The scarcity of drawings by Rubens after the model in the early 1620s is not so easily explained as the diminishing number of compositional drawings. In his many painted works of these years—the Medici cycle, the ceiling paintings for the Jesuit church (today Saint Charles Borromeo) in Antwerp, the series on the lives of Achilles and Constantine the Great, and many individual paintings—dozens and dozens of new figures appear, but we know of only one or two drawings after the model from this period.[103] Were they lost as a group early on? Did Rubens not need any? It has been argued, for instance, that the paintings of the Medici cycle contain many quotations after classical sculptures.[104] Perhaps Rubens was indeed able to come up with the figures he needed with the help of his large drawings collection, which was an inventory of almost every famous ancient statue. The *Study of a Seated Woman Turned to the Right* (cat. no. 109) is a rare late drawing by Rubens from the model. This sheet is exceptional, however, since it is drawn, unusually, mostly in red (rather than black) chalk; the sitter's attitude is so natural that one doubts there was any deliberate posing; and there is no picture for which it was the preparatory drawing. It is in a way comforting that from this later period we have only this one extraordinary study. It would be disconcerting if we had, on the contrary, only one "normal" model study, because that would imply that Rubens continued making drawings after the model as usual and that they were indeed lost early on.

Yet Rubens did not abandon drawings after the model altogether. A special group of nine figure studies from the early 1630s has been preserved (see cat. nos. 90–92); they are all related to one painting, today called the *Garden of Love*, but in Rubens's time known as *Conversation à la mode* (Conversation of Young Women). There is no evidence of such careful preparation by Rubens since his studies for the *Raising of the Cross* of 1610–11.[105] The painting is something of a novelty, because it depicts the old medieval theme of the garden of love—in this case, especially of married love—but the clothes, the hairstyles, and the architecture of the garden pavilion are obviously seventeenth-century. One is inclined to think that Rubens felt the need to make figure studies precisely because he transplanted the scene to "modern times." It is as if Rubens the history painter wanted to get a grip on modern, *à la mode* clothing. The great attention to costume sets these drawings apart from Rubens's earlier drawings, in which the models rendered were almost nude and in which the right posture and the appropriate facial expression were of the essence. The *trois crayons* technique also distinguishes these drawings from the artist's earlier drawings after the model. Although Rubens had been using this technique more often in his later work, he usually reserved the red chalk for flesh parts; in the *Garden of Love* studies he also used it for textiles, as one can see in the dazzling red mantle in *Young Man Descending Stairs* (cat. no. 92). Stylistically, these sheets show a freedom and boldness unparalleled in Rubens's earlier drawings from the model. Although the sheets are more drapery studies than proper studies from the model, the artist did pay attention to the faces, and in the end there is a beautiful equilibrium between the features of the faces and those of the body. The mastery of the three chalks, a facility and daring of line, and a tenderness of human gesture and emotion make the studies for the *Garden of Love* truly magnificent.

While compositional drawings and drawings after the model significantly declined in the 1620s, one category in Rubens's drawn (and painted) oeuvre grew: portraits. During his years in Italy Rubens—young and looking for new clients—had painted several portraits, but once back in Antwerp he engaged less often in portraiture, which in the general hierarchy of painting was the lowest of the pictorial genres. From the 1620s, however, a steady stream of portraits left the artist's studio. Rubens at that time was an internationally acclaimed painter, and from 1621 he was also a highly esteemed diplomat, who had the run of the courts in London, Paris, and Madrid. Princes were eager to have their portraits painted by Rubens, and of course the diplomat could not refuse. The artist portrayed almost all the rulers of the aforementioned courts, including many members of their immediate family and people in their entourage (see cat. nos. 76–80). At more or less the same time, Rubens started on a sequence of portraits of his own family (see cat. nos. 81–86, 88).

The surviving drawings for Rubens's early portraits executed in Italy, as noted above (see the discussion under "Drawings for Portraits"), display an array of different techniques in a variety of media. Since from the 1620s on Rubens drew portraits mainly in chalk, a comparison of one of his early portrayals in chalk with a later portrait drawing may help us discern something of the artist's development in this genre. Juxtaposing the *Portrait of Ferdinando Gonzaga* of 1601–2 (fig. 17) with *Nicolaas Rubens Wearing a Red Felt Cap* of 1625–27 (cat. no. 85), one does not need to be a connoisseur to see how dramatically the artist's style changed, from careful and precise—many lines are repeated several times in the Gonzaga portrait—to confident and loose. The handling of the light, and consequently the depth, is definitely more convincing in the later drawing. Even the mise-en-page of

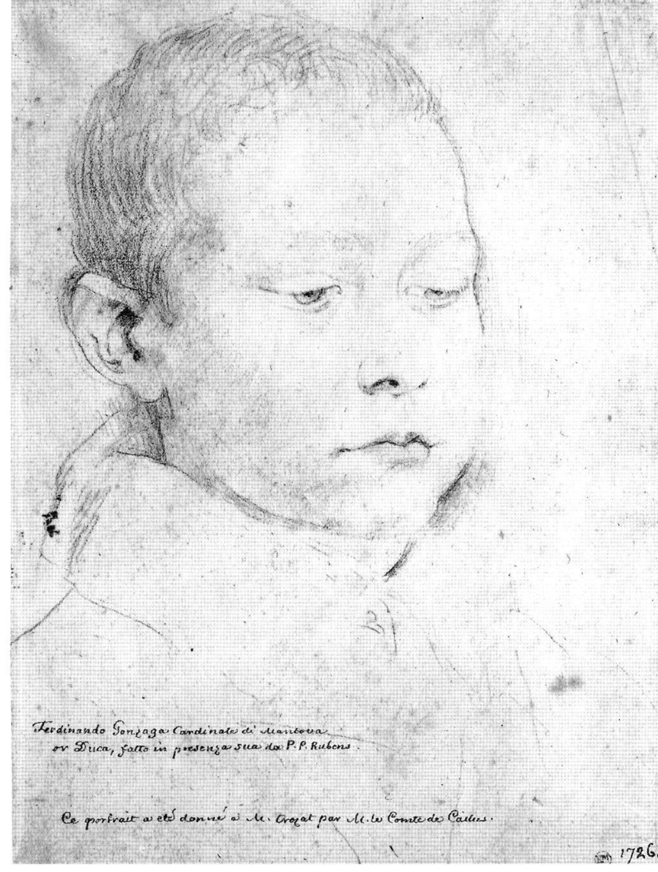

Fig. 17. Peter Paul Rubens, *Portrait of Ferdinando Gonzaga*, 1601–2. Black and red chalk, 224 x 160 mm (8 13/16 x 6 5/16 in.). Nationalmuseum, Stockholm (1917/1863)

Nicolaas's portrait seems more daring than that of Ferdinando's. One has to keep in mind, of course, that portraying one's own child is rather different from portraying a prince and the son of one's employer, which Ferdinando's father, the Duke of Mantua, was to Rubens in Italy. And it must be admitted that another drawing from the mid-1620s, for a more official portrait, *George Villiers, 1st Duke of Buckingham* (cat. no. 77), is not as loosely drawn as the portrait of Nicolaas; still, it betrays the same accurate and confident way of drawing, lack of pentimenti, and attention to the play of light on the face. Furthermore, one detects an attempt at subtle psychological insight into the sitter. If Ferdinando is purely a physical presence, Nicolaas and Buckingham are persons with at least a hint of character—pouting lips for the boy and an assured attitude for the English nobleman.

It is in the compositional drawings, drawings from the model, and drawings for portraits that one can follow Rubens's stylistic development, because the artist continued to make these types of drawings throughout his career. Other drawing activities (retouching old master drawings, or overseeing the making of preparatory drawings for reproductive prints and correcting them) and types of drawings (landscapes, designs for book illustrations and title pages) at which Rubens excelled are less suitable for observing changes over time, because there may be too few works in a particular genre, because Rubens's contributions are not always entirely clear, or because he made the sheets within a relatively short period of time.

Recent Developments in the Connoisseurship of Rubens's Drawings

Julius Held published his two-volume *Rubens: Selected Drawings* in 1959, and a revised, enlarged edition in 1986. To a large extent it remains the standard work today. The brilliant introduction is still the best way to get acquainted with the master's drawings. Held's dating of the works, moreover, has proved to be correct time and again. Nonetheless, differences of opinion have inevitably arisen here and there, discoveries have been made, drawings have entered the public domain and at last can be properly examined, and certain drawings have been studied in more depth. These additions to and modifications of the existing scholarship have changed (and are still changing) our idea of Rubens as a draftsman. Without aiming to be exhaustive, we will address the more important findings and suggestions concerning Rubens's drawn oeuvre that have occurred during the last two decades.

One of the most exciting events for Rubens scholars was the appearance on the art market in 1987 of eleven previously unknown anatomical drawings by Rubens; a twelfth study came to light in 1999.[106] Thanks to the *cantoor* copies by Rubens's pupil Willem Panneels, today in Copenhagen, we had been aware that Rubens kept a book of anatomical drawings; the "new" drawings confirmed the existence of his *Anatomy Book* and were in turn anchored in his oeuvre by the Copenhagen copies. The sheets are now scattered among various collections; some show complete male figures, singly or in small groups, while others are studies of arms and hands in often rather awkward arrangements (see cat. no. 16). The media—primarily pen and brown ink, but also black and red chalk—and technique recall those of Rubens's early drawings from his middle to later years in Italy, between about 1602 and 1608, making it likely that they originated during that time. In this respect, the newly found sheets confirm our picture of Rubens in Italy as a young artist who took his profession very seriously, dedicating himself to mastering proper figure drawing not only by copying Renaissance prototypes and classical sculptures but also by studying anatomy.

In 1999 the city of Antwerp purchased, on behalf of the Museum Plantin-Moretus and the Stedelijk Prentenkabinet, a small book with Rubens's earliest extant drawings, his copies after the *Dance of Death* woodcuts designed by Hans Holbein the Younger.[107] With this acquisition a part of Rubens's drawn oeuvre was retrieved for the city where the artist spent most of his life (Rubens as a draftsman is not well represented in Belgian collections, as most of his drawings left the country early on). This interesting group of early drawings is now accessible publicly for the first time since its discovery in 1972. In 2000 they were the focus of an exhibition at the Rubenshuis. An excellent essay by Michael Kwakkelstein in the accompanying catalogue examines the role of copying prints in the training of artists during the Renaissance.[108] Rubens's early training clearly followed established tradition.

Three heretofore unknown drawings by Rubens after two famous antique sculptures, one drawing of the *Laocoön* and two of the *Centaur Tormented by Cupid* (see cat. no. 20), were discovered in the Wallraf-Richartz-Museum, Cologne, in 2000. All three are on large sheets of paper, drawn in black chalk only. In 2001 Uwe Westfehling, head of the Graphische Sammlung of the Cologne museum, published them, correctly, as works by Rubens.[109] In execution the drawings are very close to the well-known group of Rubens's copies after antique statuary in the Ambrosiana, Milan, among which is another depiction of the *Laocoön*.[110] Moreover, both drawings of the *Centaur Tormented by Cupid* correspond exactly to copies by Panneels in the Copenhagen *cantoor.* Together with a previously known drawing in Moscow with another view of the *Centaur* from the right (cat. no. 21), the two sheets support the often-stated claim that, when possible, Rubens preferred to make several drawings, from different angles, of a single sculpture.

Yet another Rubens drawing after an antique sculpture, a copy after the *Belvedere Torso,* was discovered on the verso of the *Virgin and Child Adored by Saints* (cat. no. 34) in The Metropolitan Museum of Art, New York, when the Museum acquired the sheet in 2002. In execution the drawing resembles the anatomical study in red chalk of a *Nude Male Figure Reaching up to the Right* (private collection).[111] The drawing is the only one known by Rubens showing the *Belvedere Torso* from the back (Rubens drew the sculpture at least once from the front).[112] It offers additional evidence that Rubens was in the practice of making multiple drawings of the sculptures he copied. Of great interest is that in this drawing Rubens completed the *Torso* by adding a head with curly hair—to date, the most illuminating example of how Rubens went about "breathing life," as he put it, into marble sculpture (see the discussion above under "Rubens's Copies"). His use of red chalk—a rather unusual medium for the artist when copying sculpture—may have been prompted by his urge to give the *Torso* a more lifelike appearance.

Rubens's oeuvre lost four drawings after the antique when Arnout Balis reattributed them to Anthony van Dyck in 2001.[113] Except for the *Portrait Statue as Ceres* (British Museum, London), which had been doubted earlier,[114] the others—the *Roman Couple in the Guise of Venus and Mars* (State Hermitage Museum, Saint Petersburg), the *Togatus with Portrait Head of Nero* (Institut Néerlandais, Paris), and the *Greek Philosopher*, also called the *Arundel Homer* (Kupferstichkabinett, Berlin)—had been published as recently as 1994 as Rubens originals.[115] While we do not entirely agree with the attribution of all four drawings to Van Dyck, we support their removal from Rubens's oeuvre. If we compare them to drawings after the antique that we consider securely attributed to Rubens, we see that the artist (or artists) drew the antique works in a detached way, making no effort to "breathe life" into them, as Rubens required of such drawings. Their removal clarifies our notion of Rubens's approach to copying after antique sculpture.

One of the important recent Rubens rediscoveries is the drawing of a *Man on Horseback* (cat. no. 13), officially presented to the Staatliche Graphische Sammlung, Munich, in 1996. For almost seventy years this drawing was in a private collection and hardly accessible. The last to have properly studied it were the Viennese art historians Gustav Glück and Franz Martin Haberditzl, who included it in their 1928 catalogue of Rubens's drawings. The drawing is rather unusual, as it is drawn on an exceptionally large sheet—it is the largest Rubens drawing known—and in great detail with a fine pen. The drawing was extensively discussed by Thea Vignau-Wilberg in an article in 1998 and in a small book in 1999,[116] and was shown in an exhibition at the Prado, Madrid (2001–2), organized by Alejandro Vergara.[117] At the Prado the Munich drawing was shown next to Rubens's 1603 painting of the *Duke of Lerma on Horseback* (fig. 48) and another, much smaller drawing traditionally attributed to Rubens of a *Man on Horseback* (Louvre, Paris). Ultimately, it became clear that the Paris drawing, which until then had been considered the primary drawing for Rubens's equestrian portrait of Lerma, could not hold its own next to the Munich sheet, which exhibited all the characteristics of an early Rubens work made in preparation of the 1603 painting and not, as had been previously suggested, after the painting. The Munich sheet is now generally regarded as the *modello* that Rubens submitted to his patron the Duke of Lerma for approval. Opinions about the Paris drawing are still mixed; in our opinion, the smaller sheet is a *ricordo,* by someone close to Rubens, of the Lerma portrait prior to its completion (see cat. no. 13).

Two other portrait drawings, both of Genoese noblewomen and supposedly dating from Rubens's years in Italy, need to be mentioned briefly. One, in the Pierpont Morgan Library, New York, is well known; the other one, in a private collection, is unpublished.[118] The New York drawing relates to Rubens's portrait of *Brigida Spinola Doria* (National Gallery of Art, Washington, D.C.), dated 1606; the second example records (rather than prepares) Rubens's portrait of *Giovanna Spinola Pavese (?)*, in a private collection, as well as what is now believed to be a lesser version, in the Muzeul Naţional de Artă al României, Bucharest.[119] Stylistic similarities indicate that the drawings may be by the same artist—not Rubens, but perhaps a compatriot, since the notes concerning color on the New York drawing are in Flemish.[120] In both drawings the entire composition, including the architecture, is depicted, which would be unusual for Rubens. Furthermore, the palazzo in the New York drawing is rendered incompletely and without definition, which gives the work the appearance of a copy. (Parts of the balustrade appear particularly inept.) The fine, fluidly drawn pen lines that one observes in Rubens's *Man on Horseback* drawing (cat. no. 13) are absent, and the washes do not indicate light and shade as they usually do in the master's drawings. It is also strange, for a Rubens drawing, that the annotations in Flemish concerning color are in the building rather than on the garments. It is tempting to attribute the two drawings to Deodaat del Monte (1582–1644), a pupil of Rubens who accompanied the artist to Italy, but he is unknown as a draftsman.[121]

We also question the attribution to Rubens of two other drawings likewise believed to date from the artist's Italian period: *Saint Catherine* (Metropolitan Museum of Art, New York) and *Saints Gregory, Domitilla, Maurus, and Papianus* (Musée Fabre, Montpellier); the latter was already doubted by Hans Vlieghe in 1973 and by David Freedberg in 1978.[122] Both sheets, extensively washed, have been considered preparatory drawings for Rubens's altarpiece of 1606–8 for the church of Santa Maria in Vallicella, Rome. However, their technique and supposed function are fundamentally at odds with the master's drawn oeuvre as it is known today. We believe that when Rubens applies wash to a drawing it is always in direct interaction with the pen. Wash and pen are used to enhance the outlines of limbs and garments, thus creating solid figures and eventually introducing depth to a composition. In the *Saint Catherine* drawing in New York, however, there are very few pen strokes, and these are added at will and in a rather haphazard fashion. The Montpellier sheet may contain more pen work, but it is still basically a wash drawing and highly finished. It is more reminiscent of a record of an artwork than of a drawing in preparation for one.

Four of the above-mentioned drawings, the Louvre *Man on Horseback*, the Morgan Library *Portrait of a Lady, Saint Catherine,* and *Saints Gregory, Domitilla, Maurus, and Papianus*, figured prominently in Held's two editions of *Rubens: Selected Drawings*. It is therefore not surprising that their removal from Rubens's oeuvre has repercussions for our notion of Rubens's development during his stay in Italy between 1600 and 1608. The full-length *Portrait of a Lady* and *Man on Horseback* are now being "replaced," so to speak, by one highly finished and very refined drawing for a portrait, the *Man on Horseback* in Munich (cat. no. 13). The removal from Rubens's graphic oeuvre of the two wash drawings of *Saint Catherine* and *Saints Gregory, Domitilla, Maurus, and Papianus* leaves the more traditional sheets made in preparation for the altarpiece, like those in the British Museum, London; in the Musée Condé, Chantilly; and in the Albertina, Vienna (cat. no. 18).[123] It seems, as a result of this rather drastic diminishment, that in his approach to creating a work of art the young Rubens was in some respects more methodical and conventional in style and technique than was previously thought.

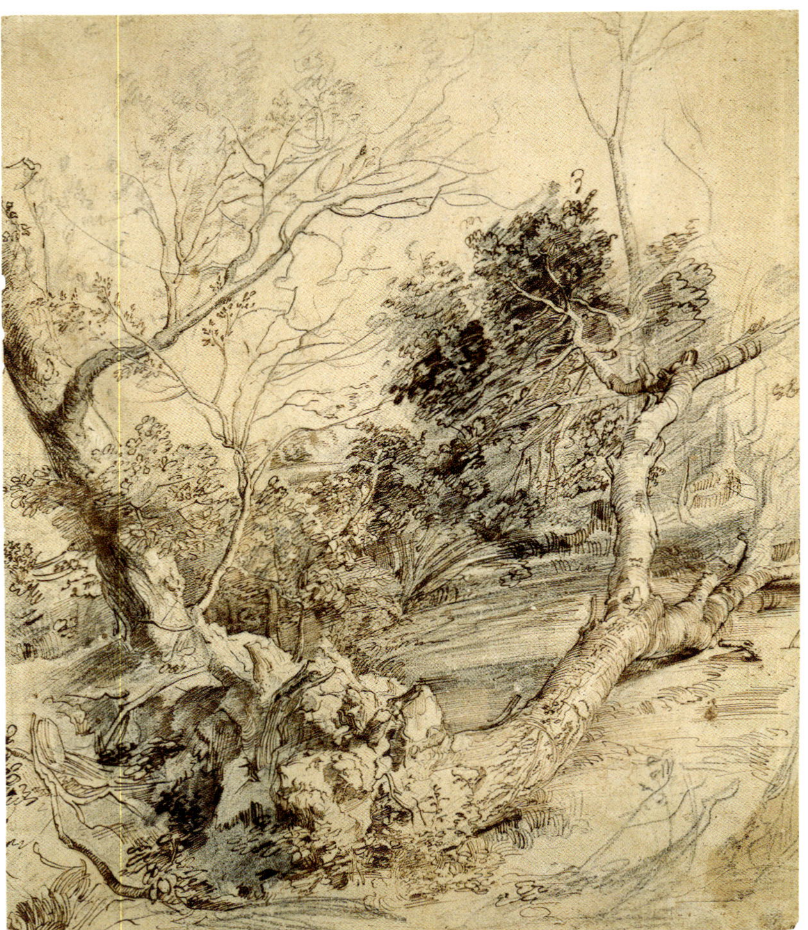

Fig. 18. Peter Paul Rubens (?), *Landscape with Fallen Tree*, ca. 1618. Black chalk and pen and dark brown ink, traces of heightening with white, on pale buff paper, 582 x 489 mm ($22^{15}/_{16}$ x $19^{1}/_{4}$ in.). Département des Arts Graphiques du Musée du Louvre, Paris (20.212)

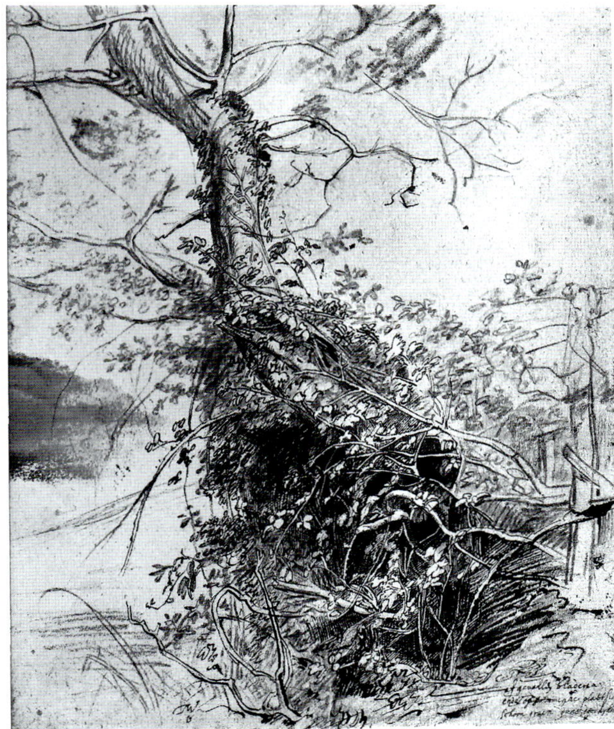

Fig. 19. Peter Paul Rubens (?), *Dying Tree, Covered with Brambles*, ca. 1618. Pen and brown ink over red and black chalk, touched with brown wash and yellow and blue chalk, 352 x 298 mm ($13^{7}/_{8}$ x $11^{3}/_{4}$ in.). The Duke of Devonshire and the Chatsworth Settlement Trustees, Chatsworth (1008)

In our opinion, two drawings from the late 1620s that figure prominently in Held's catalogues require a reassessment as well: *Virgin and Child Adored by Saints* in Stockholm (fig. 80) and *Studies for Saint George and the Princess* in Berlin.[124] Both sheets were considered preparatory for paintings now in Antwerp (fig. 77) and London, respectively, but both are executed in a technique that is unusual for Rubens in drawings of this kind: an extensive underdrawing in black chalk, gone over with pen and brush and finished with a layer of wash in different shades of brown, results in (especially in the Stockholm sheet) a muddy, hard-to-read drawing without depth. (Already in 1959 Held considered the layer of wash in the Stockholm drawing "somewhat disturbing" and suggested that it "might have been added by a later hand.")[125] Rubens's preliminary drawings for compositions were usually done with the pen only, sometimes enhanced with wash. The recently discovered *Virgin and Child Adored by Saints* in New York (cat. no. 34 recto), also for the painting in Antwerp, is a prime example. The New York drawing is

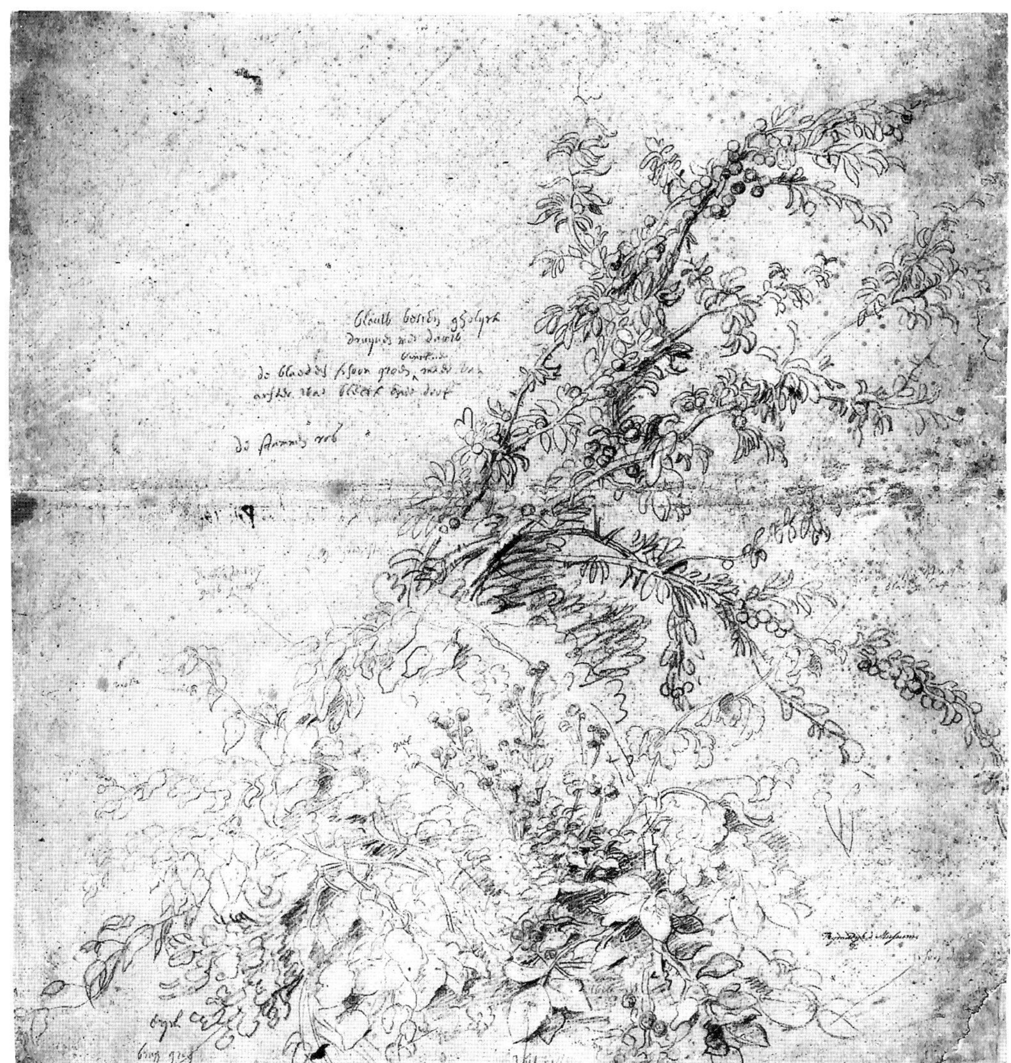

Fig. 20. Peter Paul Rubens, *Study of Blackthorn with Bramble and Other Plants*, ca. 1620. Black, white, and red chalk, and yellow watercolor on brown paper, 495 x 545 mm (19½ x 21⁷⁄₁₆ in.). The Samuel Courtauld Trust, Courtauld Institute of Art Gallery, London (D.1978.PG.63)

completely different from the Stockholm and Berlin sheets: it has some areas that are difficult to read, but generally it is clean, and the forms are solid and well defined. In addition, on the verso of the Stockholm drawing we find individual studies, all in a different technique, something that is not found, so far as can be established, in Rubens's extant graphic oeuvre. These unusual features seem to support removing the Stockholm and Berlin drawings from the artist's oeuvre. In all likelihood, the Stockholm *Virgin and Child Adored by Saints* was drawn by an assistant who had access to an earlier stage of Rubens's preliminary work for the Antwerp altar. Our inability to suggest an artist as author of the drawings in Stockholm and Berlin underscores how relatively little we still know about the draftsmanship of some of Rubens's close associates.

The most startling recent development in the connoisseurship of Rubens's drawings came in 1999, when Martin Royalton-Kisch organized an exhibition at the Rubenshuis, Antwerp, and the British Museum, London, of landscape drawings and watercolors by Anthony van Dyck. Kisch included in his show three much admired landscape drawings that for more than a century had unanimously been thought to be by Rubens—and attributed them to the young Van Dyck. He dated them about 1618–20, when Van Dyck worked in Rubens's studio. The drawings are the *Landscape with Fallen Tree* (fig. 18), the *Dying Tree, Covered with Brambles* (fig. 19), and the *Fallen Tree Lying by a Pool* at Chatsworth.[126] The key reason for Kisch's assigning these drawings to Van Dyck is the inscription on the *Dying Tree,*

Covered with Brambles, which in Kisch's opinion is by Van Dyck.[127] The inscription reads: "afgevallen bladeren / ende op sommighe plaetsen / schoon gruen gras doorkyken" (fallen leaves and in some places fresh green grass peep through).

In our opinion, Kisch's argument that the inscription is by Van Dyck and thus the drawing is most likely by him as well is not that solid. Although it bears a certain resemblance to Van Dyck's, the handwriting has a rather general character. Furthermore, the observations are similar to those we know from other landscape drawings by Rubens, such as *Study of Blackthorn with Bramble and Other Plants* (fig. 20) and *Trees Reflected in Water at Sunset* (cat. no. 104). Rubens wrote his comments in his Flemish script, which is difficult to decipher, and one might therefore ask whether such an inscription was originally found on the *Dying Tree, Covered with Brambles* as well but then transcribed in a humanist handwriting (possibly by Van Dyck) to make it more intelligible. One should also remember that in the seventeenth and eighteenth centuries annotations of all sorts were added to drawings. *Dying Tree Covered with Brambles* itself includes, along the right edge of the recto, another annotation in pen and brown ink in a different (unfortunately, illegible) seventeenth-century hand, which has not been discussed in the literature on the drawing. A translation into English of Rubens's Flemish inscription was added by another hand to *Trees Reflected in Water at Sunset* (cat. no. 104).

The stylistic comparison that Kisch makes between *Landscape with Fallen Tree* (fig. 18) and Van Dyck's elaborate study of the *Taking of Christ* in Hamburg[128] is a stronger argument for reattributing the three landscape drawings to Van Dyck. The angular and hurried underdrawing in black chalk and the strong diagonal slant created in the more distant foliage in the *Landscape* drawing indeed call to mind the sheet in Hamburg. However, the elaborate technique of the Hamburg drawing is also exceptional for Van Dyck, and one could argue that the *Landscape* inspired the young assistant to make the drawing now in Hamburg, especially since one does find in other Rubens drawings a similar use of black chalk, for example, in *A Man Threshing beside a Wagon, Farm Buildings Behind* (cat. no. 98), also from about 1618, and *Saint Gregory Nazianzenus* (Fogg Art Museum, Cambridge), from 1620.[129]

Two of the three nature studies Kisch attributed to Van Dyck are closely related to paintings by Rubens. The *Landscape with Fallen Tree* reappears in the *Landscape with a Boar Hunt* in Dresden, generally dated 1616–18, while the *Fallen Tree Lying by a Pool* is repeated in *Ulysses and Nausicaa* (Palazzo Pitti, Florence), painted in the first half of the 1630s.[130] According to Kisch, the Dresden painting, in which the fallen tree is the focal point around which the boar hunt progresses, is largely by Van Dyck.[131] Van Dyck was indeed indispensable to Rubens in the late 1610s, but did the pupil compose the master's paintings as well? It is perhaps not impossible, but it would be the only known example. Would Rubens have sold the painting in 1627 to as important a collector as George Villiers, 1st Duke of Buckingham, if Van Dyck had been the primary author? Kisch speculates that Rubens was able to use *Fallen Tree Lying by a Pool* for a painting dating from 1630–35—some fifteen years after the drawing was made—because the study was retained in his studio or because he had made a drawing of the same motif himself. Again, this may be possible, but it seems a bit of a stretch.

If Kisch is correct, the oeuvre of Van Dyck, who despite all the recent attention never was a true landscapist, would be enriched by a stunning group of three landscape drawings—two of them of a very large size, which is rather unusual for Van Dyck—that show a beauty and an eye for (literally low-to-the-ground) details that were not repeated in later works, at least not with such grandeur. Conversely, in the oeuvre of Rubens, who was a great landscapist with about forty painted landscapes, the three drawings fit easily with nature studies such as the very large sheet *Study of Blackthorn with Bramble and Other Plants* (fig. 20), which bears an inscription, definitely added by Rubens in his Flemish script, similar to that on *Dying Tree, Covered with Brambles* (fig. 19).[132] The black-chalk technique and the function of some of the drawings as preparatory studies for paintings make them comparable to Rubens's drawings after the model. The addition to some of pen and brown ink does not really affect the argument. It seems to us better to keep the three drawings under the name of Rubens, though with a question mark. This puzzling matter deserves more discussion. Indeed, as we present this exhibition, twenty-five years after the last major exhibitions of Rubens's drawings took place, it is our hope that new scrutiny of Rubens's drawings and new scholarship will continue to deepen and refine our knowledge of Rubens as a draftsman.

1. Huvenne 1993, pp. 21–24.
2. For Rubens's testament, see Held 1986, p. 16.
3. Konrad Renger in Munich 1990–91, p. 87, doc. 3, and p. 97, doc. 36.
4. Quoted in Carmen C. Bambach, "Introduction to Leonardo and His Drawings," in New York 2003, p. 8.
5. Hans Lützelburger made the woodcuts after Holbein's designs. In 1999 the Museum Plantin-Moretus and Stedelijk Prentenkabinet, Antwerp, acquired the drawings by Rubens after Holbein's *Dance of Death*; they are now bound as a small book, in an eighteenth-century red morocco-leather binding. For Rubens's complete drawings after Holbein, see Antwerp 2000 and Lille 2004, no. 1.
6. See Belkin 2000, p. 96 and fig. 39 (color ill.).
7. Van der Meulen 1994, vol. 2, nos. 76–93, vol. 3, figs. 145–64 *(Laocoön)*; vol. 2, nos. 14–24, vol. 3, figs. 31, 33–52 *(Hercules Farnese)*; vol. 2, no. 71, vol. 3, fig. 136 *(Farnese Bull)*.
8. Ibid., vol. 2, no. 1, vol. 3, fig. 3 *(Apollo Belvedere)*; vol. 2, no. 3, vol. 3, fig. 7 *(Seated Bacchus)*; vol. 2, nos. 25, 26, vol. 3, figs. 53, 55 *(Hermes Belvedere)*; vol. 2, nos. 28, 29, vol. 3, figs. 58, 59, 61 *(Silenus Leaning against a Tree Trunk)*.
9. See Jan Garff and Eva de la Fuente Pedersen in Copenhagen 1988; and Antwerp 1993, with contributions by various authors. For a discussion of the *cantoor* in Rubens's house, see Jeffrey M. Muller and Fiona Healy in Antwerp 2004b, pp. 59–62, 298–309.
10. Rubens met Goltzius only later, in 1612, when Rubens traveled to Haarlem; see Huigen Leeflang in Amsterdam–New York–Toledo 2003–4, p. 21 and p. 310, n. 68.
11. Van der Meulen 1994, vol. 2, no. 77, vol. 3, fig. 150 (Staatliche Kunstsammlungen, Kupferstich-Kabinett, Dresden), vol. 2, no. 81, vol. 3, fig. 153 (Biblioteca Ambrosiana, Milan).
12. In his unpublished Latin treatise *De Imitatione Statuarum* (On the Copying of Sculpture) Rubens wrote: "I am convinced that in order to achieve the highest perfection [in art] one needs a full understanding of the statues, nay a complete absorption in them; but one must make judicious use of them and before all avoid the effect of stone. For many neophytes and even some experts do not distinguish stuff from form, stone from figure, nor the exigencies of the marble from its artistic use. . . .Whoever can make this distinction with wise discretion should indeed welcome the statues in a loving embrace." See Stechow 1968, p. 26, and Van der Meulen 1994, vol. 1, pp. 77–78.
13. See London 1977a, no. 14, ill.; Held 1986, no. 39, pl. 23.
14. See note 12 above.
15. See Helen Braham in London 1988–89, p. 50, under nos. 58, 59. For the provenance and recent discussion of the sketchbook, see notes 63 and 64 below.
16. Bellori 1672 (1968 ed.), p. 301; M. Jaffé 1977, pp. 101–2.
17. Van der Meulen 1994, vol. 2, no. 168a, vol. 3, fig. 322, as Rubens; Lille 2004, no. 41, ill., as Rubens; Nico van Hout in Antwerp 2004c, p. 110, fig. 79, as anonymous, retouched by Rubens.
18. "Si ha da avertire che l'opra riuscerebbe molto diversa da questi scizzi, li quali sono fatti leggierissimamente da primo colpo per dimostrar solo il pensiero, mà poi si farebbono li dissegni come anco la pittura con ogni studio e diligenza." Lugt 1949, no. 1007, pl. XII; Paris 1978, no. 8, ill.; d'Hulst and Vandenven 1989, no. 39, fig. 87.
19. Held 1986, p. 28.
20. See Bauer and Bauer 1999, pp. 520–30. See Vasari 1568 (1906 ed.), vol. 5, p. 528, or vol. 1, pp. 174–77: "gli schizzi . . . chiamiamo noi una prima sorte di disegni che si fanno per trovar il modo delle attitudini, ed il primo componimento dell'opra; e sono fatti in forma di una macchia, ed accennati solamente da noi in una sola bozza del tutto" (Sketches are in artists' language a sort of first drawing made to find out the manner of the pose, and the first composition of the work. They are made in the form of a blotch, and are put down by us only as a rough draft of the whole; English translation from Vasari 1907, p. 212). See also Held 1963a, pp. 86–87.
21. Held 1963a, p. 89, and Held 1986, p. 29.
22. Held 1986, no. 124, pl. 124.
23. J. R. Martin 1968, no. 19a, fig. 108 *(Saint Athanasius)*, no. 25a, fig. 133 *(Saint Gregory Nazianzenus)*. As Held (1986, p. 125, under no. 147) observed, the *Saint Athanasius* drawing is somewhat inferior in quality to the *Saint Gregory* sheet.
24. Held 1986, no. 156, pl. 151.
25. See Bauer and Bauer 1999, pp. 520, 526–29, and Joanna Woodall in London 2003–4a, pp. 9–10.
26. The different approaches in the Protestant Northern Netherlands and the Catholic Southern Netherlands to depicting the female nude are discussed in Volker Manuth, "'As stark naked as one could possibly be painted . . .': The Reputation of the Nude Female Model in the Age of Rembrandt," in Edinburgh–London 2001, pp. 47–53, and in Thøfner 2004, pp. 1–33.
27. "But Sir Peter Rubens told mee that at his being in Italy, divers of his nation had followed this Academicall course for twenty Yearses together to little or noe purpose. Besides these dull, tedious and heavy wayes doe ever presuppose *Animam in digitis* [literally, where the spirit rests in the fingers, i.e., where the skill of their fingers is primary, as in dry, mechanical drawings], a man whose soule hath taken up his Lodging in his fingers ends, and meanes to sacrifice his spirits and time for a Life and a day in this study onely." Norgate 1997, pp. 108, 209–10, n. 307.
28. 's-Hertogenbosch–Rome 1992–93, no. 20, ill. Rubens adapted the seated shepherd in the Fermo *Adoration of the Shepherds* (M. Jaffé 1989, no. 79, 1608) thirty years later in the Torre de la Parada series; see Alpers 1971, no. 40b, fig. 158, and no. 46b, fig. 157.
29. To reach their goal the Carracci established their own academy, the Accademia del Disegno or the Accademia del Naturale, later the Accademia degli Incamminati (see M. Jaffé 1977, pp. 54–56, and Held 1986, p. 66, under no. 7).
30. Annibale Carracci's study *The Giant Cacus* in The Metropolitan Museum of Art, New York (inv. 1972.118.244), was attributed to Rubens until 1956. See Bean 1979, no. 98, ill. Michael Jaffé (1956a, pp. 12–16) reattributed it to Annibale.
31. Rooses 1910, pp. 221–22. See also Arnout Balis, "'Fatto da un mio discepolo': Rubens's Studio Practices Reviewed," in Tokyo 1993, pp. 97–127.
32. See Baudouin 1992, pp. 78–85, figs. 58–60, and Vynckier 1992, pp. 159–61, figs. 135, 141.
33. Magurn 1955, p. 38, letter 12, November (?) 1603, sent by Rubens from Valladolid, Spain, to Annibale Chieppio, Vincenzo Gonzaga's secretary of state, in Mantua.
34. See Hervey 1921, p. 175, and Held 1986, pp. 32–33.
35. For the painting in Munich, see M. Jaffé 1989, no. 652, 1620; Renger and Denk 2002, pp. 272–75, no. 352.
36. Held 1986, no. 145, pl. 144.
37. M. Jaffé 1989, no. 879, 1626–27.
38. Held 1986, no. 200, pl. 191.
39. M. Jaffé 1989, no. 1400, ca. 1639.
40. For Rubens's possible involvement with etching, see Renger 1975, pp. 166–72, and Nico van Hout, "Rubens aquafortiste?" in Antwerp 2004c, pp. 70–75.
41. Judson and Van de Velde 1978, vol. 1, nos. 1–5, figs. 41–46; Van der Meulen 1994, vol. 1, pp. 97–113, text ills. 51, 54, 57, 59, 61.
42. In addition, Rubens designed thirteen title pages for books on politics and history, nine for books about archaeology and philology, and five for volumes of poetry and emblems. He designed only one title page for a scientific publication. See Held 1986, p. 37.
43. See Judson and Van de Velde 1978, vol. 1, pp. 43, 50.
44. For Moretus's letter to Cordier, see Judson and Van de Velde 1978, vol. 1, p. 27, vol. 2, p. 385, and Deborah-Irene Coy and Julius S. Held in Williamstown 1977, p. 34, no. 19. Moretus's aim was apparently to politely decline the commission, for Rubens could work much faster if need be. For example, on June 8, 1634, Moretus reported to Benedict van Haeften that he would ask Rubens to prepare a design for Van Haeften's *Regia Via Crucis* "with haste"; Rubens had it ready on August 16. See Held in Williamstown 1977, pp. 38–39, nos. 26–28.
45. For Rubens's payments, see Judson and Van de Velde 1978, vol. 1, p. 27. For Rubens's library, his interest in books, and his acceptance of books in exchange for his designs, see Antwerp 2004a.
46. Proof impressions of the title page and five illustrations for the *Breviarium Romanum* with Rubens's retouches are preserved in the Bibliothèque Nationale, Paris; Judson and Van de Velde 1978, vol. 2, figs. 82, 84, 91, 93, 96.

47. Magurn 1955, p. 400, letter 237, August 16, 1635.
48. Bellori 1672 (1976 ed.), pp. 13–14.
49. Carl Depauw in Antwerp–Amsterdam 1999–2000, nos. 1–3.
50. Broos 1989, pp. 34–55; Monbeig Goguel 1988, pp. 821–35.
51. In the late-seventeenth and early-eighteenth centuries—during the height of classicism—Rubens's retouched Italian drawings may have been admired even more than his own drawings. See the essay by Michiel C. Plomp in this publication.
52. Jeremy Wood in Edinburgh–Nottingham 2002. See also Wood 1994.
53. Hind 1923, no. 32, pl. V; London 1977a, no. 49, ill.; Antwerp 2004b, no. 88, color ill.
54. Piles 1677, p. 218. See also Held 1986, p. 48.
55. Held 1986, no. 22, pl. 22.
56. A. W. F. M. Meij, with Maartje de Haan, in Rotterdam 2001, no. 21, ill.
57. Jeremy Wood suggested that Rubens added the wash in the early 1630s (see Edinburgh–Nottingham 2002, no. 12).
58. For the *Fight for the Standard,* see Anne-Marie Logan in New York 2003, no. 135, ill.
59. Vasari's description of Leonardo's *Battle of Anghiari,* in which the crossed swords are mentioned, may have inspired Rubens. See Joannides 1988, p. 80.
60. Anne-Marie Logan in New York 2003, no. 135. Earlier, Karl Suter (1937, pp. 83–85, 1615) and Julius Held (1986, no. 49, ca. 1612–15) also suggested a later date.
61. Held 1986, p. 27.
62. For Quellinus's inventory, which was begun at his death on November 7, 1678, and continued in March 1679, see Duverger 1984–, vol. 10, p. 369: "Een teeckenboeck van Rubbens [drawing book of Rubens] / Een cleyn teeckenboecken van 71 bladeren met root crijt [a small drawing book of 71 pages, in red chalk (also by Rubens?)] / Noch een cleyn boecken van Rubbens met Architectuer" [another small book of Rubens, with architecture].
63. At the time of the fire, the *Pocket Book* was in the possession of André-Charles Boulle (1642–1732), cabinetmaker to the French court. Rubens's first son, Albert, did not inherit it after Rubens's death in 1640, as had been thought until recently. Rather, Rubens appears to have presented the book to the canon Antoon Tassis (d. May 11, 1651). It is likely that de Piles acquired the book through the Flemish art dealer Matthijs Musson, who was involved in the dispersal of the canon's estate. This probably happened in 1676, the year de Piles initiated his correspondence with Rubens's nephew, Philip. De Piles must have owned the *Pocket Book* by 1699, when he quoted from it in his *Abrégé de la vie des peintres.* See Balis 2001, pp. 11–40 (pp. 15–16 for the provenance).
64. For a recent discussion of the *Pocket Book,* see Balis 2001. (Balis is preparing the *Pocket Book* for publication in the Corpus Rubenianum Ludwig Burchard series.) For a concordance of the various manuscripts with passages copied from the *Pocket Book,* see Laneyrie-Dagen 2003, app. 1, pp. 162–95.
65. "Vn libro di sua mano, in cui si contengono osseruationi di ottica, simmetria, proportioni, anatomia, architettura, & vna ricerca de' principali affetti, ed attioni cauati da descrittioni di Poeti, con le dimostrationi de' pittori. Vi sono battaglie, naufragi, giuochi, amori, & altri passioni e auuenimenti, trascritti alcuni versi di Virgilio, e d'altri, con rincontri principalmente di Rafaelle, e dell'antico." See Bellori 1672 (1968 ed.), pp. 300–301.
66. Held 1986, p. 66, under no. 7.
67. Held (ibid., p. 67, under no. 7) supposed that Rubens began the *Pocket Book* before leaving for Italy in 1600.
68. Sale cat., London, Christie's, July 6, 1987, lots 57–67, ills. (introductory text by Michael Jaffé). See also note 106 below.
69. Piles 1699, pp. 166–68.
70. The sale catalogue of the library of Albert Rubens, who had inherited his father's books, listed Vesalius's *Opera Anatomica* (Basel, 1555). See Arents 2001, p. 345.
71. Copenhagen 1988, nos. 84, 107, 162, 216, pls. 86, 109, 164, 218.
72. The *Costume Book* is published in Belkin 1980.
73. For the *Mémoriaux,* see Comblen-Sonkes and Van den Bergen-Pantens 1977.
74. Held 1951, pp. 286–91.
75. Belkin (in Antwerp 2000, p. 102) dates the *Costume Book* ca. 1610–13.
76. Rott 2002, p. 18. See also L. Bauer 1992, pp. 224–43.
77. Arents 2001, nos. 29, 30, 35.
78. For the two drawings in the Pierpont Morgan Library, see Held 1986, nos. 125, 126, pls. 106, 107, and Stampfle 1991, nos. 308, 309, ill. For the drawing in the British Museum, see Held 1986, no. 127, pl. 125, ca. 1617–20.
79. Erwin Mitsch in Vienna 1977b, nos. 32, 34, ill.
80. For the tradition of copying prints, see Kwakkelstein 2000, pp. 35–62.
81. For his well-known drawing after Stradanus, showing two tuba players, Rubens used two different prints by Adriaen Collaert (1560–1618) after compositions by Stradanus. This drawing, now in the Museum Boijmans Van Beuningen, Rotterdam (Rotterdam 2001, no. 3, ill.), is the only sheet that can be related to an early painting by Rubens (and Jan Brueghel the Elder), the *Battle of the Amazons* in Schloss Sanssouci, Potsdam (see M. Jaffé 1989, no. 7, ca. 1598).
82. The *Portrait of Archduke Albert of Austria as a Cardinal* in the Albertina, Vienna, was for a long time considered to be a possible collaboration between Van Veen and the young Rubens. The latter was supposed to have drawn the border (see Vienna 1977b, no. 1, ill.). We agree with Held (1980, p. 527, n. 7), who attributed the entire sheet to Van Veen.
83. For instance, Van Veen's designs for illustrations to the *Quinti Horatii Flacci Emblemata* in the Pierpont Morgan Library, New York, clearly show pen-and-brown-ink outlines and hatchings (see Stampfle 1991, nos. 113–215, ill.).
84. The idea that Rubens may have been influenced by Van Veen to make oil sketches is Held's (1980, p. 8). For oil sketches by Van Veen, see Foucart 1985, p. 101; Starcky 1988, nos. 181–90, ill.; Stampfle 1991, nos. 113–215, ill. pp. 65–99; and sale cat., London, Christie's, July 6, 2004, nos. 161, 162 (colored oil sketches).
85. For Van Veen's grisailles with underlying scribbles, see Lassalle 1972, pp. 280–81 (Rouen), and sale cat., Paris, Tajan and Hôtel Drouot, July 4, 2002, lots 26–29, 32, ill. Several of these grisailles bear Latin inscriptions, in pen and brown ink.
86. This possibility is suggested in Kwakkelstein 2000, p. 37 (with bibl.).
87. Belkin 2000, pp. 98, 105–6.
88. Held 1986, no. 12, pl. 13; Luijten in New York–Fort Worth–Cleveland 1990–91, no. 43, ill.; Rotterdam 2001, no. 8, ill.
89. Lugt 1949, no. 1065, pl. XLIII; Edinburgh–Nottingham 2002, no. 46, color ill. p. 26.
90. London 2003–4a, pl. 8.
91. Edinburgh–Nottingham 2002, p. 67, under no. 46.
92. For Rubens's copies after Michelangelo's prophets and sibyls from the Sistine Chapel ceiling, see Lugt 1949, nos. 1040–47, pls. XXXVI–XXXIX; Paris 1978, nos. 83–90, ills.; Edinburgh–Nottingham 2002, nos. 9, 10, ill.
93. Edinburgh–Nottingham 2002, p. 26.
94. Jeremy Wood (in ibid., 2002, no. 12) also dates Rubens's *Nude Youth Turning to the Right* to 1606, although he suggests that the artist added the red wash in the early 1630s. Held (1986, no. 22), however, dates the sheet 1601–5.
95. For the drawing in Rome, see note 28 above.
96. Edinburgh–Nottingham 2002, p. 19.
97. For the *Study of a Nude Man,* Ashmolean Museum, Oxford, see Held 1986, p. 91, under no. 55; Judson 2000, no. 20h, fig. 72; Rotterdam 2001, p. 108, under no. 18, fig. 1.
98. The practice of preparing paintings with painted sketches in oil probably developed largely in Italy. Rubens's teacher Van Veen was in all likelihood one of the first Northern artists who made many oil sketches and grisailles (see Held 1980, pp. 7–8; for Van Veen's oil sketches, see notes 83–85 above).
99. For the compositional drawings for the Medici cycle, see Held 1986, nos. 158, 159, 160, pls. 157–59; for the oil sketches, see Held 1980, nos. 52–79, pls. 53–81, colorpl. 10.
100. Held 1986, no. 159, pl. 157.
101. Ibid., no. 99, pl. 100, and Rotterdam 2001, no. 16, ill.
102. Held 1986, no. 184, pl. 179.
103. The dating of the drawing after the model *Study for Mercury Descending* (Victoria and Albert Museum, London) to the early 1620s, to which

Held (1986, no. 157, pl. 153) adhered, is not certain, however. Van Gelder (1978, p. 457) established that a watermark in the London drawing is datable to 1614. He also pointed out that the study was used in Rubens's painting of the *Four Evangelists* (Bildergalerie, Schloss Sanssouci, Potsdam; M. Jaffé 1989, no. 259, ca. 1614).

104. Held 1986, p. 57.
105. It is not known if the *Garden of Love* drawings from the model were preceded by the usual oil sketch. Rubens seems to have made the painting for himself. This circumstance perhaps diminished the need for an oil sketch, since there was no patron to whom he was required to submit it for approval. For more on the creation of the *Garden of Love* painting and its preliminary drawings, see cat. nos. 90–93.
106. Sale cat., London, Christie's, July 6, 1987, lots 57–67 (see also note 68 above). For the twelfth anatomical drawing by Rubens, see sale cat., London, Christie's, July 6, 1999, lot 223 (ex coll. Ludwig Burchard).
107. See note 5 above.
108. Kwakkelstein 2000, pp. 35–62.
109. Westfehling 2001, pp. 200–222.
110. See Van der Meulen 1994, vol. 2, nos. 76, 81, 91–93, vol. 3, figs. 145, 153, 163, 164.
111. Holm Bevers in Berlin and other cities 1999–2000, no. 40, color ill., ca. 1605–10.
112. Rubens's frontal view of the *Torso* is preserved in the Rubenshuis, Antwerp (Van der Meulen 1994, vol. 2, no. 37, vol. 3, fig. 75, and Lille 2004, no. 17, ill.). Two additional views of the *Torso* from the front (probably after a replica or cast rather than the statue) are known in the *cantoor* copies in Copenhagen (Van der Meulen 1994, vol. 2, no. 38, copy 1, 2, vol. 3, figs. 78, 79).
113. Arnout Balis, "Van Dyck's Drawings after the Antique," in Vlieghe 2001, pp. 29–42.
114. Van der Meulen 1994, vol. 2, no. 62, vol. 3, fig. 119, as Rubens (?).
115. Ibid., vol. 2, no. 50, vol. 3, fig. 93 *(Greek Philosopher);* vol. 2, no. 51, vol. 3, fig. 95 *(Togatus);* vol. 2, no. 99, vol. 3, fig. 175 *(Venus and Mars).*
116. Vignau-Wilberg 1998, pp. 275–87; Vignau-Wilberg 1999.
117. For the catalogue of the exhibition, see Madrid 2001–2.
118. For the Morgan Library drawing, in pen and brown ink, see Held 1986, no. 29, pl. 32, and Stampfle 1991, no. 298, ill. The drawing in a private collection is executed in black chalk, pen and brush and brown ink and brown wash; it measures 287 x 180 mm. We thank Nicolas Schwed, Christie's, Paris, for making the drawing available for study.
119. For the Washington painting, see M. Jaffé 1989, no. 56. For the Bucharest painting (oil on canvas, 247 x 147 cm), see Piero Boccardo in Genoa 1997, no. 22, ill. (not in M. Jaffé 1989). Another, closely related, version of the latter painting, also possibly representing Giovanna Spinola Pavese, has become known. However, the sitter is slightly older (Piero Boccardo and Anna Orlando in Genoa 2004, no. 120, ill.).
120. Jeremy Wood informs us that he no longer believes that the New York drawing may be a copy by Van Dyck after the Washington painting. He maintains his doubts about its attribution to Rubens, however (Wood 1980, p. 19, and e-mail of April 2004). Kerry Downes also suggested that the New York drawing might be a copy by Van Dyck, drawn about 1621, after the painting (see Downes 1980, p. 46, pl. 22). Both Wood and Downes objected to the poor rendering of the architecture, and Wood questioned the color notes. Egbert Haverkamp-Begemann, too, questions the attribution of the New York drawing to Rubens (oral communication).
121. Strangely, none of Rubens's preliminary drawings or oil sketches for his Genoese portraits seems to have survived. Even if his Genoese patrons kept them, that does not explain their disappearance. Piero Boccardo, director of the Galleria di Palazzo Rosso in Genoa, has never encountered such works during his extensive explorations of the Genoese archives. Only in the collection of Marcello IV Durazzo (1821–1904), who gave his collection to the city of Genoa in 1848, was there one drawing of a female figure attributed to Rubens; this drawing was stolen before the end of the nineteenth century, however, leaving no trace (Piero Boccardo, letter, April 8, 2004).
122. Held 1986, no. 32, pl. 33 *(Saint Catherine),* and no. 33, pl. 39 *(Saints Gregory, Domitilla, Maurus, and Papianus).* For the disattribution of *Saints Gregory, Domitilla, Maurus, and Papianus,* see Vlieghe 1973, p. 57, under no. 109f; Freedberg 1978, p. 90, n. 19; Logan 1987, p. 69.
123. London 1977a, no. 30a, ill. (*Saints Domitilla, Nereus, and Achilleus,* British Museum); Held 1986, no. 41, pl. 40 (*Saints Gregory, Maurus, and Papianus,* Musée Condé).
124. Held 1986, no. 171, pl. 169 *(Virgin and Child Adored by Saints),* and no. 177, pl. 171 *(Studies for Saint George and the Princess).* For *Saint George,* see also Lille 2004, no. 110.
125. Held 1959, no. 53, and Held 1986, no. 171.
126. *Landscape with Fallen Tree:* Held 1986, no. 115, pl. 113, ca. 1617–19. *Dying Tree, Covered with Brambles:* Held 1986, no. 116, pl. 116, ca. 1618–20; M. Jaffé 2002, vol. 1, no. 1157. *Fallen Tree Lying by a Pool:* Held 1986, no. 117, pl. 117, ca. 1617–19; M. Jaffé 2002, vol. 1, no. 1156.
127. Martin Royalton-Kisch in Antwerp–London 1999a, pp. 13–21, and nos. 1 (with inscription), 2, 3, ill. The attribution of the drawings to Van Dyck is supported by Jaco Rutgers (1999, p. 58). Carl Depauw (in Antwerp–Amsterdam 1999–2000, p. 63, fig. 3) illustrates the Chatsworth *Dying Tree, Covered with Brambles* as a work by Van Dyck, as does Nicolas Barker in the most recent catalogue of works from Chatsworth (Memphis and other cities 2003–5, no. 66, ill., ca. 1615–20. Renger (in Essen 2003, pp. 332, 333, fig. 6) accepts the attribution to Van Dyck of the *Landscape with Fallen Tree.*
128. Kisch in Antwerp–London 1999a, p. 18, fig. 11.
129. Held 1986, no. 147, pl. 146.
130. For the Dresden painting, see Adler 1982, no. 18, fig. 53, and M. Jaffé 1989, no. 401. For the Florence painting, see K.d.K., ed. Oldenbourg 1921, no. 354, 1630–35, and M. Jaffé 1989, no. 1063, 1630–35.
131. Kisch in Antwerp–London 1999a, pp. 13–14.
132. *Willow Tree:* Held 1986, no. 119, pl. 120. *Study of Blackthorn with Bramble and Other Plants:* Adler 1982, no. 71, fig. 157, before 1620; London 1988–89, no. 37, ill. In his inscription on the study Rubens observes that "the leaves [are] bright green shimmering but at the back a bit pale and dull," or "the backs of the leaves [are] lighter."

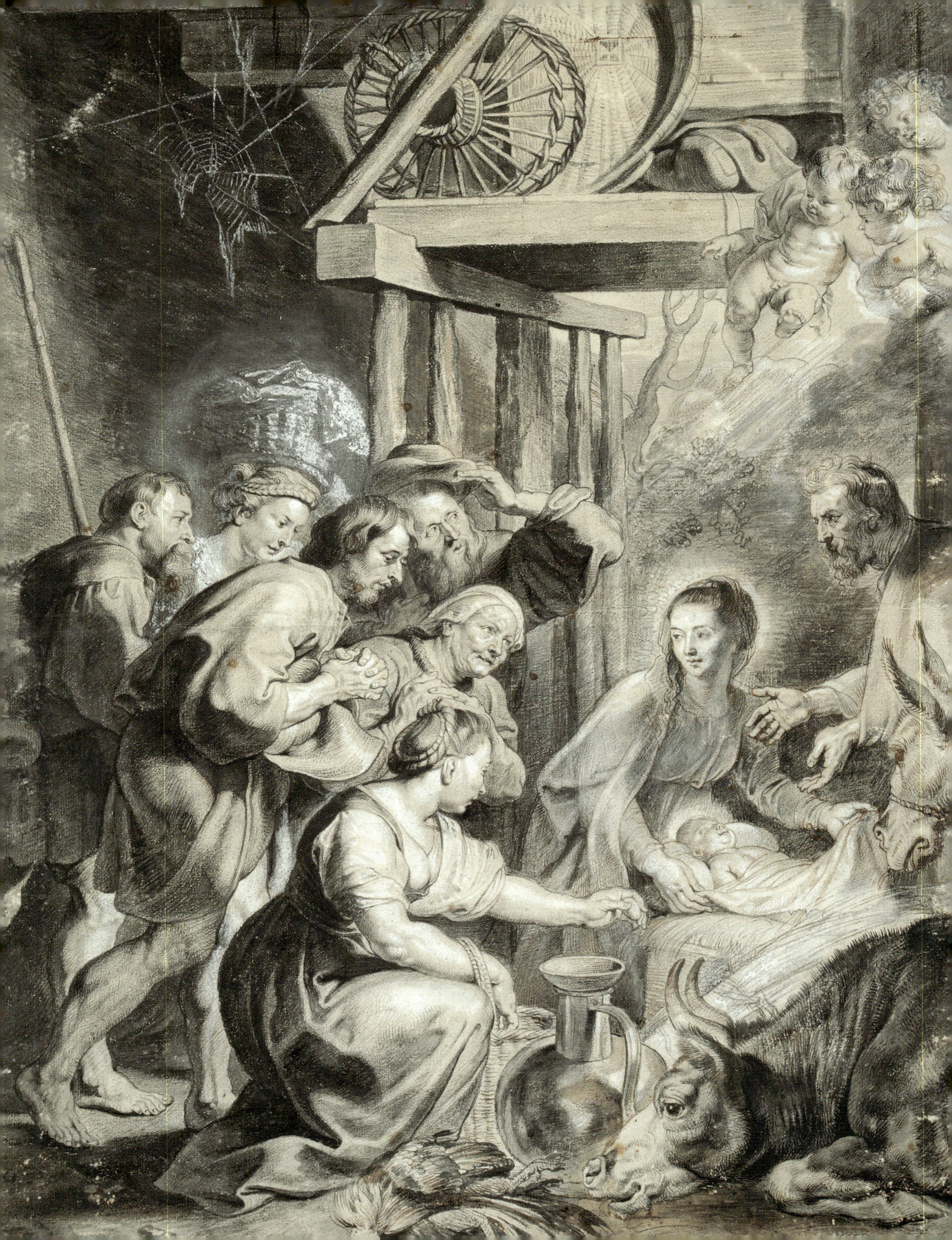

COLLECTING RUBENS'S DRAWINGS

In 1657, seventeen years after Peter Paul Rubens's death, virtually all his drawings were still together, in the possession of the artist's family. In 2005, almost 350 years later, Rubens's drawings are scattered throughout the world. The largest concentrations are to be found in public collections in Vienna, Paris, and London. Other important groups are in museums in Rotterdam, Berlin, Saint Petersburg, New York, and Los Angeles. A part of his studio collection, consisting mainly of drawings by pupils, found a permanent home in Copenhagen. Ironically, Rubens's native soil can't boast of any major holdings of the artist's drawings or those of his pupils. This essay will follow the diaspora of the work of the great Flemish draftsman. It will be a journey through several centuries and various countries, among collectors of all ranks. Above all, it will be an encounter with the history of taste.

The 1657 Auction and Its Aftermath

Rubens was in all likelihood keen to keep his working material, including his drawings, safe together in his studio, invisible to the outside world. It is well known how, rather than surrender the sketches that he used for a certain commission, he painted a second large altarpiece for the patron (such was the choice given to him in the contract).[1] Although the preparatory works in this instance were probably oil sketches, one can assume he acted in the same way to safeguard his drawings. In addition, Rubens amassed a large quantity of other artists' drawings, for immediate study (he reworked many of them; see cat. nos. 114–117), for inspiration, and certainly also for aesthetic pleasure.[2] Most of them were by sixteenth-century Italian masters, like Michelangelo (1475–1564), Raphael (1483–1520), and Giulio Romano (1499?–1546) and their schools, but there were also works by Northern artists, like Hans Holbein the Younger (1497/98–1543), Bernaert van Orley (ca. 1488–1541), and Pieter Coecke van Aelst (1502–1550) and their schools. Among all the art treasures that Rubens brought together in his Antwerp house, his drawings collection, consisting of his own work and that of others, was definitely one of the greatest assets. It should be realized, however, that the collection was simultaneously an often-consulted, indispensable part of the studio.

The importance Rubens attached to his drawings collection becomes clear from the stipulations he laid out in his testament. Although the original document is lost, we are well informed about its provisions:

> *[T]he drawings which he had collected and made he ordered to be held and preserved for the benefit of any of his sons who want to follow him in the art of painting, or, failing such, for the benefit of any of his daughters who might marry a recognized painter; thus they should be kept until the youngest of his children should have reached his eighteenth year. If by that time none of his sons should have followed him in his art and none of his daughters should have married a recognized painter, the drawings should be sold and the receipts divided in the same manner as his other assets.*[3]

Rubens's youngest child, Constantia Albertina, was born on February 3, 1641, so the sale of drawings had to wait until after February 3, 1659, when she turned eighteen. However, Constantia entered a monastery before August 1657, leaving

Fig. 21. After Peter Paul Rubens, likely retouched lightly by Rubens, *The Adoration of the Shepherds,* ca. 1619. Black chalk, brown and black wash, pen and dark brown ink on beige paper, heightened with white body color, outlines traced with the stylus, 563 x 437 mm (22 3/16 x 17 3/16 in.). Département des Arts Graphiques du Musée du Louvre, Paris (20.309)

no reason to delay the auction any longer. (The next-youngest child, Peter Paul, was born in 1637.) As none of Rubens's sons or sons-in-law had followed in his footsteps, the family could sell the collection in the summer of 1657. Unfortunately, no sale catalogue or other documentation of this important event survives. The only certainty is that the drawings sale raised the large sum of 6,557 florins and 16 stuivers.[4]

Before examining the aftermath of the 1657 auction it may be illuminating to put Rubens's drawings collection and sale in a somewhat larger perspective. Rubens's eagerness to keep all his drawings together, as well as the provisions laid out in his testament, fit a long-standing tradition. Drawings—compositional designs, figure studies, landscape sketches, and so on—were usually treasured objects in a studio, as artists continuously went back to them, for inspiration, borrowing, or teaching. Wealthy artists like Rubens often added other people's drawings to their own, creating a veritable artistic gold mine. (Rubens went even further, building a princely collection of paintings and antique sculpture, but that is an issue we will not address here.)[5] It goes without saying that by absorbing the great works of his predecessors or contemporaries the artist learned a great deal. In addition, unlike prints, which were widely circulated, drawings are unique, so if an artist copied certain elements from them in his own work it would not be so easily noticed. For these reasons many artists collected other artists' drawings and, most important, carefully stored their own work. Eventually such a studio collection was conscientiously handed down to the next generation.[6] As Rubens was a prolific draftsman, who in addition was wealthy and widely traveled and had an open mind for art from other countries and other centuries, his collection probably was large and very diverse.

Meanwhile, a passion for drawings slowly but surely emerged among nonprofessionals, the so-called amateurs. This interest probably started in Italy in the sixteenth century, and soon spread north of the Alps. Not surprisingly, Rubens quickly had a role in this new development. For instance, Thomas Howard, 2nd Earl of Arundel (1585–1646), one of the most prominent art collectors of the seventeenth century and one of the first major drawings collectors in England, seems to have engaged Rubens in his hunt for drawings. Arundel asked for the artist's assistance in the acquisition of drawings by Michelangelo (or copies after them).[7] Furthermore, the earl seems to have been interested in sketches by Rubens himself. In 1619 Edward Norgate, one of Arundel's agents, begged for drawings from Rubens, probably on Arundel's behalf: "first and sleight drawings either of landskips or any such kind as might happily be procured for a word, they being things never sold but given to friends that are leibheffers, you know to whom they would be most welcome."[8] Whether Norgate succeeded in acquiring such "first and sleight drawings" by Rubens is unknown, but the attempt is telling.[9]

Another early drawings collector was Antoine Triest, the bishop of Ghent (1576–1657). He seems to have been successful in procuring drawings from Rubens at an early stage. In 1623 this powerful cleric, whose portrait Anthony van Dyck had painted, for whom David Teniers the Younger (1610–1690) worked in the mid-1640s, and who apparently had a large art collection, helped Rubens considerably in the resolution of an impasse concerning the commission of an altarpiece for Ghent cathedral.[10] The sheets we know Triest owned are Italian drawings retouched by Rubens, including works by Giulio Romano, Titian (ca. 1487/90–1576), and Perino del Vaga (1501–1547) or their schools.[11] How the bishop was able to obtain these works and when he acquired them remain unclear. Given Triest's apparently genuine interest in art and his powerful influence on commissions, it is tempting—although pure speculation—to think that Rubens offered him the drawings as a kind of bribe. All that is certain is that Triest, who died on May 28, 1657, was one of the few privileged persons to obtain something from Rubens's collection before it was officially broken up in the summer of 1657.

At the 1657 auction it was Johannes Philippus Happaert (d. 1686), a canon of the Onze-Lieve-Vrouwekerk in Antwerp and also an art dealer, who did a good stroke of business. He is supposed to have spent "6000 florins at the auction of *Rubens's* goods [i.e., Rubens's drawings]."[12] As the sale as a whole raised 6,557 florins and 16 stuivers, this means that the Antwerp canon bought almost the entire collection. The inventory made up after Happaert's death gives an idea of his possessions.[13] Some hundred framed artworks are mentioned. Apart from a drawing each by Raphael and Polidoro, these were all paintings and oil sketches, mostly by Flemish artists, as can be gleaned from the artists' names occasionally given. Rubens's name occurs most often, with 14 entries. Among the hundreds of works the inventory lists in Happaert's drawings and prints collection were drawings by Leonardo (12), Michelangelo (14), Raphael (23), Brueghel (12; by which Brueghel is not always specified), and Abraham van Diepenbeeck (6), as well as two albums with drawings by Maerten de Vos. Again Rubens scores highest, with 92 sheets and an unspecified "little book with some sketches *[crabbelingen]*."[14] As impressive as this amount may seem, it can be only a small portion of the riches Happaert once had, as Rubens's studio collection must have contained hundreds and hundreds of drawings by his own hand. In the course of time the Antwerp canon must have sold most of them.

That Happaert was an important dealer, mainly in prints and drawings, in the 1670s is evident from the diary of Constantijn Huygens the Younger (1628–1697), secretary to Stadholder William III (later king of England). (Happaert probably was already dealing earlier.) In April 1678 Huygens wrote that Happaert "ne voulut jamais me vendre son dessein de trois femmes nues de Rosso ou de Rubens apres luy."[15] In all likelihood he was referring to the drawing *Three Nude Women Holding Garlands* (fig. 12), by an artist from the circle of Francesco Primaticcio (1504/5–1570).[16] The reason that Happaert did not sell the sheet to Huygens is unknown. However, Happaert did sell the sheet sometime in the next decade or so to another major collector of drawings, the Flemish artist Prosper Henry Lankrink (1628?–1692). Lankrink's collector's stamp, PHL, is clearly visible in the lower right hand corner, just to the left of the caryatid on the far right.[17]

Lankrink, who was born in Antwerp and who left for London probably in the mid-1660s, must have been a buyer *en gros* from Happaert. One hundred and twenty drawings by Rubens, or retouched by him, can be traced to Lankrink.[18] Apart from drawings preparatory for prints, virtually every aspect of Rubens's draftsmanship was represented in Lankrink's collection: compositional studies, drawings from the model, portraits, landscapes, copies of other artists' work, and retouched drawings.[19] Not only the quantity but also the high quality is noteworthy. Lankrink owned, for instance, the *Portrait of Isabella Brant* (cat. no. 82), two *ignudi* after Michelangelo (see fig. 11) and *Landscape with Wattle Fence* (all British Museum, London), *Kneeling Male Nude Seen from Behind* (cat. no. 35), and *Young Woman with Crossed Hands* (Museum Boijmans Van Beuningen, Rotterdam). Minor sheets or possible misattributions are relatively rare. Examples of the latter category seem to be *Fall of the Damned* (Collection Frits Lugt, Institut Néerlandais, Paris), which has a caricature-like appearance rather unusual for Rubens, and *Rubens with His Family Walking in a Garden* (fig. 22), which is a copy after the well-known painting now in The Metropolitan Museum of Art, New York.[20] In Lankrink's collection straightforward copies after sixteenth-century Italian drawings, or Italian drawings retouched by Rubens, exceeded the rest by far. This taste for Italian work was in keeping with the general trend in Europe in the middle of the seventeenth century.[21]

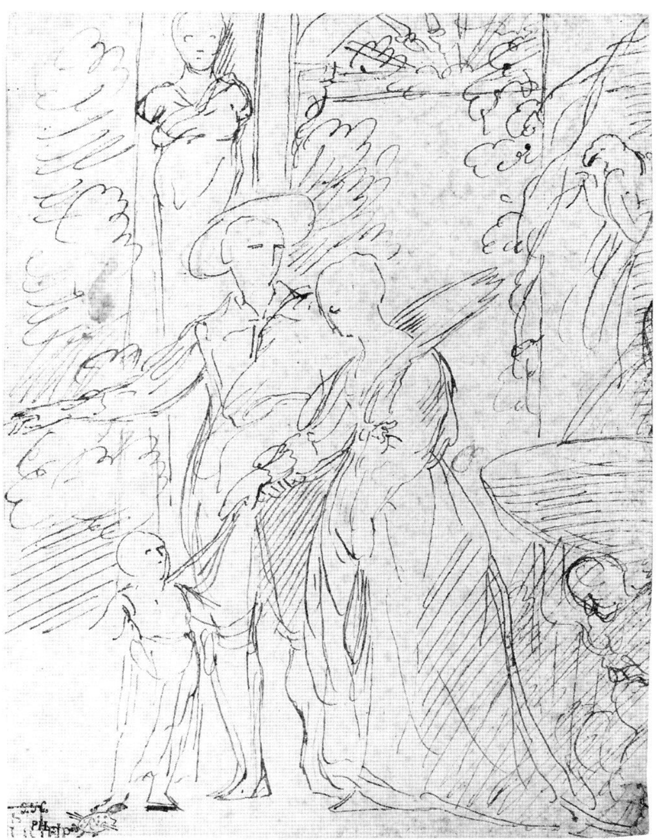

Fig. 22. After Peter Paul Rubens, *Rubens with His Family Walking in a Garden*, ca. 1650. Traces of black chalk, pen and brown ink, 185 x 141 mm (7 5/16 x 5 9/16 in.). Fitzwilliam Museum, Cambridge (PD. 44-1961)

Another prominent collector who seems to have bought drawings by Rubens on a large scale from Happaert was Everhard Jabach (1618–1695), an affluent German-born banker and collector who moved to Paris in 1638. Still in Germany, at the age of nineteen, Jabach had already been in contact with Rubens, commissioning from him an altarpiece in memory of his father for the high altar of Saint Peter's at Cologne. Whether this resulted in any drawings for Jabach is unknown.[22] Altogether Jabach owned probably about eighty drawings that he thought were by Rubens or his immediate circle. Jabach sold a large part of his drawings collection, including forty-nine exceptional Rubens drawings, to Louis XIV in 1671. Most of these drawings ended up in the Louvre, Paris. Since Jabach continued collecting afterward—in 1695 he had twenty-seven Rubens drawings—it is possible that the Parisian banker did not buy the Rubens drawings *en bloc*, but had dealings with Happaert over a longer period of time.[23]

As was fashionable at the time, Jabach was chiefly interested in Italian drawings, but he made exceptions for certain Northerners, like Rubens and Paul Bril (1554–1626). Jabach had a great predilection for highly finished drawings (a penchant we'll see time and again), not for the sketches praised in Arundel's circle. The drawings Jabach valued most, his so-called *dessins d'ordonnance*, were complete compositions; a gold border was added to them and they were pasted in albums. The wealthy collector even hired an artist who "finished" drawings when they were considered incomplete.[24] Sketches, figure studies, or drawings of animals and flowers—what Jabach called the "rubbish" (*le rebut*) of his collection—did not receive such treatment. In view of this preference, it is not surprising that Jabach acquired many preparatory sheets for Rubens's reproductive prints: detailed drawings after his paintings, very often made by Rubens's pupils and usually only retouched by the master (see fig. 21). Jabach owned sixteen of these impressive sheets. Another indication of his love of finished drawings were the carefully drawn copies he had by Rubens after Italian masters (among them a beautiful group after Michelangelo; see cat. no. 3) and the large group of Italian drawings Rubens reworked.[25] The Rubens drawing owned by Jabach that is probably the most esteemed today is the large *Baptism of Christ* (cat. no. 14). Rather surprisingly, at the time this compositional study for Rubens's monumental altarpiece was thought to be by Anthony van Dyck.

Two of Rubens's most talented collaborators, Jan Boeckhorst (ca. 1604–1668) and Erasmus II Quellinus (1607–1678), possessed groups of drawings by Rubens. Whether they were acquired from Happaert is unknown. The older, Boeckhorst, owned a complete series of early Rubens drawings: forty-four scenes copied from Hans Holbein the Younger's *Dance of Death* (Stedelijk Prentenkabinet, Antwerp; see fig. 3).[26] Boeckhorst's extended inventory makes clear that he was a wealthy man, but unfortunately it gives no information on the number or nature of his artworks. (We know that he owned Rubens's series after Holbein from the testimony of the eighteenth-century connoisseur Pierre-Jean Mariette.) As the sale of Boeckhorst's collection in 1668 lasted twelve days and raised the considerable sum of 6,026 guilders, the collection must have been very important, and it probably contained Rubens drawings beyond the copies after Holbein.[27] The inventory of the collection of Quellinus, who was a close friend of Boeckhorst, is more informative. Among many other things, it lists about 170 works by Rubens, including two (perhaps three) complete sketchbooks.[28] It is difficult to properly evaluate the Rubens works in Quellinus's obviously major collection, since media such as painting, oil sketch, or drawing are very often not distinguished. Strangely, an exception seems to have been made for Rubens's "scribbles" *(crabbelingen),* a type of drawing that seems hardly of interest to anybody other than the maker, as they are usually rather sketchy. The notary who described Quellinus's inventory recorded twenty-four of these *crabbelingen* by Rubens (see cat. nos. 30–34). Contemporary artists were probably fascinated by them. The German artist Matthäus Merian the Younger (1621–1668) is also known to have owned quick sketches attributed to Rubens, apparently a small group of half a dozen sheets.[29]

There is one final ensemble of Rubens drawings that seems to have survived the ravages of time intact (although some in the group were apparently separated from the others between their initial sale and today). In the Albertina, Vienna, there are at least twenty drawings that show a special coherence, in terms not only of quality and technique but also of subject matter—they are portraits and drawings from the model—such that one has to conclude that they belong together. In addition, quite a few of them are annotated "P. P. Rubbens" or "Rubbens" in pen and brown ink, in a seventeenth-century hand (or share other seventeenth-century annotations in red chalk; see cat. nos. 11, 58, 59, 77, 78, 81, 83, 84, 86, 87), clear evidence that these drawings were together at an early stage, perhaps since their making. Some of the sheets are portraits of members of the Rubens family, including the artist's sister-in-law Susanna Fourment (cat. no. 83), his son Nicolaas (cat. nos. 81, 85, 86), and, possibly, his daughter Clara Serena (cat. no. 84). Therefore, one wonders—but this is speculation—whether at the 1657 sale these drawings formed one lot that was bought (for the 557 florins not spent by Happaert?) by someone in Rubens's family. Strangely, however, Albert of Sachsen-Teschen (1738–1822), the founder of the Albertina, seems not to have acquired the twenty drawings as one ensemble. The majority of these portraits and model drawings came into his possession in 1796 through an exchange with the imperial Hofbibliothek, in Vienna—a provenance only recently revealed. Among them were portraits of Marie de Médicis, George Villiers, 1st Duke of Buckingham (cat. no. 77), and Don Diego Messía (Mexía), 1st Marquis of Leganés (cat. no. 78), as well as several drawings from the model, such as *Study of Saint Catherine* (cat. no. 58), *Study for the Christ Child* (cat. no. 59), and *Young Man Carrying a Ladder* (cat. no. 66).[30] The *Study of the Christ Child* and *Study of a Young Woman (Helena Fourment [?])* (cat. no. 96) are the only sheets with a Hofbibliothek provenance that might depict members of Rubens's family, which leaves open the possibility that Albert acquired the family portraits as a group sometime during his governorship of the Austrian Netherlands, between 1780 and 1792. The aforementioned seventeenth-century inscriptions are undeniable testimony to the close connection of the family portraits with the Hofbibliothek drawings, but for the time being it remains a mystery how this group of drawings was split up and brought together again.

England

Rather surprisingly, two of the best-known collectors of drawings in seventeenth-century England, Nicholas Lanier (1588–1666), an active agent for the king's painting collection, and Peter Lely (1618–1680), the portraitist, seem to have had little interest in Rubens's drawings. In keeping with the general taste for sixteenth-century Italian drawings, they owned some of his copies after Italian masters and retouched sheets.[31] (Their adherence to fashion makes it all the more apparent how Arundel, a contemporary of Lanier, and Lankrink, at one time an assistant to Lely, broke new ground with their interest in Rubens's own sketches.) Lely made one curious exception, however: his collector's stamp appears on a title-page design by Rubens for a commentary on the Pentateuch (cat. no. 51). This drawing is intriguing, not only because it is a genuine Rubens sheet from Lely's collection, but also because it was at the time the one and only circulating title page design by Rubens. (His numerous title-page designs appeared on the market only in the middle of the eighteenth century; see below.) The English inscription in a seventeenth-century hand makes clear that an English collector, possibly Lely himself, used the sheet as a title page for an album or portfolio of his own. This not very respectful treatment of the drawing is probably typical for the second half of the seventeenth century in England, when a taste for Flemish drawings was only just developing. With regard to Rubens, this attitude would change in the following century.

In the first half of the eighteenth century it was the distinguished writer, connoisseur, and painter Jonathan Richardson Sr. (1665–1745) who had the most extensive collection of Rubens drawings in England. Some 115 sheets by the Flemish draftsman or from his circle carry one of the two collector's marks employed by Richardson. In his collection nearly all genres were represented: loose sketches, figure studies, landscapes, portraits, copies after early Netherlandish masters, Italian masters, and the antique, and retouched drawings. Apart from the thirty small medal drawings (formerly in the Lankrink collection), retouched Italian sheets and sketches were the greatest in number. The former were, as said earlier, highly fashionable, the latter in all likelihood less so. Whether Richardson had a genuine interest in quick sketches is unknown.[32] The portraits in Richardson's collection were nearly all of Rubens's family: his brother-in-law Pieter Hecke; his wives Isabella Brant (cat. no. 82 recto) and Helena Fourment (four portraits); his daughter Isabella Helena; and Rubens himself (fig. 1) were represented; there were three portraits of his son Frans Rubens. Furthermore, Richardson owned Lankrink's *Rubens with His Family Walking in a Garden* (fig. 22).[33] Obviously, these family-related works by Rubens were popular at the time. Some descriptions of the drawings' subjects—as we read them in Richardson's 1747 auction catalogue—seem to have sprung from an all-too-inventive mind. One work, said to show "*Rubens* as a satyr, and his wife," is perhaps to be identified with the drawing *Pan and Syrinx* (British Museum, London), based on a composition by Raphael or his school. It carries Richardson's collection mark in the lower right corner.[34] Whether this is the drawing listed in the catalogue or not, the idea that Rubens could depict himself as a satyr is a sign of how some eighteenth-century English connoisseurs thought of Rubens as a kind of primitive Flemish boor. They would never think or say such a thing about sixteenth-century Italian artists.

Richardson's son, Jonathan Richardson Jr. (1694–1771), who, unlike his father, traveled through Europe on several occasions, and who collaborated on his father's writing, was also an eminent collector, although on a smaller scale. Only

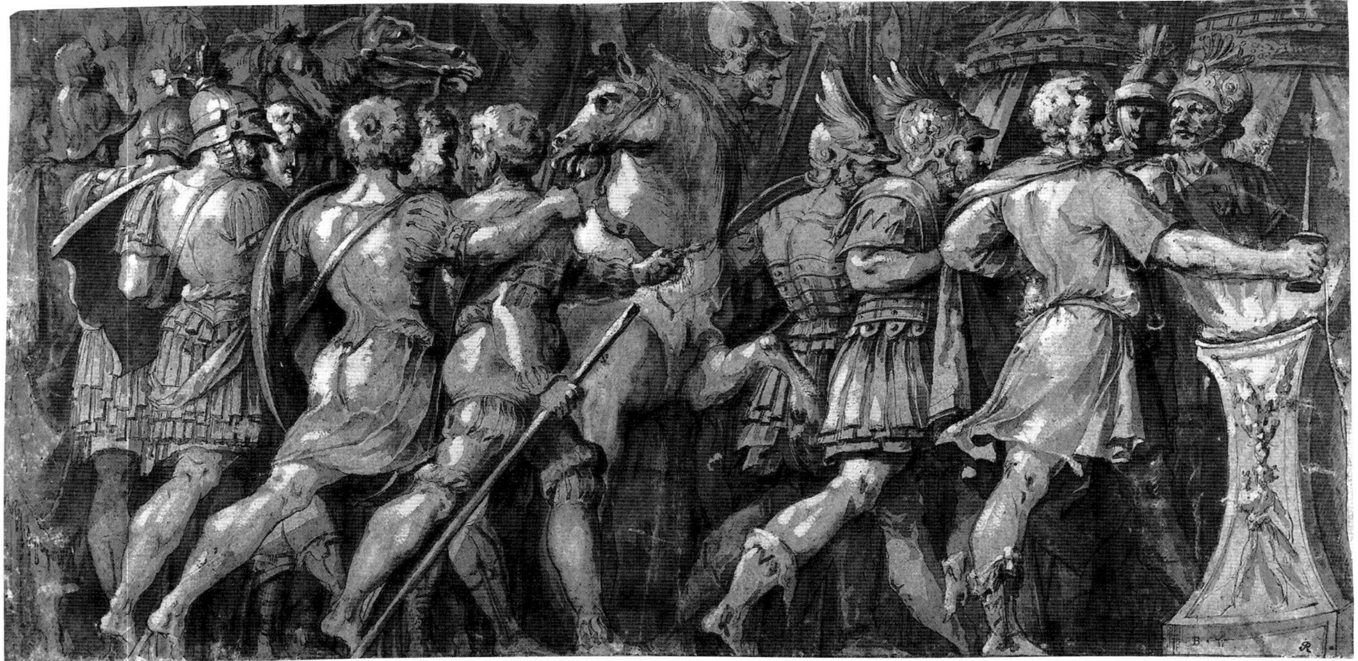

Fig. 23. After Polidoro da Caravaggio, *The Fortitude of Mucius Scaevola,* probably 16th century with reworkings probably from the 18th century. Pen and brown wash, heightened with touches of white and greenish gray oil pigment, 200 x 399 mm (7⅞ x 15¹¹⁄₁₆ in.). The Ashmolean Museum, Oxford (P II 484)

twelve drawings by Rubens (or his school) carry his collector's mark; four of them are from his father's collection. Great finds by Richardson Jr. are the drawings *Seated Young Woman with Raised Hands* (a study for the *Garden of Love;* cat. no. 90), the *Raising of Lazarus* (Kupferstichkabinett, Berlin), and *Diana* (Courtauld Institute of Art Gallery, London).[35]

The Richardsons were among the first drawings collectors who wrote extensively about art, connoisseurship, and their own collections. From their publications it is obvious that they were Italophiles. That they nonetheless collected Rubens is perhaps not so surprising, as by the nature of his work he is virtually half-Italian. Still, the attitude of the Richardsons was rather ambivalent. Statements like "Rubens was Great, but rais'd upon a *Flemish* idea" or "*Rubens's* People are as it were of Another Countrey; one sees not Nature Improv'd by the Antique, but a Sort of Nature, not the Best" make clear that, for their taste, Rubens did not idealize enough, or did not idealize in the way of their beloved sixteenth-century Italian masters.[36] Of course, Richardson Sr. greatly appreciated Rubens's retouched Italian drawings; he had several very good examples in his collection. Writing about the relationship between a retouching and the original, he stated that a "[reworked] Drawing looses not its first Denomination, 'tis an Original still, made by two several Masters'"—a remarkably subtle characterization, especially when compared to his son's blunt assessment of a retouched drawing: "something damaged by Time, and Rubens."[37] Eventually, Richardson Sr. seems to have been betrayed by his susceptibility to these retouched drawings. For instance, he valued very highly a drawing after Polidoro da Caravaggio, *The Fortitude of Mucius Scaevola* (fig. 23), deeming it a "Capital Drawing" by Polidoro himself. On the back of the mount he described how he bought it from the dealer Richard Gibson and repeated Gibson's view, apparently endorsing it, that the drawing was "superior to the rest of his [Gibson's] Pollidores, touched by Rubens." The general consensus today, however, is that the drawing is not an original but a copy after Polidoro and that Rubens did not work on it. It has even been suggested that the retouchings originated with Gibson, who, apparently well aware of Richardson's penchant for such reworkings, deceived his client.[38] Whether that is true or not, it is obvious that almost one hundred years after Rubens's studio sale the retouched Italian sheets were still valued very highly, perhaps even more than his own drawings.

The sale of Richardson Sr.'s collection in 1747 offered his pupil and son-in-law Thomas Hudson (1701–1779) a great opportunity to acquire many drawings, among which were numerous works by Rubens. Eventually, Hudson is believed to have acquired half of the Rubens drawings owned by Richardson.[39] From elsewhere he added several other important Rubens drawings, including *Woman with a Fan* (Louvre, Paris) and Rubens's *Self-Portrait* (fig. 1).[40] Hudson, who was later the teacher of the young Joshua Reynolds (1723–1792), can be seen as the link between Richardson Sr. and Reynolds, the two greatest drawings collectors in England in the eighteenth century. However, while Hudson clearly appreciated drawings from the Low Countries (although quantitatively Italian drawings still prevailed in his collection), Reynolds stuck to the traditional preference for Italian drawings.[41] His group of Rubens drawings was relatively small, about twenty sheets. There were some excellent pieces, though as a whole his collection seems a little dull compared to what his countrymen had achieved.

Several smaller English collectors like John Barnard (d. 1784), Clayton Mordaunt Cracherode (1730–1799), and William Esdaile (1758–1837), incidentally all nonartists, showed a nearly equal interest in draftsmen from north and south of the Alps. A rare case was John Perceval, 1st Earl of Egmont (1683–1748), who seems to have had hardly any Italian drawings. Egmont may have been the first owner of a series of beautiful colored landscapes that for a long time were thought to be by Rubens (see fig. 24); their attribution is still unresolved, as a relation to Rubens or his school is not obvious.[42] As it was Egmont who in all likelihood had Rubens's name written on the sheets, he is perhaps the perpetrator of the attribution. Apparently a lover of Northern drawings, he does not seem to have been the keenest connoisseur.[43] Esdaile and Barnard definitely knew their material better, including their Rubens drawings. Two drawings in this exhibition were once part of Barnard's collection (cat. nos. 27, 47).

Thomas Lawrence (1769–1830), the most prominent collector of drawings in England about 1800, maintained the traditional preference for Italian works. Yet, again like the earlier artist-collectors Richardson Sr. and Hudson, Lawrence amassed a very large group of Rubens's drawings. The group numbered well over 130 sheets, with all genres represented. In Lawrence's collection we encounter many sheets we have seen in earlier collections and others for the first time, including—for English collectors—a new genre: title-page designs. Lawrence had no less than six of these refined designs by Rubens.[44] He was also able to assemble a beautiful group of figure studies for Rubens's *Garden of Love* painting (fig. 137),

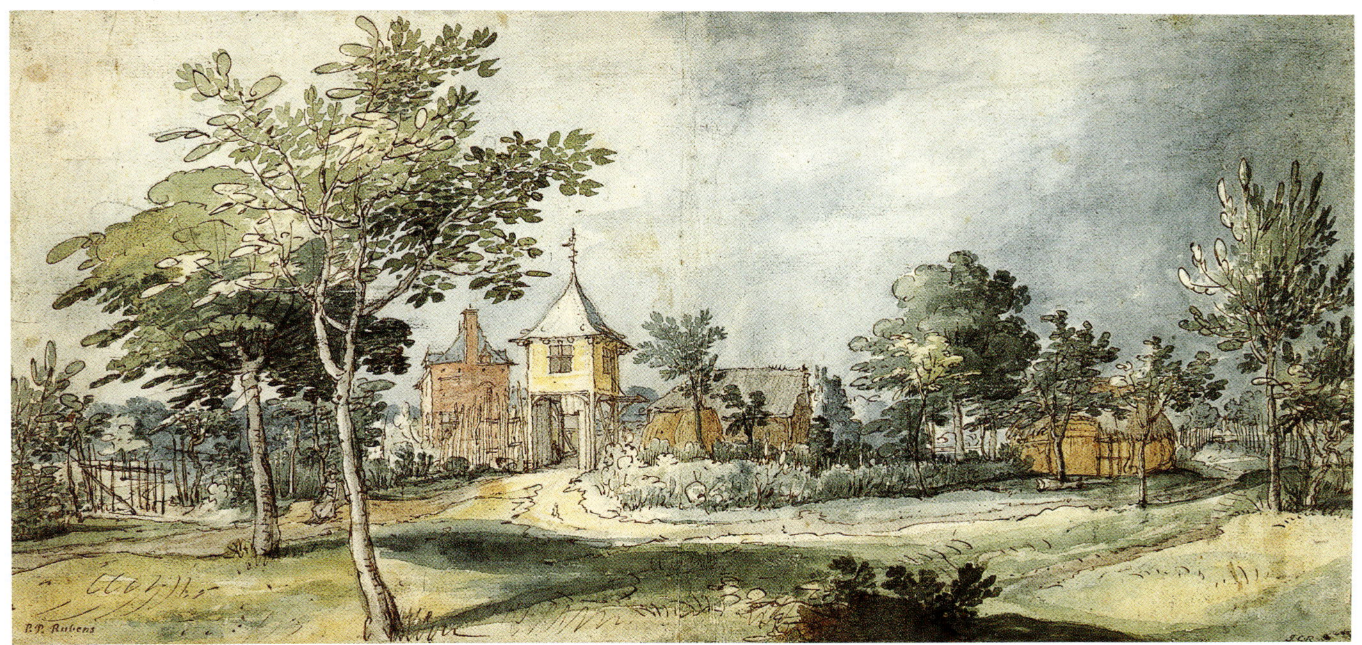

Fig. 24. Circle of Peter Paul Rubens, *Landscape with Farm Buildings: "[Het] Keyzers Hof,"* 1606–10. Pen and brown ink, watercolor in blue, green, yellow, and red, over faint indications in black chalk, 232 x 481 mm (9⅛ x 18 15/16 in.). The Pierpont Morgan Library, New York (I, 231)

among them *Young Man Embracing a Young Woman* (cat. no. 91) and *Young Man Descending Stairs* (cat. no. 92). Two sheets in this group carry marks of earlier English collectors, Richardson Jr. and Hudson.[45] The surfacing in England in rapid succession of these *Garden of Love* studies suggests that they had remained as a group since the 1657 sale. (It only makes sense, of course, that Rubens would have kept them together in his studio.) Another interesting group of figure studies still together in Lawrence's collection were related to Rubens's large Antwerp altarpiece the *Raising of the Cross* (fig. 87; cat. nos. 37–40); they probably came from the Dutch artist Jacob de Wit (1695–1754; see below). Spectacular individual sheets in Lawrence's collection included *Hercules Strangling the Nemean Lion* (Clark Art Institute, Williamstown),[46] *Man on Horseback (Study for the Portrait of the Duke of Lerma;* cat. no. 13), and *Lioness Seen from the Rear, Turning to the Left* (cat. no. 47).

Lawrence left no writings describing his motives or any ideas related to collecting, but a list of his framed drawings has survived, which allows some insight into his taste. Not surprisingly, most of the fifty-eight framed drawings were Italian. Of the thirteen framed Rubens drawings, only two are considered authentic today: the *Man on Horseback* (cat. no. 13) and the *Lioness* (cat. no. 47). Several of the others were designs for prints merely retouched by Rubens, like the *"Coup de Lance"* and the *Descent of the Holy Spirit* (both British Museum, London). Four large colored drawings were copies after Rubens's famous painting *Fall of the Damned*, also at the British Museum; their author is unknown.[47] Two were misattributions: *Our Lady of Sorrows* (incorrectly identified as *Saint Teresa*), now in the collection of Mr. and Mrs. G. Bagnani, Toronto, and *Head of a Negro Woman* (fig. 25);[48] both sheets exhibit similarities with Rubens's paintings, but not so much with his drawings, and again, their author is unknown. This peculiar gathering should not surprise us too much, as it fits a larger fashion: the great love for picture drawings. We saw this earlier in Jabach's distinction between *dessins d'ordonnance* and the *rebut* of his collection. For Lawrence the requirement may have been stronger, since (unlike Jabach) he used his drawings to decorate his walls. At any rate, all Lawrence's framed sheets were complete compositions or highly finished, usually both. Despite the high praise for the sketch—a recurring topos probably of classical origin[49]—we see time and again how collectors in previous centuries were attracted above all by picturelike drawings (their love for Rubens's retouched Italian drawings amounts to the same thing). In Samuel Woodburn's 1835 sale catalogue of Lawrence's collection, praise abounds for drawings that are finished to some degree—"very fine, and highly finished," "exquisitely finished," "splendid effect, highly finished"—while only rarely does a compliment seem to refer to a sketchier sheet: "a superb drawing, full of energy and spirit." Nonetheless, *Hercules Strangling the Nemean Lion,* the drawing about which this phrase was written, is a complete composition and largely worked out in detail.[50]

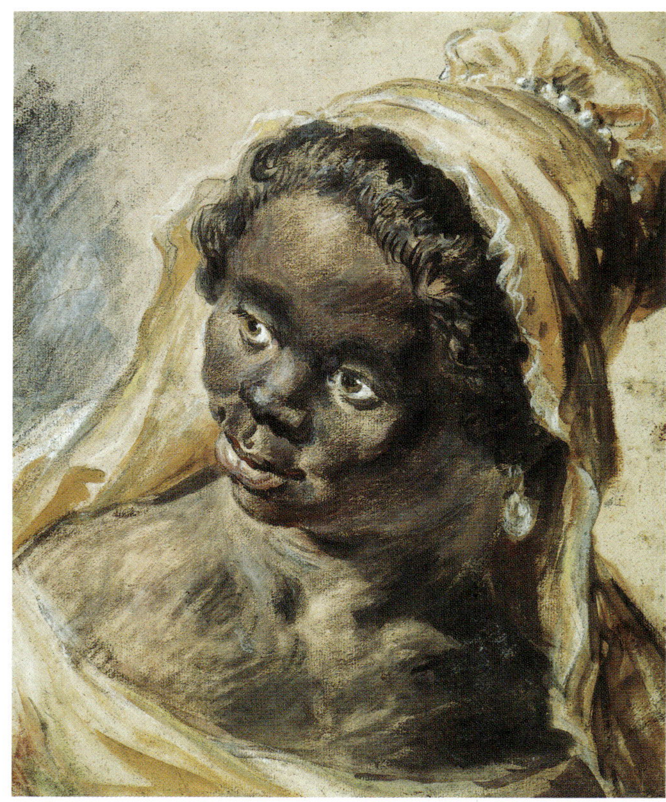

Fig. 25. Rubens follower, *Head of a Negro Woman,* probably 18th century. Body color, 485 x 390 mm (19⅛ x 15⅜ in.). The British Museum, London (1897-4-10-13)

Although Lawrence had made arrangements to preserve his collection for the British nation, his wishes were not followed, and his large collection was sold in several auctions. Despite this great loss, there are many wonderful drawings by Rubens in the United Kingdom, owing largely to the existence of the British Museum. This eminent institution received major donations or was able to acquire complete collections under favorable conditions. There were six drawings by

Rubens (or attributed to him) in the founding collection of Sir Hans Sloane (1660–1753). More important with respect to Rubens were the collections of Richard Payne Knight (1750–1824) and John Malcolm of Poltalloch (1805–1893), which came to the museum shortly after the collectors' respective deaths.[51] Other bequests that contained Rubens drawings came from William Fawkener in 1769, Clayton Mordaunt Cracherode (1730–1799), and George Salting (1835–1909). In 1935 the National Gallery deposited on loan sixteen drawings by Rubens (and his school) and by Anthony van Dyck from the Robert Peel collection. In 1994 these sheets, which included the print designs *"Coup de Lance"* and *Descent of the Holy Spirit* mentioned above, as well as the beautiful *Lioness* (cat. no. 47), were formally transferred to the British Museum, enriching the institution with an extremely interesting group of drawings by or related to Rubens.[52]

France

Roger de Piles (1635–1709), amateur artist and collector, was the great champion of Rubens in France in the last quarter of the seventeenth century (he was the art theorist who led the debate on *dessin* and *coloris*), and it is not surprising that he owned an interesting ensemble of drawings by the Flemish master. De Piles had direct contact with Rubens's family, as he corresponded with Philip Rubens, the nephew of the artist. He did so in order to obtain biographical data about Rubens that he needed for his *Dissertation sur les ouvrages des plus fameux peintres* (1681). In all likelihood Philip Rubens was the source of several items from the artist's estate that De Piles owned: Rubens's *Pocket Book*, his *Costume Book,* and an album of drawings with ninety-four studies of heads (which are now attributed to Rubens's workshop).[53] Rubens's once-celebrated *Pocket Book,* a book that he kept from 1601/2 into the mid-1630s, is now known only in several incomplete transcripts. It was almost totally destroyed by fire in 1720; the *Studies for Hero and Leander* (cat. no. 10) in Edinburgh may be a surviving sheet. Today, the *Costume Book* is kept in the British Museum and the drawings from the album are scattered in various collections.[54] It would be interesting to know what proportion of De Piles's collection was made up of Rubens drawings—he apparently also had several loose sheets—and how many works he owned by other artists. Unfortunately, there is little information about the art theorist's collection.[55]

After De Piles's death a part of his collection, including Rubens's *Costume Book* and the album with the studies of heads, was bought by Pierre Crozat (1665–1740), one of the most illustrious drawings collectors of all time.[56] The collections of Antoine Triest, in Ghent, and Everard Jabach, in Paris, were also important sources for Crozat. We are relatively well informed about Crozat's collection because his drawings are described in his auction catalogue, in which about 320 drawings by Rubens are listed. This number includes the ninety-four head studies—the album was taken apart at the 1741 sale—and forty-three drawings from the *Costume Book.* Still, it is a staggering amount, with well over one hundred true "compositions de Rubens" and well over forty retouched drawings. Among the *compositions* were impressive sheets like the *Crucifixion of Saint Peter* (Basel), the *Descent of the Holy Spirit* (London), and one of the two drawings for prints after the *Garden of Love* (cat. no. 93). Many of the sheets, including the three just mentioned, were large, well-finished drawings preparatory for prints—works that are now generally thought to be by Rubens's pupils and only retouched by the master. It is noteworthy that Crozat's auction catalogue is the first in which we encounter book-related designs by Rubens. Apparently, this distinct group within Rubens's drawn oeuvre had somehow remained together until the beginning of the eighteenth century.[57]

Crozat, whose collection consisted mostly of Italian drawings, obviously had a special taste for the art of the Flemish draftsman. We do not know exactly what Crozat thought of his Rubens drawings, but we have the commentary of one of his close friends, Pierre-Jean Mariette (1694–1774). A bookseller and publisher, Mariette was himself an important collector of drawings and an eminent art connoisseur. He organized many art auctions, especially of prints, and in 1741 he oversaw the auction of Crozat's collection. The catalogue that Mariette produced for that sale—a standard work in auction catalogue literature—contains many illuminating asides. For instance, Mariette commented on Rubens as a retoucher, stating that Rubens used only mediocre or damaged sheets after great draftsmen for these reworkings, changing them heavily according to his taste, eventually transforming them almost into an invention of his own.[58] According to twenty-first-century scholarship, Mariette seems to be correct in his claim that Rubens usually retouched only minor drawings. The extent to which Rubens's hand can be discerned in a

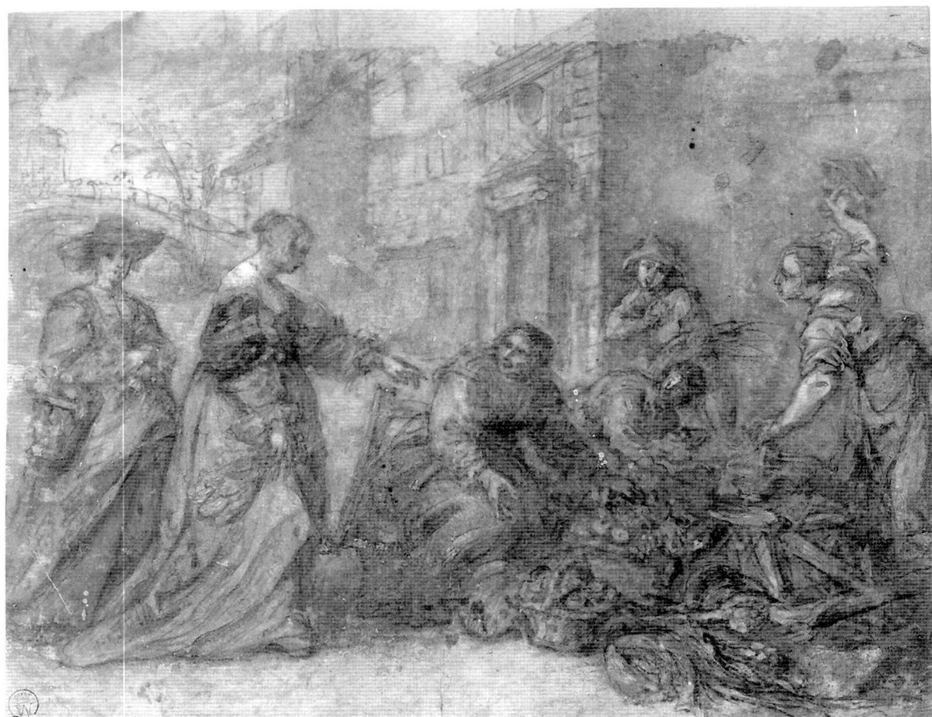

Fig. 26. Flemish school, 17th century (attributed to Jan Boeckhorst), *Women Visiting the Vegetable Market.* Black chalk, pen and brown ink, brown wash heightened with white on tan paper, 155 x 191 mm (6⅛ x 7½ in.). Photograph courtesy of Sotheby's, Inc. © 1981

number of drawings is still a matter of considerable debate.

In the Crozat sale catalogue Mariette also discussed the master's drawing style in general. In Rubens's slight sketches, he said, "the core and the spirit [une ame & un esprit] denote the speed with which he [Rubens] conceived and executed his ideas." However, according to Mariette, when Rubens created his drawings in a neater way—maintaining their spirit but making them more regular *(reglé)*—he attained, with the help of *peinture* and *clair-obscur,* truly accomplished works.[59] Mariette clearly favored the latter. This preference is manifest in the way he catalogued Crozat's Rubens drawings, giving more attention to a sheet if it was more finished, and in his own collection of Rubens drawings, where again we encounter many preparatory drawings for prints (several from Crozat) and other well-finished sheets, among them the charming *Women Visiting the Vegetable Market* (fig. 26), which, however, is not by Rubens but probably by one of his pupils.[60] In the Crozat catalogue Mariette concluded his description of Rubens's drawing style as follows: "Son goût de Dessein n'est point celui de l'antique, Rubens répresentoit la nature telle qu'il la voyoit dan son païs; mais c'étoit toujours avec une verité, & même avec une science, ausquelles les personnes qui ne sont touchés que de belles formes, ne peuvent refuser leur admiration."[61] In other words, even classicist, Italophile art connoisseurs could not deny Rubens his due.

Mariette's (and probably also Crozat's) positive view of Rubens differs considerably from the judgment, in 1722, by Jonathan Richardson Sr., who dwelled on the Flemish background of the artist and criticized Rubens for not idealizing enough. This difference of opinion, between collectors equally taken with Italian art, must have to do with the Rubens works they knew and, ultimately, with their own drawing collections. It is conceivable that Richardson knew Lankrink's collection. Since he owned many drawings with Lankrinks's collector's mark, it has been suggested, plausibly, that he attended the two Lankrink sales in 1693 and 1694. Mariette knew the Crozat collection extremely well, of course, and probably also the French royal collection in the Louvre, acquired from Jabach in 1671. If we compare these illustrious collections, and those of Richardson and Mariette, it is obvious that, according to currently accepted attributions, there were far more genuine Rubens drawings in England than in France. In France the preparatory sheets for prints—made by Rubens's pupils and merely retouched by the master—dominated.[62] Mariette's judgment must have been influenced by this imbalance. Of course it is speculation, but one wonders whether he might have shared Richardson's opinion, had he only known the works by Rubens in England.

In time, however, the preference in France in the eighteenth century for highly finished drawings by "Rubens" yielded to concern and even condemnation. At some point Mariette realized—as we know from his posthumously published writings—that Giovanni Pietro Bellori had written in 1672 that Rubens had his pupil Anthony van Dyck make preparatory drawings and oil sketches for prints. Mariette had no difficulty believing this.[63] However, it was Antoine-Joseph Dezallier d'Argenville (1680–1765), another French connoisseur and drawings collector, who wrote in 1745: "The finished drawings that pass as works by him [Rubens] are in fact made by the engravers after his paintings; Rubens only contributed some assured strokes *[quelques coups hardis]*."[64] Strangely, however, although most connoisseurs and collectors must have been aware of Dezallier's allegation, they apparently did not wish to believe it. Dezallier himself continued to consider his *Martyrdom of Saint Lawrence* (fig. 27), a highly finished drawing after a composition by Rubens, a genuine work by the master; it is now believed to be possibly by Van Dyck.[65] And in the 1776 sale of Mariette's collection, highly finished drawings, very often preparatory works for prints—like *Sanherib* (Albertina, Vienna), *Queen Tomyris with the Head of Cyrus* (cat. no. 55), and the two *Garden of Love* sheets (cat. nos. 93, 94)—still commanded the highest prices. One gets the feeling that at least some of the collectors did not see the difference between a work by Rubens and one by a pupil. How else are we to explain the fierce debate, also at the Mariette sale, over a genuine, very beautiful Rubens drawing, the *Holy Family with the Infant Saint John the Baptist* (fig. 28)? In the auction rooms of Basan, in Paris, there seem to have been lengthy discussions about this sheet, a rare case of an engraver's drawing made entirely by Rubens. At the time some people seem to have been convinced that it was by Abraham van Diepenbeeck (1596–1675), an artist who worked for Rubens in the late 1620s and the 1630s.[66] By contrast, a colored drawing, *Landscape with Mired Wagon* (Metropolitan Museum of Art, New York), that is, at least to twenty-first-century eyes, obviously a copy does not seem to have aroused any suspicion.[67]

During the Revolution many private art collections in France were confiscated by the state. As a result, several beautiful and important Rubens sheets, such as *The Vestal Tuccia, Self-Portrait* (fig. 1), *Woman with a Fan, Kneeling Woman, Walking Child,* and *Landscape with Fallen Tree* (fig. 18), eventually ended up in the Louvre. With the addition of these drawings, almost invariably marked with the stamps of English collectors, the collection in the Louvre—which at the time consisted mainly of elaborate drawings for prints—became more balanced. Then there was silence. In the nineteenth century (and also in the twentieth) in France there appears to have been no particular interest in Rubens's drawings. Prominent collectors like Dominique Vivant-Denon (1747–1825) and Jean-Baptiste-Joseph Wicar (1762–1834) do not seem to have had any affinity for his work. French collectors at this time tended to have very broad taste and looked into work, like that of the Italian or Flemish Primitives or even Dutch seventeenth-century artists, that had hardly been explored in preceding centuries. It seems to be almost an accident to encounter a Rubens work in a French drawings collection at this time, such as in those of Aimé-Charles-Horace His

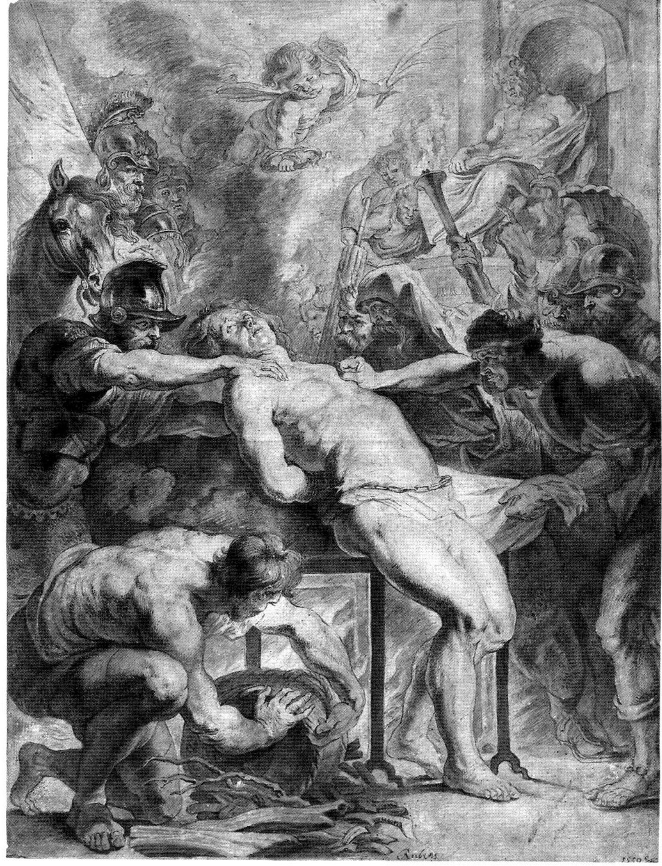

Fig. 27. Ascribed to Anthony Van Dyck, *The Martyrdom of Saint Lawrence*, ca. 1618–19. Brush and gray and brown wash over black chalk, traces of body color, 377 x 279 mm ($14\frac{13}{16}$ x 11 in.). Courtauld Institute of Art Gallery, London (D.1978.PG.327)

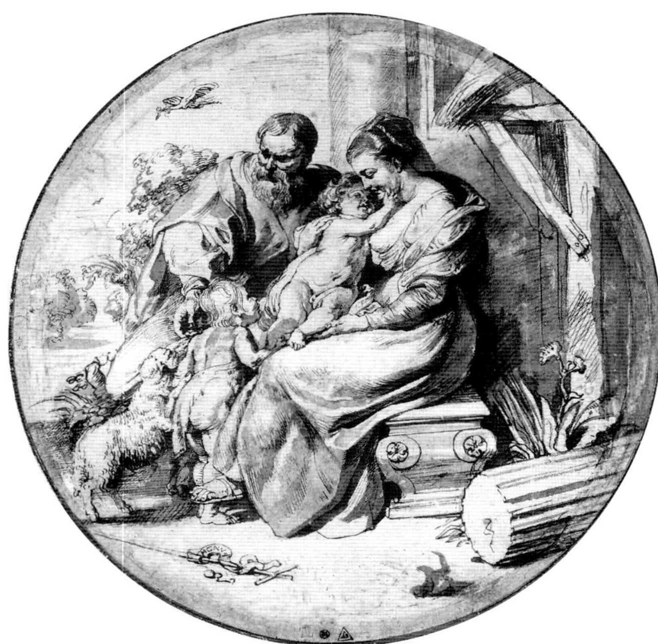

Fig. 28. Peter Paul Rubens, *Holy Family with the Infant Saint John the Baptist*, ca. 1615–17. Pen and brown ink and wash, over black chalk, outlines traced with the stylus, diam. 201 mm ($7^{15}/_{16}$ in.). The British Museum, London (1860.16.16.89)

de la Salle (1795–1878) and Xavier Atger (1758–1833). Both men gave a large part of their drawings collections to public institutions, the former to the Louvre, the latter, who owned the beautiful *Susanna* (cat. no. 29), to the Medicine Faculty in Montpellier (and thence to the Musée Atger).[68]

German-Speaking Countries

There probably were not many Rubens drawings in Germany in the seventeenth century. Two artists, Joachim von Sandrart (1606–1688) and his pupil Matthäus Merian the Younger (1621–1687), are known to have had some. Describing his drawings and prints collection in the 1670s, Sandrart mentioned Rubens's name in the one album that was devoted to German and Netherlandish drawings. As there were twenty-one artists' names given for that album (and additional unspecified artists), it seems unlikely that Sandrart's Rubens group was large. One Rubens drawing from Sandrart's collection is still known: the *Adoration of the Shepherds* in the Collection Frits Lugt, Institut Néerlandais, Paris.[69] Merian's relatively small collection, which contained half a dozen sketchy pen drawings by Rubens, was acquired by the ruling Prussian family, the house of Brandenburg, at the end of the seventeenth century. The attribution of most of the sheets has been doubted, however, and Merian probably kept the authentic Rubens drawing *A Knight and a Lady* (cat. no. 6) as a work by Israhel van Meckenem (ca. 1440/45–1503).[70] There was a lot of interest at the various German courts in Rubens's paintings, but his drawings were evidently not equally sought after, neither in the seventeenth nor in the eighteenth century. For instance, the Kupferstichkabinett in Berlin (where the Brandenburg collection also found a home) started seriously acquiring Rubens drawings only during the directorship of Friedrich Lippmann (1876–1903). It was especially with the acquisition in 1902 of the collection of Adolf von Beckerath (1834–1915)—which included the *Continence of Scipio* (cat. no. 33)—that the Berlin Rubens group came into its own.[71]

The most substantial group of Rubens drawings in Germany was (and still is) to be found in Dresden. Most of them, today in the Kupferstich-Kabinett, were acquired during the reign of Friedrich August I, elector of Saxony (later Augustus II, king of Poland; 1670–1733). In 1723 and 1726 several albums of drawings were acquired by Johann Heinrich von Heucher, the first head of the Dresden print room, at the autumn fair in Leipzig, containing altogether thirty-six drawings under the name of Rubens. In 1728 the Wagner collection was added, consisting of about ten thousand sheets.[72] This important collection—assembled by the Leipziger Gottfried Wagner (1652–1725)—consisted mostly of German and Netherlandish material. Among the Rubens works were anatomy studies, drawings after the antique, and an oil sketch, *Saint Roch as Patron of the Plague-Stricken.* As the last was specifically mentioned in the records of Heucher (he did not single out any other work), it must have been considered a significant piece. Now recognized as a rather crude copy, the oil sketch testifies to German collectors' interest in the more painterly—entirely in line with the predilections we have encountered in France and England in the eighteenth century.[73]

There were also important drawings collectors in the Habsburg Austrian empire, like Count Carl Cobenzl (1712–1770), Prince Charles de Ligne (1759–1792), and Duke Albert of Sachsen-Teschen (1738–1822). All three had lived for a long time in the Austrian Netherlands, and one wonders whether their love for collecting drawings was somehow influenced by their stay, because the Netherlands (especially the northern part) had a rich tradition of collecting drawings (see below).

Cobenzl, the minister plenipotentiary of Austria, knew the Netherlands, north and south, well, as he had studied in Leiden and lived from 1753 on in Brussels. His collection, numbering well over thirty-five hundred sheets, consisted mostly of Flemish works. There were dozens of Rubens drawings among them, some of high quality, like the *Portrait of the Daughter of Balthasar Gerbier* (Hermitage, Saint Petersburg) and the *Descent from the Cross* (cat. no. 9).[74] However, there were also several drawings that do not stand the test of twenty-first-century critique, like the colored drawing the *Stoning of Saint Stephen,* also in Saint Petersburg.[75] This sheet, representing the central section of a Rubens triptych now in the Musée des Beaux-Arts, Valenciennes, seems to have been highly valued not only by Cobenzl. In 1766 Cassiodore de Monchaux, the grand prior of the abbey near Valenciennes where the Rubens triptych was hanging at the time, had Louis-Joseph Watteau (1731–1798) make copies after the wings on the same scale and in the same technique as Cobenzl's sheet. De Monchaux presented them to Cobenzl, who could thus re-create the triptych, as it were. Cobenzl's collection is still intact, as it was bought by Catherine II of Russia in 1768 and transferred to the Hermitage, in Saint Petersburg. De Ligne operated a major publishing house at the château de Beloeil, Haincourt, in the Austrian Netherlands. Although he died young, De Ligne amassed a collection of about six thousand sheets, among which there were many drawings by the greatest artists. Unfortunately, in the case of Rubens—there were twenty-seven sheets in the collection—De Ligne seems not to have been a great connoisseur. By twenty-first-century standards, most of these drawings, usually showing complete compositions, are copies or are now attributed to Rubens's pupils. A known exception is *Madonna with Saint George* (Albertina, Vienna), a drawing after Correggio retouched by Rubens.[76] Again, it seems to be the penchant for complete compositions or finished drawings that led this eighteenth-century collector astray.

We have an idea what Rubens drawings were owned by De Ligne because seventeen of them are now in the Albertina, Vienna. Duke Albert of Sachsen-Teschen, the founder of the Albertina, bought them at the De Ligne auction in 1794, a clear indication that Albert believed De Ligne's attributions.[77] (De Ligne and Albert, incidentally, had known each other well from their shared time in the Southern Netherlands.) Moreover, in the catalogue of Albert's entire collection made in 1822 after his death, only two Rubens sheets were branded copies, and the De Ligne drawings were not among them.[78] The 1822 catalogue is interesting for other reasons, as well. Albert's ensemble of drawings by Rubens—in the end he had acquired about 125 sheets—was described according to subject matter, first biblical (Old Testament followed by New Testament), then mythological, and finally landscapes and (portrait) studies. Almost all the historical subjects have an individual entry; the studies and the portraits do not. Almost at the end of the seven pages in the catalogue dedicated to Rubens one encounters the following:

> *Seize Portraits parmi lesquels ceux du Duc de Buckingham et son Epouse, celui de la Reine Marie de Medicis, et celui de la Soeur de Rubens.*
>
> *Quarante sept pieces représentant des Bustes, têtes et différentes études.*[79]

At the time this division according to subject matter (within an artist's oeuvre) was the usual way prints were catalogued; drawings were not usually catalogued so rigidly. (Today, quality and chronology would be the criteria for cataloguing a large group of drawings by a single artist.) What is most telling, however, not to mention ironic, is that most of the historical drawings on which the catalogue lavished so much attention were of the low caliber of De Ligne's drawings, while many of the "portraits . . . bustes, têtes et différentes études" are now considered some of Rubens's finest drawings. The Rubens drawings catalogue published by the Albertina in 1977 is almost a complete inversion of Albert's 1822 catalogue: the studies and portraits are in the front, in full-page color reproductions, while the history drawings are in the back, in black and white and often two to a page.[80]

There can hardly be any doubt that the order of Rubens drawings in the 1822 catalogue and the rejection of only two sheets as copies date from Albert's lifetime. Albert had started as a print collector on a large scale, under the guidance of the very systematic print connoisseur Giacomo Durazzo; they must have adopted a similar system for Albert's drawings. Furthermore, the 1822 catalogue was made within two months.[81] It is unlikely that the order of the 13,600 drawings that had to be described was changed within that brief time or that anyone undertook research to check the authenticity of the drawings (if, indeed, there was any inclination to do so). We will probably never know if Albert would have wanted a proper description of each study and each portrait—in other words, if he properly valued them. Given the general fashion for complete compositions and finished drawings, it seems unlikely that he did. Even if he did appreciate them, however, one cannot escape concluding that in the eighteenth century connoisseurship of Rubens drawings in Austria and in the Southern Netherlands (where Albert and De Ligne probably bought many of their drawings and where Pierre Wouters had a comparable collection; see below) was, generally, not at the highest level.

The Netherlands

When Rubens was born in 1577 the Netherlands were still part of the empire of the Spanish Hapsburgs. This changed in 1579, when the ten southern provinces formed an alliance with Spain, and the seven northern provinces joined together against Spain. The Dutch Republic (the seven United Provinces in the north) was officially recognized only in 1648.

Information concerning seventeenth-century Netherlandish collectors of Rubens drawings is scarce. As we have seen, the Antwerp dealer Happaert acquired basically all Rubens's drawings at the sale of the artist's estate in 1657, but he seems to have sold them largely to foreigners, like Lankrink and Jabach. Constantijn Huygens tried to buy the "Rosso-Rubens" drawing (fig. 12) from Happaert, but to no avail. Whether he succeeded in other instances is unknown. His close friend Jan van der Does, heer van Bergesteyn (ca. 1635?–1704), seems to have had more luck: he owned at least nine drawings by Rubens.[82] Most of them seem to have been Italian drawings retouched by Rubens—*God the Father* (cat. no. 116) was one of them—exactly the type of work that, as we have seen time and again, early drawings collectors most appreciated. The collection mark of Nicolaes Flinck (1646–1723), another eminent drawings collector about 1700, has not been found on any major Rubens drawing.[83]

More is known about eighteenth-century collectors in the Netherlands and their treasures, because more auction catalogues, inventories, and other collector's paraphernalia survive. A special example of the last category is an elaborate drawn title page that prefaced a volume of drawings by Rubens, as is indicated by the elegantly written text in the center of the page (fig. 29). This anonymous sheet, largely copied after Rubens's design for the title page to Frans Verhaer's *Annales Ducum seu Principum Brabantiae* (History of the Duchy or Principality of Brabant), proudly states that the album belonged to Johannes Baptista Jacobs (b. 1672), a bookseller and art lover in Antwerp.[84] This Jacobs was the owner of at least four drawings albums, all containing Flemish drawings, that have miraculously survived intact. Jacobs also had at least two volumes with Italian drawings.[85] We have no information about exactly which Rubens drawings the Antwerp collector owned. In 1723 his son Jacobs Jr. seems to have sold most of the Northern drawings to John Perceval,

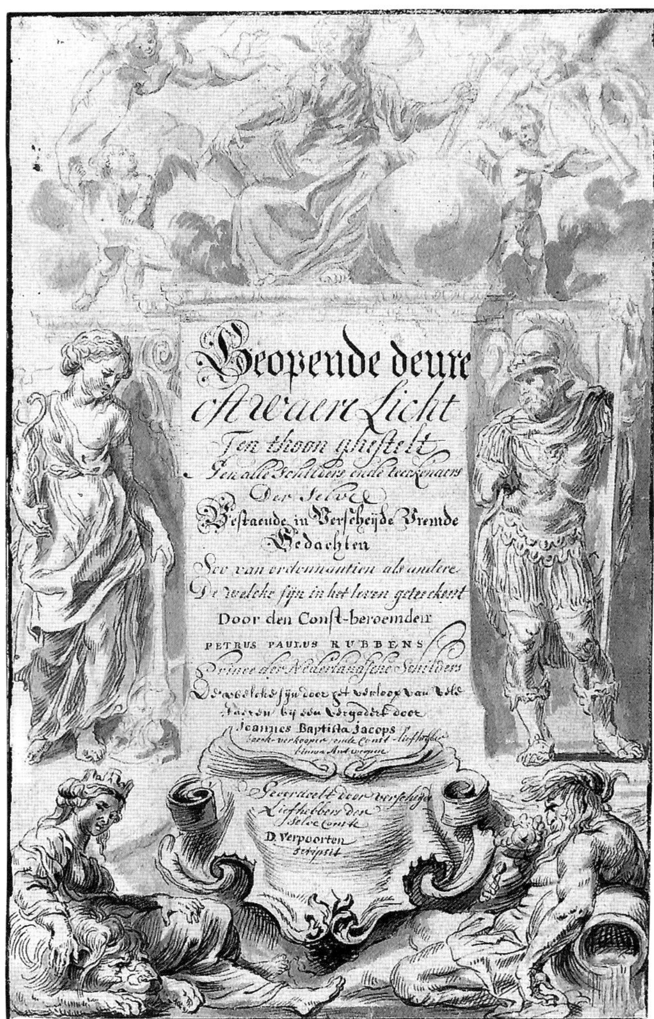

Fig. 29. After Peter Paul Rubens, *Title Page for an Album with Rubens Drawings* (after Rubens's design for title page to Frans Verhaer, *Annales Ducum seu Principum Brabantiae*), probably ca. 1700. Pen and gray ink, with gray-brown wash, over graphite, indented for transfer, 290 x 179 mm (11 7/16 x 7 1/16 in.). The British Museum, London (1985.7.13.2)

Earl of Egmont (1683–1748), so that one could speculate that the drawings in Egmont's collection attributed to Rubens were once the property of the Jacobs family, in all likelihood including the watercolor landscape series in which *Landscape with Farm Buildings* (fig. 24) figures.[86] However, we are not sure when these sheets were attributed to Rubens, as the inscription "P. P. Rubens" on them seems to originate with Egmont. Furthermore, Egmont probably also bought from other sources.

In the eighteenth century the Dutch Republic was rich in drawings collectors. Although Flemish drawings were not their top priority, several collectors, such as Samuel van Huls, Gosinus Uilenbroek, Valerius Röver, Cornelis Ploos van Amstel, and Dirk Versteegh, had interesting groups of drawings by Rubens.[87] The Hague burgomaster Van Huls stands out, with a large ensemble of about a hundred drawings by Rubens. The short descriptions in his 1736 auction catalogue unfortunately make it hard to identify them. However, as only one Rubens drawing in his collection, the *Assumption of the Virgin,* was framed and described as an "excellent dessin," it is logical to assume it is the same as a costly *Assumption of the Virgin* by Rubens that circulated among several Dutch collections during the century and that recently ended up in the Getty Museum (cat. no. 53). Uilenbroek was the first known owner of eleven large Rubens sheets depicting the life of Christ: preparatory drawings for illustrations in the *Breviarium Romanum* (Roman Breviary). At Uilenbroek's sale in 1741 the group, among them *All Saints* (cat. no. 50), was dispersed.[88] Röver owned several Italian drawings that Rubens had worked on—as Röver put it, "Rubenisato"—among them Zuccaro's *God the Father* (cat. no. 116). Ploos possessed great documentation: two drawings series by Jacob de Wit (for a total of fifty sheets) showing the complete now-lost ceiling decorations by Rubens for the Jesuit church in Antwerp (today Saint Charles Borromeo). Furthermore, the Amsterdam collector had several loose sheets, like the Getty *Assumption* (cat. no. 53), the *Adoration of the Magi* (possibly cat. no. 49), *Title Page for Oliver Bonartus* (Albertina, Vienna), and *Saint Francis Kneeling, Receiving the Infant Christ* (Courtauld Institute of Art Gallery, London).[89] Versteegh was able to acquire two impressive studies for the *Raising of the Cross* (probably cat. nos. 38, 39), two versions of *Cattle in Pasture* (see cat. no. 101), and the drawing, rather popular at the time, but now dismissed, *Portrait of a Young Woman with a Ruff* (British Museum, London).[90]

There were of course also Dutch collectors with only small groups of drawings by Rubens. Some of them owned important sheets, however. Hendrik van Eyl Sluyter (1739–1814), for example, was the proud possessor of the *Portrait of Nicolas Trigault in Chinese Costume* (cat. no. 73) and the two exceptional drawings, by Rubens and Christoffel Jegher (1596–1652/53), based on the *Garden of Love* (cat. nos. 93, 94). The presence in the Dutch Republic of the *Garden of Love* sheets, previously in the collections of Jabach, Crozat, and Mariette, is a rare case in which drawings of such caliber were "bought back" by Northern collectors. Usually in the eighteenth century, the traffic was one-way—richer countries like England and France were buying out the Netherlands.[91] Eventually, the *Garden of Love* drawings wound up back in the hands of foreign dealers and were exported again. Since 1958 both sheets have been in the Metropolitan Museum, New York, where in 1999 Van Eyl Sluyter's Trigault portrait (cat. no. 73) also ended its journey.

The aforementioned Dutch eighteenth-century artist and collector Jacob de Wit, who was heavily influenced by Rubens, occupied a category of his own. During his formative years De Wit lived in Antwerp with his godfather, Jacob (or Jacomo) de Wit, a dealer in paintings. There the young artist studied paintings by Rubens firsthand. He also probably started to collect Rubens's works. Eventually De Wit had an important ensemble of works by Rubens, with no less than sixteen paintings, several lifesize, among them two predella paintings from Rubens's early Antwerp altarpiece the *Raising of the Cross* (fig. 87).[92] Furthermore, he owned, according to his 1755 auction catalogue, about seventy-five drawings by Rubens, eight of them studies for "the large Cross," in all likelihood the Antwerp *Raising of the Cross* altarpiece, for which several studies are known (cat. nos. 37–40).[93] This might be another example of how figure studies related to a particular project (like the studies made for the *Garden of Love*) had been sold together and, more important, had probably previously been kept together by Rubens in his studio. De Wit owned or had access to at least some of the studies for the *Raising of the Cross,* for he retouched one of them and copied another. The somewhat randomly applied dark washes indicating shaded areas in *Crouching Man Seen from the Back* (cat. no. 38) are typical of De Wit.[94] Similar washes distinguish De Wit's copy *Christ Being Crucified* from Rubens's original *Study for the Figure of Christ* (cat. no. 37), both now in the Fogg Art Museum, Cambridge.[95]

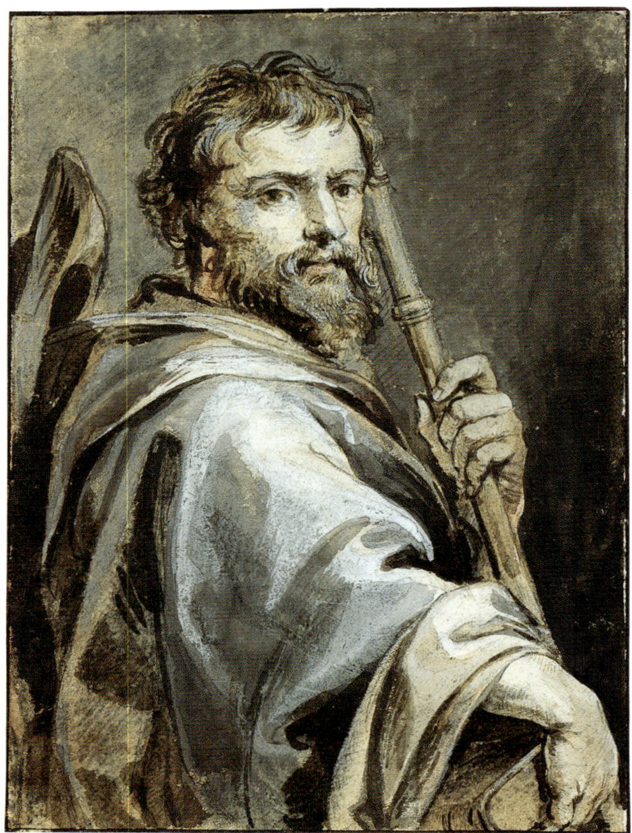

Fig. 30. Unknown Rubens pupil (possibly Nicolaes Ryckmans), retouchings here attributed to Jacob de Wit, *Saint James the Greater,* probably 1620–26, probably retouched ca. 1720–54. Black chalk, watercolor, heightened with white body color, outlines traced with the stylus, 176 x 130 mm (6 15/16 x 5 1/8 in.). Albertina, Vienna (8220)

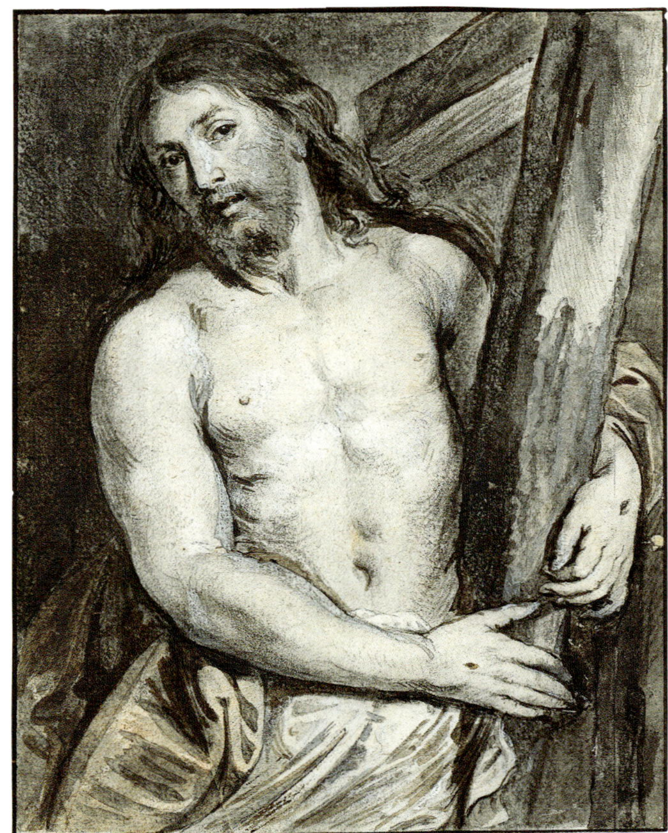

Fig. 31. Unknown Rubens pupil (possibly Nicolaes Ryckmans), retouchings here attributed to Jacob de Wit, *Christ as Salvator Mundi,* probably 1620–26, probably retouched ca. 1720–54. Black chalk, watercolor, heightened with white body color, outlines traced with the stylus, 175 x 134 mm (6 7/8 x 5 1/4 in.). Albertina, Vienna (8214)

Rubens himself was a champion in retouching old master drawings, although he normally used drawings of little quality, and in doing the same De Wit was perhaps following the master's lead.[96] In the 1755 auction catalogue of De Wit's collection, about fifteen drawings, basically all by seventeenth-century Flemish artists, are described as being "finished" by him. Rubens is mentioned only four times among them, but these were probably not the only Rubens sheets that De Wit had retouched.[97] In other eighteenth-century Dutch sale catalogues, too, we encounter Rubens drawings retouched by De Wit.[98] Recently, one such sheet, a finished colored drawing mentioned in a 1759 Amsterdam auction, was identified in the English royal collection at Windsor: *Diogenes in Search of an Honest Man.*[99] In the eighteenth century the drawing was described as by Rubens and De Wit, as if it were a collaboration. Whether there is a sketch by Rubens underneath in the *Diogenes* is unclear; the work seems to be entirely by De Wit. A case in which De Wit indeed seriously retouched seventeenth-century drawings from the circle of Rubens is the *Christ and the Apostles* series in the Albertina, Vienna. These thirteen drawings were used by Nicolaes Ryckmans (known 1616–26) for thirteen prints, as the contours are indented for transfer.[100] The delicate reworking with watercolor, however, and the heightening with white body color and the black washes in the shadows betray the hand of De Wit (figs. 30, 31).[101] He probably did not add his retouches in order to deceive anyone. Reworked drawings could be signed on the verso or just outside the framing lines. Later owners (perhaps not with the best of intentions) pasted the drawings down or cut off these signatures. In addition to "finishing" Rubens drawings, De Wit made slight changes in copies after compositions by Rubens. That such sheets as *Diana and Her Nymphs Returning from the Hunt* (fig. 32) and the *Miracle of Saint Walburga* (Albertina, Vienna) have in the course of time been attributed to Rubens or his school indicates how close De Wit came to his admired example.[102]

De Wit's activities to "finish" drawings by Rubens make clear that in the Dutch Republic, as elsewhere, the master's most finished works were the most prized. This is corroborated by Christiaan Josi's comments on Rubens's drawings, published in 1821. Josi (1768–1828), a Dutch art dealer and connoisseur who lived and worked for a long time in England, went on at length about Rubens's finished drawings.[103] Arguing against an unnamed person (easily recognizable, however, as Antoine-Joseph Dezallier d'Argensville) who had claimed that Rubens never completed his drawings and that all finished Rubens drawings were actually by his pupils, Josi admitted that some drawings attributed to Rubens were in fact by pupils or engravers. These included, he almost sneered, "la plupart des dessins encadrés qu'on voit sous le titre de ce grand maître dans la salle d'Apollon au Louvre à Paris; qui sont exécutés lourdement, sans esprit et sans touché." But, Josi continued, there were certainly drawings that Rubens started and also beautifully finished himself. According to the Dutch connoisseur, they were distinguished by their spirit and ardour and by the freedom and swiftness of their execution. He mentioned six drawings as examples: the two *Garden of Love* sheets (cat. nos. 93, 94), the *Assumption of the Virgin* (cat. no. 53), *Christ on the Cross* (cat. no. 56), *Queen Tomyris with the Head of Cyrus* (cat. no. 55), and a folio title page unknown today. All six are now considered drawings that Rubens retouched; still they were well chosen, as they do indeed come close to genuine Rubens works (and certainly closer than the Paris works Josi denigrated), because the corrections by Rubens are more elaborate than usual. Finally, Josi called attention to Rubens's chalk drawings—his portraits and his figure studies. Although he stated explicitly that these studies were highly esteemed by collectors, he spent only a few words on them.[104]

Apart from Cobenzl, De Ligne, and Albert of Sachsen-Teschen, mentioned above, local collectors of drawings in the Austrian Netherlands (initially allied with Spain, the Southern Netherlands became Austrian after the War of the Spanish Succession, in 1701–14) are hard to find. The collection of Pierre Wouters (d. before 1797) in Brussels seems to be exceptional. This priest and canon of the collegiate church of Saint Gomer in Lier (near Antwerp) had a large collection of more than 2,000 drawings, among them about 120 by Rubens. From the available descriptions, however, one doubts that their quality was good. There were many highly finished

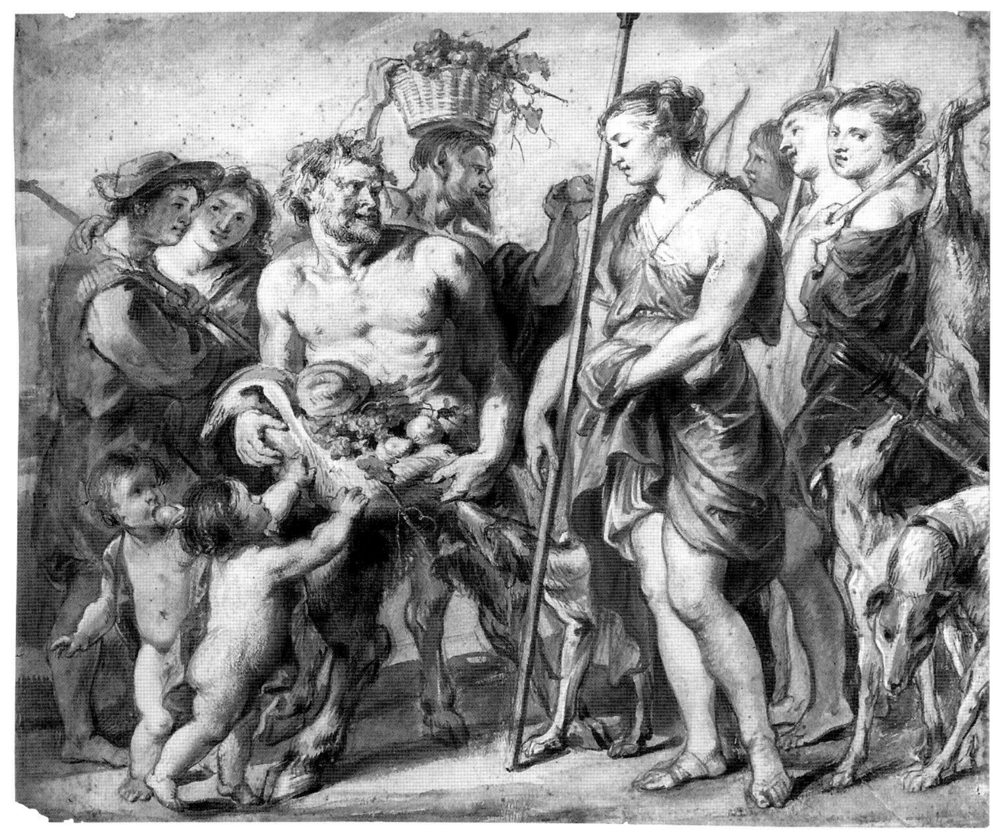

Fig. 32. Attributed to Jacob de Wit, *Diana and Her Nymphs Returning from the Hunt*, ca. 1730–50. Black and red chalk, brush and brown wash, body color, 342 x 407 mm (13 7/16 x 16 in.). Fitzwilliam Museum, Cambridge (2235)

complete compositions, executed in black and red chalk; drawings with elaborate brown washes; and drawings on blue paper. This all sounds rather atypical for Rubens. Furthermore, the few Rubens drawings that have been associated with the Wouters collection, like the *Penitent Magdalen* (art market), the *Three Graces* (Museum Boijmans Van Beuningen, Rotterdam), and the *Bull Hunt* (Collection Frits Lugt, Institut Néerlandais, Paris),[105] are now usually categorized as Rubens school rather than as Rubens originals.

After the fall of Napoleon, the Northern and the Southern Netherlands were united for fifteen years. But in 1830 the Belgian Revolt created two separate kingdoms, the Netherlands and Belgium. The most important collectors of Rubens drawings in the Netherlands during this era were probably King William II (1792–1849) and Carel Joseph Fodor (1801–1860). In their collecting activities both went against the grain; as it had been in the eighteenth century, seventeenth-century Dutch art was still the chief desire of most Netherlandish collectors. William II, well known for the international orientation of his paintings collection—in which the Flemish Primitives were especially prominent—had a small but fabulous collection of old master drawings. The latter consisted mostly of Italian sheets, by Leonardo, Raphael, and Michelangelo, but it also contained thirty-six drawings by Rubens. Most, if not all, of them came from Sir Thomas Lawrence, acquired through Samuel Woodburn in 1835.[106] Among them was the impressive *Man on Horseback* (cat. no. 13), which formed the central part of a large tableau that included two additional Rubens drawings, *Queen Tomyris with the Head of Cyrus* (cat. no. 55) and the *Feast of Herod* (cat. no. 57). William had them framed together "dans un grand écran en bois des Indes, sculpté avec elegance."[107] The *Man on Horseback* is a rare youthful masterpiece by Rubens himself, while the other two are late works retouched by the master. The five beautiful drawings from the model for the *Garden of Love* (cat. nos. 90, 91) are authentic. Although most of William's collection had to be sold after his death, two of the Rubens drawings are still owned by the Dutch royal family: *Fight for the Standard* (today no longer accepted as Rubens) and *Nude Man with Raised Arms* (cat. no. 39).[108]

At the sale of William II's collection, Fodor, an Amsterdam coal magnate, walked away with most of the *Garden of Love* studies. They fitted into Fodor's small ensemble of Dutch and Flemish old master drawings. As Fodor spent most of his money on finished old master drawings and contemporary French works, also highly accomplished, he may not have considered his Rubens acquisition major.[109] But taste changes, and the *Garden of Love* studies are now among the most cherished works in the Amsterdams Historisch Museum, the final home of Fodor's collection.

In the meantime, Rubens had become a national symbol of the new Belgian state, established in 1830. In 1840 a grandiose national celebration was held for the bicentenary of the artist's death, and a statue of him was erected in Antwerp. This renewed interest in Rubens seems to have resulted more in systematic study of the artist's work than in collecting activities. Max Rooses (1839–1914), the author of the monumental *L'oeuvre de Rubens* (1886–92) and the first curator of the new Plantin-Moretus Museum, Antwerp, was a modest collector of drawings by Flemish artists. In 1905 he donated his collection to the Plantin-Moretus Museum. Unfortunately, his stylistic judgment of Rubens was not faultless, and his choices therefore were not always the best. Clement van Cauwenberghs, an Antwerp collector from about 1900, had a better hand at buying. His entire collection, including Rubens's beautiful drawings the *Last Communion of Saint Francis, Henry IV,* and *Hercules Strangling the Nemean Lion* (cat. no. 110), was aquired by the Plantin-Moretus Museum. Together with a small book (acquired by the museum in 1999) containing Rubens's earliest extant drawings, his copies after the *Dance of Death* woodcuts designed by Hans Holbein the Younger (see fig. 3), the former Cauwenberghs sheets are among the rare Rubens drawings that one can admire today on the artist's native soil.[110]

Epilogue: The Twentieth and Twenty-First Centuries

During the twentieth century it became more difficult for collectors, including museums, to find any drawings by Rubens, let alone important ones. With this rarity, prices rose to astronomical heights. Still, there have been collectors, connoisseurs, and museum curators who have been able to bring together interesting groups of drawings by Rubens.

In 1978 the Courtauld Institute of Art Gallery, London, received the collection of Count Antoine Seilern (1901–1978), with thirty-two paintings and twenty-four drawings by or connected with Rubens.[111] Seilern, an art historian himself, who had written his thesis on Rubens at the end of the 1930s, was Austrian by birth, but moved from Vienna to London in 1939. He assembled a group of works that exemplify almost all aspects of Rubens's oeuvre. Among the drawings, the dazzling portrait of Helena Fourment (fig. 10) is probably the most appealing. Other imposing works are *Study for the Bath of Diana, Modello for a Title Page to Cordelius's "Commentaries on Saint Luke,"* and the *Conversion of Saint Paul.* The last was apparently cut in two after the sale of Lankrink's collection. Although the left half had been owned by the Ashmolean Museum, Oxford, since 1940, Seilern was able to reunite them. No less than seven sheets in Seilern's collection carried Lankrink's stamp.[112] This is not a coincidence; the drawings once owned by the early Flemish-English collector are usually of high quality, and for the most part they are sketches rather than finished drawings. Seilern had an obvious liking for sketches by Rubens, be they drawn or painted. At the same time, the Rubens sketch in general was emerging as the subject of serious scholarship, literature, and exhibitions.[113]

Frits Lugt (1884–1970), internationally famous for his learning and connoisseurship, especially in regard to drawings, created a spectacular collection, now housed in the Hotel Turgot in Paris (together with the Institut Néerlandais). Judging from his writing and his drawing collection (and from the way he stored it), it is obvious that in a way the Dutch Lugt emulated his eighteenth-century compatriots. However, Lugt did not neglect Flemish draftsmen, as eighteenth-century Dutch collectors had often done in their great admiration for their own ancestors. Lugt brought together a beautiful array of drawings from the Southern Netherlands (indeed, the first public exhibition at the Institut Néerlandais, mounted after his death, was called "Flemish Drawings of the Seventeenth Century from the Collection of Frits Lugt"). There were twenty Rubens drawings, among them *Woman Holding a Dish, Portrait of Lucas van Leyden, Lansquenets Carousing* (cat. no. 113 recto), and the retouched Giulio sheet, *Hylas.*[114] Perhaps not suprisingly, Lugt had acquired most of them before 1950. After that, prices went sky-high.

Interest in old master drawings came relatively late to the United States. At the Fogg Art Museum, in Cambridge, Paul J. Sachs and Agnes Mongan were in charge in the first half of the twentieth century. As they were more or less building up a collection from scratch, they bought very widely. Still, they were able to acquire a few good Rubens drawings, such as *Head of Nero Caesar Augustus, Two Apostles,* and *Study for the Figure of Christ* (cat. no. 37).[115] The last was given to the museum by Paul Sachs. In 1956 the Fogg Art Museum organized the first exhibition in the United States of drawings and oil sketches by Rubens (all from American collections). Other American institutions, like the recently opened National Gallery of Art, in Washington, D.C., and the Pierpont Morgan Library and The Metropolitan Museum of Art, in New York, were trying to catch up with drawings exhibitions and acquisitions. The Morgan Library already owned a small group of Rubens's drawings, since the collection of the English painter and *marchand-amateur* Charles Fairfax Murray (1849–1919) had been bought *en bloc* by John Pierpont Morgan in 1910. It contained, for example, *Daniel in the Lion's Den* (cat. no. 45), the *Adoration of the Magi, Angel Blowing a Trumpet, Facing Right,* and *Jesuit Priest in Chinese Costume.* The library began to augment the group in the mid-1950s, adding, for instance, works from Rubens's circle like *Study for the Portrait of Marchesa Brigida Spinola Doria* (1954) and *Sleeping Lion* (1977). A lucky strike came in 1957, when the library acquired *Angel Blowing a Trumpet, Facing Left* and thus reunited Rubens's two complementary design drawings for the facade of the Jesuit church in Antwerp. These two sheets had last been together in the sale of the collection of Jonathan Richardson Sr. in 1747. In 1984 two copy drawings Rubens made after Tobias Stimmer, *Meeting of Abraham and Melchisedek* and *Job's Wife and Judith and Holofernes* (cat. no. 1), increased the library's Rubens collection.[116]

About 1950, The Metropolitan Museum of Art had only a few Rubens drawings, such as *Alcibiades Interrupting the Symposium* and the *Presentation in the Temple,* both of which had entered the collection as works by Anthony van Dyck. A great stroke was the acquisition in 1958 of the two large *Garden of Love* drawings previously in the collections of Crozat, Mariette, and Van Eyl Sluyter (cat. nos. 93, 94). After that, however, little happened. This changed when George R. Goldner became curator in charge of the Museum's Department of Drawings and Prints in 1993.[117] Under his tenure the holdings of Northern European drawings are being considerably enlarged. Building up a representative selection of Northern European draftsmanship is a rewarding but not easy task in times when high-quality master drawings on the art market are scarce and when prices can be astronomical. Nevertheless, many important old master drawings have been added to the collection of The Metropolitan Museum of Art in the last ten years. In the case of Rubens one encounters stunning acquisitions, like *The Prophets David and Daniel* (1995; cat. no. 114), *Anatomical Studies* (1996; cat. no. 16), *Susanna* (1998; cat. no. 25), *Portrait of Nicolas Trigault in Chinese Costume* (1999; cat. no. 73), *Sermon in a Village Church* (2000; cat. no. 107), and the *Virgin and Child Adored by Saints* (2002; cat. no. 34). This group beautifully spans almost the entire career of Rubens and represents almost all his drawing techniques and all the functions his drawings played. This great interest at the Metropolitan Museum in the drawn work of the Flemish artist makes it all the more appropriate that the first large exhibition in the United States solely devoted to Rubens drawings is being presented here.

1. J. R. Martin 1968, p. 214. Rubens's letters also make clear how conscientious he was about shutting his studio when he was away (see Huvenne 1993, p. 21).
2. M. Jaffé 1964–66; Muller 1989, pp. 21–22; Wood 1994, passim; Belkin 2004, pp. 310–13.
3. Quoted from Held 1986, p. 16. For the original Flemish text, see Génard 1895, p. 139.
4. Rooses 1897, p. 56.
5. For Rubens's collections of paintings and antique sculpture, see Antwerp 2004b, p. 87, and Healy 2004, pp. 260–63.
6. Held 1963a, p. 74.
7. See Wood 1988, p. 10. A few drawings associated with Rubens claim an Arundel provenance: for example, a copy after a drawing by Giulio Romano, retouched by Rubens, in the art trade (ibid., p. 10, n. 12).
8. Edward Norgate to William Trumbull, December 3, 1619, quoted in Howarth 1985, p. 55, and p. 231, n. 3. This interest in "first and sleight drawings" is in keeping with the well-known praise for quick sketches by Arundel's librarian, Franciscus Junius, in his *Painting of the Ancients* (1638): "many who have a deeper insight in these arts, delight themselves as much in the contemplation of the first, second, and third draughts which great Masters made of their workes as in the workes themselves" (see Held 1963a, pp. 85–86; see also Plomp 2002, p. 35).
9. Also telling is the use of the word "leibheffers" (a misspelling of the Dutch *liefhebbers*, "amateurs"). It is a clear indication of how at the beginning of the seventeenth century the Netherlands had a leading role in the development of the new interest in drawings. For early Dutch collectors, see Plomp 2001–2, pp. 22–26.
10. For Triest, see M. Jaffé 1977, p. 43; for the 1623 commission, see Held 1980, p. 548, under no. 400. For portraits by Van Dyck and Teniers of Triest, see Vienna 1977b, no. 133, ill., and Margret Klinge in Antwerp 1991, nos. 76, 77.
11. See Van Gelder 1965, pp. 5–20.
12. Wood 1994, pp. 333–34.
13. For the inventory of Happaert's goods, see Duverger 1984–, vol. 11, doc. 3754, pp. 370–82.
14. Ibid., p. 374.
15. Huygens 1881, p. 238. For Happaert, see also Amsterdam–Ghent 1982–83, p. 36, and Wood 1994, p. 334.
16. For *Three Nude Women Holding Garlands*, in the Museum Boijmans Van Beuningen, Rotterdam, see the essay "Peter Paul Rubens as a Draftsman" in this publication. For earlier opinions on the attribution of the drawing, see M. Jaffé 1956b, p. 318 ("finished" by Prosper Henry Lankrink; see also note 21 below); Logan and Haverkamp-Begeman 1978, p. 94 (earlier copy drastically retouched by Rubens); Rotterdam 2001, no. 21, ill. (autograph Rubens).
17. For Lankrink's collector's stamp, see Lugt no. 2090 (and suppl.).
18. Belkin 1994, p. 113, n. 14. For Lankrink's paintings collection, see "Lankrink's Collection" 1945, pp. 29–35. There were 464 paintings in all, including 18 originals by Rubens and 4 copies. It is possible that Lankrink's Rubens drawings numbered more than 120—we have only the stamps to go by. Affixed to a drawing now in the British Museum is a small scrap of paper with Lankrink's stamp (Held 1986, no. 142, pl. 140). It was probably cut off when the sheet was (heavily) "restored." The conscientious saving of the collector's stamp in this case is probably exceptional. In other cases the stamp was probably just cut off and thrown away.
19. Wood 1988, p. 12.
20. *Fall of the Damned,* black chalk, pen and brown ink, 429 x 307 mm; Collection Frits Lugt, Institut Néerlandais, Paris, inv. 2250. For *Rubens and His Family Walking in a Garden,* see Cambridge 1981–82, pp. 8–9 (as Anthony van Dyck), and Liedtke 1984, vol. 1, p. 182 (as copy). An attribution to Matthias Jansz. van den Bergh (1615–1687) should perhaps be considered; compare, for example, his summary copy drawing of the family portrait in the Kupferstichkabinett, Berlin (Bock and Rosenberg 1930, vol. 1, p. 82, no. 2232, vol. 2, ill.). Before accusing Lankrink of misattributions, one should keep in mind that we don't know under which artists' names he filed his drawings.
21. On collecting Italian drawings, see Van Gelder and Jost 1985, pp. 206–11; Dethloff 1992, p. 204; Plomp 2002, pp. 29–40. Additions in some of the Italian drawings that Rubens retouched have been rather unconvincingly attributed to Lankrink. It has been suggested that Lankrink, after having "finished" such a drawing, used his collector's stamp as his signature (see M. Jaffé 1956b, p. 318; Müller Hofstede 1964, p. 15; Rotterdam 2001, p. 347, under no. V5). It is not necessarily the case, however, that Lankrink himself ever applied the mark to the works in his collection. Roger North, for instance, put Peter Lely's collector's stamp on the drawings only just before the Lely sale (see Lugt, p. 388, under no. 2092); the same probably applies to Nicolaes Flinck's stamp (see Plomp 2001–2, pp. 91–92). Several Lankrink drawings give the impression of having been cut and stamped afterward, at the time of the sale (see London 1977a, no. 46, ill., and Oxford–London 1988, p. 59, under no. 16). The same practice of cutting a drawing and later putting the collector's stamp on it was probably followed at the Lely sale (see Dethloff 1992, p. 198).
22. For Jabach, see Py 2001. The Rubens school drawing now in Basel, the *Martyrdom of Saint Peter,* which shows the same composition as the Cologne altar, was in Everhard Jabach's collection and later in that of his grandson Michael (see Falk 1992, pp. 178–79, fig. 1).
23. Py 2001, p. 12. Until recently it was believed—following Mariette (1851–60, p. 70)—that Jabach acquired all his Rubens drawings at the 1657 sale (see note 4 above). However, Wood (1994, p. 333) found that Happaert must have been the main buyer at the 1657 sale.
24. Monbeig Goguel 1988, pp. 821–35.
25. For Jabach's Rubens drawings in the Louvre, Paris, see Lugt 1949, nos. 1009, 1010, 1027, 1028, 1035, 1036, *1037*, 1038, 1040–47 (eight drawings after Michelangelo), 1049–56, *1057*, *1060*, 1061, 1066, *1068*, 1070, 1075–77, 1079–80, 1082, 1085, 1103, 1106–10, 1126, 1128, *1129*, 1130, 1133–35, *1136*, 1137, *1139–40*, 1147, *1148*, 1149, 1157, 1161, 1169–70, 1185, 1219–20, 1229, 1255, 1257, 1258, 1264–65. The numbers in italics are also drawings that stem from Jabach, although Lugt does not mention them as such (I thank Bernadette Py, of the Musée du Louvre, who brought this to my attention).

For Jabach's post-1671 drawings, see Py 2001, p. 12, nos. 271–80, 461, 538–40, 543, 544, 580–83, 1003–5, 1165–67.

26. See Belkin 2000, pp. 79–80.

27. For the provenance of Rubens's drawings series after Holbein, see ibid., pp. 76–81. For the results of the Boeckhorst auction, see Antwerp–Münster 1990, p. 24.

28. Duverger 1984–, vol. 10, doc. 3333, pp. 347ff. (p. 359: "Boeren en Boerinnen crabbelinge Rubbens" [see cat. no. 103]; p. 369: "Een teeckenboeck van Rubbens / Een cleyn teeckenboecken van 71 bladeren met root crijt / Noch een cleyn boecken van Rubbens met Architectuer" (a drawing book by Rubens / a small drawing book of seventy-one pages, in red chalk [also by Rubens?] / another small book by Rubens, with architecture).

29. See Konow 1940, pp. 58–63, and Berlin 1977, nos. 1, 4, 5, 17, 19, 21, 23(?), 27, ill. The attribution to Rubens of most of these drawings has been doubted, however (see Logan 1987, p. 67). Merian probably kept the sheet *A Knight and a Lady* (cat. no. 6) as a work by Israhel van Meckenem (ca. 1440/45–1503).

30. For Albert's exchange with the Hofbibliothek, see Barbara Dossi in Toronto–New York 2000, pp. 56–57. The Rubens drawings that came from the Hofbibliothek are Vienna 1977b, nos. 9, 11–17, 20–22, 24, 27, 28, 33, 37, 39, 40, 44, 45, 50, 52, 53, 59, 67, 102, 116, ill. I thank Heinz Widauer and Marianne Bisanz-Prakken, both from the Albertina, Vienna, who helped me with this provenance.

31. For Lanier, see Wood 1988, pp. 10–11; for Lely, Dethloff 2003, p. 127.

32. Richardson did say that the sketch was "at the very pinnacle of art" (see Finsten 1993, p. 54). Such a denomination, however, is probably a topos (see Held 1963a, pp. 86–90).

33. For Richardson's ownership of four drawings of Rubens's second wife, Helena Fourment, see Wood 1988, p. 12; Held 1986, nos. 146, pl. 143 (Hecke), 149, pl. 154 (Isabella Brant), 222, pl. 212 (Frans Rubens). For all three portraits of Frans Rubens owned by Richardson, see Rotterdam 2001, p. 348.

34. Sale of Jonathan Richardson Sr., London, Cock, January 22 and following days, 1747, p. 38, lot 54: "Five [drawings] *Rubens* as a satyr, and his wife, *P. Veronese, Guido etc.*" For the *Pan and Syrinx* drawing in the British Museum, see Edinburgh–Nottingham 2002, no. 26, ill.

35. Held 1986, no. 132, pl. 126 *(Lazarus)*, no. 220, pl. 210 *(Diana)*.

36. Richardson 1725, p. 206, and Richardson 1722, p. 351; quoted in Wood 1988, pp. 8, 13. Comparing portraits by Rubens and Anthony van Dyck, Richardson seemed to prefer the latter: "Son [Rubens] Dessein étoit plus grand, mais aussi peu correct, & aussi éloigné du meilleur goût *Italien* & de l'Antique, que celui de son Disciple [Van Dyck]" (Richardson 1728, vol. 1, p. 29). Richardson's sometime dislike of Rubens's portraits is evident in his comment on Rubens's portrait of his first wife, Isabella Brant (cat. no. 82 recto), a drawing that he himself owned: "le Visage est un des plus desagréables que j'aie jamais vus; & je suis sûr, qu'il l'est plus qu'il n'étoit nécessaire pour la faire ressembler, quelque laide qu'elle fût éfectivement." (Richardson 1728, p. 28).

37. Richardson 1719, pp. 175–76, quoted in Wood 1988, p. 9; Richardson 1722, vol. 1, p. 79. See also Logan 1987, p. 65.

38. Richardson 1725, p. 60, and Wood 1988, p. 9. See also Brigid Cleaver in Oxford–London 1988, p. 56, under no. 15.

39. For Hudson's acquisition of Rubens drawings at the 1747 Richardson sale, see Wood 1988, p. 14 (with bibl.).

40. Held 1986, no. 207, pl. 201 *(Woman with a Fan)*, no. 225, pl. 207 (Rubens's *Self-Portrait*).

41. For Hudson, see Lugt no. 2432, and London 1979, nos. 67–78, ill. (with intro.). For Reynolds, see Martin Royalton-Kisch, "Rubens as a Collector," in London 1978, pp. 61–75, and, for Reynolds's apparent lack of enthusiasm for Rubens's drawings, Held 1980, vol. 1, p. 7, n. 5.

42. See Martin Royalton-Kisch in Antwerp–London 1999a, pp. 46–47 (with bibl.). Kisch attributes the entire series to Gillis Claesz d'Hondecoeter (ca. 1570–1638).

43. For Egmont as a collector, but not a great connoisseur, see Haverkamp-Begemann and Logan 1970, vol. 1, p. xii. The authors did not pay attention to the English annotations on the drawings from the Egmont Albums, which may well have originated with Egmont. We encounter the same handwriting on other drawings that were once in his collection, including two sheets now in the British Museum, London (Hind 1923, pp. 32–33, nos. 105, 107, pl. XIV). I thank Martin Royalton-Kisch, of the British Museum, for his help in this matter.

44. Judson and Van de Velde 1978, vol. 1, nos. 10a, 39a, 46a, 51b, 55a, 61b, figs. 56, 131, 155, 175, 191, 209.

45. The *Seated Young Woman with Raised Hands* in Berlin (cat. no. 90) has the collector's mark of Richardson Jr. The *Figure Study of a Standing Woman (Helena Fourment?)*, formerly in the Franz Koenigs Collection and now in the Pushkin State Museum, Moscow, carries Hudson's collector's mark (see Elen 1989, no. 521). According to Samuel Woodburn, more *Garden of Love* studies came from Hudson (for example, cat. nos. 90, 91), but they do not carry his collector's mark (see London 1835, nos. 46–48).

46. London 1977a, no. 63, ill.

47. Ibid., nos. 90–93 (four drawings connected with the *Fall of the Damned)*, 162 *("Coup de Lance")*, 166 *(Descent of the Holy Spirit)*, ill.

48. Judson 2000, no. 42, copy 1, fig. 128 *(Our Lady of Sorrows)*; Hind 1923, p. 32, no. 104, pl. XIII *(Head of a Negro Woman)*.

49. Held 1963a, pp. 90–91.

50. London 1835, no. 31. See also London 1977a, no. 63, ill. (*Hercules Strangling the Nemean Lion*, Sterling and Francine Clark Art Institute, Williamstown).

51. For the six Rubens drawings from Sloane's collection, see Hind 1923, pp. 16–47, nos. 32, 115, 116, 125, 126, pls. V, XVI, XVII, and London 1977a, no. 46, ill. For Payne Knight's and Malcolm's Rubens drawings, see London 1977a, passim. On Malcolm as a drawing collector in general, see London 1996, passim.

52. Fawkener (Hind 1923, pp. 9–47, nos. 10, 51, 52, 127, 129), Cracherode (Hind 1923, pp. 7–45, nos. 5, 7, 14, 18, 27, 108, 121, pls. IV, XV), Salting (Hind 1923, p. 15, nos. 28, 30). For drawings from the Peel collection, see Popham 1935–36, pp. 10–18.

53. For de Piles's correspondence with Philip Rubens, see Ruelens 1883, pp. 157–75, and Teyssédre 1965, p. 228. These items were still with the artist's family and not sold at the 1657 sale probably because they belonged to the papers and books ("written as well as printed") bequeathed to Albert, the antiquarian among Rubens's children (for this bequest, see Génard 1896, pp. 253–55).

54. For Rubens's *Pocket Book*, which was almost completely lost in a fire that consumed most of the important drawings and prints collection of the cabinetmaker André-Charles Boulle (1642–1732), see M. Jaffé 1966, vol. 1, p. 302, and London 1988–89, pp. 50–51, under nos. 58, 59; for the *Costume Book*, Belkin 1980; for the album with figure heads, Eidelberg 1997.

55. One loose Rubens sheet that de Piles owned was "la chûte des Anges qui l'a été [gravé] par Soutman" (Mariette 1741, lot 829; see also Hollstein 1949–, vol. 27 [1983], p. 227, no. 8). The only other artist for whom we have numbers is Rembrandt; it seems that de Piles owned about three hundred sheets by him (Schatborn 1981, pp. 41–42).

56. For Crozat, see Hattori 1997 (p. 181 mentions the acquisition of the De Piles collection) and Hattori 2003. Rubens's *Pocket Book* was probably not acquired by Crozat, as it formed part of Boulle's collection in 1720 (see note 54 above).

57. How many frontispieces and title pages were in Crozat's collection is not clear, as they are not described individually. However, two lots in Crozat's catalogue—together comprising twenty-eight drawings—contained a substantial number of them (Mariette 1741, lots 824, 826).

58. For Rubens's retouching and restoring of old master drawings, see Logan and Haverkamp-Begemann 1978, pp. 94–96. For a Salviati drawing from the collections of Crozat and Mariette (with an inscription by the latter) that Rubens heavily retouched (and to which he added a whole corner), see London–Paris–Bern–Brussels 1972, no. 74, pl. 40.

59. "Dans ses plus legeres Esquisses, ce grand Maître met une ame & un esprit, qui dénotent la rapidité avec laquelle il concevoit & executoit ses pensées. Mais lorsqu'il les met au net, alors, sans rien perdre de cet esprit, qui devient seulement plus reglé, il y ajoute tout ce qu'un homme qui possedoit dans un éminent degré les differentes parties de la peinture, & singulierement celle du clair-obscur, étoit capable d'imaginer pour en faire des ouvrages accomplis" (Mariette 1741, pp. 97–98, under lot 845).

60. For Mariette as a collector, see Paris 1967; for *Women Visiting the Vegetable Market,* Held 1985, p. 35, n. 6. Mariette praised highly the preparatory works for prints. He stated that there is no reason to be surprised by the perfect prints: "les beaux modéles qu'ils [the engravers] avoient devant les yeux, les y conduisoient" (Mariette 1741, p. 96, under lot 835).
61. Ibid., p. 98, under lot 845.
62. With Rubens paintings it is the other way around, as in the eighteenth century France (and Germany) were better off than England; see Hans Vlieghe in *The Dictionary of Art,* ed. Jane Turner (New York, 1996), vol. 27, p. 301.
63. Mariette 1851–60, vol. 5, p. 70. Bellori (1672 [1968 ed.], p. 308) specifically mentioned the *Battle of the Amazons,* for which, he said, Anthony van Dyck made the engraver's drawing, now in Christ Church, Oxford. For the drawing and Vorsterman's print, see Antwerp–Amsterdam 1999–2000, no. 4, ill.
64. Dezallier d'Argenville 1745–52, vol. 2, p. 145: "Les desseins finis qui passent pour être de lui, ont été faits par des graveurs d'après ses tableaux; Rubens y donnoit seulement quelques coups hardis." In his 1762 edition Dezallier changed "engravers" to "his pupils and above all Vandyck." In a footnote he said that this should be a warning to collectors—he himself had been deceived two times—and he refered the reader to a section where he stated that "drawings that are too finished rarely are original" (Dezallier d'Argenville 1762, vol. 1, p. lxii, vol. 3, p. 295).
65. Labbé and Bicart-Sée 1996, no. 1559, ill. We will probably never know if this was perhaps one of his two mistakes (see note 64 above).
66. Held 1986, p. 9, no. 103, pl. 99.
67. Ibid., p. 41, n. 26, fig. 7.
68. For Atger, see Lugt no. 38; for His de la Salle, Lugt nos. 1332, 1333, and Lugt 1949, no. 1022.
69. Sandrart is known to have had two art collections. The first he discarded in 1645 (see Klemm 1986, p. 339). For the second one, see Sandrart 1925, p. 333. For Rubens's *Adoration of the Shepherds* in the Collection Frits Lugt, Institut Néerlandais, Paris, see Haarlem–Paris 2001–2, vol. 2, no. 69, ill.
70. See note 29 above.
71. For the history of the Rubens drawings collection in the Berlin Kupferstichkabinett, see Berlin 1977, p. 10. For Rubens drawings from the Beckerath collection, see Berlin 2002–3, nos. 93, 94, ill.
72. For the 1723 and 1726 acquisitions, see Christian Dittrich in Dresden–Vienna 1997–98, p. 14. For Wagner, see Dittrich 1987, pp. 7–38.
73. For the oil sketch in Dresden of Saint Roch, see Dittrich 1987, pp. 8–9, fig. 2.
74. Held 1986, no. 178, pl. 175 *(Portrait of the Daughter of Balthasar Gerbier).* For Cobenzl, see Lugt no. 2858b and Brussels–Rotterdam–Paris 1972–73, pp. ix–xi.
75. Brussels–Rotterdam–Paris 1972–73, no. 89, pl. 90, and Vlieghe 1973, no. 146c, fig. 114.
76. For the "Rubens" drawings owned by De Ligne, see Vienna 1977b, nos. 36, 47, 48, 58 (Correggio), 74, 81, 82, 108, 109, 129, 154–158, 160–162, ill.
77. See note 76 above.
78. Vienna 1977b, nos. 84, 110, ill. (see pp. 251–58 for the 1822 inventory, and p. 258 for the copies).
79. Quoted from ibid., p. 257. See also Erwin Mitsch in ibid., pp. viii–ix.
80. *Die Rubenszeichnungen der Albertina: Zum 400. Geburtstag.* See Vienna 1977b.
81. The landscape painter Franz Rechberger (1771–1841) compiled the 1822 catalogue. A friend and colleague of Adam von Bartsch, Rechberger acquired quite a reputation as a connoisseur (see Barbara Dossi in Toronto–New York 2000, p. 31).
82. The Delft collector Valerius Röver (1686–1739) mentioned in the handwritten inventory of his art collection (now in the Universiteitsbibliotheek van Amsterdam [inv. II A 18; see Mendes da Costa 1902, p. 231, no. 1446a]) that he acquired nine Rubens drawings from Bergesteyn (see album 6: eight sheets; album 39: one sheet).
83. For possible Rubens drawings with Flinck's collector's mark, see M. Jaffé 2002, vol. 1, nos. 965, 969, 1144, 1152, ill. Another indication that there were not many Rubens drawings in the Dutch Republic about 1700 is the relatively limited supply offered by the art dealer Jan Pietersz. Zomer (1641–1724). His sales catalogue, dating from 1720–24, contains only about a dozen sheets by Rubens (in the portfolios G, W, Y, Z, DD, and 44). I have come across only one drawing associated with Rubens with Zomer's collector's mark (Lugt no. 511): *Portrait of Charles V* (black and red chalk, pen and black ink, 157 x 136 mm; Amsterdams Historisch Museum, inv. TA 10376). Although attributed by the museum to Jacob de Wit, the sheet was not included in the recent catalogue Oud and Van Oosterzee 1999. I thank Norbert Middelkoop, of the Amsterdams Historisch Museum, for his help in this matter.
84. Having long owned Rubens's design for the title page to Frans Verhaer's *Annales Ducum seu Principum Brabantiae,* after which the Jacobs title page was copied (Hind 1923, p. 18, no. 38, pl. VI), the British Museum, London, acquired the Jacobs title page in 1985 (inv. 1985-7-13-2). Jane Shoaf Turner and Felice Stampfle gathered information on Jacobs, also calling attention to the British Museum title page (see Stampfle 1991, p. 103).
85. Stampfle 1991, p. 103.
86. For *Landscape with Farm Buildings,* see ibid., no. 322, ill., and Martin Royalton-Kisch in Antwerp–London 1999a, pp. 46–47.
87. If not otherwise indicated, the information in this paragraph comes from Plomp 2001–2, pp. 232–36, and Plomp 2002, pp. 258–61.
88. At the same time other book illustrations by Rubens, like the title pages in the Crozat collection, surfaced. It seems that these book-related drawings remained together in an as-yet-unknown collection, becoming available to individual collectors only in the early eighteenth century.
89. Stampfle 1991, no. 305 *(Adoration of the Magi),* ill.; Vienna 1977b, no. 69 *(Title Page for Oliver Bonartus),* ill.; London 1988–89, no. 35 *(Saint Francis Receiving the Infant Christ),* ill.
90. London 1977a, no. 159, ill., and Held 1986, p. 14, fig. 3.
91. The dealer Christiaan Josi (1768–1828) mentioned how his colleague Pieter Fouquet brought the two *Garden of Love* drawings to Amsterdam at the end of the eighteenth century and sold them to the collector Jan Gildemeester (1744–1799). After the Van Eyl Sluyter sale in 1814 Josi took both drawings to England (see Josi 1821, n.p. [under Rubens], and also cat. nos. 93, 94).
92. Heiland 1969, p. 422. For the two predella paintings, the *Miracle of Saint Walburga* and *Angels Carrying the Dead Body of Saint Catherine of Alexandria,* see Judson 2000, no. 23, fig. 88, and no. 25.
93. Sale of Jacob de Wit, Amsterdam, De Leth and Van Schorrenberg, March 10, 1755, Album C, lots 21–27 (no. 26 contains two sheets).
94. J. Q. van Regteren Altena suggested already in 1938 that *Crouching Man Seen from the Back* was worked over by De Wit (see Judson 2000, no. 20i). Michael Jaffé wrote in 1956 (1956b, p. 318): "the familiar blackish wash of J. de Wit shades Mr Chr. P. van Eeghen's splendid life-study." For De Wit's retouching Rubens drawings, see Staring 1958, pp. 110–11, and Held 1986, p. 49, n. 35. For De Wit's retouching a drawing by Jacob Jordaens, see Te Rijdt 2001, pp. 34–37. Comparable drawings entirely by De Wit with the same kinds of washes, applied in the same way, are in the Kunsthalle, Bremen, in the Prentenkabinet der Universiteit, Leiden (see Amsterdam 2003, pp. 21–23, ills.), and in Otterlo (Otterlo, Rijksmuseum Kröller-Müller 1959, no. 125, fig. 55).
95. For Rubens's original and De Wit's copy, see Judson 2000, nos. 20b, fig. 65 (De Wit; from the Winthrop collection), and 20c, fig. 66 (Rubens; from the Sachs collection); Judson attributed both sheets to Rubens. Already in 1958 J. Q. van Regteren Altena suggested that De Wit added the washes on the Winthrop sheet. Three years later Frits Lugt attributed the Winthrop drawing entirely to De Wit (Fogg Art Museum files). Judson did not mention either of these opinions.
96. In the seventeenth and eighteenth centuries, retouching old master drawings was nothing exceptional. In France, for example, Jabach hired an artist to "finish" some of his treasured drawings (see note 24 above). The English collector John Perceval, 1st Earl of Egmont (1683–1748), also seems to have employed someone to add washes to a great many of his drawings (see Haverkamp-Begemann and Logan 1970, vol. 1, pp. xii–xiii). In the Dutch Republic in the eighteenth century, too, contemporary artists finished old master drawings (see Broos 1989, pp. 34ff). Discussing the retouching practice in Holland in the eighteenth century, Te Rijdt (2001, p. 37) distinguishes lucrative retouching for dealers from personal retouchings for private enjoyment and learning.

97. Sale of Jacob de Wit, Amsterdam, De Leth and Van Schorrenberg, March 10, 1755, Album F, lots 8: "Christ Showing His Wounds to His Disciples by P. P. Rubens, retouched by J. de Wit"; 13: "Crucifix by Rubens; and retouched by J. de Wit"; F22: "Two Females Heads by Rubens, retouched by J. de Wit"; 35: "A ditto [female head] by Rubens, retouched by J. de Wit." For more Rubens (school) drawings finished by De Wit and probably owned by him, see notes 101 and 102 below. The Rubens school drawing *Two Prisoners,* in the Louvre (Lugt 1949, no. 1177), was also retouched by De Wit.

98. Sale of B. Hagelis, Amsterdam, De Leth, March 8, 1762, Album N, lot 1162: "Rubens and His Wife as a Shepherd and a Shepherdess, by Rubens and De Wit"; sale of P. Yver, Amsterdam, March 31, 1788, Album D, lot XX: "The Annunciation, powerfully drawn and beautifully washed by Rubens and retouched by J. de Wit"; sale of D. de Jongh, Rotterdam, Van Rijp . . . Van Leen, March 26, 1810, Album Y, lot 2: "A Head of Young Man by Rubens, retouched by J. de Wit"; sale of Hendrik van Eyl Sluyter, Amsterdam, Van der Schley . . . De Vries, September 26, 1814, Album L, lot 8: "A Church Gathering: Two Bishops, One Cardinal and Another Religious Person, red chalk, black ink, indigo, heightened with white on gray paper by Rubens and De Wit"; sale of Jan Gildemeester, Amsterdam, Van der Schley . . . Pruyssenaar, November 24, 1800, Album B, lots 13: "Last Supper, pen and black ink by PP Rubens and J. de Wit"; 14: "Christ Is Saying to the Sick, Take Your Bed and Walk, artfully executed with the pen, black ink, and wash by the same masters [Rubens and De Wit]"; sale of J. de Bosch, Amsterdam, October 5, 1767, Album D, lot 245: "Maria de Medicis, with black chalk and black ink, by Rubens and finished by J. de Wit."

99. See White and Crawley 1994, no. 439, ill. For the 1759 description of the drawing as by Rubens and De Wit, see Plomp forthcoming.

100. For *Christ and the Apostles* in the Albertina, see Vienna 1977b, nos. 87–99, ill. For Ryckmans's prints, see Hollstein 1949–, vol. 20 (1978), pp. 204–5, nos. 15–28.

101. The Vienna series of *Christ and the Apostles* might have come from De Wit's collection. It has been argued that De Wit retouched only drawings in his own collection (see Te Rijdt 2001, p. 37). In De Wit's sale catalogue, a series of *Christ and the Apostles* is described, though not as by Rubens and retouched by De Wit but as by De Wit alone (see sale of Jacob de Wit, Amsterdam, De Leth and Van Schorrenberg, March 10, 1755, Album E, lot 16: "Thirteen pieces, being Christ and the Twelve Apostles, very elaborate with black chalk and black ink, drawn by the same artist [Jacob de Wit]").

102. Michael Jaffé attributed the drawings in Cambridge and Vienna to Jacob Jordaens (see Ottawa 1968–69, nos. 160, 252, ill.). These attributions have not been universally accepted (see Haverkamp-Begeman 1969, p. 177; d'Hulst 1974, vol. 2, nos. B19, D8). The clear contours, the love of (cross)-hatchings, and the almost abstract rendition of the hair in the *Miracle of Saint Walburga* are typical for De Wit's chalk drawings, as one can judge from his works in the Rijksprentenkabinet, Amsterdam (see Amsterdam 1995, p. 149, fig. 113, p. 175, pl. XV). Most of the figures in *Diana and Her Nymphs Returning from the Hunt,* like the two androgynous men on the left, the chubby putti in the foreground, and the stately but girlish nymphs on the right, are characteristic for De Wit; we find them often in his paintings (see Staring 1958, figs. 46, 47, 53, 92, 94). The *Miracle of Saint Walburga* was made after a Rubens painting De Wit owned himself (see note 91 above). Both sheets are possibly to be identified with drawings (both under the name of Rubens) in the De Wit sale (see sale of Jacob de Wit, Amsterdam, De Leth and Van Schorrenberg, March 10, 1755, Album C, lots 8: "A Saint in a Ship, with a Very Turbulent Sea" and 10: "Some Nymphs with Satyrs, done in colors."

103. Josi 1821, n.p. Josi reproduced one drawing by Rubens, *Saint Francis Kneeling, Receiving the Infant Christ,* now in the Courtauld Institute of Art Gallery, London (see London 1988–89, no. 35, ill.).

104. "Ces études sont très estimées des amateurs." Josi tells us as well that he owns two figure studies for the *Garden of Love* (see Josi 1821, n.p. [under Rubens]).

105. For the *Penitent Magdalen,* see sale, London, Christie's, July 7, 1998, lot 270, ill.; for the *Three Graces* in Rotterdam, see Rotterdam 2001, p. 354, MB 5125, ill.; and for the *Bull Hunt* in the Collection Frits Lugt, Paris, see Balis 1986, no. 26, copy 8.

106. For William II's art collections, see Hinterding and Horsch 1989, passim.

107. Sale of William II, The Hague, De Vries / Roos / Brondgeest, August 12–20, 1850, lot 282. Eventually the three drawings were withdrawn from the sale on behalf of William's daughter, Sophie (1824–1897), the Grand Duchess of Sachsen-Weimar-Eisenach. For the drawings' provenances, see cat. nos. 13, 55, 57.

108. For the complete group of *Garden of Love* model drawings, see Schapelhouman 1979, p. 103. For the *Fight for the Standard* in the Dutch royal collection, see Anne-Marie Logan in New York 2003, pp. 671–78, under no. 135.

109. For Fodor's collection, see Broos 1981, p. 7, and Hamilton–New York–Amsterdam 1985–86, pp. 9–13.

110. For the *Last Communion of Saint Francis* and *Henry IV,* see Antwerp 1971, nos. 61, 65, pls. 5a, 5b, 9, and Held 1986, no. 135, pl. 128. For Rubens's drawings after Holbein's *Dance of Death,* see Antwerp 2000 and Lille 2004, no. 1.

111. For Seilern and his collections, see Van Claerbergen 2003–4, pp. 23–30. For Seilern's Rubens paintings and especially the drawings, see London 1988–89, passim.

112. Seilern 1955, nos. 57 *(Conversion of Saint Paul),* 64 *(Helena Fourment),* 65 *(Diana).* For Lankrink, see London 1988–89, nos. 24, 25, 30 (stamped twice), 39, 41, 43 (as "ascribed to Van Dyck"), ill.

113. Van Claerbergen 2003–4a, p. 26.

114. London–Paris–Bern–Brussels 1972, no. 72, pl. 35 *(Hylas),* no. 81, pl. 37 *(Lucas van Leyden),* no. 84, pl. 42 *(Woman Holding a Dish),* no. 85, pls. 44, 45 *(Lansquenets Carousing).*

115. Cambridge, Mass.–New York 1956, nos. 21 *(Two Apostles),* 27 *(Head of Nero Caesar Augustus).*

116. For all the Rubens drawings in the Pierpont Morgan Library, New York, mentioned, see Stampfle 1991, nos. 294, 295, 305, 308–10, ill.

117. Previously, Goldner had bought equally well for the J. Paul Getty Museum, Los Angeles; see Goldner 1988, nos. 90–94, ill., and Goldner and Hendrix 1992, nos. 85, 86, ill.

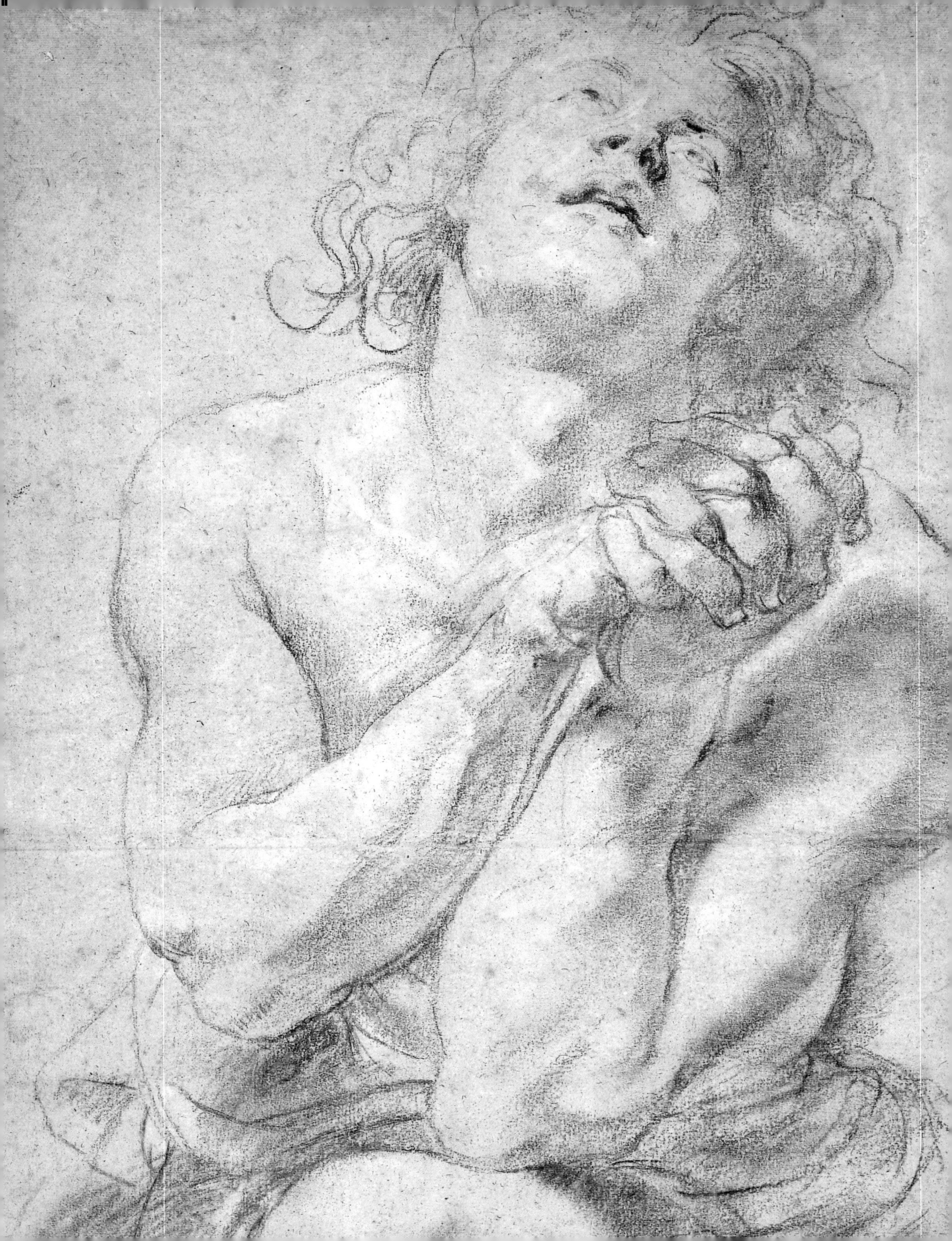

CATALOGUE

RUBENS'S BEGINNINGS

1. *Job's Wife and Judith and Holofernes,* ca. 1596–97

Pen and brown ink, 188 x 127 mm (7 7/16 x 5 in.)
Inscribed by the artist in pen and brown ink at lower right: *sy taster int doncker naer* (she gropes for it in the dark)

The Pierpont Morgan Library, New York; Gift of Otto Manley (1984.46)

PROVENANCE: Charles Fairfax Murray (1849–1919), London (for unknown reasons not included in John Pierpont Morgan's acquisition in 1909); Victor Ezekiel (his sale, London, Sotheby's, February 7, 1956, lot 1659; parcel of drawings to Koblitz); Baron Koblitz; Dr. Edmund Schilling (1888–1974), London; Otto Manley (d. 1989), Scarsdale, New York; gift to the Pierpont Morgan Library.

LITERATURE: Lugt 1943, pp. 109, 111, fig. 16; Held 1959, no. 156, pl. 166, and p. 53; Held 1986, no. 5, pl. 5; Stampfle 1991, no. 294, ill.; Held 1993, p. 297, no. 294.

EXHIBITION: Basel 1984, no. 101, fig. 144.

Rubens's earliest known drawings are copies after prints by Hans Holbein the Younger (1497/98–1543), Jost Amman (1539–1591), and Tobias Stimmer (1539–1584). He copied the images on this sheet from Stimmer's *Neue künstliche Figuren Biblischer Historien,* the so-called Stimmer Bible, published in Basel in 1576. This widely disseminated and popular picture Bible consists of 168 woodcuts by Stimmer (134 scenes from the Old Testament, 34 from the New Testament), accompanied by brief moralizing texts in rhyme by Johann Fischart, called Mentzer (1546–1590). The importance of Stimmer's woodcuts to Rubens can be gauged from his recommendation, in 1627, to the young German painter and writer Joachim von Sandrart (1606–1688) to copy from Stimmer's "jewel" (*Kleinod*), as Rubens confessed he had done in his youth.[1]

On the present sheet Rubens united two women from the Old Testament, Judith and Job's wife. The scene in the lower half of the sheet is taken from the Book of Judith in the Stimmer Bible (fig. 33) and shows Judith preparing to cut off the head of the slumbering Assyrian commander Holofernes and thus deliver the Jews. The drawing gives no indication of the darkened tent in which Stimmer's scene takes place, and Rubens explained Judith's outstretched right arm in a brief inscription in his native Flemish: *sy taster int doncker naer,* or, she gropes for it (the head of Holofernes) in the dark. Rubens omitted the maidservant who assisted Judith in her gruesome deed; in Stimmer's woodcut she kneels directly behind her mistress. (Rubens returned to the theme of Judith and Holofernes a number of times; see, for example, cat. no. 27.)

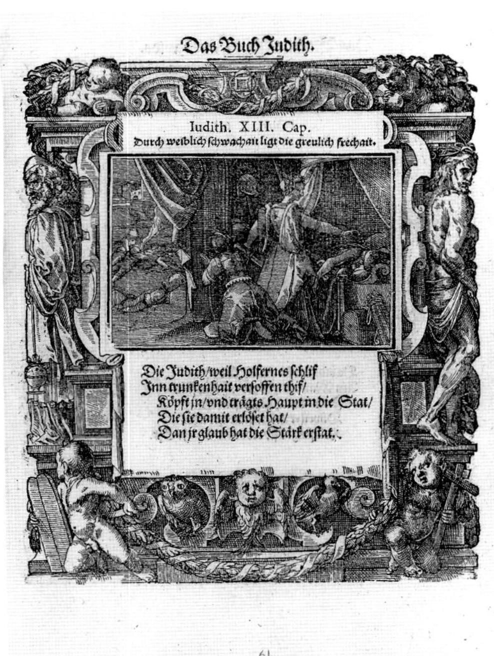

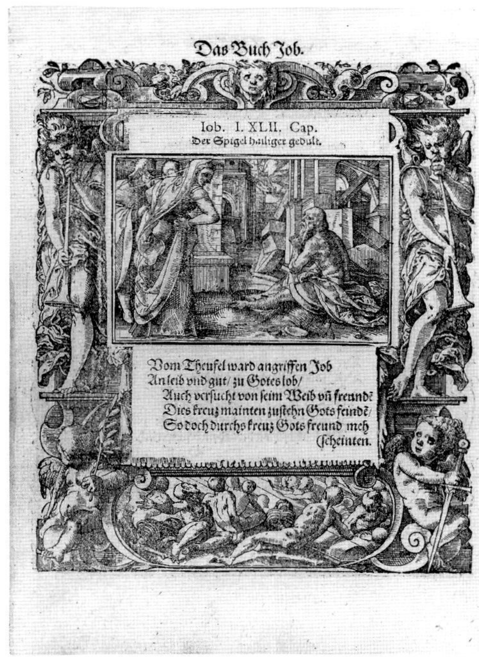

Fig. 33 (left). Tobias Stimmer, *Judith and Holofernes,* 1576. Woodcut, 209 x 155 mm (8 1/4 x 6 1/8 in.). From Tobias Stimmer, *Neue künstliche Figuren Biblischer Historien* (Basel, 1576), XIII, leaf O IV. The Metropolitan Museum of Art, New York; Harris Brisbane Dick Fund, 1945 (45.42.2)

Fig. 34 (right). Tobias Stimmer, *Job and His Wife,* 1576. Woodcut, 20.9 x 15.5 cm (8 1/4 x 6 1/8 in.). From Tobias Stimmer, *Neue künstliche Figuren Biblischer Historien* (Basel 1576), I.XLII, leaf Q II verso. The Metropolitan Museum of Art, New York; Harris Brisbane Dick Fund, 1945 (45.42.2)

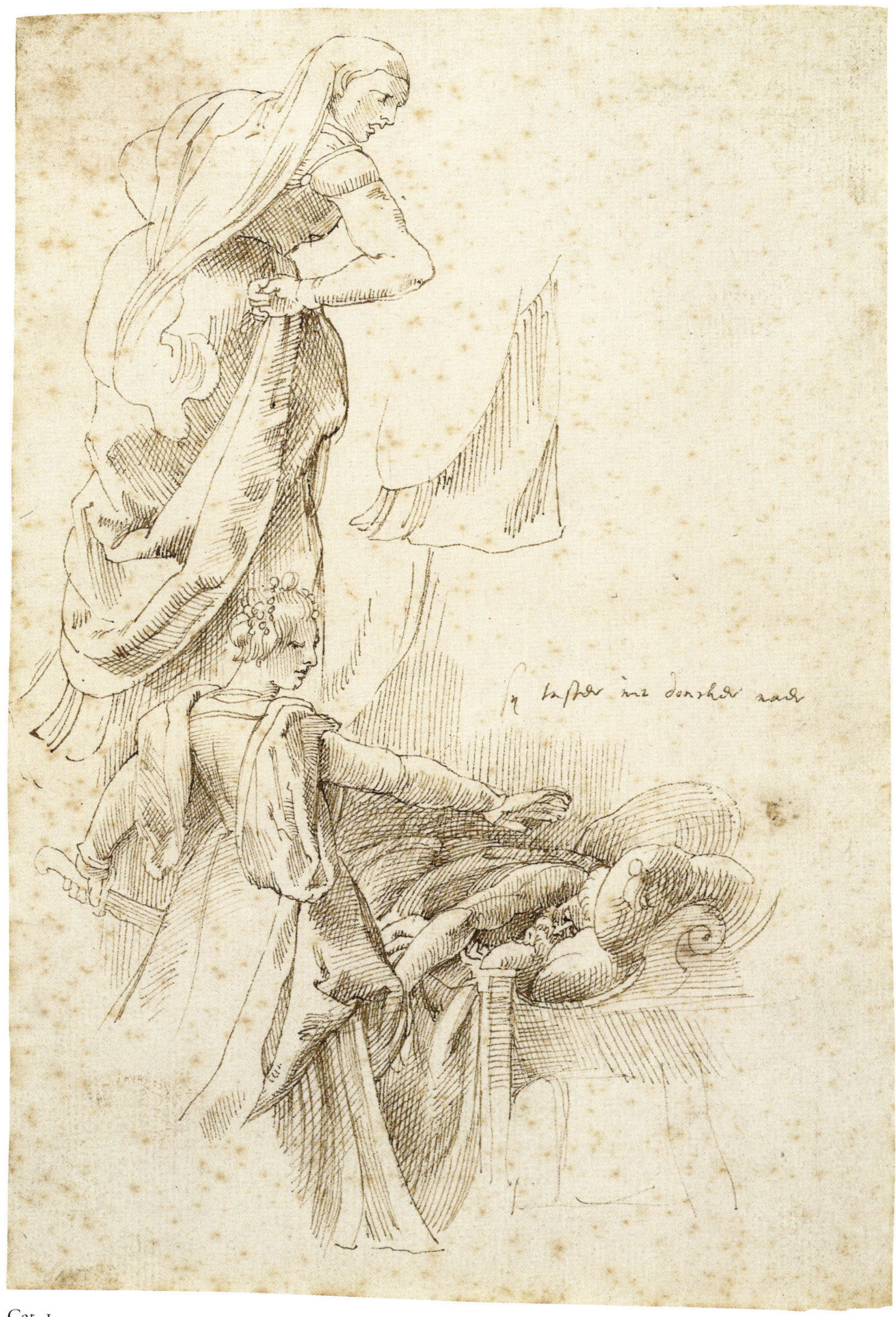

Cat. 1

In the upper half of the sheet Rubens copied Job's wife from an illustration for the Book of Job in the Stimmer Bible (fig. 34). The woodcut shows her berating her husband, whom the accompanying German text describes as "the mirror of holy patience" (*der Spigel hailiger gedult*) but whom Rubens omits. In all likelihood Rubens drew Judith and Holofernes first and Job's wife second. Running out of room for the latter's dress, which is partially obscured by Judith's head, Rubens sketched the complete hem of the dress in the center of the sheet.

Rubens's copies in pen and brown ink are about double the size of the figures in the woodcuts from the Stimmer Bible. The lines of his pen are much more fluid, undulating, and refined than the stiff printed lines of Stimmer's woodcuts and do not slavishly follow their model. Rubens's lines have a greater degree of differentiation as a consequence of the varied pressure he applied to the quill pen. It was not Rubens's intention to imitate the woodcut technique. As a young apprentice, he copied prints such as Stimmer's primarily in order to learn the artist's trade.

A significant feature of Rubens's artistic career is already evident in this early drawing: Rubens is highly selective, using copying to build a repertory of visual material and taking from a composition only that which catches his interest. At times he rearranges the details into an entirely new image, as in his copy after figures from engravings in Hendrick Goltzius's Passion series (see cat. no. 2).

1. Sandrart 1925, p. 106; see also pp. 102–3. Lugt (1943) was the first to identify a sizable group of copies by Rubens after Stimmer, among them anonymous or misattributed drawings in the Louvre, Paris; the Museum Boijmans Van Beuningen, Rotterdam; and the Pierpont Morgan Library, New York. For a recent discussion of the entire group, see Stampfle 1991, pp. 136–37, under no. 294. A recent search for the two or three drawings in this group that Lugt (1943, p. 108) thought were in the Albertina, Vienna, was unsuccessful.

2. *Pilate,* ca. 1597–99

Pen and brown ink, 196 x 133 mm ($7^{11}/_{16}$ x $5^{1}/_{4}$ in.)
Annotated by Johann Friedrich Städel in pencil on verso: *très rare / Henricus Goltzius penna delin. // No. 27*

Graphische Sammlung im Städelschen Kunstinstitut, Frankfurt am Main (806)

PROVENANCE: Johann Friedrich Städel (1728–1816), Frankfurt.

LITERATURE: Burchard and d'Hulst 1963, no. 10, pl. 10; Reznicek 1992, p. 121, fig. 117.

EXHIBITION: Frankfurt 2000, no. 24, ill.

On this sheet Rubens assembled into a new scene figures copied from two engravings by Hendrick Goltzius (1558–1617). He drew with a very fine pen, carefully but not slavishly imitating the technique of engraving. Rubens copied Pilate, seated on a throne, and the two attendants standing to either side of him, from Goltzius's *Christ before Pilate,* the fifth print in his Passion series, monogrammed and dated 1596 (fig. 35).[1] In so doing, however, Rubens made notable modifications. He moved Goltzius's scene closer to the fore, lowering the dais of Pilate's throne, depicting the man seen from the back in the right foreground in three-quarter rather than full length, and

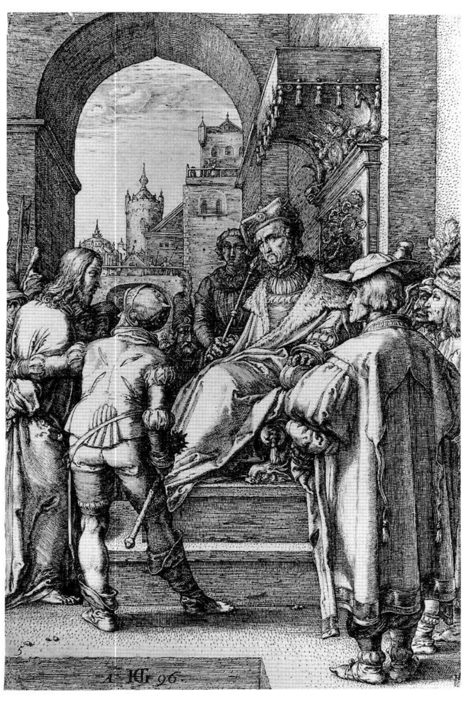

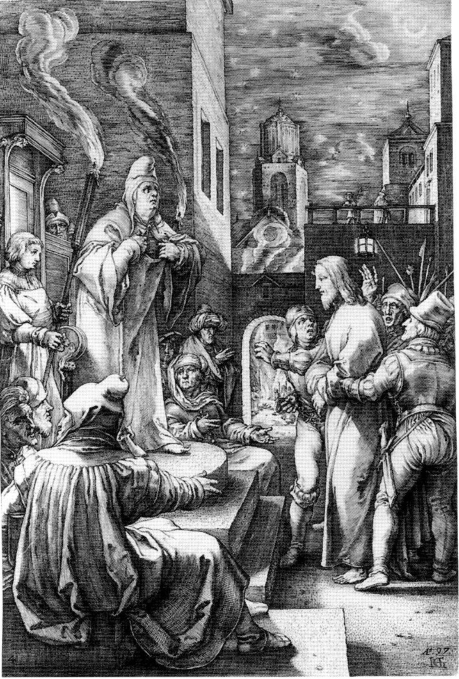

Fig. 35 (left). Hendrick Goltzius, *Christ before Pilate.* Engraving, 196 x 133 mm ($7^{11}/_{16}$ x $5^{1}/_{4}$ in.). No. 5 in Passion series, 1596. The Metropolitan Museum of Art, New York; The Elisha Whittelsey Collection, The Elisha Whittelsey Fund, 1951 (51.501.167[5])

Fig. 36 (right). Hendrick Goltzius, *Christ before Caiaphas.* Engraving, 196 x 133 mm ($7^{11}/_{16}$ x $5^{1}/_{4}$ in.). No. 4 in Passion series, 1597. The Metropolitan Museum of Art, New York; The Elisha Whittelsey Collection, The Elisha Whittelsey Fund, 1951 (51.501.167[4])

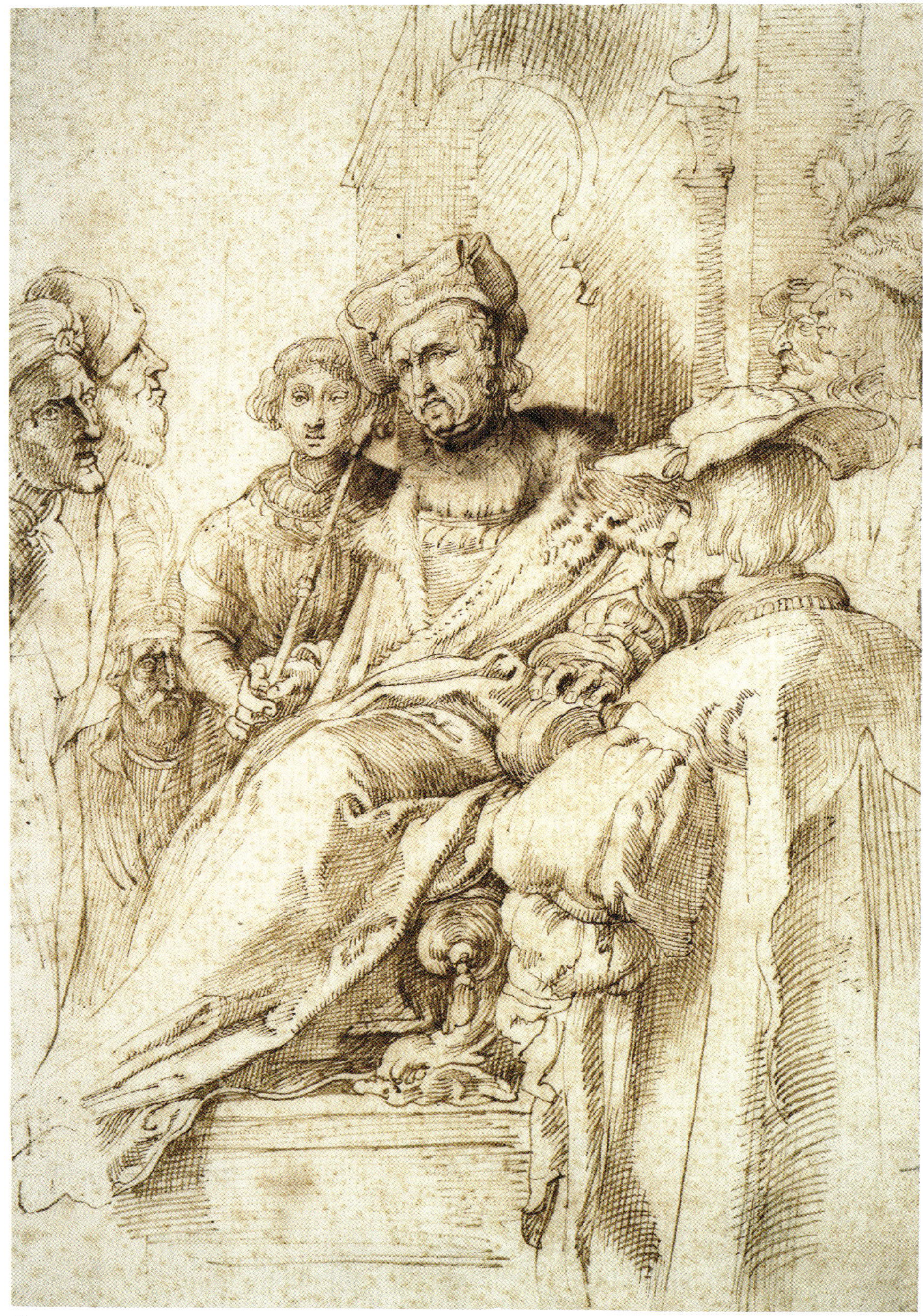

Cat. 2

leaving out the archway in the background. Although Rubens retained Goltzius's focus on Pilate and the figures surrounding him, he omitted the figures of Christ and the soldier at the left of the print, replacing them with two male onlookers. Rubens copied these spectators from *Christ before Caiaphas,* Goltzius's fourth engraving in the Passion series, dated 1597, where they sit at the lower left (fig. 36).[2] In Rubens's drawing, the men stand.

Without much hesitation or many noticeable corrections, Rubens arranged Goltzius's figures in new spatial relationships, in a new composition. Indeed, Rubens pieced together the quotes from Goltzius so well that at first glance his copy appears as if it were taken in its entirety from a single print. Such regrouping and rearranging of details from various sources reveal a complex working procedure that goes beyond mere copying; the present drawing, therefore, is probably slightly later than Rubens's copies after Tobias Stimmer (see cat. no. 1). It is impossible to know if Rubens had in mind a specific use for this new composition, or was simply exercising his imagination.

Rubens was deeply impressed when he saw Goltzius's engravings of the Passion, soon after their publication in Haarlem between 1596 and 1598, if one can judge from the existence of three related drawings by Rubens that are today in the Louvre, Paris, all dating from the late 1590s.[3] One drawing is another copy of the figure of Caiaphas from *Christ before Caiaphas.* In the second Rubens copied a figure from the *Flagellation of Christ,* the sixth print of the series, and in the third he copied most of the *Entombment,* the eleventh, penultimate print in Goltzius's series. Rubens probably saw Goltzius's Passion series when he was an apprentice in the studio of Otto van Veen (1556–1629) from the mid-1590s until 1598. Prints traveled very fast; furthermore, Van Veen, who was from Leiden, had close ties with the Northern Netherlands.

To attribute copies to a specific artist is exceedingly difficult, since in Rubens's time copying after prints was traditionally practiced during an artist's formative years, when his personal style was not yet developed. When the German collector, bibliophile, and philanthropist Johann Friedrich Städel owned the present drawing, he believed it to be Goltzius's preliminary design for one of his engravings, as he noted in his inscription on the verso. (Goltzius's original drawings are in the Museum der Bildenden Künste, Leipzig.)[4] In 1921 Otto Hirschmann correctly identified the drawing as a copy after Goltzius's Passion engravings but did not recognize Rubens's hand in it. The first to associate the drawing with Rubens was J. Q. van Regteren Altena, in 1939;[5] his opinion is unanimously accepted today.

1. Hollstein 1949–, vol. 8, pp. 10–11, no. 25. For a recent discussion of Goltzius's Passion series, see Amsterdam–New York–Toledo 2003–4, no. 80.
2. Hollstein 1949–, vol. 8, pp. 10–11, no. 24.
3. Lugt 1949, nos. 1123, 1121, 1122, pl. LVI.
4. Reznicek 1961, pp. 249–50, nos. 33–44, figs. 262–73.
5. Hirschmann 1921, p. 21.
6. In a lecture at the Congress of History of Art, London (Burchard and d'Hulst 1963, p. 24).

MICHELANGELO BUONARROTI

3. *Studies for the Libyan Sibyl,* recto; *Studies for the Libyan Sibyl and a Small Sketch for a Seated Figure,* verso, ca. 1512

Red chalk, recto; charcoal or black chalk, verso, 289 x 214 mm (11⅜ x 8 7/16 in.); cut on all sides, triangular section at right margin made up
Annotated in pen and light brown ink at lower left: *di M . . . gelo bonarroti . . .;* at upper right: *58;* unidentified paraph annotated in pen and darker brown ink at lower center

The Metropolitan Museum of Art, New York; Purchase, Joseph Pulitzer Bequest, 1924 (24.197.2)

Provenance: Buonarroti family, Florence; Everhard Jabach (1618–1695), Cologne and Paris; Carlo Maratti (?, 1625–1713), Rome; Andrea Procaccini (1671–1734), Rome (La Granja de San Ildefonso); Aureliano de Beruete, Madrid; purchased in Madrid from Beruete's widow by the Metropolitan Museum in 1924.

Literature: Bean 1982, no. 131, ill. (with bibl.); Hirst 1988, p. 67; Perrig 1991, pp. 50–51, fig. 8 (recto) [copy]; Bambach 1997, p. 69.

Exhibitions: New York 1965–66, no. 36, ill.; Washington 1988, no. 16, ill.; Florence–Philadelphia 1996–97, no. 39, ill.

The work of Michelangelo (1475–1564) had a great influence on Rubens. It is likely that during his first trip to Rome, in 1601–2, Rubens visited the Sistine Chapel, in the Vatican, and viewed the ceiling frescoes that Michelangelo had painted for Pope Julius II between 1508 and 1512. Among the frescoed figures is the Libyan Sibyl (fig. 37), painted near the altar during the last phase of work on the ceiling. Michelangelo must have prepared many of the preliminary drawings for the vault proper of the Sistine Chapel early on, in late 1510, but it is likely that he continued working on the figures of the altar wall until close to the frescoes' completion in October 1512.[1]

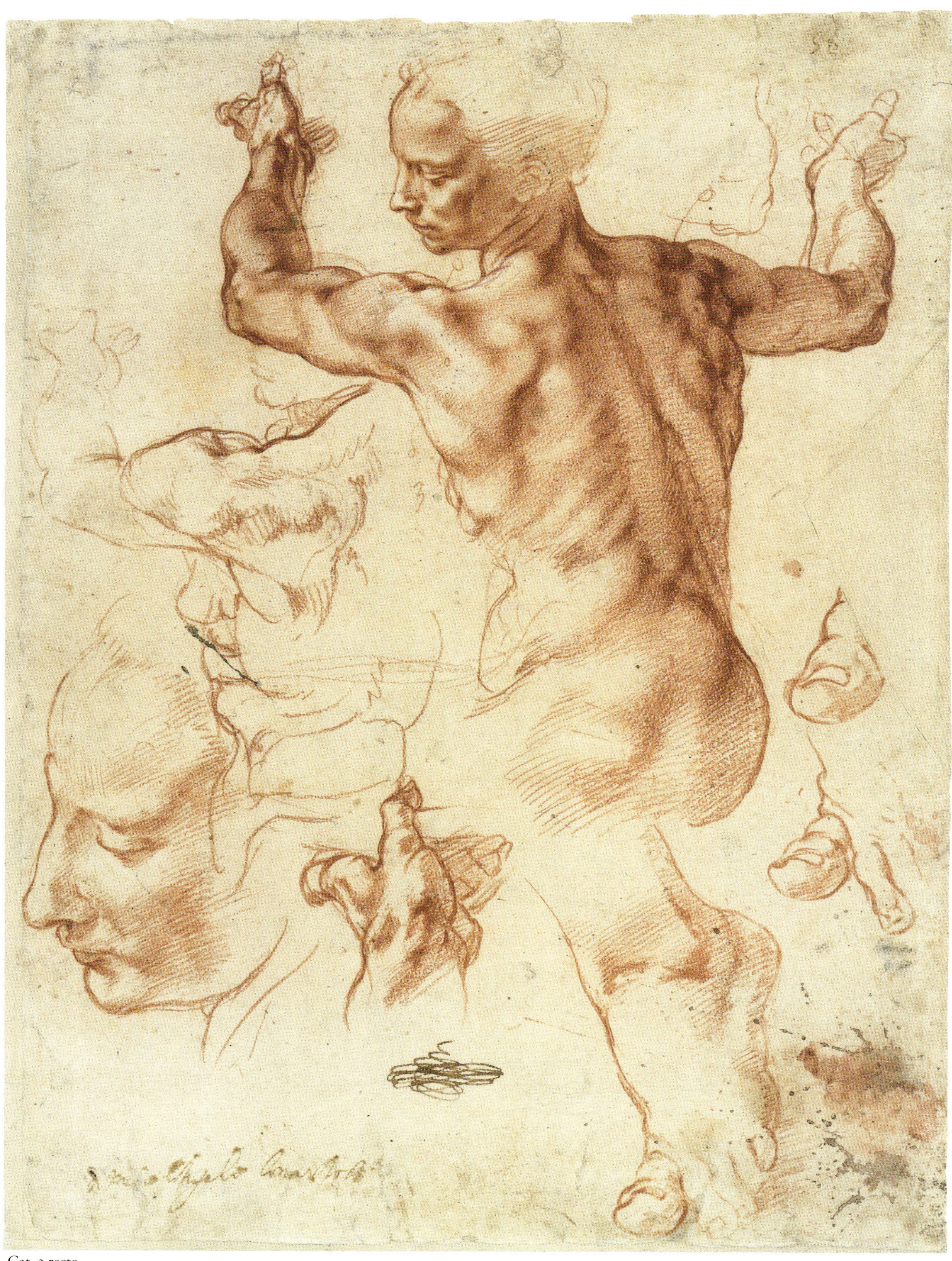

Cat. 3 recto

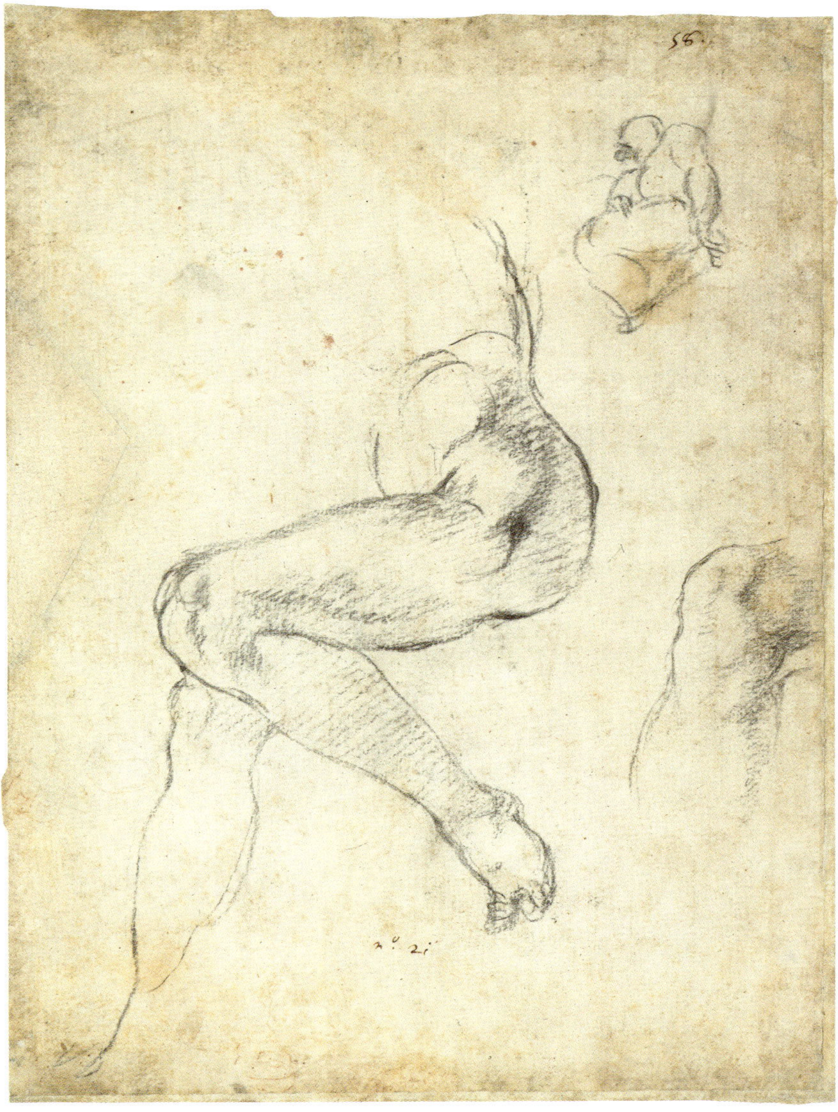

Cat. 3 verso

Michelangelo prepared the Libyan Sibyl in the studies on this double-sided sheet, including a highly finished study of the sibyl's nude upper body on the recto. As was his custom, Michelangelo drew the female figure from a male model. Michelangelo's training as a sculptor is evident in the precise articulation of the musculature and the figure's formal balance. Elsewhere on the recto the artist studied the sibyl's head and left foot, and he drew a second, outline sketch of the torso. On the verso, Michelangelo drew the sibyl's lower torso and legs, with a small sketch of a seated figure at the upper right. The change in medium, from red chalk on the recto to charcoal or black chalk on the verso, may mean that the two sides of the sheet were drawn at different times.

A drawing after the Libyan Sibyl (cat. no. 4) is one of eight known drawings by Rubens after sibyls and prophets from the Sistine ceiling. In his rendering Rubens displays the same attention to anatomical accuracy as Michelangelo does in his studies on the New York sheet. Drawings by Italian masters, if not those of Michelangelo himself, are certainly the source of many features of Rubens's drawings, including the use of red chalk, the working of both sides of a sheet, and the careful, individual study of parts of the human body.

Rubens may even have owned autograph drawings by Michelangelo. Johannes Philippus Happaert, a canon of the Onze-Lieve-Vrouwekerk in Antwerp and also an art dealer, purchased almost all of Rubens's drawings when they were sold in August 1657. In Happaert's 1686 inventory, fourteen Michelangelo drawings were listed; some of these may have come from Rubens's collection.[2] In addition, two Michelangelo drawings in the Albertina, Vienna, have long been thought to have been in Rubens's possession: one of a nude youth, in red chalk, for the *ignudo* frescoed above the Persian Sibyl in the Sistine ceiling,[3] the other of a nude man seen from the back, in black chalk, associated with Michelangelo's studies for the *Battle of Cascina*.[4]

1. We thank Carmen C. Bambach, curator in the Department of Drawings and Prints at The Metropolitan Museum of Art, for a chronology of Michelangelo's work on the Sistine ceiling.
2. Wood 1994, p. 347, n. 6.
3. Birke and Kertész 1992–, vol. 1, no. 120 (with bibl.).
4. Ibid., no. 123 (with bibl.).

4. *The Libyan Sibyl,* 1601–2

Black and red chalk, bottom corners missing and made up, strip 46 mm wide added at bottom, 525 x 336 mm (20⅝ x 13¼ in.)

Département des Arts Graphiques du Musée du Louvre, Paris (20.227)

PROVENANCE: Everhard Jabach (1618–1695), Cologne and Paris (Lugt 2959; not in his inventory; among the "dessins de rebut" [Rubens]); entered the French royal collection in 1671; museum mark (Lugt 1886).

LITERATURE: Morel d'Arleux, inv. MS 1, no. 237 [Michelangelo]; Reiset 1866, no. 568; R., vol. 5, no. 1391; Glück and Haberditzl 1928, no. 20, pl. 20; Lugt 1949, no. 1044, pl. XXXVI; Burchard and d'Hulst 1963, no. 20, pl. 20; Edinburgh–Nottingham 2002, pp. 25–26; Joannides 2003, no. 259, ill.

EXHIBITION: Paris 1978, no. 87, ill. [Rubens?].

This drawing after Michelangelo's Libyan Sibyl (fig. 37) is one of eight large drawings that Rubens made after six of the seven prophets depicted on the Sistine ceiling and two of the five sibyls; today, all of the drawings are in the Louvre, Paris.[1] The drawings' degree of finish varies, indicating that Rubens probably worked on them during a number of sessions. He most likely began the series shortly after his arrival in Rome in late July 1601 and may have finished it before returning to Mantua in April 1602.

Although the authorship of the eight copies after Michelangelo has at times been disputed, in our opinion their attribution to Rubens is secure.[2] They may be the "drawings of Michael Angelos roofe" that the English collector Thomas Howard, 2nd Earl of Arundel, sought to acquire from Rubens in 1636.[3] It has been established, moreover, that several of these drawings are on paper with a watermark that is also found on Rubens's recently discovered copies after antique sculpture, in Cologne, as well as on Rubens's copy after the *Belvedere Torso* in the Rubenshuis, Antwerp.[4]

Rubens began this drawing with a sketch in fine black chalk, still visible in the headband of the sibyl and in the pages of the open book she holds. In a softer black chalk he then modeled the figure with controlled, dense parallel hatching built up in layers, leaving white areas to indicate the highlights. Rubens used red chalk for the sibyl's flesh and some locks of her hair, as well as for the ample gown that is folded back over her lap. He also applied strokes of red chalk to the naked upper bodies of the putti in the background at the left. With a darker, possibly wet, red chalk he added accents along the contours of the sibyl's body, enhancing her musculature. (The rendering of the muscles can be compared to that in Rubens's copy, also in red chalk, after the *Belvedere Torso* [cat. no. 34 verso]). In some areas along the back of the figure the fine chalk strokes merge so seamlessly that Rubens may have used some stumping. Rubens added a strip at the bottom of the sheet in order to complete the sibyl's right foot.

Rubens did not slavishly imitate Michelangelo in his drawing. Rather, he focused on what was important to him—the figure of the sibyl—and paid less attention to other elements of the composition: the putti beside her and the chair covered with her cloak behind her. At the right of the drawing, moreover, he added ornamentation that is not in the fresco and seems to be his own invention. In addition, Rubens increased the tilt of the sibyl's head slightly and made her lean forward more.

It has often been wondered if, in his copies after Michelangelo's prophets and sibyls, Rubens drew in the Sistine Chapel itself or worked from an intermediate source. Recently,

Paul Joannides suggested that Rubens copied from other drawn copies.[5] This would of course have been much easier for the artist. Joannides's arguments for such a procedure, however, are not so strong. The simplification of architectural details in Rubens's drawings, Joannides's main argument against Rubens's having copied directly from Michelangelo's frescoes, is not particularly illuminating, since in his copies Rubens always concentrated on details that were of interest to him, not on the complete composition. The anonymous sixteenth-century Italian drawings that Joannides mentions as possible examples for Rubens are of rather inferior quality, and it is doubtful that Rubens would have worked from them.[6] Finally, the eight drawings in the Louvre would be the only known copies by Rubens after other people's drawings. Rubens drew many copies after sculptures, paintings, and prints,[7] but we do not know of any instance where he copied drawings by other artists. He seems to have preferred to retouch them (see cat. nos. 114–117). All in all, we support the theory that the artist made the impressive series now in Paris while he was in Rome, in the Sistine Chapel.

1. All are from the collection of Everhard Jabach and were sold to Louis XIV of France in 1671. Copies after the seventh prophet and three other sibyls may once have existed as well. See Lugt 1949, pp. 22–23, nos. 1040–1047, ill.
2. According to Arlette Sérullaz in Paris 1978, p. 86, in 1827 Morel d'Arleux inventoried them as by Michelangelo; according to Joannides 2003, p. 324, he inventoried them as "d'après Michel-Ange." Reiset (1866) associated them with Rubens, an attribution that Frits Lugt (1949) strongly supported and that has been accepted since, although at times with some reservation, for example, by Sérullaz in Paris 1978, p. 87.
3. The earl's interest in the drawings is mentioned by the painter Balthasar Gerbier in a letter to Rubens of October 29, 1636. Rooses and Ruelens 1887–1909, vol. 6, pp. 168–69, and Oxford–London 1988, p. 10.
4. For the drawings in Cologne and Antwerp and their watermarks, see Westfehling 2001, p. 102.
5. Joannides 2003, p. 312, under no. 229 and pp. 324–25, under no. 25. Joannides dates Rubens's Sistine series to 1600, when the Flemish artist was in Italy but had not yet visited Rome.
6. Ibid., pp. 324–25, under no. 259: sale, London, Phillips, July 7, 1999, lots 120 (black chalk heightened with white; 395 x 256 mm), 121 (black chalk with brown wash heightened with white; 398 x 261 mm), ills., and a sheet in the Detroit Institute of Arts (see Detroit Institute of Arts 1992, pp. 273–74, no. A10, ill.).
7. It is unlikely that Rubens worked after prints for his Sistine series. The ones available at the time after the main figures from the Sistine ceiling, such as those by Cherubino Alberti (1553–1615) or Adamo Scultori (fl. 1566–80), are small and provide less detail than we see in Rubens's copies (see Rome 1991, pp. 84–90, 113–16). One might add that, judging from the known examples, Rubens used pen and ink when he copied from prints (see cat. nos. 1, 2), rather than chalk.

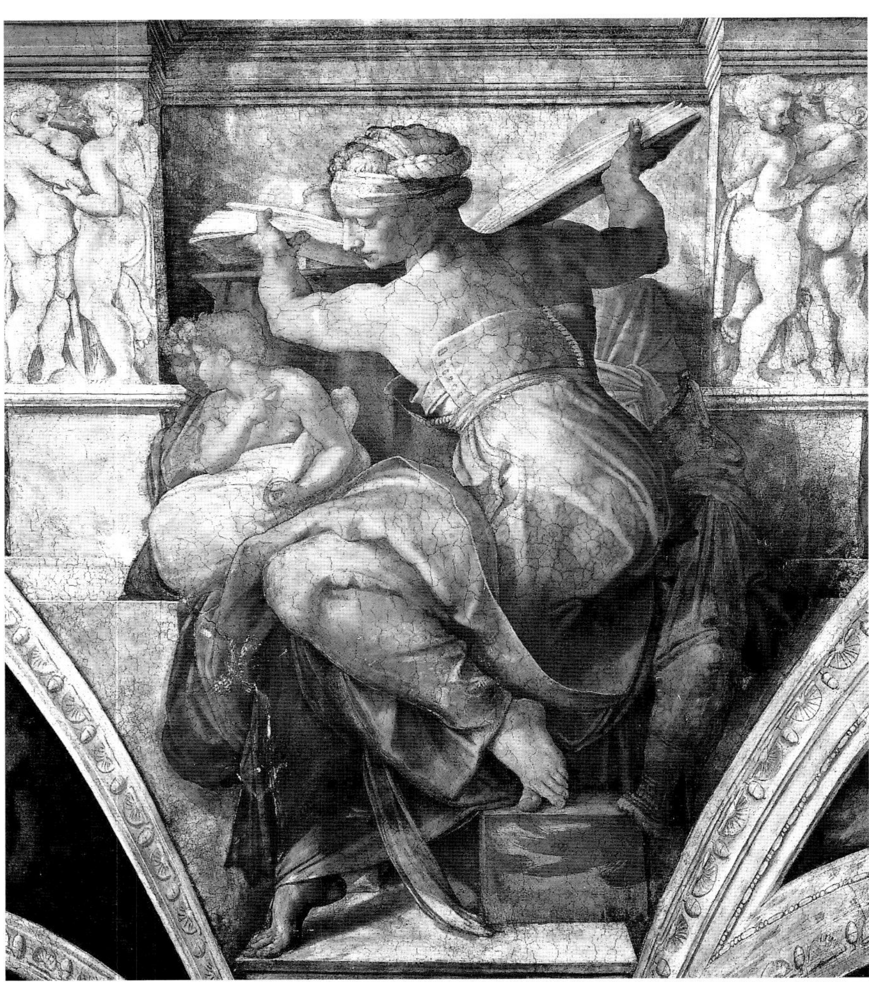

Fig. 37. Michelangelo, Detail of Libyan Sibyl from the Sistine Chapel ceiling fresco, 1508–12. Vatican City

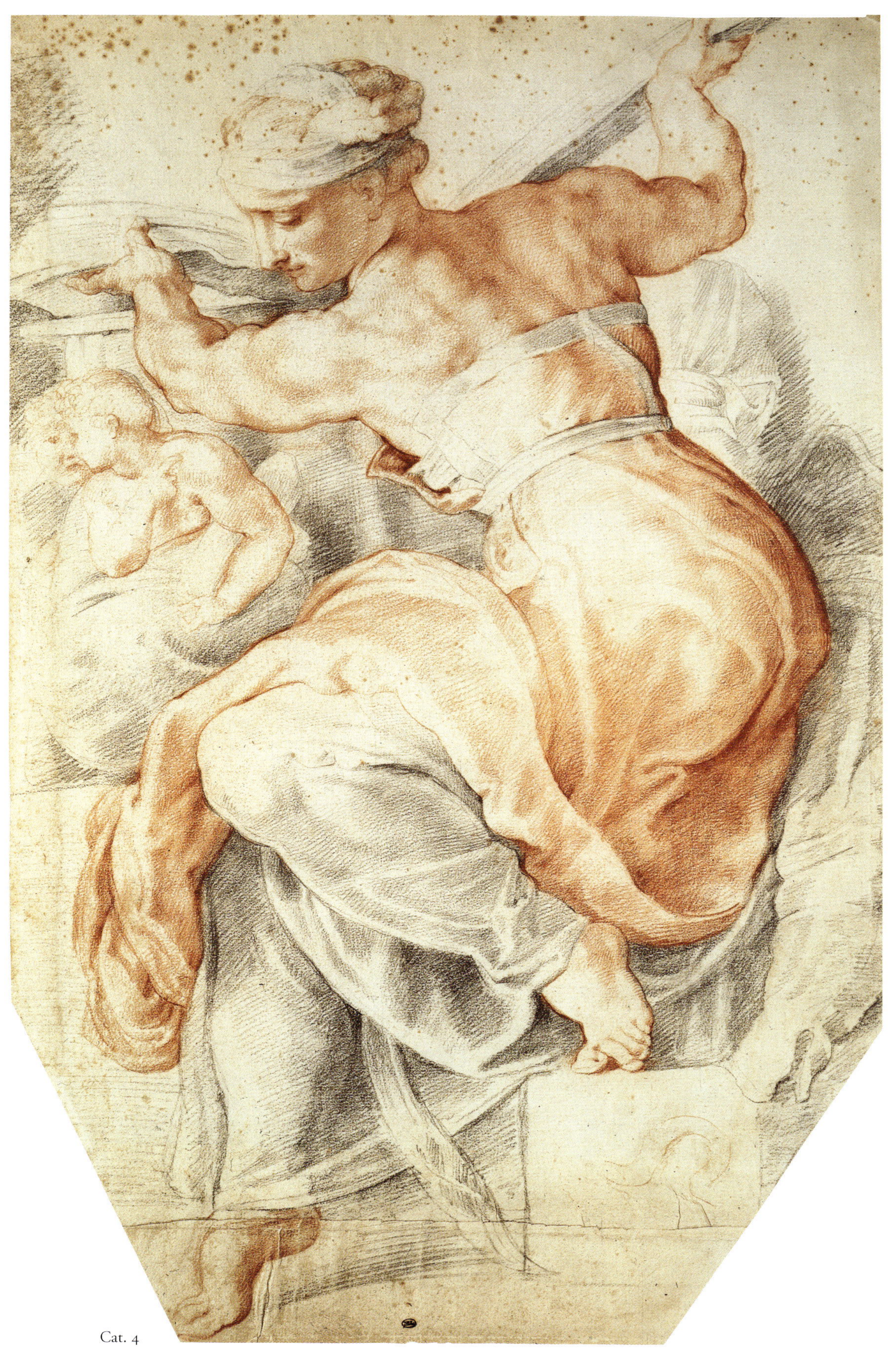

Cat. 4

5. *Eleven Studies of Women's Headdresses,* ca. 1609–12

Pen and brown ink, 202 x 314 mm (8 x 12⅜ in.)

Herzog Anton Ulrich-Museum, Braunschweig (Z 171)

PROVENANCE: Probably purchased by Charles I, Duke of Braunschweig (1713–1780); probably confiscated by Napoleon's army in 1806, returned to Braunschweig in 1815.

LITERATURE: Held 1959, no. 162, pl. 165; Held 1960, pp. 264–69, fig. 10; Burchard and d'Hulst 1963, no. 3, pl. 3; Sonkes 1969, pp. 51–53, no. B8, pl. 11a; Held 1986, no. 64, pl. 64.

EXHIBITION: Antwerp 1977, no. 124, ill.

Rubens was interested in the study of costumes and documented them in his *Costume Book* (British Museum, London), dated about 1609–12, that is, immediately following his return to Antwerp from Italy in late 1608.[1] In this sketchbook Rubens drew studies of late medieval costumes of the Netherlands, Burgundy, and Germany as well as figures in Turkish, Persian, and Arabic dress. He copied many of the costumes from the *Mémoriaux* of Antonio de Succa (before 1567–1620), a Flemish painter who at the behest of Archduke Albert and Archduchess Isabella traveled throughout Flanders making sketches of tomb sculptures, painted portraits, and miniatures, among other objects, to document the genealogy of the archducal family.[2] For Rubens, the *Costume Book* was a visual resource for possible application in his paintings.

In all probability the present drawing originally belonged to the *Costume Book,* but was later separated.[3] The uniformity of the studies in size and subject matter supports this surmise. The heads are copied not from De Succa, however, but from other sources.

The head in the lower left corner is based on the Tiburtine Sybil on the left wing of the *Bladelin Altarpiece* by Rogier van der Weyden (1399/1400–1427), now in the Gemäldegalerie, Berlin.[4] The precise whereabouts of this altarpiece in the first decades of the seventeenth century are unknown. But wherever it was, it seems unlikely that Rubens would have copied only the sibyl's head on a page with ten unrelated ones. Rather, Rubens probably made his copy from an intermediate source. In his drawing Rubens followed the headdress of Rogier's sibyl closely, but tilted the face upward more.

The first four heads from the left in the upper row and the last two in the lower appear to derive from Heinrich Vogtherr's *Kunstbüchlin,* a pattern book first published in Strasbourg in 1537 and last in 1610.[5] There are discrepancies, however, between Vogtherr's prints and Rubens's studies: for example, the veils of the first two headdresses at the right in the bottom row are more extended than those of their prototypes (figs. 38, 39). More important, all of Rubens's heads are reversed from Vogtherr's. Since prints usually reverse the direction of the preliminary image, both Rubens and Vogtherr may have worked from a common early-sixteenth-century Netherlandish source, possibly another pattern book. This pattern book or sketchbook—possibly by Jan Mostaert (1474–1555?)—in all likelihood included a drawing after Rogier's Tiburtine Sibyl as well as studies of heads.[6]

1. Hind 1923, no. 119. See also Belkin 1980.
2. Today, the De Succa *Mémoriaux* album, which is incomplete, is in the Bibliothèque Royale Albert Ier, Brussels. See Comblen-Sonkes and Van den Bergen-Pantens 1977.
3. Belkin 1980, pp. 44, 58, and no. 45, fig. 232.
4. De Vos 1999, pp. 242–48, no. 15, ill.
5. Held 1960, pp. 264–69, fig. 10.
6. Belkin 1980, pp. 177–78.

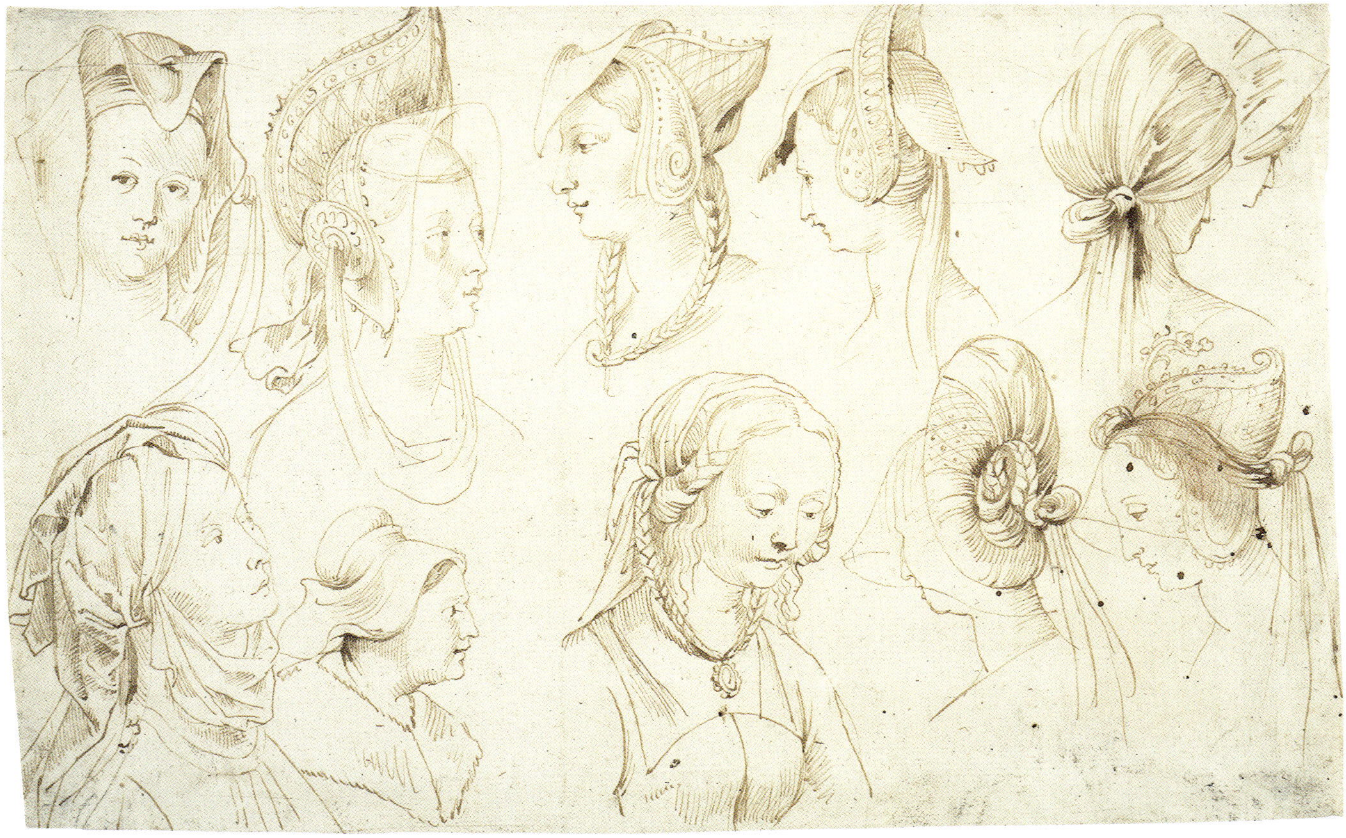

Cat. 5

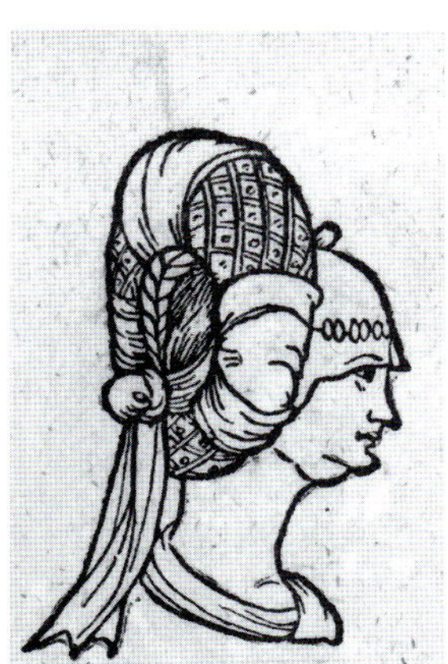

Fig. 38. Heinrich Vogtherr, *Woman's Head,* 1537. Woodcut, 188 x 145 mm ($7\frac{3}{8}$ x $5\frac{11}{16}$ in.). From Heinrich Vogtherr, *Ein Fremb'ds und wunderbares Kunstbüchlin* (Strasbourg, 1538), p. Biii recto. The Metropolitan Museum of Art, New York; Rogers Fund, 1919 (19.62.2)

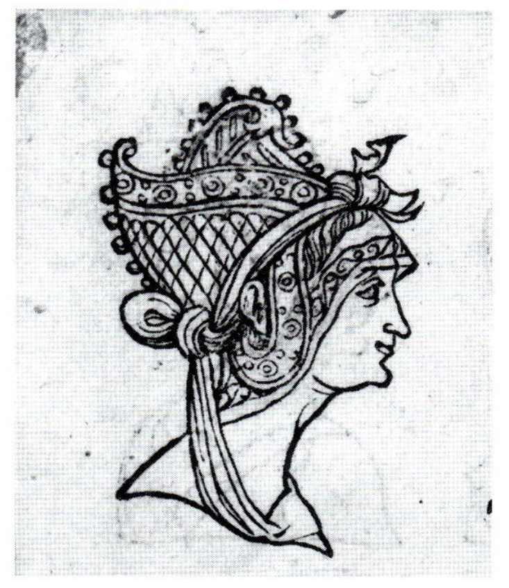

Fig. 39. Heinrich Vogtherr, *Woman's Head,* 1537. Woodcut, 188 x 145 mm ($7\frac{3}{8}$ x $5\frac{11}{16}$ in.). From Heinrich Vogtherr, *Ein Fremb'ds und wunderbares Kunstbüchlin* (Strasbourg, 1538), n. p. [p. 4 verso]. The Metropolitan Museum of Art, New York; Rogers Fund, 1919 (19.62.2)

6. *A Knight and a Lady*, ca. 1609–12

Pen and brown ink, 200 x 139 mm (7⅞ x 5 7/16 in.)
Staatliche Museen zu Berlin, Kupferstichkabinett (KdZ 3243)

PROVENANCE: Matthäus Merian the Younger (1621–1687), Frankfurt; Friedrich Wilhelm, Elector of Brandenburg (1620–1688), Berlin; Friedrich Wilhelm I of Prussia (1688–1740), Berlin (Lugt 1631); in the 18th century in the Royal Library, Berlin; since 1814 in the Akademie der Künste; in 1831 transferred to the Royal Print Room, founded that year.

LITERATURE: Bock and Rosenberg 1930, p. 253, no. 3243; Held 1959, no. 157, pl. 167; Burchard and d'Hulst 1963, no. 8, pl. 8; Held 1986, no. 65, pl. 63.

EXHIBITION: Berlin 1977, no. 17, ill.

With a fine pen Rubens copied this youthful couple from the fifteenth-century engraving *A Knight and a Lady* by Israhel van Meckenem (ca. 1440/45–1503; fig. 40).[1] He gave the figures slightly more volume than in the print and a more self-assured presence. The pentimento in the right leg of the knight indicates that the leg was initially thicker and heftier, closer to Rubens's own ideal. Interested in the couple's costume rather than in copying the engraving per se, Rubens omitted from his drawing the scrollwork and banderoles that surround the couple in the print.

In type and execution, the drawing resembles the costume studies that Rubens recorded in his *Costume Book* (British Museum, London; see cat. no. 5),[2] but it does not seem to have been a part of it. The sheet is slightly smaller than the leaves of the *Costume Book,* and it shows a single couple rather than, as in the sketchbook, multiple studies. The drawing nonetheless most likely dates from about 1609–12, when Rubens assembled the *Costume Book*.[3]

1. Hollstein 1949–, p. 193, no. 501.
2. Hind 1923, no. 119. See also Belkin 1980.
3. In 1986 Held revised his dating of the drawing, from before 1600? to 1608–12, that is, after Rubens had returned to Antwerp from Italy; the revised date is closer to the date of about 1610–14 that Held suggested for the *Costume Book* studies. Hans Mielke (in Berlin 1977, p. 60) preferred a date of 1610–15 for them.

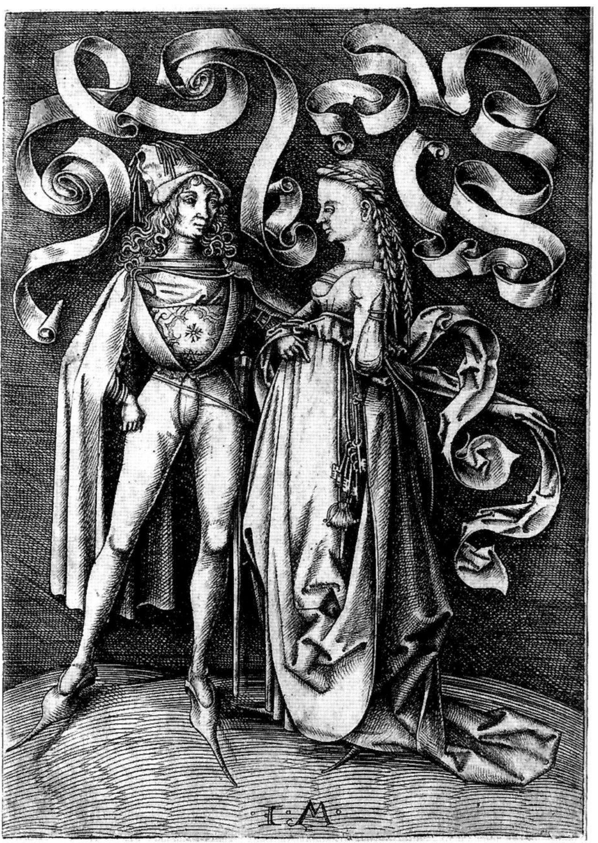

Fig. 40. Israhel van Meckenem, *A Knight and a Lady*, ca. 1495–1503. Engraving, 161 x 110 mm (6 5/16 x 4 5/16 in.). National Gallery of Art, Washington, D.C.; Rosenwald Collection (1943.3.157 [B2712])

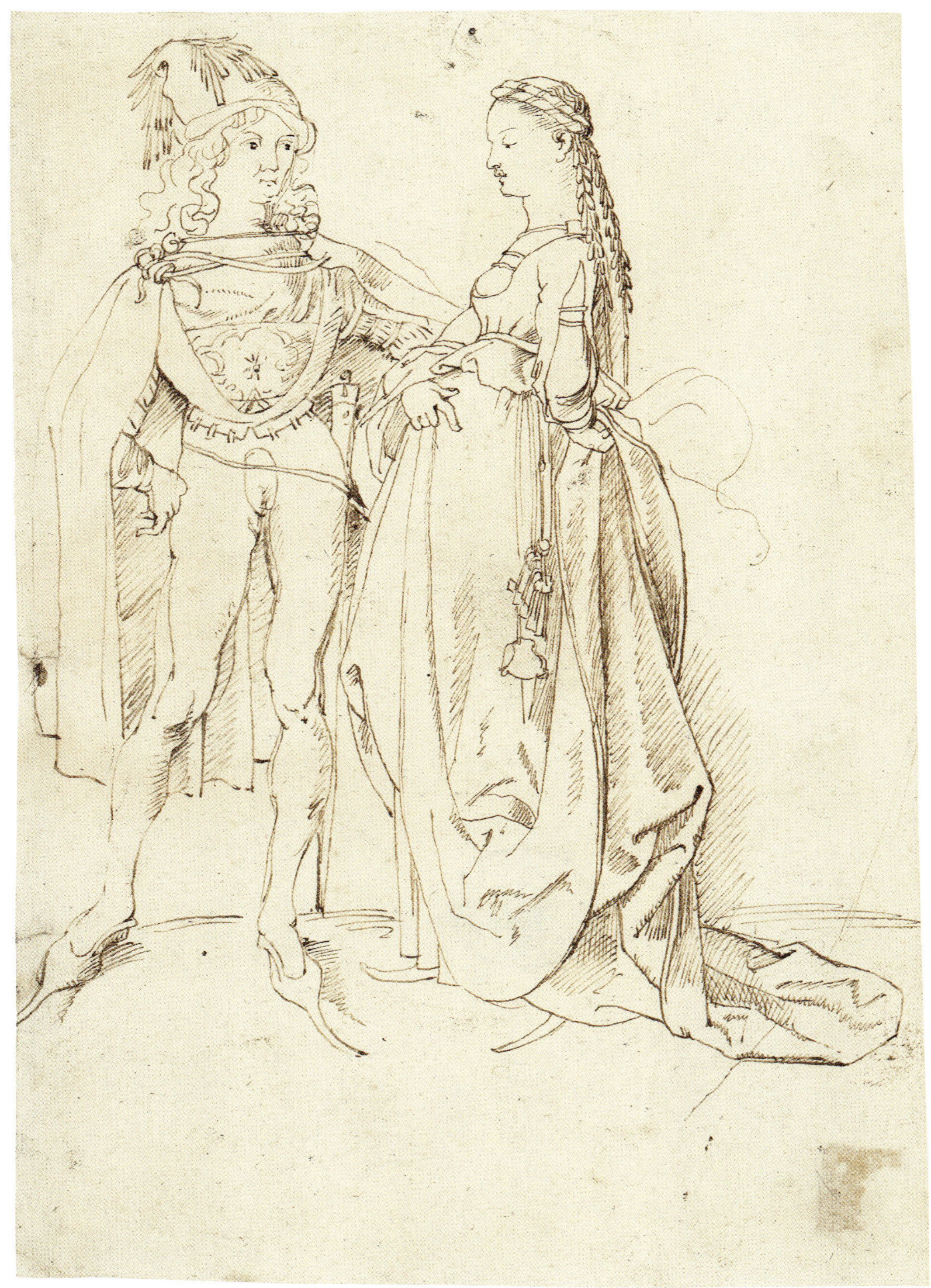

Cat. 6

7. *Studies of Women,* autumn 1628

Red and black chalk, heightened with white chalk, 449 x 289 mm (17 11/16 x 11 3/8 in.); lower right corner replaced

The J. Paul Getty Museum, Los Angeles (82.GB.140)

PROVENANCE: Prosper Henry Lankrink (1628?–1692), London (Lugt 2090); Dr. Nicolaas Beets, Amsterdam; A. S. Drey, Munich; Dr. Gollnow, Stettin; Dr. Anton Schrafl, Zurich (sale, Christie's, London, December 9, 1982, lot 78).

LITERATURE: Glück and Haberditzl 1928, no. 3, pl. 3; Held 1959, under no. 64; Burchard and d'Hulst 1963, no. 158, pl. 158; Held 1986, p. 56, no. 175, pl. 5; Goldner 1988, no. 94, ill.

EXHIBITION: Wellesley–Cleveland 1993–94 (Wellesley only), no. 55, ill.

There probably was no painting by Titian in Antwerp when Rubens was learning his profession, and Rubens would have known Titian's work only through reproductive engravings and woodcuts. His first encounters with the original work of the great Venetian painter would have occurred in 1600, when he visited Venice and when he began his service at the Gonzaga court in Mantua.

In 1603 Rubens visited Spain, carrying gifts from the Duke of Mantua to King Philip III. He was impressed by the "most beautiful" (*bellissime*) paintings by Titian, Raphael, and others in the royal collections in Madrid and at the Escorial. He wrote to Annibale Chieppio, Gonzaga's secretary of state, describing the paintings' quality and quantity and noting particularly (in the margin) the large number of Titians: "del Titiano–quantità."[1] When Rubens made his second visit to Madrid and the Spanish royal collections, between mid-September 1628 and April 1629, he did so on another diplomatic mission, this time to negotiate a treaty between England and Spain. During this stay of seven-odd months in Madrid he is said to have copied every Titian painting owned by the king, which would have come to several dozen paintings. Today some twenty copies by Rubens after Titian are known.[2]

The studies after Titian on this sheet are not arranged in any apparent order. The large female figure in the upper third of the drawing is one of Diana's companions, copied from *Diana and Actaeon* (fig. 41), and the study directly below shows the head of Diana, in black chalk, and her raised left arm, in red chalk.[3] Rubens copied the female head at the bottom center from *Venus and Adonis* (Prado, Madrid).[4] The remaining three heads, the two at the right in red and some black chalk and the third at the top left in black chalk, are based on the *Diana and Callisto* (now in Edinburgh).[5] As he copied from Titian's paintings, Rubens made a few subtle changes. The most obvious modification here is in the center of the drawing, where he lowered Diana's arm just enough to allow for a full view of her face. The detailed rendering of the women's heads and intricately arranged hair recalls Rubens's sketches, twenty years earlier, of women's heads and fanciful headdresses (cat. no. 5).

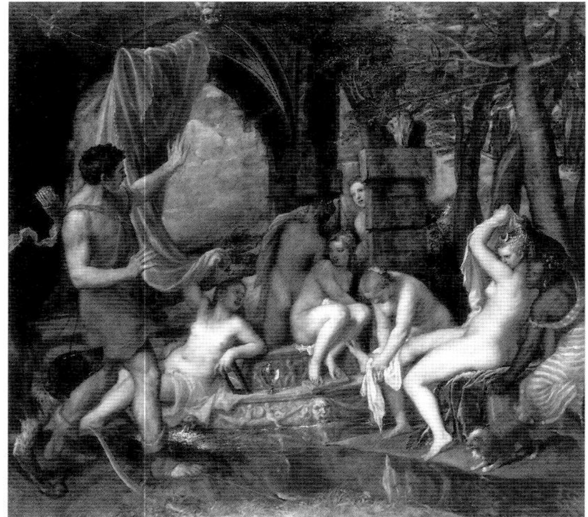

Fig. 41. Titian, *Diana and Actaeon*, 1556–59. Oil on canvas, 184.5 x 202.2 cm (72 5/8 x 79 5/8 in.). National Gallery of Scotland, Edinburgh (NGL 58.46)

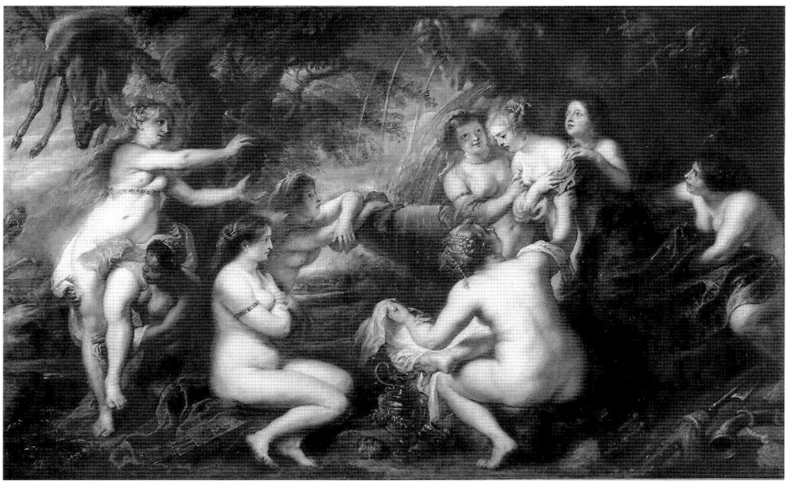

Fig. 42. Peter Paul Rubens, *Diana and Callisto,* ca. 1638–40. Oil on canvas, 202 x 323 cm (79 1/2 x 127 3/16 in.). Prado, Madrid (1671)

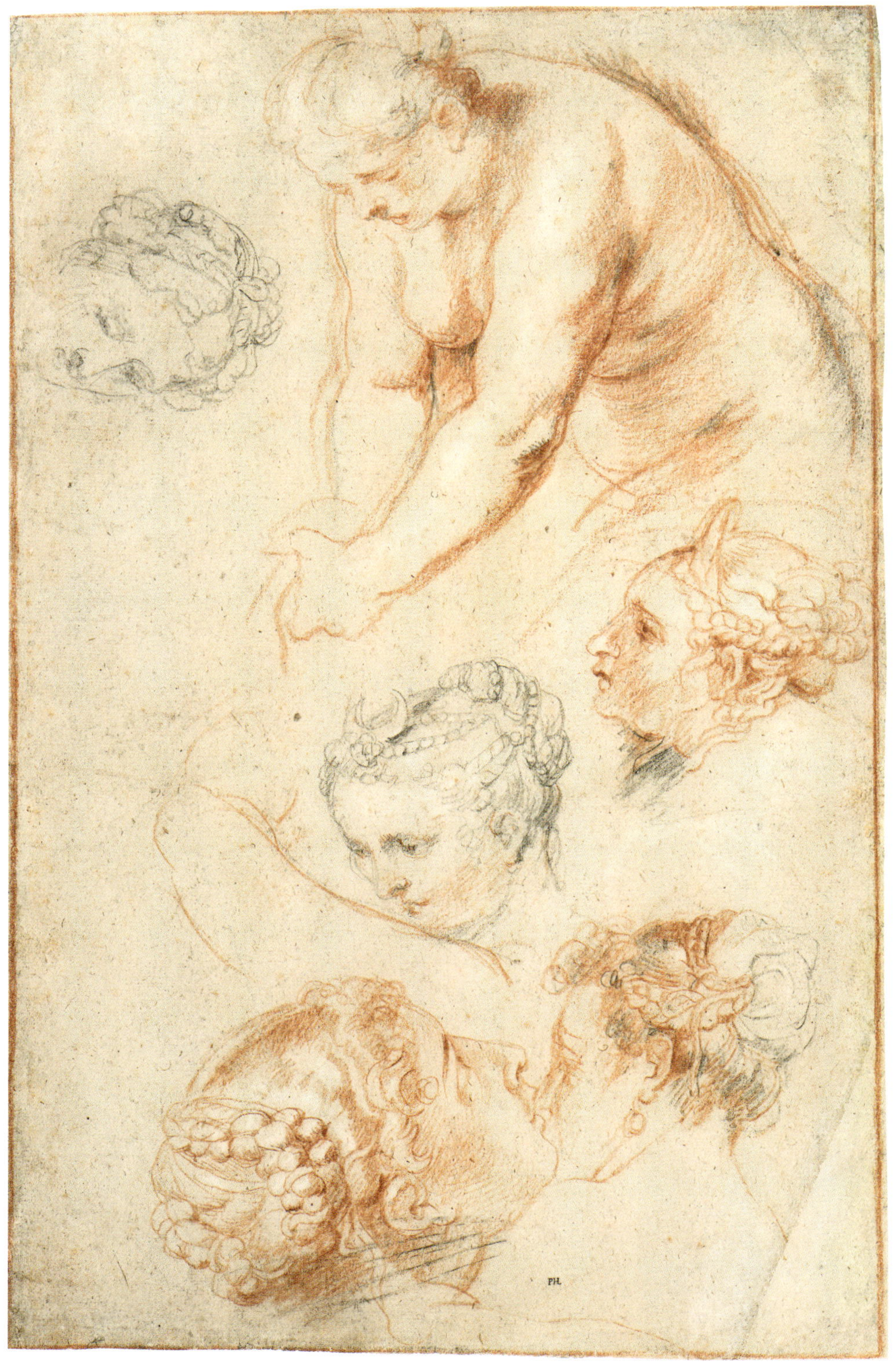

Cat. 7

Rubens may have executed these studies in the autumn of 1628, during an early visit to the Titian gallery in the Spanish royal collection, possibly to obtain permission for making full-scale painted copies of the three works studied on the sheet.[6] He probably took all the painted copies back with him to Antwerp, where they remained in his collection until Philip IV purchased most of them from his estate between 1640 and 1645.[7]

Rubens returned to the heads and figures recorded in the present drawing for his own version of *Diana and Callisto* of about 1638–40 (fig. 42).[8] The figure of Callisto, at the right of Rubens's painting, is reminiscent of the study of Diana's companion at the top of the present sheet. For the head of the nymph kneeling below Callisto, holding up her clothes, Rubens used almost unchanged the head of Venus sketched at the bottom center of the sheet. Besides the *ricordi* in this drawing, Rubens of course had his painted copies after Titian's originals to work from.[9]

1. Rooses and Ruelens 1887–1909, vol. 1, p. 146, letter 31; Magurn 1955, p. 33, letter 8, May 24, 1603.
2. The assertion that Rubens copied all the paintings by Titian in the Spanish royal collection was made by Francisco Pacheco (1564–1644), the teacher and father-in-law of Diego Velázquez (1599–1660). Pacheco 1638 (1956 ed.), p. 153, and Held 1986, p. 137. For Rubens's painted copies after Titian, see M. Jaffé 1989, pp. 76–79, and Muller 1989, p. 182.
3. Wethey 1969–75, vol. 3, pp. 138–41, no. 9, pl. 142.
4. Ibid., pp. 188–90, no. 40, pl. 84.
5. Collection of the Duke of Sutherland, on loan to the National Gallery of Scotland, Edinburgh; ibid., pp. 138–41, no. 10, pl. 143.
6. M. Jaffé 1971, p. 43.
7. Muller 1989, pp. 103–4, nos. 43–45. For Philip IV's purchase of copies after Titian and other paintings from Rubens's estate, see also Vergara 1999, pp. 144–58.
8. K.d.K., ed. Oldenbourg 1921, no. 433; M. Jaffé 1989, no. 1352, 1637–38.
9. Rubens's copy after Titian's *Diana and Callisto* has survived, in the collection of the Right Hon. The Earl of Derby. M. Jaffé 1989, no. 978, ca. 1630. His copies after Titian's *Diana and Actaeon* and *Venus and Adonis* are lost.

ITALY, 1600–1608

8. *Three Groups of Apostles in a Last Supper,* recto; *Three Sketches for Medea and Her Children,* verso, 1600–1604

Pen and brown ink, 296 x 439 mm (11 11/16 x 17 1/4 in.)
Inscribed by the artist in pen and brown ink on recto at top right of center: *Gestus magis largi longiq[ue] / brachijs extensis* (the gestures [to be] larger and broader with arms extended), *A* [twice] *lag.*; on verso: *vel Medea respiciens Creusam ardentem et Jasonem velut Insequens . . .* (?) (Medea looking back at the burning Creusa and at Jason as if [?] pursuing. . . [?]); and in red chalk on right: *Creusa arden[s?]* (Creusa burning).

The J. Paul Getty Museum, Los Angeles (84.GA.959)

PROVENANCE: Probably purchased ca. 1723 by William, 2nd Duke of Devonshire, Chatsworth; by descent to the 11th Duke of Devonshire (sale, London, Christie's, July 3, 1984, lot 53, ill.).

LITERATURE: Held 1959, nos. 7 recto and 7 verso, pl. 7, and under nos. 6, 12, 13; Burchard and d'Hulst 1963, no. 34, pl. 34, and under no. 35; Held 1986, no. 19, pl. 19; Goldner 1988, no. 90, ill.; Judson 2000, no. 3, figs. 4, 5; M. Jaffé 2002, p. 148, no. 1147, ill. (recto), and p. 146, under no. 1146.

EXHIBITIONS: Cologne 1977, no. 25; London 1977a, no. 25.

On the recto Rubens shows the Apostles at the Last Supper, huddled in three tight-knit groups in intense conversation as they react to Christ's announcement of a traitor among them. These studies are closely related to Rubens's *Five Groups of Figures for a Last Supper* at Chatsworth (fig. 43). The two sheets were likely drawn one soon after the other. The drawing in Chatsworth probably came first, since certain shared figures —in particular, the disciple perched on a stool at the left and the apostle pointing toward himself at the upper right—are developed in greater detail in the Getty studies. These two figures are examples of Rubens's borrowing from the work of other artists. The seated disciple was probably taken from Caravaggio's *Calling of Saint Matthew* (1599–1600; Contarelli Chapel, San Luigi dei Francesi, Rome); the figure appears several times in Rubens's early drawings[1] as well as in two early paintings by him of the *Judgment of Paris* (Akademie der Bildenden Künste, Vienna, and National Gallery, London). The pointing disciple recalls Marcantonio's engraving of the *Last Supper* after Raphael.[2] There is no known painting by Rubens to which the Getty and Chatsworth *Last Supper* studies relate.[3]

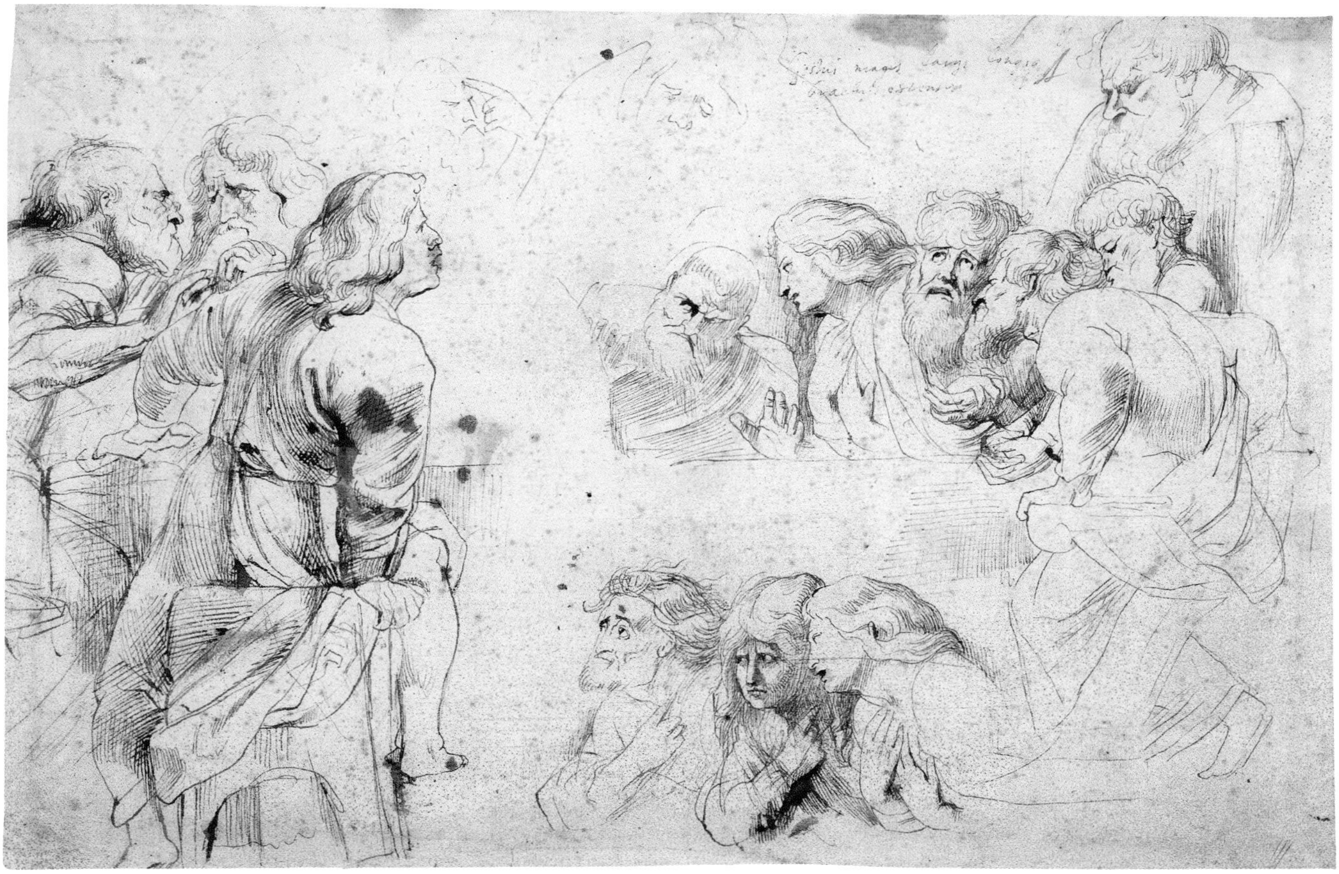

Cat. 8 recto

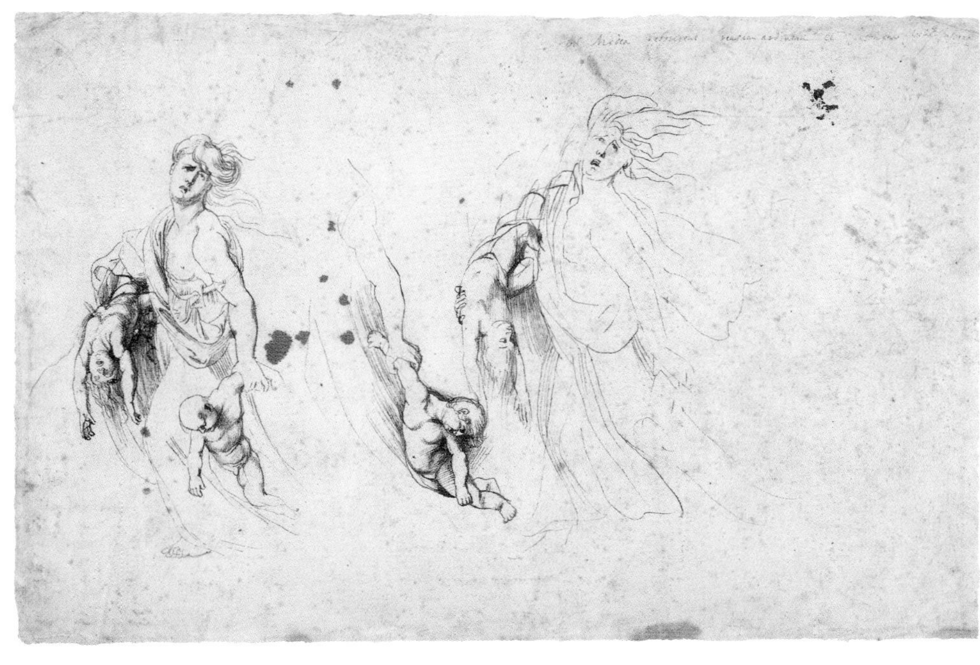

Cat. 8 verso

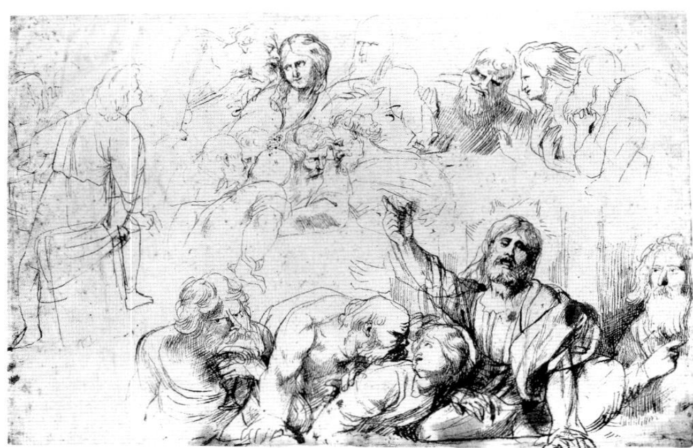

Fig. 43. Peter Paul Rubens, *Five Groups of Figures for a Last Supper,* 1600–1604. Pen and brown ink and touches of brown wash on cream paper, 283 x 444 mm (11⅛ x 17½ in.). The Duke of Devonshire and the Chatsworth Settlement Trustees, Chatsworth (1007A)

On the verso of the Getty sheet Rubens sketched three studies of Medea, the Greek sorceress of myth, carrying her dead children. After Medea helped Jason obtain the Golden Fleece, she married him and bore him two children. When he deserted her to marry Creusa, she gave Creusa an enchanted wedding gown, which burned her to death. Finally, the vengeful Medea killed her own children. Here, Rubens represented the crazed Medea carrying one dead child and dragging the other. Medea was usually depicted not on foot, as in these studies, but, rather, riding in a chariot, as Rubens himself drew her in a study now in the Museum Boijmans Van Beuningen, Rotterdam.[4]

Although they differ in subject matter, the recto and verso of the present sheet can be dated to 1600–1604, the early years of Rubens's sojourn in Italy (1600–1608).[5] In execution the recto and the related studies at Chatsworth strongly resemble drawings that Rubens made during his stay in Italy, particularly his *Descent from the Cross* in the Hermitage (cat. no. 9), which is here dated about 1601–2, when the artist first visited Rome. The figural types on both recto and verso and their emotionally charged expressions are also in keeping with works Rubens created in Italy rather than after his return to Antwerp in late 1608. Rubens's unconcealed quoting from other artists and his explanatory inscriptions in Latin reflect a student inspired by his encounter with Italian art.

1. See *Figure of Paris,* the verso of the *Death of Dido (Suicide of Thisbe),* Louvre, Paris (Paris 1978, no. 2, ill.), and *Sketch of a Baptism of Christ and a Figure of a Man,* the verso of *Alcibiades Interrupting the Symposium,* Metropolitan Museum of Art, New York (Held 1956, p. 124, fig. 31).
2. Oberhuber 1978, p. 41, no. 26. See also Held 1986, p. 73.
3. Monballieu (1965, pp. 183–205) associated the two sheets with a *Last Supper* commission of 1611 and dated both between April 6 and July 25, 1611. Rubens never completed the commission, however, probably due to a lack of funds from the magistrates of Sint Winoksbergen who wanted the altarpiece for the church of the Benedictine abbey in their city.
4. Held 1986, no. 16, pl. 16; Rotterdam 2001, no. 5. Rubens made the drawing while serving at the Gonzaga court in Mantua. He copied the scene of Medea riding in a chariot from an antique sarcophagus that is still in the Palazzo Ducale in Mantua today.
5. This dating follows that of Julius Held and other writers, contrary to an opinion Anne-Marie Logan expressed in 1985 when she associated the Getty *Last Supper* studies with the Sint Winoksbergen commission (see note 3 above); conversation cited in Goldner 1988, no. 90.

9. *The Descent from the Cross,* ca. 1601–2

Pen and brush and brown ink and brown wash over preliminary drawing in black chalk, 435 x 380 mm (17⅛ x 15 in.)

Inscribed by the artist in pen and brown ink at top left: *Vide(n)tur (?) ex Daniele Volterrano / Unus qui quasi tenens tamen reli(n)quit / Item alius qui diligentissime / descendit ut laturus opem* (One sees [?] with Daniele da Volterra / one who, as if holding, nevertheless lets go / and another who carefully / descends to support the [precious] weight [?])[1]
Annotated at bottom right, partially legible: *Rubens*

The State Hermitage Museum, Saint Petersburg (5496)

Provenance: Count Carl Cobenzl (1712–1770), Brussels (Lugt 2858b, in his mount); purchased from him in 1768 by Catherine II of Russia (1729–1796) for the Hermitage, Saint Petersburg (Lugt 2061).

Literature: Held 1959, no. 3, pl. 4; Burchard and d'Hulst 1963, no. 37, pl. 37, and under no. 36; Kuznetsov 1974, pl. 22; Held 1986, no. 15, pl. 14; Judson 2000, no. 43a, fig. 136; Alexei Larionov in London 2003–4a, pp. 35–39, pl. 2.

Exhibitions: Cologne 1977, no. 26a, ill.; Padua–Rome–Milan 1990, no. 56; New York 1998–99, no. 64, ill.; Toronto 2001, no. 94, ill.; London 2003–4a, no. 2.

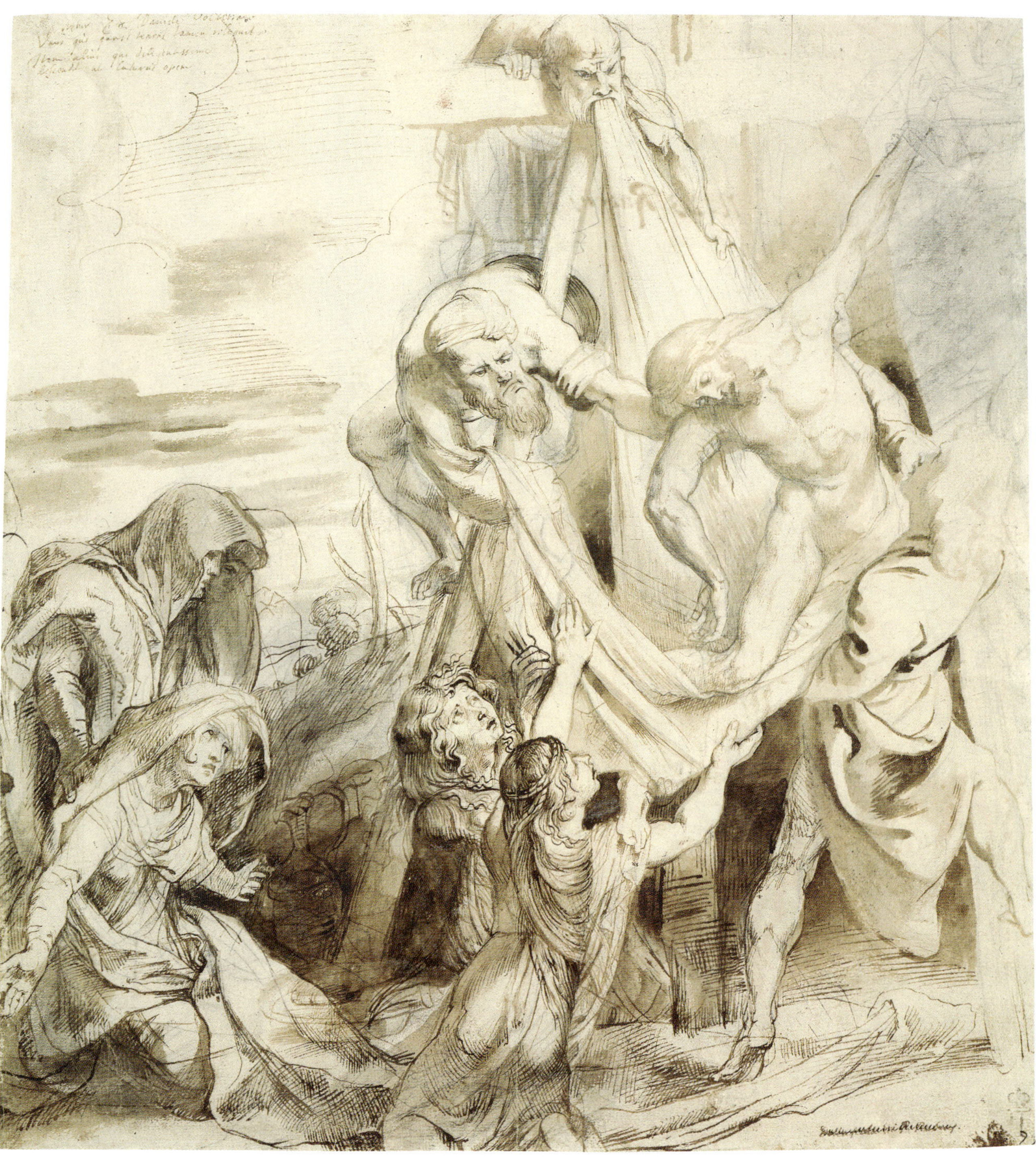
Cat. 9

This study is the earliest of Rubens's many representations in drawings, oil sketches, and paintings of the Descent from the Cross. Rubens began in black chalk and reworked the composition in ink, except for portions at the top right. Unfortunately, the drawing must have been cropped, since at the right the beginning of a ladder and a man's hand grasping Christ's left arm are still clearly visible. Furthermore, above Saint John the Evangelist, the figure on the right holding Christ's body, one sees a round form that may be a remnant of a second figure on the ladder at the right. He completed the drawing with wash, to introduce light and dark areas and to cover pentimenti, such as a basin and pitcher next to the ladder at the left. The vigorous pen strokes show many alterations, especially in the figure of a veiled, mourning woman at the left; she originally stood farther to the right and bent her head lower toward the grieving Virgin Mary, whom she supports. Mary Magdalen, kneeling at the base of the Cross, initially turned away in grief and buried her head in her hands.

Rubens's fragmented inscription in Latin at the top left refers to the Italian artist Daniele da Volterra (ca. 1509–1566) and probably to his well-known fresco of the *Descent from the Cross* in the Orsini Chapel in Santa Trinità dei Monti, Rome, painted in the mid-1540s. (Today, the composition is clearer in Daniele's preparatory drawing, in the Louvre, Paris, than in the badly damaged fresco.)[2] The meaning of the inscription is not clear; it may indicate that Rubens was considering more figures on the ladder, as in Daniele's fresco.[3] The drawing with its inscription is evidence both of Rubens's close attention to the art he saw in Rome and of his creation, in emulating it, of works of his own.[4]

The sheet has been dated to before 1600, about 1600–1602, and 1611–12, depending on whether the writer considers the drawing preparatory for Rubens's early *Descent from the Cross,* painted about 1602 for Santa Croce in Gerusalemme, Rome (now known only in a copy in Grasse), or for the monumental altarpiece of 1611–14 painted for Antwerp Cathedral (fig. 93).[5] A date of 1601–2, during Rubens's first visit to Rome, when he was recording subjects of interest to him and building a visual library for future use, seems the most likely. The confident pen strokes, the dense cross-hatching to model the figures, and the types of figures (especially the Magdalen, Nicodemus, and the man holding the shroud with his teeth) closely link this drawing to Rubens's *Anointing of Christ* (fig. 14), dated about 1600–1602.[6] Rubens's explanatory inscription in Latin at the top of the drawing is also typical of the years when he was first discovering the riches of Rome.

It was Rubens's habit to have continual recourse to his drawings, and this was the case with the present sheet. Rubens reused the arrangement of the drawing's main figures in his *Descent from the Cross* altarpiece for Antwerp Cathedral. The figure of Saint John supporting Christ's body also reappeared later, in Rubens's *Descent from the Cross* in Lille of about 1617.[7]

1. The translation of the inscription is from Held 1986, p. 71.
2. For Daniele's preparatory drawing and fresco, see Florence 2003–4, pp. 70–79, nos. 8–12, ill.
3. Judson 2000, p. 171.
4. Held (1986, no. 15) cited another possible source for Rubens's drawing, "the first thought of a Descent from the Cross by Daniele da Volterra" in the collection of G. Huquier, sold in Amsterdam in 1761. He even suggested that Rubens might have owned the drawing. Burchard and d'Hulst (1963, p. 67) stressed the influence of Ludovico Cigoli's painting of the *Descent from the Cross* (Palazzo Pitti, Florence).
5. According to Bialostocki (1964, pp. 512–13), the drawing predated Rubens's first stay in Italy. Burchard and d'Hulst (1963, p. 68), Judson (2000, p. 17), and Alexei Larionov (in London 2003–4a, pp. 35–39) consider it preparatory to the Antwerp *Descent from the Cross* of ca. 1611–12.
6. Held 1986, no. 12, pl. 13; Rotterdam 2001, no. 8.
7. M. Jaffé 1989, no. 434.

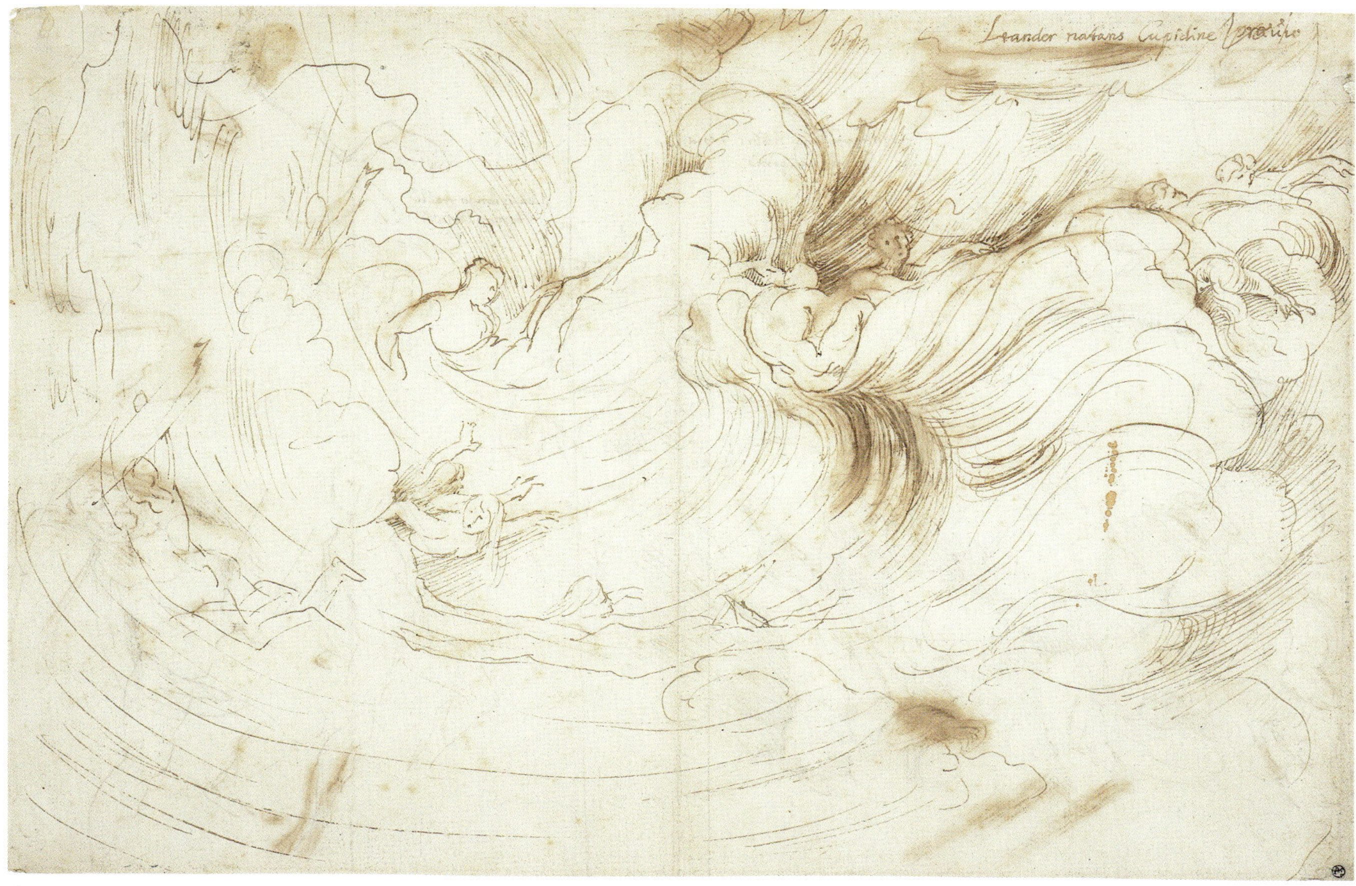

Cat. 10 recto

10. *Studies for Hero and Leander,* recto; *Battle Scene between the Greeks and Amazons and Studies for Samson,* verso, ca. 1601–3

Pen and brown ink and brown wash, recto; pen and brown ink, verso, 204 x 306 mm (8 x 12$^{1}/_{16}$ in.)
Inscribed by the artist in pen and brown ink on recto at top right: *Leander natans Cupidine praevio* (Leander swimming, urged on by Cupid); on verso at top left: *Sol* (sun); at left of center: *ad pedes lúx clarior* (at their feet the light is brighter); at top left of center: *Maxima púlvis núbis instar / aút Caliginis* (the greatest dust like a cloud or fog); at top right of center: *púlvis longo tractu / a tergo albescit* (the dust from being drawn out in a trail that turns white at the rear).
Annotated in pencil at bottom center: *Luca Cambiaso*

National Galleries of Scotland, Edinburgh (D 4936)

PROVENANCE: Pierre-Jean Mariette (1694–1774), Paris (Lugt 1852; his sale, Paris, Basan, November 15, 1775–January 30, 1776, possibly p. 154, no. 1005); Hans M. Calmann (1899–1982), London (purchased in 1969).

LITERATURE: M. Jaffé 1970a, pp. 42–51, pls. 41, 42; Andrews 1985, vol. 1, pp. 69–70, vol. 2, figs. 464, 465; M. Jaffé 2002, p. 134, fig. 20 (verso).

EXHIBITION: London 1977a, no. 11, ill.

In the lively pen sketch on the recto Rubens depicted an episode from the story of Hero and Leander, famous lovers from Greek mythology. Leander, a young man from Abydos, swam the Hellespont nightly in order to visit his beloved Hero, a priestess of Aphrodite at Sestos, who illuminated Leander's way with a light from her tower. One night, the winds of a storm extinguished the light, and Leander drowned. Seeing his body, Hero threw herself from her tower into the sea. In his drawing Rubens represented Leander's desperate struggle as

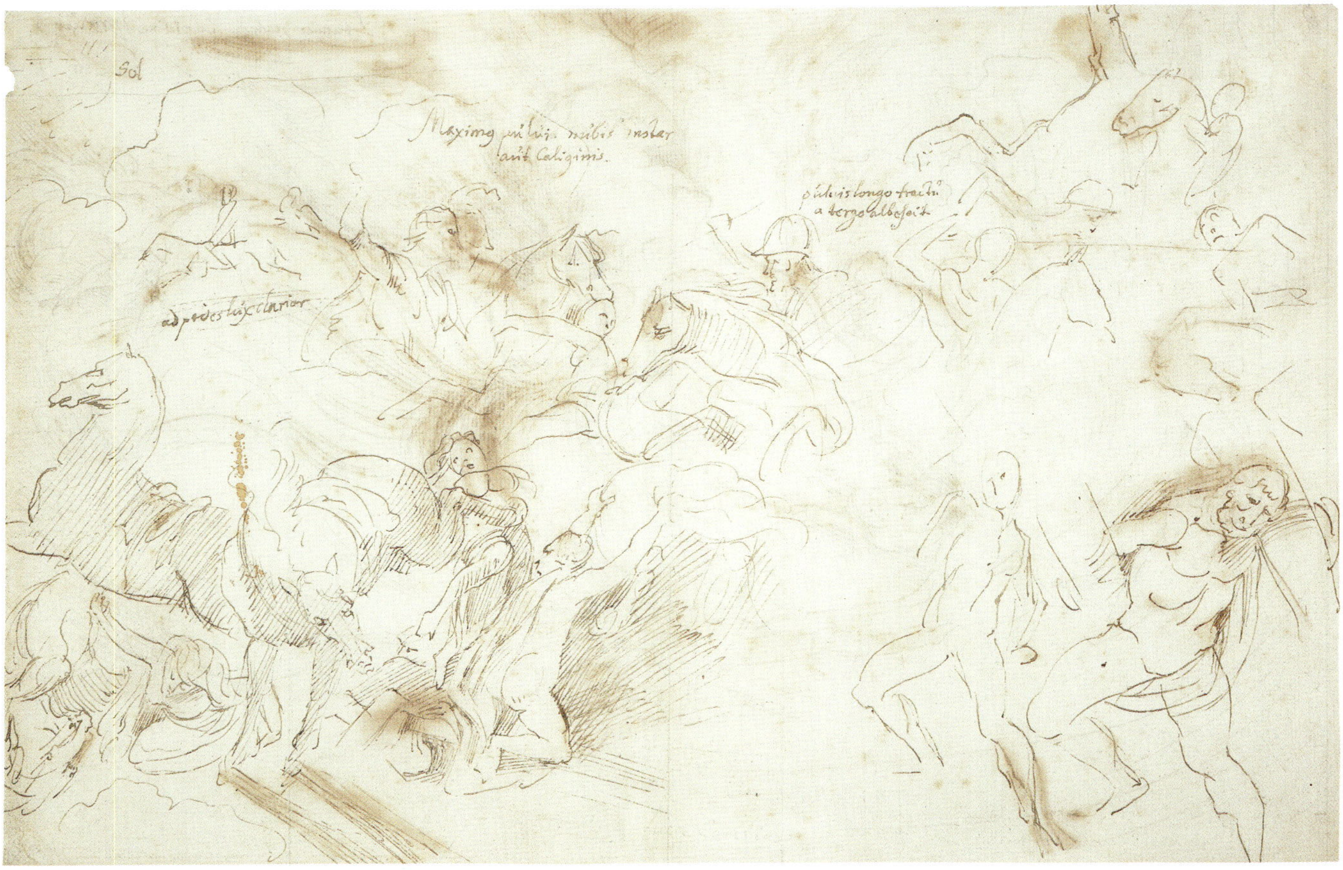

Cat. 10 verso

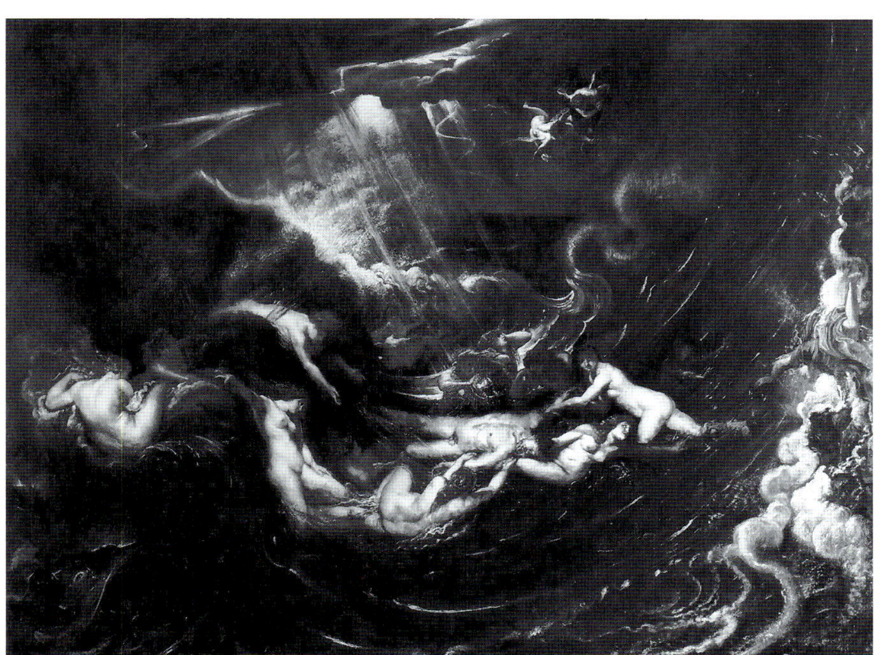

Fig. 44. Peter Paul Rubens, *Hero and Leander*, ca. 1604–5. Oil on canvas, 95.9 x 128 cm (37¾ x 50⅜ in.). Yale University Art Gallery, New Haven; Gift of Susan Morse Hilles (1962.25)

a tall wave prepares to break over him. The tail of a fish supports Leander's upper body, keeping his head above water, while eleven Nereids battle the waves in an attempt to rescue him. The heavy, turbulent sea recalls Leonardo da Vinci's *Deluge* drawings of about 1515–17.[1] Indeed, according to Roger de Piles (1635–1709)—the French critic and early biographer of Rubens—when Rubens was in Madrid in 1603 he may have seen some of Leonardo's drawings including the *Deluge* ones, at the home of Pompeo Leoni (ca. 1533–1608), a sculptor at the Spanish royal court.[2]

The drawing relates to Rubens's painting *Hero and Leander* of about 1604–5 (fig. 44),[3] which, however, depicts a later moment in the story. Nereids surround the drowned Leander and guide his body toward the shore. The despondent Hero, absent from the drawing, plunges into the sea upon seeing Leander's lifeless body. Nonetheless, many compositional elements of the drawing appear in the painting, with slight adjustments. The Nereid at the upper right, clinging to the crest of a wave, appears to the left of center in the painting; the Nereid at the lower left, holding on to a post, is at the right of the painting, supporting Leander's right arm. The fish has become a whale in the painting, at the bottom left corner.

The quick sketches Rubens jotted down on the verso are of two unrelated subjects: a battle between the Greeks and Amazons and, at the lower right, the Old Testament figure Samson. Neither sketch relates to any known painting by Rubens, although some of the figures reappear in Rubens's related, more finished compositional drawing of the *Battle of the Greeks and Amazons* (cat. no. 12) and in his well-known painting of about 1618 (fig. 46).

Rubens's explanatory inscriptions in Latin on the verso are all related to the effects of light and, specifically, to the interplay of light and dust. If it is the case that the drawing was inspired by the work of another artist, the inscriptions may be references to features of the original battle scene. It is interesting to note that Leonardo had written about effects of light and dust on the battlefield, including dust-laden air and ground dust stirred up by galloping horses, in his projected treatise on painting, the *Libro di pittura*.[4] Rubens could have seen the *Libro* at Pompeo Leoni's house, at the same time that he saw the *Deluge* drawings. This entire sheet seems to reflect Rubens's study of Leonardo, since the *Hero and Leander* on the recto may have been instigated by Leonardo's advice in the *Libro* about painting deluges.[5]

The two studies at the bottom right of the verso depict Samson wrapping his arms around columns in the temple of the Philistines, in preparation for pulling down the edifice. The figure of Samson is also recorded on folio 15v of the so-called *Antwerp Sketchbook* of about 1615–20 at Chatsworth, attributed to Anthony van Dyck, which in turn seems to be based in part on Rubens's lost early sketchbook, the *Pocket Book*.[6] The largest portion of the *Pocket Book* is surmised to date from Rubens's stay in Italy, between 1600 and 1608, and the exploratory nature of the drawing on this double-sided sheet accords with Rubens's work from the early years of that sojourn. This sheet may, therefore, have survived from the *Pocket Book*.

1. Ten of Leonardo's *Deluge* drawings are today in the Royal Library, Windsor Castle.
2. Piles 1699, pp. 166–68; New York 2003, no. 116, ill.
3. M. Jaffé 1970a, pp. 42–51, fig. 1; M. Jaffé 1989, no. 51, ca. 1605.
4. Carmen C. Bambach in New York 2003, p. 482. For Leonardo's *Libro di pittura*, see J. P. Richter 1939, vol. 1, pp. 348–50, and J. P. Richter 1977, vol. 1, pp. 31–36.
5. J. P. Richter 1977, vol. 1, pp. 355–57.
6. See M. Jaffé 1966, vol. 2, fol. 15v, and M. Jaffé 1970a, pp. 46–47.

11. *Jan Woverius*, July 1602

Black, red, and traces of yellow chalk (on forehead and cheek), heightened with white chalk, stumped, brush and brown ink, pen and dark brown ink (eyes and nostril) on brownish paper, 296 x 243 mm (11⅝ x 9 9/16 in.)
Annotated in pen and brown ink, in a seventeenth-century hand, at bottom right: *Rubbens*

Albertina, Vienna (8264)

PROVENANCE: Duke Albert of Sachsen-Teschen (1738–1822), Vienna (Lugt 174).

LITERATURE: R., vol. 5, no. 1537; Glück and Haberditzl 1928, no. 42, pl. 42; Huemer 1977, no. 50, fig. 130.

EXHIBITIONS: Cologne 1977, no. 35, ill.; Vienna 1977b, no. 3, ill.; Padua–Rome–Milan 1990, no. 61, ill.

The lawyer Jan Woverius (Jan van den Wouwere; 1576–1639) was a friend of Rubens and his older brother, Philip, and, like Philip, a student of Justus Lipsius (Joest Lips; 1547–1606), the influential Flemish humanist and philosopher who taught at the universities in Jena, Leiden, and Louvain. In early July 1602, during Rubens's service as court painter to the Gonzaga in Mantua, he and his brother visited with Woverius in Verona, as we learn from a letter from Philip to Woverius.[1] Many years later, Rubens commemorated the meeting in *Justus Lipsius and His Pupils,* painted about 1611–12 (fig. 45).[2] There, Woverius is seated at the right, next to Lipsius; Rubens portrayed himself at the far left, behind Philip, who holds a quill pen. About 1610, Rubens dedicated the first reproductive print after his painting of the so-called Large *Judith* (now lost) to Woverius (fig. 67).

This portrait of Woverius[3] is most likely a souvenir of Rubens and Woverius's 1602 meeting in Verona. The delicate application of the chalk strokes recalls the drawings by Federico Barocci (ca. 1535–1612), whose work Rubens must have seen during his stay in Italy.[4] The sheet does not relate to any known painting by Rubens, although a "portrait of Mr. Van den Wauwer *[sic],* believed to be painted by Rubens" was listed in the 1678–79 inventory of the collection of Rubens's collaborator Erasmus II Quellinus (1607–1678).[5]

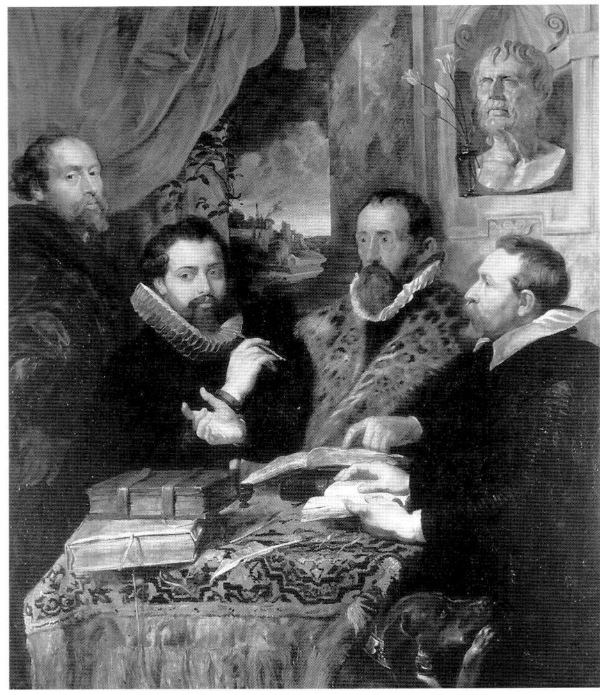

Fig. 45. Peter Paul Rubens, *Justus Lipsius and His Pupils,* ca. 1611–12. Oil on panel, 167 x 143 cm (65¾ x 56 5/16 in.). Palazzo Pitti, Florence

The annotation "Rubbens," in pen and brown ink in a seventeenth-century hand, is found on a number of Rubens's drawings that are today in the Albertina, Vienna.[6] The shared annotation may be evidence that this group of drawings remained intact from 1657, when Rubens's drawings were auctioned, until their acquisition by Albert of Sachsen-Teschen, the founder of the Albertina.

1. Rooses and Ruelens 1887–1909, vol. 1, pp. 51–58, letter 11.
2. Palazzo Pitti, Florence; M. Jaffé 1989, no. 153, ca. 1611–12.
3. Müller Hofstede (1965d, pp. 106–8, fig. 159) was the first to identify Woverius as the sitter.
4. Ibid.
5. Duverger 1984–, vol. 10, p. 349: "Een Conterfeytsel van d'heer Van den Wauwer men meynt Rubbens geschildert."
6. Cat. nos. 59, 70, 71, 83, 84, 86, 87, and inv. 8308.

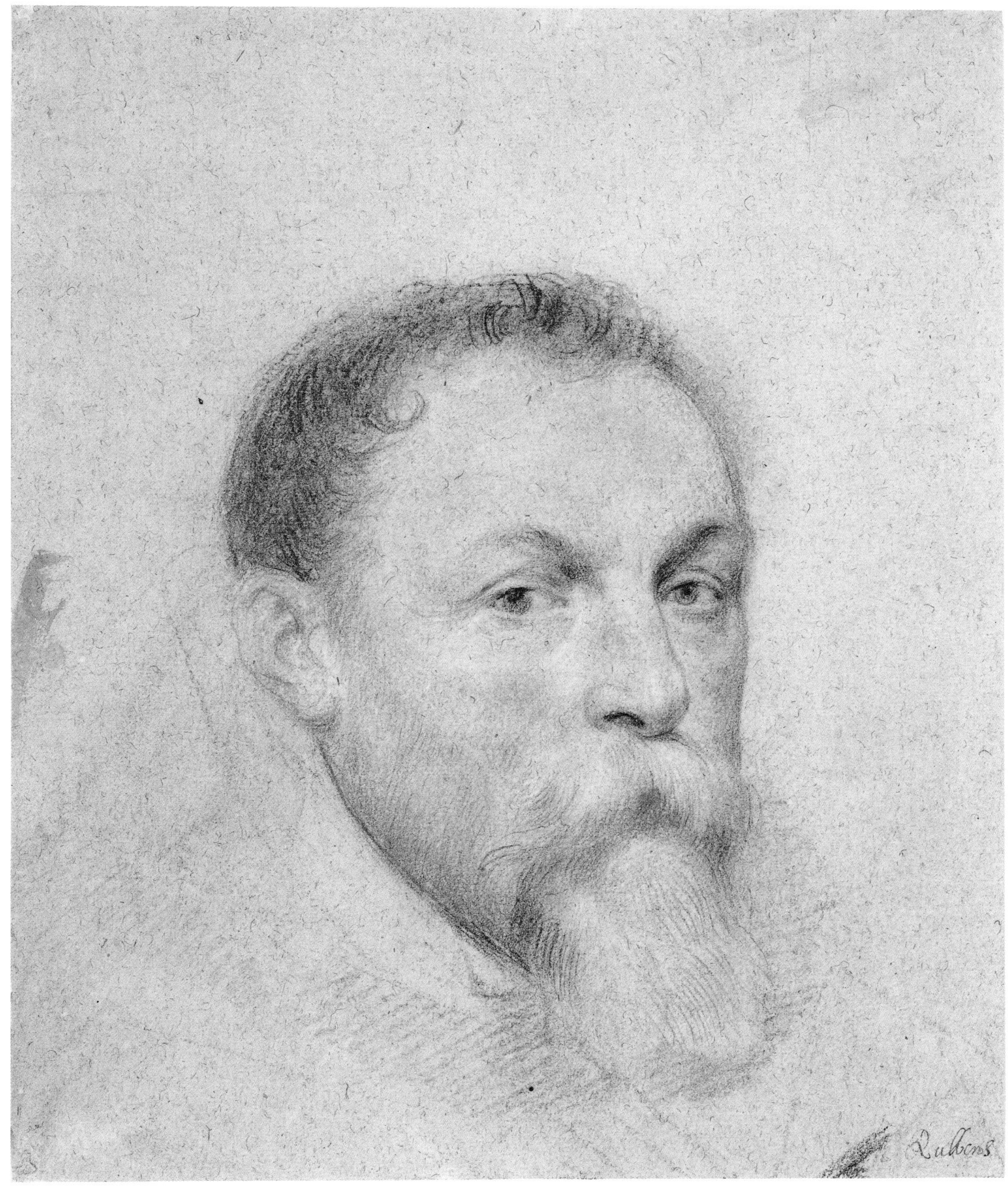

Cat. 11

12. *Battle of the Greeks and Amazons,* ca. 1602–4

Pen and brown ink over traces of graphite, 251 x 428 mm (9⅞ x 16⅞ in.)

The British Museum, London (1895.9.15.1045)

PROVENANCE: Jonathan Richardson Sr. (1665–1745), London (Lugt 2184); John Bouverie (ca. 1723–1750), London (Lugt 325);[1] Sir John Charles Robinson (1824–1913), London (Lugt 1433); John Malcolm of Poltalloch (1805–1893), London (Lugt 1780); John Wingfield Malcolm (sold in 1895 to the British Museum).

LITERATURE: R., vol. 5, no. 1548; Hind 1923, no. 24; Held 1959, no. 2, pl. 2, under nos. 1, 3, 21, and p. 64; Burchard and d'Hulst 1963, no. 50, pl. 50; M. Jaffé 1970a, pp. 46–47, fig. 4; Held 1986, no. 9, pl. 9.

EXHIBITIONS: Cologne 1977, no. 24, ill.; London 1977a, no. 21, ill.

Four representations by Rubens of a battle between the mythological Greeks and Amazons survive: two drawings, a sheet in Edinburgh (cat. no. 10 verso) and the present sheet in London, and two paintings, an early one, of about 1598, in Potsdam[2] and the more famous painting, of about 1618, in Munich (fig. 46).[3] The drawings relate to the paintings more in theme and motifs than in composition.

Additional Rubens drawings of battle scenes appear once to have existed, judging from references in old inventories, especially that of Erasmus II Quellinus (1607–1678), a collaborator with Rubens in the 1630s. In the portion of Quellinus's inventory drawn up on March 24, 1679, three "quick sketches of battle scenes" *(crabbelinge Battalien)* by Rubens are mentioned,[4] as well as a drawing of a *Battle of the Amazons* for which Rubens's authorship was considered doubtful.[5]

On this sheet Rubens defined the general outlines of the scene in an initial draft in graphite, then drew over it with a fine pen. The few pentimenti, visible in the rearing horse at the left and in the left arm of the Amazon trying to restrain it, establish that the drawing is a fairly finished compositional drawing. The battle does not develop parallel to the picture plane; instead, the figures seem to be coming straight at the viewer, as they do in the 1598 Potsdam *Battle of the Amazons.* Rubens's fascination with the horse in violent motion, and with the animal's role in battle as both supporter and adversary of man, is evident. (He had displayed the same interest in the copies he drew in the late 1590s after the illustrations by Jost Amman [1539–1591] for a 1580 edition of Flavius Josephus.)[6] The Amazon thrown to the ground and the Amazon thrown off her horse in the foreground are reminiscent of two early drawings by Rubens depicting the Death of Dido, the mythological queen of Carthage; one is in the Louvre, Paris (fig. 47), the other at Bowdoin College, Maine.[7] The angular, rather coarse cross-hatching at the right recalls Rubens's drawing of the

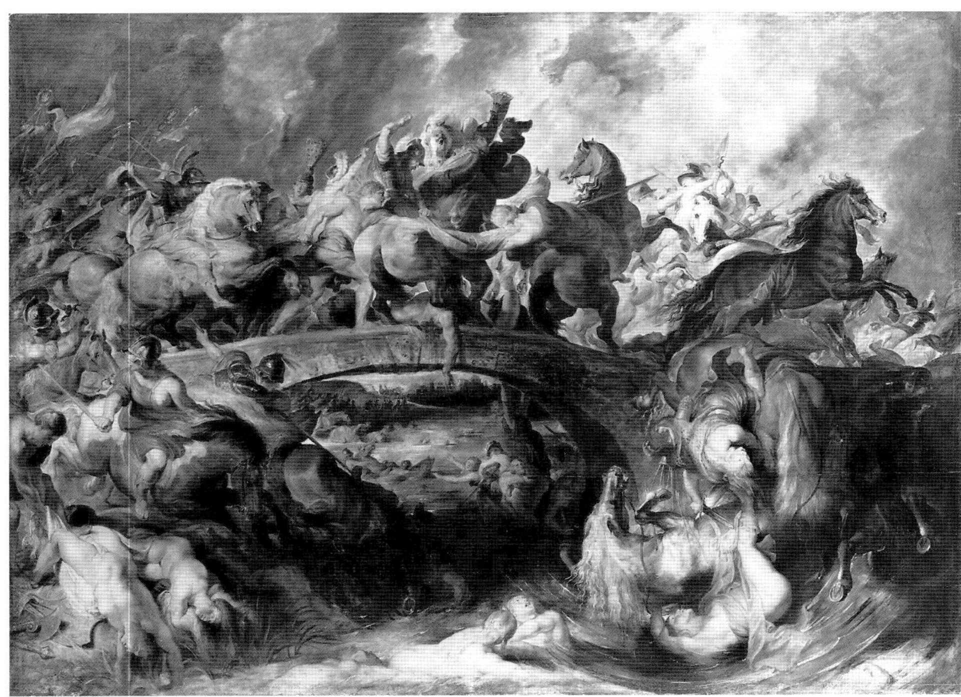

Fig. 46. Peter Paul Rubens, *Battle of the Amazons,* ca. 1618. Oil on panel, 120.3 x 165.3 cm (47⅜ x 65$^{1}/_{16}$ in.). Bayerische Staatsgemäldesammlungen, Alte Pinakothek, Munich (324)

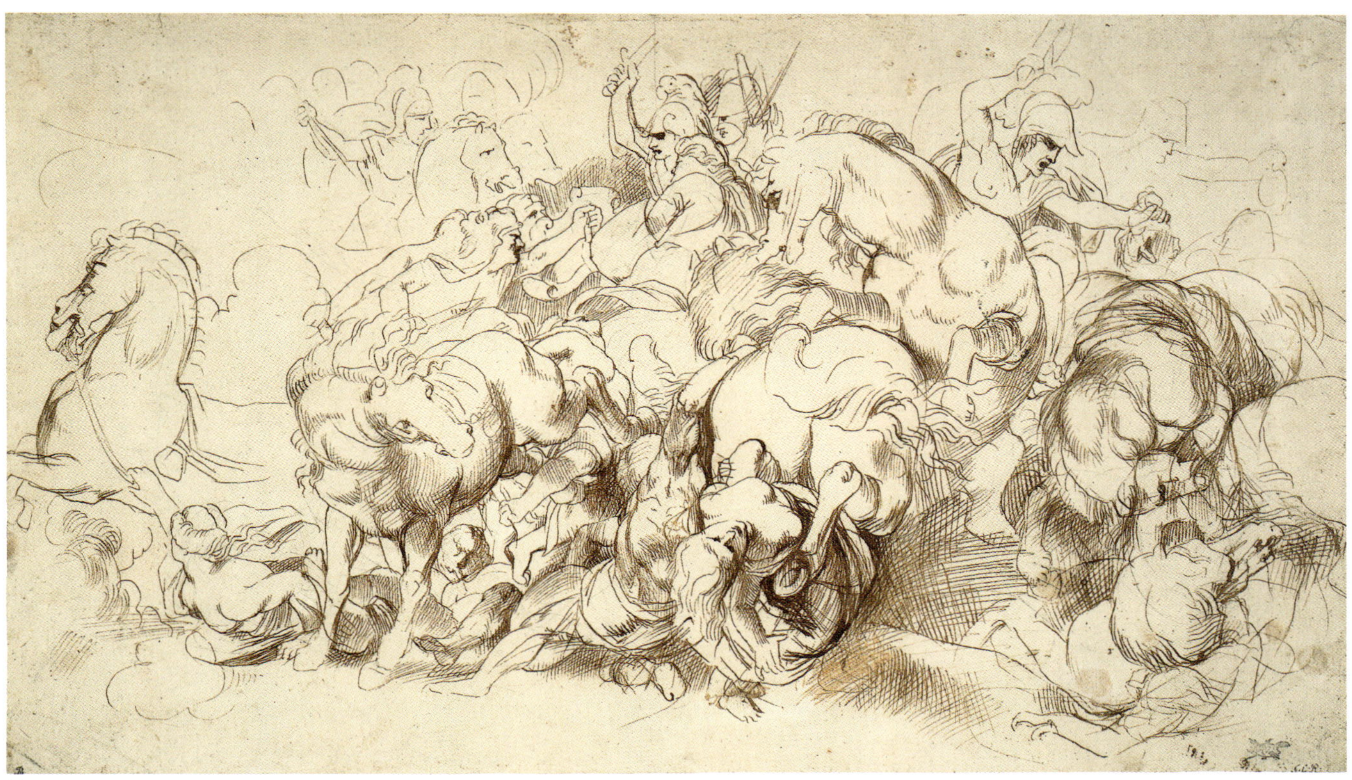

Cat. 12

Descent from the Cross in the Hermitage (cat. no. 9). The *Dido* and *Descent* drawings are dated to the early years of Rubens's stay in Italy. We suggest a similar date, about 1602–4, for the present drawing.

Rubens must have preserved the sheet for later use, since basic motifs formulated here are found in the Munich *Battle of the Amazons;* they include the Amazon holding the severed head of a Greek, the stumbling horse at the right, and the horse in profile fleeing the scene (in reverse and at the right in the painting). Horses reminiscent of those seen here also found their way into paintings with other subjects, such as the *Death of Decius Mus* (1616; Liechtenstein Museum, Vienna), the *Defeat of Sanherib* (ca. 1617; Alte Pinakothek, Munich), and the *Conversion of Saint Paul* (ca. 1616–17; formerly Berlin, destroyed in World War II). The two fighting horses in the drawing were most likely inspired by Leonardo da Vinci's *Fight for the Standard,* the central portion of his lost mural of the *Battle of Anghiari* (commissioned about 1503 for the Sala del Gran

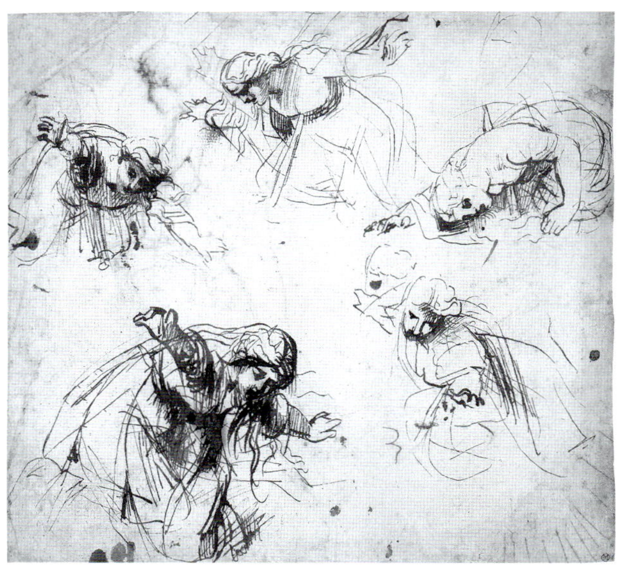

Fig. 47. Peter Paul Rubens, *Studies for the Death of Dido,* 1602–4. Pen and brown ink, 194 x 207 mm (7⅝ x 8⅛ in.). Département des Arts Graphiques du Musée du Louvre, Paris (19.916)

Consiglio of the Palazzo della Signoria, Florence), which in the early 1600s Rubens may have known from a drawn copy or an engraving.[8]

The present drawing is probably later than the *Battle Scene between the Greeks and Amazons* in Edinburgh (cat. no. 10 verso) and probably served a different function. The more spontaneous rendering in Edinburgh resembles a *prima idea,* a jotting down by Rubens of his initial ideas. In contrast, the London drawing is a more finished compositional study and was perhaps a preliminary drawing to a work that was never realized.

1. Turner 1994.
2. Held 1983, pp. 21–25; M. Jaffé 1989, no. 7 (ca. 1598).
3. K.d.K., ed. Oldenbourg 1921, no. 196; M. Jaffé 1989, no. 295 (ca. 1615); Renger and Denk 2002, p. 350, no. 324 (ca. 1618).
4. Duverger 1984–, vol. 10, pp. 359, 366.
5. Ibid., p. 360: "Slacht van d'Amasone dubieus de Rubbens."
6. Louvre, Paris (Paris 1978, no. 55, ill., with several copies on one sheet).
7. Louvre, Paris (ibid., no. 2, ill.), and Bowdoin College Museum of Art, Brunswick, Maine (Becker in Brunswick, Me., and other cities 1985–86, no. 13, ill.). See also Held 1986, nos. 24, 25, pls. 24, 25, both dated ca. 1602–5. For the subject of the drawings in Paris and Brunswick, see Elizabeth McGrath in London 1981–82, p. 214.
8. For an Italian sixteenth-century copy after Leonardo's *Fight for the Standard,* restored and reworked by Rubens, probably about 1615 or between 1612 and 1615, see Anne-Marie Logan in New York 2003, pp. 671–78.

13. *Man on Horseback (Study for the Portrait of the Duke of Lerma),* September 1603

Pen and brown ink, brush and brown wash over black chalk, heightened with white, 761 x 410 mm (30 x 16⅛ in.); strip of paper 88 mm wide added at top; horizontal crease through center

Staatliche Graphische Sammlung, Munich (1983.84 Z)

PROVENANCE: Spanish collection (according to Sir Thomas Lawrence); Sir Thomas Lawrence (1769–1830), London (listed in his inventory among the framed drawings: "Rubens. 46. Charles the 5th on Horseback, a grand fine drawing, pen & bistre"); William II of the Netherlands (1792–1849), The Hague (listed in his sale, The Hague, August 12–20, 1850, as part of lot 282, as "Charles V on Horseback," but withdrawn in favor of Sophie, Grand Duchess of Sachsen-Weimar-Eisenach, daughter of William II); grand dukes of Sachsen-Weimar-Eisenach; Graphische Sammlung, Schlossmuseum, Weimar (ca. 1928–ca. 1944); private collection, southern Germany (bought in 1948 at the sale of the grand ducal property and bequeathed to the Staatliche Graphische Sammlung in 1983).

LITERATURE: R., vol. 5, no. 1504; Glück and Haberditzl 1928, no. 47, pl. 47; Huemer 1977, no. 20b, fig. 70; Vignau-Wilberg 1998, pp. 275–87; Thea Vignau-Wilberg 1999; Sarah Schroth in Madrid 2001–2, pp. 31–46, 60–67; Thea Vignau-Wilberg in Madrid 2001–2, pp. 21–29, 54–59.

EXHIBITIONS: Munich 1995–97, no. 9, ill.; Madrid 2001–2, no. 2.

In early March 1603 Duke Vincenzo Gonzaga sent Rubens from his court in Mantua to Spain, to escort gifts for King Philip III and members of the Spanish court. Among the gifts were paintings, some of which were rain-damaged upon Rubens's arrival in Valladolid in late May. Rubens was able to restore all but one, for which he substituted a painting of his own, made on the spot, the *Democritus and Heraclitus* (Museo Nacional de Escultura, Valladolid). Rubens's painting caught the attention of the Duke of Lerma, Philip III's chief minister and *valido,* or favorite. Don Francisco Gómez de Sandoval y Rojas (1553–1623), 5th Marquess of Denia and 4th Count of Lerma, was created 1st Duke of Lerma in 1599. Lerma was an avid collector, and at the time of Rubens's visit to Spain his art collection was second only to the king's.[1]

Lerma commissioned a painting from Rubens, eventually settling on an equestrian portrait of himself.[2] On September 15, still in Spain, Rubens wrote in a letter that he was at work "to satisfy the taste and demand of the Duke of Lerma . . . by a great equestrian portrait."[3] By November Rubens had finished the portrait of Lerma—the artist's first equestrian portrait—which he signed and dated: "P. P. Ruebens f. 1603" (fig. 48).[4] The painting was installed at Huerta de la Ribera, Lerma's estate outside Valladolid, amid portrait busts of Roman emperors and adjacent to a gallery that displayed paintings of Roman emperors on horseback. Probably at the time when the proper place to hang the picture was established, Rubens decided, or was asked, to expand the painting at the top. To integrate this relatively large addition and to hide the seam in the canvas, the artist cleverly introduced into the image tree branches and overhanging foliage. Rubens's portrait of the Duke of Lerma is so

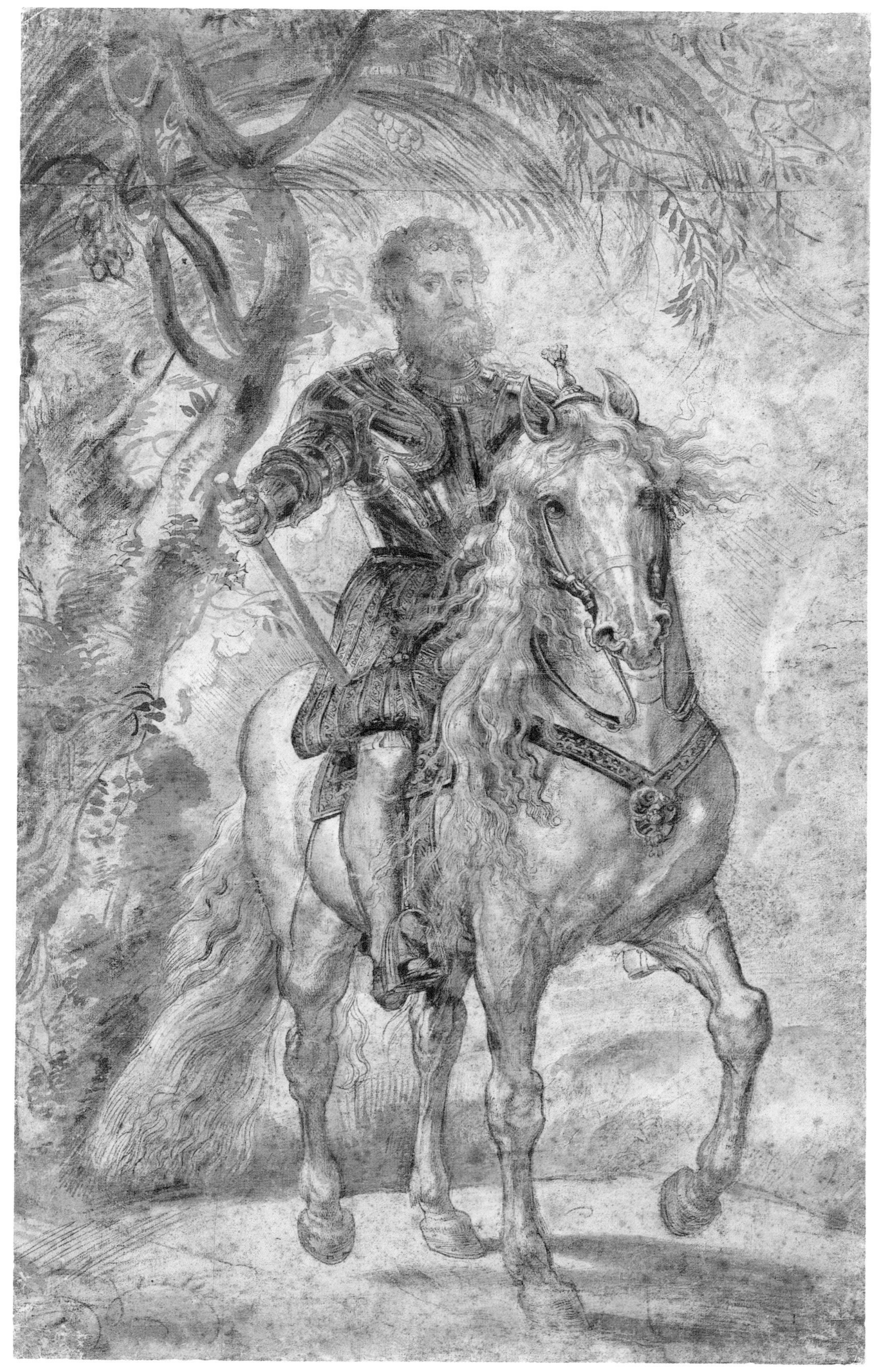

Cat. 13

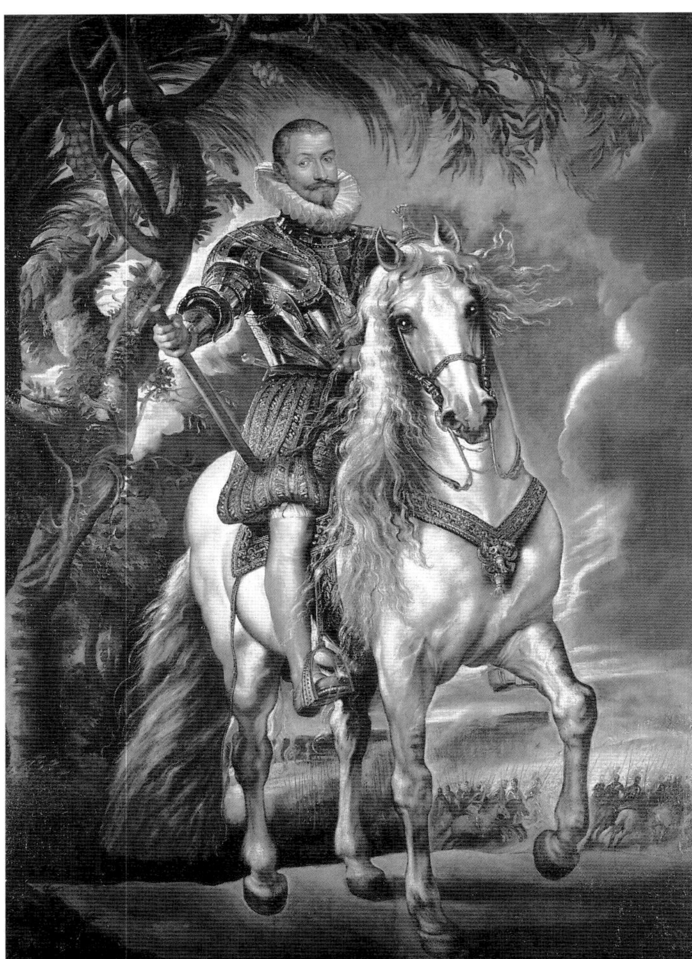

Fig. 48. Peter Paul Rubens, *The Duke of Lerma on Horseback*, November 1603. Oil on canvas, 289 x 205 cm (113¾ x 80¹¹⁄₁₆ in.). Prado, Madrid (3137)

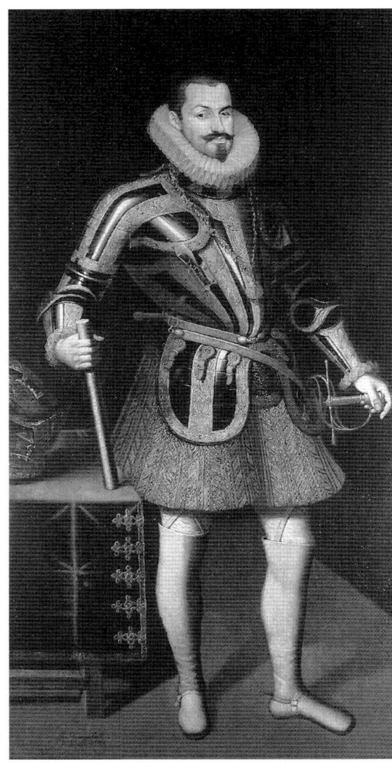

Fig. 49. Juan Pantoja de la Cruz, *The Duke of Lerma,* ca. 1600. Oil on canvas, 190 x 110 cm (74¹³⁄₁₆ x 43⁵⁄₁₆ in.). Palacio Tavera, Toledo (P [3]-1)

large, the vantage point so low, and the subject so elevated above the viewer that Lerma is virtually on a par with a king.

This exceptionally large, highly finished drawing was in all likelihood Rubens's proposal, or *modello,* for the 1603 equestrian portrait of Lerma. Strangely, however, the man's head in the drawn *modello* and the head in the painting are not the same. The drawing shows a man with curly hair and a beard, and without the ruff collar the man in the painting wears. However, Spanish etiquette dictated that, as in the painting, the duke wear short-cropped hair, a trimmed mustache, and a goatee. Thus it cannot be said that the drawing does represent Lerma, just with more hair and a beard.[5] The man in the drawing has yet to be identified convincingly. It has been said that he was a groom, used as a stand-in for the duke; it has been proposed that he represents a Roman emperor—not surprising in view of the Duke of Lerma's interest in imperial Rome and his collection of paintings and portrait busts of Roman emperors.[6] The armor shown in the drawing is clearly Lerma's, however, and it is difficult to reconcile contemporary armor with the head of a Roman emperor.

Lerma's position at court required him to remain always in the company of the king, making it unlikely that he sat for Rubens's portrait of him. Rather, Rubens probably copied the duke's head from Lerma's official portrait by Juan Pantoja de la Cruz (fig. 49), which in October 1603 was in the duke's villa in Ventosilla.[7] The artist most likely painted Lerma's head, including the ruff collar, directly into his unfinished painting.

The drawing has been widely studied only since the mid-1990s, when the Staatliche Graphische Sammlung in Munich acquired it (previously, it had been known only from photographs). Until then, an almost identical drawing, of a *Man on Horseback,* in the Louvre, Paris,[8] was considered the preparatory drawing for the Lerma portrait. However, the Munich drawing is not only clearly the more accomplished work but also the only one of the two drawings securely attributable to Rubens. So precise is the execution of the

Munich sheet that it has been thought, incorrectly, that the drawing was a design for a print made after the painting rather than a preliminary study for it.[9] The drawing was enlarged at the top with a strip of the same type of paper as the rest of the sheet.[10]

In contrast, the initial draft in chalk in the Louvre drawing, half the size of the Munich drawing, is rather rigid; the pen lines are coarser than in the Munich drawing, and the cross-hatching for the modeling is cruder. The so-called pentimento in black chalk along the horse's neck and left leg is more likely evidence of an inept draftsman than of rethinking by Rubens. The Louvre drawing contains no new ideas (indeed, it lacks the strap that hangs, in both the Munich drawing and the painting, from the saddle at the left) but depends on the *modello* in Munich, even reproducing the bearded, curly-haired man in place of Lerma (though, strangely, on a separate piece of paper attached to the drawing).[11] In all likelihood, the sheet in the Louvre is a *ricordo,* by another artist, of the state of the Lerma portrait before Rubens finished the painting.[12]

1. Lerma even tried to retain Rubens at the Spanish court, rather than let him return to Mantua. For the Duke of Lerma as a collector, see Schroth 1990.
2. At one time, Lerma may have wanted Rubens to paint a Roman emperor on horseback, probably because the painting was meant to join the many pictures of Roman emperors already in Lerma's collection. Sarah Schroth in Madrid 2001–2, p. 61.
3. Magurn 1955, p. 37, letter 11.
4. M. Jaffé 1989, no. 36, 1603; only the Paris drawing (see note 8 below) is mentioned as a preliminary study.
5. Sarah Schroth in Madrid 2001–2, p. 61.
6. Ibid., pp. 61, 64.
7. Ibid., p. 65.
8. Lugt 1949, no. 1018; Paris 1978, no. 1, ill. In an exhibition at the Prado, Madrid, the Paris sheet and the present drawing were exhibited side by side, next to Rubens's equestrian portrait of Lerma; they are discussed in the accompanying publication, Madrid 2001–2.
9. Lugt 1949, under no. 1018.
10. Thea Vignau-Wilberg in Madrid 2001–2, pp. 21–29, 57. She observes (p. 57) that the handling of line and wash on both pieces of paper is identical, proving that the strip was there during the work process. She thinks that the strip may have been there from the beginning.
11. As Vignau-Wilberg (ibid., p. 57) notes, the Louvre drawing originally must have been larger at the top.
12. The Munich drawing probably stayed with the duke in Spain (the *modello* usually remained with the person commissioning the work of art); according to Thomas Lawrence, a previous owner, the drawing came from Spain. According to Paris 1978, the Louvre drawing came from the collection of Everhard Jabach (1618–1695). This is not so, however. As Bernadette Py kindly informed us (letter, January 12, 2004), the drawing does not appear in any inventory of Jabach's collection. The *Man on Horseback* is included for the first time in the French royal inventory of 1752–53 and therefore entered the royal collection sometime before 1752, as Lina Propeck of the Louvre established (e-mail communication). The previous owner is unknown.

14. *The Baptism of Christ,* ca. 1604

Black chalk, squared in black chalk, corrected and heightened with white; a few small, irregularly shaped pieces of paper pasted onto the sheet as restorations or corrections after the squaring, 486 x 767 mm (19⅛ x 30¼ in.)

Département des Arts Graphiques du Musée du Louvre, Paris (20.187)

PROVENANCE: Everhard Jabach (1618–1695), Cologne and Paris (Lugt 2959; mounted with gold band; Inventaire 5, 201, "dessins d'ordonnance" [Van Dyck]); entered the French royal collection in 1671; Prioult (Lugt 2953, with number 201); museum mark (Lugt 1899, 2207, 1886).

LITERATURE: Morel d'Arleux, inv. MS 6, no. 8743; Reiset 1866, no. 548; R., vol. 5, no. 1343, pl. 384; Glück and Haberditzl 1928, no. 50, pl. 50; Lugt 1949, no. 1009, pl. XIV; Held 1959, no. 11, pl. 12, and pp. 66–67, 69, 127; Burchard and d'Hulst 1963, no. 29, pl. 29, and p. 36; Kuznetsov 1974, pl. 20; Held 1986, no. 28, pl. 28; White 1987, pp. 31–32, pl. 43; Von zur Mühlen 1998, pp. 115–21.

EXHIBITIONS: Paris 1978, no. 4, ill.; Antwerp 1993, no. 90, pl. 17.

Rubens's most important commission while serving Vincenzo Gonzaga, Duke of Mantua, from 1600 until 1608 was for three paintings for Santissima Trinità, the Jesuit church in Mantua. The duke's mother, Eleonora of Austria, had been instrumental in bringing the Jesuits to Mantua and, together with her husband, Duke Guglielmo Gonzaga (r. 1550–87), founded Santissima Trinità. The decision to decorate the main chapel with three paintings was made in 1597 by Duke Vincenzo Gonzaga. He was anxious to have the chapel completed, since his mother, who died on August 5, 1594, had been buried before its altar. The Jesuit chapter in Rome apparently helped select the paintings' subjects, which were *Vincenzo Gonzaga and His Family Adoring the Holy Trinity* (fig. 51),[1] the central canvas; the *Baptism of Christ,* for the left wall (fig. 50); and the *Transfiguration* (Musée des Beaux-Arts, Nancy) for the right.[2]

Rubens may have received the commission fairly soon after his arrival in Mantua, possibly before June 1601, when Vincenzo

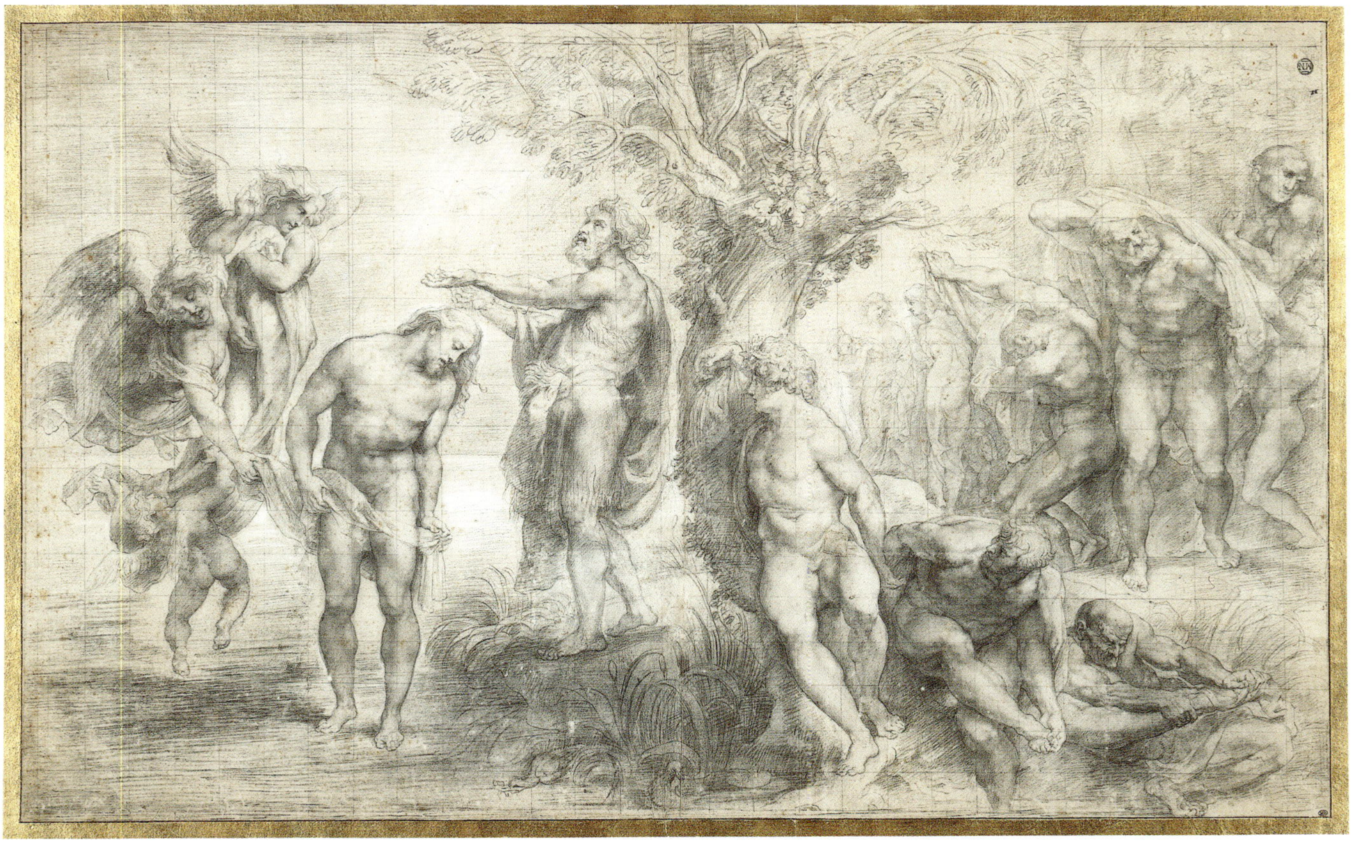

Cat. 14

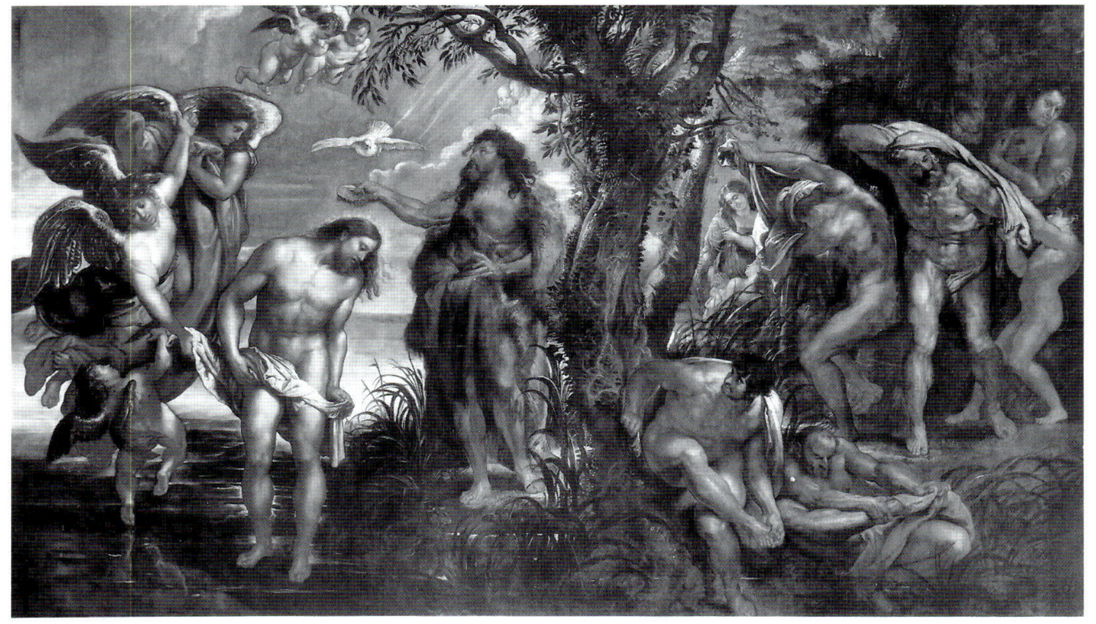

Fig. 50. Peter Paul Rubens, *The Baptism of Christ*, 1604. Oil on canvas, 411 x 675 cm ($161\frac{13}{16}$ x $265\frac{3}{4}$ in.). Koninklijk Museum voor Schone Kunsten, Antwerp (707)

Gonzaga left for the Turkish war. Shortly thereafter, in mid-July, Rubens traveled to Rome; he returned to Mantua by April 1602, for about ten months. He must have begun work on the paintings for the chapel before Duke Vincenzo sent him on a mission to Spain in March 1603. After his return to the Gonzaga court in late spring 1604, Rubens finished the paintings relatively quickly, as they were unveiled on Sunday, June 5, 1605, the Feast of the Holy Trinity.

Rubens drew this detailed compositional study in preparation for his monumental *Baptism of Christ* (today in the Koninklijk Museum voor Schone Kunsten, Antwerp; fig. 50)[3] for the chapel's left wall. The exceptionally large drawing is the only known study for the painting. The sheet is one of only two in Rubens's oeuvre, moreover, where he experimented with the cartoon, a type of preliminary drawing that had been frequently employed by sixteenth-century Italian artists but that he never adopted, preferring the colored sketch in oil on panel. The earlier Italian artists had produced full-size cartoons on a one-to-one scale; Rubens's drawing, in contrast, is more akin to a *cartonetto,* or small cartoon. (For Rubens's second known cartoon, see catalogue number 17.)

Although the drawing is fully squared for transfer, Rubens did not reproduce the composition in its entirety in the painting but, rather, introduced a number of changes.[4] The most dramatic difference is in the center foreground of the painting, where the youth leaning against the tree in the drawing is omitted, allowing Rubens to increase the size of the remaining figures and move them closer to the center. In addition, in the painting Rubens altered the figure of Saint John the Baptist and the act of baptism itself. Saint John baptizes Christ not with water cupped in his hands but with water scooped up in a shell. The dove symbolizing the Holy Spirit is barely indicated in the study, appearing faintly in a beam of light above the Baptist's hands; it is clearly rendered in the painting, however, hovering over Saint John's hand as he baptizes Christ. In Rubens's painting the Baptist alone is aware of its presence.[5]

Many figures on the sheet testify to Rubens's study of classical and Renaissance works of art. Rubens adapted the seated youth in the right foreground of the drawing—who joins the two halves of the composition—from a sketch he made during his first visit to Rome (1601–2): a copy after an antique sculpture based on a Greek original by Lysippos (?), then still in the Medici collection in Rome.[6] The seated man drying his feet, to the right of the youth, was obviously inspired by another statue that Rubens had copied: the famous *Spinario,* a Roman copy after a Greek original of a boy pulling a thorn from his foot.[7] The standing male figures discarding their clothes at the right of the composition are heavily indebted to Michelangelo's *Last Judgment* in the Sistine Chapel. One is also reminded of Rubens's drawing after Michelangelo's *Saint John the Baptist,* known today only from the counterproof by Willem Panneels (ca. 1600–1634) in the *cantoor,*[8] and his copy after Michelangelo's *ignudo* in the British Museum (fig. 11).[9] Some of the figures, especially the four bathers at the right, seem to have been inspired by Michelangelo's now-lost cartoon for the *Battle of Cascina* mural (commissioned about 1504 for the Sala del Gran Consiglio, Palazzo della Signoria, Florence). Indeed, Rubens may have seen a portion of the cartoon; according to Giorgio Vasari, fragments of Michelangelo's work were in the collection of Uberto Strozzi, a "gentiluomo mantovano" (Mantuan nobleman), in the sixteenth century.[10]

1. M. Jaffé 1989, no. 41. The painting is still in the Palazzo Ducale, Mantua, in a mutilated state.
2. Ibid., no. 43. For a reconstruction of the choir of the chapel, see Von zur Mühlen 1998, fig. 32.
3. M. Jaffé 1989, no. 42.
4. The thorough squaring of the drawing into 29 horizontal and 18 vertical rows varies between 25 and 28 mm, with an additional 5-mm-wide band at the top and bottom. Nico van Hout, curator at the Koninklijk Museum voor Schone Kunsten, Antwerp, kindly informs us (e-mail communication, November 2003) that there are no marks along the edges of the *Baptism of Christ* painting in Antwerp that might correspond to the squaring of this drawing.
5. Von zur Mühlen 1998, p. 119.
6. Van der Meulen 1994, no. 3, fig. 7. Rubens must have gained access to the Medici collection thanks to Vincenzo Gonzaga's wife, Eleonora de' Medici; his allusion to this statue may have been intentional.
7. Rubens's drawings after the *Spinario* (Palazzo dei Conservatori, Rome) are in the British Museum, London; in the Museé des Beaux-Arts, Dijon; and formerly in a Swedish private collection, sold, London, Christie's, July 8, 2003, lot 96.
8. Copenhagen 1988, no. 251, pl. 251.
9. Held 1986, no. 22, pl. 22.
10. De Tolnay 1943–, vol. 1, p. 211; Vasari 1962, p. 27.

15. *Study for a Halberdier,* 1604

Black and some red chalk (face and right hand), touches of pen and brown ink and light gray-brown wash, heightened with white body color, on light gray paper, 407 x 260 mm (16 x 10¼ in.)
Annotated in pen and brown ink at bottom right: *Rubens*

Bibliothèque Royale Albert Ier, Brussels (SV 95843)

PROVENANCE: Prosper Henry Lankrink (1628?–1692), London (Lugt 2090); Joseph van Haecken (Lugt 1516; sale, Langford, January 17–20, 1758); Michael Jaffé (1923–1997), Cambridge (sale, London, Sotheby's, November 11, 1965, no. 56); acquired by the Bibliotheque Royale Albert Ier.

LITERATURE: Held 1959, no. 72, pl. 82, and pp. 66, 73; Elizabeth McGrath in London 1981–82, pp. 214–21; Held 1986, no. 27, pl. 30; Von zur Mühlen 1998, pp. 99–118.

EXHIBITIONS: Cologne 1977, no. 38, ill.; Düsseldorf–Cologne 1979, no. 12, ill.; Tokyo 1982, no. 62, ill.

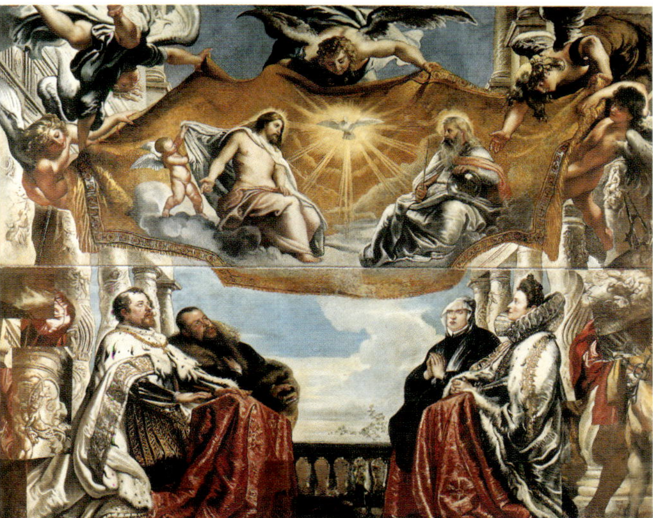

Fig. 51. Peter Paul Rubens, *Vincenzo Gonzaga and His Family Adoring the Holy Trinity,* ca. 1604. Oil on canvas, 430 x 700 cm (169⁵⁄₁₆ x 275⁹⁄₁₆ in.). Galleria del Palazzo Ducale, Mantua

Rubens's immense painting *Vincenzo Gonzaga and His Family Adoring the Holy Trinity,* of about 1604, was commissioned for the main chapel of the Jesuit church of Santissima Trinità in Mantua.[1] (For the circumstances of the commission, see the discussion under catalogue number 14.) During the French occupation of Mantua in 1797, the Jesuit church was used for storage; in 1801 the painting was moved to a depot and cut up. The main fragments of Rubens's picture are today in the Palazzo Ducale in Mantua (fig. 51). In the lower fragment, members of the ducal family kneel in adoration of the Holy Trinity; Vincenzo Gonzaga and his father, Guglielmo, are on the left, and their wives, Eleonora de' Medici and Eleonora of Austria, respectively, are on the right. Rubens's painting had originally included portraits of a third generation of the ducal family—the children of Vincenzo and Eleonora de' Medici—as well as at least five halberdiers.

This large study of a halberdier is Rubens's preliminary drawing for a guard who once stood at the lower right, of a type that the artist may have observed at the court in Mantua. One can discern in the mutilated painting the halberdier's left leg and puffed breeches more or less the way Rubens had drawn them in this study. In a reconstruction of the painting by Ugo Bazzotti, a Swiss guard stands in front of the halberdier, obscuring his midsection.[2]

The drawing is one of Rubens's earliest studies for a single figure. With a broad, greasy black chalk, Rubens drew over an earlier draft in a drier, finer black chalk. His heavy lines show few corrections or changes. In execution the study resembles Rubens's 1601–2 black-chalk studies for the *Raising of the Cross* (cat. no. 30 verso and fig. 16), where one finds the same emphasis on contour lines filled with coarse parallel hatching; the figures in those studies are, like the halberdier, awkward and almost two-dimensional. Indeed, Rubens gave so little attention to the head of the halberdier and to his hands and legs that the drawing is essentially a costume study.[3] The guard's right hand is especially angular, lacking the free, flowing lines that one observes in Rubens's later figure studies in chalk.

1. M. Jaffé 1989, no. 41. The painting measured about 4.3 x 7 m.
2. Bazzotti's reconstruction is reproduced in Limentani Virdis and Bottacin 1992, p. 46. Von zur Mühlen 1998, fig. 23.
3. L. de Pauw-de Veen in Brussels 1969, p. 252.

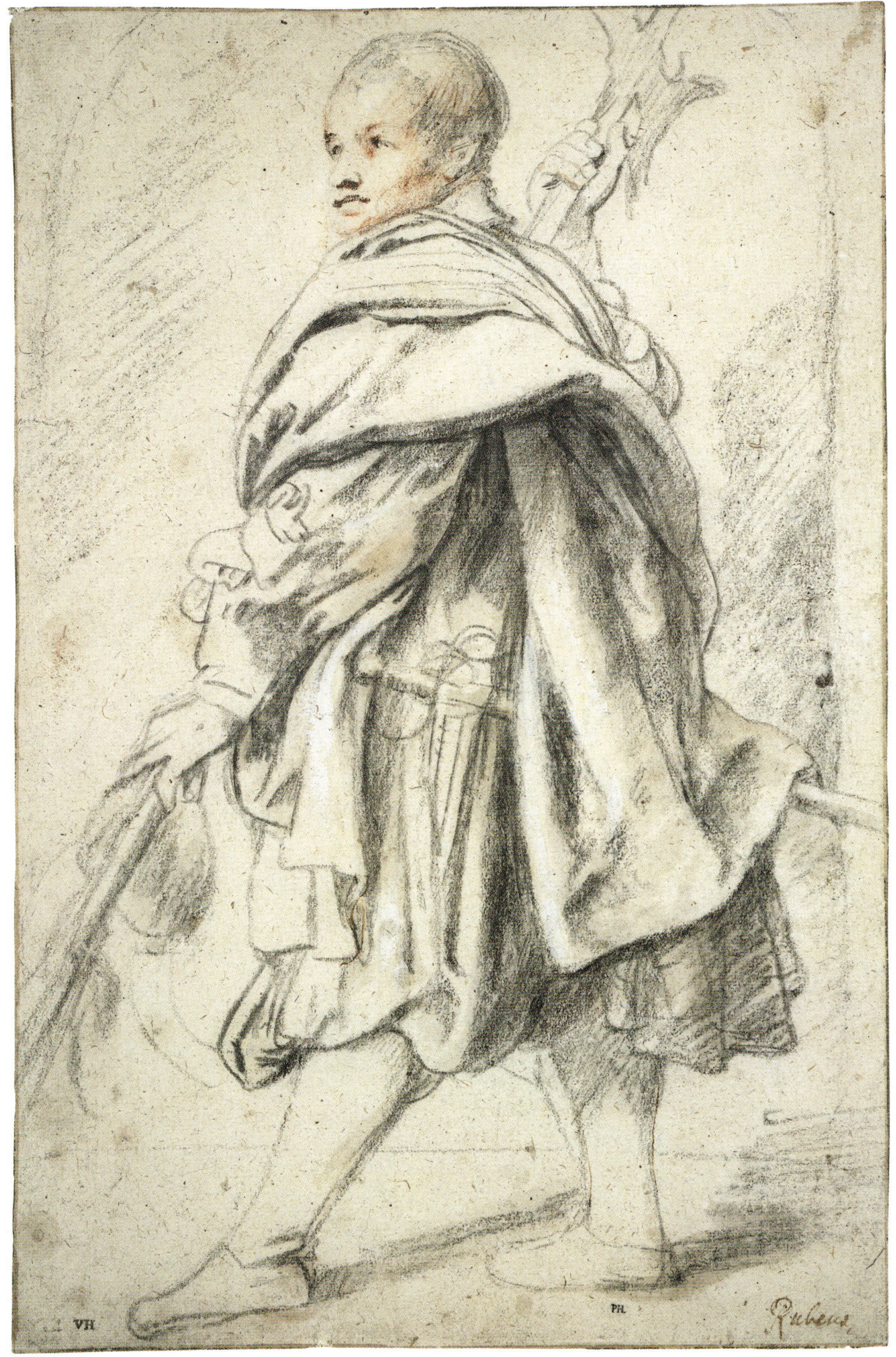
Cat. 15

16. *Anatomical Studies: A Left Forearm in Two Positions and a Right Forearm,* ca. 1600–1605

Pen and dark brown ink, 278 x 186 mm (10 15/16 x 7 5/16 in.)

The Metropolitan Museum of Art, New York; Rogers Fund, 1996 (1996.75)

PROVENANCE: Pierre Crozat (1665–1740), Paris (?; Mariette mentions écorchés in the Crozat collection); Sir Roger Newdegate V (apparently acquired on the Continent in 1738–40), Newdegate Settlement, London (sale, London, Christie's, July 6, 1987, lot 66, ill.); Bernard Quaritch Ltd., London; Hazlitt, Gooden and Fox, London, 1992.

LITERATURE: R., vol. 5, no. 1229, 11; M. Jaffé 1987, pp. 58–61, 80–81; Copenhagen 1988, pp. 78–81.

EXHIBITION: Antwerp 1993, no. 2, ill.

This drawing is one of eleven anatomical studies by Rubens that came to light only in 1987.[1] The group had been in the collection of Sir Roger Newdegate V, who apparently purchased them on the Continent during his grand tour in 1738–40. In 1999 a twelfth sheet became known.[2]

Some of these studies are drawn in pen and brown ink, as is the present drawing; in others brown wash has been added; in a few Rubens used black or red chalk only. The use of a variety of materials is an indication that he probably worked on them over time. Several of the drawings focus on arms, while others depict figures in motion. A number of sheets feature écorché

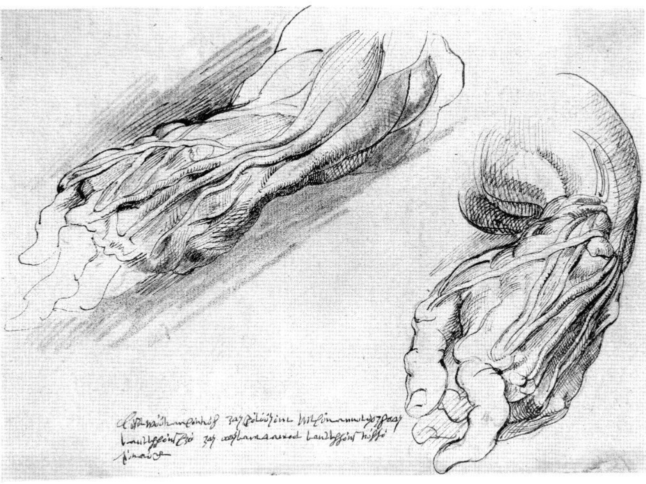

Fig. 52. Willem Panneels after Peter Paul Rubens, *Flayed Left Forearm in Two Positions,* ca. 1628–29. Black and red chalk, pen and brown and black ink on beige paper, 153/156 x approx. 106 cm (6/6 1/8 x approx. 4 3/16 in.). Rubens Cantoor, Den Kongelige Kobberstiksamling, Statens Museum for Kunst, Copenhagen (KS GB 6158)

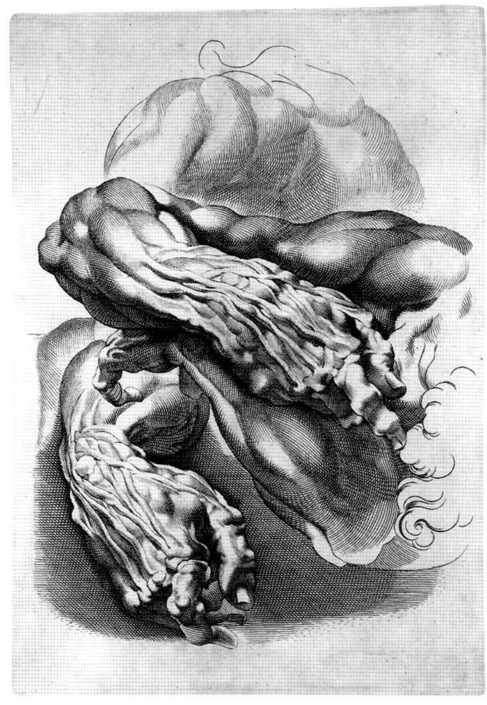

Fig. 54. Paulus Pontius, *Anatomical Study of Three Arms and Two Hands,* ca. 1649. Etching, 324 x 214 mm (12 11/16 x 8 7/16 in.). The Metropolitan Museum of Art, New York; The Elisha Whittelsey Collection, The Elisha Whittelsey Fund, 1951 (1.501.7111[10])

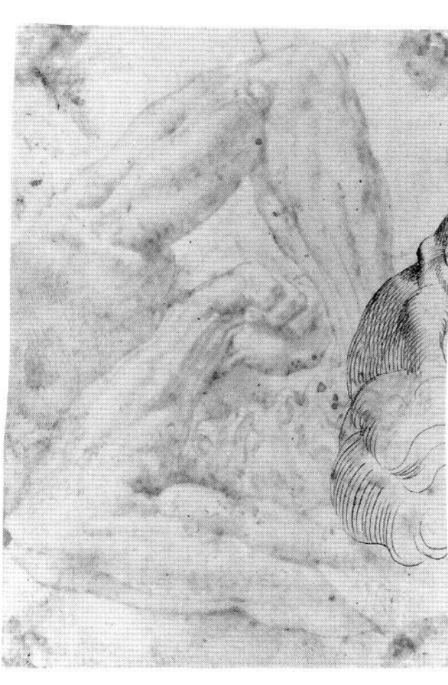

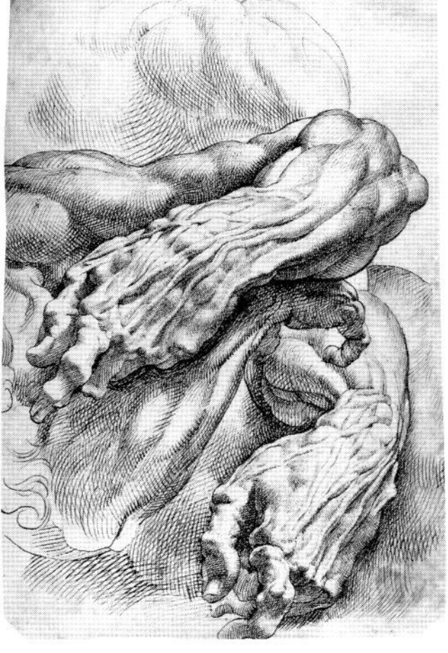

Fig. 53. Rejoined anatomical drawings by Peter Paul Rubens. Right: cat. no. 16. Left: Peter Paul Rubens, *Two Anatomical Studies of a Left Arm,* ca. 1600–1605. Pen and brown ink, 268 x 189 mm (10 9/16 x 7 7/16 in.). Private collection, United States

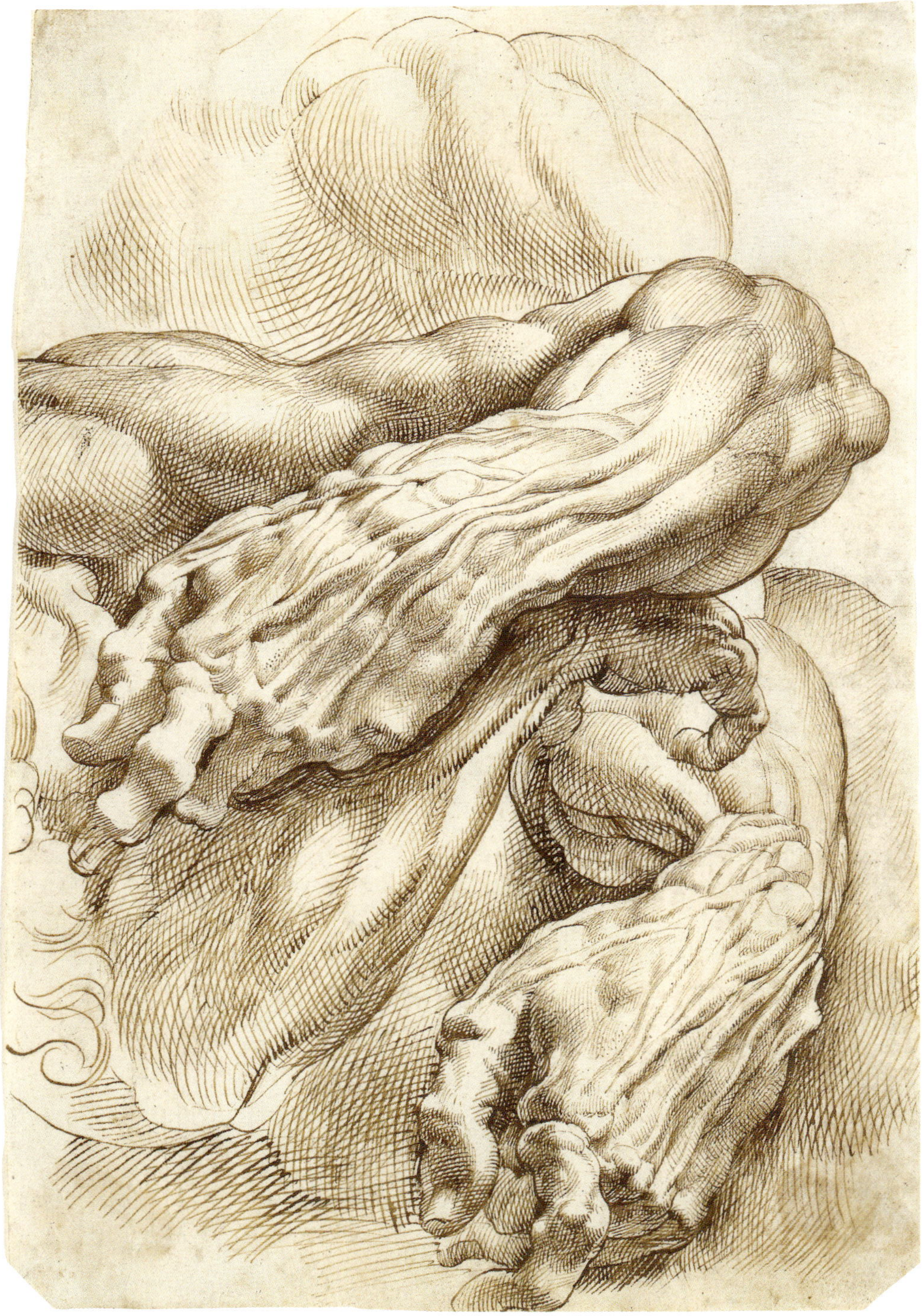

Cat. 16

figures in poses that resemble those of small bronzes by, among others, the Dutch sculptor Willem van Tetrode (ca. 1525–1580). Rubens may have been familiar with Tetrode's bronze of an écorché man now in a private collection.[3]

Not all scholars have accepted the newly discovered anatomical studies as autograph works by Rubens.[4] It is true that these drawings stand apart from the artist's other early works. Nonetheless, the attribution of the present drawing to Rubens is supported by a sheet by Willem Panneels (ca. 1600–1634), one of Rubens's students from about 1624 and a resident in Rubens's house while the artist was away during 1628 and 1629. On his sheet (fig. 52) Panneels copied two of the forearms in the present drawing, with a notation that they were after Rubens's original. His inscription reads: "I copied these two hands from

Rubens's anatomy book which I also fetched from Rubens's *cantoor.*"[5] (Panneels noted on several other anatomical drawings that he made during his stay in Rubens's house that they, too, were copies after originals in Rubens's "annotomibock." This *Anatomy Book* was taken apart after Rubens's death and the sheets were dispersed.)[6] The present drawing was also engraved by Paulus Pontius (1603–1658) and included in Rubens's so-called *Drawing Book,* published after his death, which included prints after Rubens's drawings and oil sketches.

Rubens's anatomical studies probably date from his initial years in Mantua, 1600–1605, since such exercises belong to an artist's early training.[7] We know from Roger de Piles, moreover, that Rubens was fascinated by the anatomical studies by Leonardo da Vinci that he most likely saw in 1603, when he traveled to Spain at the behest of the Duke of Mantua.[8] In late 1605 Rubens went to Rome, where his copying after antique sculpture expanded his interest in anatomy.

On the present sheet Rubens drew an intricate composition of three arms and two torsos. Originally, the torso on the left ended in a head of curly hair, which extended onto the adjoining page of Rubens's sketchbook. The drawing of the remainder of the head has recently been located on the verso of another anatomical study by Rubens, today in a private collection. Rubens's original composition is evident when that sheet and the one in the Metropolitan are joined together (fig. 53). The head also appears in a copy of the drawing at the Wellcome Library for the History and Understanding of Medicine, London,[9] apparently made while the *Anatomy Book* was still intact.

The copy in the Wellcome Library is probably Pontius's design for his etching after Rubens's original drawing. Its contours are traced for transfer and its measurements correspond closely to the New York drawing.[10] (Pontius would have made a tracing of Rubens's sheet in order not to damage the original with stylus incisions, which were necessary in order to transfer the composition to the copperplate in preparation for the printing process.) Eventually, for reasons now unknown, Pontius omitted from his etching the top of the head and the neck on the second sheet. His print, therefore, reproduces exactly the drawing in the Metropolitan Museum (fig. 54).

1. M. Jaffé 1987, pp. 58–61, 80–81.
2. *Anatomical Studies of Three Nudes,* black chalk, pen and brown ink, brown wash, right corners cut, 291 x 191 mm; ex coll. Ludwig Burchard; sale cat., London, Christie's, July 6, 1999, lot 223, ill. in color. A copy after this drawing (sale, London, Sotheby's, June 29, 1926, lot 115) was in the collection of Pierre Crozat (1665–1740); it is inscribed with the number assigned to it by Pierre-Jean Mariette (1694–1774) when he prepared Crozat's collection for auction in 1741. That at least one of Crozat's sheets was a copy may explain Mariette's dismissive comment, in the *Abecedario,* about the écorché drawings in Crozat's collection (Mariette 1851–60, vol. 5, p. 141).
3. See, for example, his écorché of ca. 1562–67 in the Hearn Family Trust, New York; Amsterdam–New York 2003, p. 125, no. 31, ill.
4. Garff and Pedersen (in Copenhagen 1988, p. 81) suggested that the studies were made by an Italian artist, such as Bartolomeo Passarotti, or drawn by Paulus Pontius in preparation for engravings.
5. Ibid., p. 78, no. 82: "dese twee handen heb ick geteekent uit den annotomibock van Rubbens, die ick oock van't cantoor van Rubens hebbe gehaelt."
6. See Jeffrey M. Muller, "Rubens' Anatomieboek / Rubens' Anatomy Book," in Antwerp 1993, pp. 78–94.
7. Piles 1715, p. 162. See also Muller 1989, p. 15, n. 35, and Muller in Antwerp 1993, p. 82. Drawings by Leonardo were in the collection, in Madrid, of the court sculptor Pompeo Leoni (ca. 1533–1608).
8. Michael Jaffé (1987, p. 61) dated the group 1605–10, while Jeffrey M. Muller (in Antwerp 1993, p. 78) dated them 1600–1608.
9. Inv. 28636 i. Pen and dark brown ink over a faint underdrawing in black chalk, 302 x 252 mm, laid down; ex coll. the Marquis de Boilleul (annotation on verso of mount); annotated in pen and brown ink at bottom right: "P P Rubens."
10. The London drawing measures 215 mm up to the vertical fold at the left, which corresponds more or less with the measurements of the print.

17. *Study for the Circumcision,* early 1605

Black and some red chalk, squared in pen and brown ink at 55-mm or 27.5-mm intervals, with numbers 1–12 along bottom; 45-mm-wide strip added at top with 9-mm overlap, horizontal fold through center of sheet, trimmed at both sides, laid down, 410 x 322 mm (16 1/8 x 12 11/16 in.)

National Museums Liverpool (The Walker) (WAG 1995.215)

Provenance: Richard Houlditch (d. 1736), Hampstead (Lugt 2214; initials "RH" in ink in lower right corner; "No. 35" in pen and brown ink on mount at bottom right, possibly his number; "1756" in pen and brown ink on verso of mount may indicate date drawing was mounted; his sale, London, February 12–14, 1760); probably William Roscoe, Liverpool (his sale, Liverpool, Winstanley, September 1816, lot 483, for £1.01, as a "Capital drawing by Rubens"); bt. Slater; Charles Robert Blundell of Ince (1761–1837), near Liverpool; thence by descent to Colonel Joseph Weld of Lulworth Manor, Dorset (d. 1994); acquired by

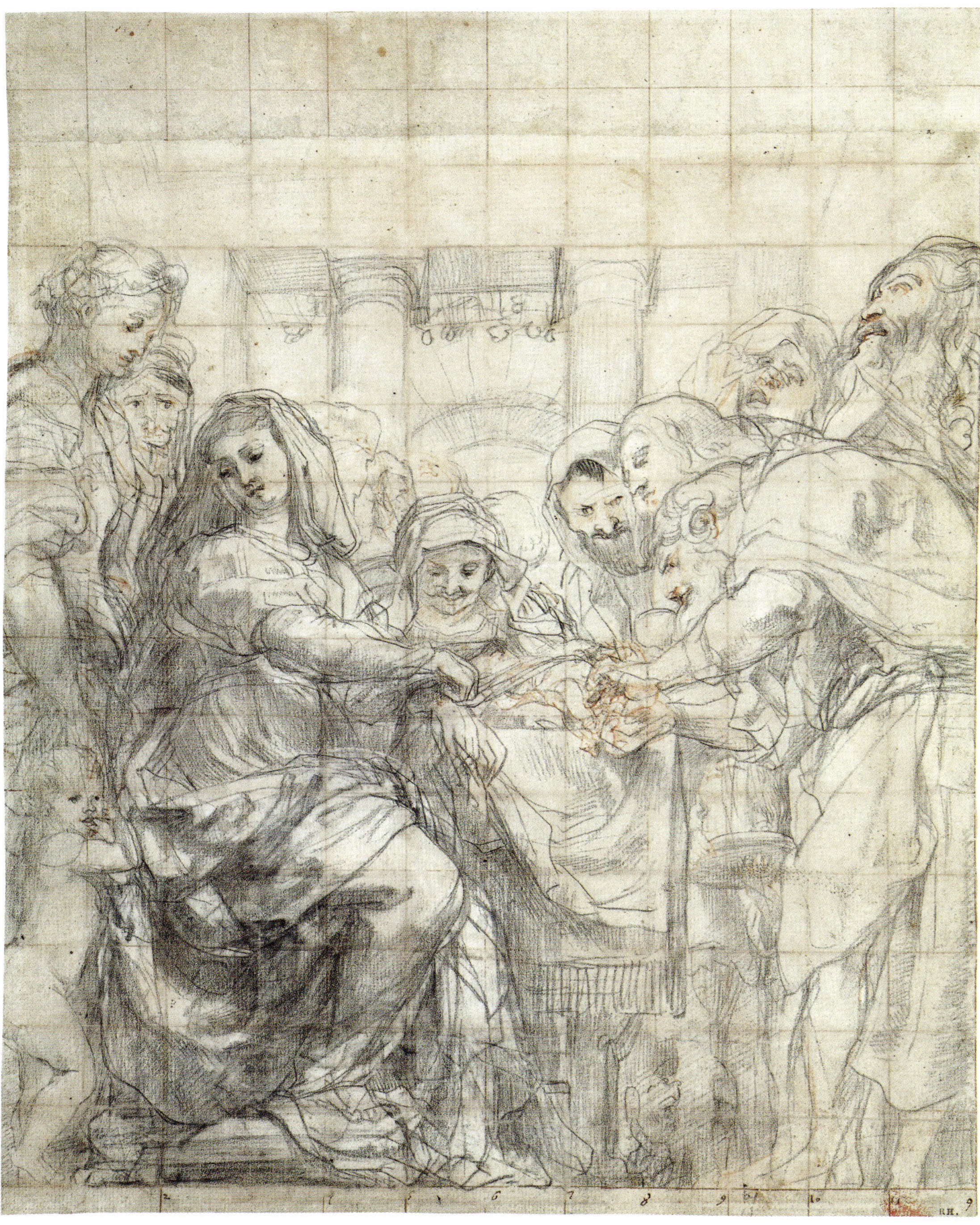

Cat. 17

the Walker Art Gallery from his executors through Christie's by private sale in 1995.

LITERATURE: M. Jaffé 1988, pp. 525–27, fig. 39; M. Jaffé 1989, under no. 53; Göttler 1997, pp. 796–844, fig. 3; Göttler 1999, pp. 10–31.

EXHIBITION: Liverpool–London 1998–99, no. 78, ill.

In late 1604[1] Rubens was commissioned to paint a *Circumcision of Christ* altarpiece for the Jesuit church in Genoa, Santi Ambrogio e Andrea. He received the commission directly from the church's founder, Padre Marcello Pallavicini, SJ (1560–1625).[2] The Pallavicini family belonged to the wealthy Genoese nobility. Rubens was acquainted with Padre Marcello's younger brother, Marchese Nicolò Pallavicini (1563–1619), who was the

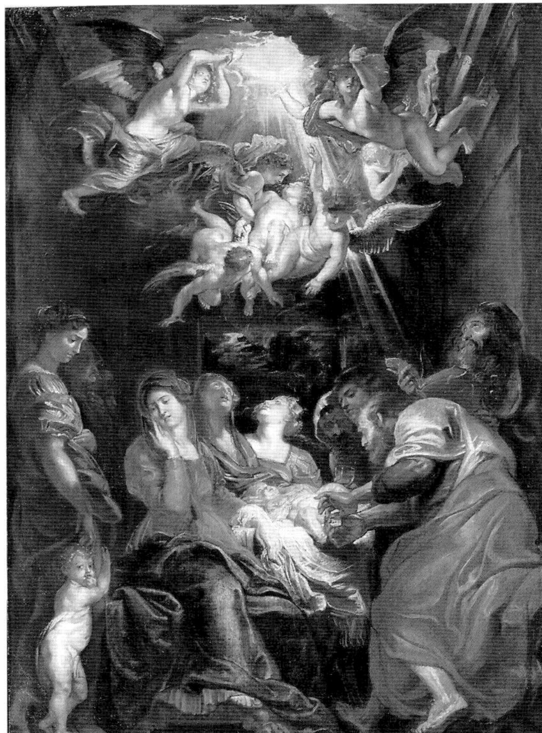

Fig. 55. Peter Paul Rubens, *The Circumcision of Christ*, 1605. Oil on canvas, fastened to wood, 105 x 74 cm (41 5/16 x 29 1/8 in.). Gemäldegalerie der Akademie der Bildenden Künste, Vienna (GG 897)

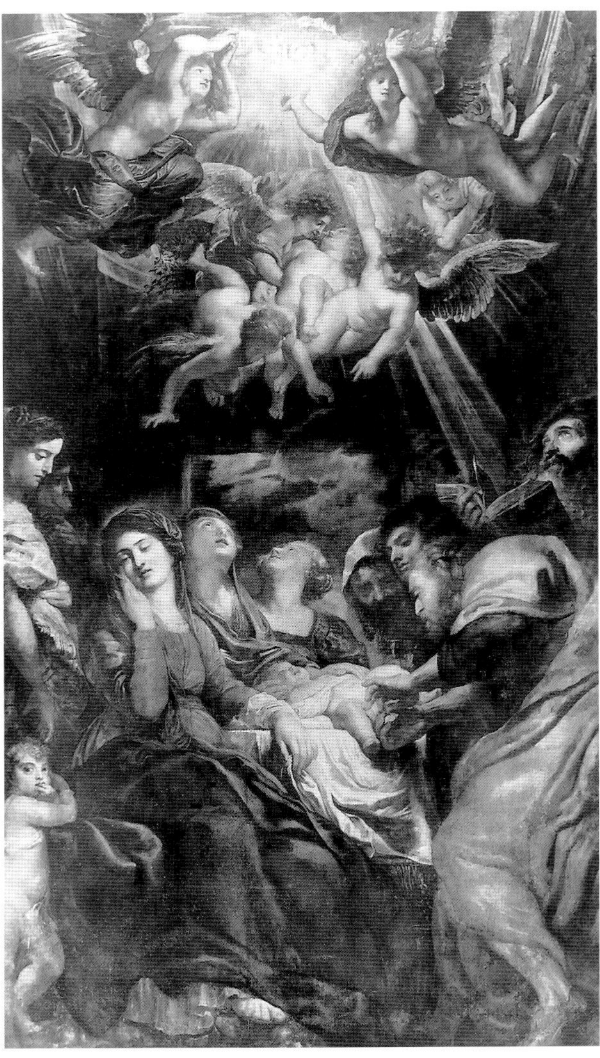

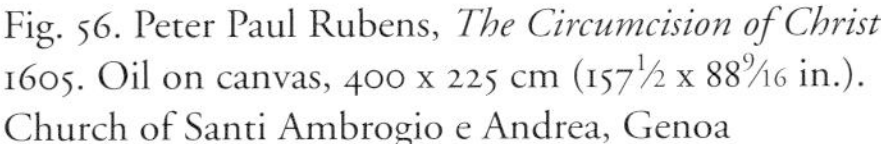

Fig. 56. Peter Paul Rubens, *The Circumcision of Christ*, 1605. Oil on canvas, 400 x 225 cm (157 1/2 x 88 9/16 in.). Church of Santi Ambrogio e Andrea, Genoa

banker to the Gonzaga in Mantua. The marchese and Rubens may have met first early in 1604, when Rubens passed through Genoa on his return from Spain in order to claim compensation for the expenses incurred during his mission to the Spanish court on behalf of the Duke of Mantua.[3]

It is likely that Rubens began work on the altarpiece once he had completed his three monumental paintings for Santissima Trinità in Mantua, which were dedicated on June 5, 1605 (for these paintings, see the discussion under catalogue number 14). Since Rubens was staying in Rome by November 1605 it is generally assumed that he painted the *Circumcision* altarpiece for Genoa there during the fall and winter and had it shipped to Santi Ambrogio e Andrea late in 1605.[4] The altarpiece probably was inaugurated on January 1, 1606, the Feast of the Circumcision.

Rubens must have made many preliminary studies before arriving at this finished compositional drawing of the *Circumcision.* After squaring the sheet with pen and brown ink, the artist transferred the design to an oil sketch on canvas (fig. 55),[5] which in turn was the *modello,* or final sketch, for the altarpiece (fig. 56).[6] The drawing was enlarged at the top, but the added area remained blank; in the *modello* and in the finished altarpiece, the Hebrew name Jeshua appears at the top in a stream of light issuing from heaven and surrounded by angels. This drawing and the slightly earlier *Baptism of Christ* sheet of about 1604 (cat. no. 14)—both carefully worked out in black chalk, highly finished, and fully squared, ready for transfer—are exceptional in Rubens's oeuvre. They are the only known examples of a cartoon among the stages in Rubens's production.

According to Jewish belief, circumcision on the eighth day after a boy is born marks the moment when the child enters the covenant between God and the Jewish people. At this time he is given his name, which contains his spiritual destiny. The New Testament (Luke 2:21) describes how Christ was circumcised on the eighth day after he was born and "his name was called Jesus [i.e., Saviour]." The Circumcision of Christ was a favorite subject for the high altar in Jesuit churches: it was the occasion not only when he received the name that the Jesuits adopted for their order (the Society of Jesus) but also when he spilled blood for the first time—an allusion to his ultimate spilling of blood in atonement for mankind.

In Rubens's drawing the Christ Child rests on a pillow atop a wooden table covered with a large cloth. The Virgin Mary is seated prominently in the foreground at the left, turning away from the sight while she holds the Child's swaddling clothes in both hands. The mohel performing the procedure is wearing a tallith, or prayer shawl. Joseph, who will name the Child following the circumcision, is depicted at the far right, holding a prayer book and looking heavenward. Still uncertain in the drawing are the placement and orientation of some of the bystanders in the background—the second female figure standing at the left, the young women in the center looking heavenward, and the male figure at the right shielding his eyes are only summarily sketched. The name giving is followed by a kiddush, or blessing, pronounced over wine by the mohel. In the drawing the wineglass is only lightly indicated, next to the mohel's face. The lower right section of the drawing is indistinctly drawn. Among the outlines one can identify a small dog and a child holding a tablet. Neither reappears in the *modello* or the altarpiece.

Rubens made many changes in the *modello* and the finished altarpiece. One alteration is in the depiction of the Virgin. She no longer holds the Child's swaddling clothes in her hands; instead, she raises her right hand to her face, to pull her veil across it, in a gesture reminiscent of that of the so-called *Pudicitia,* an antique sculpture in the collection of Ciriaco Mattei (1546–1603) that Rubens in all likelihood saw during his 1601–2 stay in Rome. In the *modello* and the final altarpiece, moreover, a ray of light from above shines down on Joseph's prayer book; in the drawing there is no such reference to the heavenly guidance of Joseph. Rubens also changed the setting of the circumcision scene in the *modello.* The rounded archway and columns in the background of the drawing are replaced by a square opening revealing a cloudy morning sky. Rubens replaced the elderly woman, possibly Elizabeth, bending over the Child, with two young women looking heavenward toward the apparition of the name of Jesus. Finally, Rubens altered the position of the mohel: in the drawing he is standing, bent over the Child, while in the oil sketch and the altarpiece he appears to be sitting.

The additions in red chalk in the present drawing, superimposed over the black chalk, relate directly to changes introduced in the oil sketch and therefore must be by Rubens. These additions are most noticeable in the women in the center looking upward, in the position of the mohel's hands, and in the faces of the men at the right. It is possible that the present drawing was an intermediary step, and that Rubens subsequently completed another compositional study before proceeding to the *modello.*

1. Rubens probably did not receive the official commission until after the high altar was consecrated, on October 26, 1604. P. Giulio Negrone, SI, *Historia domus professae Societatis Jesu Genuae institutae in ecclesia Sancti Ambrosii sub Nomine Sanctissimo Jesu.* Anno 1603. Ms. Archivium Romanum Societatis Iesu (A.R.S.I., Med. 81, sv. 1605, c. 27), quoted in Genoa 1977–78, under no. 5, p. 225.
2. M. Jaffé 1988, p. 523. For the history of the Church of Santi Ambrogio e Andrea (also known as the Chiesa del Gesù), see Göttler 1997, pp. 796–844.
3. Nicolò Pallavicini became a close friend and, in 1618, godfather to Rubens's son Nicolaas. Sometime after 1612, he commissioned from Rubens an altarpiece representing Saint Ignatius of Loyola for a chapel in the north transept of Santi Ambrogio e Andrea, where it remains today.
4. Genoa 1977–78, p. 225.
5. Held 1980, no. 331, pl. 326, ca. 1605; M. Jaffé 1989, no. 53, 1605. According to Held (1980, p. 459), the letters in the beam of light were probably added to the altar painting later, by a different hand.
6. K.d.K., ed. Oldenbourg 1921, no. 21; M. Jaffé 1989, no. 54, 1605.

18. *Adoration of the Image of the Virgin and Child,* shortly after April 24, 1608

Pen and brown ink and brown wash, corrected with white body color (primarily between the putti) and heightened with white (in the clouds below), over traces of graphite; center line, lines along the top, left, and right side of sheet drawn with the ruler in black chalk and completed with wash, 268 x 152 mm (10½ x 6 in.)

Albertina, Vienna (8231)

PROVENANCE: Pierre-Jean Mariette (1694–1774), Paris (Lugt 1852; his sale, Paris, F. Basan, 1775, no. 1002); Hofbibliothek, Vienna; Duke Albert of Sachsen-Teschen (1738–1822), Vienna (Lugt 174; Altes cahier: "N° 1002 du Catalogue de Mariette vient du Cabinet de L'Empereur").

LITERATURE: R., vol. 5, under no. 1432 [not Rubens]; Glück and Haberditzl 1928, no. 54, pl. 54; Held 1959, no. 17, pl. 19, and under no. 74; Incisa della Rocchetta 1962, p. 173, n. 14; M. Jaffé 1963, p. 231, fig. 26; Müller Hofstede 1966b, pp. 9–10, 18, 40–42, 58, fig. 4; Held 1986, no. 42, pl. 43; Danesi Squarzina 1990, pp. 7–38, fig. 20; Rome 1995, pp. 150–73, fig. 163; Von zur Mühlen 1998, pp. 172–73.

Exhibitions: Vienna 1977b, no. 5, ill.; Padua–Rome–Milan 1990, no. 65, ill.; Brussels–Rome 1995, no. 174, ill.

"When the finest and most splendid opportunity in all Rome presented itself, my ambition urged me to avail myself of the chance. It is the high altar of the new church of the Priests of the Oratory, called S[anta] Maria in Vallicella—without doubt the most celebrated and frequented church in Rome today, situated right in the center of the city, and to be adorned by the combined efforts of all the most able painters in Italy." With these words, written from Rome on December 2, 1606, Rubens appealed to Annibale Chieppio, the agent of his employer, the Duke of Mantua, to be allowed to remain in the Eternal City to paint the altarpiece.[1] The commission for the high altar in Santa Maria in Vallicella, or the Chiesa Nuova, which Rubens had received a few months earlier from the Oratorian Fathers, was by far his most prestigious to date.

This commission is one of the best documented and has been the subject of much discussion among scholars, since Rubens eventually painted two different altarpieces.[2] It all started in August 1606 with the decision of the Oratorian Fathers—a lay order founded in 1564 by Saint Philip Neri—that the miraculous image of the Madonna della Vallicella, a fourteenth-century fresco, should be moved to the high altar of their church and that a new altar painting should be commissioned. Shortly afterward, Rubens received and signed a contract specifying that the altarpiece would show the miraculous image of the Madonna della Vallicella above a group of six saints: Gregory (Pope Gregory the Great), Maurus, Papianus, Domitilla, Nereus, and Achilleus. Although the Oratorians rejected Rubens's first version, the *Madonna della Vallicella Adored by Gregory, Domitilla, and Other Saints,* now in Grenoble,[3] in January 1608 they asked Rubens to submit a new design that would insert the miraculous image into the altarpiece as if it were a relic. At a meeting of the Oratorians on April 24, 1608, Rubens offered to divide the composition of the earlier altarpiece into three distinct pictures, with the central one placed over the high altar, and the other two against the lateral apse walls. To reduce the glare, Rubens was to paint the three pictures in situ on slate. He was also asked to submit sketches for

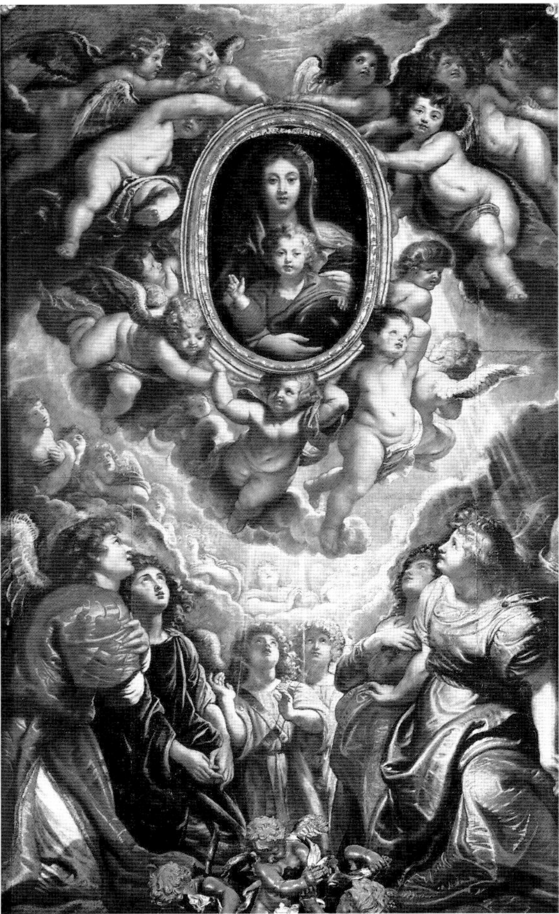

Fig. 57. Peter Paul Rubens, *The Virgin and Child Adored by Angels*, May–October 1608. Oil on slate, 425 x 250 cm (167⁵⁄₁₆ x 98⁹⁄₁₆ in.). Chiesa Nuova, Rome

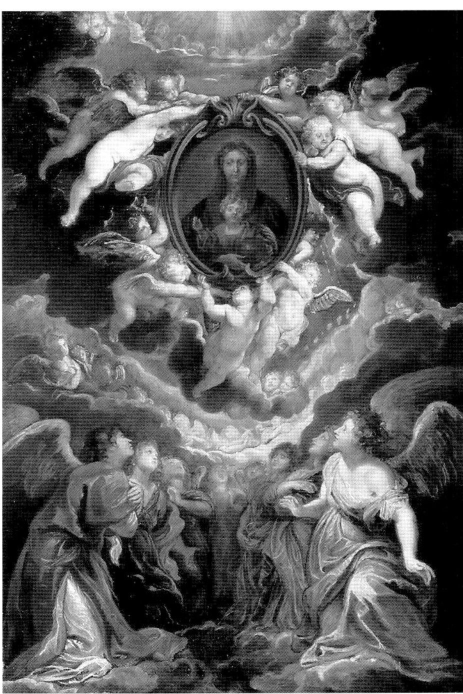

Fig. 58. Peter Paul Rubens, *The Image of the Virgin Adored by Angels,* April–May 1608. Oil on canvas, 87 x 58 cm (34¼ x 22¹³⁄₁₆ in.). Akademie der Bildenden Künste, Vienna (GG 629)

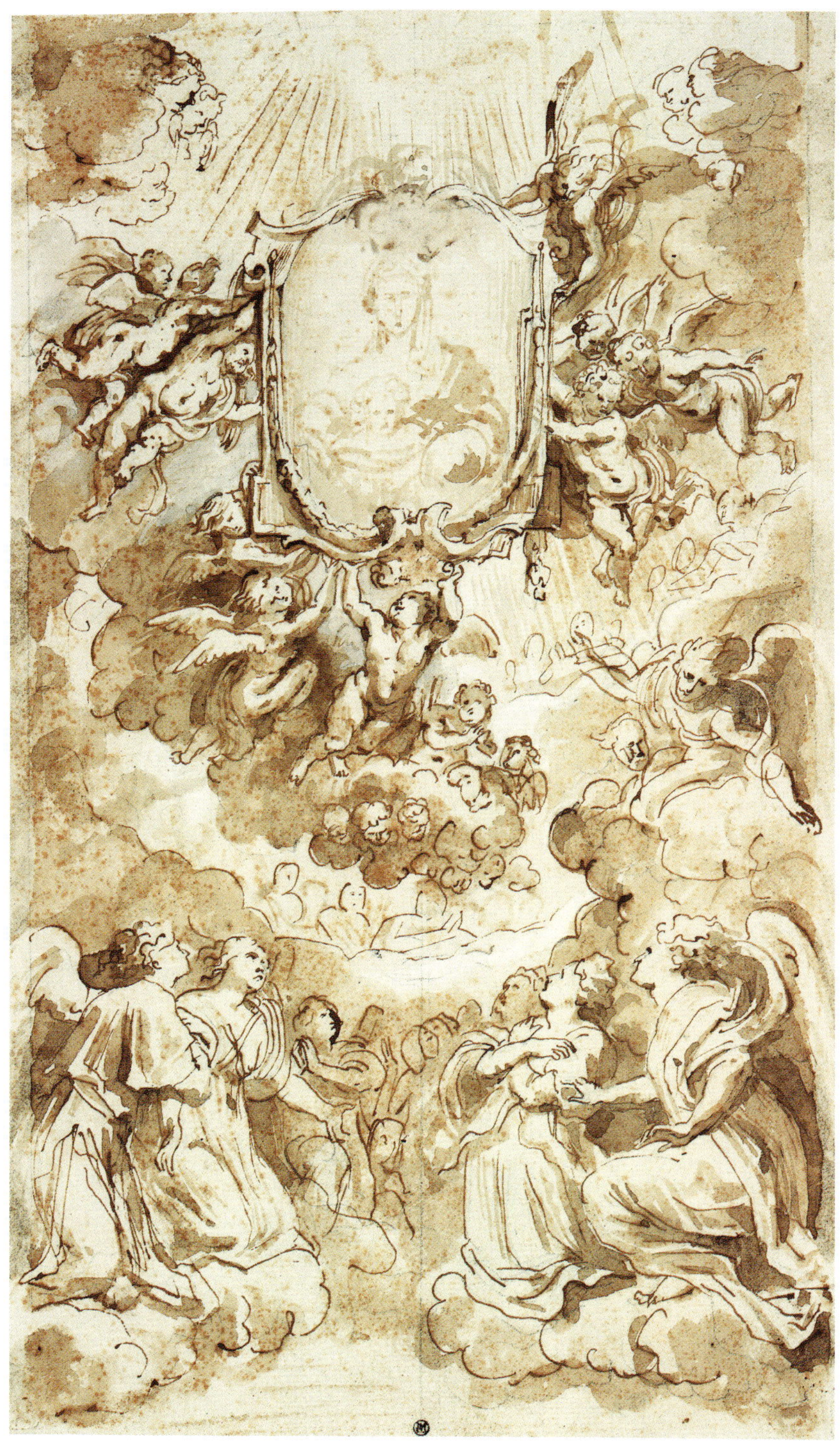

Cat. 18

approval, which he must have done before May 13, 1608.[4]

In his revised design Rubens distributed the original composition over three separate slate panels: the Virgin and Child adored by angels were to be in the center, Saint Gregory between Saints Maurus and Papianus on the left, and Saint Domitilla accompanied by Saints Nereus and Achilleus on the right. He also incorporated the Madonna della Vallicella fresco into the upper section of the central painting; an opening was cut into the slate with the fresco placed into the wall behind it. For the days when the miraculous image was to remain hidden (it was shown only on special religious occasions), Rubens painted an image of the Madonna and Child on copperplate to cover the fresco.

The small pen sketch in the Albertina is a preliminary study for the revised central altarpiece (fig. 57). It shows how well Rubens could visualize a complicated event in a clear, clean design with relatively few corrections. Three clusters of joyous small angels carry the framed image of the Madonna della Vallicella aloft, while six large angels kneel in adoration on clouds below, three on either side, arranged diagonally in two converging rows. An additional angel at the right of center hovers on another cloud and points to the miraculous image being carried heavenward. Rubens drew the image of the Madonna with the brush only. He offered the Oratorians two options for the frame: an ornate one with scrolls (at the left), and a simpler one with rectangular protrusions (at the right). Rubens elaborated on the right-hand solution in more detail in a drawing today in the Pushkin Museum, Moscow,[5] which therefore must follow the Albertina study.

Once the Oratorians had approved the composition proposed in the present drawing, Rubens proceeded to paint the oil sketch, or *modello* (fig. 58).[6] Although he retained the overall composition, he enlarged the group of kneeling angels to eight and dramatically increased their size. The angel in the foreground at the right now directs the attention of the viewer toward the miraculous image of the Madonna, while the floating angel that he had included in the drawing at the right of center is omitted. In the final altarpiece Rubens's image of the Madonna and Child is placed slightly lower to align it better with the trecento fresco of the Madonna della Vallicella that by March 10, 1608, had been inserted into the wall behind the altar.

1. Magurn 1955, p. 39, letter 14; Rooses and Ruelens 1887–1909, vol. 1, p. 354, letter 89.
2. For an excellent overview of the commission, see Held 1980, pp. 537–45, nos. 396–98; for more recent investigations, see Von zur Mühlen 1990, 1996, and 1998.
3. K.d.K., ed. Oldenbourg 1921, no. 23; M. Jaffé 1989, no. 64, 1607.
4. On that day the initial payment for slate was approved, which meant that Rubens's revised design had been approved. Held 1980, pp. 538–39; Incisa della Rocchetta 1962, p. 173.
5. *The Miraculous Image of the Madonna della Vallicella Supported by Angels,* inv. 7098. Held 1986, p. 84, under no. 42.
6. Held 1980, no. 397, pl. 387; M. Jaffé 1989, no. 76.

COPIES AFTER THE ANTIQUE

19. *Three Figures from a Roman Sarcophagus,* ca. 1606–7

Black chalk, 281 x 416 mm (11 1/16 x 16 3/8 in.)
Inscribed by the artist in pen and brown ink at top left: *Socrates procul dubio* (Socrates without doubt); at top right: *Xantippe quae stomachatur / vide os columnatum* (Xantippe in one of her moods / see her pillared face)
Annotated in pen and brown ink at bottom left: *Rubbens*

The Art Institute of Chicago; The Leonora Hall Gurley Memorial Collection (22.2002)

PROVENANCE: Dr. C. D. Ginsburg (1831–1914), Palmer's Green (Lugt 1145); Leonora Hall Gurley (1831–1903), Chicago (collector's mark at lower left; not in Lugt); donated in 1922 by the William F. E. Gurley Foundation.

LITERATURE: Held 1959, no. 160, pl. 169, and p. 45; McGrath 1983b, p. 232, nn. 23, 24, fig. 43a; Held 1986, no. 21, pl. 21; Van der Meulen 1994, vol. 2, no. 138, fig. 269.

EXHIBITIONS: Cambridge, Mass.–New York 1956, no. 5, pl. 2; Cologne 1977, no. 62, ill.; Birmingham 1978, no. 36, ill.

On this sheet Rubens recorded in black chalk three draped figures from a Roman sarcophagus of the early third century A.D. with representations of "the nine Muses and other figures."[1] The artist drew the two muses now believed to represent Polyhymnia and Urania, who flank a bearded male figure, in the same sequence in which they appear on the right side of the sarcophagus but omitting the columns separating them. He must have seen the sarcophagus in the garden of the villa of the collector Ciriaco Mattei (1546–1603), during one of his trips to Rome (1601–2; 1605–8), as Phyllis Pray Bober first established.[2] Today the sarcophagus is in the Museo Nazionale Romano Terme di Diocleziano, Rome.[3]

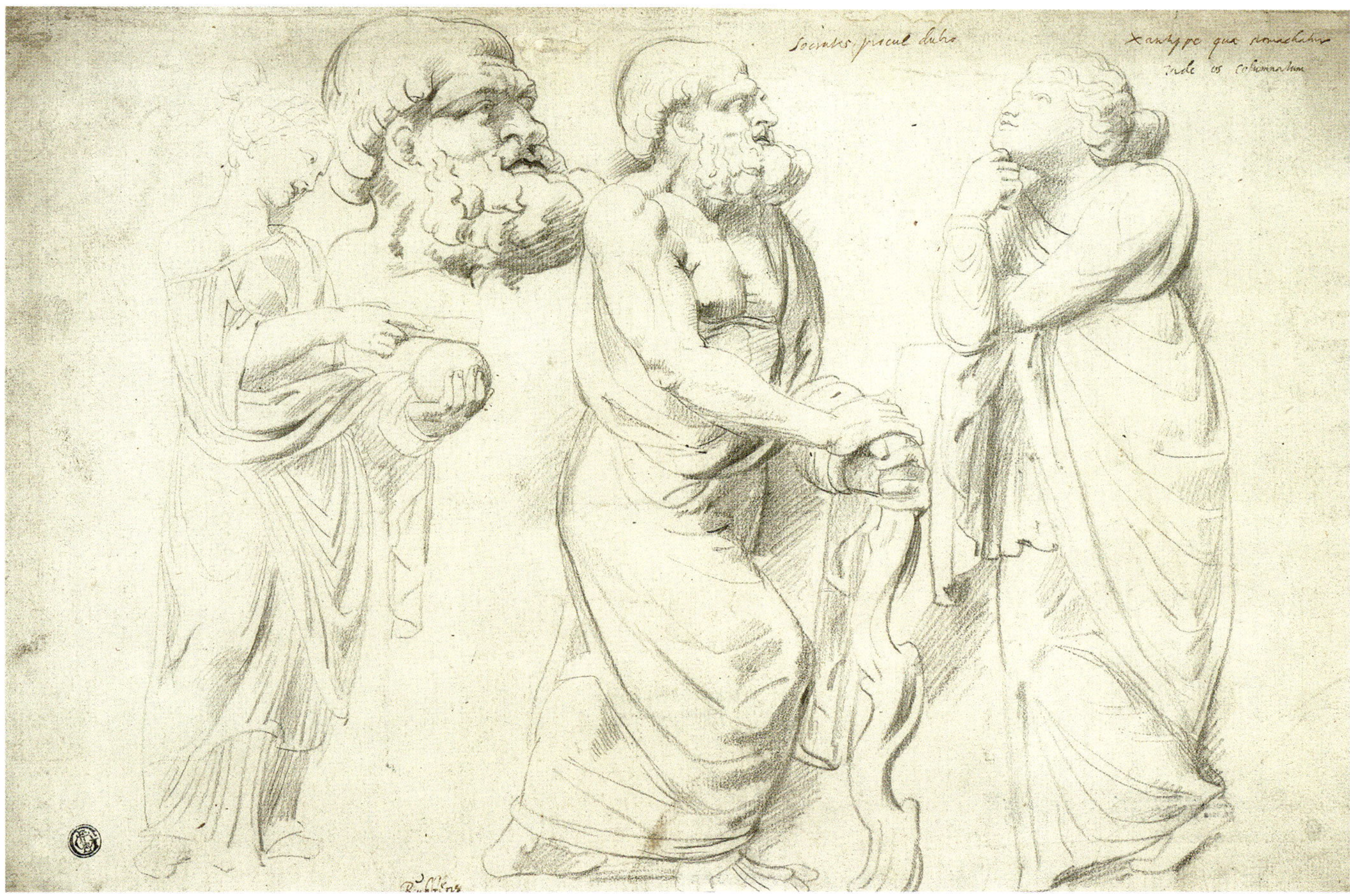

Cat. 19

Various interpretations have been put forth regarding Rubens's inscriptions at the top. His identification of the bearded man as Socrates is plausible since this figure does resemble antique portraits of the Greek philosopher; more puzzling is Rubens's interpretation of the muse with her chin resting on her hand as Xantippe, the cantankerous wife of Socrates. Rubens characterized her in his inscription as "in one of her moods,"[4] and he continued with "vide os columnatum" (look how the bone resembles a column), which can be translated more freely as "see her pillared face." Since Rubens was a good antiquarian, these comments were probably made tongue-in-cheek rather than seriously.[5] Such a reading is encouraged by Rubens's ironical addition of "procul dubio" next to Socrates' name.[6] Julius Held discovered a closely related passage, "notice the pillared face," in Plautus's comedy *Miles Gloriosus* (The Braggart Warrior) that Rubens may have alluded to here, since the artist literally raised the "pillared" face in the drawing by means of the hand so that it would be clearly understood.[7] During the early part of Rubens's second stay in Rome (1605–8) it would not have been out of the ordinary for him to allude to Plautus, since at this time he was working on illustrations for his brother Philip's *Electorum Libri Duo* (published by the Plantin Press in Antwerp in 1607), where Plautus is cited often. Because of this association, a date for the drawing of about 1606–7 seems likely.

1. The sarcophagus is described thus in the 1614 inventory of the Mattei collection. See Lanciani 1902–12, vol. 3, p. 94; Van der Meulen 1994, vol. 2, p. 159, n. 2.
2. Bober cited in Held 1986, p. 73.
3. Inv. 80711. Wegner 1966, pp. 50–52, no. 128, pls. 84, 87–89; M. E. Micheli in Museo Nazionale Romano 1979–, vol. 1, pt. 8:1, pp. 51–57, ill.
4. McGrath 1983b, p. 232.
5. As suggested by McGrath (1983b) and Held (1986), in contrast to Müller Hofstede in Cologne 1977, p. 266, no. 62.
6. McGrath 1984, pp. 89–90, n. 78.
7. *Plautus*, vol. 3, ll. 209–12, Loeb Classical Library (London, 1924), pp. 142–43.

20. *Centaur Tormented by Cupid, Seen from the Left,* ca. 1606–8

Black chalk, 481 x 371 mm ($18^{15}/_{16}$ x $14^{5}/_{8}$ in.)

Wallraf-Richartz-Museum–Fondation Corboud, Cologne (Z 5887)

PROVENANCE: Probably from the collection of Ferdinand Franz Wallraf (1748–1824), Cologne.

LITERATURE: Westfehling 2001, pp. 200–222, fig. 28.

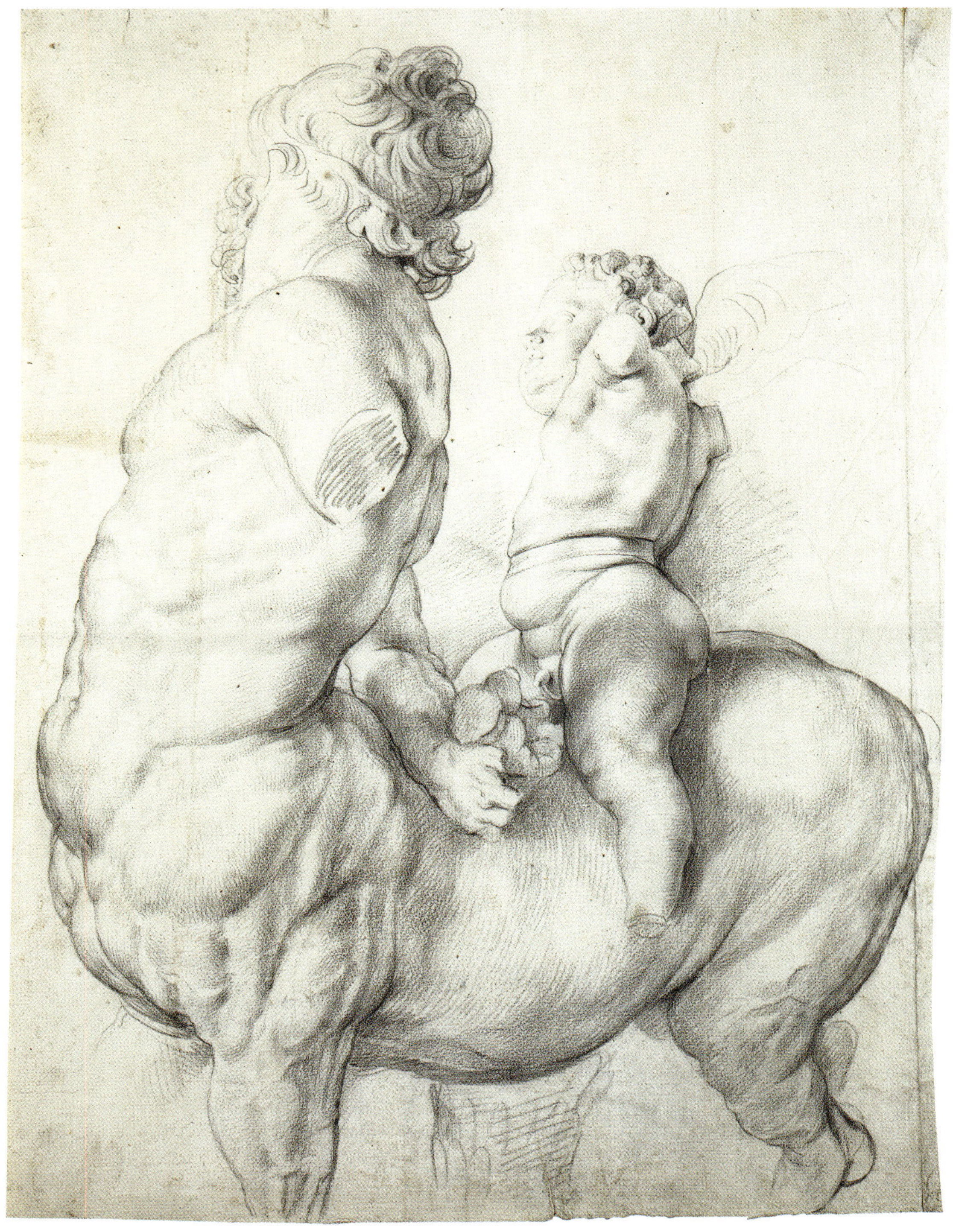

Cat. 20

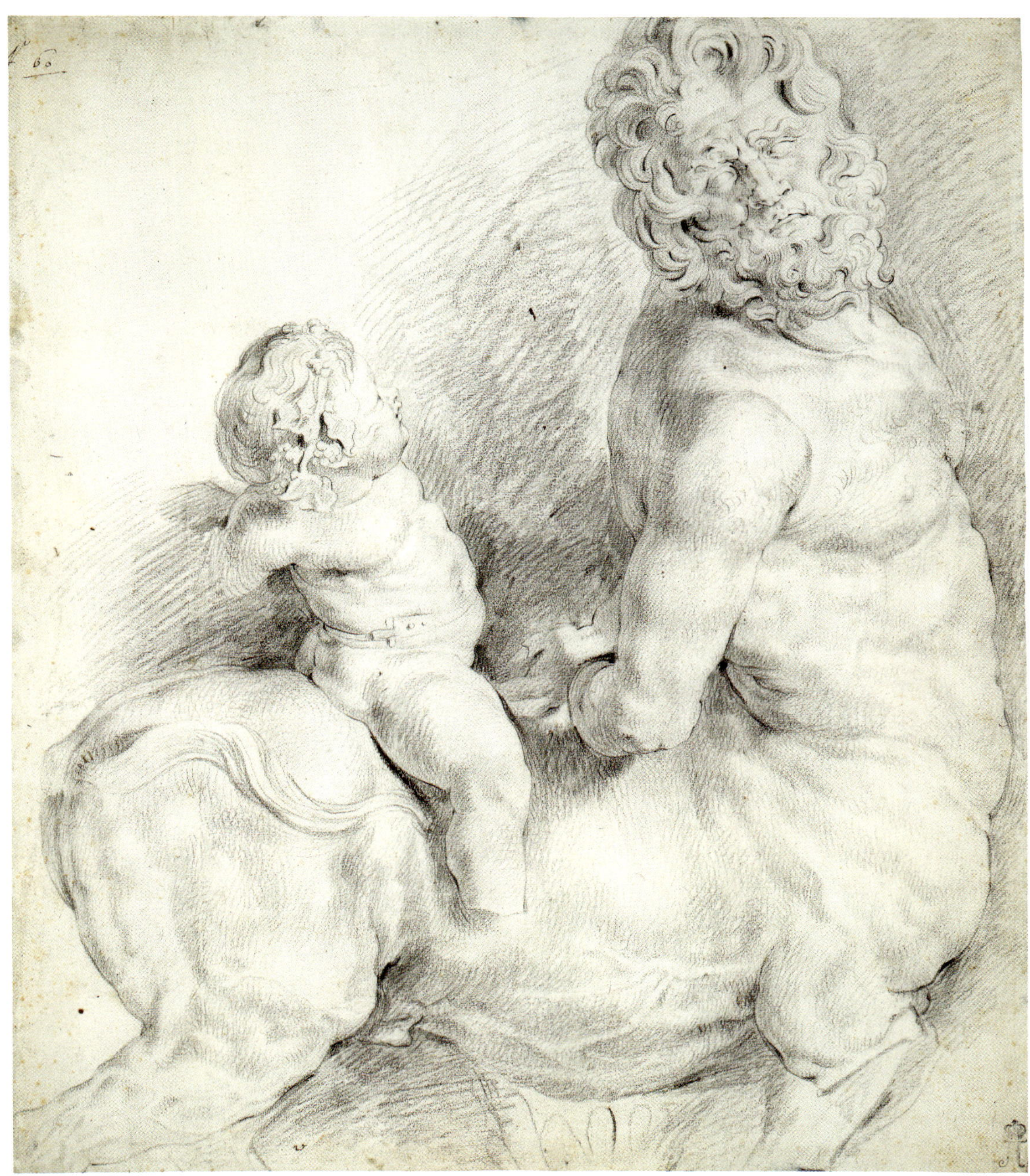

Cat. 21

21. *Centaur Tormented by Cupid, Seen from the Right,* ca. 1606–8

Black chalk and greasy black chalk, heightened with white chalk, 463 x 397 mm (18¼ x 15⅝ in.); laid down on Cobenzl mount
Annotated in pen and brown ink at upper left: *60*; at bottom left: *27*

The State Pushkin Museum of Fine Arts, Moscow (7099)

PROVENANCE: Count Carl Cobenzl (1712–1770), Brussels (in his mount; Lugt 2858b); purchased from him in 1768 by Catherine II of Russia (1729–1796) for the Hermitage, Saint Petersburg (Lugt 2061); transferred to the Pushkin Museum in 1930.

LITERATURE: Kuznetsov 1974, pl. 12; Van der Meulen 1994, vol. 2, no. 65, fig. 124; Westfehling 2001, pp. 200–207, fig. 34.

EXHIBITIONS: Antwerp 1993, no. 48, pl. 13; New York 1998–99, no. 62, ill.

The marble sculpture of the *Centaur Tormented by Cupid,* believed to be a Hadrianic copy of a bronze original of the second century B.C.,[1] was one of the most celebrated statues in Rome (fig. 59). The centaur, with his hands tied behind his back, is at the mercy of the mischievous Cupid riding on his back. The marble was supposedly discovered in Rome at the beginning of the seventeenth century, near the Hospital of San Giovanni in Laterano,[2] and thereafter was probably in the collection of Scipione Borghese.[3] Scipione Caffarelli-Borghese (1576–1633) began collecting art in 1605, the year he was created a cardinal. Rubens must have been among the first to have access to the Borghese collection and to study it. His drawings after the *Centaur*—at least five once existed—likely date from his second visit to Rome, between 1605 and 1608.[4] Rubens's drawings of the *Centaur* are of special interest since they show the statue in its unrestored state and are the oldest known records of it: Cupid's arms and wings, and the centaur's arms and right foreleg, are missing, while a sculpted tree trunk was apparently added below the centaur's belly for support. (Rubens's interest was also caught by the most admired statue in the Borghese collection, the *Dying Seneca,* or *Borghese Fisherman.* For two drawings by Rubens after that statue, see catalogue numbers 22, 23).

The *Centaur Tormented by Cupid, Seen from the Left* (cat. no. 20) and another copy after the *Centaur,* this one showing the sculpture from the right, were discovered in 2000, when the Wallraf-Richartz-Museum moved to new quarters.[5] On this sheet Rubens positioned the sculpture on the sheet with broad outlines in black chalk (he even quickly sketched Cupid's missing wings). Then he worked up the drawing with short strokes and cross-hatching to add volume. He painstakingly copied even the veins in the rump to create a finely modeled, highly finished work of art.

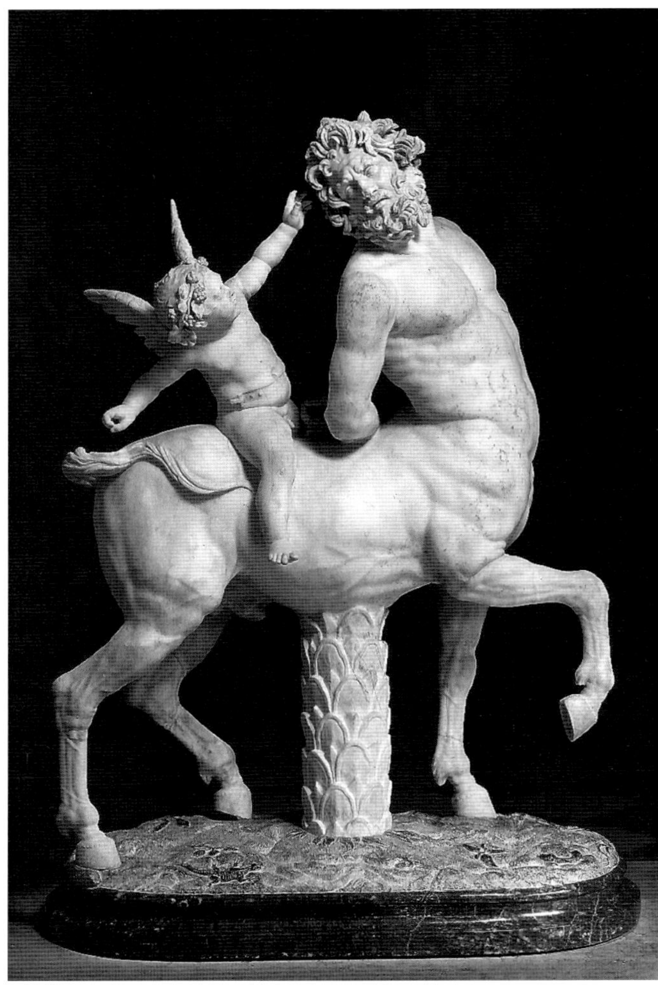

Fig. 59. Hadrianic copy after 2nd century B.C. bronze original, *Centaur Tormented by Cupid.* Marble, h. 147 cm (15⅞ in.). Musée du Louvre, Paris; Borghese Collection (MA 562)

In the *Centaur Tormented by Cupid, Seen from the Left,* Rubens seems to have been interested in recording the marble sculpture per se. In the *Centaur Tormented by Cupid, Seen from the Right* (cat. no. 21), however, the artist stressed the interplay of the figures, captured in the bearded centaur's pleading look backward at the mischievous Cupid.

The two recently discovered drawings in Cologne of the *Centaur Tormented by Cupid* are documented through copies in the *cantoor* group of drawings in the Statens Museum for Kunst, Copenhagen, that Willem Panneels (ca. 1600–1634) made after them while he stayed in Rubens's house, possibly as early as 1624, more likely in 1628–29. When Panneels copied catalogue number 20 in the 1620s, he did not use black chalk as Rubens had; instead, he selected red chalk (fig. 60).[6] This deviation may serve as a reminder that one cannot deduce from a Panneels copy after a lost Rubens original whether Rubens used black or red chalk when copying after the antique. (For his *Copy after the "Belvedere Torso"* [cat. no. 34 verso] Rubens used red chalk; for his copy after that drawing, Panneels used pen and ink.) Rubens's drawing of the *Centaur* seen from the back is known only through Panneels's copy, on which he noted that he took the "original of this centaur from the Rubens *cantoor.*"[7] Panneels also made several copies of Cupid alone.

Rubens returned to catalogue number 20 many years later. During his work designing the *Life of Achilles* tapestry cycle, shortly after 1630, he referred to it for the scene of *Achilles Being Educated by the Centaur Chiron* (Museum Boijmans Van Beuningen, Rotterdam).[8]

1. Haskell and Penny 1981, pp. 179–80, no. 21, fig. 93.
2. Martinelli 1644, pp. 111–12; Van der Meulen 1994, vol. 2, p. 84, n. 2.
3. See Van der Meulen 1994, vol. 2, p. 84, n. 3.
4. Van der Meulen (ibid., p. 84) dated the drawings to the summer of 1606.
5. A third study by Rubens after the antique—*Laocoön and His Younger Son, Seen from the Front*—was found at the same time. Uwe Westfehling (2001, pp. 200–222) published all three drawings. He also investigated watermarks and paper type. The latter seems consistent with that of at least three drawings made by Rubens in Rome, the *Copy after the "Belvedere Torso"* (Rubenshuis, Antwerp) and the copies after Michelangelo's prophets *Zacharias* and *Daniel* from the Sistine Chapel ceiling (Louvre, Paris; Lugt 1949, nos. 1040, 1045, ill.).
6. Copenhagen 1988, p. 137, no. 175, pl. 177; Westfehling 2001, fig. 29.
7. Copenhagen 1988, p. 41, no. 4, pl. 4: "het princepaelvandesen sentaurushebbe ickoock / vant cantoorgehaelt."
8. M. Jaffé 1989, no. 1030, 1630–32. For a recent discussion of the *Achilles* series, see Rotterdam–Madrid 2003–4, pp. 74–82, no. 2.

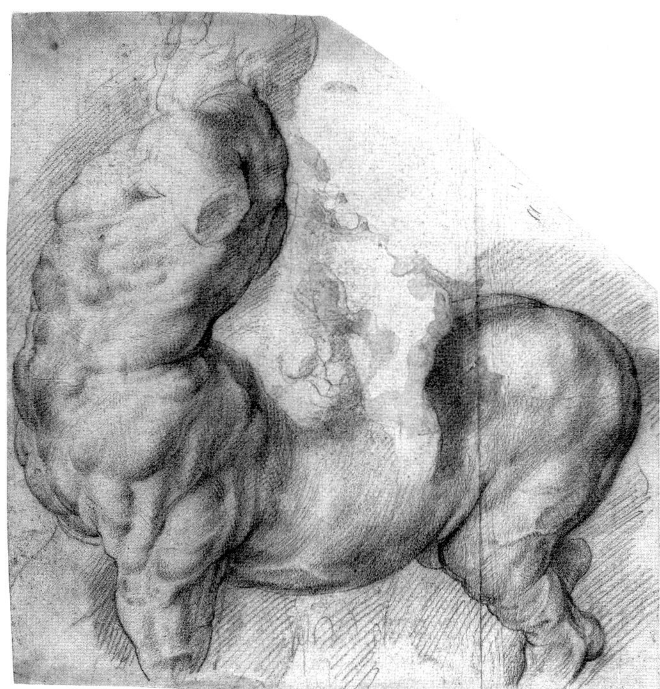

Fig. 60. Willem Panneels after Peter Paul Rubens, *Centaur Tormented by Cupid*, ca. 1628–29. Red chalk, 332 x 340 mm (13$^{1}/_{16}$ x 13$^{3}/_{8}$ in.). Rubens Cantoor, Den Kongelige Kobberstiksamling, Statens Museum for Kunst, Copenhagen (III, 14 [G73])

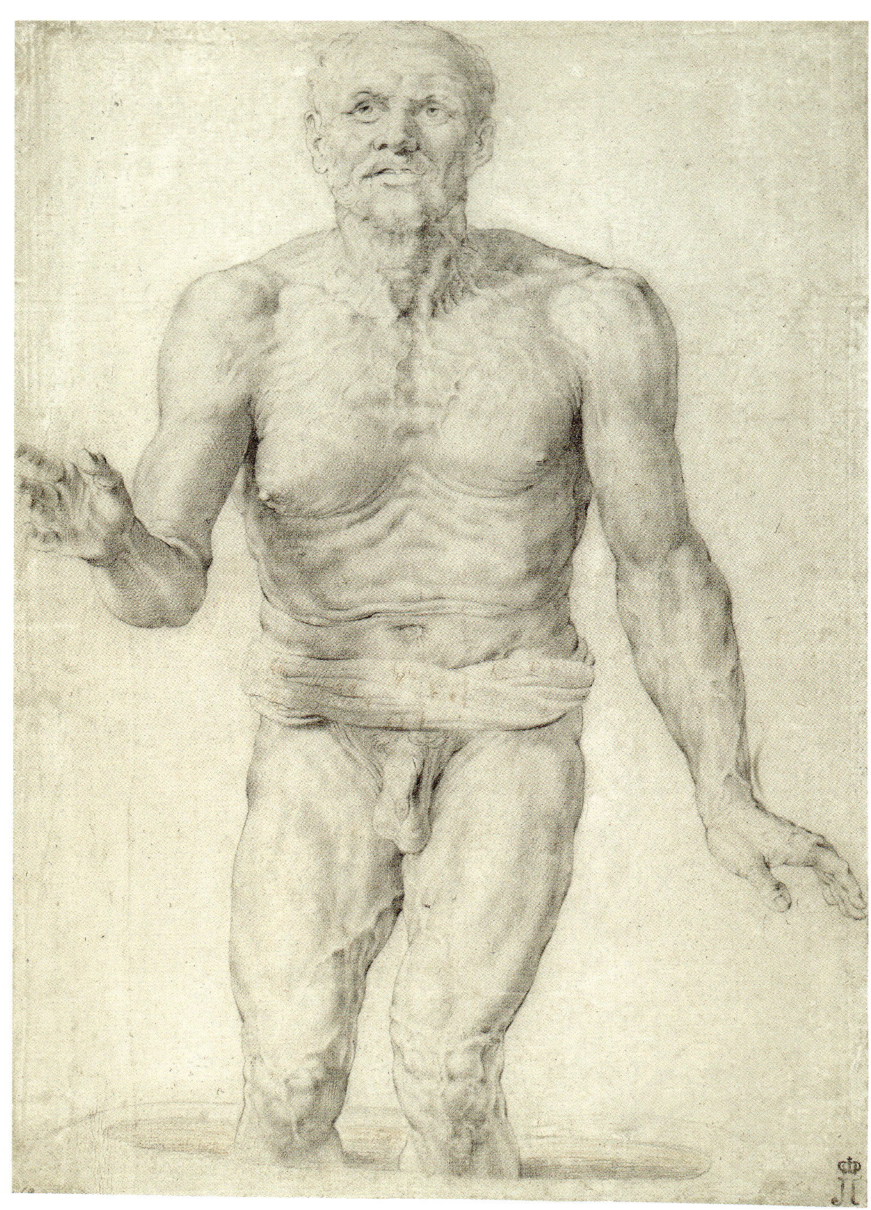

Cat. 22

22. *Dying Seneca (The Borghese Fisherman; The African Fisherman) Seen from the Front,* ca. 1606–8

Black chalk, 460 x 320 mm (18⅛ x 12⅝ in.)
Annotated in pencil at bottom left: *10*

The State Hermitage Museum, Saint Petersburg (5499)

PROVENANCE: Count Carl Cobenzl (1712–1770), Brussels (Lugt 2858b); purchased from him in 1768 by Catherine II of Russia (1729–1796) for the Hermitage, Saint Petersburg (Lugt 2061); sale, Leipzig, Boerner, April 29, 1931, lot 208, pl. 18 (withdrawn).

LITERATURE: Rooses 1900b, p. 201; Glück and Haberditzl 1928, no. 26, pl. 26; Judson and Van de Velde 1978, p. 163, n. 2 [copy]; Van der Meulen 1994, vol. 2, no. 8, vol. 3, fig. 22 [copy].

EXHIBITIONS: Retretti 1991, p. 134, ill.; Toronto 2001, no. 99, ill.; London 2003–4a, p. 118, no. 50, ill.

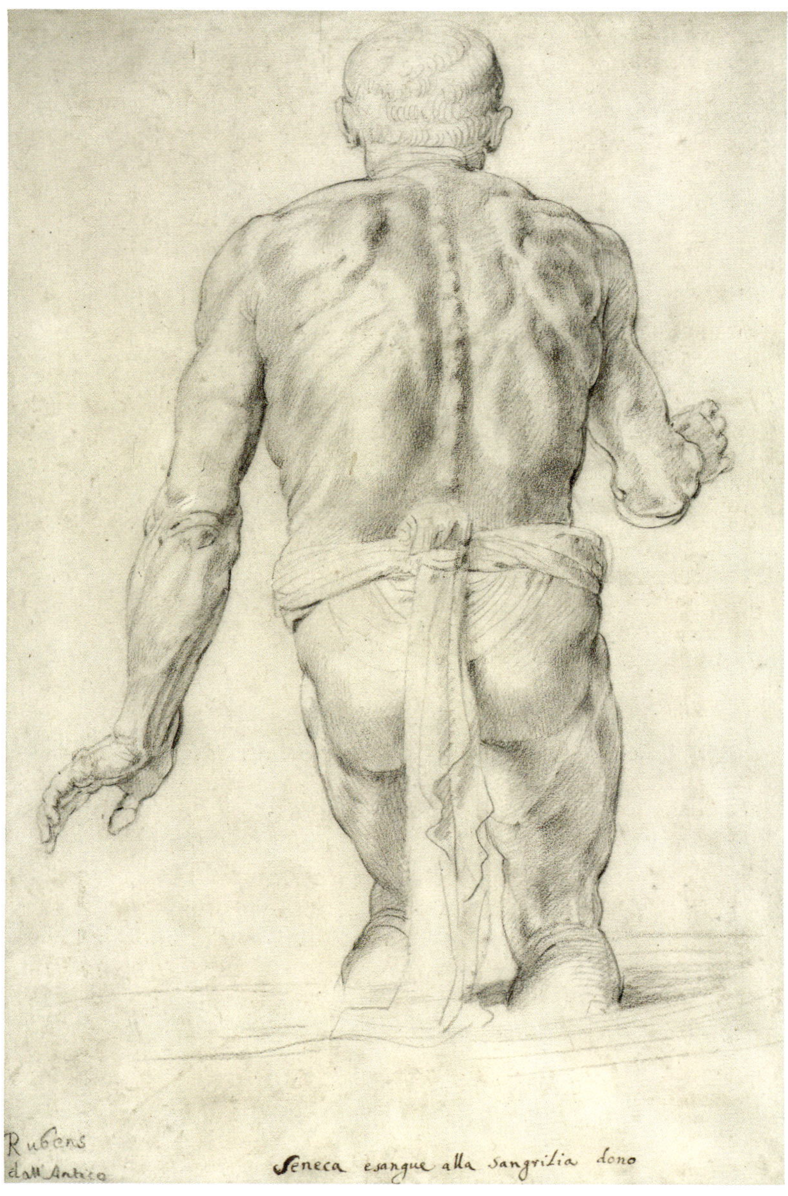

Cat. 23

23. *Dying Seneca (The Borghese Fisherman; The African Fisherman) Seen from the Back,* ca. 1606–8

Black chalk, 473 x 314 mm (18⅝ x 12⅜ in.)
Annotated in black chalk at bottom left: *Rubens / dall' Antico;* by Padre Sebastiano Resta in pen and brown ink at bottom center: *Seneca esangue alla sangrilia dono*

Private collection

PROVENANCE: Maximiliaen Labbé, Mechelen (d. 1675); acquired before 1684 by Padre Sebastiano Resta (1635–1714), who mounted it in an album that he presented to Philip V of Spain in or shortly after 1701; Philip V of Spain (1683–1746); Orléans collection?; Horace Walpole, Earl of Orford (1717–1797), London and Strawberry Hill, Twickenham; his sale, London, Robins, June 8, 1842, lot 1262 (bought by Tiffin: "A folio, containing upwards of 100 drawings . . . specimens by . . . Rubens . . . in Morocco, bearing the royal arms of Spain"); sale, London, Christie's, November 22, 1966, no. 119, ill. (as no. 16 from an album with the shelf number V, bearing the Spanish coat of arms comprising the arms of the duchy of Milan [used from 1700 until 1714], containing 109 drawings); Agnew's, London.

LITERATURE: Wood 1990, p. 7, fig. 4 and cover; Van der Meulen 1994, vol. 2, no. 13, vol. 3, fig. 30.

EXHIBITION: Wellesley–Cleveland 1993–94, no. 39, ill.

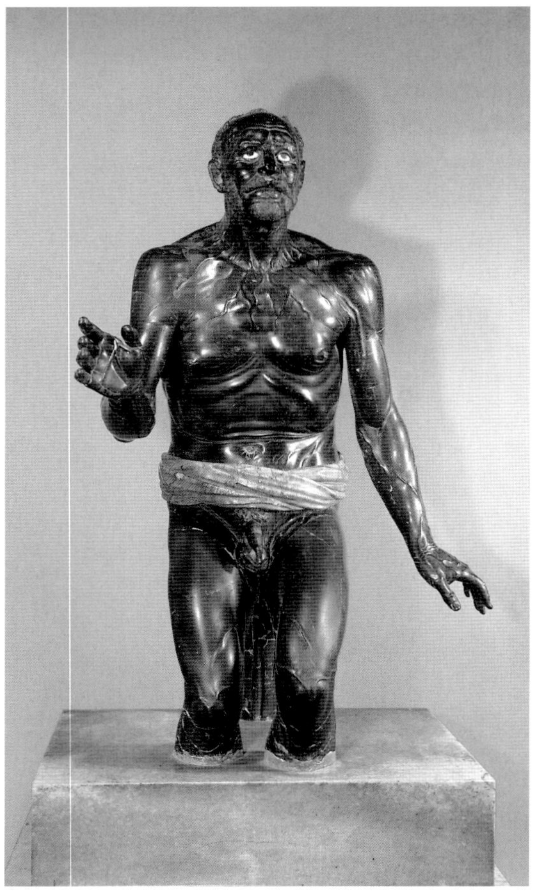

Fig. 61. Roman 2nd-century copy after a Hellenistic original, *An African Fisherman (Dying Seneca).* Black marble, enamel, and alabaster, h. 118 cm (46 7/16 in.). Musée du Louvre, Paris; Borghese Collection (MA 1354)

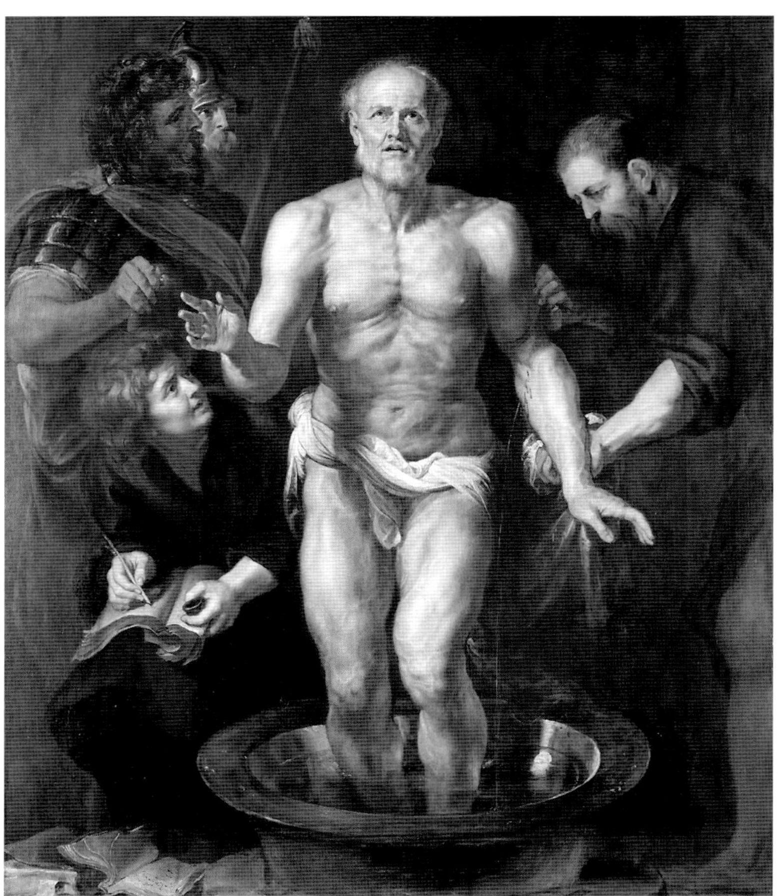

Fig. 62. Peter Paul Rubens, *The Death of Seneca*, 1612–13. Oil on panel, 181 x 152 cm (71 1/4 x 59 13/16 in.). Bayerische Staatsgemäldesammlungen, Alte Pinakothek, Munich (305)

Among the more heroic death scenes from classical history is that of the Roman statesman and Stoic philosopher Lucius Annaeus Seneca (4 B.C.?–A.D. 65). In A.D. 65 the emperor Nero forced Seneca, his former tutor, to commit suicide for alleged participation in a conspiracy against him. Seneca obliged by opening his veins so that he would bleed to death. However, as the blood did not flow quickly because of old age, he also took poison, and finally stood in a tub of hot water to accelerate the process. While performing this act, he assembled his friends around him and called for a scribe to dictate a long discourse.[1]

Seneca's writings were widely read in Europe in the seventeenth century. Justus Lipsius (Joest Lips; 1547–1606), a distinguished Flemish humanist and the teacher of Rubens's brother Philip, translated his works.[2] In a group portrait now in the Pitti Palace, Florence (fig. 45), Rubens painted himself in the company of Lipsius, Philip, and another student of Lipsius's, Jan Woverius; a bust of Seneca owned by Rubens appears prominently at the right.[3]

From the time of its excavation in the second half of the sixteenth century, the statue shown in these two drawings was one of the most admired antique sculptures in Rome. Initially thought to depict Seneca during his suicide, the sculpture is a copy from the second century after a lost Hellenistic original, preserved in the Louvre, Paris, since 1807 (fig. 61).[4] Only in the late eighteenth century was it realized that the sculpture represents neither the famous Stoic philosopher nor a dying man. In all likelihood, it is even not a portrait but a generic depiction of an old man, possibly—as the figure's pose seems to suggest—a fisherman. Since the man's facial features are vaguely African and since the statue is made of dark brown marble, the work has been called the *African Fisherman.*

Rubens drew the statue, then probably still in the collection of Duke Giovanni Altemps (d. 1620) in Rome, at least six times from different angles, working his way completely around it. Besides catalogue numbers 22 and 23, a drawing in the Hermitage—of lesser quality—depicts the statue from the front;[5] another drawing, again in Saint Petersburg, shows it from the back, turned slightly to the left; and a sheet in the Ambrosiana, Milan, shows it from the side facing to the left.[6] Two additional drawings by Rubens are lost and known only from copies in the so-called Rubens *cantoor* in Copenhagen. One depicts the statue from the front, but turned to the left, while the second shows it almost in mirror image, facing to the right.[7] In every version, Rubens included the motif of a basin, which may be the elaborate black marble tub that was added below the sculpture in September 1602.[8] This would date these drawings to Rubens's second Roman sojourn, from November 1605 until October 1608, possibly more specifically to the summer of 1606 when the artist devoted himself to the study of antique models.[9]

For all the drawings after the so-called Seneca, Rubens used black chalk. None of the six sheets shows many pentimenti. The careful execution, with fine hatching to record the smallest anatomical details, reflects the amount of time that Rubens spent on his task. The drawing that studies the sculpture from the back (cat. no. 23) has a slightly more fluid line and shows the artist going over some of the contours.

Rubens's purpose in copying the statue appears to have been twofold: to carefully observe the anatomy of the figure and to consciously record a famous antique work. His close study of the so-called Seneca vividly reveals the artist trying to absorb and commit to memory every facet of the sculpture. It clearly reflects his belief that "in order to attain the highest perfection in painting, it is necessary to understand the antiques [i.e., antique sculpture], nay, to be so thoroughly possessed of this knowledge, that it may diffuse itself everywhere," as he wrote in his unpublished treatise *De Imitatione Statuarum* (On the Copying of Sculpture).[10]

Back in Antwerp, Rubens would use the frontal view of the marble sculpture for his 1612–13 painting of the *Death of Seneca,* now in Munich (fig. 62).[11] Rubens made use of the image once more for an illustration in the 1615 edition by Justus Lipsius of *L. Annaei Senecae Philosophi Opera, quae Exstant Omnia,* with engravings by Cornelis Galle the Elder (1576–1650), published by the Plantin Press in Antwerp.[12]

The bottom of catalogue number 23 bears an annotation by Sebastiano Resta (1635–1714), a friar in the order of the Oratorians. Resta spent his life collecting drawings from his cell in Santa Maria della Vallicella, Rome. It is notable that he was able to acquire drawings by Rubens relatively early, in the 1680s, for the majority of the drawings were kept together in the artist's estate until 1657 and afterward were mostly sold in large groups to Northern collectors (see the essay by Michiel C. Plomp in this publication). Resta bought these drawings indirectly, from Maximiliaen Labbé (d. 1675), a Flemish sculptor who brought them to Italy after he had inherited them at Rubens's death in 1640.[13] There were probably more drawings of the so-called Seneca in the group bequeathed to Labbé, for in addition to catalogue number 23, Resta also once owned the sheet now in the Ambrosiana, and in a letter of 1684 he mentioned that he knew of two further, related examples.[14]

1. Tacitus *Annales* 15.60–64.
2. Morford 1991; Morford 1998, pp. 387–89. See also Huemer 1996, pp. 29–54.
3. The bust was one of Rubens's prized possessions. Van der Meulen 1994, vol. 2, pp. 135–36, under no. 117, vol. 3, fig. 218. For Rubens's drawing of Woverius (1576–1639), see catalogue number 11.
4. The Duke of Altemps, the sculpture's first owner, had the statue restored. Later it was in the collection of Cardinal Scipione Borghese (thus the alternative title *Borghese Fisherman*). See Haskell and Penny 1981, no. 76, and Van der Meulen 1995, p. 34, n. 3a.
5. Judson and Van de Velde 1978, pp. 160–64, nos. 31, 31a, 31b; Van der Meulen 1994, vol. 2, nos. 8–9, vol. 3, figs. 22, 23. The version in Saint Petersburg (inv. 5500) has at times been described as a copy after catalogue number 22, possibly by a member of Rubens's circle, a suggestion made most recently by Alexei Larionov (in Toronto 2001, under no. 99). We know that Rubens was traveling in Rome with a fellow artist from Antwerp, Deodaat del Monte (1582–1644), but no securely attributed drawings by the latter have been identified.
6. Van der Meulen 1994, vol. 2, no. 11, vol. 3, fig. 24, and vol. 2, no. 7, vol. 3, fig. 21.
7. Ibid., vol. 2, no. 10, vol. 3, fig. 26 (copy), and vol. 2, no. 12, vol. 3, figs. 28, 29 (copies 1, 2). For a discussion of Rubens's drawings and paintings of Seneca, see also Iris Kockelbergh in Antwerp 1993, pp. 108–15.
8. The invoice dated September 1602 for adding the basin was discussed by Andreas Thielemann in his unpublished lecture "Die Seneca-Statue, Kunstmuster und Studienobjekt," at the Rubens symposium in Cologne on December 6, 2002. The invoice is published in Scoppola 1987, p. 295.
9. According to a letter Philip Rubens wrote on July 29, 1606, on his brother's behalf to Annibale Chieppio, the agent at the Gonzaga court in Mantua. Rooses and Ruelens 1887–1909, vol. 1, p. 346, letter 85; Van der Muelen 1994, vol. 1, p. 42.
10. Roger de Piles published this passage from Rubens's manuscript in his *Cours de peinture par principes* (Paris, 1708); English translation 1743, p. 86. See Stechow 1968, p. 26.
11. K.d.K., ed. Oldenbourg 1921, no. 44; M. Jaffé 1989, no. 179; ; Renger and Denk 2002, pp. 386–89, no. 305. Another version of this painting, also from 1612–13, is in the Prado, Madrid (see M. Jaffé 1989, under no. 179, and Braunschweig 2004, no. 49).
12. The design for this illustration is in the Pierpont Morgan Library, New York (inv. I,234b); Stampfle 1991, no. 317.
13. For Labbé, see Arnout Balis, "'Fatto da un mio discepolo': Rubens's Studio Practices Reviewed," in Tokyo 1993, p. 120, n. 39.
14. Wood 1990, pp. 7, 9, 39, app. 1, 2.

24. *Antique Cameo with Claudius and Agrippina*, ca. 1622

Pen and brown ink, 148 x 223 mm (5 13/16 x 8 3/4 in.)
Inscribed by the artist in pen and brown ink at top left: *Claudius et Agrippina;* at top right: *Anpekolo bellissimo col fundo scuro / et le figure berettine c[h]iare tra lazurro / et il bianco / Et li serpenti colle summita dalle vesti / et li cappelli e la corazza del Imperatore / di bellissimo sardoni [c]o;* below in Flemish, also by the artist, in another color ink and a thinner pen: *het vuerste handeken van het vrauwken wat meer / wt steken ende verscheyden van het ander;* within the cameo at left: *pezzo moderno*

Staatliche Museen zu Berlin, Kupferstichkabinett (KdZ 3374)

PROVENANCE: Samuel Woodburn (1786–1853), London (his sale, London, Christie's, June 12, 1860, lot 1437); George Salting (1835–1909), London (presented to the Staatliche Museen in 1888).

LITERATURE: R., vol. 5, no. 1407; Glück and Haberditzl 1928, no. 24, pl. 24; Bock and Rosenberg 1930, p. 251, no. 3374, pl. 181; Held 1959, under no. 21 and p. 45; Burchard and d'Hulst 1963, under no. 14; Held 1986, p. 39 and under no. 60; Van der Meulen 1994, vol. 1, pp. 94, 136, 138, vol. 2, no. 165, vol. 3, fig. 310.

EXHIBITION: Berlin 1977, no. 31, ill.

In October 1621 Rubens received a letter from the French scholar Nicolas-Claude Fabri de Peiresc (1580–1637) in Paris, inquiring whether Peiresc might borrow the artist's drawing after the Gemma Augustea, one of the most famous cameos of the time.[1] The loan of this design, now in the Sankt Annen-Museum, Lübeck,[2] initiated a plan to jointly publish a book reproducing some twenty-five to thirty outstanding gems, from both Rubens's own collection and elsewhere. Rubens was to supply the drawings for the engravings, while Peiresc was to write the accompanying texts.[3]

Among the surviving drawings for the unrealized project is the present pen-and-ink study of a cameo that Rubens believed to represent the Roman emperor Claudius and his wife Agrippina in a chariot drawn by two winged dragons. (Today the cameo is thought to depict another of Claudius's wives, Messalina. As Peiresc conceded in a letter to Rubens of November 3, 1623, antique representations of Agrippina and Messalina were difficult to distinguish.)[4] Judging from the detailed notations on the sheet, Rubens must have been drawing after the antique Roman cameo itself, which is now in the Cabinet des Médailles, Bibliothèque Nationale, Paris (fig. 63).[5] He recorded it close to its actual size and carefully described the various colorings of the gem. The inscription at the right, in Italian (for Peiresc's benefit), states that "the figures are light grayish blue, between blue and white against a dark ground; the snake, with the raised parts of the clothes, the hair, and the cuirass of the emperor, are of the most beautiful sardonyx [rust-brown]." To this Rubens added, in his native Flemish, "the woman's hand in front is more extended and different from the other one." In her left hand Agrippina is actually holding a poppy capsule. Rubens also indicated that the section at the left is "modern" (*pezzo moderno*): the emperor's position leaning backward, his right arm, his billowing mantle, and the upper-left portion of the chariot are Rubens's invention.

The drawing was never engraved, but we know from Peiresc's partial description of the cameo preserved among his manuscripts that it was meant to be included in the gem book.[6] The cameo apparently entered the royal collection in Versailles in 1684 from the treasury of a French church,[7] where Rubens most likely copied it, probably during his 1622 visit to Paris, where he traveled in connection with the commission for the Medici cycle of paintings for the Luxembourg Palace. During those weeks Rubens met several times with Peiresc, who mentioned the project to another collector of gems, Pompeo Pasqualino, in Rome, in a letter of January 26, 1622.[8] Therefore, Rubens's drawing most likely dates from early 1622.[9]

Rubens's interest in glyptic art is first documented during his stay in Italy, when he visited the collection of Lelio Pasqualino (the uncle of Pompeo) in Rome probably between 1605 and 1608 and recorded works that were of interest to him in his travel diary.[10] During his lifetime Rubens collected a sizable number of gems, possibly including one that is today in The Metropolitan Museum of Art, New York, and that Peiresc identified as representing the Return of Odysseus (fig. 64).[11]

1. Today the cameo is in the Kunsthistorisches Museum, Vienna; Van der Meulen 1994, vol. 2, pp. 176–80, fig. 312.
2. Inv. AB245; ibid., no. 164a, pp. 179–80, vol. 3, fig. 314.
3. David Jaffé (1997, p. 182) suggested that the project had a dual purpose: to promote gems Rubens wanted to sell—an aim evident in Rubens's selection of those to be engraved—and to publish all the antique gems, cameos, and glass then known, in order to preserve the images.
4. Rooses and Ruelens 1887–1909, vol. 3, p. 261, letter 351; Van der Meulen 1994, vol. 2, p. 181.
5. Babelon 1897, no. 276; Megow 1987, p. 207, no. A86, fig. 27.3.
6. Bibliothèque Nationale, Paris; transcribed in Van der Meulen 1994, vol. 1, pp. 185–86, app. 4.3.3.
7. Oudinet 1736, pp. 278–79, pl. 10, as Germanicus and Agrippina the Elder, represented as Ceres and Triptolemos quoted by Van der Meulen 1994, vol. 2, p. 181, n. 2.
8. Bibliothèque Nationale, Paris; transcribed in Van der Meulen 1994, vol. 1, pp. 178–80, app. 3.
9. Glück and Haberditzl (1928, no. 24, pl. 24) placed the drawing in Rubens's Italian years 1600–1608.
10. Only a few pages have been preserved in a French translation in the Cabinet des Médailles, Bibliothèque Nationale, Paris; see Van der Meulen 1994, vol. 1, p. 27, and a transcription on pp. 153–57, app. 1, 1–3.
11. See G. Richter 1956, no. 635, pl. 71, as the Return of Orestes; Van der Meulen 1994, vol. 1, p. 142, text fig. 65, as Phaedra and Hippolytus.

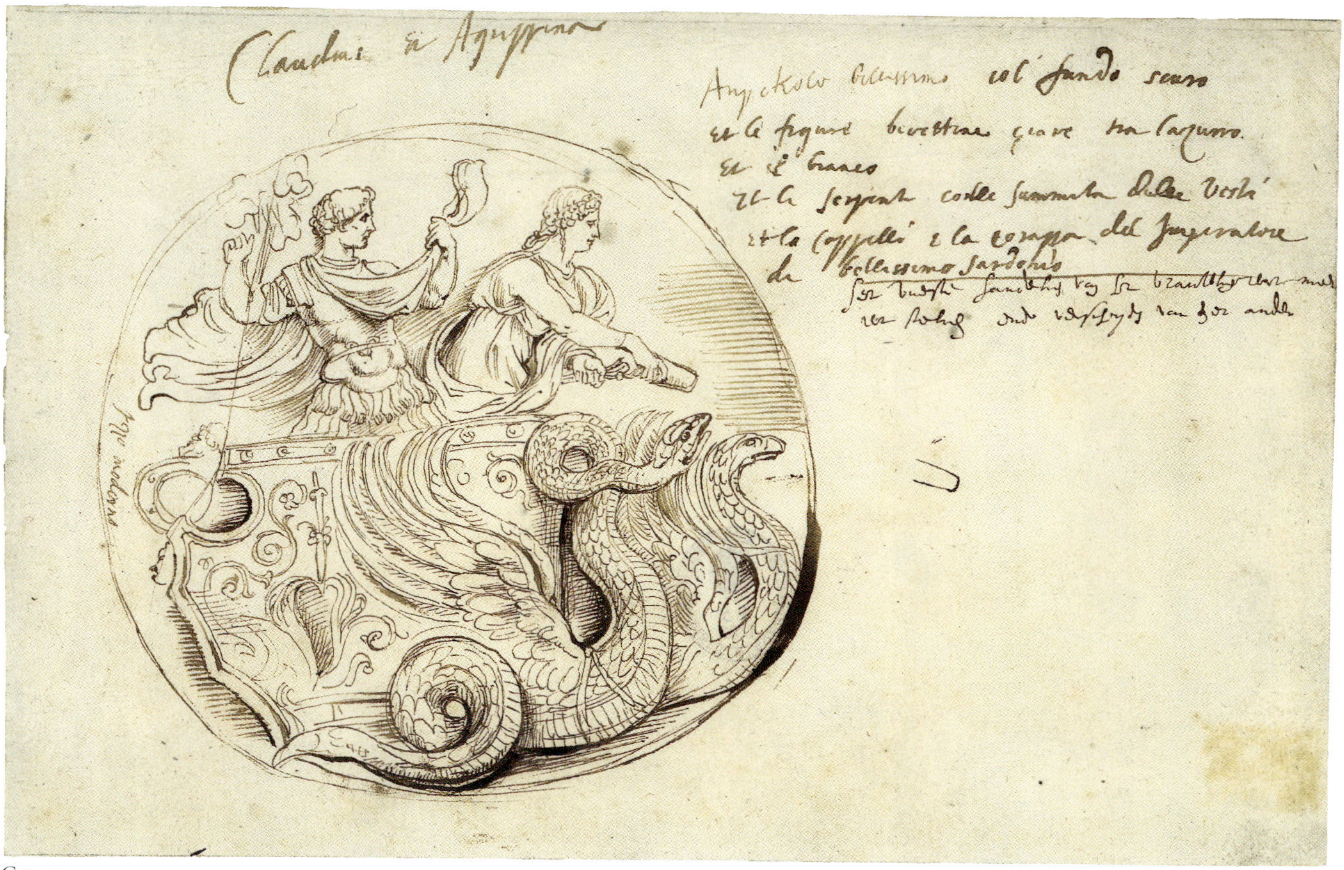

Cat. 24

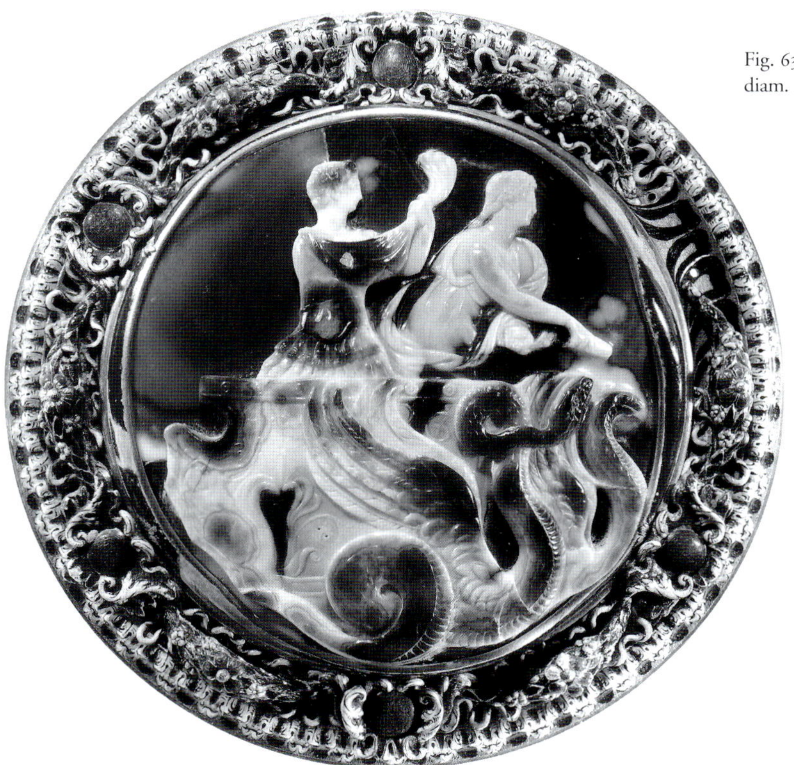

Fig. 63. Roman, *Claudius and Messalina on a Dragon Chariot.* Cameo, diam. 12.2 cm ($4^{13}/_{16}$ in.). Bibliothèque Nationale de France, Paris (Bab. 276)

Fig. 64. Roman, *The Return of Orestes (?).*Cameo, two-layered glass paste, 34.9 x 42.9 cm ($13^{3}/_{4}$ x $16^{7}/_{8}$ in.). The Metropolitan Museum of Art, New York; Gift of J. Pierpont Morgan, 1917 (17.194.16)

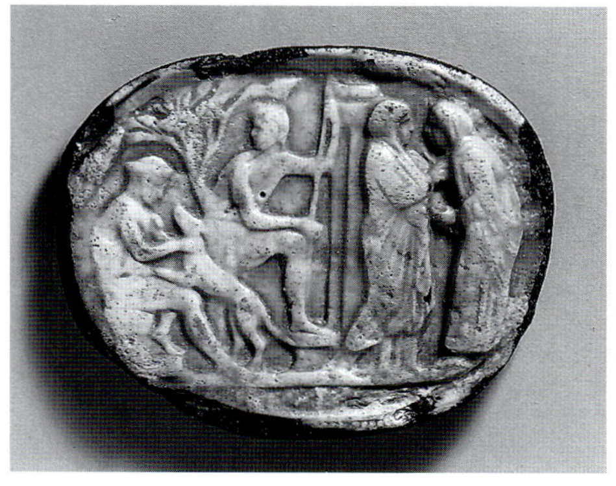

COMPOSITIONAL DRAWINGS

25. *Susanna*, 1607–11

Pen and brown ink, brush and brown wash on off-white laid paper, 175 x 152 mm (6⅞ x 6 in.)

The Metropolitan Museum of Art, New York; Purchase, Anonymous Gift, in memory of Frits Markus, 1998 (1998.74)

PROVENANCE: Private collection, Germany; Thomas Le Claire Kunsthandel, Hamburg, 1998.

LITERATURE: *MMAB* 1998, p. 26, ill.

EXHIBITION: New York 1998, no. 10, ill.

The story of Susanna in the Apocrypha tells how two elders conspired to seduce Susanna, the beautiful wife of Joachim, a wealthy Jew in Babylon. When they surprised her bathing alone and demanded sexual favors, she rejected them. The elders then falsely accused Susanna of adultery. A conflict in the men's testimony, however, betrayed their lie and revealed Susanna's innocence. Thus the elders, rather than Susanna, were put to death. No fewer than three paintings of Susanna were hanging in Rubens's house at the time of his death in 1640,[1] and seven paintings of Susanna and the Elders are extant.[2] The figure of Susanna can be understood as a symbol either of chastity or of silence, since she did not speak up to declare her innocence.[3] At the same time, however, the theme of Susanna and the Elders was considered piquant. In a letter of May 12, 1618, to the English diplomat and collector Sir Dudley Carleton, Rubens offered a painting of Susanna, calling it a "galanteria," whose subject was "[neither] sacred nor profane although taken from the Holy Scriptures."[4] Carleton replied that he hoped the *Susanna* would be beautiful enough to titillate even old men,[5] indicating, perhaps, his desire that the painting depict the then-popular theme of unequal love (*turpe senilis amor*) from Ovid's *Amores*.

The drawing in New York, which Rubens sketched quickly in pen, adding wash for modeling and depth, cannot be related specifically to any of Rubens's known Susanna paintings, although the pose of Susanna is similar in two of them. The earlier one is that in the Galleria Borghese, Rome (fig. 65), dated about 1607–8.[6] The later work, in the Nationalmuseum, Stockholm, Rubens signed and dated 1614.[7] A pentimento in the drawing is almost identical to the position of the right arm of Susanna in the Galleria Borghese painting, indicating that the drawing may date as early as 1607–8, that is, during Rubens's second stay in Rome. However, the handling of the pen and the color of the wash are very close to those of the study for the *Presentation in the Temple* in The Metropolitan Museum of Art, New York (cat. no. 30 recto), suggesting a date soon after Rubens's return to Antwerp, that is, 1609–10. Another study showing Susanna in a more dynamic pose (cat. no. 29 recto) likely dates from this period as well. The sheet in New York demonstrates how difficult it is to assign specific dates to Rubens's drawings when no related works by the artist are known.

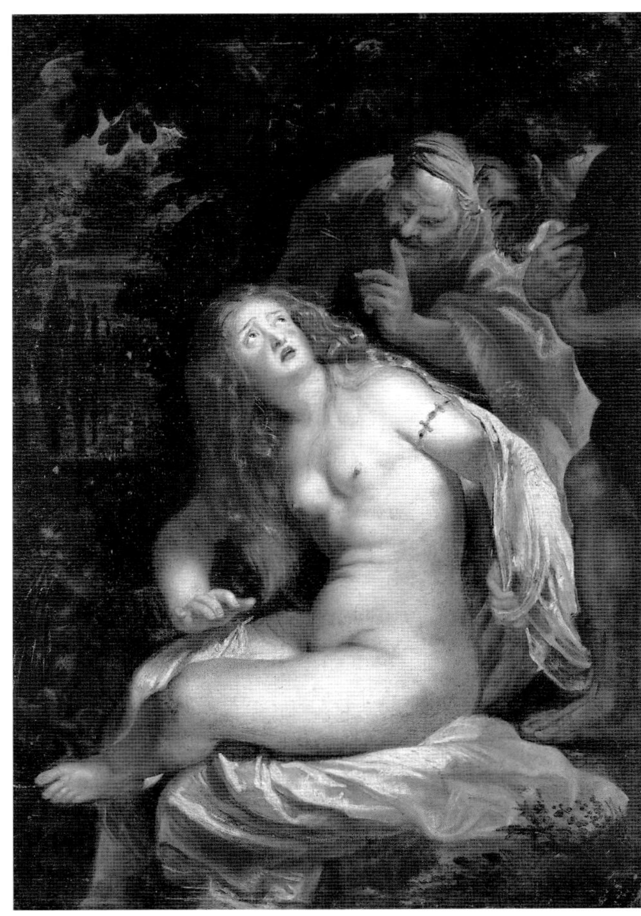

Fig. 65. Peter Paul Rubens, *Susanna and the Elders*, ca. 1607–8. Oil on canvas, 94 x 67 cm (37 x 26⅜ in.). Museo Galleria di Villa Borghese, Rome (277)

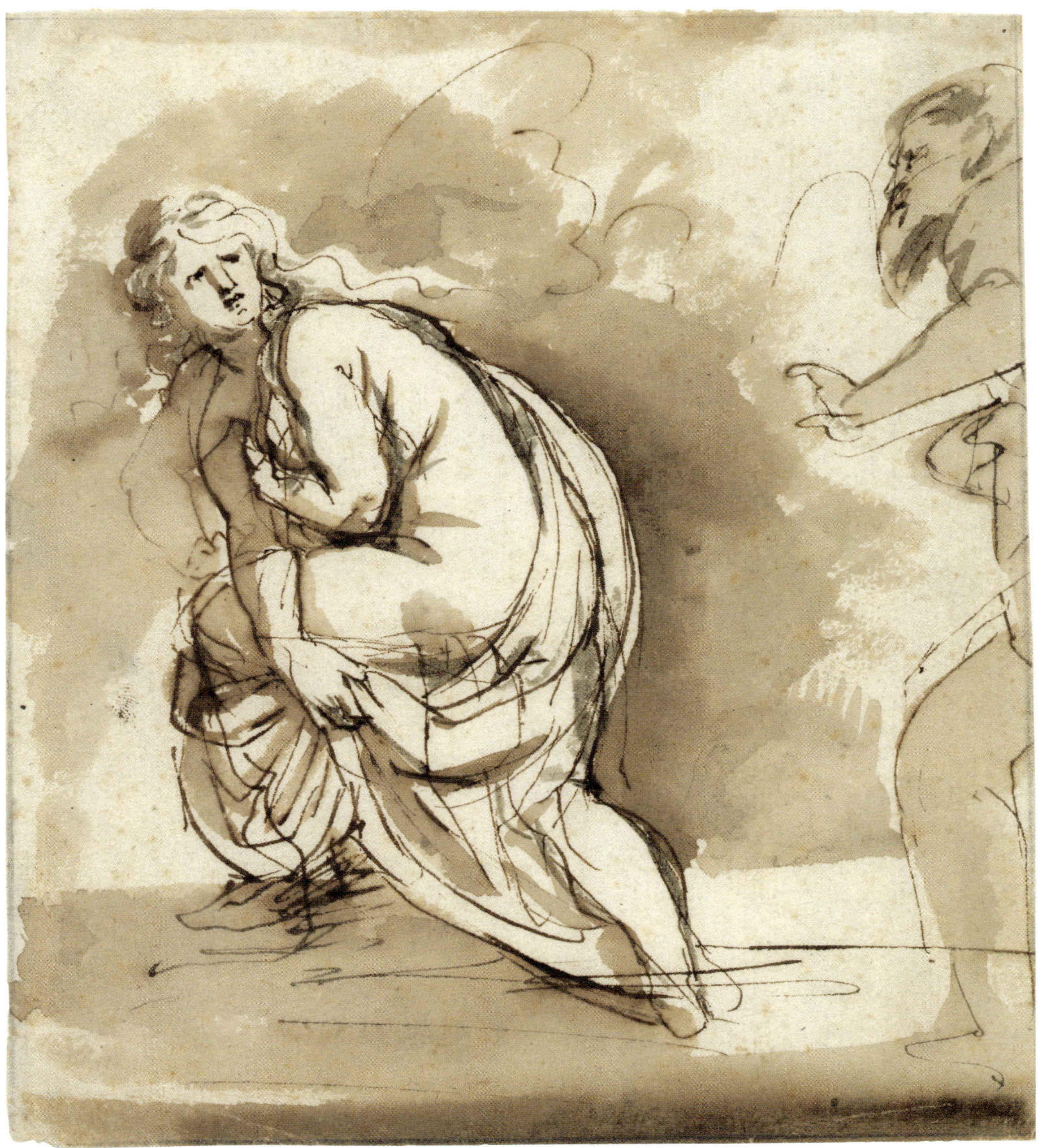

Cat. 25

1. Muller 1989, p. 115, no. 99, p. 123, nos. 161, 162.
2. The seven paintings are in the Galleria Borghese, Rome (K.d.K., ed. Oldenbourg 1921, no. 19, left; M. Jaffé 1989, no. 70, 1607–8); State Hermitage Museum, Saint Petersburg (M. Jaffé 1989, no. 101, ca. 1609); Real Academia de Madrid (K.d.K., ed. Oldenbourg 1921, no. 32; M. Jaffé 1989, no. 112, 1609–10); Nationalmuseum, Stockholm (K.d.K., ed. Oldenbourg 1921, no. 75; M. Jaffé 1989, no. 232, signed and dated 1614, and no. 552); Alte Pinakothek, Munich (K.d.K., ed. Oldenbourg 1921, no. 411; M. Jaffé 1989, no. 1348, ca. 1636–39); and whereabouts unknown (M. Jaffé 1989, no. 477).
3. Bleyerveld 2000–2001, p. 223.
4. Rooses and Ruelens 1887–1909, vol. 2, p. 150, letter 168. For the interpretation of the subject, see McGrath 1984, pp. 73–90.
5. Ibid., p. 165, letter 171, May 22, 1618: "hà da esser bella per inamorar anco li Vecchij."
6. K.d.K., ed. Oldenbourg 1921, no. 19, left; M. Jaffé 1989, no. 70, 1607–8.
7. K.d.K., ed. Oldenbourg 1921, no. 75; M. Jaffé 1989, no. 232, 1614.

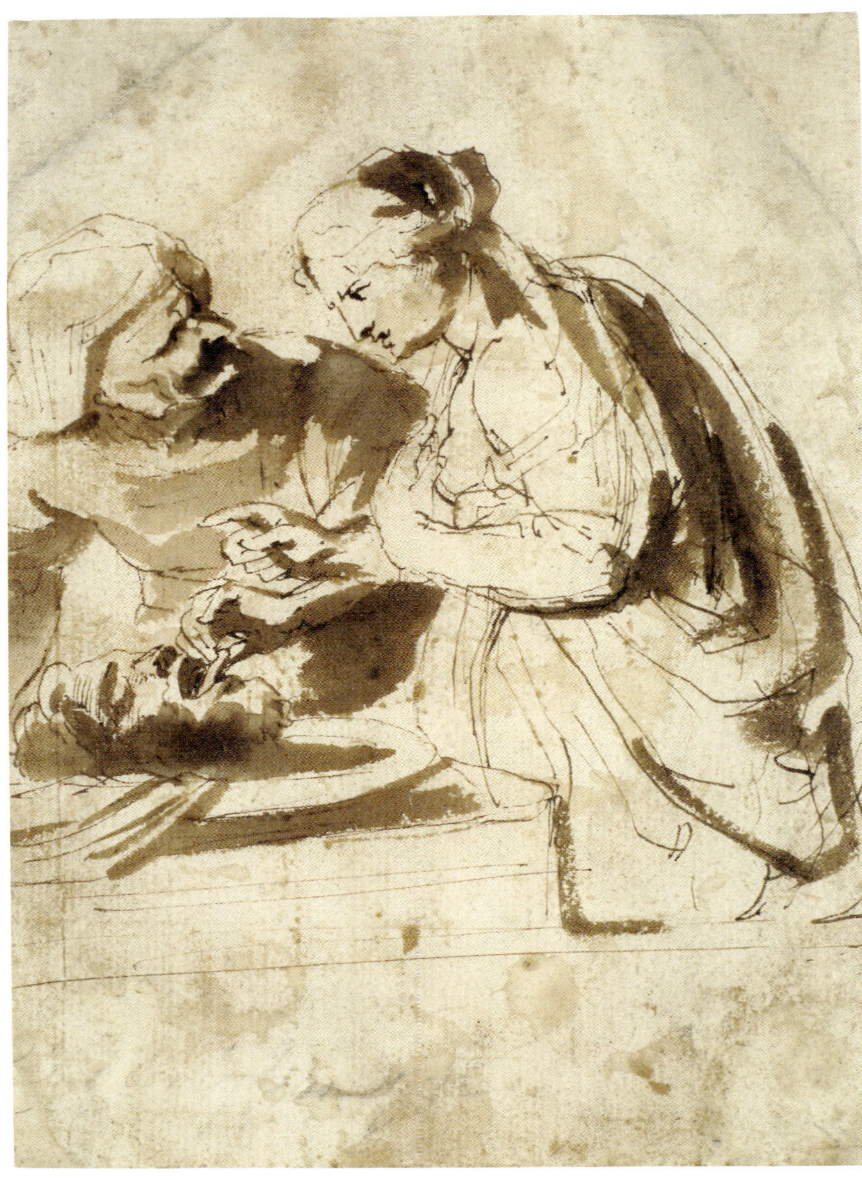

Cat. 26 recto

26. *Salome with the Head of John the Baptist,* recto; *David with the Head of Goliath,* verso, ca. 1609

Pen and brown ink and brown wash, traces of writing in black chalk at bottom left, recto; pen and brown ink, verso, 183 x 130 mm (7³⁄₁₆ x 5⅛ in.); triangular pieces cut off at top corners and made up

Amsterdams Historisch Museum (A18 085)

PROVENANCE: Henry Oppenheimer (1859–1932), London (sale, London, Christie's, July 10–14, 1936, lot 238A [Van Dyck, *Judith with the Head of Holofernes*]); bought by J. Q. van Regteren Altena on behalf of the Fodor Museum; transferred in 1975 with the Fodor Museum collection to the Amsterdams Historisch Museum.

LITERATURE: Burchard and d'Hulst 1963, no. 42, pl. 42, and under no. 133; Hubala 1978, pp. 145–47, fig. 5; Schapelhouman 1979, no. 61, ill.; Held 1980, under no. 414; Peter C. Sutton in New York 1999, under no. 27, fig. 3.

EXHIBITIONS: Antwerp 1977, no. 128, ill.; Lyons 1980, no. 56, ill.

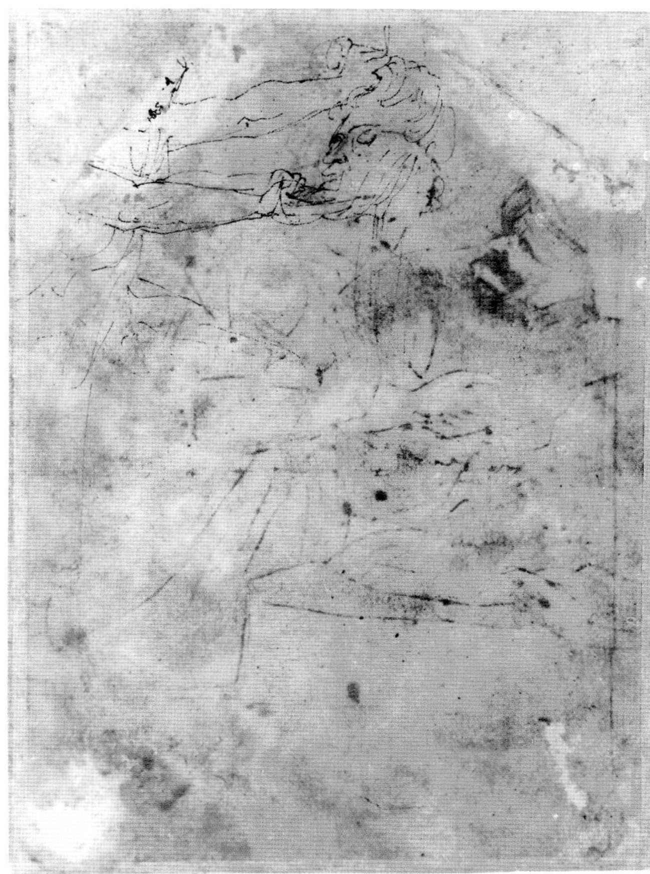

Cat. 26 verso

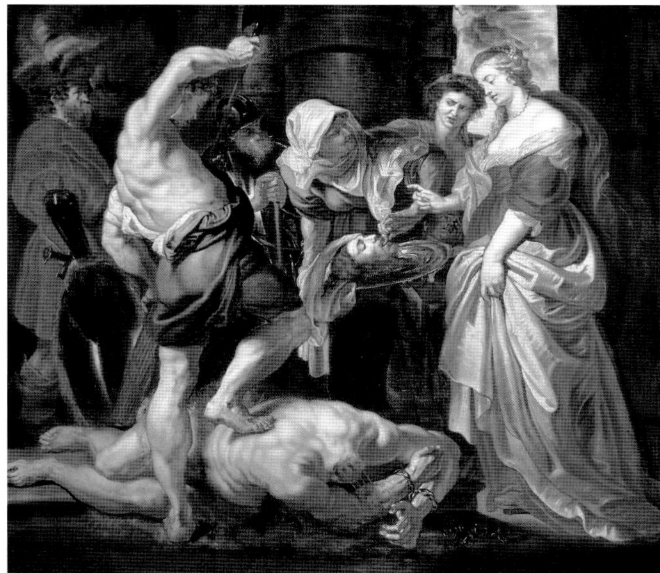

Fig. 66. Peter Paul Rubens, *The Beheading of Saint John the Baptist,* 1609. Oil on panel, 94 x 102 cm (37 x 40 3/16 in.). Private collection, United States

At the wedding banquet of Herodias and King Herod, Herod was so taken by the beautiful dancing of Salome, his new stepdaughter, that he offered her anything she wished as a reward.[1] At her mother's urging, Salome asked for the head of John the Baptist, who had reproached Herod for his illicit marriage to Herodias, his brother's wife. The king fulfilled Salome's wish and had John's head delivered to her on a silver platter. That moment is depicted in this drawing, although Rubens added to the drama by having Salome make an admonishing gesture toward the Baptist's head and the servant pull at his tongue.

Rubens sketched the composition quickly with a fine pen and then added accents with a broad brush and brown wash, possibly to show it to a potential client. The sheet, which has been cut at the left, represents an early idea for Rubens's *Beheading of Saint John the Baptist,* which resurfaced only in 1998 and is now in a private collection in the United States (fig. 66).[2] In the painting Rubens presented the full, brutal scene, with the executioner sheathing his sword after decapitating the Baptist, whose body with chained hands is prostrate at Salome's feet. As in the Amsterdam drawing, Salome makes an admonishing gesture toward the severed head and the old female servant pulls at the tongue.

Nothing is known of the commission of this violent painting; however, it appears to have been popular, for a number of copies after it have been preserved. One copy in Dresden, by Hieronymus II Francken (1578–1623), is dated 1609,[3] thus furnishing a date *ante quem* for Rubens's original and this related drawing, namely, the same year, sometime soon after Rubens's return to Antwerp from Italy on December 11, 1608. The Amsterdam drawing has been associated with still another variant of this subject, a half-length painting of *Salome and Herodias with the Head of John the Baptist* by Gerard Seghers (1591–1651), supposedly after a Rubens original of about 1611, now lost.[4]

In the seventeenth century, representations of the Beheading of John the Baptist were often interpreted as appeals to the example of virtue *(exemplum virtutis),* reminding the viewer to be vigilant and especially to be wary of the caprices of cunning women and their power to betray and humiliate. Rubens later painted the related *Feast of Herod* (fig. 156), in which Herodias pierces the tongue of John the Baptist, since he had spoken against her marriage. A drawing by Rubens of this subject is included in the exhibition (cat. no. 57).

The present drawing is similar in technique, style, and execution to two other compositional drawings, which are equally dramatic in subject matter: the *Judith Killing Holofernes* in Frankfurt (cat. no. 27) and the *Susanna* in Montpellier (cat. no. 29). This manner of drawing proved to be very influential on Rubens's younger assistant and collaborator Anthony van Dyck (1599–1641). Most of Van Dyck's historical drawings look very much like these early works by Rubens. Consequently, over the past centuries a number of early Rubens drawings have been attributed to Van Dyck, this sheet among them. In the 1930s J. Q. van Regteren Altena was the first to recognize the difference between Rubens's and Van Dyck's drawings, and he correctly attributed catalogue numbers 26 and 27 to Rubens.

The faint pen drawing on the verso, probably contemporary with the recto, depicts David, his left leg bent, forcefully fixing the severed head of Goliath onto a stake. No painting by Rubens of this subject is known.

1. The story of Salome is found in Mark 6:14–29 and in Matthew 14:1–12, as well as in Flavius Josephus (ca. 37–ca. 100), *Antiquitates Judaicae*, book 18.
2. M. Jaffé 1989, no. 115, ca. 1609–10; sale cat., Sotheby's, New York, January 30, 1998, lot 137, color ill., 94 x 101.8 cm. After restoration, the work was exhibited at Otto Naumann Ltd. in New York (New York 1999, no. 27, color ill.). D. Jaffé and Bradley 2003, pp. 13–14, fig. 24.
3. Inv. 855; oil on copper, 38.5 x 33.5 cm. Staatliche Kunstsammlungen, Gemäldegalerie, Dresden. Härting 1989, p. 168, fig. 148.
4. Müller Hofstede 1966a, p. 442, n. 42; Bieneck 1992, no. A1, ca. 1612–14, color ill. Seghers's painting omits the pulling of the tongue. Bieneck dated the work to Seghers's Italian sojourn (ca. 1611–20), which would mean that the artist would have had to work from a drawn copy after catalogue number 26; there is such a copy, attributed to Seghers by Börje Magnusson, in the Nationalmuseum, Stockholm (inv. 1655/1875; pen and brown ink and brown wash over black chalk, 152 x 158 mm; Stockholm 1977, no. 36). The Stockholm copy proves that the present drawing was cut rather severely at the left and to a lesser extent at the right.

27. *Judith Killing Holofernes,* ca. 1609–10

Pen and brown ink and brown wash, 206 x 160 mm (8⅛ x 65/16 in.)

Graphische Sammlung im Städelschen Kunstinstitut, Frankfurt am Main (15 690)

PROVENANCE: John Barnard (d. 1784), London; Sir Thomas Lawrence (1769–1830), London (Lugt 2445; in his mount [Van Dyck]); Samuel Woodburn (1786–1853), London (sale, London, Christie's, June 5, 1860, no. 361 [Van Dyck]); R. P. Roupell (1798–1886), London (Lugt 2234; his inscription in pen on mount: "R. P. R. van Dyck. Judith slaying Holofernes. Barnard, Sir Thos. Lawrence, one of the selected fifty for Woodburn's Exhibition in 1853," and in pencil: "34"); Robert Low (1838–1909), London (Lugt 2222); Johann Friedrich Lahmann (d. 1937), Dresden; acquired by the Städelsches Kunstinstitut in 1935.

LITERATURE: Held 1959, no. 15, pl. 16, under nos. 13, 14, and p. 67; Burchard and d'Hulst 1963, no. 47, pl. 47; Held 1986, no. 48, pl. 48; d'Hulst and Vandenven 1989, no. 50a, fig. 110, and pp. 106, 159–60.

EXHIBITION: Frankfurt 2000, no. 27.

This is the earliest of Rubens's drawings and paintings on the theme of Judith and Holofernes.[1] Judith, a beautiful and pious Jewish widow, saved her people from the Assyrians by killing their commander, Holofernes, whose army laid siege to her city. As described in the Apocrypha, Judith, accompanied by her maidservant, Abra, ventured into the enemy's camp, where they were apprehended and taken to Holofernes, to whom Judith offered her assistance. Eventually, Judith accepted

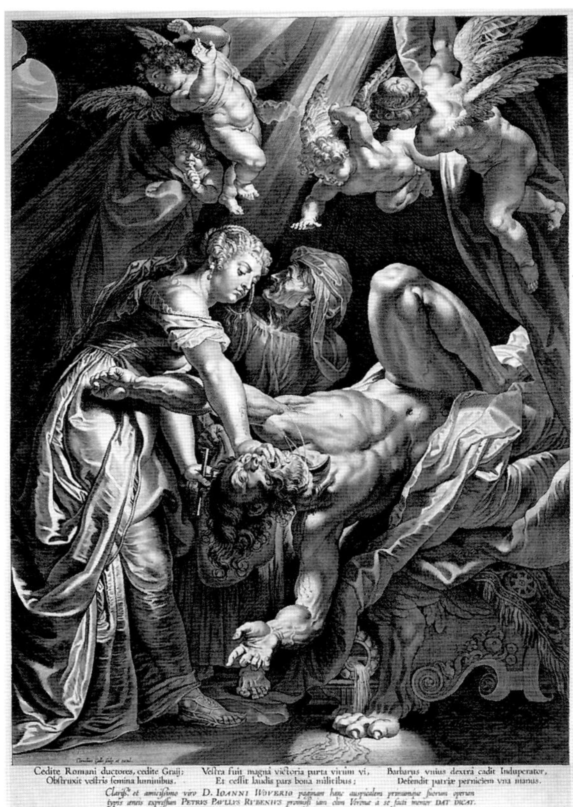

Fig. 67. Cornelis Galle the Elder, *Judith Beheading Holofernes,* ca. 1611. Engraving, 542 x 374 mm (215/16 x 14¾ in.). The Metropolitan Museum of Art, New York; The Elisha Whittelsey Collection, The Elisha Whittelsey Fund, 1951 (51.501.7000)

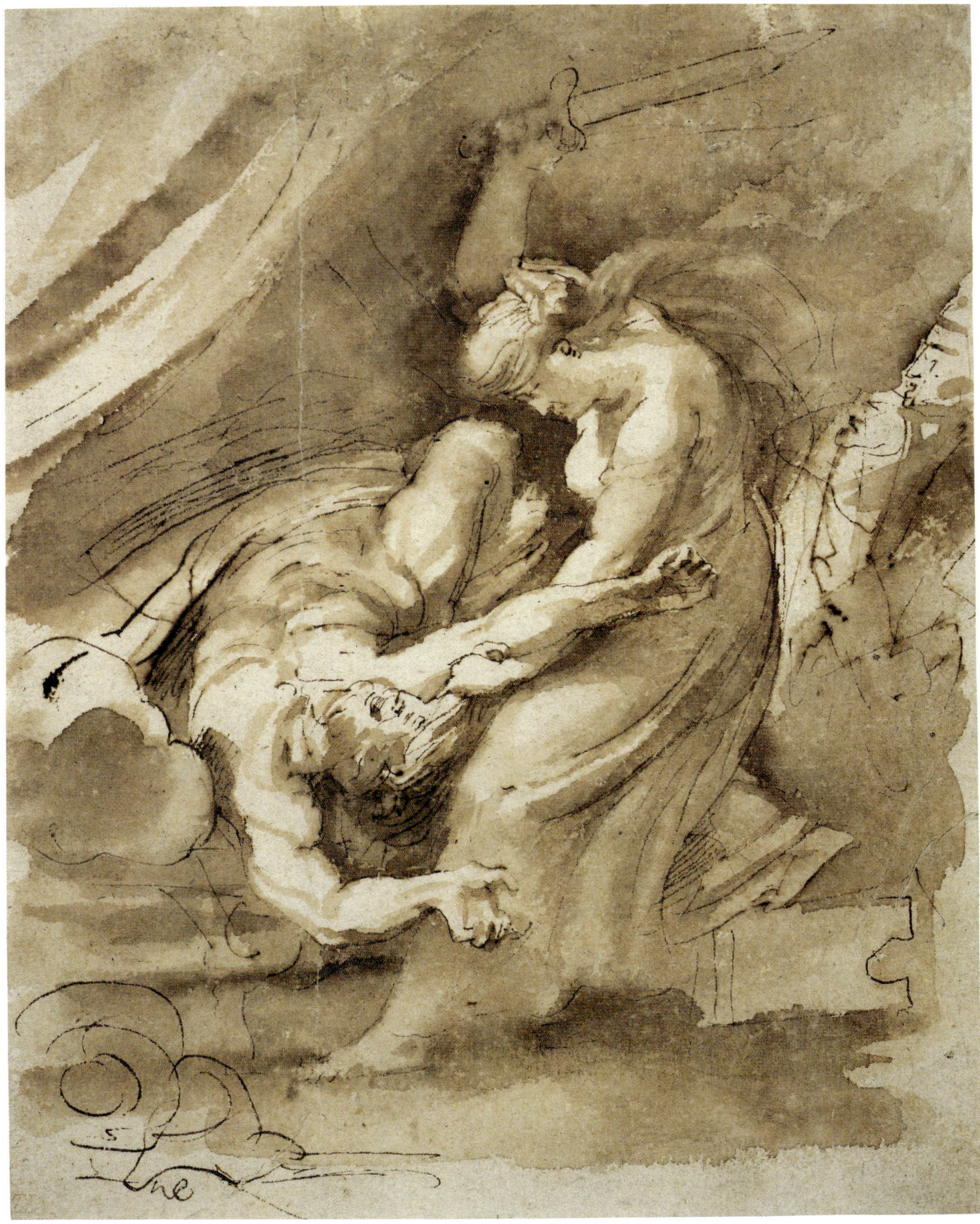

Cat. 27

Holofernes' invitation to dine with him in his tent at night. When Holofernes fell asleep, Judith seized his sword and cut off his head, which she then hid in a basket and carried back to her people in triumph. Rubens's quick pen sketch shows the dramatic moment when Judith raises the sword to cut off Holofernes' head, which she grabs by the hair. The Assyrian commander's twisted body is seen in strong foreshortening, his arms raised in agony, while the maidservant looks on from the background at the right. Rubens added wash to indicate the darkness of the tent but left white areas to represent light falling on the victim and his executioner.[2]

This quick compositional pen sketch relates to the so-called Large *Judith*,[3] a painting known through the engraving by Cornelis Galle the Elder (1576–1650) and a few painted copies.[4]

Galle's engraving is the first known reproductive print after a Rubens painting (fig. 67).[5] The present drawing most likely reflects an early idea for Rubens's lost painting, which has been dated either between 1605 and 1608, during his second visit to Rome, or shortly after his return to Antwerp, that is, about 1609–10. The latter dating is the more logical, since the drawing is close stylistically to *Samson and Delilah* of about 1609–11 (see cat. no. 28). Rubens chose a slightly later moment in the story for the final composition; in Galle's print after the lost painting, Judith is already in the process of cutting off Holofernes' head.

Rubens represented Judith and Holofernes several times in drawings, as we may conclude from three references in the inventory of Rubens's collaborator Erasmus II Quellinus (1607–1678). Listed among the drawings are a "crabbelingh, Rubbens. Noch 2 Judith," another "Judith ende Holofernes," and "Verscheyde Judith ende Holofernes Rubbens."[6] This dramatic sheet in Frankfurt may be one of the drawings from Quellinus's estate.

1. Besides the present drawing and the painting known from Galle's engraving, two paintings by Rubens, in Braunschweig and Florence, represent Judith holding the severed head of Holofernes (M. Jaffé 1989, no. 453, ca. 1617, and no. 665, ca. 1620–22; Braunschweig 2004, nos. 1, 2).
2. The drawing was attributed to Anthony van Dyck until J. Q. van Regteren Altena recognized it as a work by Rubens. See Held 1959, under no. 15.
3. M. Jaffé 1989, no. 85, ca. 1609. A "small" Judith does not seem to exist.
4. The best painted copies are in the Dexia Bank, Brussels (oil on canvas, 152 x 107 cm; K.d.K., ed. Oldenbourg 1921, p. 30), and in the museum at Carpentras, France (oil on canvas, 114 x 88 cm).
5. Schneevoogt 1873, p. 10, no. 79; Hollstein 1949–, vol. 7, p. 49, no. 31. Rubens dedicated the engraving to his friend Jan Woverius (1576–1639), to commemorate their meeting in Verona in 1602, when Rubens was in the service of the Duke of Mantua. For a portrait of Woverius by Rubens, see catalogue number 11.
6. Inventory of March 22, 1679; listed in Denucé 1932, pp. 285, 287, 289, and in Duverger 1984–, vol. 10, pp. 359, 362, 364.

28. *Samson and Delilah,* recto; *Indistinct Sketches,* verso, ca. 1609–11

Pen and brown ink and brown wash, recto; pen, verso, 164 x 162 mm (6⁷⁄₁₁ x 6⅜ in.)
Annotated in pen and brown ink at bottom left: *V.D.*

Private collection, The Netherlands

PROVENANCE: Reinier Willem Petrus de Vries (1841–1919), Amsterdam.

LITERATURE: Held 1959, no. 24, pl. 21; Burchard and d'Hulst 1963, no. 46, pl. 46; Kuznetsov 1974, pl. 27; Held 1986, no. 51, pl. 53; d'Hulst and Vandenven 1989, no. 31a, fig. 75, and pp. 111, 113–14, 116, 118.

EXHIBITION: Antwerp 1977, no. 129, ill.

The drawing on the recto depicts an episode from the Old Testament story of Samson and Delilah, from chapter 16 of the Book of Judges. The Jewish hero Samson is in love with the beautiful Delilah. Bribed by the leaders of the Philistines, enemies of the Jews, Delilah tries to discover the secret of Samson's great strength. Finally, she learns that the source of his power is his long hair, which he has let grow since birth in order to express his covenant with God. When Samson falls asleep in her lap, Delilah betrays him by calling for a Philistine to cut off his locks, thus depriving him of his might and permitting his capture. God gives him strength one more time, however, and with his bare hands he pulls down the temple of the Philistines in which he is imprisoned, destroying himself along with his persecutors.

Here, Rubens concentrated on the figures of Samson, Delilah, and the Philistine carefully cutting the hair. At the left, an old woman illuminates the scene with a candle. Vaguely indicated in a doorway in the right background are accomplices waiting to take Samson prisoner. Rubens developed the composition further in an intermediary oil sketch on panel (fig. 68).[1] There, the artist added space above the figures, introduced a baldachin-like drapery over the bed, and lowered and moved the Philistine to the left, between Samson and Delilah, so that the figures form a tightly knit group. Rubens also extended Delilah's right leg, which is bent in the drawing. The statuette of Venus and the blindfolded Cupid in a niche in the background wall alludes to the cause of Samson's downfall and identifies Delilah as a woman of easy virtue. The final painting (fig. 69) varies little from the oil sketch; only the shape of the composition has changed, from a square format to a more horizontal one.[2]

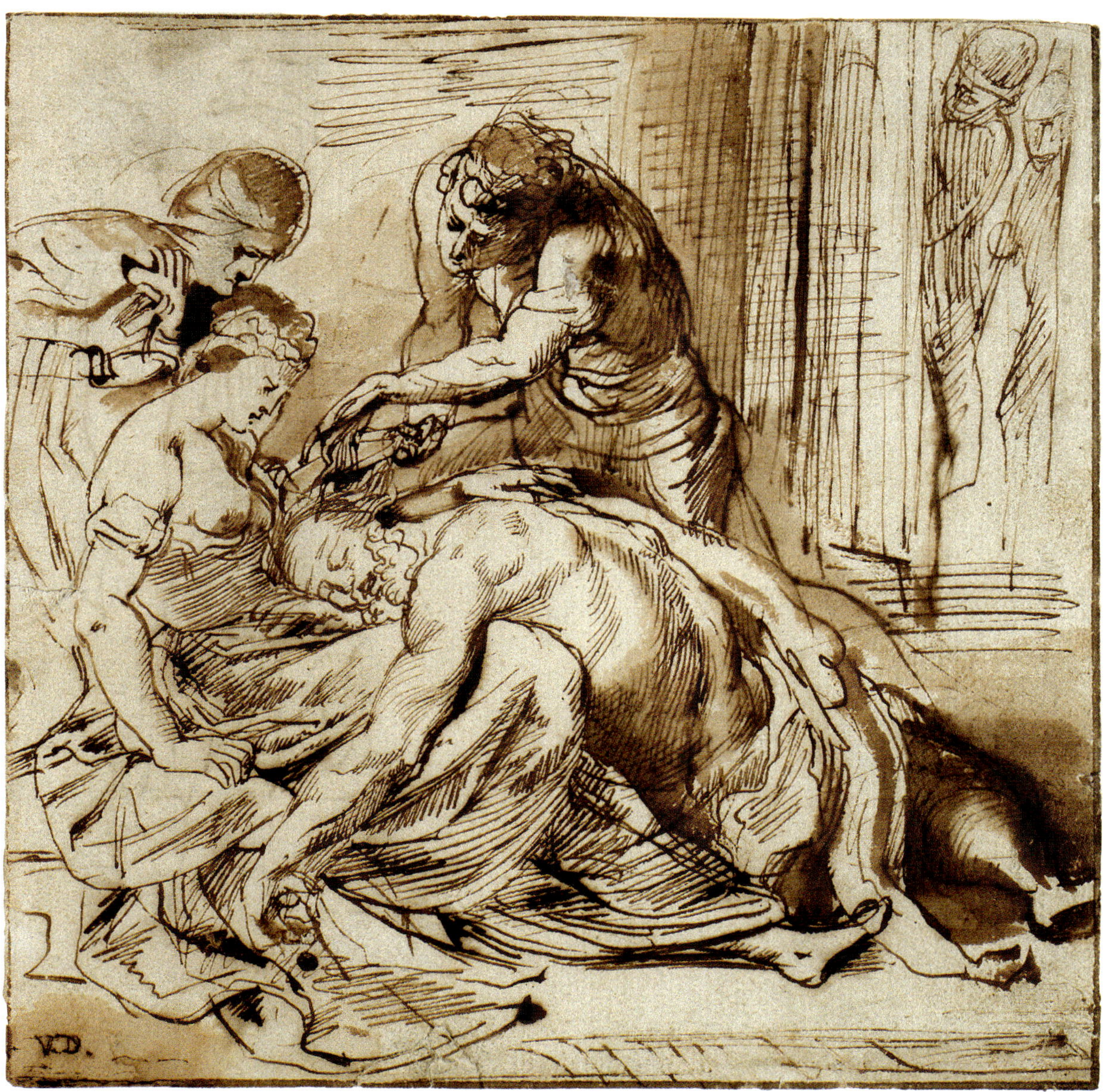

Cat. 28 recto

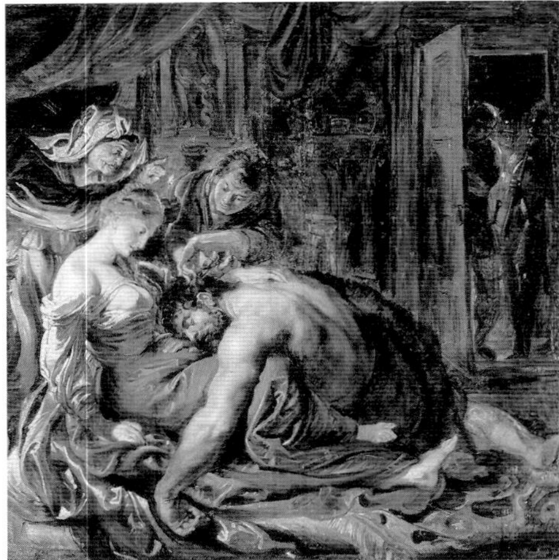

Fig. 68. Peter Paul Rubens, *Samson Asleep in Delilah's Lap,* ca. 1609–11. Oil on panel, 51.8 x 50.6 cm (20⅜ x 19 15/16 in.). Cincinnati Art Museum; Mr. and Mrs. Harry S. Leyman Endowment (1972.459)

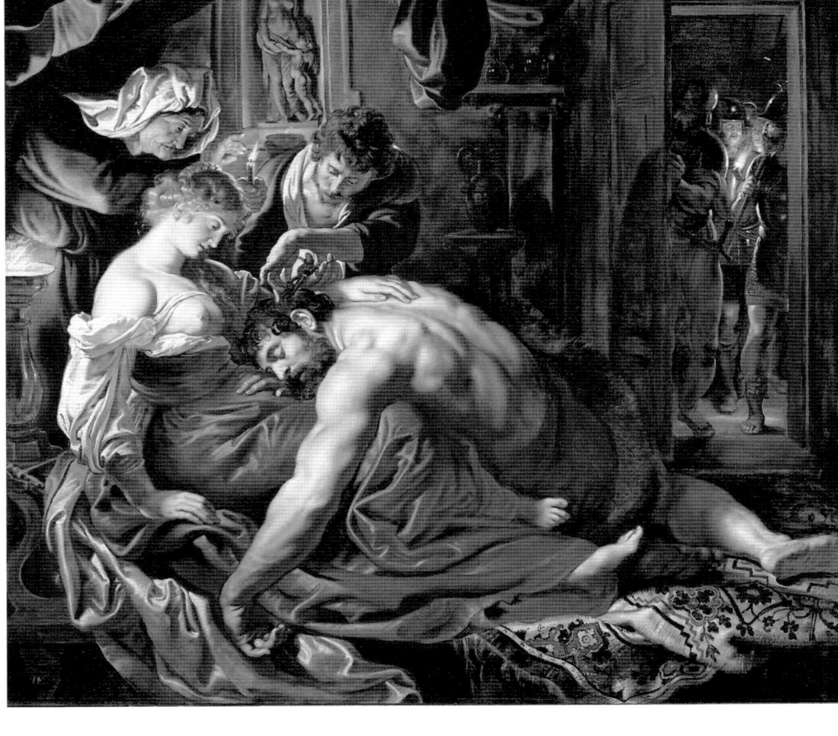

Fig. 69. Peter Paul Rubens, *Samson and Delilah,* ca. 1609–11. Oil on panel, 185 x 205 cm (72 13/16 x 80 11/16 in.). National Gallery, London (NG 6461)

This progression from drawing to oil sketch to finished painting provides one of the earliest and clearest examples of Rubens's working procedure. From his *primi pensieri,* or first thoughts, on paper, most often sketched in pen and brown ink, he proceeded to a more detailed *modello* painted in oil on panel to be shown to the patron, before starting on the final work. In this instance, we know the identity of a very early owner of the painting: Nicolaas Rockox (1560–1640), a former mayor of Antwerp, who became a friend and important patron of the artist. *Samson and Delilah,* now in London, hung in the large parlor room (de groote Saleth) of the Rockox house on the Keizerstraat. Frans Francken II (1582–1642) depicted it in his painting *Banquet at the House of Burgomaster Rockox,* where it appears prominently over the mantelpiece (fig. 70).[3]

Jacob Matham (1571–1631), the stepson and student of the artist and printmaker Hendrick Goltzius, engraved Rubens's

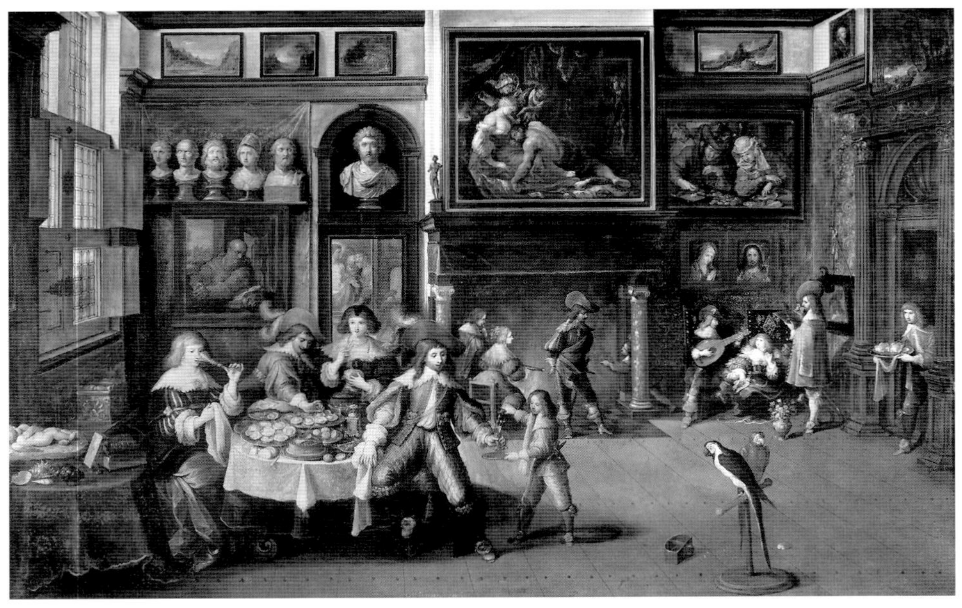

Fig. 70. Frans Francken II, *Banquet at the House of Burgomaster Rockox,* ca. 1630–35. Oil on panel, 62.3 x 96.5 cm (24½ x 38 in.). Bayerische Staatsgemäldesammlungen, Alte Pinakothek, Munich (858)

Samson and Delilah in reverse, perhaps as early as 1611.[4] He based his engraving on the Cincinnati oil sketch rather than the painting in London. It is the only print Matham produced after a Rubens composition and is among the earliest known reproductive prints after Rubens. Matham—rather than Rubens—published the engraving and added the dedication to Nicolaas Rockox, which mentions that Rockox owned the original.

The painting and this preliminary drawing have traditionally been dated to the period immediately following Rubens's return to Antwerp, that is, after about 1609.[5] Here, we accept David Jaffé's suggestion that the painting—and implicitly the drawing—might date as late as 1611, since an impression of Matham's *Samson and Delilah* in the British Museum, London, bears the date 1611. Thus we date the present sheet about 1609–11.

The pen sketches on the verso are indistinct and thus are not illustrated here.

1. Held 1980, no. 312, pl. 309, first half of 1609; M. Jaffé 1989, no. 89, ca. 1609.
2. M. Jaffé 1989, no. 90, ca. 1609.
3. Inv. 858; Renger and Denk 2002, p. 202, no. 858, ca. 1630–35. See also De Staelen 2004, pp. 367–69.
4. Hollstein 1949–, vol. 11, p. 216, no. 11.
5. This dating was roughly corroborated by a recent dendrochronological analysis at the National Gallery, London, which established that one of the planks of the *Samson and Delilah* has the same felling date, 1600, as a plank in Rubens's 1610 *Raising of the Cross* in Antwerp Cathedral. D. Jaffé 2000, pp. 22–23.

29. *Susanna,* recto; *David and Goliath,* verso, ca. 1610–12

Pen and brush and brown ink and brown wash, recto; pen and brown ink, verso, 219 x 159 mm (8⅝ x 6¼ in.)
Annotated by Xavier Atger in pen and brown ink on recto at bottom left: *Rubens fecit;* in pen and black ink at bottom center: *=Susanna au bain=;* by another hand in pen and brown ink at bottom right: *P. P Rubens* (partly covered by mount)
Annotated perhaps by Xavier Atger in pen and brown ink on verso at bottom center: *David et G[olia]t[h];* in pencil at bottom right: *P P Rubens fecit;* in black chalk (?) at top left: *80;* at top right: *30;* in pencil (?) at bottom left: *2½*

Musée Atger, Montpellier (MA 245)

PROVENANCE: Xavier Atger, Paris (1758–1833); gift to the Medicine Faculty, Montpellier, in 1829; 1907, Musée Atger; museum mark (Lugt 38).

LITERATURE: Held 1959, no. 20, pl. 17, and pp. 67–68 (recto), no. 26, pl. 28, under nos. 25, 29, and p. 69 (verso); Burchard and d'Hulst 1963, no. 70, pl. 70, and under no. 71 (recto and verso); Kuznetsov 1974, pl. 34 (recto), pl. 40 (verso); Held 1986, no. 52, pl. 52 (recto), no. 63, pl. 62 (verso); d'Hulst and Vandenven 1989, no. 59a, fig. 154 (recto), no. 37, fig. 84 (verso); Nicq 1996, p. 10, no. MA 245 (recto and verso).

EXHIBITION: Montpellier 1997, nos. 80 (verso), 81 (recto), ill.

Of the various figures of Susanna that Rubens painted or drew, this is by far the most dramatic. With a dynamic, sweeping gesture, the naked Susanna grasps a large cloth in an attempt to shield herself from the view of the elders and frantically tries to escape their grasp. (For the story of Susanna and the elders, see the discussion under catalogue number 25.) One outstretched arm of an elder—and perhaps two faces—can be seen at the extreme left of the drawing. Rubens first quickly drew the figure of Susanna in pen. He then went over her form with a brush and brown ink and added the landscape with a waterfall at the right. A pentimento of the left leg, stretching farther to the left, is visible.

The drawing may reflect an early idea for Rubens's *Susanna and the Elders* of about 1610, now in the Real Academia de Bellas Artes de San Fernando, Madrid.[1] The expansive gesture and the active pose of Susanna, although toned down, are repeated in the painting, albeit in reverse. Another more or less similar figure is found in a *Susanna and the Elders* painted by Rubens about 1609 (fig. 71),[2] indicating that the artist was preoccupied with this type for several years. It is possible that Rubens received commissions for these various Susanna paintings shortly after his return to Antwerp from Italy in late 1608.

The verso of the drawing represents *David and Goliath.* The rapid pen sketch in the center shows David pinning the prostrate Goliath between his legs. David holds the sword with both hands above his right shoulder, ready to strike. At the upper right, Rubens drew the figure of David once more: this time David extends his arms above his head in order to deliver an even more ferocious blow. Rubens adapted the latter figure for the man swinging a baby above his head in a recently rediscovered early masterpiece of the *Massacre of the Innocents,* now in a private collection.[3] This muscular, dynamic figure appears regularly in Rubens's works of 1609–12, almost like a signature.

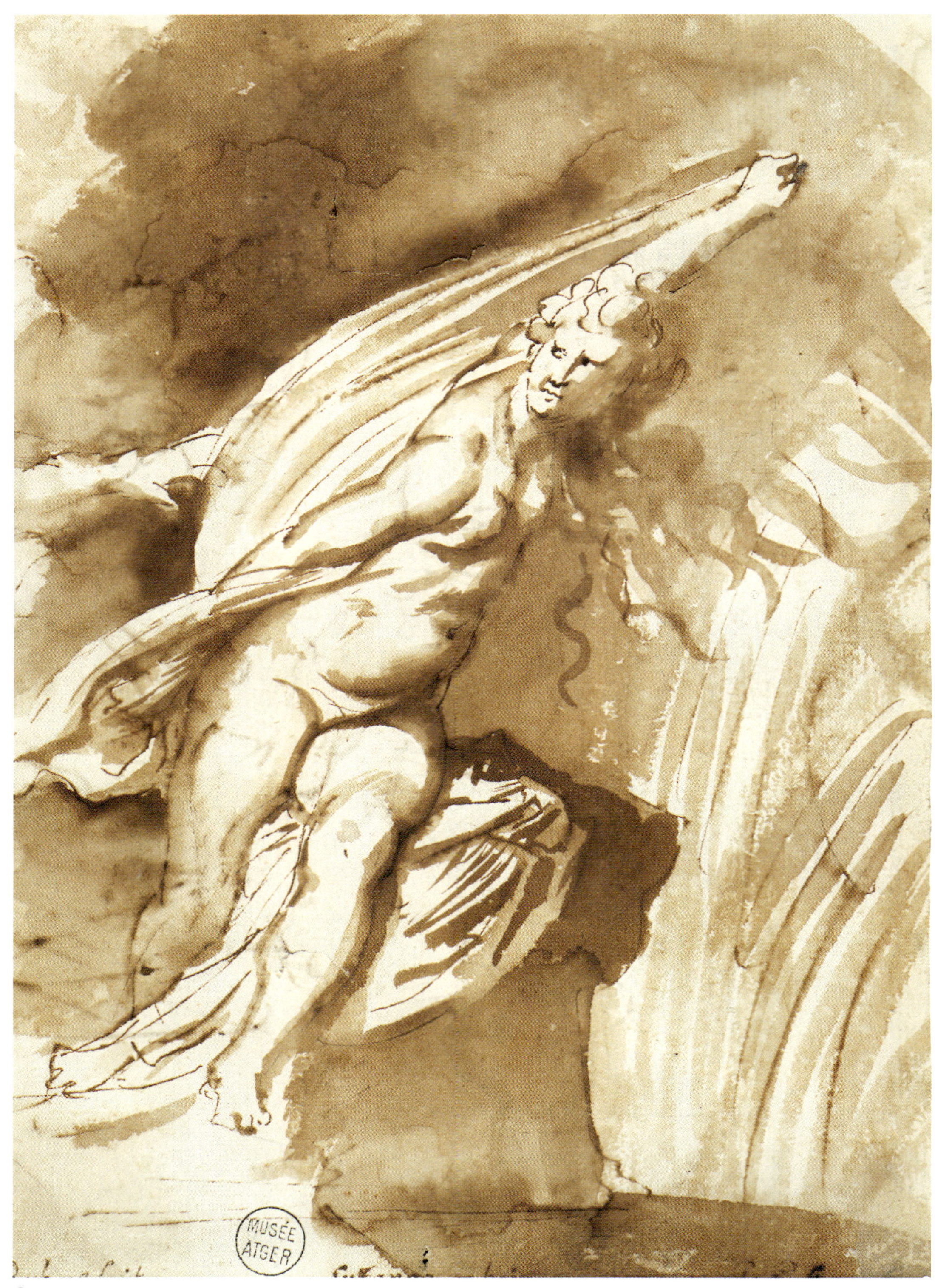

Cat. 29 recto

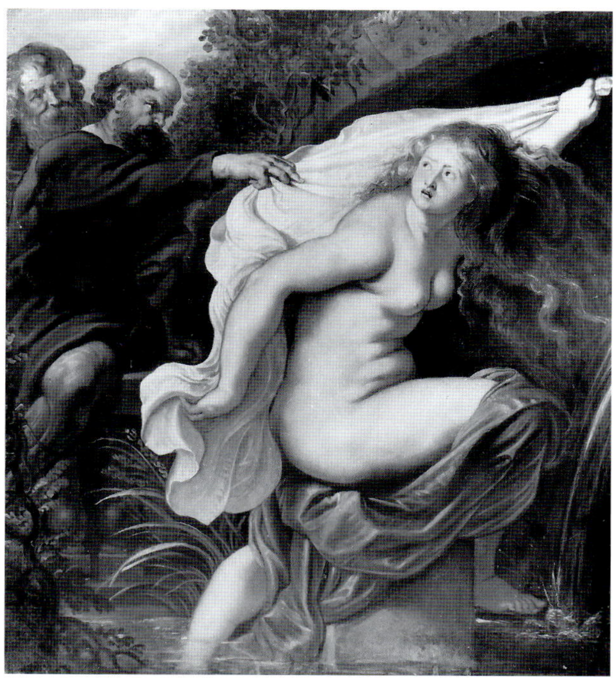

Fig. 71. Peter Paul Rubens, *Susanna and the Elders*, ca. 1609. Oil on panel, 123 x 108 cm (48 7/16 x 42 1/2 in.). The State Hermitage Museum, Saint Petersburg (7080)

The Philistine cutting off Samson's hair in a drawing of *Samson and Delilah* (cat. no. 28 recto) is of the same type.

The *David and Goliath* drawing relates to another, somewhat more elaborate study in Rotterdam, which is the same size and also drawn in pen and brown ink.[4] The two drawings likely date from the same time. On the Rotterdam sheet Rubens depicted a slightly later moment in the story, when David, grabbing Goliath by the hair to keep his head up, decapitates the giant. Despite Rubens's obvious interest in the subject, no corresponding painting is known. A date of about 1610–12 for the present drawing, both recto and verso, seems likely.

1. K.d.K., ed. Oldenbourg 1921, p. 32; M. Jaffé 1989, no. 112, 1609–10.
2. M. Jaffé 1989, no. 101, ca. 1609; according to d'Hulst and Vandenven (1989, p. 206, under no. 60), the painting is a copy.
3. M. Jaffé 1989, under no. 114, 1609–10; D. Jaffé (2003, p. 3, fig. 1) dated the painting ca. 1611–12.
4. Inv. V 41, pen and brown ink, 219 x 160 mm; Rotterdam 2001, no. 13, ill. in color.

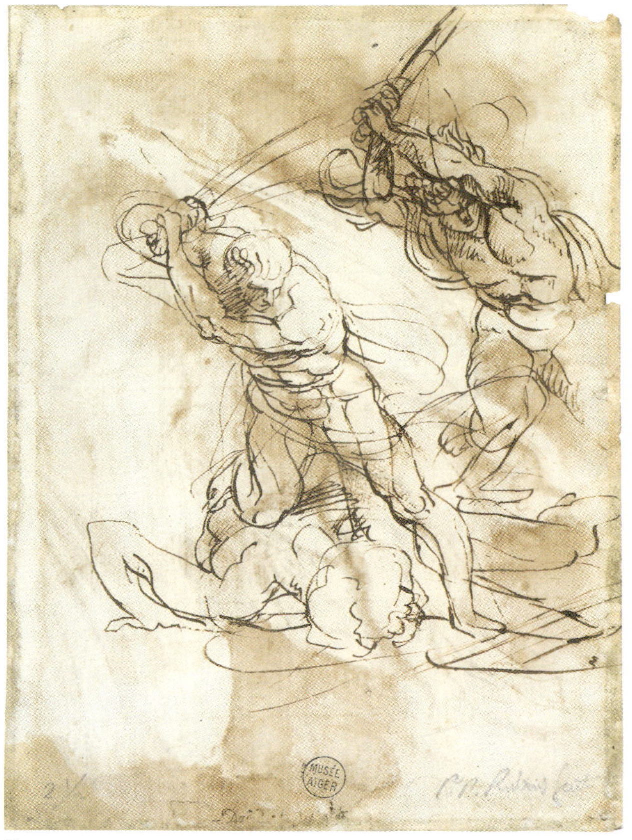

Cat. 29 verso

30. *The Presentation in the Temple,* recto, March–September 1611; *Study of Man's Leg and Elbow,* verso, 1601–2

Pen and brown ink and brown wash on pale tan paper, recto; black chalk and touches of brush and grayish brown wash, verso, 214 x 142 mm (8⁷⁄₁₆ x 5⁹⁄₁₆ in.)

The Metropolitan Museum of Art, New York; Gift of Mr. and Mrs. Janos Scholz, 1952 (52.214.3)

PROVENANCE: Mr. and Mrs. Janos Scholz, New York.

LITERATURE: Held 1959, no. 28 (left), pl. 34 and fig. 50, under nos. 27, 70, and pp. 24, 69–70, 130; Burchard and d'Hulst 1963, under nos. 55, 60, 61; Held 1986, no. 72 (left),, pl. 73; Judson 2000, under no. 20g, fig. 70, no. 45b, fig. 154.

EXHIBITIONS: Cambridge, Mass.–New York 1956, no. 11, pl. 7; Antwerp 1977, no. 136, ill.; Wellesley–Cleveland 1993–94, no. 43, ill.

While Rubens was finishing the *Raising of the Cross* altarpiece (fig. 87, cat. nos. 37–40) for the church of Saint Walburga in Antwerp, he was approached in March 1611 by the Arquebusiers' (Crossbowmen's) Guild for a *Descent from the Cross* triptych to grace the altar in its chapel in Antwerp Cathedral.[1] His friend Nicolaas Rockox, president of the guild and a former mayor of Antwerp, was probably instrumental in securing this important commission. (Rubens portrayed Rockox among the faithful on the inner right wing of the completed altarpiece.) The contract was signed on September 7, 1611. A year later the central section of the three-panel altarpiece was ready. The wings, however, were not delivered to the cathedral until February and March 1614. The altar was dedicated on July 22, 1614 (fig. 93).[2]

The unity of Rubens's *Descent from the Cross* altarpiece is derived from the name of the Arquebusiers' patron saint, Christopher—from Christophorus, meaning "bearer of Christ" (according to legend, Christopher carried the Christ Child on his back across a river). This idea of the physical support of Christ is clearly expressed in the central panel, the *Descent from the Cross,* in the way that Christ is gently lowered and held, most notably, by Saint John; in the *Visitation* scene (the left panel) with the Virgin Mary carrying Christ in her womb; and in the *Presentation in the Temple* scene (the right panel) with Simeon holding the swaddled Child in his arms.

It is surprising that only four drawings related to this elaborate triptych seem to have survived: a sheet of studies of heads and hands in the Albertina (cat. no. 44) and one sheet each in the Musée Bonnat, Bayonne;[3] the Metropolitan Museum, New York (the present drawing); and the Courtauld Institute of Art Gallery, London.[4] However, the last three sheets, all with drawings on both recto and verso, originally formed one large sheet that was cut at an unknown date: on the recto were studies for

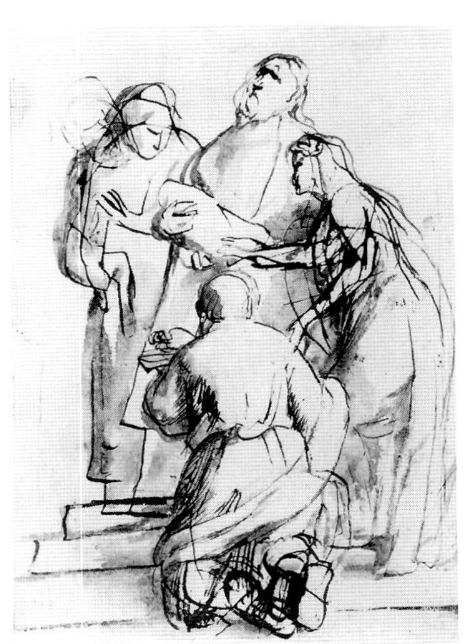

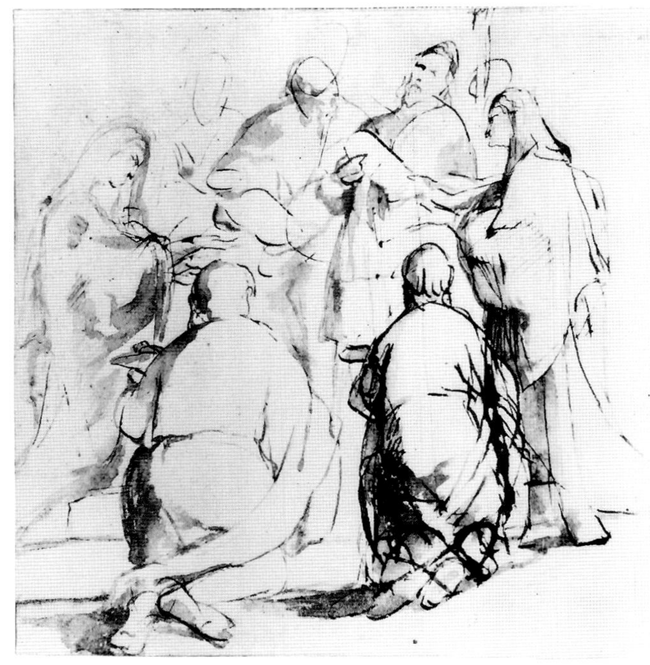

Fig. 72. Peter Paul Rubens, *Studies for the Presentation in the Temple* (reconstruction), 1611. Left: cat. no. 30 recto. Right: pen and brown ink and brown wash, 242 x 238 mm (9½ x 9⅜ in.). Courtauld Institute of Art Gallery, London; bequeathed by Count Seilern as part of the Princes Gate Collection (D 1978.PG.60 recto)

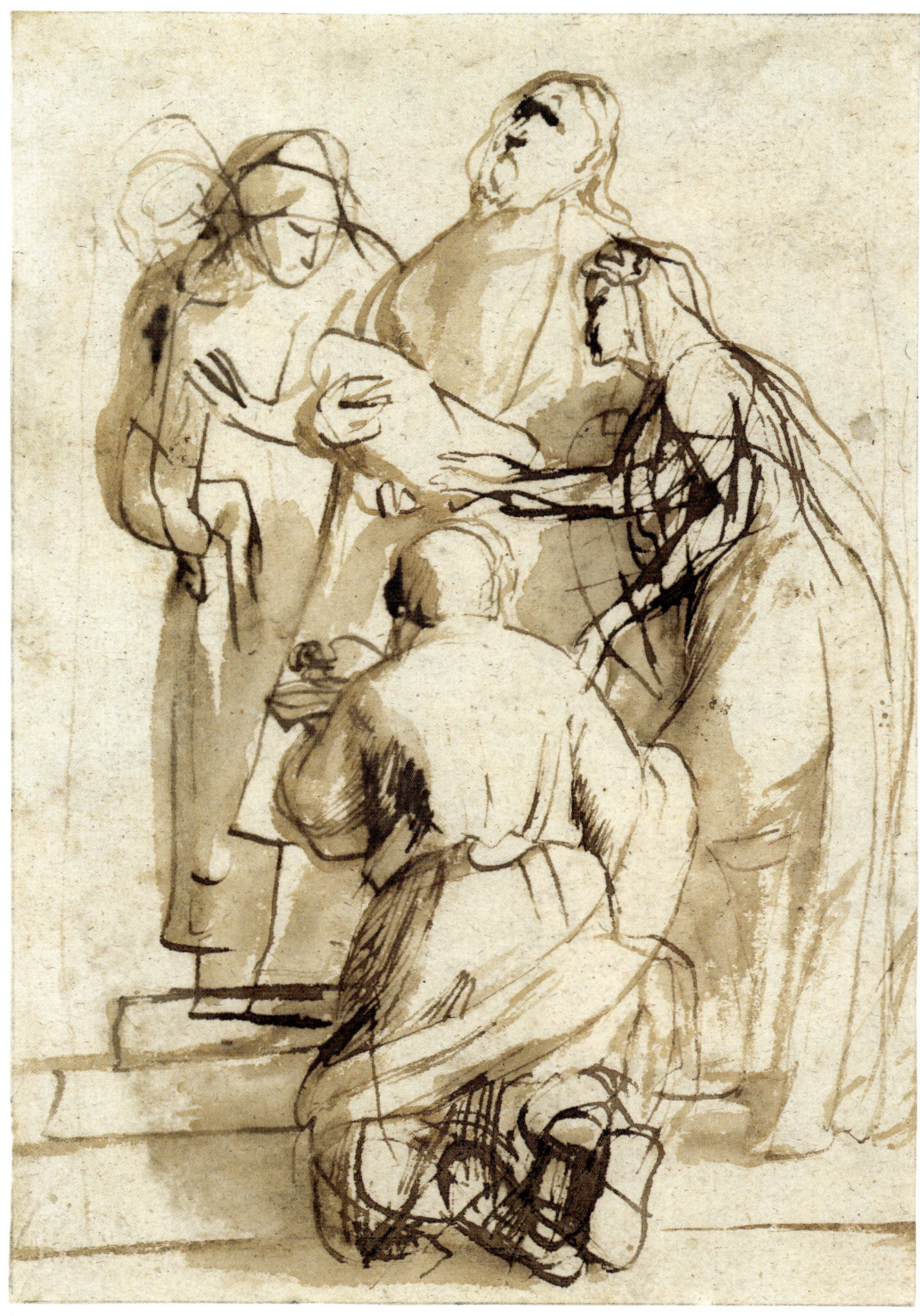

Cat. 30 recto

the *Descent from the Cross* altarpiece—for the *Visitation* (fig. 6) and the *Presentation in the Temple* (cat. no. 30 recto, fig. 72); on the verso were studies of a man holding the shaft of the Cross (cat. no. 30 verso, fig. 16), made by Rubens in connection with an earlier altarpiece (see below). Consequently, there are actually only *two* surviving studies by Rubens for the *Descent from the Cross* altarpiece, which contains well over twenty-five figures. Rubens likely made many more preliminary drawings.

The small study on the recto of the Metropolitan sheet is a preliminary drawing for the lifesize figures in the *Presentation in the Temple,* on the inner right wing of the *Descent from the Cross* altarpiece. The reduction in the number of figures to the Virgin, Joseph, Simeon, and Hannah, grouped around the Child, may be an evolution from the pen sketch on the

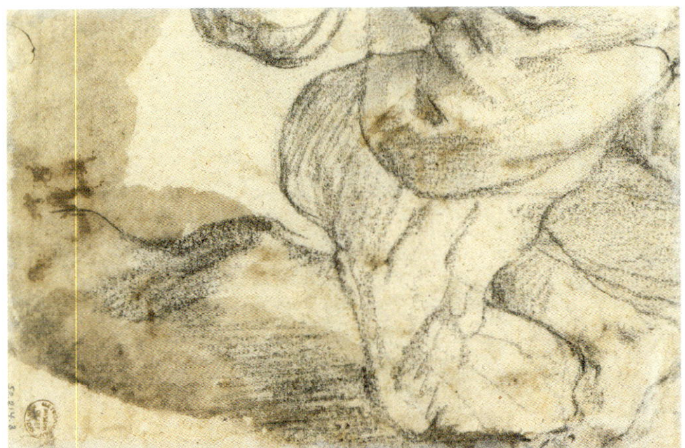

Cat. 30 verso

fragment in London (fig. 72, right), reflecting a change in the altar's dimensions.[5] Here, Rubens was primarily trying to establish the proper interaction of the principal figures. In a mixture of pen and wash, he created a group closely arranged around the prophet Simeon, who holds the swaddled newborn. The Virgin Mary leans forward, extending her right arm toward the Child and touching Him, while her left hand rests lightly on Joseph's shoulder, thus clearly including him in the company. Joseph, kneeling in front, turns slightly to the left, which allows the viewer to see that he is carrying a dove. This is a composition in progress, however, for Rubens made several noticeable alterations: he adjusted the inclination of the head of the prophetess Hannah at the left, the placement of Joseph's feet, and the gestures of the Virgin. In the subsequent oil sketch (fig. 94)[6] and in the final altar wing (fig. 93), Rubens depicted the Virgin standing at the right next to Joseph, who presents two doves. Simeon, holding the Christ Child, has been turned to face the Virgin diagonally in front of him, while Hannah has been moved between them in the background. The Virgin no longer touches Joseph but extends both arms and hands toward the Child, expressing her fear of handing Him to Simeon.

On the verso of the Metropolitan sheet, the leg and elbow of a man, drawn in black chalk, are illegible without the adjoining section in London; placed together, the two fragments reveal a man holding a thick shaft. The remaining section in Bayonne completes the very large sheet that, reconstructed, reveals two studies of a man bearing down on a long pole or wooden shaft (fig. 16). Rubens most likely drew them over two pages of an open sketchbook. Losses in the center of the reconstructed sheet probably occurred when these pages were torn out. These were, in all likelihood, Rubens's preliminary drawings for the man bearing down on the shaft of the Cross in his *Raising of the Cross* for the church of Santa Croce in Gerusalemme, Rome, painted in late 1601 or early 1602.[7] This altarpiece has not survived, but it is known through a copy in Grasse Cathedral.[8]

It is illuminating to compare these black-chalk figure studies with those Rubens drew almost ten years later for the Antwerp *Raising of the Cross* altarpiece (cat. nos. 37–39). The two-dimensional and angular figures here are replaced in the later drawings with lifelike ones, with bulging muscles that suggest the strain of lifting the Cross; instead of flat, uniform hatching to indicate volume, curved lines follow the forms of the figures, making them appear more realistic. The handling of the black chalk on the versos of the fragments in Bayonne, London, and New York is much closer to that of another early black-chalk drawing, the 1604 *Study for a Halberdier* (cat. no. 15).

The disparity in date between the recto and the verso of the sheet is in keeping with the artist's working habits. Throughout his career Rubens returned to earlier drawings that he preserved for reuse when appropriate. He was also careful not to waste paper, which was expensive, and in all likelihood he used the other side of his drawings for related subjects. Since Rubens painted the *Raising of the Cross* and the *Descent from the Cross* within a relatively short time span, he may have filed the drawings close together.

1. K.d.K., ed. Oldenbourg 1921, no. 52; M. Jaffé 1989, no. 189a–e, 1612 for the *Descent from the Cross,* 1614 for the wings.
2. For the relevant documents in the city archive in Antwerp, see R., vol. 2, pp. 114–16, and Nieuwenhuizen 1962, pp. 27–33.
3. Inv. 1438; 265 x 360 mm; Held 1986, no. 71, pl. 72.
4. Inv. PG 60; 242 x 238 mm; ibid., no. 72 right, pl. 73.
5. Rubens drew the Bayonne and Courtauld studies for the *Visitation* and the *Presentation in the Temple* in a horizontal format rather than in the narrow, vertical format of the Metropolitan's study and the final wing of the triptych, a disparity that prompted Held (1980, p. 493, under no. 358, and p. 446, under no. 320) to argue that the dimensions of the altar may have been changed after its commissioning, and that Rubens may have followed these studies in pen with an oil sketch, now lost, in a more horizontal format.
6. Held 1980, no. 358, pl. 354, ca. 1612–13; M. Jaffé 1989, no. 137, 1612–13.
7. First proposed by Evers (1943, p. 137, fig. 10) and supported here. Judson (2000, no. 45b) dated the drawing to about 1610–11, thus associating it with Rubens's *Raising of the Cross* in Antwerp Cathedral—a highly unlikely proposition.
8. K.d.K., ed. Oldenbourg 1921, no. 2, right; M. Jaffé 1989, no. 19a. See Maeyer 1953, pp. 75–83. For additional information on this copy, see Von zur Mühlen 2001, pp. 105–35.

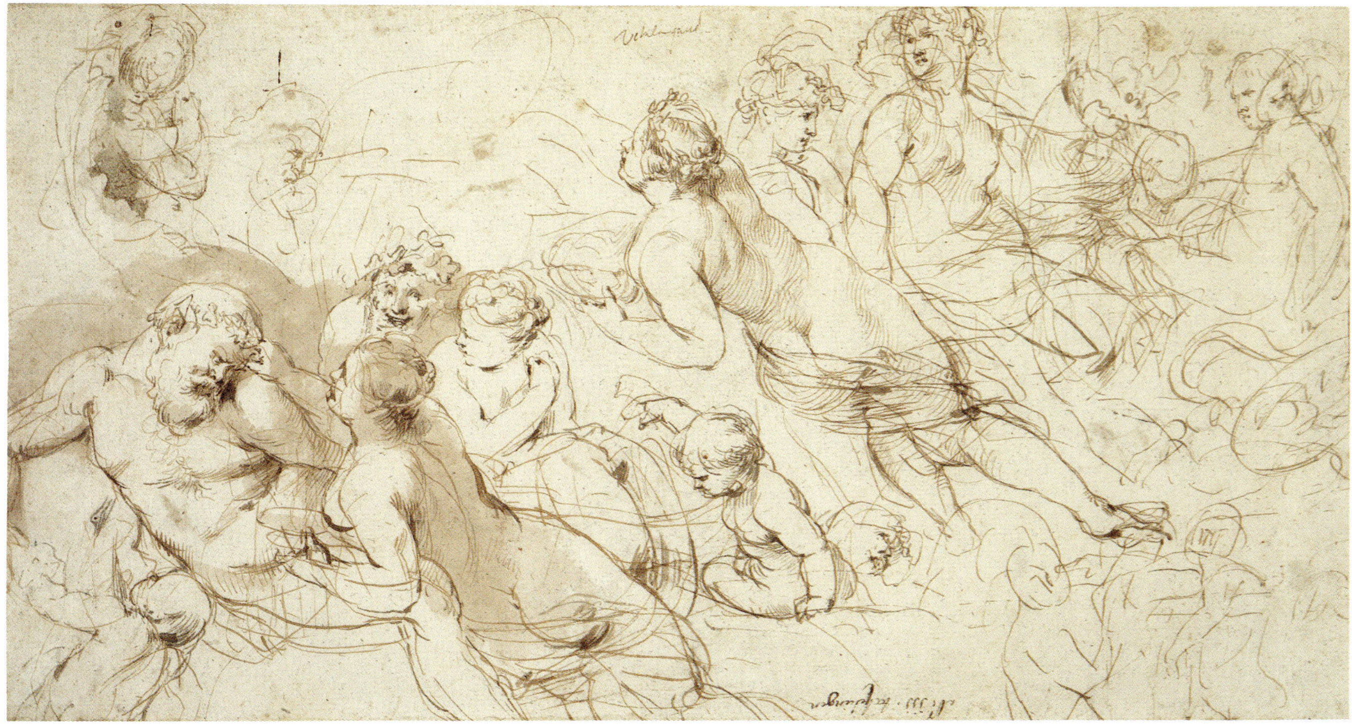

Cat. 31 recto

31. *Studies for Silenus and Aegle,* recto; *Various Studies,* verso, ca. 1612–14

Pen and light and dark brown ink and brown wash, recto; pen and grayish brown ink and gray wash, verso, 281 x 508 mm (11⅙ x 20 in.)
Inscribed by the artist in pen and brown ink at top center: *Vi[e]tula gaud[ium]* (Vitula, goddess of joy)
Annotated in pen and brown ink along bottom edge, upside down: *No jjj—tekeningen.*

Lent by Her Majesty Queen Elizabeth II, Royal Library, Windsor Castle (6417)

PROVENANCE: George III of England (1738–1820), London (inventory A, p. 105: "Of Rubens . . . Silenus and Bacchanalian Women").

LITERATURE: Glück and Haberditzl 1928, no. 188, pl. 188 (recto); Held 1959, no. 29, pl. 30 (recto) and pp. 21, 22, 45, 70; Burchard and d'Hulst 1963, no. 51, pl. 51; Kuznetsov 1974, pl. 25; Balis 1986, no. 2a, fig. 38; Held 1986, nos. 81, 82, pls. 77, 78 (recto and verso); White 1987, pp. 35, 237, pl. 55; White and Crawley 1994, no. 435, ill. (recto and verso); Alpers 1995, pp. 101–57, pl. 112; McGrath 1997, p. 19, under no. 2.

EXHIBITIONS: London 1977a, no. 58, ill. (recto and verso); Montreal–Raleigh–Indianapolis 1994–95, no. 23, ill.; London 2002–3, no. 360, ill.

In this highly dynamic drawing, Rubens spontaneously put down ideas as they flowed from his pen. Although resembling a compositional drawing, the design on the recto remains open-ended, with figures filling the entire sheet. Rubens depicted a scene from the story of Silenus and the beautiful naiad Aegle, as described by Virgil in his sixth *Eclogue* (lines 21–24): the nymphs Chromis and Mnasyllos come upon the drunken Silenus asleep and tie him up with his own garlands; when Aegle stains Silenus's forehead with crimson mulberries, he awakens and promises a song to the nymphs, and another reward to the lovely naiad, in return for his release. Here, Rubens drew Aegle staining Silenus's brow, while a small boy at the lower left ties up Silenus's hands and another child assists at the lower center. The repetition of the figures across the page anticipates Rubens's somewhat later pen sketches of reclining female nudes: the *Three Studies for Venus (?)* in the Courtauld Institute of Art Gallery, London, and the *Studies for a Last Judgment* in the Frick Collection, New York.[1]

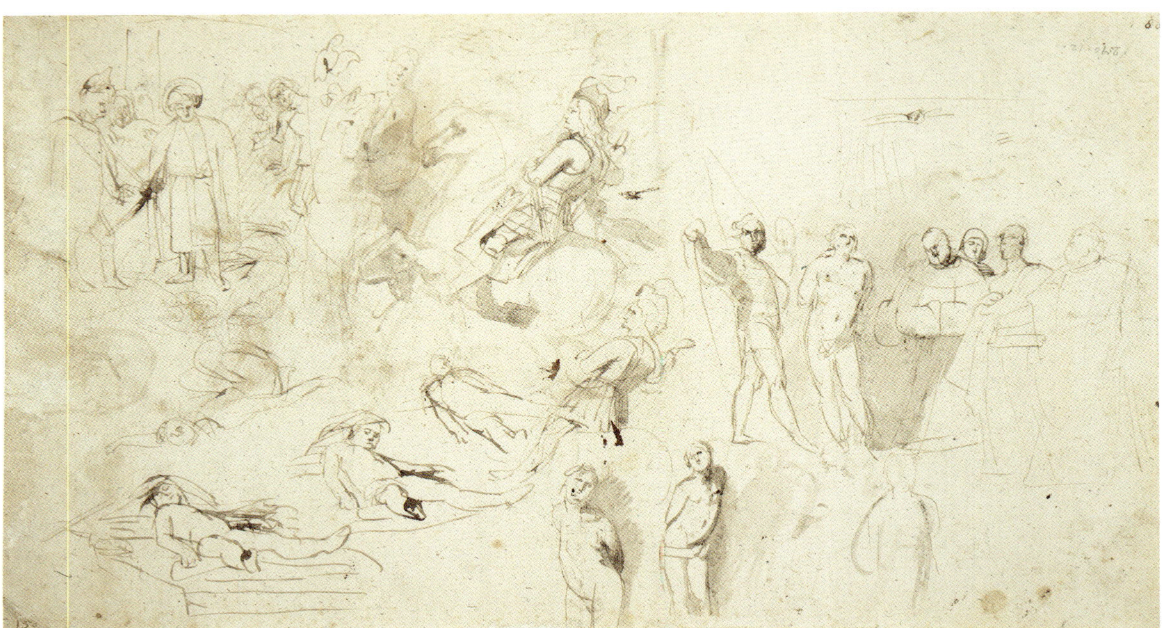

Cat. 31 verso

Rubens filled the recto of the Windsor sheet with three variations of Aegle administering to Silenus, probably beginning at the top right. There, the naiad's head and extended arm are readily visible, but her body lies underneath further, superimposed sketches. Next, the artist may have drawn the group at the lower left, where the interplay of the two protagonists is the most developed, and the slumbering Silenus is fully recognizable. (A detail of his head appears above.) A laughing satyr and a nymph witness the awakening. Here, Rubens added a thin layer of brown wash to unify the group of figures and enhance the drawing's painterly aspect. Aegle is best developed in the center, where she holds a bowl with the berries in her left hand while staining Silenus's forehead with her right; he is barely indicated with faint angular outlines above her to the left of center. Lightly drawn figures are also found at the upper left, in the center, and at the lower right of the sheet.

The drawing on the recto relates somewhat loosely to the *Bacchanal,* a painting in the Akademie der Bildenden Künste, Vienna, of about 1612–13.[2] The drawing may date from approximately the same time, about 1612–14.

Scholars have transcribed Rubens's inscription at the top center differently.[3] The latest and most plausible transcription is "Vitula [gaudium]."[4] Although not directly related to the Silenus and Aegle theme, it points to a possible source of inspiration for Rubens: Pontanus's highly popular commentary on Virgil, *Symbolarum Libri XVII Virgilii* (1599). Rubens's "Vitula gaudium" may be a reference to Vitulina, whom Pontanus describes in his book as the goddess of joy.

The drawing was lifted from its mount in 1977, on the occasion of the exhibition "Rubens: Drawings and Sketches" organized at the British Museum by John Rowlands. The verso revealed numerous figure studies in pen and ink with some wash arranged into at least four groups. Among the recognizable scenes is that at the upper left showing a turbaned man, sword in hand, standing by a decapitated figure, reminiscent of Rubens's composition of *Tomyris with the Head of Cyrus* known from both the painting in Boston (fig. 101)[5] and a drawing in a private collection (cat. no. 55). The two riders on horseback accompanied by a woman riding sidesaddle recall hunters riding armorless in Rubens's *Wolf and Fox Hunt* in the Metropolitan Museum.[6]

1. Held 1986, nos. 137, 138, 139, pls. 136–138, ca. 1618–20.
2. K.d.K., ed. Oldenbourg 1921, no. 41; M. Jaffé 1989, no. 190, ca. 1612–13.
3. Van Puyvelde (1942, no. 280) read it as "Vetula Gaud[i]a," while Evers (1943, pp. 228–30) and Held (1959, no. 29, and 1986, nos. 81, 82) read it as "Vetula gaudens," meaning an "amused old woman," although no such figure was included on the recto of the sheet.
4. As suggested by Elizabeth McGrath, quoted in Alpers 1995, p. 142.
5. K.d.K., ed. Oldenbourg 1921, no. 175; M. Jaffé 1989, no. 510, ca. 1618–19.
6. Inv. 10.37; K.d.K., ed. Oldenbourg 1921, no. 112; M. Jaffé 1989, no. 345, 1615–16.

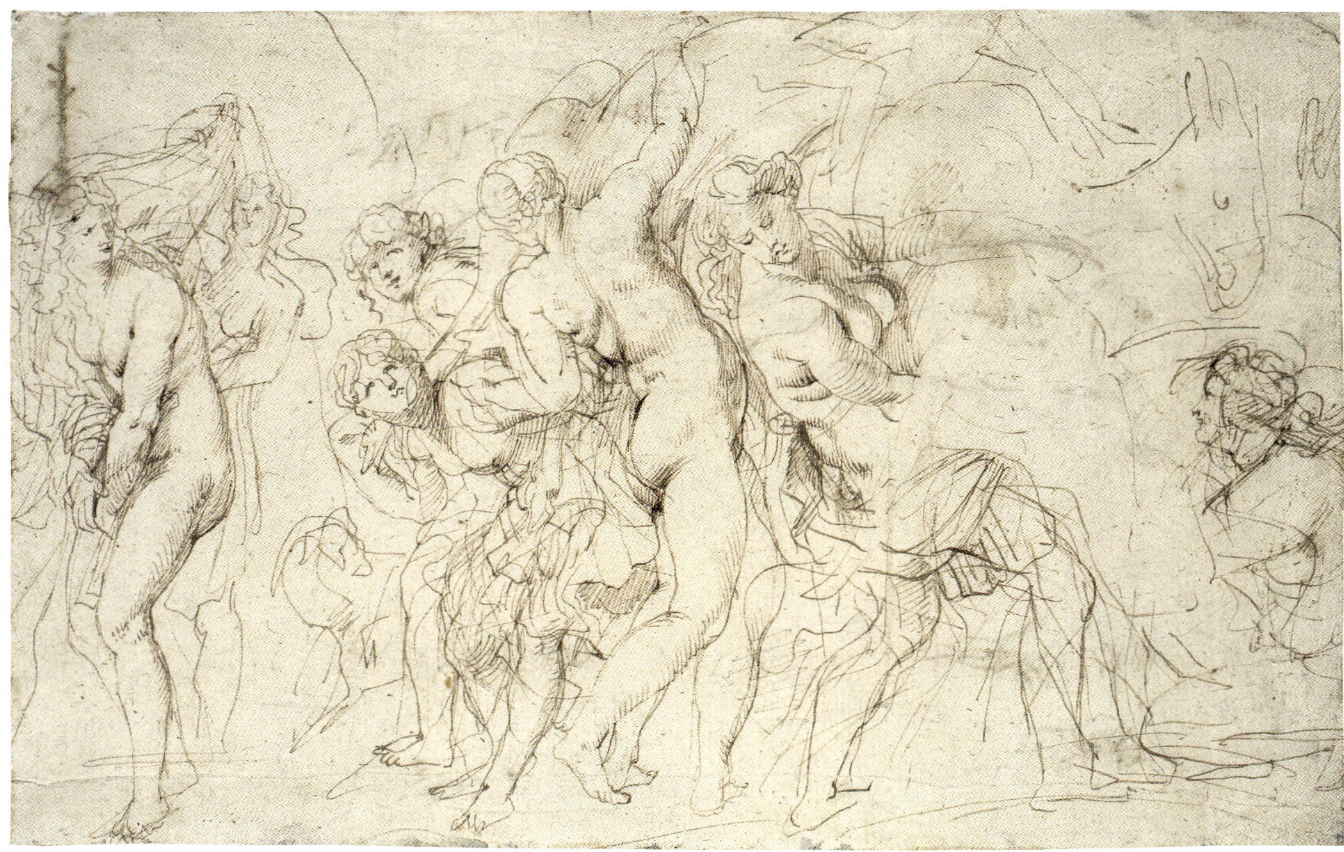

Cat. 32 recto

32. *Diana with Nymphs Unloading Deer from a Donkey,* recto; *Four Studies for Diana,* verso, ca. 1612–15

Pen and brown ink, 177 x 271 mm (7 x 10¹¹⁄₁₆ in.)

Inscribed by the artist (?) in pen and brown ink on verso at top right: *da S.Altessa (?) La S Altezza*

Rijksmuseum, Amsterdam (RP-T-1966-67)

PROVENANCE: P. Collin; Sir W. W. Krighton; J. P. Heseltine (1843–1929), London (sale, London, Sotheby, May 27, 1935, no. 192); W. Mertens, Leipzig; C. G. Boerner, Düsseldorf.

LITERATURE: Boon 1966, pp. 150–57, figs. 1, 2; Müller Hofstede 1968b, pp. 212–15 and n. 27, figs. 9, 11; Held 1976, pp. 34–46, figs. 6, 7.

EXHIBITION: Kassel–Frankfurt 2004, no. 17, ill.

The recto, full of changes and pentimenti, shows Rubens exploring possible solutions for an oil sketch or painting of Diana with nymphs unloading dead game from a donkey. Rubens quickly jotted down the female figures before adding fine cross-hatching to model their bodies. The donkey in the background and the large deer on its back are only vaguely indicated. On the verso Rubens drew four studies of Diana, naked and clothed.[1] In their pose, the nudes on the verso and the nude at the extreme left of the recto are reminiscent of two celebrated antique sculptures of the *Venus Pudica* type, the so-called *Venus Felix* (Musei Vaticani) and the *Venus de' Medici* (Uffizi, Florence).[2] In a passage in the Manuscript de Ganay attributed to Rubens and said to be based on his so-called *Pocket Book* (see cat. no. 10), the artist refers to the *Venus de Medici* as the "single supreme example in every respect for the female form, its standing posture, its beauty and all its refinements."[3] The modest pose certainly suits Diana, who in myth was surprised by the hunter Actaeon as she was bathing naked.

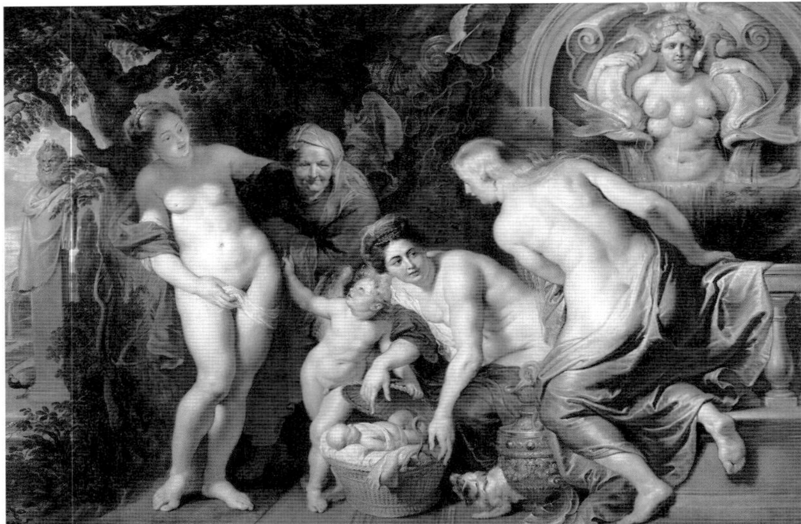

Fig. 73. Peter Paul Rubens, *The Discovery of the Infant Erichthonius*, ca. 1615. Oil on canvas, 217.8 x 317.3 cm (85¾ x 124$^{15}/_{16}$ in.). Sammlungen des Fürsten von und zu Liechtenstein, Vaduz (111)

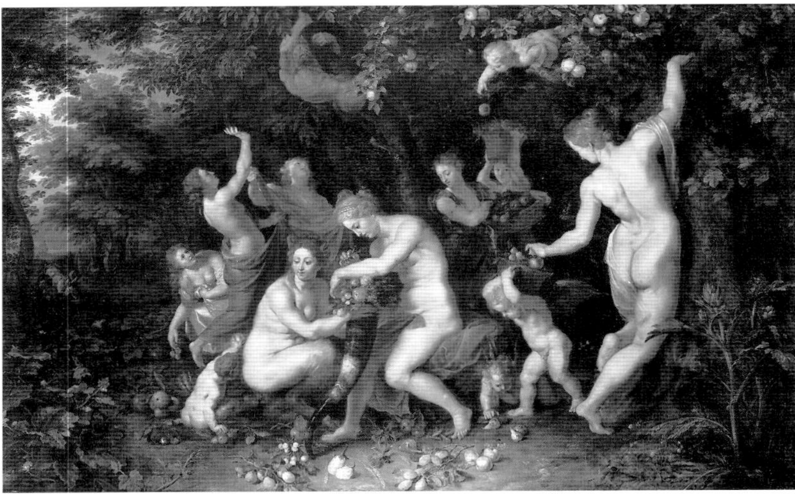

Fig. 74. Jan Brueghel the Elder and Rubens studio, *Naiads Filling the Horns of Plenty*, ca. 1612–15. Oil on panel, 67.5 x 107 cm (26$^{9}/_{16}$ x 42⅛ in.). Royal Cabinet of Paintings, Mauritshuis, The Hague (234)

On the verso Rubens explored with quick pen sketches whether Diana should cover herself with her right or left hand and whether, if dressed, she should sport a quiver, as shown at the left, or blow a hunter's horn and be surrounded by dogs, which are indicated with rough outlines at the right. The clothed Diana recalls the antique statue *Diane Chasseresse*, today in the Louvre, Paris.[4]

Here, we have a rare opportunity to observe the artist thinking with his pen, so to speak, trying out different poses. Although no painting is known in which the figures appear exactly as in this drawing, Rubens apparently did keep the sheet at hand. For example, he used one of the Diana figures on the verso for the beautiful Herse, one of Cecrops's daughters, in *The Discovery of the Infant Erichthonius* of about 1615 (fig. 73).[5]

The group of nymphs unloading the deer from a donkey, sketched over much of the recto, vaguely corresponds to a Rubens oil sketch formerly in the Kaiser Friedrich Museum in Berlin but lost since World War II.[6] Similar groups of nymphs recur in some pictures representing Diana returning from the hunt painted by Rubens (or an assistant?) and Jan Brueghel the Elder (1568–1625).[7] The nymph in the center of the sheet, gracefully reaching up to remove the dead animal, appears in a similar pose in *Naiads Filling the Horns of Plenty* (fig. 74), a painting of about 1612–15 attributed to Jan Brueghel the Elder and an assistant in the Rubens studio.[8] In this collaborative work, the artists involved were very familiar with Rubens's painting technique, and it is therefore possible that Rubens showed them pen sketches like this one. Because the nymphs unloading game and the Diana figures relate rather closely to paintings created in collaboration with Jan Brueghel, the drawing most likely dates to about 1612–15.[9]

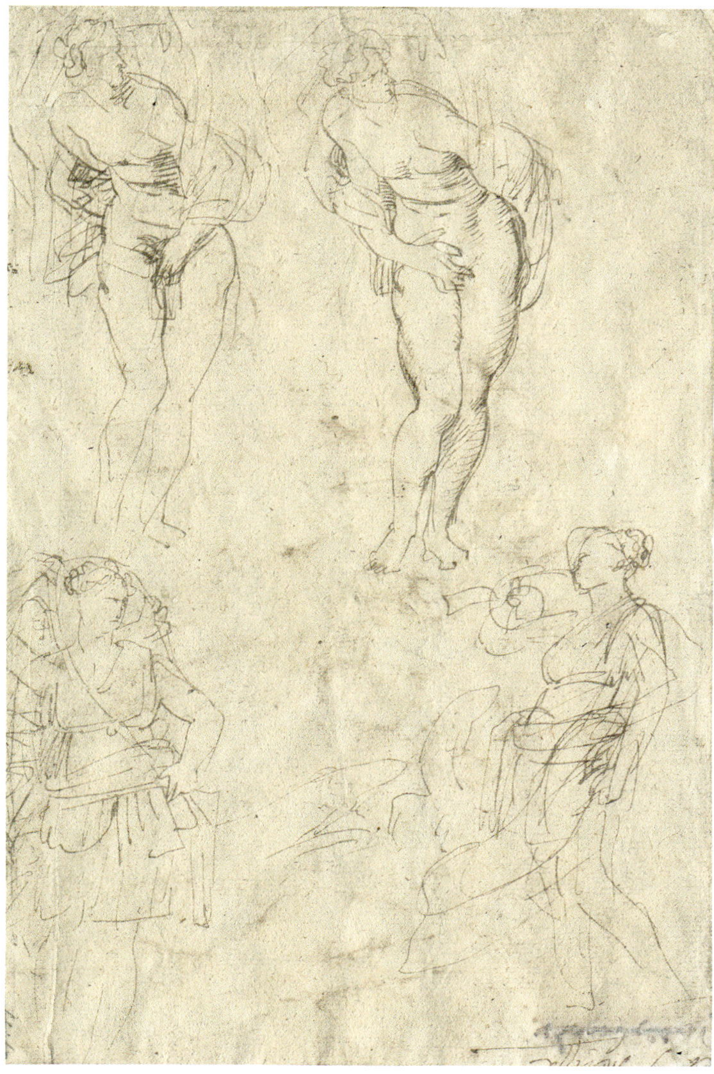

Cat. 32 verso

1. The figure was identified as Diana in Held 1976, pp. 34–46.
2. Haskell and Penny 1981, no. 87, fig. 172 (in the Belvedere Courtyard since 1523), no. 88, fig. 173 (possibly recorded in an inventory of the Villa Medici in 1598).
3. Manuscript de Ganay, fol. 23r, translated from Latin in Van der Meulen 1994, vol. 1, p. 257. For the history of the Manuscript de Ganay, see Balis 2001, p. 35, n. 14.
4. Haskell and Penny 1981, no. 30, fig. 102.
5. K.d.K., ed. Oldenbourg 1921, no. 124, 1615–17; M. Jaffé 1989, no. 320, ca. 1615. The same suggestion was made by Boon (1966).
6. Held 1980, no. 297, pl. 297, ca. 1610.
7. See, for example, *Diana Resting after the Hunt* in the Bayerische Staatsgemäldesammlungen, Munich. Müller Hofstede 1968b, p. 209, fig. 6.
8. See Broos and Wadum 1993, pp. 13–16; Wadum 1996, pp. 393–95; and Wadum 2002, pp. 473–78. The date is based on the marks of the panel maker.
9. Held (1976, p. 43) stressed the importance of the Amsterdam drawing because it documents Rubens planning a *Diana and Actaeon* possibly as a pendant to a *Diana Returning from the Hunt;* however, no such work has come to light. When Boon (1966, figs. 1, 2) first published this double-sided sheet, he associated the recto with a painting that Tobey Matthew, the agent of Sir Dudley Carleton, referred to in a letter of February 25, 1617, as a "Gruppo of dead Birds in a picture of Diana and certaine other naked Nimphes," for which Frans Snyders painted the birds; accordingly, he dated the drawing about 1617. Müller Hofstede (1968, pp. 212–13) identified this painting with a lost work representing *Diana and Her Nymphs Surprised by Satyrs,* known only through a print by J. Louys (reproduced in R., vol. 3, pl. 190). This composition, however, has nothing in common with the Amsterdam drawing.

33. *The Continence of Scipio,* ca. 1616–18

Pen and brown ink on brownish paper, old framing outline, 237 x 343 mm (9⁵⁄₁₆ x 13½ in.)
Annotated in pen and brown ink at bottom right: *9*

Staatliche Museen zu Berlin, Kupferstichkabinett (KdZ 5685)

Provenance: Richard Houlditch (d. 1736), London (Lugt 2214); Sir Joshua Reynolds (1723–1792), London (Lugt 2364); Adolf von Beckerath (1834–1915), Berlin (Lugt 2504)[1]; acquired by the Staatliche Museen in 1902.

Literature: Bock and Rosenberg 1930, p. 251, no. 5685, pl. 182; Held 1959, no. 38, pl. 40, under nos. 39, 102, and pp. 24, 70–71; Held 1986, no. 123, pl. 123; McGrath 1997, no. 49a, fig. 183, and p. 268, under no. 50.

Exhibitions: Berlin 1977, no. 24, ill.; Berlin 2002–3, no. 94, ill.

Rubens based the scene shown in this drawing on Livy's account (*Ab urbe condita* 26.50) of the Roman general Publius Cornelius Scipio Africanus (236–184/183 B.C.). After he captured New Carthage (today's Cartagena, Spain) in 209 B.C., Scipio magnanimously returned a beautiful female prisoner, her virtue unharmed, to her rightful groom, Allucius. Rubens rendered the humble young woman kneeling before Scipio, flanked by her parents and Allucius, who approaches from the left. Allucius holds his bride's right hand in a sign of betrothal, while the mother gently embraces her daughter.

The Musée Bonnat, in Bayonne, owns a similar study, although the composition is in reverse (fig. 75).[2] In both drawings, Rubens depicted Scipio seated on a throne and gesturing toward the gifts offered by the bride's parents as ransom, indicating his wish to return them, thus exemplifying liberality. Both are typical of Rubens's compositional studies executed in preparation for paintings. The scene in the Berlin drawing is less worked out, however, and shows more experimentation. The figures at the far left are barely intelligible, while the couple with their clasped hands and the surrounding figures are more carefully studied. All but one of the figures look toward the Roman general in anticipation of his decision.

Although this is a hastily drawn, initial study, Rubens had already visualized the principal actors clearly, fixing them on paper in long strokes with a rather fine pen. Even at this early stage, he differentiated between the various emotions expressed in the faces and gestures of the individuals. In the Bayonne version, Rubens gave the newly betrothed more prominence by placing them on the same dais as Scipio. The general's gesture toward Allucius is now easily understood as a sign not to proceed further but to stay with his bride. Instead of pleading, the bride's parents now express deep gratitude. Rubens thus chose a slightly later moment, after Scipio had displayed his continence and magnanimity.

Rubens did not use either of these two studies for his 1618–19 painting of the *Continence of Scipio,* which is lost but known from a related oil sketch (fig. 76) and two prints.[3] Given the stylistic evidence, the drawings in Berlin and Bayonne probably date from slightly earlier, about 1616–18.

1. When the drawing was in the collection of Adolf von Beckerath, it was attributed to Anthony van Dyck (see Berlin 2002–3, no. 94).
2. Held 1986, no. 124, pl. 124, ca. 1617–18.
3. For the oil sketch in a private collection, see Held 1980, no. 287, pl. 278, 1618–20, and Hans Vlieghe in Münster 2003, no. 34, color ill. For the engravings by Schelte à Bolswert and Jean Dambrun, see McGrath 1997, no. 49, copy 8, fig. 181, and no. 49c, copy 4, fig. 182. The second painting of the *Continence of Scipio* is known only from the description given by Roger de Piles when it was in the collection of the duc de Richelieu (1629–1715); see McGrath 1997, no. 50.

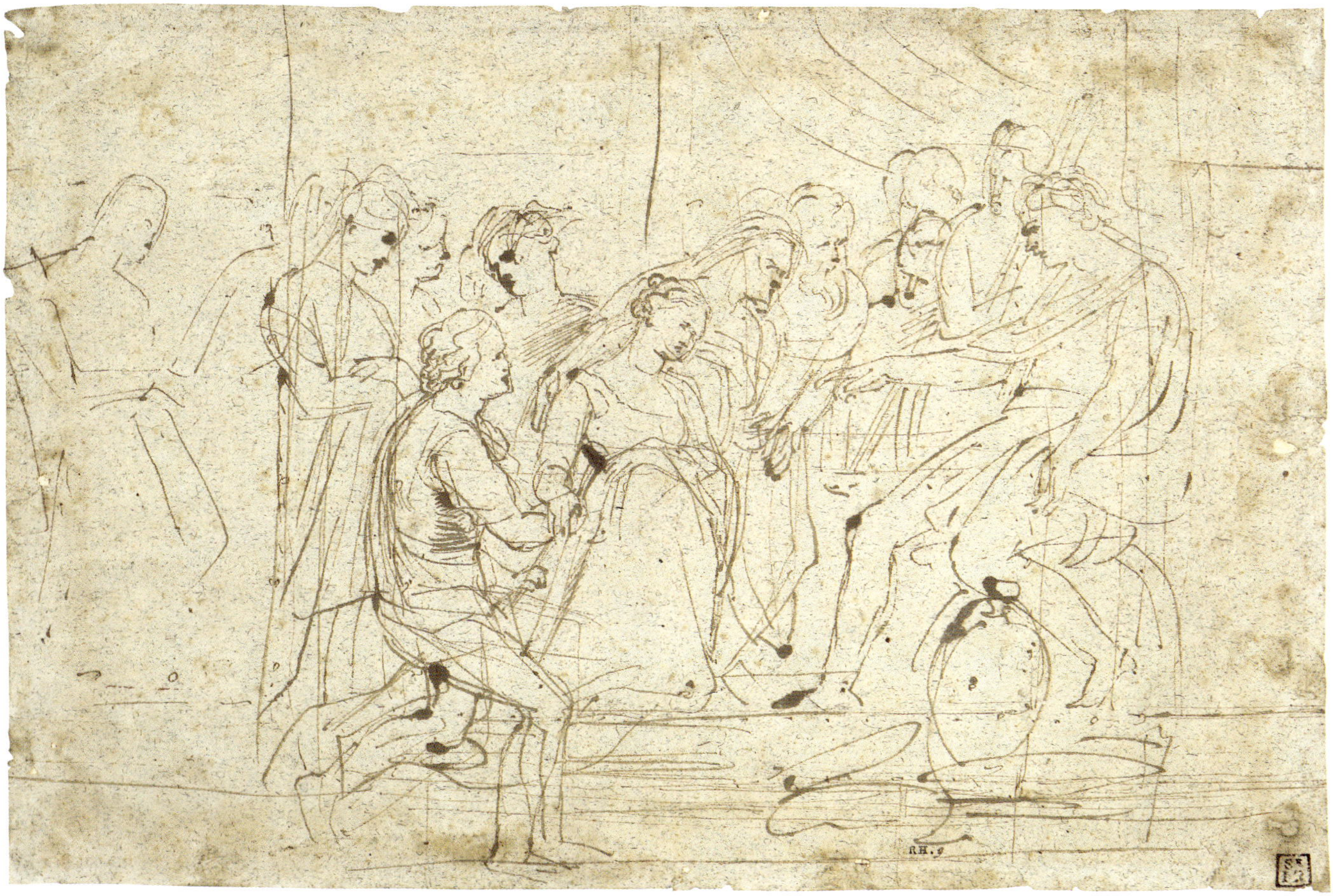

Cat. 33

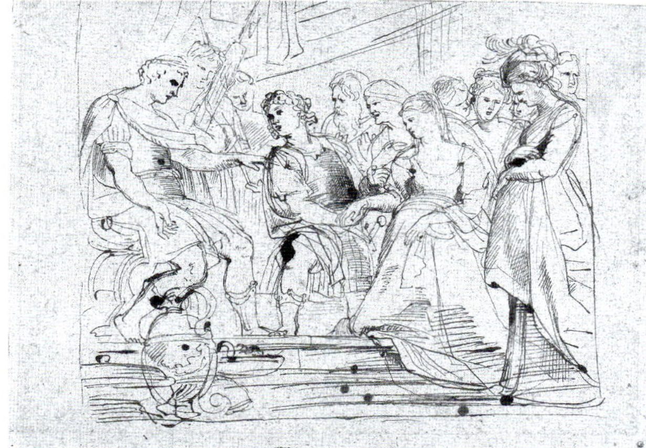

Fig. 75. Peter Paul Rubens, *The Continence of Scipio*, ca. 1616–18. Pen and brown ink, 255 x 354 mm (10 1/16 x 13 15/16 in.). Musée Bonnat, Bayonne (1436)

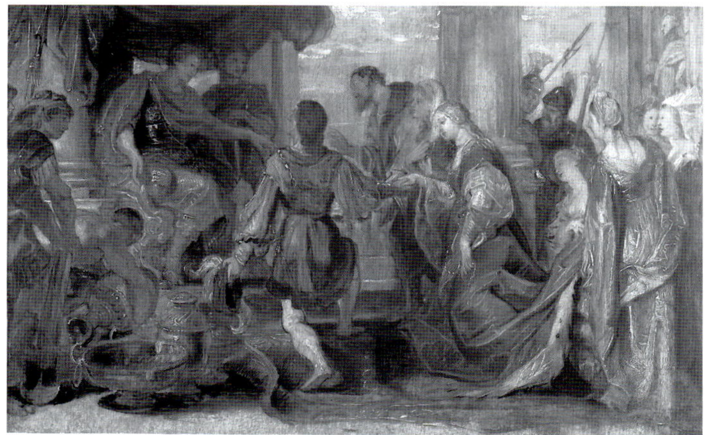

Fig. 76. Peter Paul Rubens, *The Continence of Scipio,* 1618–20. Oil on panel, 31.3 x 49.7 cm (12 5/16 x 19 9/16 in.). Private collection (CH 15)

34. *The Virgin and Child Adored by Saints,* recto, ca. 1627–28; *Copy after the "Belvedere Torso,"* verso, ca. 1601–2

Pen and brown ink, recto; red chalk, heightened with white, verso, 395 x 260 mm (15⁹⁄₁₆ x 10¼ in.)
Annotated in pen and brown ink on recto at bottom left: *P Rubens* over *N° 342*

The Metropolitan Museum of Art, New York; Purchase, 2001 Benefit Fund, 2002 (2002.12a,b)

PROVENANCE: Private collection, Paris (2000); Kunsthandel Bellinger, Munich.

EXHIBITION: London 2001, no. 17 (recto and verso), ill., verso on back cover.

This double-sided sheet, unknown until a few years ago, is one of the exceptional recent Rubens discoveries. The drawings on both recto and verso can be firmly anchored in Rubens's oeuvre. Moreover, they show the artist at two very different phases in his career.

The drawing on what is now considered the recto belongs to the group of rare compositional studies by Rubens that are described in inventories as *crabbelingen,* literally, "scratches" or "scribbles." The few remaining examples of these records of the artist's *primi pensieri,* or first thoughts, are valued today because they allow a glimpse into Rubens's creative process from the very beginning. Although Rubens's *crabbelingen* can be difficult to interpret, on the recto of the present sheet we can discern the *prima idea*—jotted down in pen and brown ink—for the *Virgin and Child Adored by Saints,* painted by Rubens for the high altar of the Antwerp church of Saint Augustine and installed in the summer of 1628 (fig. 77). Thus the drawing probably dates from late 1627 or early 1628.

These quick pen sketches provide an initial plan for the extremely large altarpiece. The seemingly haphazard arrangement of figures actually establishes much of the layout at this early stage. At the top center we see Rubens searching for the proper attitude for the Christ Child, held by the Virgin at the right and extending His hand to be kissed by Saint Catherine, who kneels below Him. The kneeling figure at the top left is most likely a detailed rendering of Catherine.[1] The figure beside the Child at the left may be Saint Joseph, who in the final painting stands on the opposite side, behind the Virgin. Prominently drawn in the lower right corner are Saints Sebastian and George, while a hastily sketched third saint (possibly an early idea for Saint Sebastian) approaches from the left. Underneath this figure Rubens had previously made a quick sketch of the Virgin and Child. Three female saints are placed in ascending order along the left edge, with the middle saint redrawn slightly higher up. These figures are all found at the far left center in the oil sketch in Frankfurt (fig. 78),[2] while in the final *modello* in Berlin

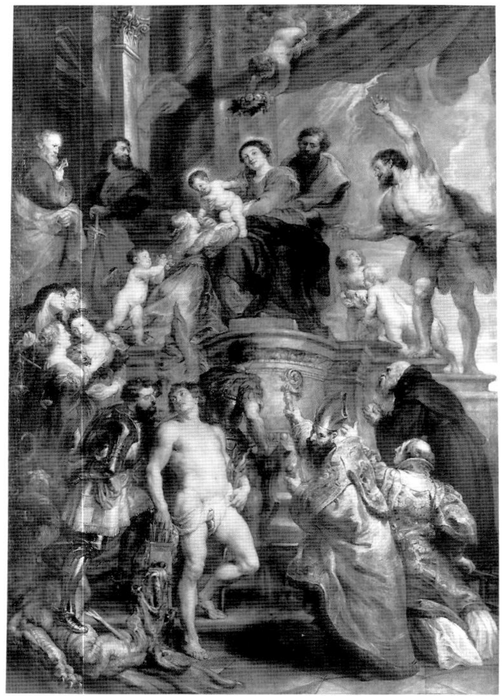

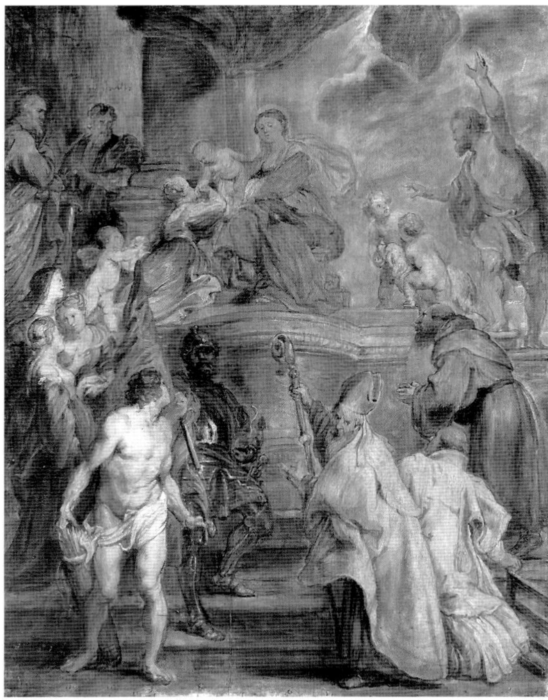

Fig. 77. Peter Paul Rubens, *The Virgin and Child Adored by Saints,* 1628. Oil on canvas, 564 x 401 cm (222¹⁄₁₆ x 157⅞ in.). Koninklijk Museum voor Schone Kunsten, Antwerp; on loan from the church of Saint Augustine, Antwerp

Fig. 78. Peter Paul Rubens, *The Virgin and Child Adored by Saints,* ca. 1627–28. Oil on panel, 63.3 x 49.5 cm (24¹⁵⁄₁₆ x 19½ in.). Städelsches Kunstinstitut, Frankfurt am Main (464)

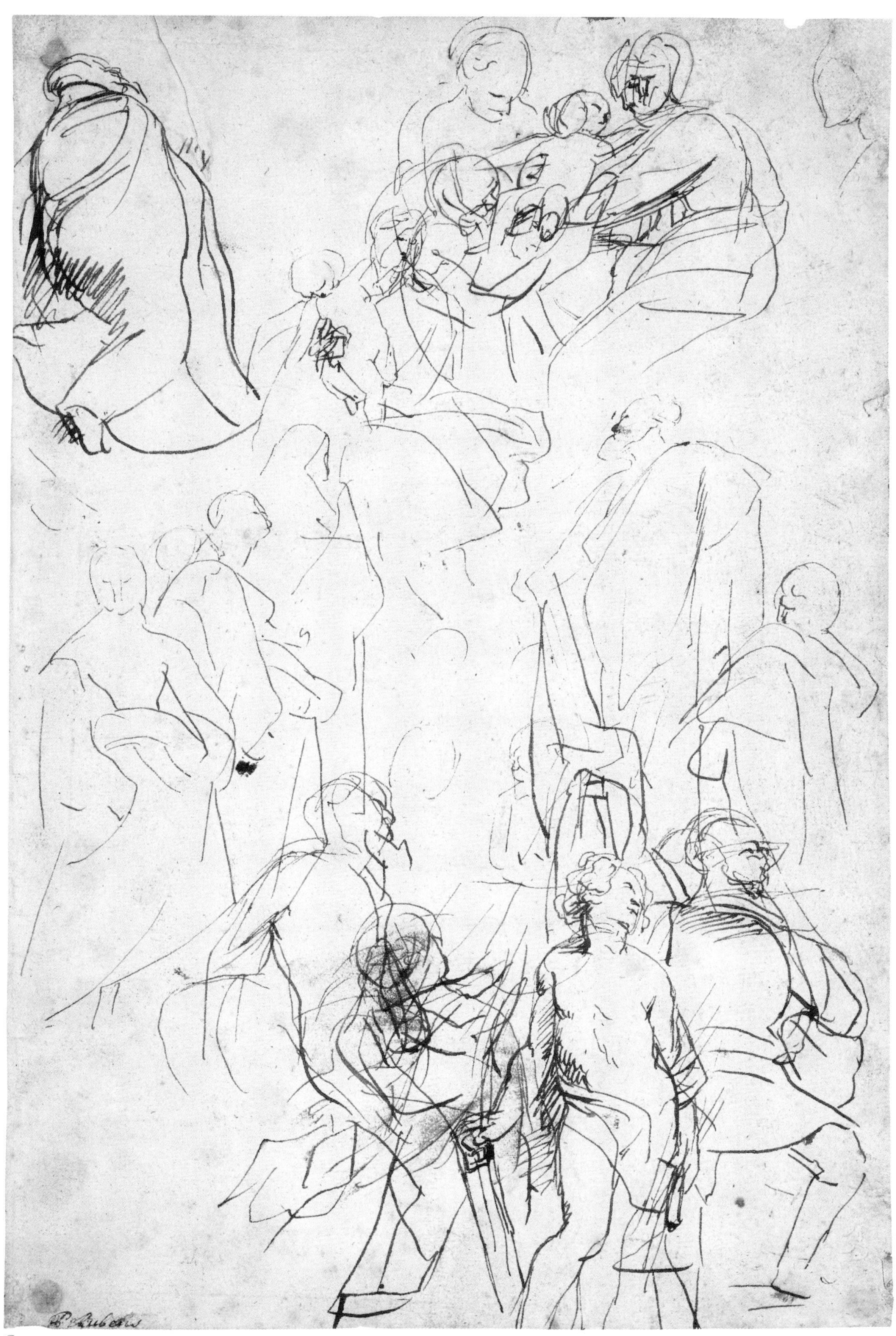

Cat. 34 recto

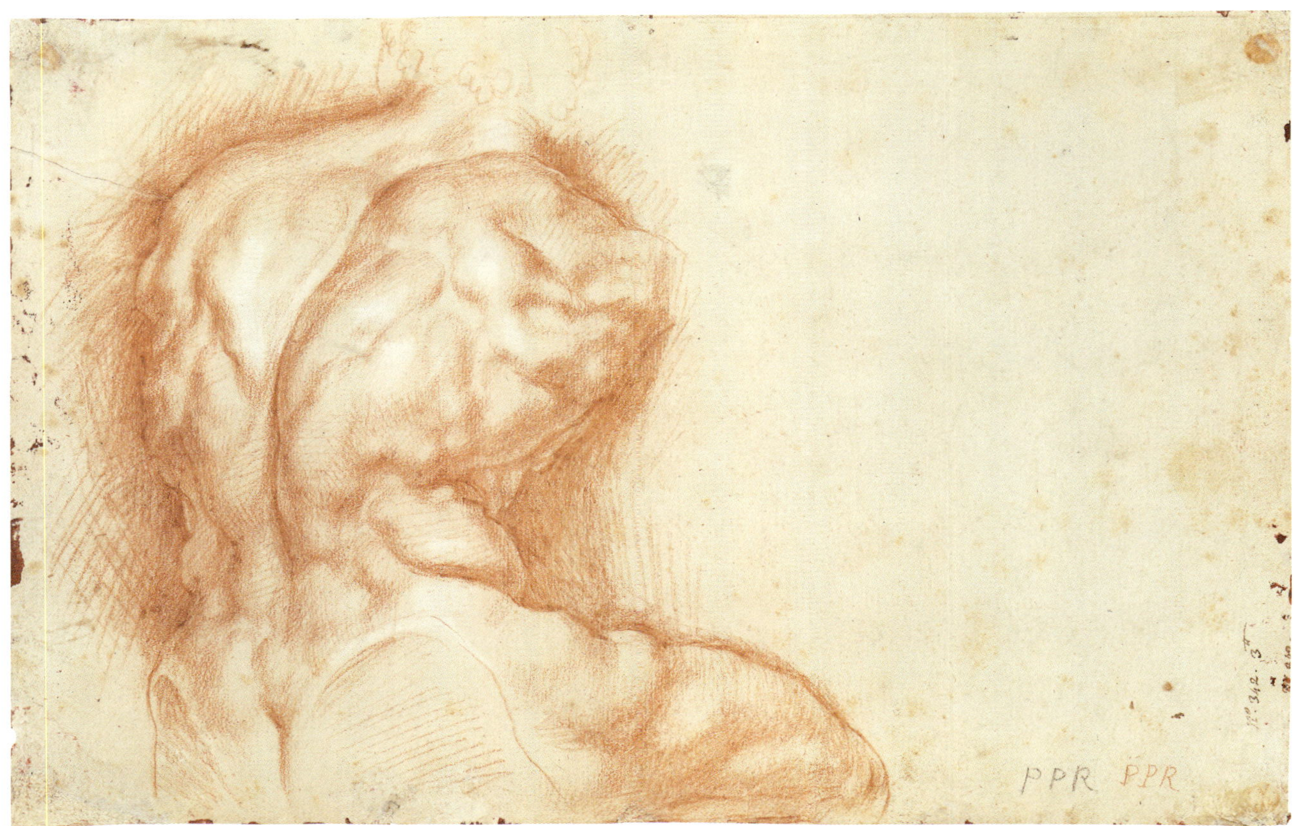

Cat. 34 verso

(fig. 79)[3] Rubens added a fourth. We can now recognize the lower pair as Saints Agnes and Apollonia (see cat. no. 68), with Mary Magdalen joining Saint Clara of Montefalcone. This is the arrangement Rubens kept in the altarpiece.

The figures on the right side of the recto are less developed than in the oil sketches and the final painting. The two standing figures above Saints Sebastian and George may be Saint Paul and Saint Peter, who were moved to the top left of the composition, beside a double column. Not present in the sketch is Saint Augustine, who stands in the lower right corner of the altarpiece pointing up to the Virgin and Child; nor do Saints William of Aquitaine, Lawrence, Nicolas of Tolentino, or John the Baptist make an appearance. Given the placement of the sketch on the verso, it does not seem likely that the sheet was cut much at the right, or in any case, enough to trim away a figure of Saint Augustine. Rubens probably added these saints due to additional patronage from other religious brotherhoods in Antwerp. (The latter helped to finance the altarpiece, which the Augustinians could not afford by themselves.) In the altarpiece most of them are featured prominently in the foreground at the right, while Saint John the Baptist appears at the upper right near the Holy Family. Rubens may have developed this side of the composition in another quick pen sketch, now lost.

This study puts into fresh perspective a sheet in Stockholm (fig. 80) that had always been considered *the* preliminary drawing by Rubens for the altarpiece.[4] The Stockholm drawing, which is closer in composition to the final painting, now appears to represent the step just prior to the earlier of the two oil sketches, the one in Frankfurt (fig. 78). Saint Sebastian and Saint George have almost the same poses and are in the same relation to each other in the Stockholm and the Metropolitan Museum drawings. William of Aquitaine does not appear in either drawing, but the Stockholm version does show Saint Augustine in very much the way he is represented in the Frankfurt oil sketch. Strangely, however, although the Stockholm drawing shows a fully developed composition, the lines seem more hesitant than those in the New York drawing.[5] Furthermore, the mixed media of black chalk with brush and brown ink differs from the technique found in Rubens's studies of this kind, such as the *Presentation in the Temple* (cat. no. 30 recto) and the *Continence of Scipio* (cat. no. 33), which are usually drawn with the pen and at times enhanced with wash. For these reasons, one cannot be entirely sure that the Stockholm drawing is by Rubens. It may

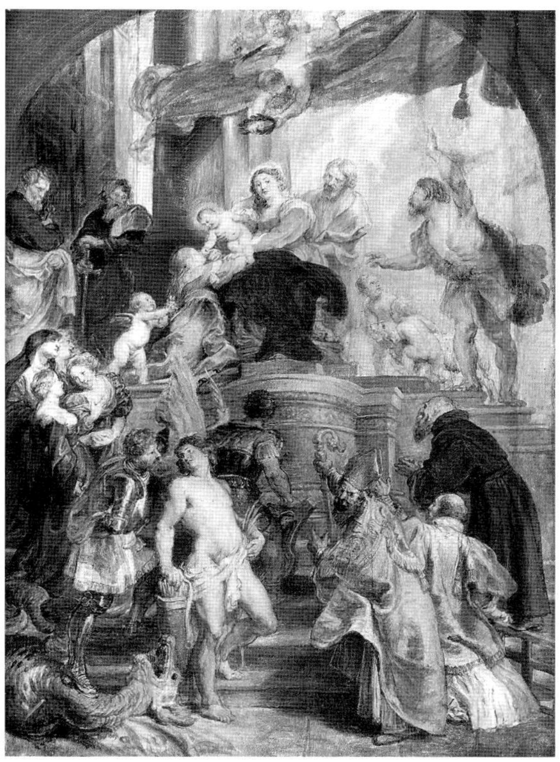

Fig. 79. Peter Paul Rubens, *The Virgin and Child Adored by Saints,* ca. 1627–28. Oil on panel, 80.2 x 55.5 cm (31 9/16 x 21 7/8 in.). Staatliche Museen zu Berlin–Preussischer Kulturbesitz, Gemäldegalerie, Berlin (780)

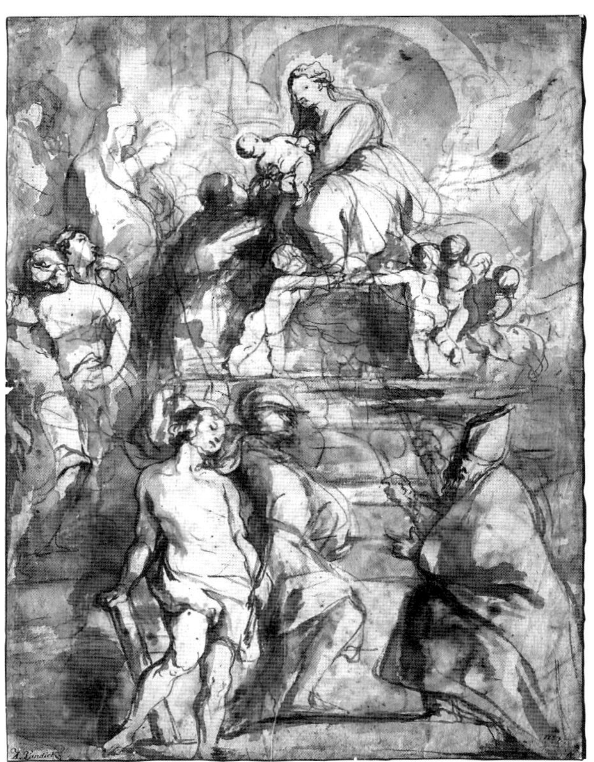

Fig. 80. Flemish 17th-century artist, *The Virgin and Child Adored by Saints*, ca. 1627–28. Pen and brush and brown ink and gray and brown wash over black chalk, 561 x 412 mm (22 1/16 x 16 1/4 in.). Nationalmuseum, Stockholm (NM H 1966/1863)

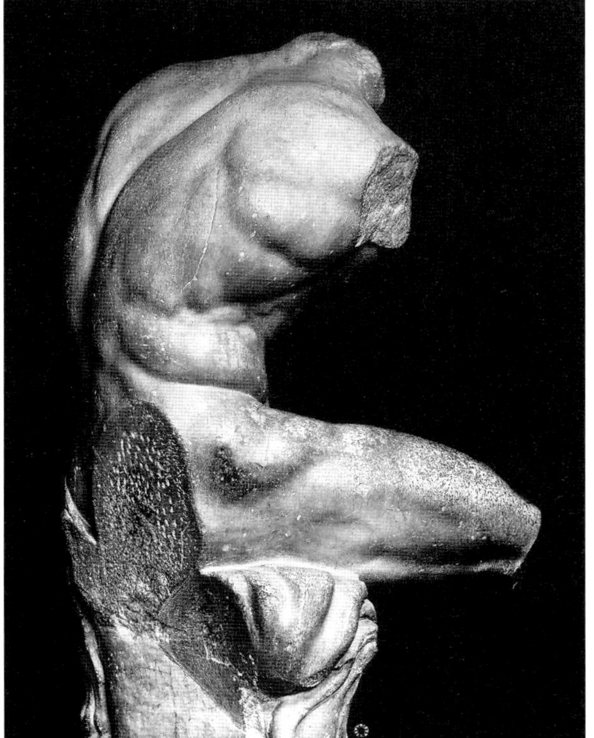

Fig. 81. Greco-Roman, *Belvedere Torso,* 1st century B.C. Marble, h. 159 cm (62 5/8 in.). Museo Pio Clementino, Vatican Museums

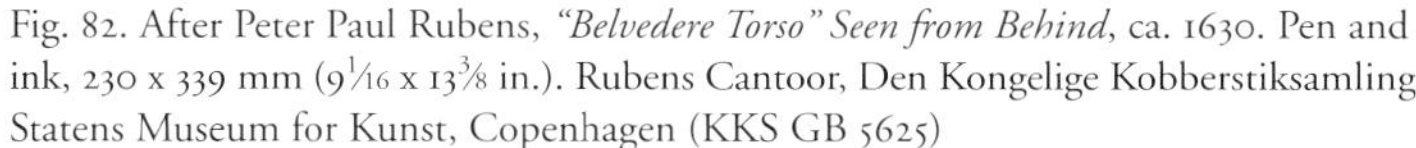

Fig. 82. After Peter Paul Rubens, *"Belvedere Torso" Seen from Behind*, ca. 1630. Pen and ink, 230 x 339 mm (9 1/16 x 13 3/8 in.). Rubens Cantoor, Den Kongelige Kobberstiksamling, Statens Museum for Kunst, Copenhagen (KKS GB 5625)

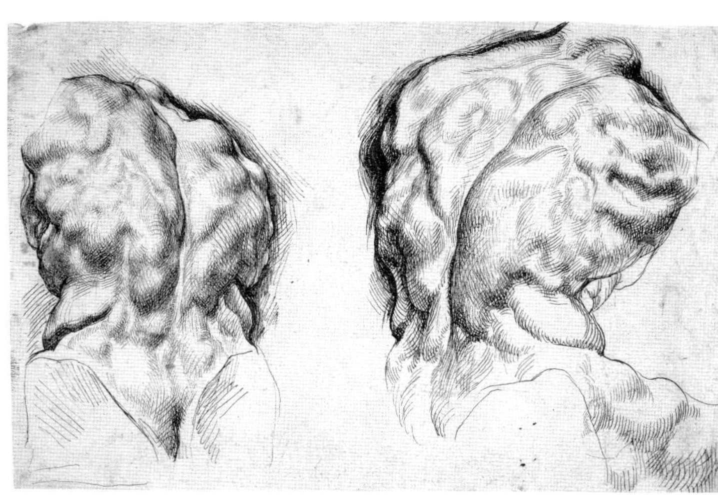

be the work of a close follower inspired by or heavily dependent on a work by the master that is probably lost.

On the verso of the Metropolitan Museum's sheet is a study based on the antique by a much younger Rubens: a back view of the *Belvedere Torso* (fig. 81), the famous sculpture from the first century B.C.[6] Rubens most likely drew the *Torso* during his first visit to Rome, in 1601–2, when he sketched other famous antique sculptures, including the *Laocoön.* (In the seventeenth century, when Rubens copied the *Torso,* then in the collection of the Colonna family, it was believed to represent *Hercules Resting.*) The delicate hatching in red chalk is found in other early Rubens drawings, for example, his copy after Michelangelo's *ignudo* (British Museum, London; fig. 11) and his study of an écorché figure (private collection).[7] Rubens probably chose to copy the white marble *Torso* in red chalk in order to simulate flesh tones. He was eager to bring life into his studies after the antique, as is clearly indicated here by the lightly sketched head with curls he added to the *Torso.*

Rubens's close-up back view of the *Belvedere Torso* relates closely to one of two studies in pen and black ink on a sheet preserved among the *cantoor* group in the Statens Museum for Kunst, Copenhagen (fig. 82).[8] Although the sheet in Copenhagen has been published as an autograph work,[9] the study at the right is probably based on the New York drawing. There cannot have been a second view of the *Torso* at the left of the New York sheet, corresponding to that on the Copenhagen sheet, since it would have had to have been cut away, and the recto composition appears to be intact.

This back view of the *Belvedere Torso* appears to have been of singular importance to Rubens, since he adapted it for several projects, including his lost anatomical treatise *De Figuris Humanis* (On the Human Body), known to us from partial copies in the Manuscripts Johnson and de Ganay, and early compositions of the *Judgment of Paris,* such as a pen sketch in the Louvre, Paris, a painting in the National Gallery, London, and an oil sketch on copper in the Akademie der Bildenden Künste, Vienna,[10] where the figure of Paris in each case reflects Rubens's study of the antique sculpture.

1. Her pose is not unlike that of Saint Augustine in Rubens's rendering of the latter in 1620, in his series of paintings for the ceiling of the Jesuit church in Antwerp (today the church of Saint Charles Borromeo). The painting was lost in a fire in 1718 and is known primarily from Rubens's oil sketch in the collection of Emil G. Bührle, Zurich (Held 1980, no. 28, pl. 32; M. Jaffé 1989, no. 622).
2. Held 1980, no. 384, pl. 375.
3. Ibid., no. 385, pl. 376.
4. Held 1986, no. 171, pl. 169.
5. At the top right in the Stockholm drawing, the artist lightly sketched another pose of the Virgin and Child that is developed on the verso, with the Child twice reaching toward the Infant Saint John rather than Saint Catherine.
6. Rubens's more familiar frontal view of the *Torso,* in black chalk, is in the Rubenshuis, Antwerp (inv. S. 109; Van der Meulen 1994, vol. 2, no. 37, fig. 75). Hendrick Goltzius (1558–1617) drew a black-chalk copy after the *Torso,* seen diagonally from behind, in Rome about 1591 (Teylers Museum, Haarlem, inv. K I 30; Amsterdam–New York–Toledo 2003–4, no. 41.2, color ill.). Reznicek (1992, pp. 121–29) has drawn attention to the similarity between Goltzius's and Rubens's back views of the *Torso.*
7. Jan and Marie-Anne Krugier-Poniatowsky, Geneva. Red chalk, 273 x 192 mm.
8. Inv. III, 59; 230 x 339 mm; Van der Meulen 1994, vol. 2, no. 39, copy, fig. 77.
9. M. Jaffé 1966, vol. 1, pl. XLVI; Müller Hofstede in Cologne 1977, no. 45, fig. K 45. Some writers have suggested that the drawing in the Copenhagen *cantoor* is a copy by Rubens after a small bronze of the *Torso* that he saw during his service in Mantua. The same is unlikely to be true of the New York drawing, however, given Rubens's use of red chalk rather than pen and ink, his usual medium for copies after small bronzes. See Schwinn 1973, p. 105.
10. For the back view of the *Torso* in the Manuscripts Johnson and de Ganay, see Van der Meulen 1994, vol. 2, under no. 39, p. 59, n. 1. For the works in Paris, London, and Vienna, see Healy 1997, pls. 1, 2, and fig. 83.

ANTWERP, 1609–15: INDIVIDUAL STUDIES

35. *Kneeling Male Nude Seen from Behind,* ca. 1609–10

Black chalk, heightened and corrected with white, 520 x 390 mm (20½ x 15⅜ in.); paper with part of arm between elbow and hand made up

Museum Boijmans Van Beuningen, Rotterdam (V52)

Provenance: Prosper Henry Lankrink (1628?–1692), London (Lugt 2090); G. Bellingham Smith, London (sale, Amsterdam, F. Muller, July 5, 1927, lot 111); Franz Koenigs (1881–1941), Haarlem (Lugt 1023a; acquired in 1927); D. G. van Beuningen, Rotterdam, acquired in 1940 and donated to the Boymans Museum Foundation in 1941.

Literature: Glück and Haberditzl 1928, no. 60, pl. 60; Held 1959, no. 75, pl. 88, under nos. 70, 76, and p. 66; Burchard and d'Hulst 1963, no. 92, pl. 92; Kuznetsov 1974, pl. 69; Held 1986, no. 54, pl. 55; Lusheck 2000, pp. 127–63, fig. 1.

Exhibitions: Antwerp 1977, no. 147, ill.; New York–Fort Worth–Cleveland 1990–91, no. 44, ill.; Rotterdam 2001, no. 11, ill.

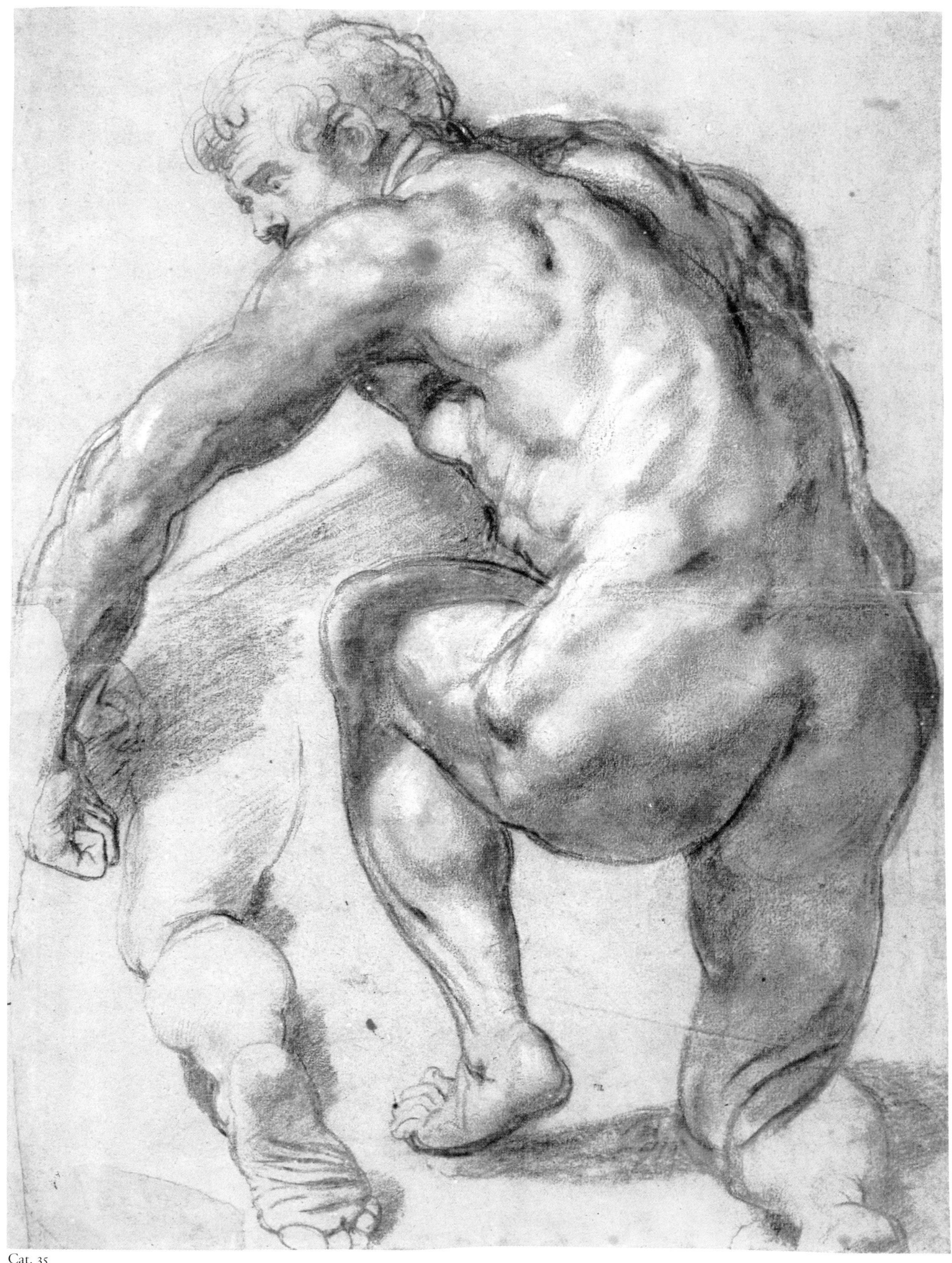

Cat. 35

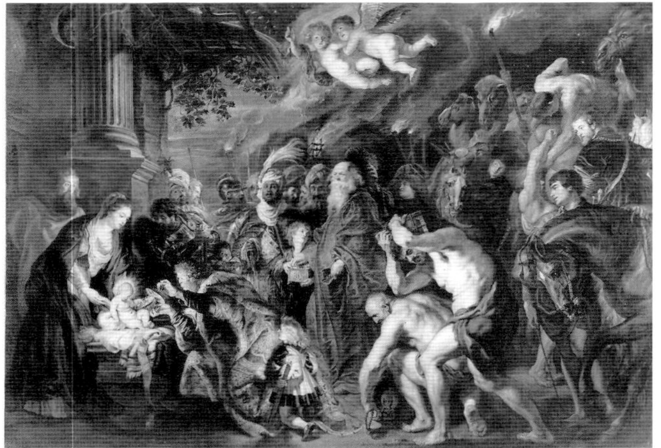

Fig. 83. Peter Paul Rubens, *The Adoration of the Magi,* 1609–10, enlarged 1628–29. Oil on canvas, 346 x 438 cm (136¼ x 172 7/16 in.). Prado, Madrid (1638)

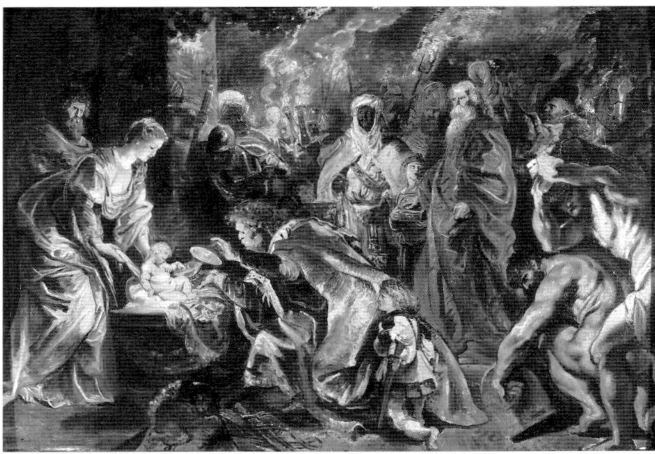

Fig. 84. Peter Paul Rubens, *The Adoration of the Magi,* 1609–10. Oil on panel, 54.5 x 76.5 cm (21 7/16 x 30⅛ in.). Groninger Museum, The Netherlands; Collection C. Hofstede de Groot (1931.0121)

This large black-chalk drawing is one of Rubens's most accomplished studies of the male nude, executed with remarkably few hesitations.[1] It prepares one of the porters bearing gifts in Rubens's *Adoration of the Magi,* today in the Prado, Madrid (fig. 83).[2] As was his practice, after painting the oil sketch (fig. 84), Rubens drew individual figure studies. This view of a kneeling man seen from behind and a comparable one in the Louvre, Paris,[3] were undoubtedly done from life. Here, Rubens concentrated on the bulging muscles on the curved back of the model and the position of his left arm.[4] In the drawing the figure is more erect, and his arm more curved, than in the oil sketch. In the final painting Rubens more or less returned to the original pose shown in the oil sketch; however, he did use the detail of the right leg and foot that he had drawn separately at the lower left of this sheet. At first sight, the right shoulder may seem anatomically incorrect, but the bulging muscles at the upper right are actually part of the foreshortened right arm, as becomes clear in the final painting. In the study Rubens paid much less attention to the lower part of the man's back, since he would eventually cover that area—as he already had in the oil sketch—with the figure of a standing porter.

Given that the *Adoration of the Magi* was commissioned in the second half of 1609 or possibly in early 1610, the Rotterdam and Paris drawings may date from then, or a little later, when the painting was in progress. However, with Rubens, a correspondence between a chalk study and a figure in a painting does not always mean that the drawing dates from the same time, for Rubens viewed his drawings as a resource and repeatedly returned to them. The sheets in Rotterdam and Paris illustrate this well. In about 1615, for example, Rubens reused the study in Rotterdam for a figure in the foreground of his *Allegory of Nature* (Museum and Art Gallery, Glasgow), although he transformed the man into a satyr.[5] Likewise, eight years after the Adoration he reused the Paris study for a slave carrying a vase at the lower right in the *Meeting of Abraham and Melchizedek* (Musée des Beaux-Arts, Caen).[6]

1. A pentimento near the left hand shows that Rubens began it first slightly higher on the sheet.
2. K.d.K., ed. Oldenbourg 1921, no. 26; M. Jaffé 1989, no. 98, 1609. A book about the painting, published by the Prado, is forthcoming (Vergara 2004).
3. Lugt 1949, no. 1030; Paris 1978, no. 16.
4. In this respect the drawing calls to mind Rubens's copies after the *Belvedere Torso,* made earlier in Rome (see cat. no. 34 verso).
5. New York–Fort Worth–Cleveland 1990–91, fig. e under no. 44. The resemblance was noted by Burchard and d'Hulst 1963, no. 92.
6. M. Jaffé 1989, no. 409, 1616–17.

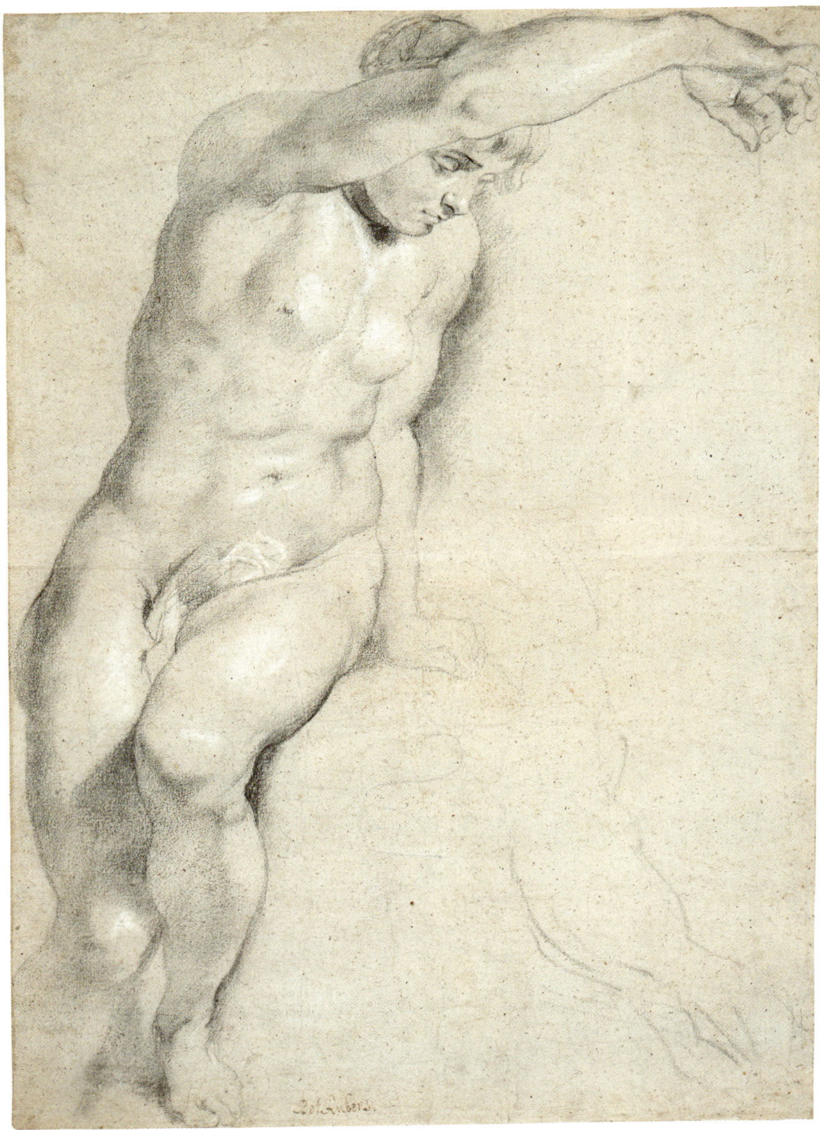

Cat. 36

36. *Female Nude: Study for Psyche,* ca. 1609–12

Black chalk, heightened with white, on buff paper, 581 x 412 mm (22⅞ x 16¼ in.)
Annotated in pen and brown ink at bottom left of center: *Del Rubens*

Lent by Her Majesty Queen Elizabeth II, Royal Library, Windsor Castle (6412)

Provenance: George III of England (1738–1820), London (possibly inventory A, p. 106: "Accademie di Diversi Autori . . . One Rubens").

Literature: Glück and Haberditzl 1928, no. 96, pl. 96; Burchard and d'Hulst 1963, no. 65, pl. 65, and under no. 29; White and Crawley 1994, no. 434, ill.

Exhibitions: Montreal–Raleigh–Indianapolis 1994–95, no. 22, ill.; London 2002–3, no. 359, ill.

During his employment in Mantua, Rubens would have seen the depiction of Cupid and Psyche painted on the ceiling of the Sala di Psiche in the Palazzo Te by Giulio Romano (1499?–1546), one of his predecessors as court painter to the Gonzaga.[1] Soon after his return from Italy to Antwerp in 1608, Rubens, possibly still impressed by the Italian master's work, painted his own *Cupid and Psyche* (ca. 1609–12). This study of

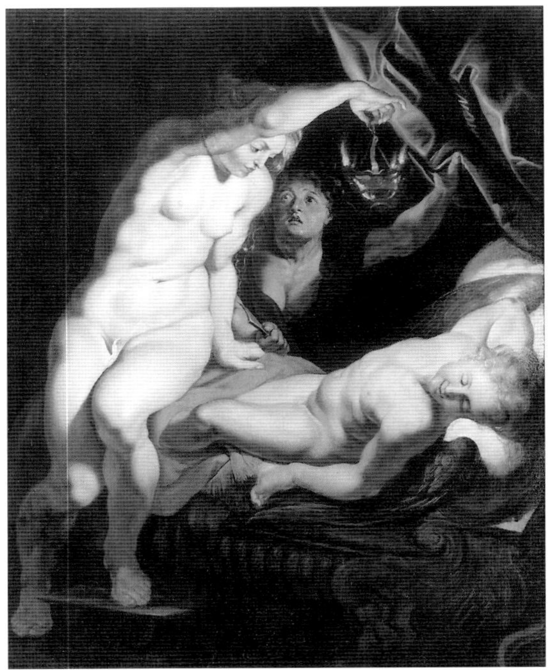

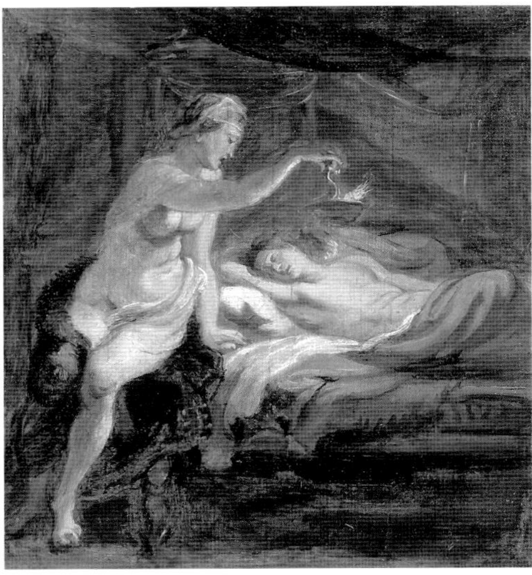

Fig. 86. Peter Paul Rubens, *Psyche and Cupid*, ca. 1636. Oil on panel, 25 x 23 cm ($9^{13}/_{16}$ x $9^{1}/_{16}$ in.). Musée Bonnat, Bayonne (CM 2)

Fig. 85. Peter Paul Rubens, *Cupid and Psyche*, ca. 1609–12. Oil on canvas, 117.5 x 92.5 cm ($46^{1}/_{4}$ x $36^{7}/_{16}$ in.). Photograph courtesy of Sotheby's, Inc. © 2002

a *Female Nude* in Windsor Castle served for the figure of Psyche in that painting, now in a private collection (fig. 85).[2]

The story of Cupid and Psyche is related in the second-century Latin narrative romance *The Golden Ass* (or *Metamorphoses*) by the writer and philosopher Lucius Apuleius. Venus, jealous of the beautiful Psyche, sends Cupid to make her fall in love with a worthless creature; instead, Cupid falls in love with Psyche and brings her to his palace. Although he warns her not to look at him when he visits her at night, she cannot resist. With an oil lamp held aloft, she illuminates the darkness to catch a glimpse of him asleep. When a drop of hot oil awakens him, however, Cupid informs Psyche that he can never return to her. Eventually, Jupiter reunites them, and their wedding is celebrated with a festive banquet attended by an assembly of the gods.

Rubens chose for his painting the moment when Psyche spies on the sleeping Cupid. In the painting Psyche carefully and gracefully raises the oil lamp with her right arm, in a pose that corresponds closely to that of the female figure in the drawing. Rubens did not redraw the truncated lower part of Psyche's right leg elsewhere on the page (as he sometimes did when he ran out of space in a figure study; see cat. nos. 35, 37), as that part of the leg would remain in shadow in the painting. Instead, he seems to have sketched at the lower right the left arm of Cupid; the marks are too slight for one to be certain, however. In the size of the sheet and Rubens's handling of the media—careful contours in black chalk with soft modeling to indicate volume, enhanced with white-chalk highlights—this drawing recalls his studies of about 1610 of male nudes for the *Raising of the Cross* (cat. nos. 37–39), as well as the study of about 1613 for the seated Daniel (cat. no. 45). These similarities also support a dating of the Windsor drawing to about 1609–12.

While Rubens may be famous for the many voluptuous female nudes in his paintings, preparatory drawings for such figures are extremely rare: this and another sheet in the Louvre (cat. no. 109) are the only known examples by him. It is doubtful, however, that Rubens made drawings of the female nude from life at all. At the time it was common for Flemish artists to draw only from male models, imitating the practice of the Renaissance masters Michelangelo and Raphael. Indeed, the rather muscular body of Psyche in the Windsor drawing suggests that Rubens here employed a male model (see also cat. no. 109).

Late in his career, about 1636, Rubens returned to this drawing in a small oil sketch of *Cupid and Psyche* (fig. 86), which he made in preparation for the decoration commissioned by Philip IV of Spain for the Torre de la Parada, his hunting lodge in Madrid. The final painting, which is today in the Prado, Madrid, was executed not by Rubens but by one of his collaborators, probably Erasmus II Quellinus (1607–1678).[3]

1. Hartt 1958, vol. 2, pls. 227, 236.
2. M. Jaffé 1989, no. 120, 1609–10; sale cat., New York, Sotheby's, January 24, 2002, lot 236, fig. 1, ca. 1611–12.
3. Inv. 1718; M. Jaffé 1989, no. 1254, 1637–38; Díaz Padrón 1995, vol. 2, p. 830, no. 1718, ill. The painting has survived only as a fragment; the figure of Psyche was cut off sometime before 1794.

37. *Study for the Figure of Christ,* ca. 1610

Black chalk and charcoal, heightened and corrected with white, on light tan paper, 403 x 297 mm (15⅞ x 11$^{11}/_{16}$ in.)

Fogg Art Museum, Harvard University Art Museums, Cambridge, Massachusetts; Gift of Meta and Paul J. Sachs (1949.3)

PROVENANCE: Jacob de Wit (1695–1754), Amsterdam (?; his sale, Amsterdam, de Leth . . . v. Schorrenberg, March 10–11, 1755, boek C, nos. 21–27); Joseph Daniel Böhm (1794–1865), Vienna (Lugt 1442); Werner Weisbach, Berlin; Goudstikker, Amsterdam; Meta and Paul J. Sachs, Cambridge, Mass. (acquired in 1927); presented to the Fogg Art Museum in 1949.

LITERATURE: Glück and Haberditzl 1928, no. 61, pl. 61; Mongan and Sachs 1940, no. 483, ill.; Burchard and d'Hulst 1963, no. 55, pl. 55; Kuznetsov 1974, pl. 28; Judson 2000, no. 20c, fig. 66.

EXHIBITIONS: Cambridge, Mass.–New York 1956, no. 8, pl. III; Wellesley–Cleveland 1993–94, no. 42, ill.

38. *Crouching Man Seen from the Back,* ca. 1610

Black chalk, with brush and gray-black wash (added by Jacob de Wit), heightened with white, 465 x 320 mm (18$^{5}/_{16}$ x 12⅝ in.)

Private collection, The Netherlands

PROVENANCE: Jacob de Wit (1695–1754), Amsterdam (his sale, Amsterdam, de Leth . . . v. Schorrenberg, March 10–11, 1755, boek C, nos. 21–27); Simon Fokke, Amsterdam (his sale, Amsterdam, v.d. Schley . . . Belli, December 6, 1784, no. 402); Cornelis Ploos van Amstel (1726–1798), Amsterdam (?); Dirk Versteegh (1751–1822), Amsterdam (?); Sir Thomas Lawrence (1769–1830), London (inventory, case 4, drawer 1, no. 44 [?]: "Study of Christ in the Act of Raising the Cross, Black Chalk, washed, superb"); Herman de Kat, Rotterdam (his sale, Rotterdam, Lamme, March 4, 1867, no. 104 [Van Dyck]); J. de Clercq, Amsterdam, 1867.

LITERATURE: Burchard and d'Hulst 1963, no. 58, pl. 58, and under no. 55; Kuznetsov 1974, pl. 29; Judson 2000, no. 20i, fig. 73.

EXHIBITION: Antwerp 1977, no. 132, ill.

39. *Nude Man with Raised Arms,* ca. 1610

Black chalk, heightened with white, 490 x 315 mm (19¼ x 12⅜ in.); triangular sections cut away at top and bottom right, irregularly cut (upper margin, 255 mm; right margin, 113 mm; bottom edge, 166 mm)
Annotated in pen and brown ink at bottom right on added piece of paper: *Rubens*

Koninklijk Huisarchief, Collection of H.M. The Queen of The Netherlands, The Hague (AT/0248)

PROVENANCE: Jacob de Wit (1695–1754), Amsterdam (?; his sale, Amsterdam, de Leth . . . v. Schorrenberg, March 10–11, 1755, boek C, nos. 21–27); Dirk Versteegh (1823), Amsterdam (his sale, Amsterdam, De Vries . . . Roos, November 3, 1823); Sir Thomas Lawrence (1769–1830), London; ?William II of the Netherlands (sale, The Hague, August 12–20, 1850, lot 303; bought in by Jean Albert Brondgeest); William III of the Netherlands; Wilhelmina of the Netherlands (1880–1962).

LITERATURE: Held 1959, no. 76, pl. 87, and under no. 70; Burchard and d'Hulst 1963, no. 56, pl. 56, and under no. 55; Kuznetsov 1974, pl. 30; Held 1986, no. 55, pl. 49; Judson 2000, no. 20d, fig. 67.

EXHIBITIONS: Antwerp 1977, no. 131, ill.; New York 1979–80, no. 120, ill.

40. *Studies of Heads and Clasped Hands,* ca. 1610

Black chalk, heightened with white chalk, on brownish paper, 389 x 269 mm (15$^{5}/_{16}$ x 10⅝ in.); cut in two from center left, separating the two pairs of hands from the two heads
Annotated in pen and brown ink at bottom right: *P. P. Rubens*

Albertina, Vienna (8306)

PROVENANCE: Gottfried Winckler (1731–1795), Leipzig; Duke Albert of Sachsen-Teschen (1738–1822), Vienna (Lugt 174).

LITERATURE: R., vol. 5, no. 1578; Glück and Haberditzl 1928, no. 64, pl. 64; Held 1959, no. 77, pl. 89, and under no. 33; Kuznetsov 1974, pl. 32; Held 1986, no. 56, pl. 59; Judson 2000, no. 20j, fig. 74.

EXHIBITIONS: Vienna 1977b, no. 7, ill.; Retretti 1991, p. 96, ill.; Pittsburgh–Louisville–Fresno 2002, no. 52, ill.

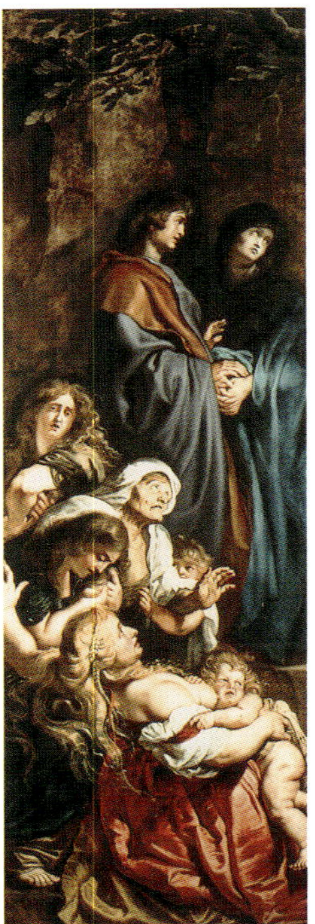
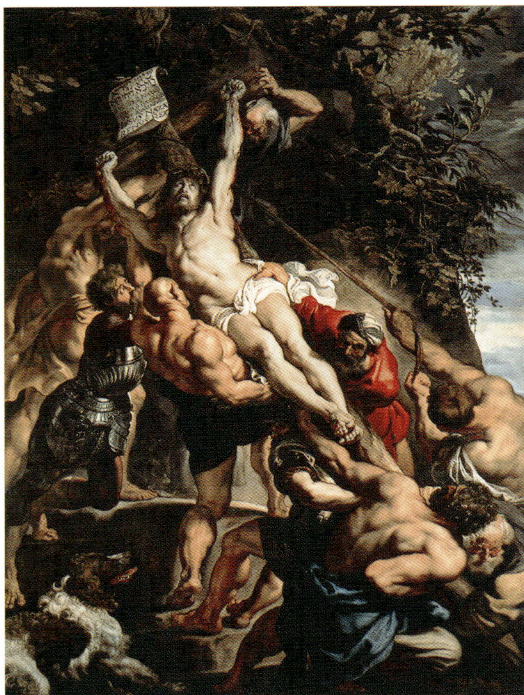
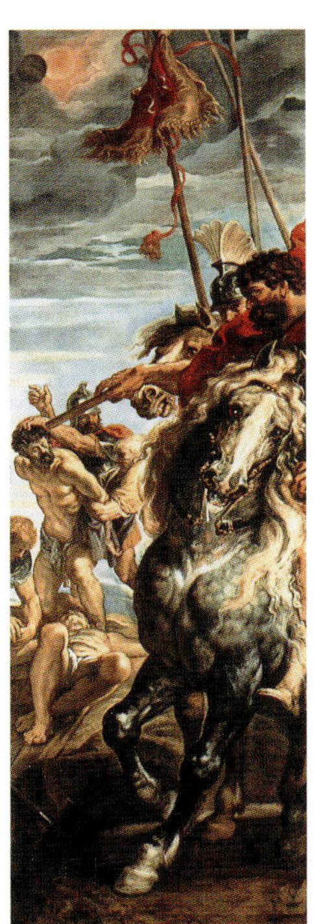

Fig. 87. Peter Paul Rubens, *The Raising of the Cross,* ca. 1610–11. Oil on panel, central panel 460 x 340 cm (181⅛ x 133⅞ in.), wings 460 x 150 cm (181⅛ x 59¹⁄₁₆ in.) each. Antwerp Cathedral

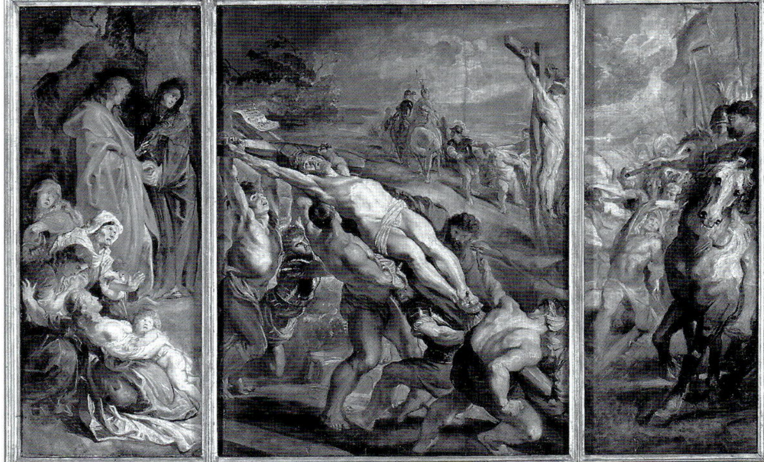

Fig. 88. Peter Paul Rubens, *The Raising of the Cross,* ca. 1610. Oil on panel, central panel 68 x 51 cm (26¾ x 20¹⁄₁₆ in.), wings 67 x 25 cm (26⅜ x 9¹³⁄₁₆ in.) each. Département des Peintures du Musée du Louvre, Service de la Récuperation, 1954, Paris (MNR 411)

In June 1610 Rubens received his first important religious commission in Antwerp, the *Raising of the Cross* triptych for the high altar of the church of Saint Walburga (now in Antwerp Cathedral; fig. 87).[1] Cornelis van der Geest (1555–1638), a wealthy spice merchant and church warden at Saint Walburga, was instrumental in securing this commission for the artist. Given the enormous size of the altarpiece, Rubens painted it in the church itself, completing it within a year. The scene of the Raising of the Cross is represented in the central panel of the triptych. The Virgin and Saint John and a group of mourning women witnessing the Crucifixion appear on the inner left wing, while the two thieves, one being nailed to a cross and the other being readied, appear on the inner right wing.

Rubens must have made many preliminary drawings for this important triptych, in which one easily counts twenty-five figures. At present, however, only five drawings are known: four figure studies for the central panel and one study of heads and hands, partly related to the inner left wing. All but the *Nude Man Seen from Behind* in the Ashmolean Museum, Oxford,[2] are included in this exhibition (cat. nos. 37–40).

The figure studies for the central panel all follow Rubens's preliminary oil sketch (fig. 88).[3] The artist must have painted

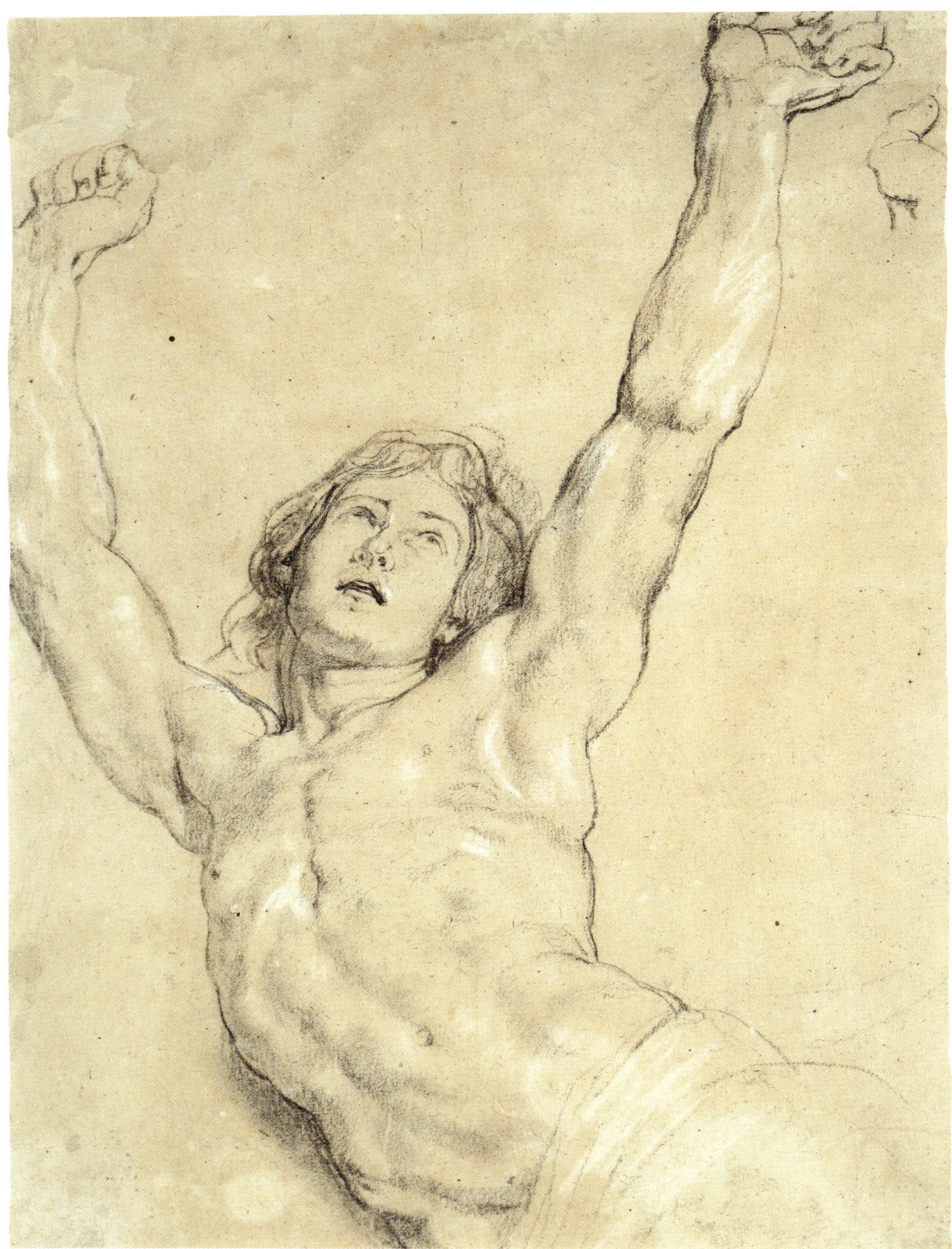

Cat. 37

this *modello* for the approval of the church authorities before June 1610, when the official contract was signed. Rubens began the individual drawings only when he needed to finalize the poses of the key figures in the triptych. In one or two instances he seemed to create these detailed figure studies at the last moment, when he was already working on the painting.

The drawing for the figure of Christ (cat. no. 37) represents a significant departure from the oil sketch. It shows Christ's body with less foreshortening, in a more erect than diagonal position, with his arms raised upward instead of extended toward the left. Since the sheet was not quite large enough, Rubens added a separate detail of the left hand and thumb at the upper right. He transferred the image, including the highlights indicated with white chalk, to the triptych, adding essentially only a beard and mustache to Christ's face. Judging from the shadow along the left side of the figure and from the faint indications of the loincloth extending horizontally across the hips, Rubens's model was lying on his back.[4]

Rubens drew the study of a crouching man (cat. no. 38) in preparation for the figure at the lower right in the central panel (fig. 7). In the oil sketch, the corresponding man stands more upright, with knees bent to counteract the strain of pulling the

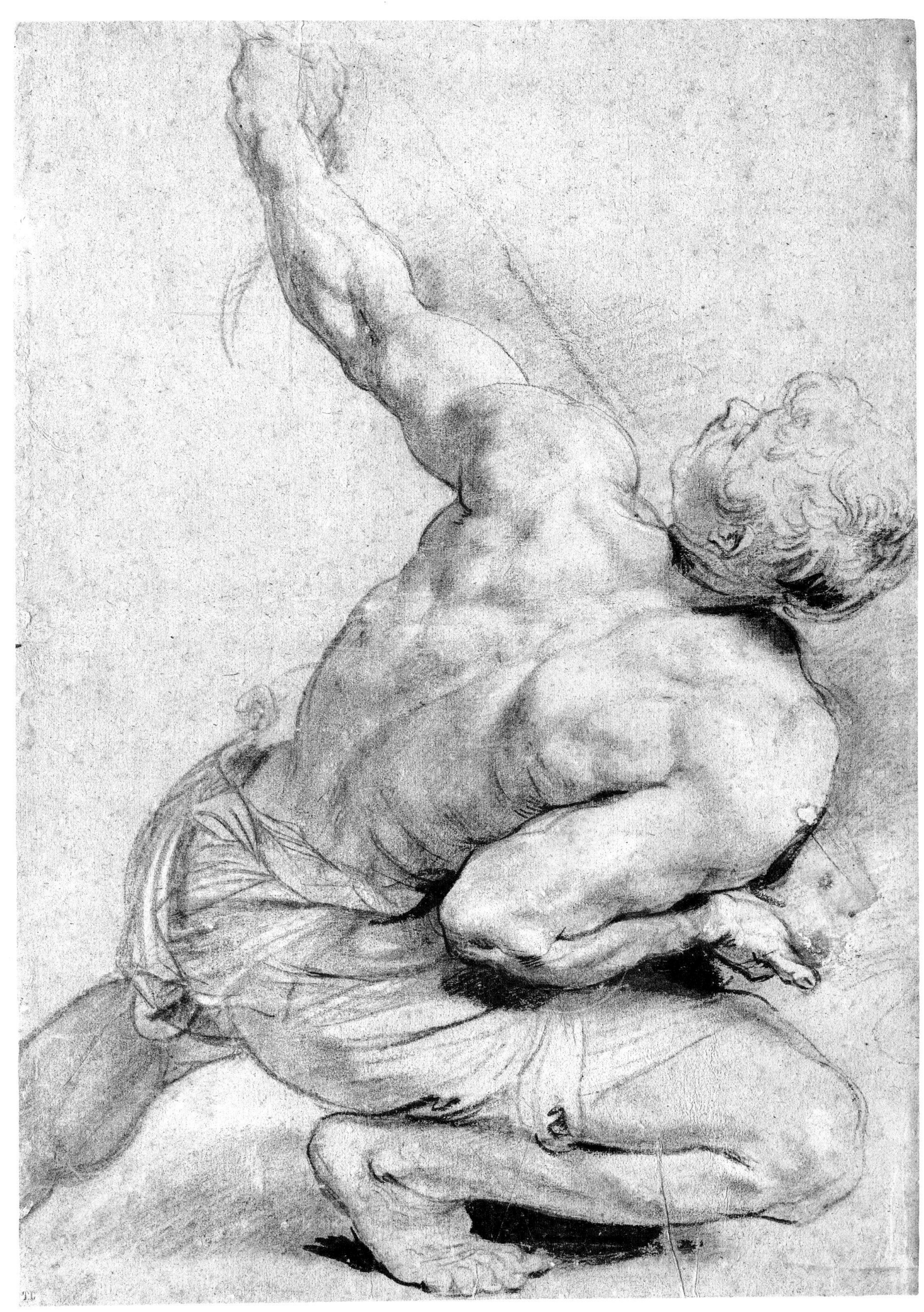

Cat. 38

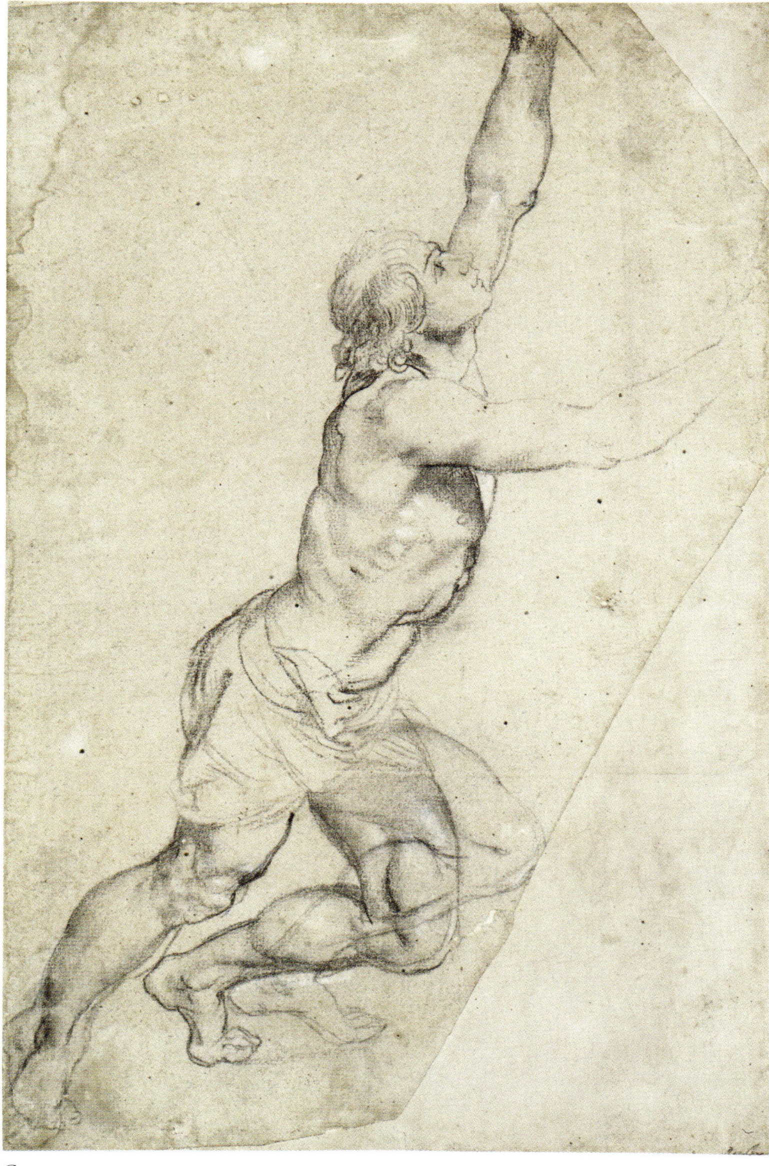

Cat. 39

rope to raise the Cross, which is very low to the ground and would require tremendous strength to lift. In the figure study, his task is entirely different. Instead of pulling the rope, the man steadies the lower end of the shaft of the Cross with both his arms and hands; this, too, requires great physical exertion, expressed in the taught play of muscles in his back. In the final painting, Rubens angled the man's right arm still further, increased the bulging muscles, and gave the figure a full head of hair and a beard. Of the three preliminary figure studies in the exhibition, this drawing is the most monumental and may belong to the last ones he drew related to the commission.

The dark washes on the drawing—for instance, below the figure's right arm and leg—are not Rubens's doing; they were added more than one hundred years later by the Dutch artist Jacob de Wit (1695–1754).[5] We encounter the same kind of shading in a number of Rubens school drawings. De Wit was a great admirer of Rubens and assembled a large collection of his paintings and drawings. In the 1755 auction catalogue of his collection, a few Rubens sheets are described as "opgetekend" (drawn upon, or worked up) by De Wit. This particular drawing is not one of these, but it was nevertheless probably in his collection, among the eight Rubens drawings described in the catalogue as related to "the large Cross" *('t groote Kruis).*[6]

The *Nude Man with Raised Arms* (cat. no. 39) is a study for the soldier at the left of the central panel of the *Raising of the Cross.* Even though in the painting the soldier's body would be largely covered by armor, Rubens studied the anatomy of a nude model. He experimented with two different positions for the

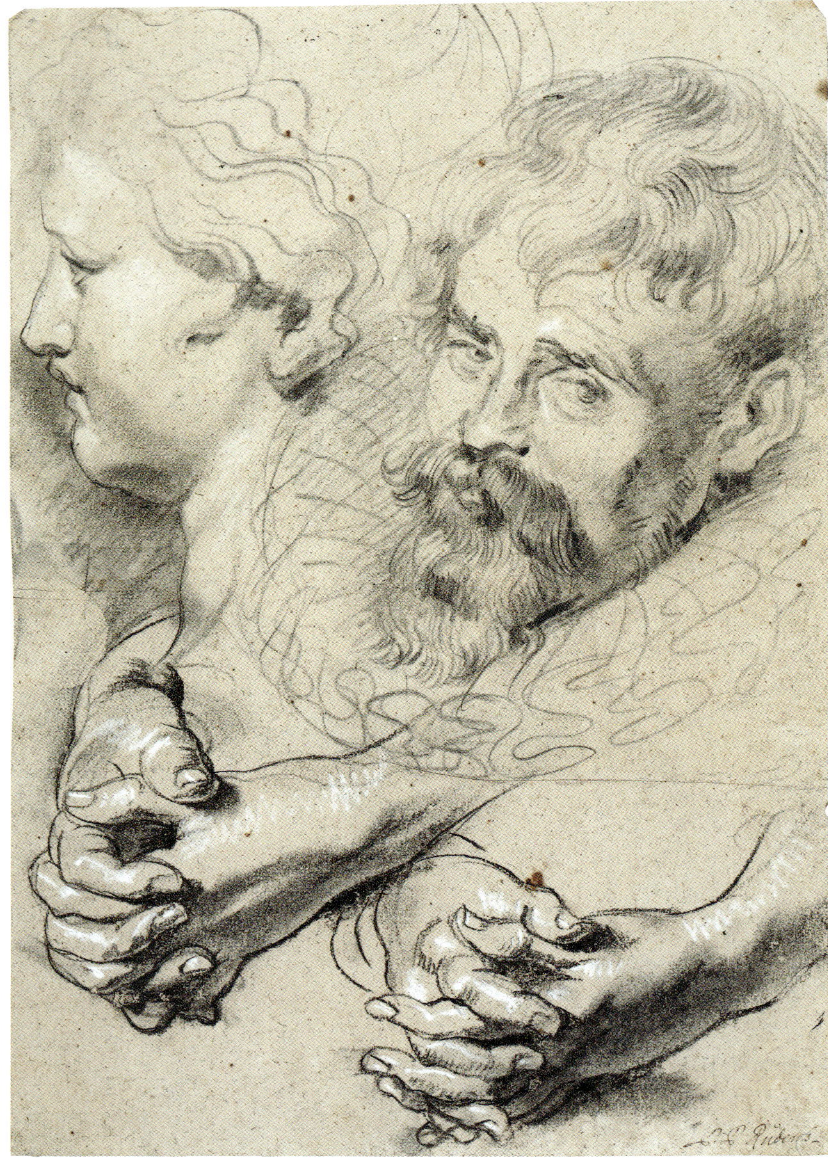

Cat. 40

left leg, the earlier one drawn more lightly. Again, the pose is a departure from the oil sketch, where the soldier is partly hidden by another figure helping to raise the Cross, and is closer to the stance exhibited by the soldier in the final triptych.

The fourth drawing in the exhibition that is associated with Rubens's *Raising of the Cross* is a sheet of studies with two pairs of clasped hands and two heads (cat. no. 40). The hands are preparatory for those of the Virgin on the inner left wing of the altarpiece.[7] Rubens apparently studied them from life, since the lower pair rests on a surface and appears to cast a shadow. Rubens chose the pair at the left for the final panel. The sheet is evidence of how carefully the artist thought about even relatively small details and prepared multiple sketches to find the most natural-looking gesture.

The hands are drawn in an oily black chalk and the head studies in a drier, grayer chalk, indicating that the two parts of the sheet may not have been sketched at the same time. The following sequence for these studies may be proposed: Rubens probably drew the head of the bearded man in a ruff collar first, since the female head and the hands respect its boundaries, followed by the female head, and ending with the hands at the bottom. The sheet was cut in two, separating the heads from the hands, but the pieces were later rejoined. After Rubens added the hands below, he applied a few accents in the oily black chalk to the female head above, strengthening her profile.[8] The woman's head has been associated with the young woman on the inner left wing of the triptych who faces the viewer.[9] In type, the face also relates to the head of the woman at the bottom of the same panel. The ruff collar of the bearded man identifies him as a contemporary of the artist, and it has been suggested that he is Cornelis van der Geest, the Antwerp merchant who had helped Rubens win the *Raising of the Cross* commission.[10] However, there is not an obvious resemblance. A more likely candidate is Jan Brueghel the Elder (1568–1625), who is portrayed by Rubens in a family portrait, painted about 1612–13.[11]

1. K.d.K., ed. Oldenbourg 1921, no. 36; M. Jaffé 1989, no. 135A, 1610; Judson 2000, no. 20, figs. 61, 63, 64, 68, 75, 76. On the outer wings Rubens represented Saints Amandus and Walburga, on the left, and Saints Catherine and Eligius, on the right (see Judson 2000, nos. 21, 22, figs. 81, 82).
2. Judson 2000, no. 20h, fig. 72.
3. Held 1980, no. 349, pl. 343; M. Jaffé 1989, no. 131, ca. 1610.
4. Baudouin (1992, p. 78) suggested that Rubens used the same model in all three figure studies shown here (cat. nos. 37–39) for the *Raising of the Cross*. We reject the opinion that a second, similar study of *Christ on the Cross* in the Fogg Art Museum (inv. 1943.524; Judson 2000, no. 20b, fig. 65) is also by Rubens. That drawing is more likely by Jacob de Wit, as first suggested by Frits Lugt in 1961 (Fogg Art Museum files, March 1961).
5. J. Q. van Regteren Altena was the first to suggest that the washes were an intervention by De Wit (letter to Ludwig Burchard, August 1938); see Judson 2000, p. 105, under no. 20i.
6. De Wit's activities as an artist, collector, and "finisher" of Rubens's drawings are discussed in the essay by Michiel C. Plomp in this publication.
7. K.d.K., ed. Oldenbourg 1921, no. 36; M. Jaffé 1989, no. 135B, 1610.
8. The sheet was trimmed especially at the top, where lines belonging to another sketch are clearly visible between the two heads.
9. Baudouin 1992, p. 83.
10. Held 1986, p. 91, under no. 56.
11. Seilern 1955, no. 18.

The Assumption of the Virgin

41. *Study of a Man Bending Forward,* recto; *Young Man in Ample Garment,* verso, ca. 1611–12

Black and red chalk, heightened with white, on light gray paper, some red chalk in the face on recto, 401 x 247 mm (15¹³⁄₁₆ x 9¹¹⁄₁₆ in.); cut irregularly at left and top

Albertina, Vienna (8300)

Provenance: Hofbibliothek, Vienna; Duke Albert of Sachsen-Teschen (1738–1822), Vienna (Lugt 174).

Literature: R., vol. 5, no. 1580; Glück and Haberditzl 1928, nos. 124, 125, pls. 124, 125 (recto and verso); Kuznetsov 1974, pl. 83; Mitsch 1977, pp. 1176–77; Freedberg 1984, no. 37a, fig. 92 (recto), no. 37b, fig. 93 (verso); Balis 1986, p. 116.

Exhibitions: Vienna 1977b, nos. 11 (recto), ill., 12 (verso), ill.; Sydney 2002, no. 48, ill.

42. *Young Woman in Profile,* recto; *Indistinct Sketches,* verso, ca. 1611–12

Black chalk, heightened with white, recto; black chalk gone over with pen and brown ink, verso, 375 x 251 mm (14¾ x 9⅞ in.)

National Gallery of Art, Washington, D.C.; Ailsa Mellon Bruce Fund (1978.18.1)

Provenance: Jonathan Richardson Sr. (1665–1745), London (Lugt 2184); Charles Rogers (1711–1784), London (Lugt 624); François Flameng (1856–1923), Paris (his sale, Paris, Georges Petit Gallery, May 26–27, 1919, lot 87, pl. 53); private collection, Paris; Slatkin Galleries, New York; acquired by the National Gallery in 1978.

Literature: Burchard and d'Hulst 1963, no. 111, pl. 111; Logan and Haverkamp-Begemann 1978, p. 92, fig. 20; Freedberg 1984, no. 37f, fig. 94; Balis 1986, p. 257; Held 1986, nos. 78, 79, pls. 86, 105.

Exhibitions: Washington 1978, p. 64, ill. on cover; Wellesley–Cleveland 1993–94, no. 46, ill.

43. *The Assumption of the Virgin,* 1612–15

Pen and brush and brown ink and brown wash, partly corrected with white bodycolor, traces of black chalk, on brown prepared paper, 292 x 231 mm (11½ x 9⅛ in.)
Annotated in pen and black ink at bottom right: *82*

Albertina, Vienna (8212)

Provenance: Duke Albert of Sachsen-Teschen (1738–1822), Vienna (Lugt 174).

Literature: R., vol. 5, no. 1437; Benesch 1959, p. 35, fig. 2 [Van Dyck]; Held 1959, no. 35, pl. 38, and p. 71; Burchard and d'Hulst 1963, no. 73, pl. 73; Kuznetsov 1974, pl. 44; Van de Velde 1975, pp. 254–58, fig. 5; Berlin 1977, pp. 65–67, under no. 20; Freedberg 1984, no. 36, fig. 86; Held 1986, no. 85, colorpl. 1.

Exhibitions: Vienna 1977b, no. 8, ill.; Vienna 1978, no. 89, ill.; Washington–New York–Vienna 1984–86, no. 35, ill.

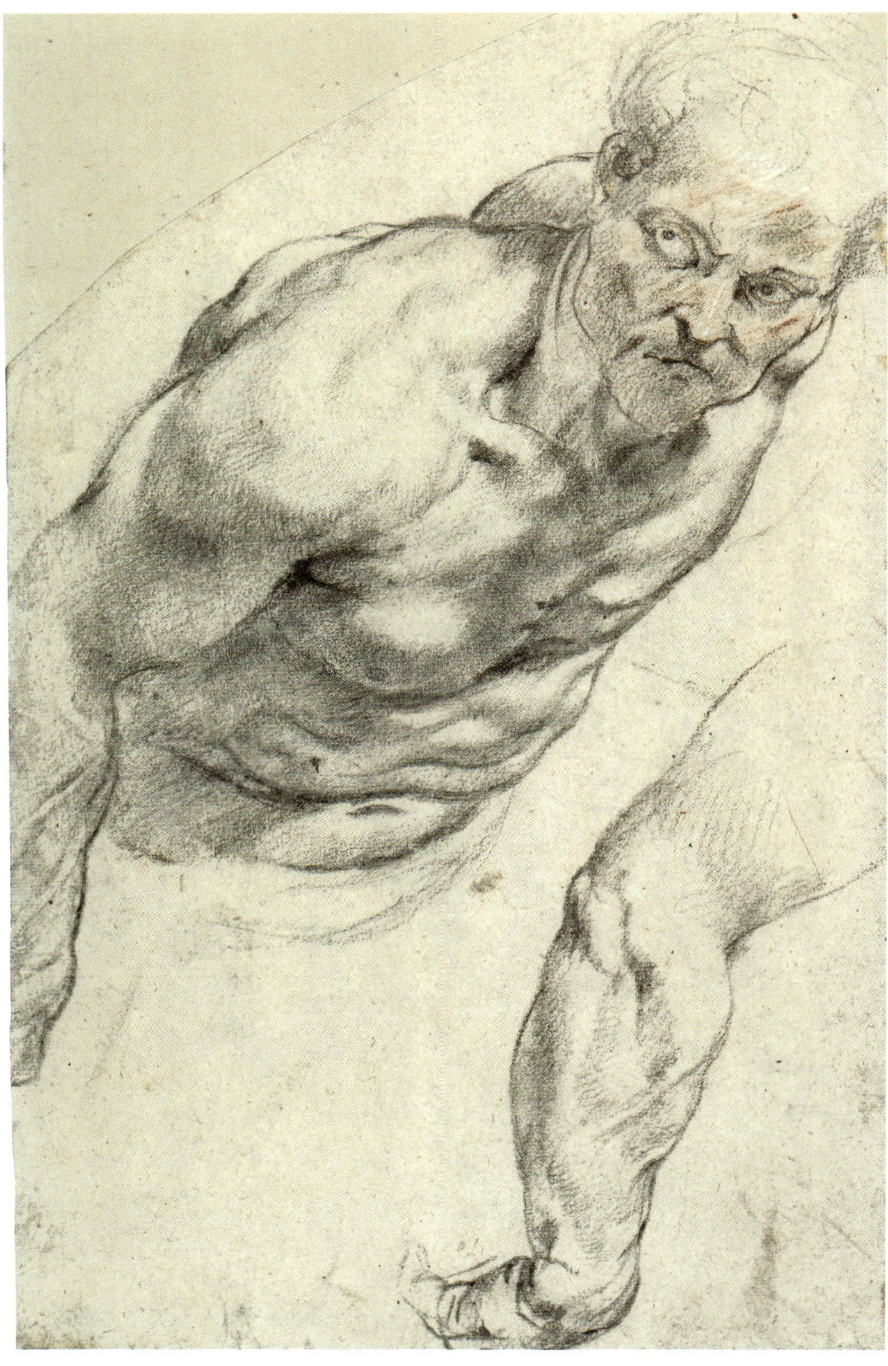

Cat. 41 recto

Rubens devoted about a dozen large altarpieces and oil sketches to the subject of the Assumption of the Virgin, an event celebrated for many centuries as an important festival of the Catholic Church. The textual source for the Assumption is not the Bible but the second-century *Liber de Transitu Virginis.*[1] There the Virgin is described as borne aloft by angels, while on the earth below, holy women and the Apostles gather around her empty tomb. Titian's famous Assumption of 1515–18 in Santa Maria Gloriosa dei Frari, Venice, surely served as the primary inspiration for Rubens's many versions. Rubens must have seen Titian's altarpiece on a visit to Venice and been struck by the powerful image of the Virgin, in the center, ascending toward God the Father, while below, separated from her by a bank of clouds, the Apostles gesture in amazement.

During the Counter-Reformation, representations of the Assumption of the Virgin were particularly popular, owing to the Church's emphasis on her veneration. It is not surprising, therefore, that Rubens created seven altarpieces depicting this

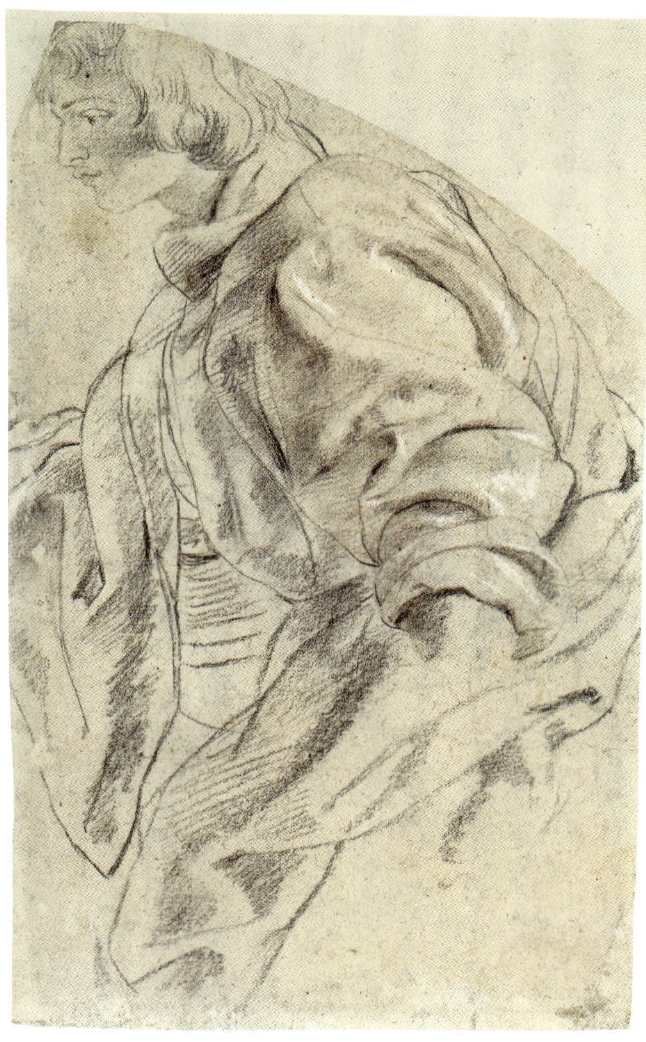

Cat. 41 verso

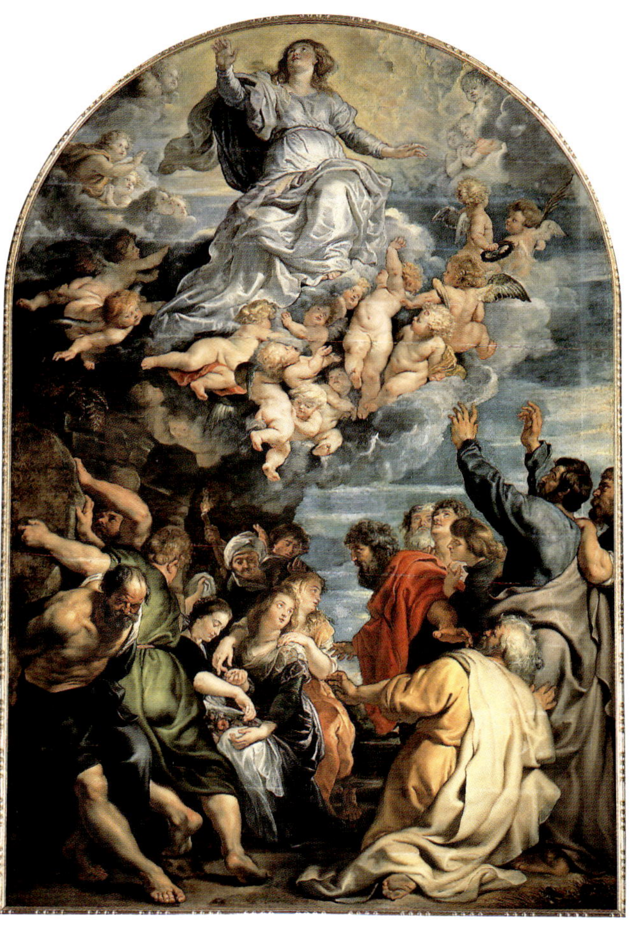

Fig. 89. Peter Paul Rubens, *The Assumption of the Virgin,* ca. 1611–13. Oil on oak panel, 458 x 297 cm (180 5/16 x 116 15/16 in.). Kunsthistorisches Museum, Vienna (GG 518)

subject, most of them with figures larger than lifesize. Five drawings associated with these paintings and their preliminary oil sketches are in the present exhibition (cat. nos. 41 recto and verso, 42, 43, 53).

The drawing of a man bending forward (cat. no. 41 recto) has been preserved in a somewhat mutilated state. In all likelihood, the study was originally one of many on a larger sheet and was cut from it by a seventeenth-century owner, perhaps in order to multiply the number of sheets in his collection or because he disliked the combination of studies on a single sheet. In doing so, he cut partly through the head of the figure of the young man on the verso.

The recto study is for the apostle in the lower left foreground of Rubens's large *Assumption of the Virgin,* today in the Kunsthistorisches Museum, Vienna (fig. 89).[2] The same figure was included in essentially the same position in the slightly earlier *modello* of the *Assumption and Coronation of the Virgin,* now in the State Hermitage Museum, Saint Petersburg (fig. 90).[3] This oil sketch and another one now lost (see below) were most likely submitted to the canons of Antwerp Cathedral on April 22, 1611, for consideration for a new painting on the high altar.[4] Although Rubens received the commission, the altarpiece was never realized, probably due to financial difficulties. In all likelihood the artist subsequently modified the upper half of his Assumption and Coronation scene for the Assumption scene in the Vienna painting. He probably began this painting soon after 1611, perhaps hoping that funds might still be raised for the Antwerp Cathedral project. The painting remained in his studio until about 1620, when members of the Houtappel family acquired and placed it in the chapel of the Virgin in the Jesuit church in Antwerp (today the church of Saint Charles Borromeo). In 1776, following the suppression of the Jesuit order, the altarpiece was added to the imperial collections in Vienna.

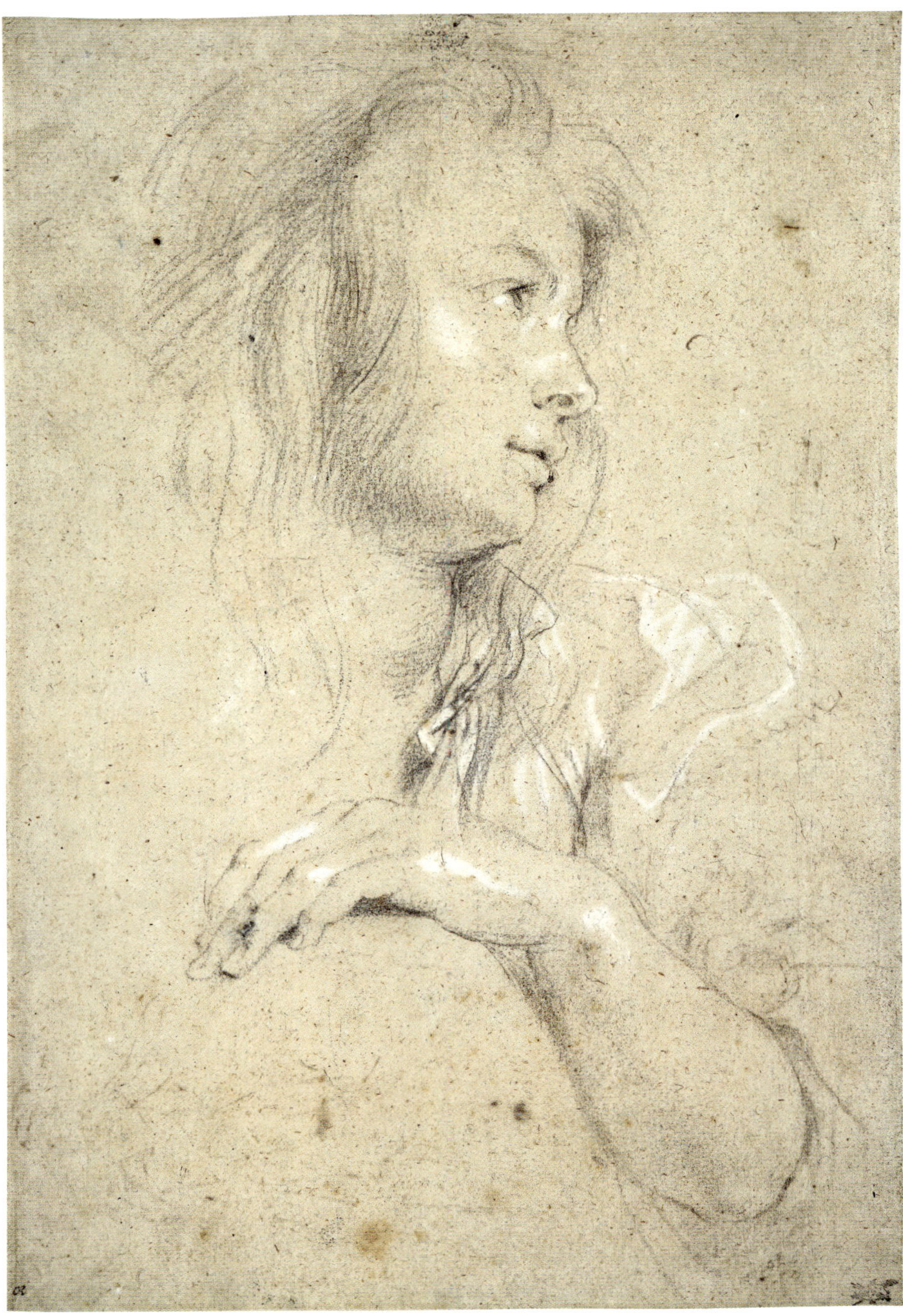

Cat. 42 recto

Although the *modello* for the Vienna *Assumption* includes the apostle at the lower left, who supports the boulder that had covered Mary's grave, Rubens the perfectionist drew the later study on the recto of catalogue number 41 from the model. The artist paid close attention to the figures in his final paintings and made detailed chalk studies like this one in order to clarify gestures and poses for himself. Here, he studied the muscles involved in the apostle's strenuous task.[5] He made a separate sketch of the figure's right arm, with the hand cupped to grasp the heavy load, but he did not incorporate it; at the left edge of the painting the right arm is cut off very much as it is in the drawing. The apostle in the *modello* is bent over and looks at the ground. In both the drawing and the final painting, his position is more erect, his brow expresses great physical strain, and his eyes meet those of the beholder.

The drawing on the verso of catalogue number 41 also shows Rubens rethinking a figure for the *Assumption* altarpiece. Apparently, the artist was not entirely satisfied in the *modello*

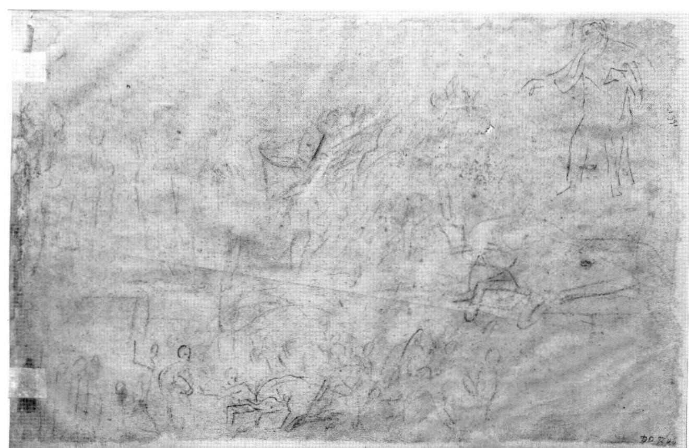
Cat. 42 verso

with the bearded apostle with open arms who appears directly opposite the women. In the drawing Rubens experimented with the apostle's pose, showing him standing almost upright and with a beardless face. Yet again, however, he changed his mind in the final painting, where the apostle is older, wears a different garment, and once again is bearded. In the end, Rubens took from the drawing only the detail of the upturned collar, though not for this apostle but for the one behind him.

Not all Rubens's figures underwent so many modifications between the preparatory chalk drawings and the final painting. For the Vienna *Assumption* the artist used almost without change the studies on a beautiful sheet in the Kupferstich-Kabinett, Dresden,[6] of the hands of the apostle with his arms thrown open and those of the apostle in the lower right foreground.

Rubens drew the sensitive study of a *Young Woman in Profile* (cat. no. 42 recto) in preparation for one of the three holy women in the Vienna *Assumption*. Made subsequent to the completion of the oil sketch, the drawing relates to the young woman beside the empty tomb of the Virgin who turns toward the group of apostles, her left hand resting on the shoulder of the woman before her. With her right hand, she points to the roses that were miraculously discovered inside the Virgin's shroud. The flowers and the apostles who watch the Virgin ascending to heaven are described in the *Golden Legend,* the popular thirteenth-century compilation of readings on the saints by Jacobus de Voragine.[7] The holy women around the tomb, frequently found in a group of three as here, are probably the women who washed the body of the Virgin and then placed it in a shroud, as described in Voragine's *Golden Legend.*[8] Of Rubens's six known preliminary sketches for the Vienna *Assumption,*[9] this one, drawn lightly in black chalk with touches of white, is by far the most delicate. On the verso, Rubens drew quick, indistinct sketches in chalk, sometimes strengthened with the pen, which are difficult to identify and place within the artist's oeuvre. They seem to include a scene with a bull and may date from about the same time as the *Young Woman* on the recto.[10]

The compositional study of the *Assumption of the Virgin* in the Albertina (cat. no. 43) is the only known drawing in which Rubens sketched the Virgin ascending to heaven. The artist's search for a satisfactory solution is evident in numerous pentimenti, especially among the putti. These were first drawn with a light brown ink, then reinforced with darker ink. Further details such as the veil billowing behind the Virgin were added with the brush, and wash was applied to suggest depth. Overall, the drawing does not display the clarity one expects of Rubens's compositional studies. The dark brown ink, the rather obvious corrections, and the heavy addition of dark wash are not characteristic of other early Rubens drawings, such as his *Adoration of the Image of the Madonna della Vallicella* of 1608 (cat. no. 18).

The sheet can be placed only approximately within Rubens's early Assumption scenes of about 1611–16. The composition seems to be an evolution from the *Assumption and*

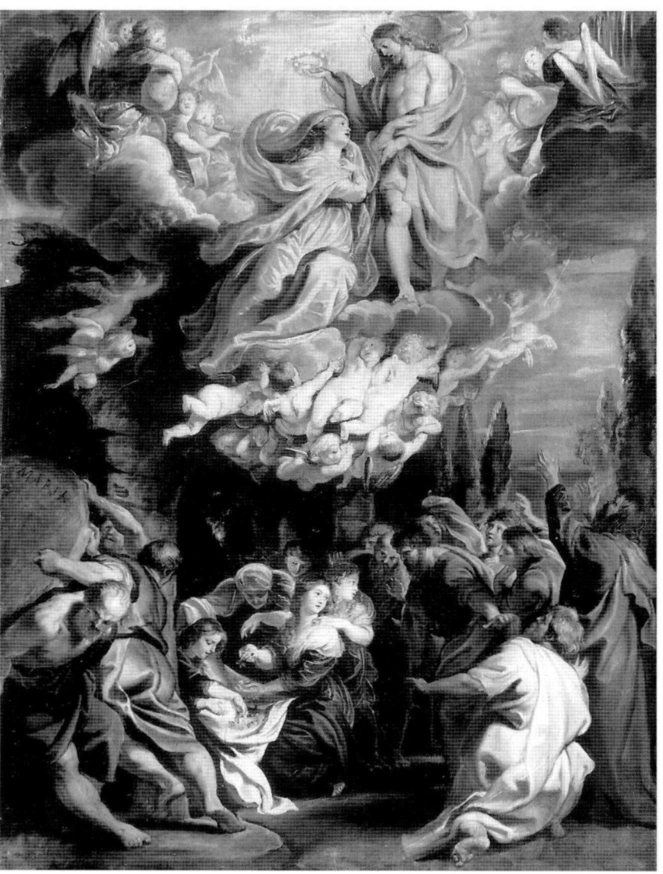
Fig. 90. Peter Paul Rubens, *The Assumption and Coronation of the Virgin,* ca. 1611. Oil on canvas transferred from wood, 106 x 78 cm (41¾ x 30 11/16 in.). The State Hermitage Museum, Saint Petersburg (1703)

Fig. 91. Peter Paul Rubens, *The Assumption of the Virgin*, ca. 1613–14. Oil on panel, 102 x 66 cm (40 3/16 x 26 in.). Collection of Her Majesty the Queen, Buckingham Palace, London (RCIN 405335)

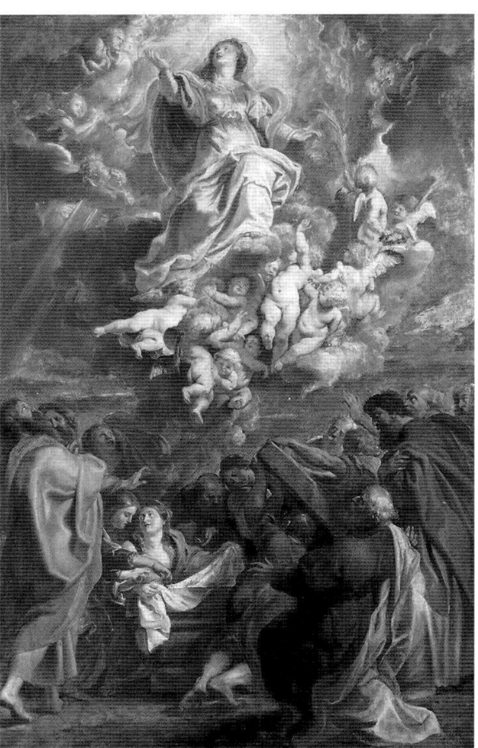

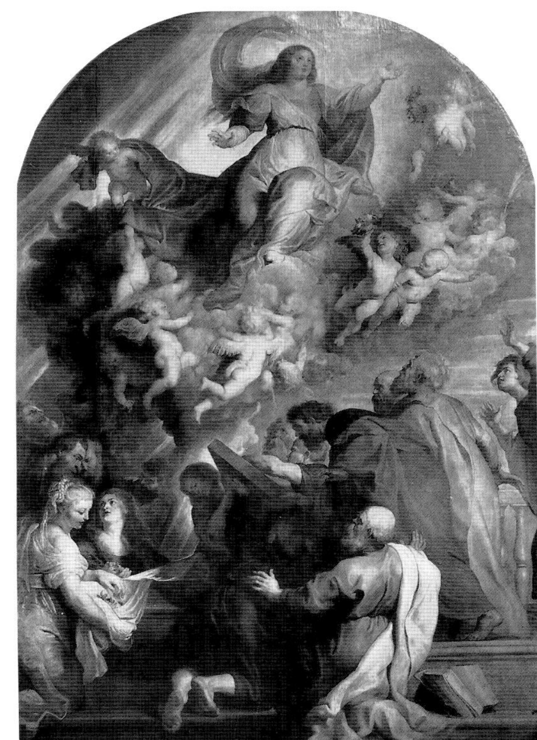

Fig. 92. Peter Paul Rubens, *The Assumption of the Virgin*, ca. 1615–16. Oil on canvas, 500 x 340 cm (196 7/8 x 133 7/8 in.). Musées Royaux des Beaux-Arts, Brussels (166)

Coronation of the Virgin oil sketch, and it has been suggested that it was made in preparation for a now-lost second *modello,* of the *Assumption,* that Rubens presented to the canons of Antwerp Cathedral.[11] Another possibility is that the drawing was an exercise for the oil sketch at Buckingham Palace (fig. 91),[12] which, in turn, is one of the preliminary works for the Vienna altarpiece. Before Rubens altered the positions of many of the angels with the brush in the drawing, their outlines in pen corresponded to those in the Buckingham Palace *modello.* To complicate things further, the pose of the Virgin resembles that of the Virgin in yet another *Assumption,* the one Rubens painted about 1615–16 for the Discalced Carmelite nuns, today in the Musées Royaux des Beaux-Arts, Brussels (fig. 92).[13] The Albertina sheet, David Freedberg has concluded, was "a working drawing which Rubens had to hand when occupied with ideas for the *Assumption* in these years [1611–16] and which may consequently be related in one way or another to all the paintings of this subject from the period concerned."[14]

Some scholars have cast doubt on the attribution of the Albertina sheet to Rubens. The Viennese art historians Gustav Glück and Franz Martin Haberditzl omitted it from their 1928 catalogue raisonné of Rubens's drawings. In 1959 Otto Benesch published the drawing with an attribution to Anthony van Dyck, which, to us, does not seem plausible. In the same year Julius Held strongly defended Rubens's authorship of the sheet in his survey of Rubens's drawings. Owing to Held's support, the drawing has been included in the Rubens literature ever since. We have reservations, however, for it is rare that it proves impossible to place a drawing in a relatively well-documented sequence in Rubens's oeuvre. Moreover, the technique and the rather dense formation of the figures on the Albertina sheet are unusual for Rubens. Nonetheless, the drawing is here tentatively included in Rubens's oeuvre.

1. Freedberg 1984, p. 138.
2. K.d.K., ed. Oldenbourg 1921, no. 206; Freedberg 1984, no. 37, fig. 87, ca. 1613; M. Jaffé 1989, no. 241, ca. 1614.
3. Held 1980, no. 374, esp. p. 510, pl. 365, ca. 1611; Freedberg 1984, no. 46, fig. 129; M. Jaffé 1989, no. 149, 1611.
4. Held 1980, p. 509, under no. 374. Held mentioned two *modelli* by Rubens and one *modello* by Van Veen.
5. The red chalk in the face was probably added by another hand.
6. Inv. C1966-64; Freedberg 1984, no. 37c, fig. 97.
7. Jacobus de Voragine, *The Golden Legend: Readings on the Saints,* trans. William Granger Ryan (Princeton, 1995), vol. 2, pp. 77–97.
8. See Freedberg 1984, pp. 138–43, for an excellent summary of the iconography.
9. Besides cat. no. 41 recto and verso, there is a double-sided drawing in the Fogg Art Museum, Harvard University, Cambridge, Mass. (Freedberg 1984, no. 37d, e, figs. 95, 96), and the aforementioned study in the Kupferstich-Kabinett, Dresden (Freedberg 1984, no. 37c, fig. 97).

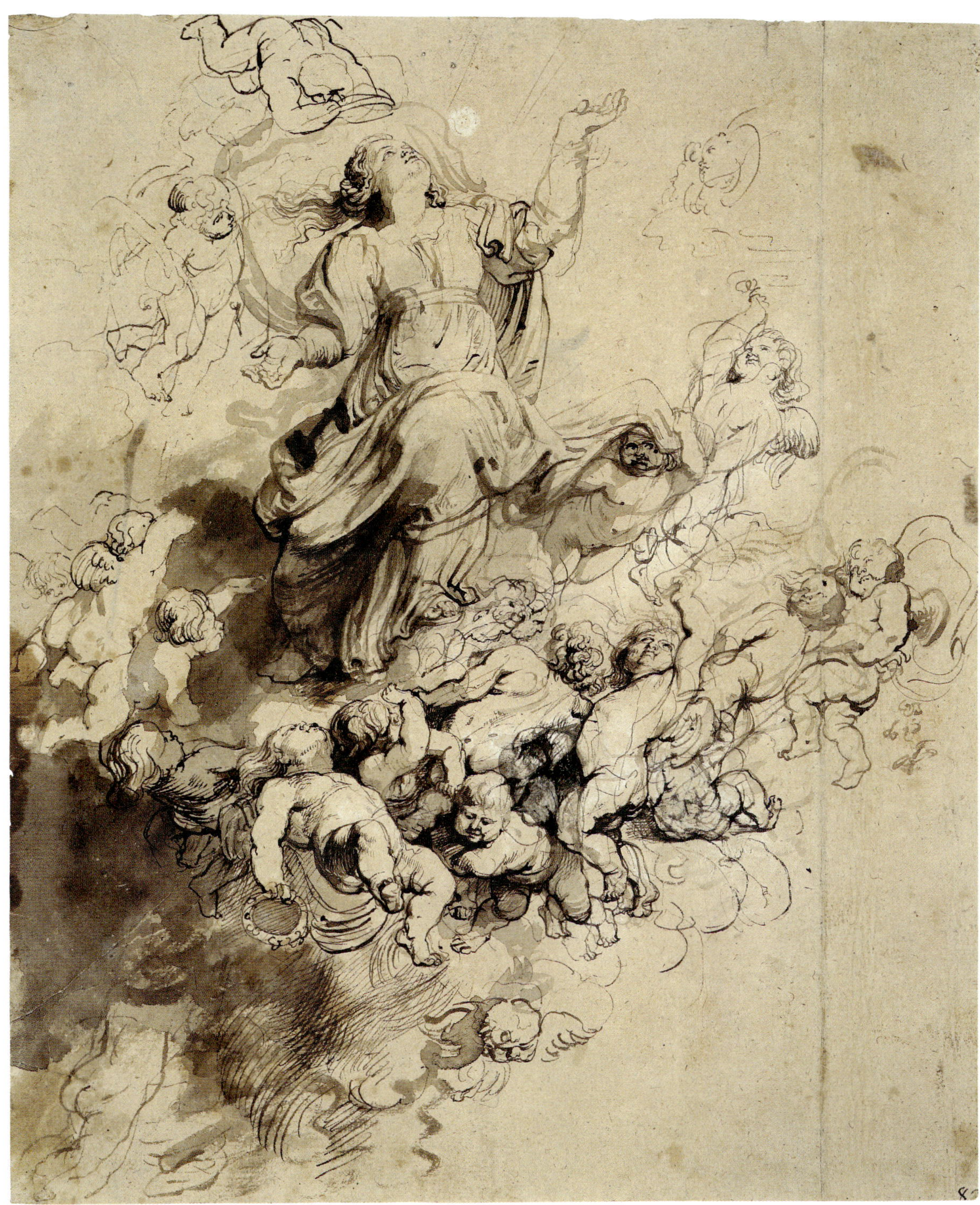

Cat. 43

10. See Balis 1986, no. 26.
11. Baudouin 1972, pp. 65–66. Baudouin identified it as a study for one of three *modelli* submitted to the canons in the spring of 1611, probably also with an Assumption scene. See Baudouin 2000, pp. 17–23.
12. Inv. RCIN 405335; Held 1980, no. 375, pl. 366, ca. 1613–14; Freedberg 1984, no. 35, ca. 1612; M. Jaffé 1989, no. 148, 1611.
13. K.d.K., ed. Oldenbourg 1921, no. 120, 1616–17; Held 1980, p. 512, under no. 375, ca. 1615–16; Freedberg 1984, no. 38, ca. 1615–16; M. Jaffé 1989, no. 382, ca. 1616.
14. Freedberg 1984, p. 148, under no. 36.

44. *Studies of Four Hands and Two Male Heads,* ca. 1613

Black chalk, heightened with white chalk, on grayish paper, 343 x 231 mm (13½ x 9¼ in.)

Albertina, Vienna (8307)

Provenance: Hofbibliothek, Vienna; in 1796 acquired through exchange by Duke Albert of Sachsen-Teschen (1738–1822), Vienna (Lugt 174).

Literature: R., vol. 5, no. 1579; Glück and Haberditzl 1928, no. 74, pl. 74; Held 1959, no. 81, pl. 90; Burchard and d'Hulst 1963, under no. 60; Kuznetsov 1974, pl. 33; Held 1980, under no. 358; Held 1986, no. 74, pl. 75; Judson 2000, no. 45d, fig. 156.

Exhibitions: Vienna 1977b, no. 9, ill.; Washington–New York–Vienna 1984–86, no. 34, ill.; Vienna–Amsterdam 1989–90, no. 47, ill.; New York and other cities 1997–99, no. 31, ill.

This sheet of studies is one of two surviving drawings for Rubens's *Descent from the Cross* altarpiece in Antwerp Cathedral (fig. 93; for a discussion of the altarpiece, see cat. no. 30). It consists of four separate studies for figures in the *Presentation in the Temple*, the inner right wing of the altarpiece. Rubens arrived at the composition in the oil sketch today in the Courtauld Institute of Art Gallery, London (fig. 94),[1] and the final painting was completed in early 1614.[2]

Using black chalk with white chalk for highlights, the artist drew the heads of Joseph (upper right) and the prophet Simeon (lower left), as well as the hands of Simeon (lower right) and the prophetess Hannah (upper left). These preliminary studies, which postdate the oil sketch, may have served as a guide to Rubens's studio assistants, who started painting the altarpiece.

While the compositional drawing in New York for the *Presentation in the Temple* (cat. no. 30) dates from 1611, the year Rubens received the altarpiece commission from the Arquebusiers' Guild, the Vienna sheet must date closer to the spring of 1613, when the panels for the wings of the altarpiece were paid for.[3]

1. Held 1980, no. 358, pl. 354; M. Jaffé 1989, no. 187, 1612–13.
2. K.d.K., ed. Oldenbourg 1921, no. 52; M. Jaffé 1989, no. 189c, 1614.
3. The panels for the wings probably were among the items the Arquebusiers' Guild paid for on May 21, 1613. See the account book published in R., vol. 2, pp. 114–15; Aerts and Nieuwenhuizen 1992, p. 41, no. 6.

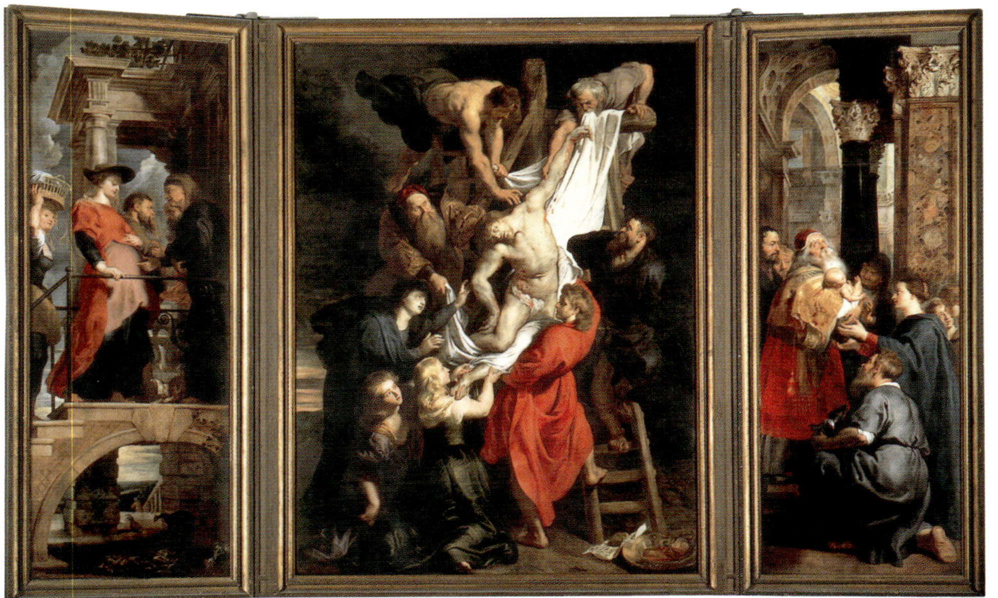

Fig. 93. Peter Paul Rubens, *The Descent from the Cross,* 1611–14. Oil on panel, central panel 421 x 311 cm (165¾ x 122⁷⁄₁₆ in.), wings 421 x 153 cm (165¾ x 60¼ in.) each. Antwerp Cathedral

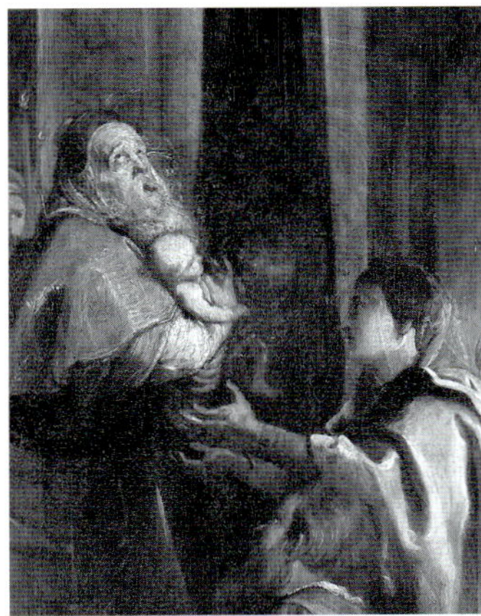

Fig. 94. Peter Paul Rubens, Detail of *The Presentation in the Temple,* 1611–13. Oil on panel, 83 x 30.4 cm (32¹¹⁄₁₆ x 11¹⁵⁄₁₆ in.). Courtauld Institute of Art Gallery, London (P.1978.PG.360)

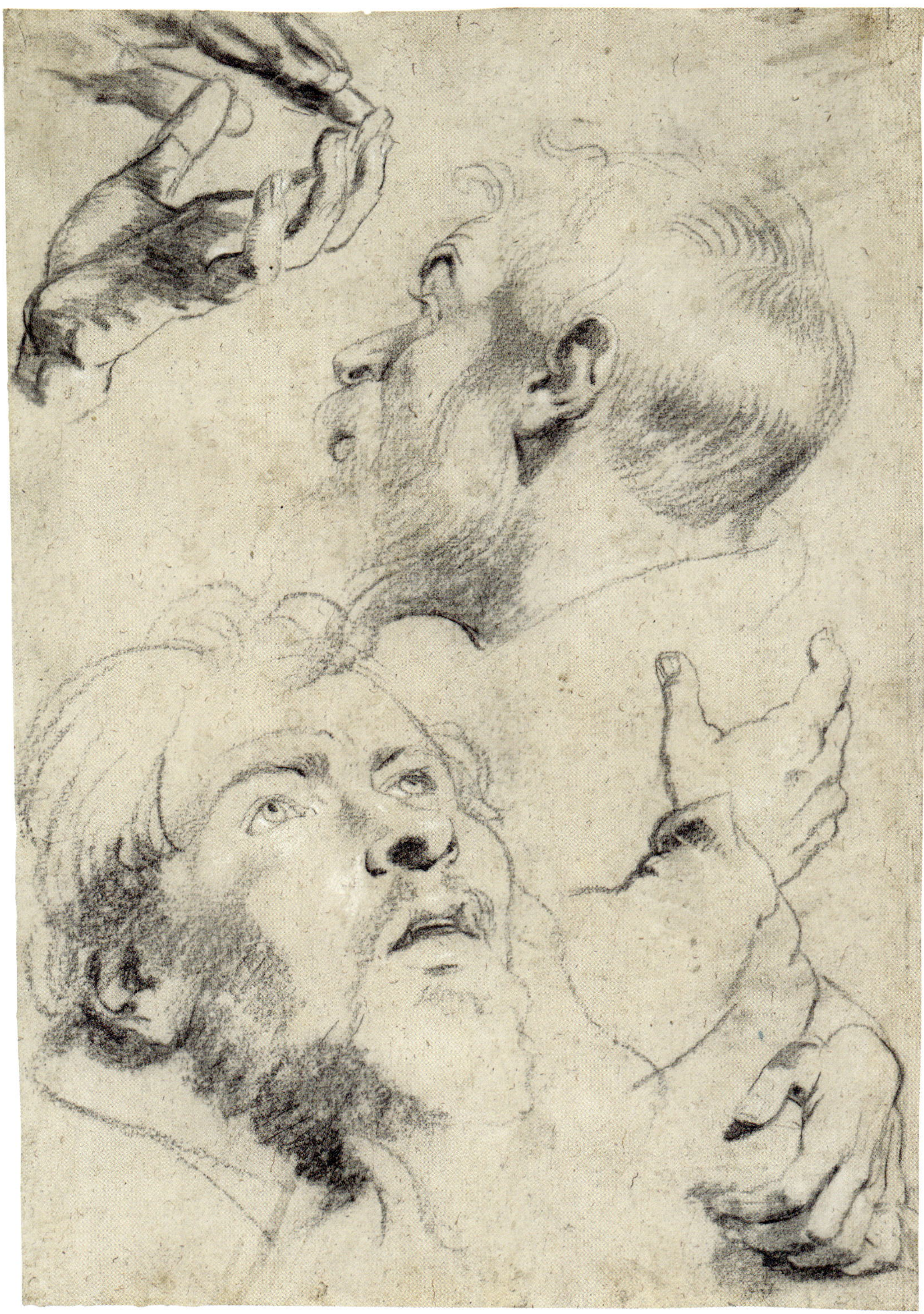

Cat. 44

Daniel in the Lions' Den

45. *Seated Male Youth,* ca. 1613

Black chalk, heightened with white chalk, on light gray paper, 500 x 299 mm (19 11/16 x 11 3/4 in.)

The Pierpont Morgan Library, New York (I,232)

Provenance: William Bates (1824–1884), Birmingham (Lugt 2604; his sale, London, Sotheby's, January 19, 1887, probably part of lot 337, "P. P. Rubens. Various Studies and Sketches" [7]); Sir John Charles Robinson (1824–1913), London (Lugt 1433); Charles Fairfax Murray (1849–1919), London and Florence; from whom purchased through Galerie Alexandre Imbert, Rome, in 1909 by John Pierpont Morgan Sr. (1837–1913), New York; his son, John Pierpont Morgan Jr. (1867–1943), New York; his gift to the Pierpont Morgan Library in 1924.

Literature: Glück and Haberditzl 1928, no. 97, pl. 97; Held 1959, no. 85, pl. 95, and p. 29; Burchard and d'Hulst 1963, no. 110, pl. 110; Kuznetsov 1974, pl. 63; Held 1986, no. 92, pl. 85; d'Hulst and Vandenven 1989, no. 57a, fig. 141, p. 190; Stampfle 1991, no. 306, ill.

Exhibitions: Cambridge, Mass.–New York 1956, no. 14, pl. 8; London 1977a, no. 69, ill.; Paris–Antwerp–London–New York 1979–80, no. 12, ill.; New York 1981, no. 59, ill.

46. *Lion,* ca. 1613

Black chalk, heightened with white, yellow chalk in background, 252 x 283 mm (9 15/16 x 11 1/8 in.)

National Gallery of Art, Washington, D.C.; Ailsa Mellon Bruce Fund (1969.7.1)

Provenance: Marquis de Gouvernet (sale, Paris, November 6–10, 1775); Conseiller Nourri (sale, Paris, February 24–March 14, 1785); Conseiller de St. Maurice (sale, Paris, February 1, 1786); George Fenwick-Owen, Lether Melton (bought in mixed lot at London, Sotheby, ca. 1930); Mrs. Denise Fenwick-Owen, London (sale, London, Sotheby, March 27, 1969, no. 86, ill.); Agnew, London.

Literature: M. Jaffé 1970b, p. 9, fig. 4, and under n. 38; d'Hulst and Vandenven 1989, no. 57h, fig. 151.

Exhibitions: Wellesley–Cleveland 1993–94, no. 44, ill.; Washington 1998, no. 74, fig. 28.

47. *Lioness Seen from the Rear, Turning to the Left,* ca. 1613

Black chalk, with touches of yellow, heightened with white oil or body color, some gray wash, laid down, 396 x 235 mm (15 9/16 x 9 1/4 in.)

The British Museum, London (1994.5.14.46)

Provenance: John Barnard (d. 1784), London (sale, London, February 21, 1787, lot 61); Sir Thomas Lawrence (1769–1830), London (Lugt 2445); Sir Robert Peel (1788–1850), London, before 1844; National Gallery, London (acquired in 1871 with the Peel collection); deposited on loan to the Department of Prints and Drawings at the British Museum in 1935 and formally transferred to the museum in 1994.

Literature: R., vol. 5, no. 1428; Hind 1923, no. 130; Glück and Haberditzl 1928, no. 99, pl. 99; M. Jaffé 1955, pp. 59–61, 64–66, fig. 4; Held 1959, p. 30, no. 83, pl. 96 and vol. 2, frontis.; Kuznetsov 1974, pl. 42; Held 1986, no. 93, colorpl. 2; d'Hulst and Vandenven 1989, no. 57g, fig. 148, pp. 190, 194, under no. 57b, and 197, under no. 57f.

Exhibition: London 1977a, no. 70, ill.

48. *Lion Resting,* ca. 1613

Black chalk and brown wash, heightened with white, background tinted in yellow, touch of green wash, 281 x 427 mm (11 1/16 x 16 13/16 in.)

The British Museum, London (Oo. 9-35)

Provenance: George Knapton (1698–1778), London; bequeathed to General Morrison (sale, London, T. Philipe, June 1, 1807, lot 745); Richard Payne Knight (1750–1824), London (Lugt 1577); bequeathed to the British Museum in 1824.

Literature: Hind 1923, no. 117, pl. XVII; Glück and Haberditzl 1928, no. 98, pl. 98; Held 1959, under no. 83; Burchard and d'Hulst 1963, under no. 110; M. Jaffé 1970b, p. 13, fig. 11; Held 1986, under no. 93; d'Hulst and Vandenven 1989, no. 57i, fig. 150, pp. 191, 194–95.

Exhibition: London 1977a, no. 68, ill.

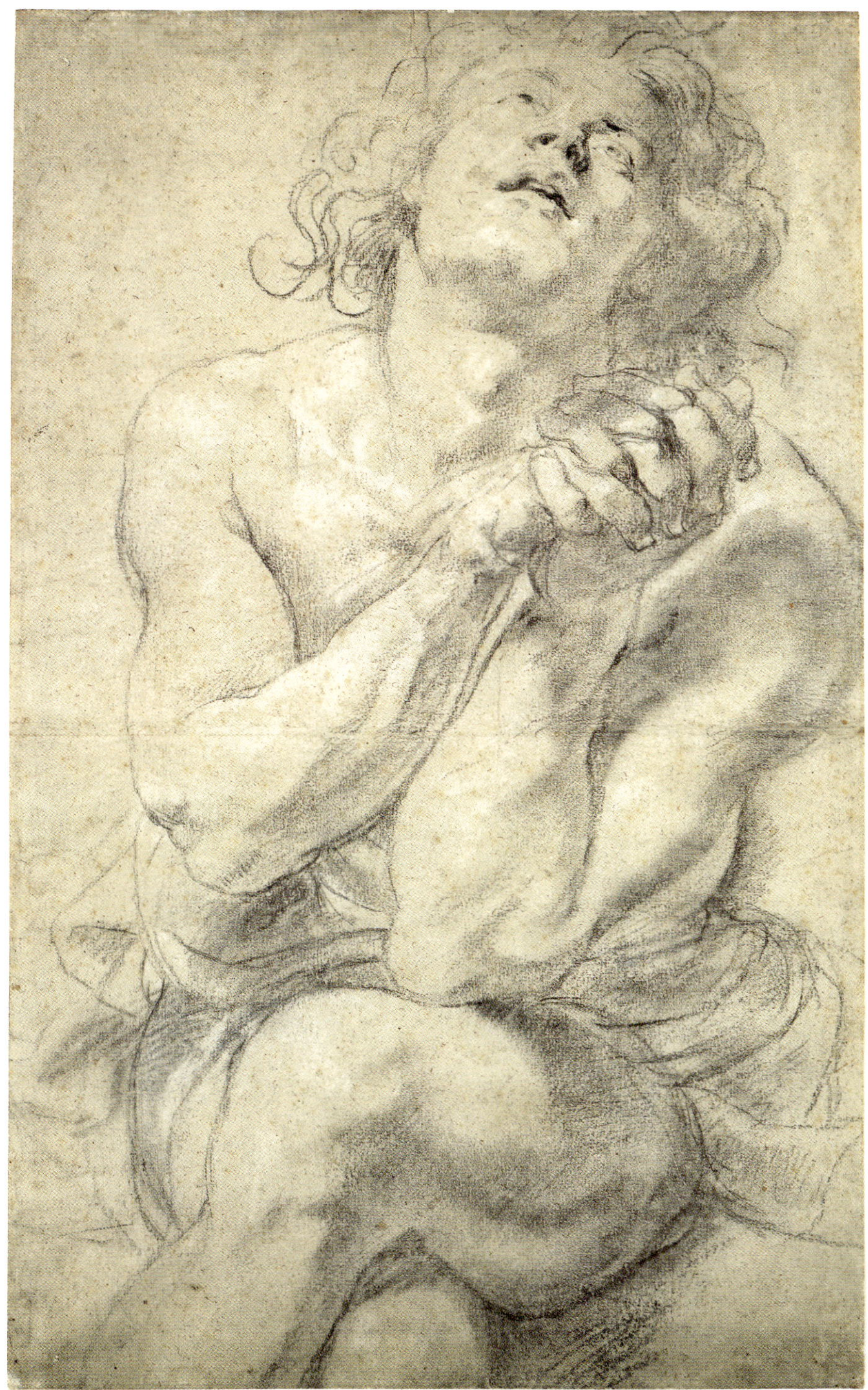

Cat. 45

Rubens drew this magnificent study of a seated youth and three equally impressive views of lions and a lioness for his painting of *Daniel in the Lions' Den,* today in the National Gallery of Art, Washington, D.C. (fig. 95).[1] According to the Old Testament story (Daniel 6:1–28), the Persian king Darius ordered that the prophet Daniel be cast into a lions' den as punishment for worshiping the God of Israel rather than the king. Rubens depicted the moment when, on the following day, the stone sealing the entrance to the den was removed and Daniel, in fervent prayer, was revealed unharmed.

Nothing is known of the circumstances surrounding the commission for the painting. We do have information, however,

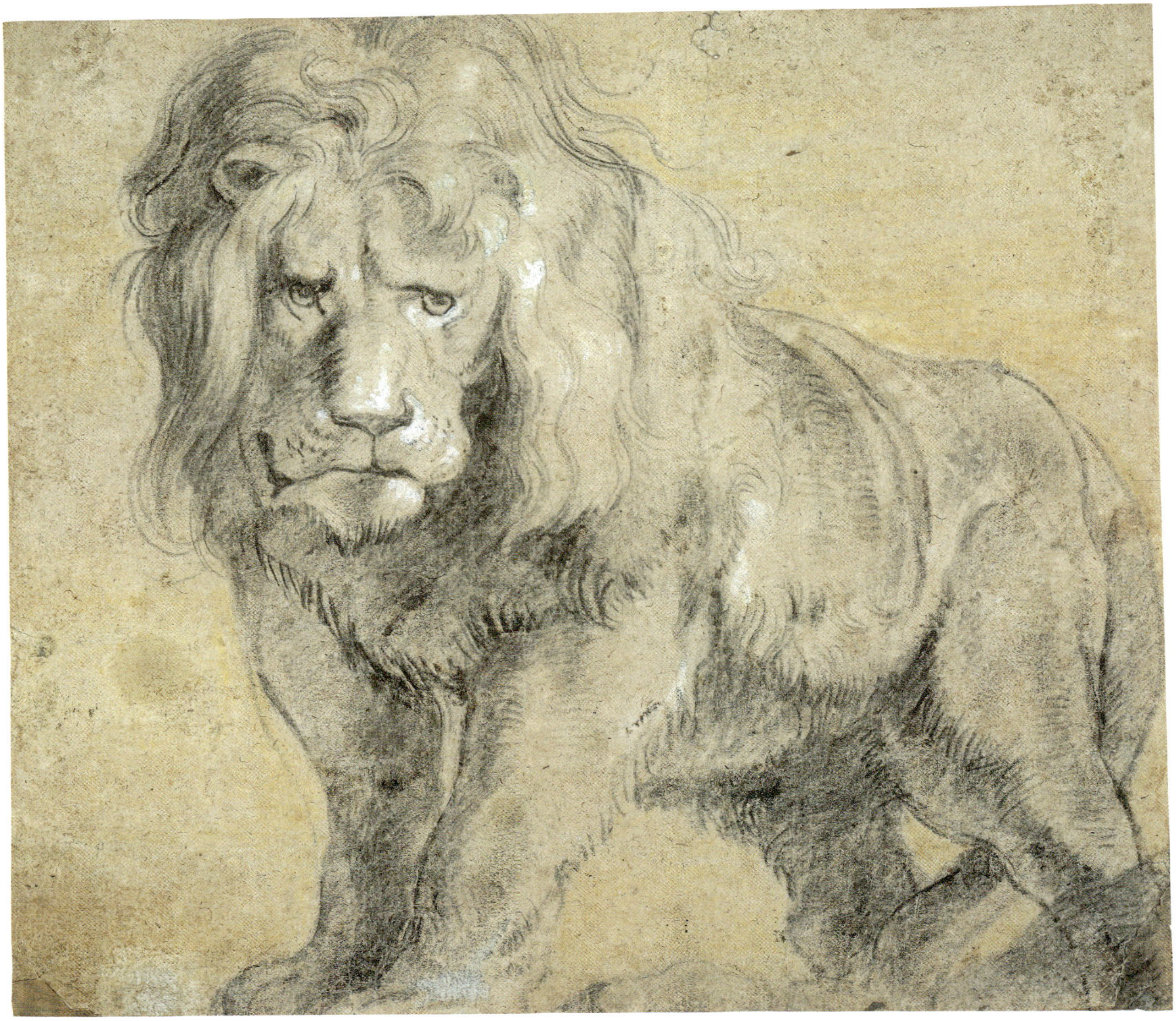

Cat. 46

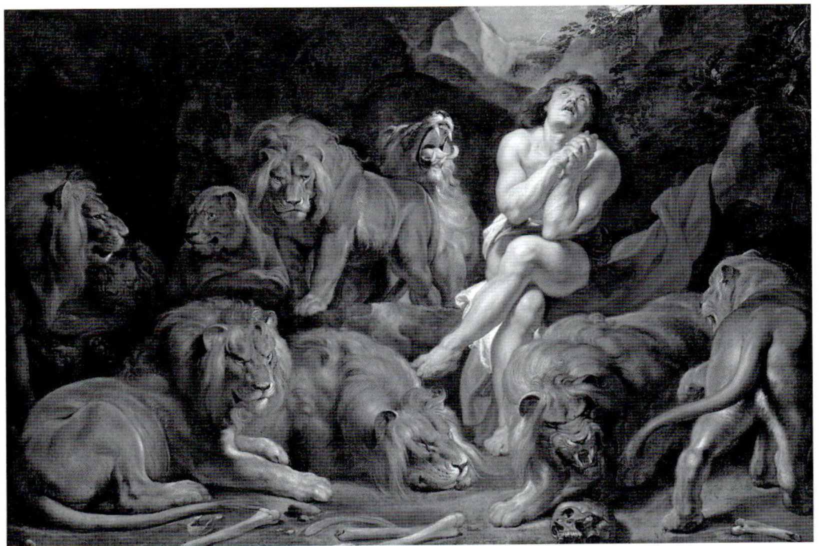

Fig. 95. Peter Paul Rubens, *Daniel in the Lions' Den*, ca. 1612–13. Oil on canvas, 224 x 330 cm (88 3/16 x 129 15/16 in.). National Gallery of Art, Washington, D.C.; Ailsa Mellon Bruce Fund, 1965 (1965.13.1 [1948])

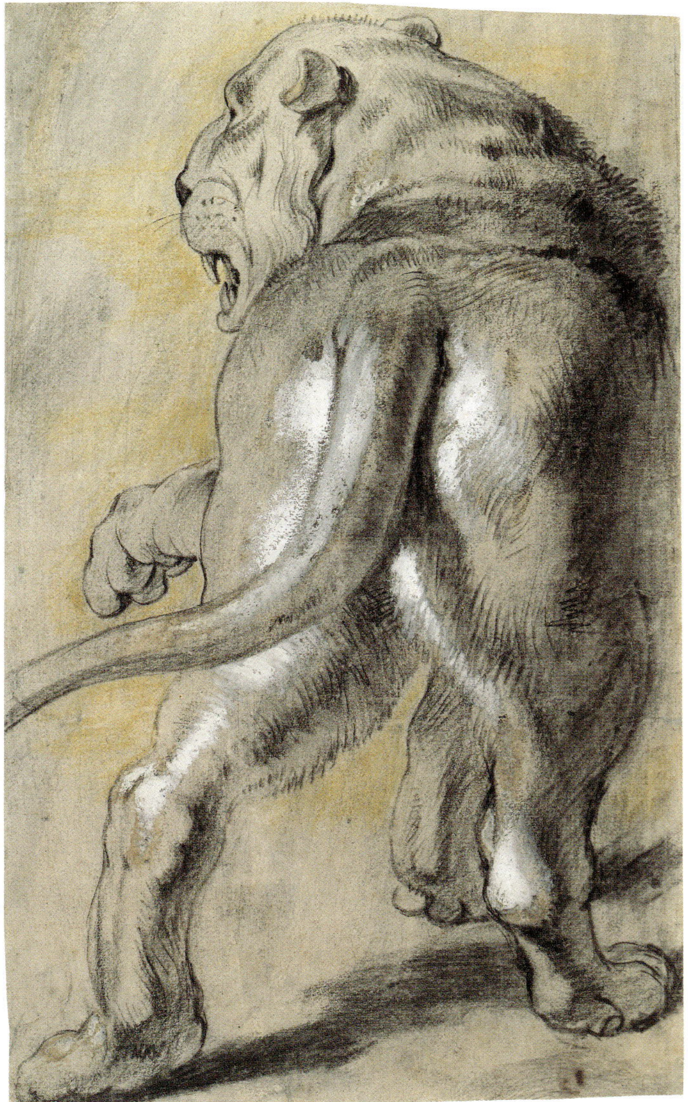

Cat. 47

about how and when it left Rubens's studio. In a letter of April 28, 1618, to the collector Sir Dudley Carleton (then serving in The Hague as the ambassador of King James I of England), Rubens described the finished canvas as follows: "Daniel among many lions, taken from life. Original entirely by my hand."[2] At the time, Rubens was negotiating an exchange of twelve paintings (produced by him alone, executed by assistants and retouched by him, or realized in collaboration with another artist) for antique marbles owned by Carleton. Rubens was successful, and the following year, his *Daniel in the Lions' Den* was recorded in Carleton's collection. The English diplomat later presented the painting to King Charles I.

On the sheet from the Pierpont Morgan Library (cat. no. 45) Rubens drew a close-up view of a seated youth in preparation for the figure of Daniel. Rubens probably sketched the youth from life, but he placed the model in an unusual pose that recalls that of the penitent Saint Jerome in a drawing of about 1585 by Girolamo Muziano (1532–1592) that may once have belonged to Rubens (today in the Louvre, Paris).[3] The young man strikes a remarkably similar pose, with crossed legs and hands joined in prayer.[4]

The male lion whom Rubens studied on the large sheet in Washington (cat. no. 46) corresponds to the animal standing calmly to the left of Daniel in the final painting. A minor change was made to the beast's left front paw, which is slightly raised in the drawing but firmly placed on a rocky ledge in the painting. With his impressive mane he appears to be the leader of the pride, towering majestically over some eleven lions and

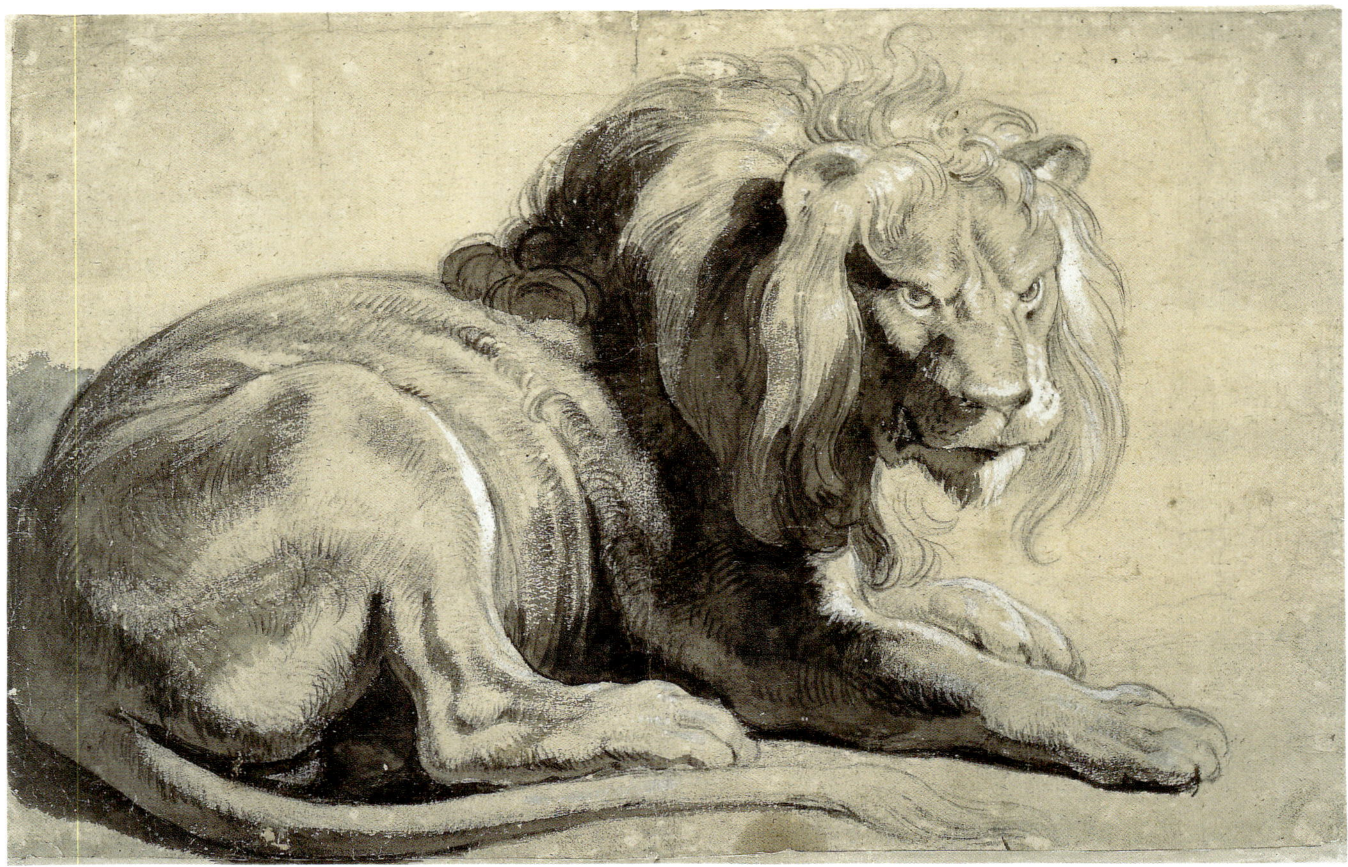

Cat. 48

facing the viewer. So lifelike are the lions in the painting that one can believe Rubens's claim, in his 1618 letter to Carleton, that he observed them in nature. He may have first made quick sketches from life, which were then worked into more elaborate studies.[5] At least two lions, named Flandria and Brabantia, were kept at the zoo in Ghent, where Rubens could have observed them. Archduke Albert and Archduchess Isabella, governors of the Southern Netherlands who in 1609 appointed Rubens their court painter, may also have had lions in their Brussels menagerie. In a 1729 anecdote, Campo Weyerman related that Rubens had a live animal brought into his studio in order to get a close-up view. When the lion was tickled to open its mouth, the beast became so enraged that it had to be killed.[6]

The powerful study of a striding lioness (cat. no. 47) is among Rubens's most memorable drawings of animals. The lioness corresponds almost exactly to the one depicted at the lower right in *Daniel in the Lions' Den.* As in the painting, the animal lifts her left front paw and the light falling on her body casts a shadow toward the right. Rubens may have developed this forceful drawing from a smaller, quick sketch of a *Retreating Lioness Seen from the Rear* (Rijksprentenkabinet, Amsterdam).[7] At some point, Rubens may have added finishing touches to the drawing in order to give it the appearance of an independent work of art. He seems to have strengthened the contours with a heavy black chalk over more lightly drawn lines, and he most likely applied the strong white highlights at this time. The same yellow chalk is found in the Washington drawing of the standing lion (cat. no. 46) and in the *Lion Resting* (cat. no. 48).

Of the many studies of lions that have been associated with *Daniel in the Lions' Den,* catalogue numbers 46 and 47 are the outstanding examples. A third preliminary drawing, in the British Museum, London (cat. no. 48), prepares the lion resting in the left foreground of the painting. Together, the sheets represent the three animals who anchor Rubens's composition.

About 1613–15 Jan Brueghel the Elder (1568–1625) painted lions that are clearly related to those of Rubens in his *Daniel in the Lions' Den.* Rubens's lioness and the snarling lion to her left appear, for example, in Brueghel's two versions of *Noah's Ark* (J. Paul Getty Museum, Los Angeles, dated 1613; Wellington Museum, Apsley House, London, dated 1615). Since Brueghel was Rubens's friend and collaborated with him on paintings in these years, he would have had access to Rubens's studio, where he could have admired *Daniel in the Lions' Den.* These borrowings make it likely that the three lion studies in the exhibition date from about 1613.

No preparatory oil sketch for *Daniel in the Lions' Den* is known. Rubens's claim to Carleton that everything in the painting was by his own hand has been received with some skepticism. If the artist really painted *Daniel in the Lions' Den* without assistants, he may well have relied on drawings by such collaborators as Frans Snijders (1579–1657) for some of the lesser lions in the background.[8]

1. M. Jaffé 1989, no. 289, ca. 1615.
2. "Daniel fra molti leoni cavati al naturale. Originale tutto di mia mano." Rooses and Ruelens 1887–1909, vol. 2, 136; Magurn 1991, pp. 59–61, letter 28.
3. Earlier, Lugt had classified the drawing as school of Rubens with the proviso that it could also be by an Italian artist (Lugt 1949, no. 1219). It was first attributed to Muziano by Michael Jaffé (1977, fig. 98).
4. A related figure of a penitent saint also appears in Cornelis Cort's engraving of *Saint Jerome in the Wilderness,* dated 1573, after Muziano's painting in the Pinacoteca Nazionale, Bologna (Hollstein 1993–, vol. 8, pt. 2, pp. 150–52, no. 116, ill.), a print that Rubens may have seen.
5. Of the eleven drawings of lions that Michael Jaffé (1970b, pp. 7–33) considered to be by Rubens himself, fewer than half are unanimously accepted today.
6. Weyerman 1729–69, vol. 1, pp. 287–89.
7. See d'Hulst and Vandenven (1989, no. 57f, fig. 149 [with bibl.]).
8. Although d'Hulst and Vandenven (1989, nos. 57b–e, figs. 142–45) accepted more than half of the lion drawings that Michael Jaffé had attributed in 1970 to Rubens (see note 5 above), Stampfle (1991, pp. 143–44, under no. 307) and others rightly questioned most of these attributions. It should be borne in mind that three lion drawings Jaffé published (1970b, pp. 13–16, figs. 12, 14, 15) bear old annotations ascribing them to Frans Snijders.

DRAWINGS FOR PRINTS AND A RELIEF

49. *Adoration of the Magi,* ca. 1612–13

Pen and brown ink and brown wash over traces of black chalk, traced for transfer, 292 x 191 mm (11½ x 7½ in.)

The Pierpont Morgan Library, New York (I,230)

PROVENANCE: Gosinus Uilenbroek (d. 1740), Amsterdam (his sale, Amsterdam, Beukelaar and Van de Land, October 23, 1741, p. 26, portefeuille Q); Jonkheer Johann Goll van Franckenstein Sr. (1722–1785), Amsterdam (Lugt 2987 [N. 972]);[1] Jonkheer Johann Goll van Franckenstein Jr. (1765–1821), Amsterdam; Pieter Hendrik Goll van Franckenstein (1787–1832), Amsterdam (his sale, Amsterdam, De Vries . . . Roos, July 1, 1833, album Q, lot 8 [to Woodburn with lot 7]); Samuel Woodburn (1786–1853), London; Sir John Charles Robinson (1824–1913), London (Lugt 1433); Charles Fairfax Murray (1849–1919), London and Florence; from whom purchased through Galerie Alexandre Imbert, Rome, in 1909 by John Pierpont Morgan Sr. (1837–1913), New York; his son, John Pierpont Morgan Jr. (1867–1943), New York; his gift to the Pierpont Morgan Library in 1924.

LITERATURE: R., vol. 5, no. 1254; Glück and Haberditzl 1928, no. 68, pl. 68; Held 1959, no. 139, pl. 151; Judson and Van de Velde 1978, vol. 1, no. 8a, pp. 142, 177, vol. 2, fig. 52; Held 1986, no. 77, pl. 76; Stampfle 1991, no. 305, ill.; Karen L. Bowen in Antwerp 1996–97, pp. 37–51, under nos. 13, 32a, 33a, pp. 178–81, tables A–D; C. van Mulders in Antwerp 1996–97, under nos. 32b, 33b.

EXHIBITIONS: Cambridge, Mass.–New York 1956, no. 12, ill.; Antwerp 1977, no. 2d; Paris–Antwerp–London–New York 1979–80, no. 11, ill.

In 1612 Rubens began to provide designs for the Plantin Press in Antwerp. Balthasar Moretus (1574–1641)—grandson of Christoph Plantin, founder of the press—was a close friend of the artist, and it must have been he who encouraged Rubens in this work during the time that he guided the press, from 1610 to 1641. We are well informed about Rubens's activity in this area, since careful account records are preserved in the archives of the Museum Plantin-Moretus, Antwerp.[2]

The designs for the folio edition of the *Missale Romanum* (Roman Missal) and the *Breviarium Romanum* (Roman Breviary), published, respectively, in 1613 and 1614, represent Rubens's largest commission for book illustrations. This *Adoration of the Magi* in the Pierpont Morgan Library, New York, and an *Ascension of Christ* (known only in a copy),[3] both for the *Missale Romanum,* were among the earliest designs that Moretus commissioned from Rubens. Derived from various books used in the early church, the missal contains prayers, benedictions, invocations, readings, and instructions for the celebration of the Roman Catholic Mass. The Plantin Press distinguished itself from its competitors by producing a greater number of rich, full-page engravings to illustrate the texts. In its 1613 edition, moreover, the ten principal images—Rubens's two illustrations and eight engravings by Marten de Vos (1532–1603)—were accompanied by an equal number of thematically related border illustrations, an innovation for the time. Rubens supplied two of the border designs.[4]

Rubens must have begun working on the missal illustrations during the summer of 1612, since Theodoor Galle (1571–1633) was paid to engrave the border designs in September of that year. (Galle was Moretus's brother-in-law and head of the Galle family's print workshop from 1612 until his death.) In the *Adoration of the Magi* Rubens represented the Virgin standing rather than sitting, which is somewhat unusual for an Adoration scene. He first drew the composition lightly in a fine pen over black chalk, to position the figures; there are few pentimenti. He then went over it more forcefully with a slightly broader pen, clearly defining the figures in the foreground. The head of the fourth man from the right, immediately behind the king standing in front, was to be omitted in the engraving; to make this correction clear for the engraver, Rubens obscured the head with landscape elements. The composition is noticeably less defined in the background, where, in keeping with common practice, it was left to the engraver to find a pleasing solution. Knowing that the image would be reversed in the print, Rubens made the Child and the kneeling king left-handed. The modeling in brush and brown wash to give the added effects of light and dark was masterfully reproduced by Galle in the engraving (fig. 96).[5]

The Plantin Press's *Missale Romanum* was well received and reprinted often. The press reused the *Adoration* for the *Breviarium Romanum* published in 1614 (see cat. no. 50).

1. More recent literature states that the Morgan Library *Adoration* was in the collections of Cornelis Ploos van Amstel and Jacob de Vos (see Stampfle 1991, p. 142). However, since the drawing does not bear the mark of either collector, it is possible that they had a (further unknown) copy, while the original drawing was handed down within the Goll family.
2. Extracts from these account books that refer to Rubens are published in Judson and Van de Velde 1978, vol. 2, app. 3, with an English translation.
3. C. van Mulders in Antwerp 1996–97, no. 33b; Karen L. Bowen in ibid., no. 32a.
4. These represent the *Tree of Jesse* (Louvre, Paris; Lugt 1949, no. 1005, pl. XI) and *Six Scenes from the New Testament* for the page opposite De Vos's *Adoration of the Shepherds* (Pierpont Morgan Library, New York; Stampfle 1991, nos. 299–304).
5. Renger 1974a, p. 131. Theodoor Galle is generally considered the engraver of the *Adoration of the Magi*. We thank Dr. Karen L. Bowen for providing us with a photograph of this engraving.

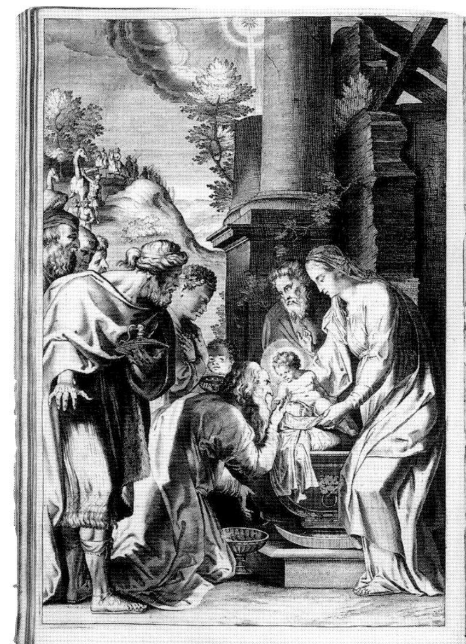

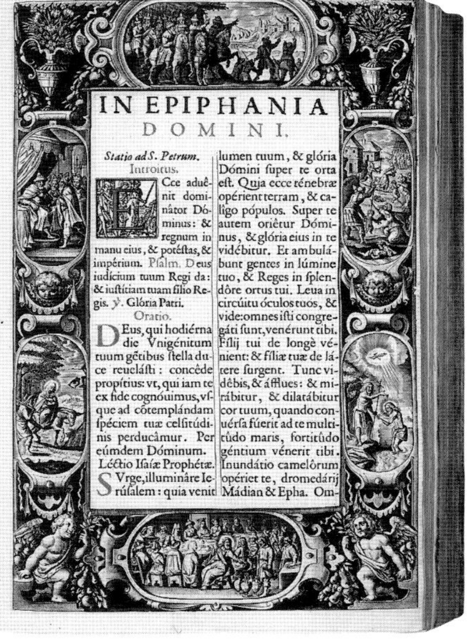

IN EPIPHANIA
DOMINI.

Statio ad S. Petrum.
Introitus.
ECce aduênit domi-
nátor Dó-
minus: &
regnum in
manu eius, & potéstas, &
impérium. Psalm. Deus
iudícium tuum Regi da:
& iustítiam tuam filio Regis. ℣. Glória Patri.
Oratio.
DEus, qui hodiérna
die Vnigénitum
tuum gẽtibus stella du-
ce reuelásti: concéde
propítius: vt, qui iam te
ex fide cognóuimus, vs-
que ad cõtemplándam
spéciem tuæ celsitúdi-
nis perducâmur. Per
eúmdem Dóminum.
Léctio Isaíæ Prophétæ.
SVrge, illumináre Ie-
rúsalem: quia venit
lumen tuum, & glória
Dómini super te orta
est. Quia ecce ténebræ
opérient terram, & ca-
lígo pópulos. Super te
autem oriêtur Dómi-
nus, & glória eius in te
vidébitur. Et ambulá-
bunt gentes in lúmine
tuo, & Reges in splen-
dôre ortus tui. Leua in
circúitu óculos tuos, &
vide: omnes isti congre-
gáti sunt, venérunt tibi.
Fílij tui de longè vé-
nient: & fíliæ tuæ de lá-
tere surgent. Tunc vi-
débis, & áfflues: & mi-
rábitur, & dilatábitur
cor tuum, quando con-
uérsa fúerit ad te multi-
túdo maris, fortitúdo
géntium vénerit tibi.
Inundátio camelôrum
opériet te, dromedárij
Mádian & Epha. Om-

Fig. 96. Theodoor Galle after Peter Paul Rubens, *The Adoration of the Magi* (left) and border design (right). Engraving, left 345 x 220 mm (13$\frac{9}{16}$ x 8$\frac{11}{16}$ in.). From the Plantin Press *Missale Romanum* (Antwerp, 1613), pp. 42–43. Museum Plantin-Moretus / Stedelijk Prentenkabinet, Antwerp (A 1546)

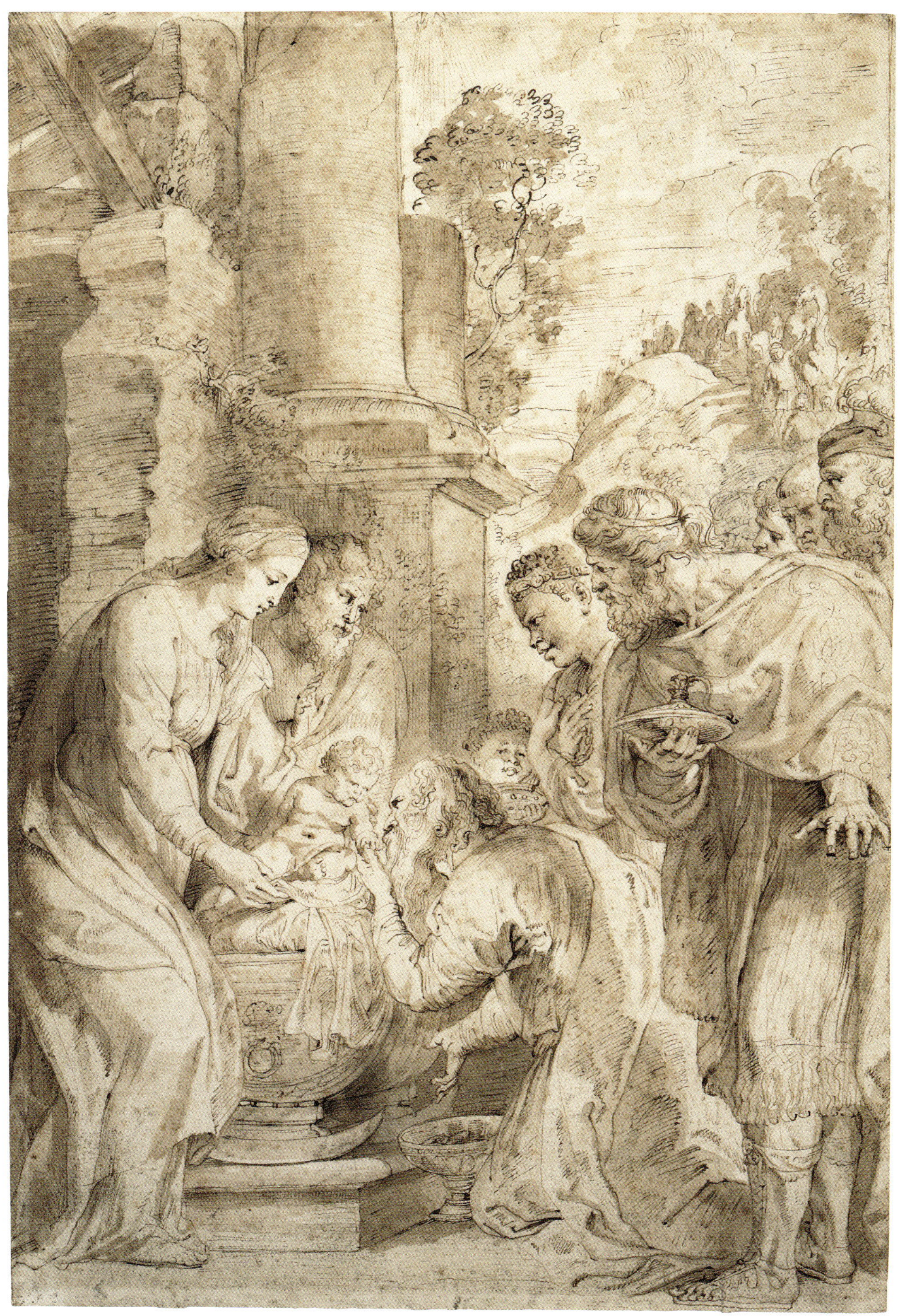

Cat. 49

50. *All Saints,* 1614

Pen and brown ink and gray-brown wash over graphite, traced for transfer, 296 x 200 mm (11⅝ x 7⅞ in.)

Albertina, Vienna (8213)

PROVENANCE: Gosinus Uilenbroek (d. 1740), Amsterdam (his sale, Amsterdam, Beukelaar and Van de Land, October 23, 1741, p. 26, portefeuille Q); Gabriel Huquier (1695–1772), Orléans and Paris (his sale, Amsterdam, Yver, September 14, 1761, lot 553); Count Moriz von Fries (1777–1826), Vienna (Lugt 2903); Duke Albert of Sachsen-Teschen (1738–1822), Vienna (Lugt 174).

LITERATURE: R., vol. 5, no. 1259, pl. 362; Glück and Haberditzl 1928, no. 70, pl. 70; Held 1959, under no. 11 and p. 26; Burchard and d'Hulst 1963, under nos. 29, 68; Judson and Van de Velde 1978, vol. 1, no. 28a, fig. 95; Karen L. Bowen in Antwerp 1996–97, pp. 37–51, under nos. 13, 32a, 33a, pp. 178–81, tables A–D; C. van Mulders in Antwerp 1996–97, under nos. 32b, 33b; Plomp 2001–2, p. 232.

EXHIBITIONS: Antwerp 1977, no. 137, ill.; Vienna 1977b, no. 10, ill.; Antwerp 1996–97, no. 33d, ill. p. 197; Sydney 2002, no. 50.

The design *All Saints* for the *Breviarium Romanum* (Roman Breviary), published by the Plantin Press in Antwerp in 1614, was the Rubens illustration used most frequently for its liturgical books. The drawing represents the entire company of saints worshiping the Holy Trinity: God the Father and Christ in heaven, and the Holy Spirit hovering between them. The Virgin, her hands clasped in prayer, stands on a bank of clouds slightly below Christ and to His left, addressing Him. Behind her are groups of male saints, including Peter and Paul. Across from them a female martyr standing on a bank of clouds addresses a group of women saints and motions toward the Trinity. Saint Gregory (Pope Gregory the Great) appears in front at the lower left, with the papal tiara beside him. At the bottom center are the martyrs Saint Lawrence, seen from the back, and Saint Stephen, who looks upward. At the right are Saints George and William of Aquitane, in armor. Saint Sebastian is seated in the lower right corner (Rubens used the same nude youth earlier for his large drawing of the *Baptism of Christ* [cat. no. 14]). Rubens included several of these figures in his 1628 altarpiece of the *Virgin and Child Adored by Saints* for the Augustinian church in Antwerp (fig. 77; for the preliminary drawing, see cat. no. 34).

The illustration of *All Saints* is one of eight by Rubens reproduced in the *Breviarium Romanum* of 1614, one of the outstanding publications of the Plantin Press. Two of the designs had been used previously, for the *Missale Romanum* published by the press the previous year: the *Adoration of the Magi* (cat. no. 49) and the *Ascension of Christ,* known only through a copy.[1] Rubens also designed the title page[2] for the breviary, a collection of psalms, readings, and hymns used in the daily service of the Roman Catholic Church. The artist finished all nine designs about March 19, 1614, for they are referred to by Jan Moretus II of the Plantin Press in a letter of that date to Jan Hasrey, a Flemish librarian residing in Madrid.[3]

Rubens received 132 florins for the eight illustrations, the frontispiece, and for two drawings of the Crucifixion that were not used.[4] Theodoor Galle (1571–1633), who is believed to have engraved all eight illustrations, was paid 65 florins on May 15 for his engraving of *All Saints*, which included the cost of the copperplate.[5] That the engraver would be paid proportionately so much more is to be explained by the length of time it took to work the plate. Moreover, Rubens drew his book illustrations only on Sundays and holidays, basically as a favor for his friend Balthasar Moretus. If Rubens had executed them during regular working hours, the price would have been at least 100 florins per drawing. He could also take his time, as Moretus usually gave him six months to complete a design.[6]

On average, the Plantin Press produced new editions of breviaries in various formats every year, with 2,000 to 3,000 copies per print run, while missals in folio were printed only every three to five years in editions of 1,300 to 1,500. During the thirty years that Moretus directed operations at the press, between 1610 and 1641, more than 33,000 missals were printed, largely for sale in Spain.[7]

Rubens also painted a small oil sketch of the subject of All Saints, which is dated to 1612–13 (Museum Boijmans Van Beuningen, Rotterdam).[8] The oil could not have been the model for Galle's engraving, however, since the print is clearly based on the Albertina drawing (which is, moreover, traced for transfer). Rather, it most likely represents an initial idea for the *All Saints* design. Rubens may have tried the composition out first in paint before translating it into a linear pen drawing to guide the engraver. A proof impression of Galle's print in the Bibliothèque Nationale, Paris, shows some corrections by Rubens, indicating the great care he took to follow a print all the way to completion.[9]

1. C. van Mulders in Antwerp 1996–97, no. 32b.
2. Moretus's plans and written instructions for the title page are in the archives of the Museum Plantin-Moretus, Antwerp. See Judson and Van der Velde 1978, vol. 1, p. 123, under no. 18a, vol. 2, figs. 75–77.
3. Rooses and Ruelens 1887–1909, vol. 2, p. 66. Jan Moretus II (1576–1618), the younger brother of Balthasar Moretus, was the business manager of the Plantin Press.

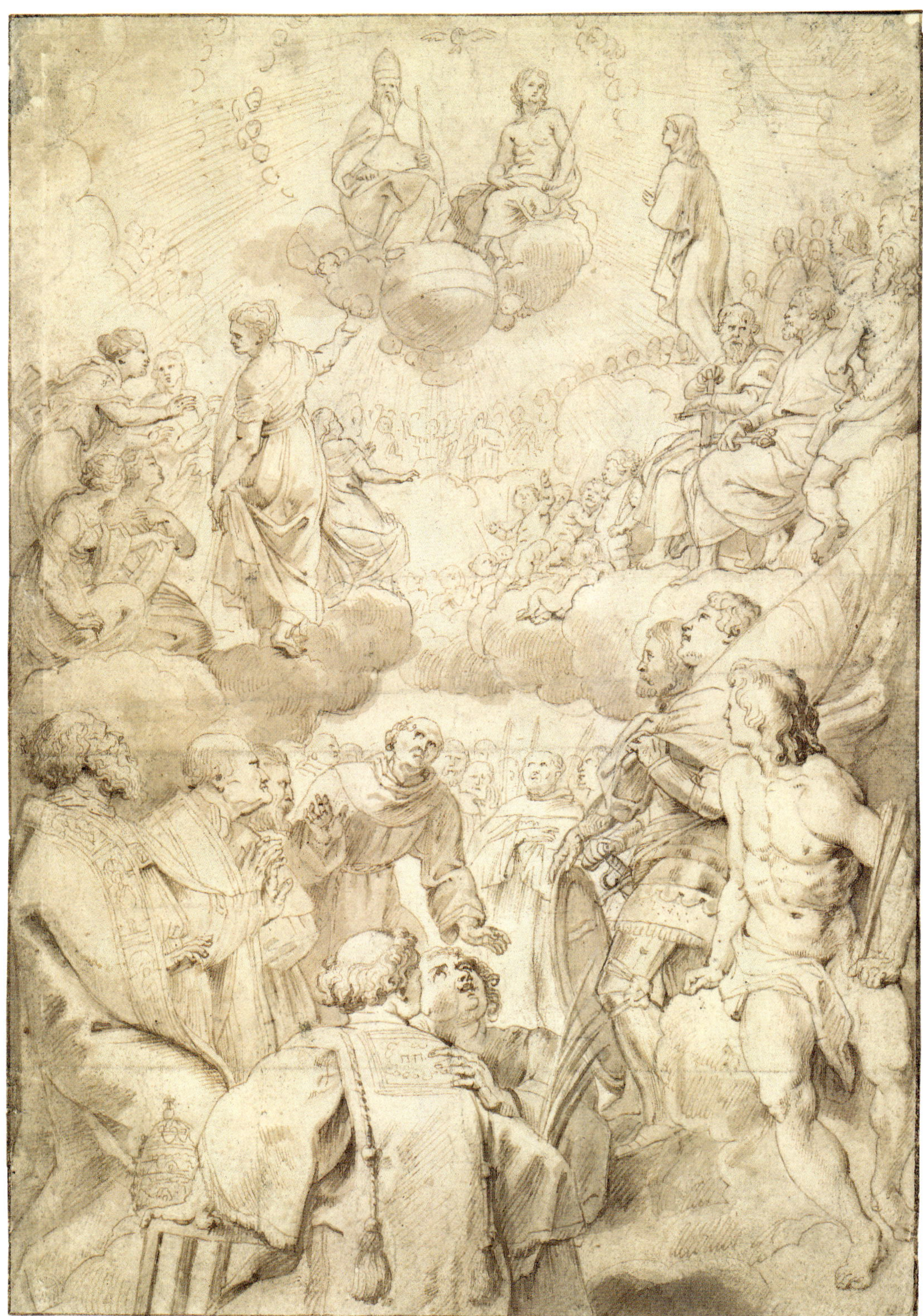

Cat. 50

4. The payment is recorded in the archives of the Museum Plantin-Moretus, Antwerp. See Judson and Van de Velde 1978, vol. 1, pp. 118–19, under nos. 18–28, and for a transcription of the document, vol. 2, pp. 447–48.
5. The payment is recorded in the archives of the Museum Plantin-Moretus, Antwerp; see Judson and Van de Velde 1978, vol. 2, p. 456, no. 20. See also Karen L. Bowen in Antwerp 1996–97, under no. 33a, p. 126.
6. Rooses and Ruelens 1887–1909, vol. 5, pp. 335–36; Judson and Van de Velde 1978, vol. 1, p. 27, vol. 2, p. 385.
7. Karen L. Bowen in Antwerp 1996–97, pp. 46–47, 126.
8. Held 1980, no. 399, pl. 389; M. Jaffé 1989, no. 205, ca. 1613.
9. Judson and Van de Velde 1978, vol. 1, no. 28b, vol. 2, fig. 96.

51. *Title Page for "Commentaria in Pentateuchum Mosis,"* ca. 1614–15

Pen and brown ink and brown wash over black chalk, partly heightened with white, traced for transfer, angel at left and medallions at right on separate pieces of paper, additions made to plinth at lower left corner, 315 x 210 mm (12⅜ x 8¼ in.)
Annotated by Peter Lely (?) in pen and brown ink at center: *A / Collection of Altars / & / Altar-Pieces, Churches / &c by y_e famous / Boromene &c / severall of them in / their propper colours. / with severall draw- / ings of Albert / Durer, Correggio / Pordenone / &c*

Department of Printing and Graphic Arts, Houghton Library, Harvard College Library, Cambridge, Mass. (TypDr 632.R755.16p Sz 3)

PROVENANCE: Sir Peter Lely (1618–1680), London (Lugt 2092); John Talman (1677–1726), Hinkworth, England (Lugt 2462); William H. Schab, New York (1942); Philip Hofer, Cambridge, Mass.

LITERATURE: M. Jaffé 1953, pp. 131–36; Deborah-Irene Coy in Williamstown 1977, pp. 103–4, no. 25; Judson and Van de Velde 1978, vol. 1, no. 36a, fig. 119; Held 1979b, p. 138, fig. 20.

EXHIBITIONS: Cambridge, Mass.–New York 1956, no. 15; Antwerp 1977, no. 7b, fig. 10; Cambridge, Mass, 1980, no. 1, ill.; Wellesley–Cleveland 1993–94, no. 47, ill.

The Flemish Jesuit Cornelius Cornelli a Lapide (Cornelis Cornelissen Vandensteen; 1567–1637) was a professor of Holy Scripture at the university in Louvain from 1596, and of Hebrew as well from 1597; in 1616 he was invited to teach in Rome. He wrote many commentaries on the Old and New Testament, including the *Commentaria in Pentateuchum Mosis* (Commentary on the Five Books of Moses). With more than one thousand pages, this exegesis of the first five books of the Old Testament became the standard text for Jesuits in the seventeenth century. Jan van Meurs and the heirs of Martin Nutius published the *Commentaria in Pentateuchum Mosis* in Antwerp in 1616. Whether Van Meurs commissioned this title page is unknown, but he obviously belonged to the same circle as Rubens and his usual publisher, Balthasar Moretus. From 1618 until 1629 Van Meurs was the partner of Balthasar Moretus at the Plantin Press. When Van Meurs started on his own in 1630, Rubens designed his printer's device.[1]

Rubens's title page to Lapide's *Commentaria in Pentateuchum Mosis* is one the most elaborate he ever designed. The artist represented Moses seated upon a pedestal displaying the two tablets of the Law. (In the engraving [fig. 97] they are inscribed with the first and fourth commandments.) Above Moses's head, encircled by the symbols of the Four Evangelists, are the Hebrew letters for God (Jehovah). The imposing architectural structure consists of an architrave, entablature, pediment, Corinthian columns, and medallions with scenes taken from the Pentateuch. Since the drawing was to be engraved, thus reproducing the image in reverse, the medallions should be read from right to left, beginning at the upper right with "God Dividing the Light from the Darkness" (Genesis 1:4), followed at the upper left with "The Passage through the Red Sea" (Exodus 14:21–28), continuing at the lower right with "The High Priest Sacrificing Fowl" (Leviticus 1:14–17), and ending at the lower left with "The Ark of the Covenant Covered by a Tent" (Numbers 4:4–6). "Moses Preaching to the People of Israel on the Plain" (Deuteronomy 1:1–3), surrounded by a cartouche, appears at the bottom center. The angel at the top left of the drawing as

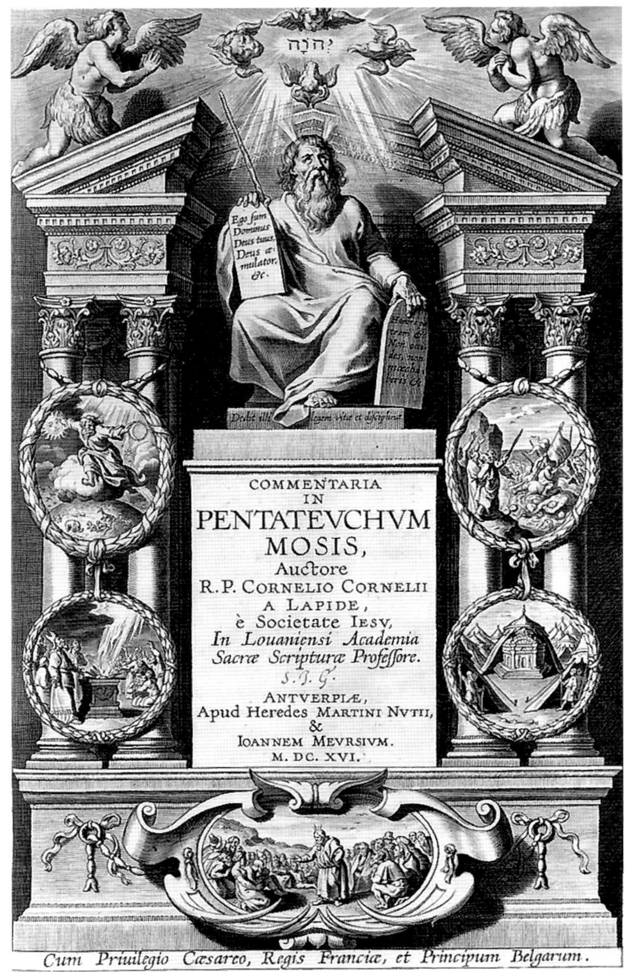

Fig. 97. Unknown engraver after Peter Paul Rubens, *Title Page for "Commentaria in Pentateuchum Mosis,"* ca. 1614–15. Engraving, 324 x 199 mm (12¾ x 7$^{13}/_{16}$ in.). Library of Congress, Washington, D.C. (BS 1225 L.35)

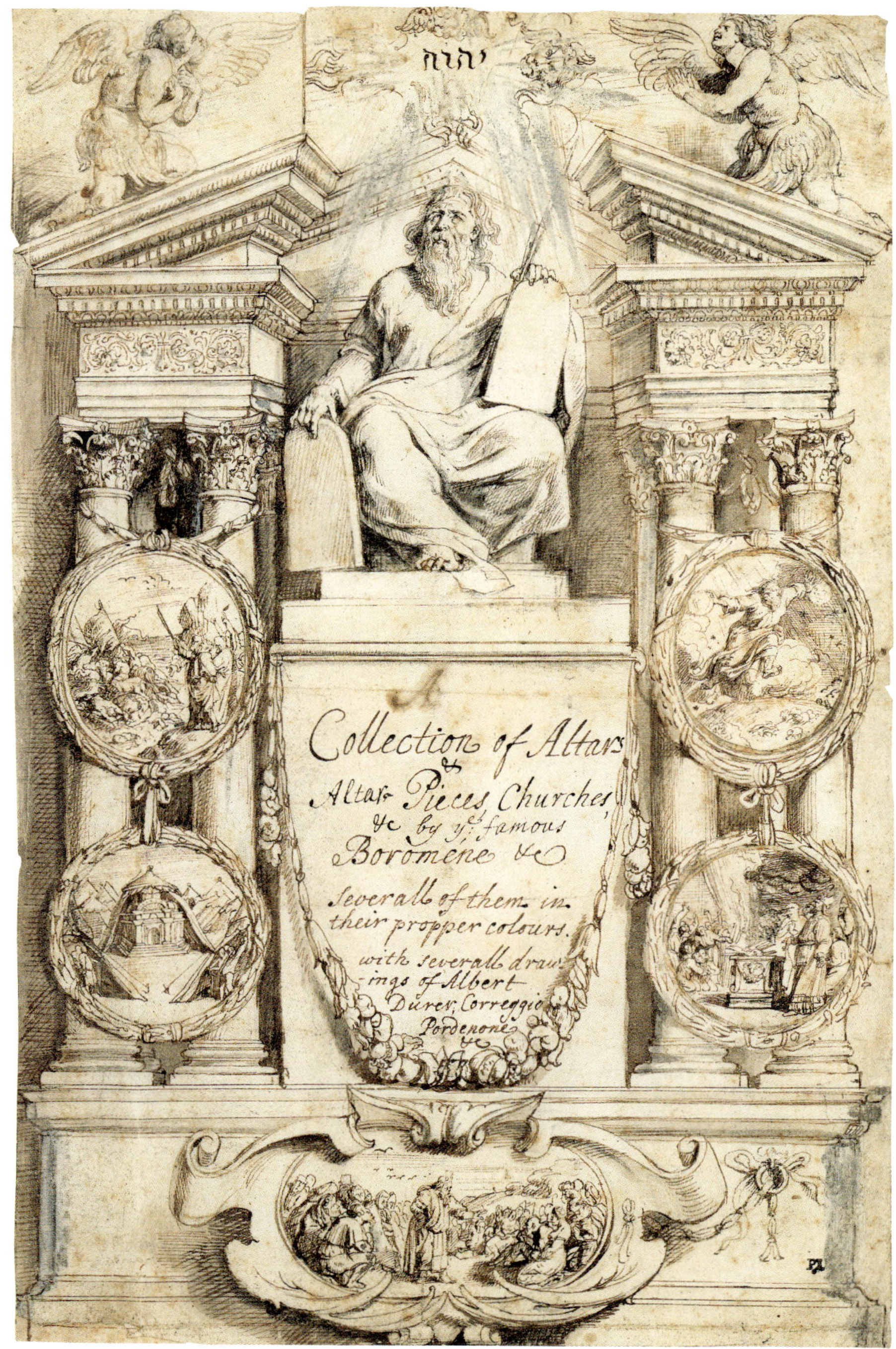

Cat. 51

well as the two medallions at the right were inserted on separate pieces of paper as corrections. Rubens drew decorative elements adorning the base of the pedestal on the right half of the drawing only, knowing that the engraver would provide a mirror image on the opposite side.

Contrary to traditional Christian iconography, Rubens represented Moses not with horns but with a bright countenance lit by rays of light emanating from above. This alludes to his radiant face after God had presented him with the tablets of the Law on Mount Sinai (Exodus 34:29–35).[2] Lapide might have asked Rubens to modify the traditional representation of Moses in accordance with his discussion in the *Commentaria in Pentateuchum Mosis* of the true meaning of the original Hebrew text. (Moses's horns derive from Jerome's incorrect

Latin translation of this passage.) The anonymous engraver, however, did not respect this interpretation and added rays simulating horns to Moses's forehead. We may infer from this change that once Rubens had submitted his design to the publisher in 1614–15 he was not involved in the engraving process, because he surely would have caught this unintended addition.

The garland of fruit and the English inscription in a seventeenth-century hand on the pedestal in the drawing were added later, after the drawing was engraved. Julius S. Held suggested that these additions were by the drawings collector and artist Sir Peter Lely (1618–1680), the first known owner of the sheet (after Van Meurs). Lely, or some other English collector, probably used Rubens's drawing as a title page for an album or portfolio of drawings in his own collection, making it a valuable document in the history of drawings collecting in England.[3]

1. For Rubens's grisalle sketch for Van Meur's printer's device in the Museum Plantin Moretus, Antwerp, see Judson and Van de Velde 1978, vol. 1, no. 60a, vol. 2, fig. 206.
2. Lawrence 1999, p. 279.
3. Held 1979b, p. 138. Lely and other English collectors of Rubens's drawings are discussed in the essay by Michiel C. Plomp in this publication.

52. *The Birth of the Virgin,* late September–early October 1620

Pen and brown ink and brown wash, 310 x 207 mm (12 3/16 x 8 1/8 in.)
Inscribed by the artist in pen and brown ink at top: *La Nativita di Nostra donna*

Hart Collection

PROVENANCE: Sale, Monte Carlo, Sotheby's, June 13, 1982, lot 114, ill.

LITERATURE: Held 1986, under no. 23, fig. 10; Renger in Munich 1990–91, pp. 62–63, fig. 35, ill.; McGrath 1991, pp. 717–19, fig. 61.

EXHIBITION: Wellesley–Cleveland 1993–94, no. 54, ill.

Rubens identified the subject matter of this drawing in his notation, in Italian, at the top of the sheet: "La Nativita di Nostra donna" (the birth of Our Lady). In the background Saint Anne rests in bed and receives well-wishers, while Joachim admires his daughter. Handmaidens in the foreground hold the baby up for him to see before swaddling her. Saint Anne is not found in the Bible; she and Joachim are first mentioned in the apocryphal Book of James (second century). The cult of Saint Anne developed later, in the Middle Ages.[1]

This is one of Rubens's best-documented drawings. In 1620 Wolfgang Wilhelm, Duke of Neuburg, Count Palatine (1576–1653), who had recently converted to Catholicism, commissioned from Rubens a *Birth of the Virgin* for the Church of Our Lady at Neuburg on the Danube (near Ingolstadt, north of Munich). On September 8, 1620, the duke wrote to his agent,

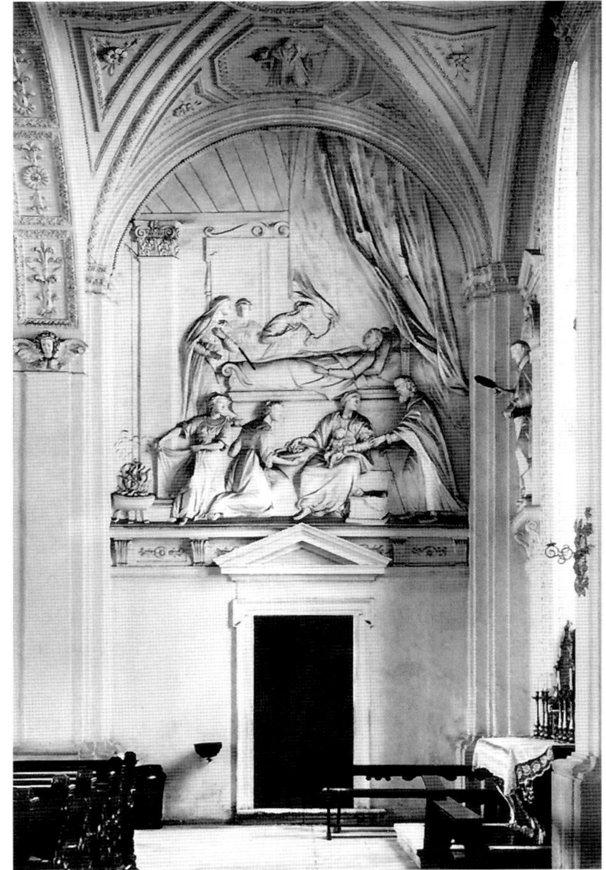

Fig. 98. Pietro Castelli, *The Birth of the Virgin*, 1620. Stucco relief, w. 440 cm (173 1/4 in.). Church of Our Lady, Neuburg an der Donau

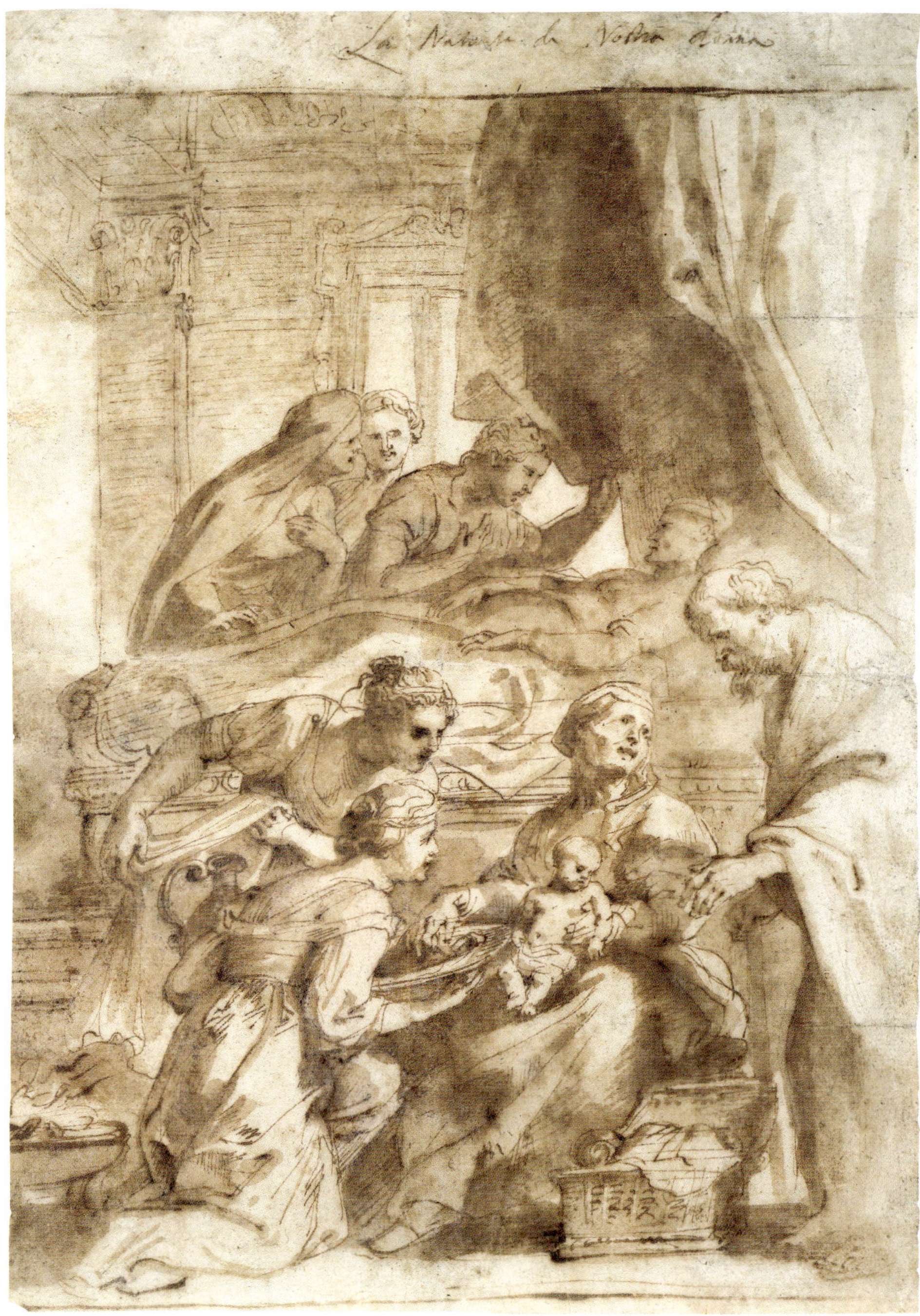

Cat. 52

Reyngodt, to inquire of Rubens whether he would be inclined to furnish a design of a nativity of the Virgin.[2] Two weeks later, on September 25, Rubens replied that he would work on a drawing over the next five or six days.[3] The agent forwarded the promised *Birth of the Virgin* to the duke on October 8,[4] which Wolfgang Wilhelm duly acknowledged receiving on October 20, stating that it pleased him ("wollgefellig").[5] The drawing's three horizontal creases are likely the result of its having been folded during its journey from Rubens to the duke.

For many years Rubens's drawing could not be connected with a specific work in the Church of Our Lady in Neuburg. In 1991, however, it was recognized as a preparatory drawing for a stucco relief.[6] This bas-relief, by Pietro Castelli, is still in the church, installed today near the entrance to the left side of the nave (fig. 98). Pietro belonged to a family of *stuccatori* recorded as working in the church between 1616 and 1620. Thus the relief must have been one of their last works for the church.[7] A related relief of the *Assumption of the Virgin,* signed by Castelli, is near the entrance to the right side of the nave. Its design is much more static than that of any *Assumption* by Rubens, so it seems safe to assume that it is not after an (unknown) design by him.

Since the *stuccatore* would not work under the artist's close supervision, Rubens was careful to provide a clear, neat drawing in pen and brown ink. His extensive use of wash to model the figures and to indicate highlights and shadows was probably also meant to guide the execution in shallow relief.[8] Rubens's unusual use of Italian for the inscription at the top was no doubt for the benefit of the Italian craftsman as well.

1. E. A. Livingstone, *Oxford Concise Dictionary of the Christian Church* (Oxford, 2000), pp. 25, 299, 306.
2. See Renger in Munich 1990–91, p. 95, doc. 30. Renger discovered and published the correspondence between the duke's agent and Rubens (sixty-seven documents). He also brought together the altarpieces that Wilhelm commissioned from Rubens, in the exhibition "Peter Paul Rubens: Altäre für Bayern" at the Bayerische Staatsgemäldesammlungen, in Munich, in 1990–91.
3. Ibid., p. 96, doc. 31: "Quant au dessein en papier de la nativité de nostre Dame ce n'est pas possible de le faire aujourdhuy mais sans doubte je le vous dévoydray entreme de cinq ou six jours affin quil puisse allier avecq l'aultre ordonné apres cestuy."
4. Ibid., p. 87, doc. 3.
5. Ibid., p. 97, doc. 36.
6. McGrath 1991, pp. 717–19, fig. 61.
7. Seitz and Lidel 1983, pp. 48–49, 68, pls. 12, 13. The relief was restored in 1721.
8. When Held first published the drawing in 1986 (under no. 23), he sensed, correctly, that it had a specific purpose. However, he thought that it recalled Rubens's designs for engravings.

PAULUS PONTIUS?, REWORKED AND RETOUCHED BY PETER PAUL RUBENS

53. *The Assumption of the Virgin,* ca. 1624

Black chalk, heightened with white, reworked and retouched by Rubens with brush and brown ink and grayish brown wash, heightened with white and gray body color and oil, and with pen and brown ink; on four pieces of paper, arched at the top; traced for transfer; laid down; traces of gold on right, left, and bottom edges, 654 x 427 mm (25¾ x 16¹³⁄₁₆ in.)

The J. Paul Getty Museum, Los Angeles (98.GG.14)

PROVENANCE: Everhard Jabach (1618–1695), Cologne and Paris (Lugt 2959; portefeuille no. 4, no. 71); Pierre Crozat (1665–1740), Paris (his number "14" at bottom right; his sale, Paris, April 10–May 13, 1741, lot 831 [Rubens]); bought by Hecquet; Jeronimus Tonneman (1687–1750), Amsterdam (his sale, Amsterdam, de Leth, October 21, 1754, album D, no 1, [Rubens]); Jacob de Wit (1695–1754), Amsterdam (his sale, Amsterdam, de Leth . . . Van Schorrenberg, March 10–11, 1755, p. 37, album D, no. 1 [Rubens]); Michiel Oudaan (ca. 1702–1766; his sale, Rotterdam, Bosch . . . Arrenberg, November 3, 1766, album M, no. 18 [Rubens]); bought by Fouquet; unidentified French collector (based on clipping from French sale catalogue, published after 1789, attached to old backing); Cornelis Ploos van Amstel (1726–1798), Amsterdam (Lugt 2034; stamp at bottom left corner of old backing; his sale, Amsterdam, Van der Schley . . . Roos, March 3, 1800, and following days, *Drawings,* album A, no. 1 [Rubens]); bought by Cornelis Sebille Roos; Hendrik van Eyl Sluyter (1739–1814), Amsterdam (his sale, Amsterdam, Van der Schley and de Vries, September 26, 1814, album N, no. 2 [Rubens]); bought by Christiaan Josi; by 1821, Heneage Finch, 5th Earl of Aylesford (1786–1859), London; possibly R. S. Holford (1808–1892), London; probably acquired by Henry Richard, 3rd Earl of Warwick (1779–1853); thence by descent (sale, London, Sotheby's, July 2, 1997, lot 54); art market, London.

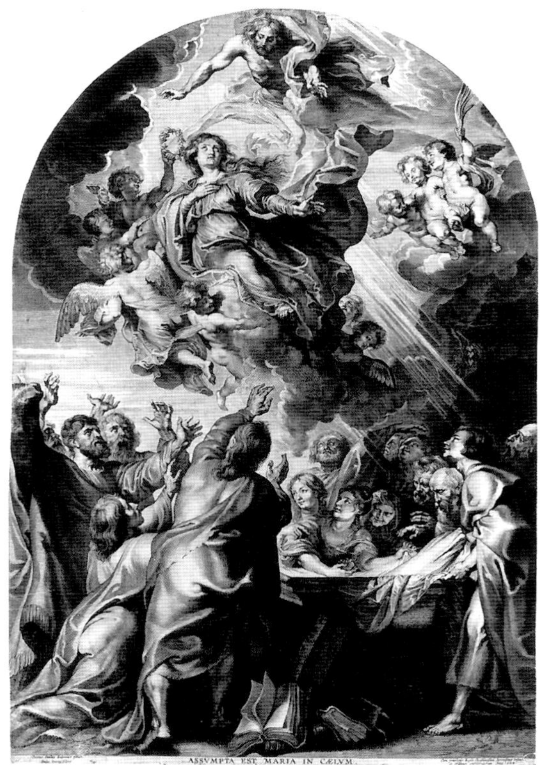

Fig. 99. Paulus Pontius, *The Assumption of the Virgin,* 1624. Engraving, 644 x 441 mm (25⅜ x 17⅜ in.) The Metropolitan Museum of Art, New York; The Elisha Whittelsey Collection, The Elisha Whittelsey Fund, 1951 (51.501.7324)

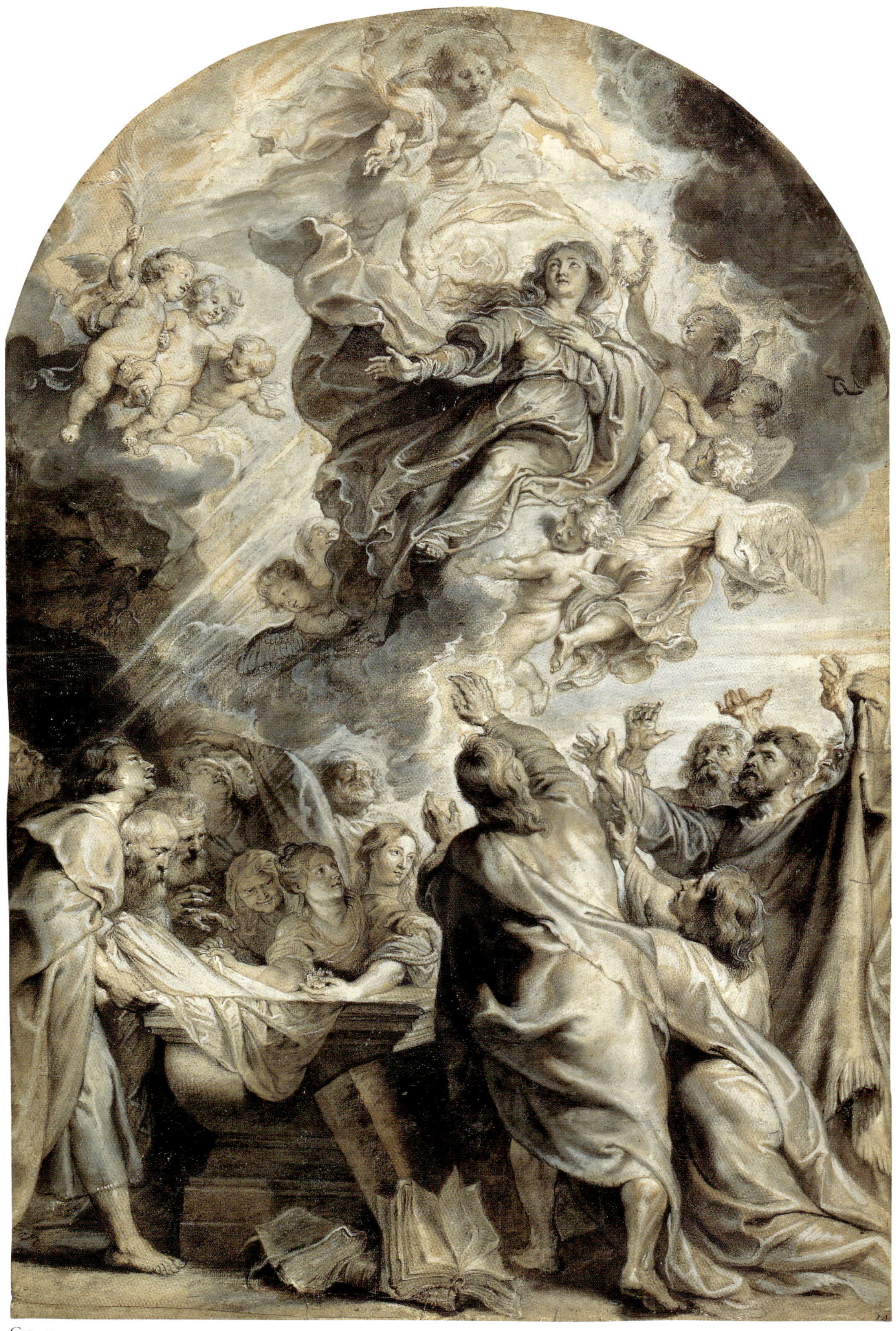

Cat. 53

LITERATURE: Freedberg 1984, pp. 164, under no. 41, 167–68, n. 1, 169, no. 41a, figs. 105, 107; Logan 1999, pp. 231–37; Py 2001, p. 98, no. 279, ill.; Turner 2001, no. 49, ill.; Plomp 2001–2, p. 232.

Rubens represented the Assumption of the Virgin repeatedly in drawings, oil sketches, and monumental altar paintings (see cat. nos. 41–43). This *Assumption of the Virgin* has become known only relatively recently, though it can be traced to the famous late-seventeenth-century collection of Everhard Jabach (1618–1695), thanks to its gold border—the same as was applied to Jabach's most highly prized drawings. In 1754 it sold for 461 guilders at the auction of the collection of Jeronimus Tonneman (1687–1750)—the highest price ever paid for a Rubens drawing in Holland until 1833, when his *Christ on the Cross* now in Rotterdam (cat. no. 56) fetched even more.[1]

In 1616–17 Rubens painted an *Assumption of the Virgin* (today in the Stiftung Museum Kunst Palast, Düsseldorf) for the Kapellekerk (Notre-Dame de la Chapelle) in Brussels, where it was installed in 1618. Several years later, in 1624, he decided to reproduce the painting in an engraving. This exceptionally large drawing served as the model for the print, by Paulus Pontius (1603–1658), one of Rubens's last and most accomplished engravers (fig. 99).[2] The engraving bears Rubens's full privilege and is dated 1624, evidence that the artist was closely involved in its execution.[3]

Differences between the design for the engraving and the painting reveal a gradual evolution of Rubens's ideas for this complex composition. The drawing, which is traced for transfer, began as a rather dry copy in black chalk with some white heightening. This phase was most likely carried out by Pontius, who then submitted his copy to Rubens for approval. At this time Rubens must have decided that he wanted to change the subject from a conventional Assumption scene into one in which Christ welcomes his mother into heaven. This necessitated enlarging the top of the drawing, which is now arched. Here, Rubens introduced the figure of Christ descending from heaven with open arms to receive the Virgin. This upper section is drawn freely in brush and brown ink, with grayish brown body color and white highlights. Much of the remaining design shows the intervention of Rubens as well. For example, he modified the veil billowing above the Virgin and inserted an apostle with raised hands at the right, thus emphasizing the spectators' astonishment at the miraculous event. These details were added with the tip of the brush dipped in brown ink. Rubens also applied light brown body color (or oil?) to the putti at the upper left, before drawing over this area with brush and brown ink. Finally, he strengthened the clouds surrounding the Virgin. The few untouched areas are at the lower left. The face of the old woman peering into the empty sarcophagus, for example, and the hands of the apostles to the right of center are drawn with black chalk alone.

Rubens gave the drawing yet another working over, possibly after Pontius showed him a proof impression of the engraving. At this stage, Rubens used a fine pen to draw additional strands of hair, for example, on the head of the woman holding roses and on the heads of the apostles at the left. He also accentuated certain faces and slightly modified the raised hand in the center of the drawing. Similar corrections are found on proofs of his prints. A counterproof of Pontius's engraving, today in the Centrale Bibliotheek van de Universiteit Gent,[4] demonstrates that Rubens made still further modifications in pen and brown ink. That this was only the second reproductive engraving by Pontius executed under Rubens's supervision may explain the unusually meticulous reworking by the master. Pontius did his best to turn this painterly *modello,* drawn largely with the brush, into the linear medium of engraving. Rubens must have been satisfied with his efforts, as the print bears the coveted privilege of the Infanta Isabella Clara Eugenia.

1. For this provenance, see Plomp 2001–2, p. 232.
2. Hollstein 1949–, vol. 17, p. 156, no. 26; 664 x 441 mm.
3. The inscription at bottom center reads: "ASSUMPTA EST MARIA IN COELUM. Petrus Paulus Rubenius pinxit. / Paulus Pontius sculpsit." At bottom left is the privilege: "Cum privilegijs Regis Christianissimi, Serenissimae Infantis / et Ordinum confederatorum. Anno 1624."
4. Freedberg 1984, p. 168, no. 41a; fig. 107.

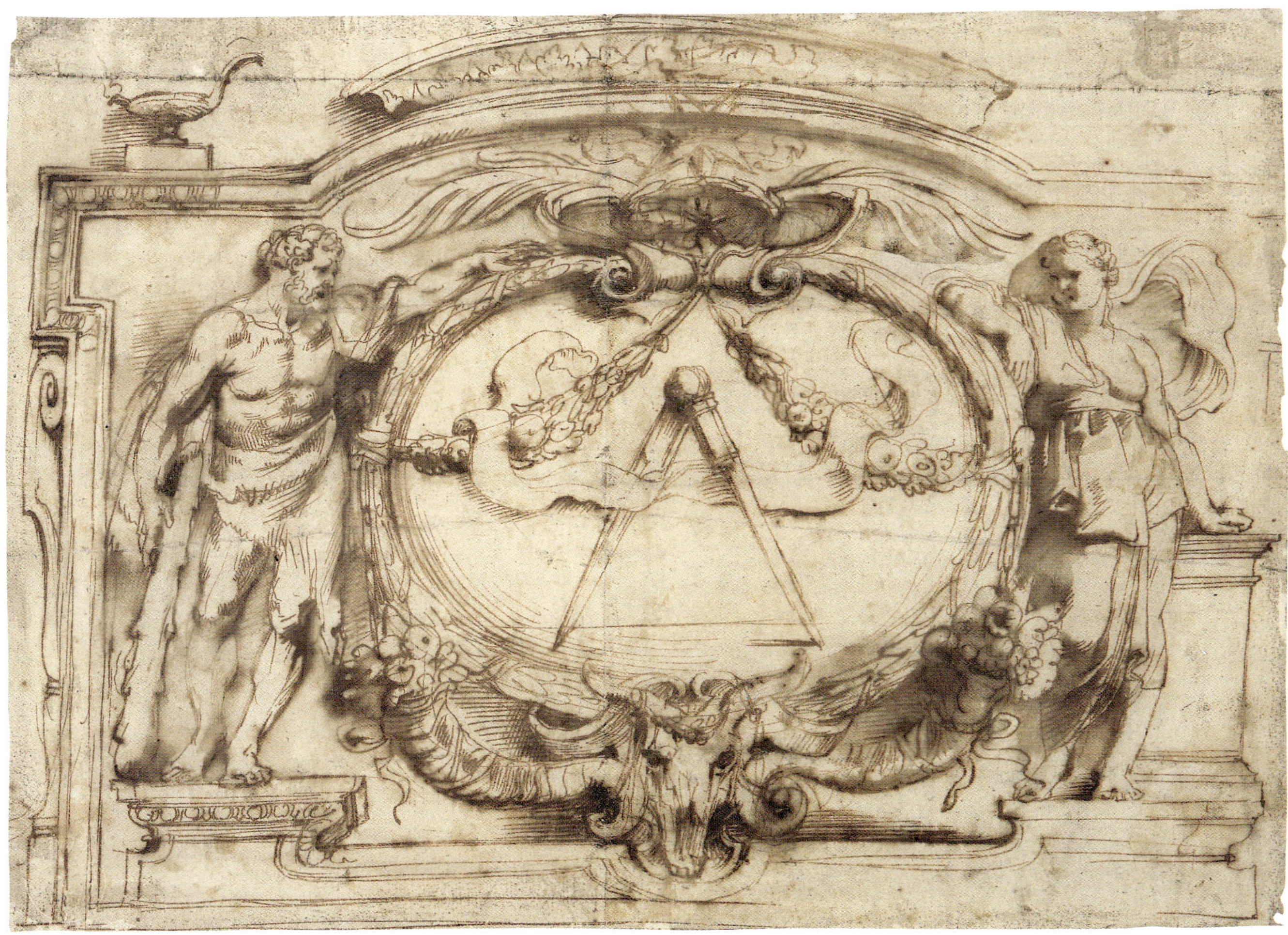

Cat. 54

54. *Design for the Emblem of the Plantin Press,* ca. 1628–30

Pen and brown ink and brown wash, 206 x 277 mm (8 3/16 x 10 15/16 in.)

Museum Plantin-Moretus / Stedelijk Prentenkabinet, Antwerp (TEK 391)

PROVENANCE: Balthasar Moretus (1574–1641), Antwerp.

LITERATURE: R., vol. 5, no. 1282; Glück and Haberditzl 1928, no. 167, pl. 167; Held 1959, no. 148, pl. 160; Burchard and d'Hulst 1963, no. 141, pl. 141; Kuznetsov 1974, pl. 139; Judson and Van de Velde 1978, vol. 1, no. 74a, fig. 255; Held 1979b, p. 122, fig. 5; Held 1986, no. 186, pl. 181.

EXHIBITIONS: Antwerp 1977, no. 30g; Birmingham 1978, no. 48, ill.; Tokyo 1982, no. 65, ill.; Antwerp 1996–97, no. 48g, ill. p. 206.

The Officina Plantiniana, or Plantin Press, in Antwerp was one of the foremost printing houses in Europe during the sixteenth and seventeenth centuries. Founded in 1555 by Christoph Plantin (ca. 1520–1589), it continued to flourish under his son-in-law Jan Moretus (1543–1610) and his grandson Balthasar Moretus (1574–1641). The latter had known Rubens since their youth, when both attended the same Latin school in Antwerp.

Rubens's design visualizes the motto of the Plantin Press, LABORE ET CONSTANTIA (through labor and constancy), which was to be written on the scroll winding through the large compass in the center. The golden compass (*Gulden Passer*) was the seal of the press. The figures of Hercules at the left and of Constantia at the right personify labor and constancy, respectively. Two fruit garlands lead up to a seven-pointed star and two palm branches. The star refers to the coat of arms of the

Moretus family, which includes a "guiding star" (*stella duce*).[1] The ox skull between the cornucopiae in the cartouche at the bottom is a reference to Piety, a symbol Rubens must have known from reading Guillaume du Choul's then-popular *Discours de la religion des anciens romains* (Discourse on the Religion of the Ancient Romans).[2]

Rubens completed the frame of the cartouche on the left side only, since the design was for a silver platter that the craftsman would complete in mirror image on the right. This piece is probably the one mentioned in a document in the Museum Plantin-Moretus archives, which records that on March 15, 1630, Balthasar Moretus paid Theodoor Galle (1571–1633) thirty-six florins for work on a silver platter after Rubens's design.[3] No work in silver with the official emblem of the Plantin Press is known today. It likely was a special commission for a piece that was primarily decorative. Since Rubens was away from Antwerp on diplomatic missions between late August 1628 and the spring of 1630, he must have either finished the design before he left Antwerp or sent the drawing from London.[4] The Plantin Press never did use the design as a printer's mark. Closest to it is a modified design that Cornelis Galle the Elder (1576–1650) provided for volumes 2–4 of Justus Lipsius's *Opera Omnia,* published by the press in Antwerp in 1637.[5]

In the portion of the inventory of Erasmus II Quellinus (1607–1678) that was drawn up on March 22, 1679, a "Labor et Constantia Rubbens crabbelinge" (a quick sketch by Rubens of a Labor and Constantia) is listed. This reference must be to an earlier, less finished draft of this composition, since the present drawing remained with the Plantin Press.[6] Quellinus became a master in the Antwerp guild in 1633–34 and collaborated with Rubens in the later 1630s, especially on designs for book illustrations.

1. Bouchery and Van den Wijngaert 1941, p. 141, n. 81.
2. Guillaume du Choul, *Discours de la religion des anciens romains* (Lyons, 1581), pp. 316–18; see Held 1986, p. 142, under no. 186.
3. Judson and Van de Velde 1978, vol. 1, pp. 308–9, under no. 74a, citing Museum Plantin-Moretus archives, Antwerp: "gesneden in een silvere talloor den passser naer Rubens."
4. Held 1986, p. 143, under no. 186.
5. Judson and Van de Velde 1978, vol. 1, p. 308, under no. 74a, fig. 254.
6. Denucé 1932, p. 286; Duverger 1984–, vol. 10, doc. 3333, p. 360.

PETER PAUL RUBENS AND STUDIO ASSISTANT

55. *Queen Tomyris with the Head of Cyrus,* ca. 1630

Pen and brown ink and gray and brown wash, touches of red watercolor, heightened with white, over a drawing by an assistant in black chalk, traced for transfer; vertical fold through the middle, 392 x 595 mm (15 7/16 x 23 7/16 in.)
Annotated in pen and brown ink at lower left: *P. P. Rubens*

Private collection, Germany

PROVENANCE: Everhard Jabach (1618–1695), Cologne and Paris (Lugt 2959; portefeuille no. 4, no. 70);[1] Pierre Crozat (1665–1740), Paris (his sale, Paris, April 10–May 13, 1741, lot 835 [Rubens]); Pierre-Jean Mariette (1694–1774), Paris (sale, Paris, November 15, 1775–January 30, 1776, lot 991 [Rubens]); Pierre François Basan (1723–1797); ?Theodorus van Duysel, The Hague (sale, Amsterdam, Van der Schley, October 11, 1784, lot 2133); sale, London, Christie's, May 11, 1791, lot 89; ?Troward, London; ?Du (or De) Roveray, London (1821); Sir Thomas Lawrence (1769–1830); acquired from his estate by Samuel Woodburn in 1835; sold in 1838 to the Prince of Orange, later William II of the Netherlands (1792–1849), The Hague (listed in his sale, The Hague, August 12–20, 1850, as part of lot 282, which included three large Rubens drawings framed together [see cat. nos. 13, 57], but withdrawn in favor of Sophie, Grand Duchess of Sachsen-Weimar-Eisenach, daughter of William II); grand dukes of Sachsen-Weimar, Weimar (lent to the Goethe-Museum, Weimar, until 1921); Joseph Fach (dealer), Frankfurt, 1951–52; Schaeffer Gallery, New York, 1959; Baroness Dorothée von Mosch (sale, London, Sotheby, November 11, 1965, no. 61, ill. [Rubens]); sale, Amsterdam, Sotheby Mak van Waay, March 21, 1977, no. 52, ill. [Rubens].

LITERATURE: Müller Hofstede 1965a, pp. 344–45, fig. 244 [Rubens]; Renger 1974a, pp. 122–75; McGrath 1997, no. 3, fig. 13 [Paulus Pontius?, reworked by Rubens]; Py 2001, pp. 97–98, no. 278, ill.

EXHIBITION: London 1835, no. 82.

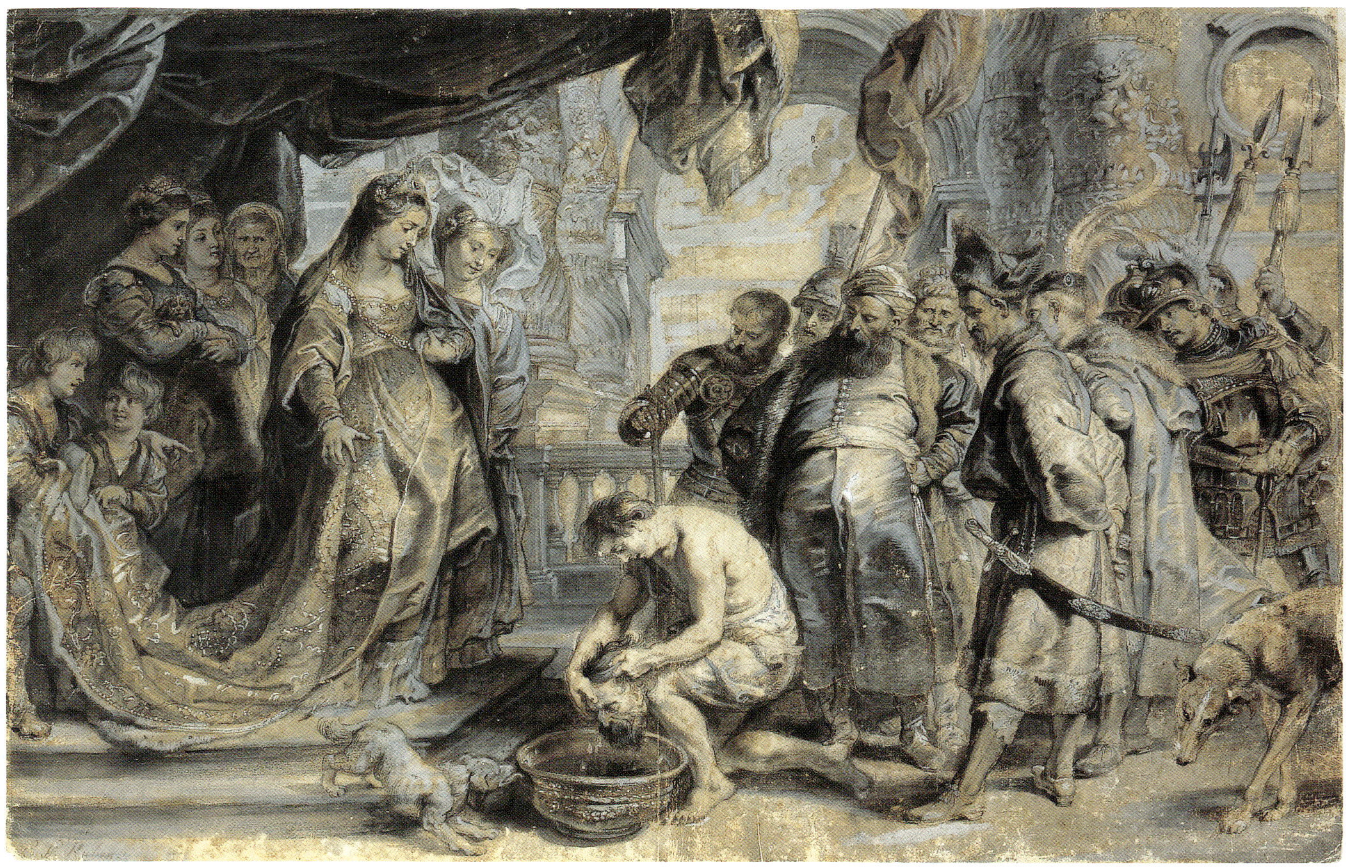

Cat. 55

This exceptionally large drawing represents Tomyris, queen of the Messagetae, a Near Eastern tribe, taking revenge on the Persian king Cyrus. According to Herodotus (*Historiae* I.212–14), who first recorded the story in the fifth century B.C., Tomyris pledged that if Cyrus failed to return her captured son alive, she would give the king his "fill of blood." Since her son died after he was captured and imprisoned, the queen held Cyrus responsible. True to her word, when the Messagetae later defeated the Persians and Cyrus was killed in battle, Tomyris had his head severed and brought to her. On this sheet Rubens depicted the queen in opulent dress, surrounded by her courtiers and watching as a servant dips Cyrus's head into a bowl filled with human blood. Her words, "Take your fill of blood that you thirsted for," are recorded in the inscription on Paulus Pontius's print based on the drawing (fig. 100).[2]

Rubens had owned a Latin edition of Herodotus's *Historiae* since 1615, and he purchased a Greek-Latin edition on June 28, 1622.[3] He represented the story of Tomyris and Cyrus in two paintings, one now in the Museum of Fine Arts, Boston (fig. 101), of about 1622–23,[4] and the other now in the Louvre, Paris.[5] In addition to this drawing for Pontius's print, a sketchy compositional study of the subject survives (Cleveland Museum of Art). The latter dates from the late 1630s and shows Rubens's initial ideas for a painting that apparently never materialized (cat. no. 112 verso).[6]

The present drawing derives from the painting in Boston. It is traced for transfer and served as the design for Pontius's engraving, which bears Rubens's full privilege and is dated 1630. There are significant changes from the painting. Most notably, Rubens enlarged the architectural setting and altered the spatial arrangement of the figures. For example, he placed Queen Tomyris and her maidservants prominently on a small platform above the men and soldiers. These changes were probably added to a studio assistant's initial drawing in black chalk that

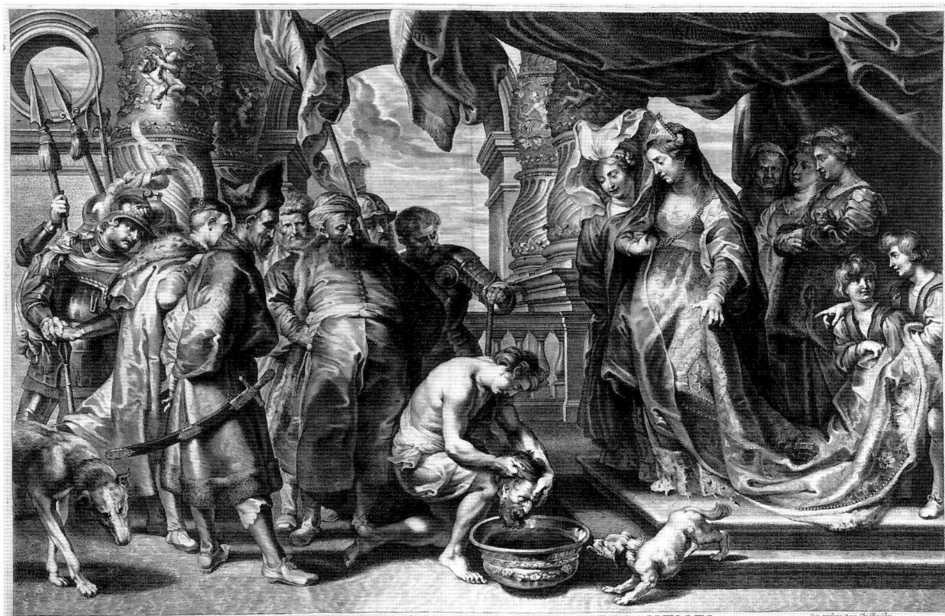

Fig. 100. Paulus Pontius, *Queen Tomyris with the Head of Cyrus*, 1630. Engraving, 405 x 485 mm ($15\frac{15}{16}$ x $19\frac{1}{8}$ in.). Private collection

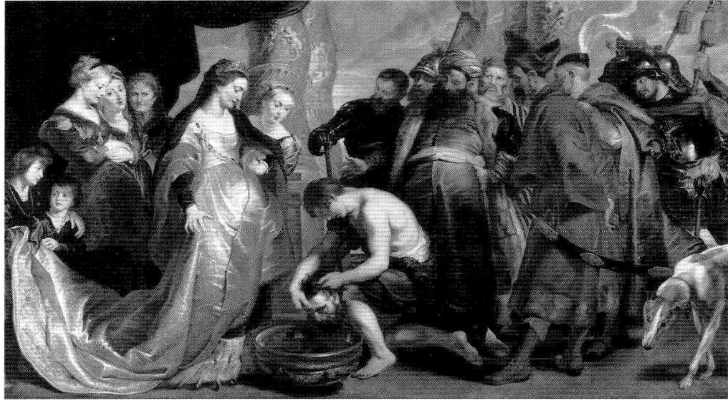

Fig. 101. Peter Paul Rubens, *Queen Tomyris with the Head of Cyrus*, ca. 1622–23. Oil on canvas, 205.1 x 361 cm ($80\frac{3}{4}$ x $142\frac{1}{8}$ in.). Museum of Fine Arts, Boston; Juliana Cheney Edwards Collection (41.40)

is now almost completely obscured by Rubens's reworkings.[7]

The assistant's drawing may date from the mid-1620s, that is, slightly later than the painting. After Rubens's return to Antwerp in early 1630 from his diplomatic missions, he published several prints, including the Pontius engraving after his design of *Tomyris and Cyrus*. Thus he likely reworked this drawing at that time.[8] Pontius took great care to reproduce the composition in his engraving, which exists in five states. Rubens closely supervised Pontius's progress, adding corrections to a proof impression of the first state.[9] Judging from some forty known copies after the Boston painting and the engraving, Rubens's Tomyris and Cyrus composition was extremely popular.[10]

1. The Jabach provenance was recently established by Bernadette Py (2001, no. 278).
2. Hollstein 1949–, vol. 17, p. 160, no. 40; 405 x 485 mm. The inscription reads: "satia te sanguine, quem semper sitisti."
3. McGrath 1997, vol. 1, p. 64.
4. M. Jaffé 1989, no. 510, 1618–19; McGrath 1997, no. 2, fig. 8.
5. M. Jaffé 1989, no. 666, 1620–25; McGrath 1997, no. 4, fig. 23.
6. We do not believe that a third drawing of the same subject in the State Hermitage Museum, Saint Petersburg (M. Jaffé 1989, no. 509, 1618–19; McGrath 1997, no. 2a, copy, fig. 9 [Rubens?]), is by Rubens.
7. Burchard suggested (and McGrath [1997, vol. 2, p. 32] follows him in this) that Rubens took a drawing for—or copy after—the Boston composition, cut it in half, and pasted the two sections back together, thereby introducing the different spatial organization with Tomyris and the women raised above the men; the engraver then copied this reworked composition for the print. However, to us, this seems too involved a process.
8. Renger 1974a, pp. 146–47.
9. London 1977b, no. 89, pl. 11.
10. McGrath 1997, no. 2 (Boston painting), copies 1–11, and no. 3 (Pontius engraving), copies 1–28.

56. *Christ on the Cross,* ca. 1630–31

Black chalk and brush and dark gray body color and touches of red ink (in eyes and left hand of Christ) and gray, white, and greenish yellow body color; traced for transfer except for upper left and right corners; squared in black chalk, on tan paper, 585 x 367 mm (23 x 14 7/16 in.)

Museum Boijmans Van Beuningen, Rotterdam (MB 5005)

PROVENANCE: Everhard Jabach (1618–1695), Cologne and Paris (Lugt 2959; his inventory, no. 64, "by P. P. Rubens, Our Lord on the cross, or the angels chasing the devil, drawn in black chalk, wash and heightening on blue paper"); Pierre Crozat (1665–1740), Paris (his sale, Paris, April 10–May 13, 1741, under lot. 834); La Live de Jully, Paris (his sale, Paris, 1770, no. 144); Johann Georg Wille, Paris (his sale, Paris, December 6–10, 1784); Jacob de Vos (1736–1833), Amsterdam (his sale, Amsterdam, J. de Vries . . . C. F. Roos, October 30, 1833, portfolio DD, no. 1); Jan Gysbert baron Verstolk van Soelen (1776–1845), The Hague (his sale, Amsterdam, J. de Vries . . . C. F. Roos, March 22, 1847, and following days, no. 499); William II of the Netherlands, The Hague (his sale, Amsterdam, August 12–20, 1850, no. 291); Gerard Leembruggen Jzn, Hillegom (Lugt 2988; his sale, Amsterdam, C. F. Roos . . . C. F. Roos, March 5, 1866, and following days, no. 532; bought in); purchased for the Museum Boijmans Van Beuningen.

LITERATURE: R., vol. 5, no. 1345, pl. 386, and under no. 291; Glück and Haberditzl 1928, no. 140, pl. 140 [Paulus Pontius?]; Judson 2000, no. 32, fig. 101; Py 2001, no. 1003.

EXHIBITION: Rotterdam 2001, no. 28, ill.

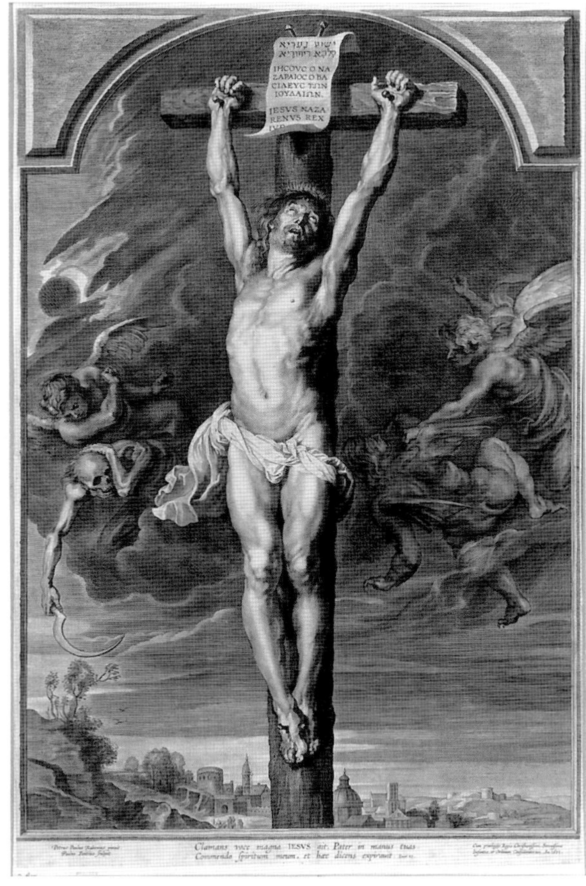

Fig. 102. Paulus Pontius, *Christ on the Cross,* 1631. Engraving, 596 x 383 mm (23 7/16 x 15 1/16 in.). The Metropolitan Museum of Art, New York; The Elisha Whittelsey Collection, The Elisha Whittelsey Fund, 1951 (51.501.3797)

This drawing is one of Rubens's most moving renderings of Christ at the moment of his most terrible suffering.[1] Rubens heavily reworked and modified an initial black-chalk drawing, probably by another hand (possibly that of Paulus Pontius [1603–1658]), that was limited to the figure of Christ, the Cross, the sky, and the distant view of Jerusalem and that ended 40 to 45 mm short of the long sides of the sheet.[2] (The initial composition does not appear to reproduce a specific painting by Rubens. Rather, it recalls numerous versions of the subject, including the painting that once hung over the door to the sacristy of the Antwerp church of the Recollects [today in the Koninklijk Museum voor Schone Kunsten, Antwerp).[3] Rubens altered the figure of Christ only slightly, but he expanded the image by widening the format of the underlying composition. With brush and grayish body color he added one angel at the left, about to strike the fleeing figure of Death with his fist, and another angel at the right, grabbing the wings of Sin (in the form of a devil) and also preparing to land a blow with his fist. (Because of these fist-fighting angels, in the eighteenth century the drawing and the engraving after it were known as *Christ "au coup de poing."*) Rubens also added the moon at the left and strengthened the clouds with gray ink and white body color. The artist finalized the composition with an arch at the top.

This heavily reworked drawing, traced for transfer, was Rubens's design for the engraving by Pontius, dated 1631 (fig. 102),[4] and must have been completed shortly before the print,

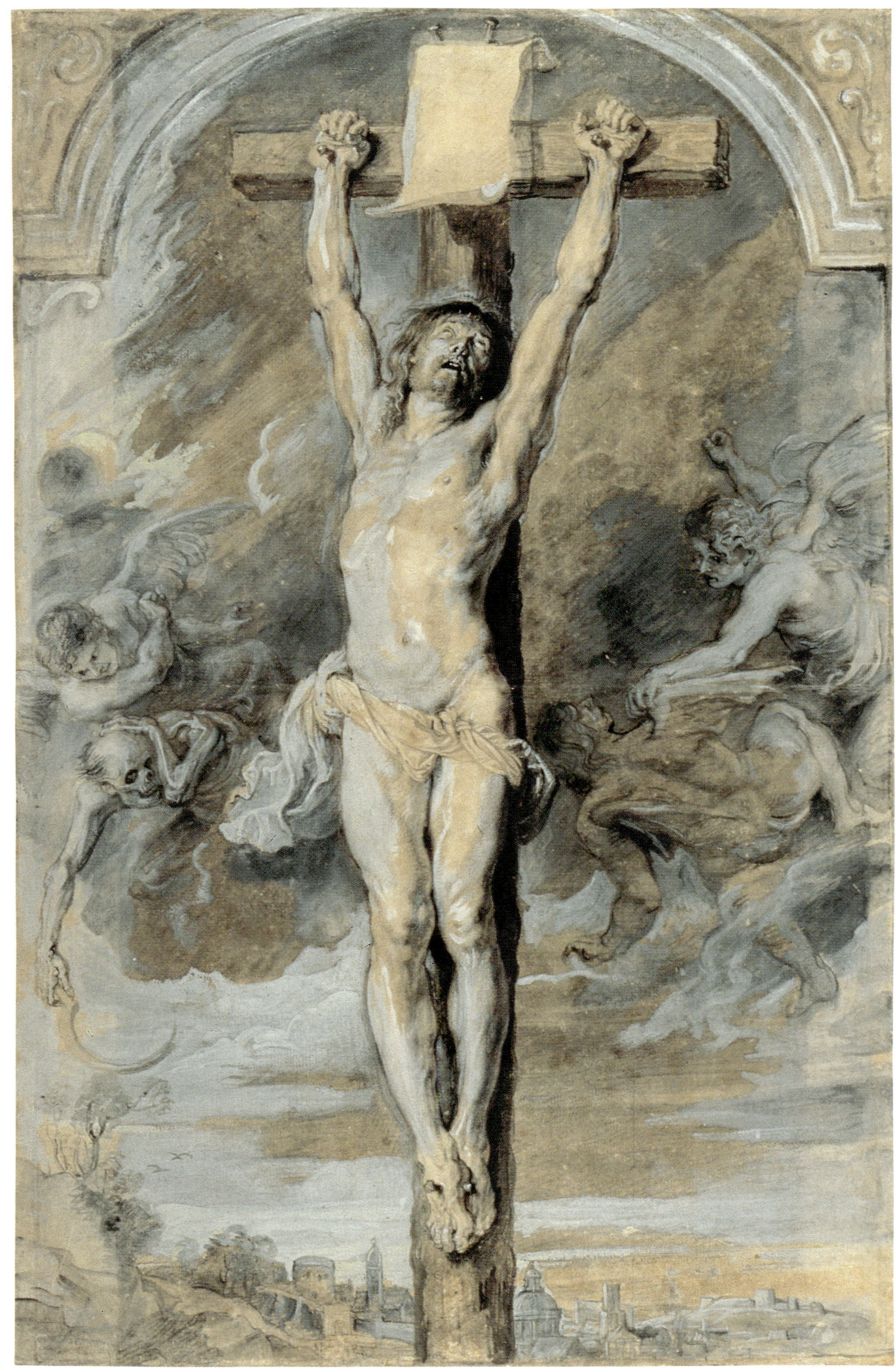

Cat. 56

or about 1630–31. The engraving differs from the drawing only in minor details, such as the trilingual inscription on the scroll attached to the top of the Cross and the gesture of the angel at the right, who restrains the devil by the arm rather than by the wing. The scrolls that decorate the sides of the arch in the drawing are absent from the print. Rubens closely supervised the progress of Pontius's engraving. In a letter of May 31, 1635, to his friend the French scholar Nicolas-Claude Fabri de Peiresc, Rubens wrote that he retouched the proofs several times.[5] On the one known proof impression of Pontius's print (Bibliothèque Nationale, Paris), Rubens added brown wash to the right side of Christ's torso and to the trees at the lower left; he introduced some white highlights (partly oxidized) in the angels, the devil, the moon, and the trees. And along the bottom edge of the sheet he wrote, in pen and brown ink, the words ultimately printed on the scroll above Christ's head: "And when Jesus had cried out with a loud voice, he said, Father, into thy hands [I commend my spirit]" (Luke 23:46).[6]

At the sale of the collection of Jacob de Vos (1736–1833) in Amsterdam in 1833, this sheet fetched the highest price paid for a Rubens drawing in Holland up to that time. (The record previously belonged to the *Assumption of the Virgin* now in the Getty Museum [cat. no. 53].)[7]

1. Glen 1977, p. 47.
2. Müller Hofstede (1965, p. 348, n. 195) considered the entire drawing to be by Rubens. Rubens also expanded an initial composition prepared by an unidentified draftsman in his *Feast of Herod* (cat. no. 57) and his *Assumption of the Virgin* (cat. no. 53).
3. Not in K.d.K., ed. Rosenberg 1905, or K.d.K., ed. Oldenbourg 1921; Glen 1977, app. pp. 252–53, no. 4, ca. 1610–12, fig. 11; M. Jaffé 1989, no. 200, ca. 1613.
4. 596 x 383 mm; Hollstein 1949–, vol. 17, p. 150, no. 11.
5. Magurn 1955, p. 398, no. 236.
6. See Judson 2000, no. 32a, fig. 103: "Luca Cap XXIII Clamans voce' magna IESVS ait Pater in manus tuas."
7. Plomp 2001–2, p. 232.

PETER PAUL RUBENS AND STUDIO ASSISTANT

57. *The Feast of Herod,* late 1630s

Brush and brown and gray wash, heightened and retouched with white body color, over a drawing by an assistant in black chalk, 476 x 718 mm (18¾ x 28¼ in.)

Private collection, United States

Provenance: Pierre Crozat (1665–1740), Paris (his sale, Paris, April 10–May 13, 1741, lot 832 [Rubens, very finished, engraved by Bolswert]); Gabriel Huquier (1695–1771), Paris (Lugt 2577; his sale, Paris, July 1–23, 1771, lot 32; sold for 301 louis d'or); Jean-Baptiste-Florentin-Gabriel de Meryan, Marquis de Lagoy (1764–1829), Paris and Saint Rémy-de-Provence (Lugt 1710; according to Lawrence exhibition, 1835; in 1820 Lagoy sold 138 of his finest drawings to Samuel Woodburn); Thomas Dimsdale (1758–1823), London (Lugt 2426; according to Lawrence exhibition, 1835); bought by Samuel Woodburn *à l'amiable* from the heirs of Dimsdale who resold the best drawings to Sir Thomas Lawrence, London (Lugt 2445; listed in his inventory, case 7, drawer 2:85.11: "A most splendid Drawing of the Feast of Herodias, highly finished, superb");[1] sold in 1838 to the Prince of Orange, later William II of the Netherlands (1792–1849), The Hague (listed in his sale, The Hague, August 12–20, 1850, as part of lot 282, which included three large Rubens drawings framed together [see cat. nos. 13, 55], but withdrawn in favor of Sophie, Grand Duchess of Sachsen-Weimar-Eisenach, daughter of William II); grand dukes of Sachsen-Weimar, Weimar, until ca. 1918; by descent until 1999; sale, London, Phillips, July 7, 1999, no. 116, ill.; Colnaghi, *An Exhibition of Master Drawings,* New York–London, 2000, no. 19, ill.

Literature: Whitfield in Washington–London 1982, p. 239, under no. 138.

Exhibitions: London 1835, no. 85 [Rubens]; New York–London 2000, no. 19, ill.

This elaborate drawing shows King Herod's birthday banquet, where Salome, the daughter of Herod's unlawful wife, Herodias, walks in with the head of John the Baptist. King Herod, seated at the right, had been so much taken by Salome's beautiful dancing that in gratitude he had promised her anything she desired. Prompted by her mother, shown here next to Herod, Salome asked for the head of John the Baptist on a platter. Herodias despised John because he had spoken against her marriage to Herod. Although greatly dismayed, the king honored Salome's request (Matthew 14).

The drawing evolved in two distinct stages. First, an assistant in Rubens's studio, possibly the engraver of the composition, Schelte à Bolswert (ca. 1585–1659), copied the master's

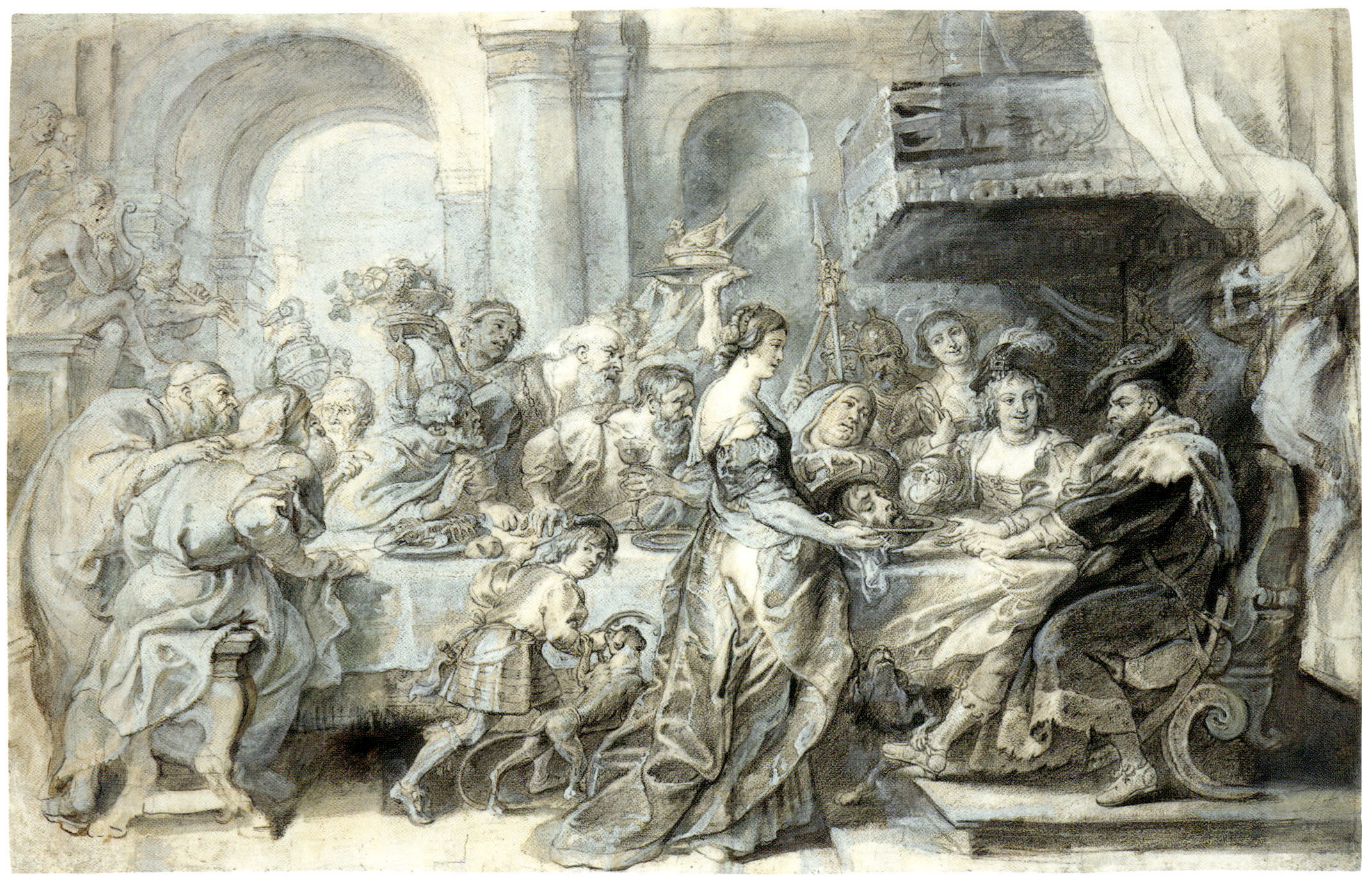

Cat. 57

painting of the *Feast of Herod* (National Gallery of Scotland, Edinburgh).[2] He left a large portion of the paper blank above and to the left, which Rubens then filled in to create a more expansive scene. The assistant's copy ends at the top right along the lower edge of the canopy over the royal couple and at the left with the attendant holding up a basket full of fruit, corresponding to the parameters of the Edinburgh painting. This initial stage was executed in an oily black chalk in a perfunctory manner, with dense hatching filling large areas. Although Rubens reworked much of this section, the assistant's drawing is still clearly visible in the figure of Herod. Rubens extended the composition at the left by about one third, showing the entire table with an additional three men, who express their horror at the sight of the severed head. A servant with a large jug stands behind them. Finally, the master added a group of musicians at the far left under an archway.

Given that the studio assistant drew his copy in the corner of a large piece of paper, it is likely that Rubens intended from the beginning to expand the composition. He sketched the new elements lightly with a dry black chalk, then reworked the entire scene with light gray body color and gray wash. (The light gray highlights in the men's garments at the left are similar to Rubens's retouches on the drawing *Fashionable Young Woman Holding a Shield* [cat. no. 117]). Obvious changes at the right are the enlargement of the dais above Herod and the curtain, which only partly obscures the boundaries of the assistant's copy in black chalk. The artist also completed Herod's chair, turning it into a massive piece of furniture. Ever the painter, he finished the design by applying accents with a brush and dark brown ink. In the end, Rubens's rethinking of the scene was so extensive that he created an entirely new composition.

As mentioned above, this drawing was engraved by Schelte à Bolswert, who began working for Rubens in 1633. As it is not traced for transfer, Bolswert likely made an intermediary copy that he used as a direct design for his engraving.[3]

The drawing's exceptional size and high finish have made it prized by collectors, and it has always been in private hands. When the collection of Gabriel Huquier (1695–1771) was sold in 1771, the drawing fetched the enormous sum of 301 louis d'or, much more than the 18 louis paid for sixty-five drawings by Rembrandt and his school.[4] The picturelike features of the drawing have also prompted collectors to frame the sheet. In 1838 the Prince of Orange, the future King William II of the Netherlands, had the sheet framed in a large tableau with two equally impressive drawings, the *Man on Horseback* (cat. no. 13) and *Queen Tomyris with the Head of Cyrus* (cat. no. 55); all three drawings are reunited in the present exhibition. The drawing became known to a wider public only briefly, in 1999–2000, when it appeared at auction in London and at Colnaghi's before being acquired once again by a private collector. Until then, it had never been reproduced, and was known primarily through Bolswert's engraving.

Both Rubens's *Feast of Herod* painting in Edinburgh and the present drawing were copied repeatedly. A contemporary copy of the latter is in the Musée Bonnat, Bayonne.[5]

1. It is unclear if the present drawing is the same as a framed *Feast of Herod* sold with drawings from the collection of Benjamin West (1738–1820), London (Lugt 419), sixteen years after West's death (sale, London, Sotheby's, May 11, 1836, lot 67, for 25 pounds, the highest price at the auction). The present drawing bears the stamp of Sir Thomas Lawrence (d. 1830), which could have been added between 1823 (after the death of the previous owner, Thomas Dimsdale) and 1834 (when Woodburn acquired the drawing from Lawrence), but it does not bear West's collector's stamp. The drawing's presence in the Lawrence collection makes it unlikely that it was also in the collection of Benjamin West. We thank Stephen Ongpin for discussing this issue of provenance.
2. M. Jaffé 1989, no. 1187, ca. 1635. By the time of Rubens's death in 1640, this painting was recorded in the collection of the wealthy Fleming Gaspar de Roomer in Naples. For Rubens's preliminary drawing for the painting, see cat. no. 112 recto.
3. 406 x 610 mm. Inscribed in the margin at the bottom: "MISITQVE ET DECOLLAVIT IOANNEM IN CARCERE ET ALLATVM EST CAPVT EIVS IN DISCO ET DATVM EST PVELLÆ ET ATTVLIT MATRI SVÆ Matthej 14 Cap. / Petr. Paul. Rubens pinxit / S.à Bolswert sculpsit; Gillis Hendricx excudit"; Schneevoogt 1873, p. 31, no. 170; Hollstein 1949–, vol. 3, p. 72, no. 13. According to Held, Bolswert's print dates to after 1644–45, thus after Rubens's death. He further argued against attributing the composition known in this print and several painted versions to Rubens himself, calling the architecture "unimaginative" and objecting to the slender Salome with a rather small head; instead he considered it the work of a follower who enlarged the composition of the Edinburgh painting. Held did not mention the present drawing in his discussion, only the painted copies with the same compositions. Held 1954, p. 122, written in reply to Burchard 1953, pp. 383–87.
4. Ongpin in New York–London 2000, no. 19.
5. Inv. 1411. Watercolor and body color over black and red chalk, heightened with white, squared for transfer, 422 x 695 mm. Although attributed to Rubens in the Bonnat inventory, and exhibited as Rubens in 1965 (Bayonne 1965, no. 3), the drawing is definitely not by Rubens. Michael Jaffé (1966a, p. 630) considered it one of the very finest copies, by Jacob Jordaens, after Rubens's *Feast of Herod* in Edinburgh; R. A. d'Hulst (1974, vol. 2, no. D1, vol. 4, fig. 598) rejected this suggestion.

ANTWERP AND INTERNATIONAL TRAVELS, 1616–35: INDIVIDUAL STUDIES

58. *Study of Saint Catherine for the "Martyrdom of Saint Catherine,"* ca. 1615–17

Black chalk, heightened with white chalk, 374 x 236 mm (14 11/16 x 9 1/4 in.); at bottom right irregularly cut, made up by another hand, and drawing completed in black chalk; horizontal fold through center
Annotated in red chalk at top: *S. Catarina*

Albertina, Vienna (8293)

PROVENANCE: Hofbibliothek, Vienna; in 1796 acquired through exchange by Duke Albert of Sachsen-Teschen (1738–1822), Vienna (Lugt 174).

LITERATURE: R., vol. 5, no. 1443; Glück and Haberditzl 1928, no. 143, pl. 143; Vlieghe 1972, no. 78a, fig. 134; Kuznetsov 1974, pl. 87; Alexis Donetzkoff in Lille 2000, pp. 174–75.

EXHIBITIONS: Vienna 1977b, no. 21, ill.; Washington–New York–Vienna 1984–86, no. 36, ill.; New York and other cities 1997–99, no. 34, ill.

This study of a young woman is Rubens's preliminary drawing for the figure of Saint Catherine in his *Martyrdom of Saint Catherine,* painted for the main altar of the church of Saint Catherine in Lille (fig. 103).[1] Saint Catherine, who lived in the fourth century, had been saved by her faith from numerous cruel tortures, but was finally sentenced to death in Alexandria. On this sheet Rubens drew only the upper body of the saint and part of her dress as he prepared her pose: looking heavenward, she kneels, awaiting her execution; her hands are bound in front of her, and her neck is exposed in readiness for the executioner's sword. In the final painting her eyes are turned more toward the viewer, and her neck is even more exposed (the executioner moves part of the collar of her dress aside). At an unknown date a large, irregular piece of the sheet was sliced away along the right edge, through the saint's dress, possibly

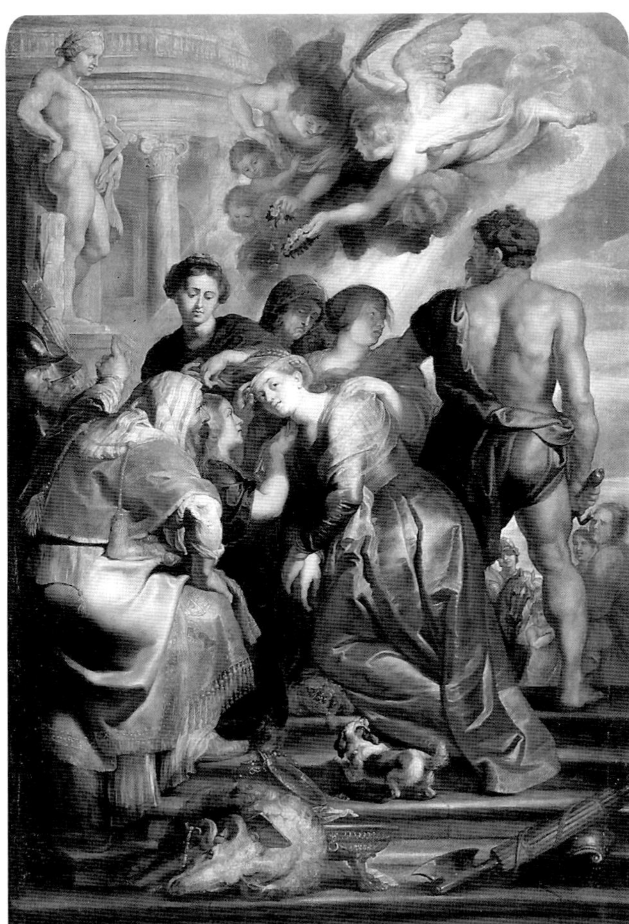

Fig. 103. Peter Paul Rubens, *The Martyrdom of Saint Catherine,* ca. 1615–17. Oil on canvas, 390 x 249 cm (153⁹⁄₁₆ x 98¹⁄₁₆ in.). Palais des Beaux-Arts, Lille (D 65-8)

because all or part of another figure appeared on the sheet, and the person who cut the drawing wanted to separate them. After the damage was done, some of Rubens's black chalk lines were extended onto a new backing sheet, to make the loss less obvious.

Rubens's *Martyrdom of Saint Catherine* altarpiece was commissioned by Jean de Seur and his wife, Marie Patyn. De Seur, a member of the Council of State in Lille since 1603, became the financier of Archduke Albert and Archduchess Isabella in 1616. He was a parishioner of the church of Saint Catherine and was buried there in 1621. His gravestone, dated June 2, 1621, is considered a terminus ante quem for Rubens's painting.[2] The drawing probably dates from about 1615–17, close in time to other black-chalk studies in the Albertina of single female figures, such as the *Young Woman Crouching, Turned to the Right* (cat. no. 63) that prepares one of Lycomedes' daughters in Rubens's *Achilles among the Daughters of Lycomedes* (fig. 108), painted with the collaboration of Anthony van Dyck (1599–1641). Rubens's studio was very busy during these years, a circumstance that might also account for the close correspondence between the present drawing of Saint Catherine and the figure of the saint in the altarpiece, which apparently is for the most part a work by the Rubens studio.

The annotation in red chalk at the top, "S. Catarina," is by the same hand that added identifications of other sitters—including George Villiers (cat. no. 77), the Marquis of Leganés (cat. no. 78), and the "Staetdochter" (cat. no. 84)—to Rubens drawings today in the Albertina.

1. K.d.K., ed. Oldenbourg 1921, no. 242; M. Jaffé 1989, no. 291, ca. 1615; Lille 2004, no. 121, ca. 1615.
2. Vlieghe 1972, no. 78.

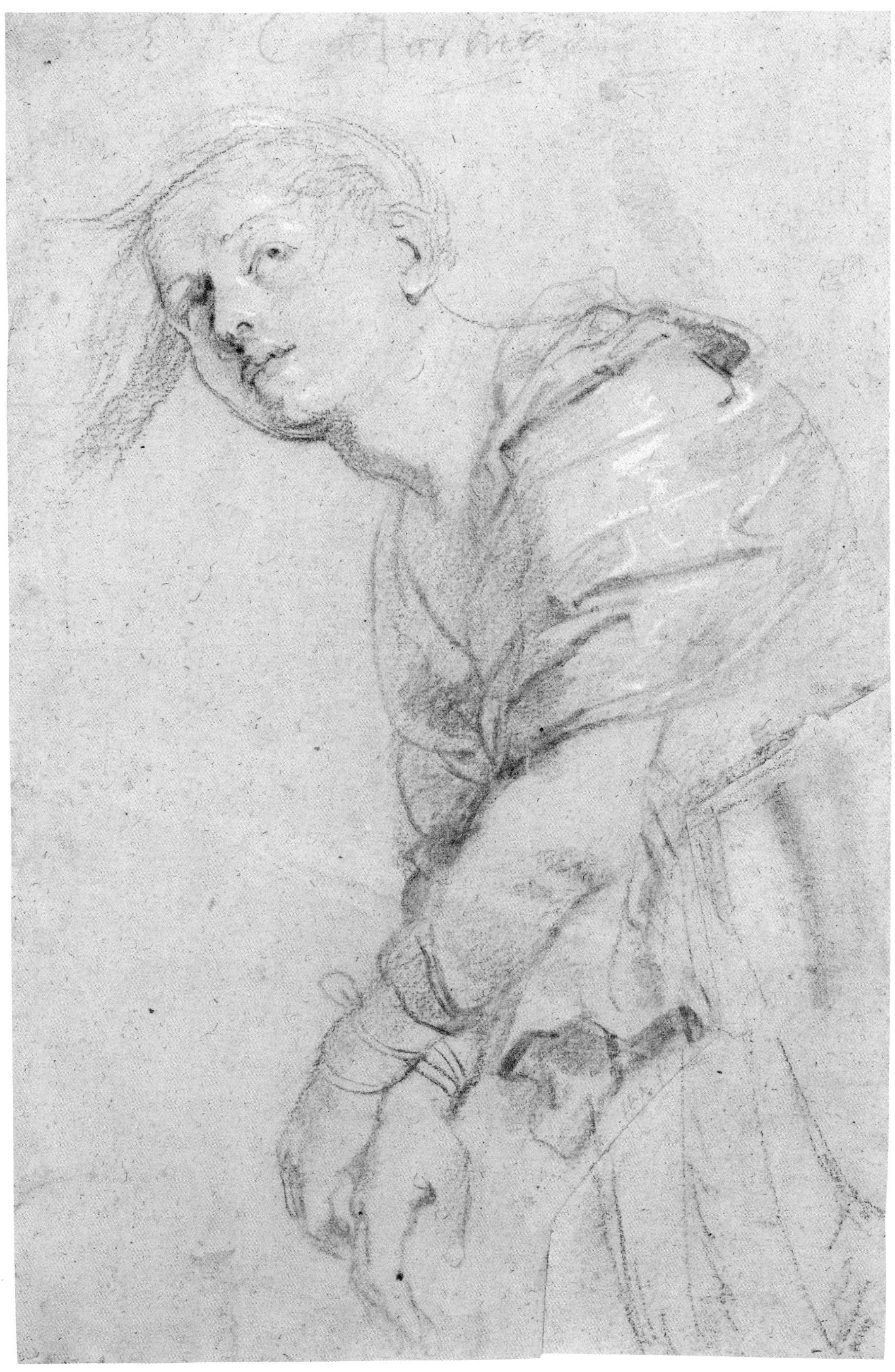

Cat. 58

59. *Study for the Christ Child,* ca. 1616

Oily black chalk, heightened with white chalk, on brownish paper, 396 x 265 mm (15 9/16 x 10 7/16 in.)
Annotated in pen and brown ink at bottom right: *Rubbens*

Albertina, Vienna (17 639)

PROVENANCE: Hofbibliothek, Vienna; in 1796 acquired through exchange by Duke Albert of Sachsen-Teschen (1738–1822), Vienna (Lugt 174).

LITERATURE: R., vol. 5, no. 1576; Glück and Haberditzl 1928, no. 86, pl. 86; Held 1959, p. 135, under no. 98; M. Jaffé 1972, p. 112; Held 1986, p. 124, under no. 144.

EXHIBITIONS: Vienna 1977b, no. 13, ill.; New York and other cities 1997–99, no. 32, ill.

The small boy in this sketch is probably Rubens's son Albert, born on June 5, 1614.[1] A supporting hand under the child's right arm steadies the boy on his feet. The child, who seems less than enthused, looks to the left with an almost mature expression of suspicion. We can see that Rubens redrew the child's shoulders, positioning them slightly higher than at first.

Rubens used this study for the Christ Child in his painting of the *Holy Family with Saint Elizabeth and the Infant Saint John the Baptist* (fig. 104),[2] which, like the drawing, dates from about 1616. In the drawing the little boy holds in his left hand what appears to be an apple, while in the painting the Child extends his left arm and hand toward the infant Saint John. Rubens also adapted this study for the body of the Christ Child in the *Virgin with Jesus and the Infant Saint John the Baptist* (fig. 126),[3] where the Child is turned more toward the left and rests his left arm on the Virgin's shoulder. For the head of the Christ Child in the same painting Rubens used the well-known study of his son Nicolaas (cat. no. 81), though without the coral necklace (in the *Holy Family* in London [fig. 104], however, the Christ Child does wear one).

The oily chalk that Rubens used for this drawing produces dark, strong lines. He employed a similar chalk in the *Study for a Halberdier* (cat. no. 15), the *Studies of Heads and Clasped Hands* (cat. no. 40), and in *Woman Kneeling, Turned to the Left* (cat. no. 62). Rubens worked with this medium only sporadically, to judge from his extant drawings, and apparently preferred drier chalk, since it allowed for softer tonalities and gradations. In addition, the greasier the chalk, the more difficult it was to erase lines.

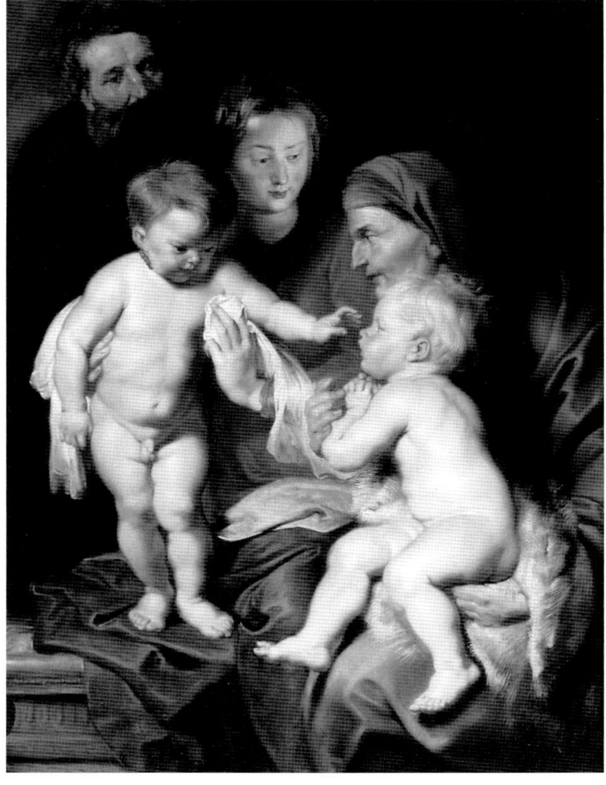

Fig. 104. Peter Paul Rubens, *The Holy Family with Saint Elizabeth and the Infant Saint John the Baptist,* ca. 1616. Oil on panel, 138 x 102 cm (54 5/16 x 40 3/16 in.). The Wallace Collection, London (P 81)

1. We owe this suggestion to Michael Jaffé (1972, p. 112).
2. K.d.K., ed. Oldenbourg 1921, no. 69, left; M. Jaffé 1989, no. 368, ca. 1616.
3. M. Jaffé 1989, no. 541, 1619–20.

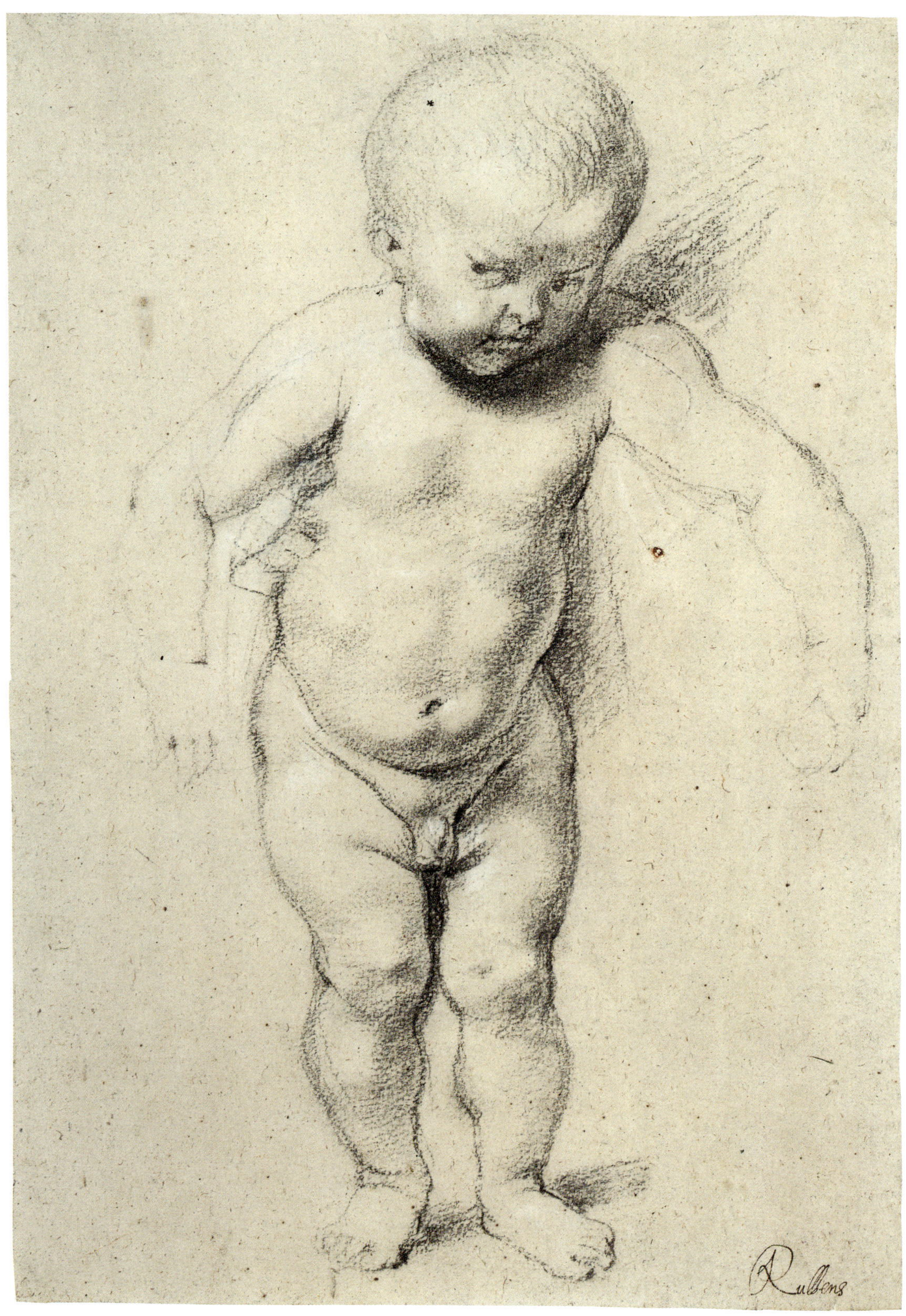

Cat. 59

60. *Young Woman Holding a Bowl,* ca. 1616

Black chalk, heightened with white chalk, on light gray paper, 347 x 307 mm ($13\frac{5}{8}$ x $12\frac{1}{8}$ in.)

Albertina, Vienna (8297)

Provenance: Hofbibliothek, Vienna; in 1796 acquired through exchange by Duke Albert of Sachsen-Teschen (1738–1822), Vienna (Lugt 174).

Literature: R., vol. 5, no. 1568; Glück and Haberditzl 1928, no. 107, pl. 107; Held 1959, no. 94, pl. 101, pp. 28–29, 73, and under no. 75; Kuznetsov 1974, pl. 85; Held 1986, no. 111, pl. 112; Judson 2000, no. 74d, fig. 221.

Exhibition: Vienna 1977b, no. 27, ill.

Rubens used great economy of line in this study of a young woman. The artist limited himself almost entirely to outlines and a few parallel hatchings to indicate shading. With fluid strokes of white chalk he highlighted the figure and indicated the shine of the woman's smooth hair. There is no hesitation, no correction in Rubens's line.

This sheet is one of three known preliminary studies of single figures[1] that Rubens drew in final preparation for his *Entombment of Christ* for the Capuchin church of Saint Géry, Cambrai (fig. 105).[2] Sébastien Briquet, canon of the cathedral of Notre Dame in Cambrai, is believed to have commissioned the altarpiece from Rubens in 1616 and to have presented it to the church, which had been dedicated on April 20, 1615. The drawing, which must date from about 1616, is Rubens's final study for Mary Magdalen, who appears at the lower right in the *Entombment,* holding a bowl to assist in the washing and anointing of Christ's body. The sheet follows the oil sketch now in Munich (fig. 106).[3] In the drawing, in contrast to the oil sketch, the Magdalen's face is rendered more in a lost profile, and her left hand, tightly holding the bowl, is seen slightly more from above, as it is in the final painting.

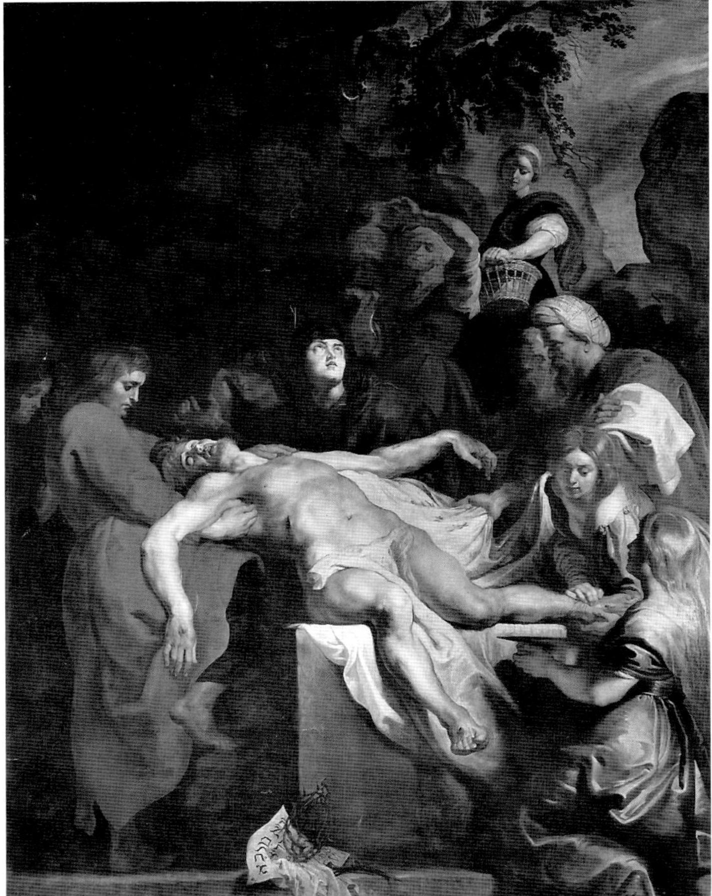

Fig. 105. Peter Paul Rubens, *The Entombment of Christ,* ca. 1616. Oil on canvas, 398 x 280 cm ($156\frac{11}{16}$ x $110\frac{1}{4}$ in.). Church of Saint Géry, Cambrai

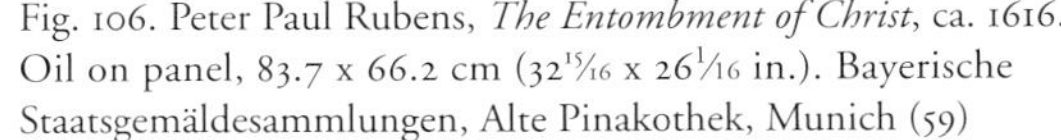

Fig. 106. Peter Paul Rubens, *The Entombment of Christ,* ca. 1616. Oil on panel, 83.7 x 66.2 cm ($32\frac{15}{16}$ x $26\frac{1}{16}$ in.). Bayerische Staatsgemäldesammlungen, Alte Pinakothek, Munich (59)

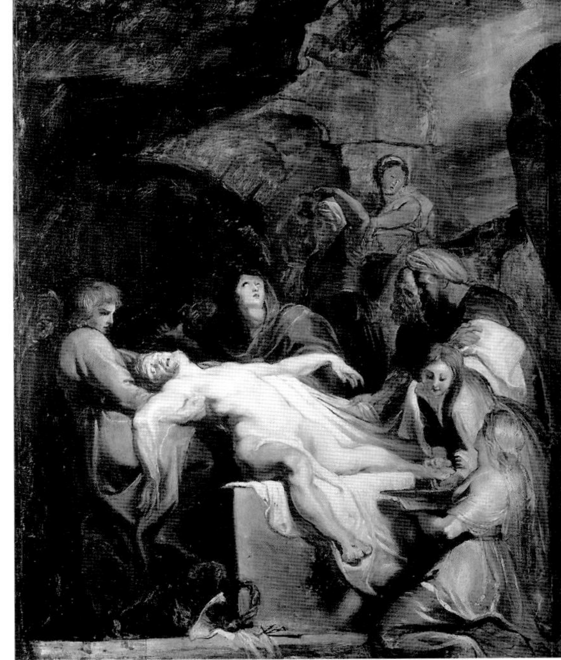

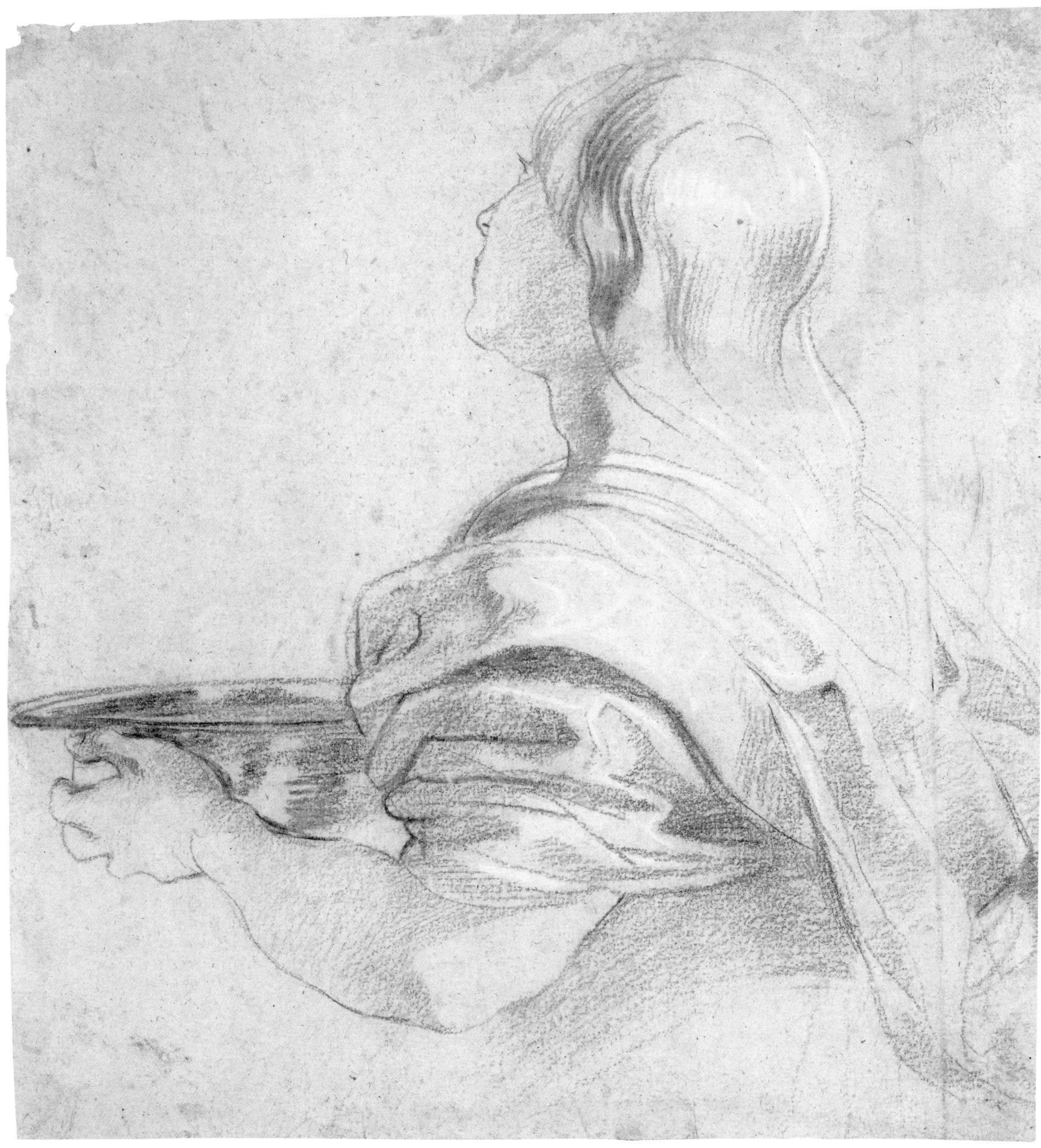

Cat. 60

1. The other two studies are for Saint John the Evangelist (Victoria and Albert Museum) and for Nicodemus, last recorded in 1939 in a private collection, Oslo (see Judson 2000, nos. 74b, 74c, pls. 218, 219).
2. M. Jaffé 1989, no. 337, 1615–17. The Cambrai altarpiece figures prominently in the center of the *Cabinet of Rubens* (Palazzo Pitti, Florence; Bodart in Florence 1977, no. 1, ill.), attributed to the Flemish painter Cornelis de Baeilleur (1607–1671).
3. K.d.K., ed. Oldenbourg 1921, no. 170; Held 1980, no. 366, pl. 358, ca. 1616; M. Jaffé 1989, no. 336, ca. 1615–16; Renger and Denk 2002, no. 59.

61. *Tartar Huntsman,* ca. 1616–18

Black chalk, heightened with white; 383 x 269 mm (15 1/16 x 10 9/16 in.) Annotated in pen and brown ink at bottom right: *del medesimo.* and (by another hand?) *Rubens 57.*

Fitzwilliam Museum, Cambridge (PD. 14-1989)

PROVENANCE: John Skippe (1742–1812), London; Mrs. A. C. Raynor Wood; by descent to Edward Holland Martin (*Catalogue of the Well-Known Collection of Old Master Drawings, Principally of the Italian School, Formed in the Eighteenth Century by John Skippe,* sale, London, Christie's, November 21, 1958, lot 278, pl. 38); Michael Jaffé (1923–1997), London (sale, London, Christie's, June 29, 1971, lot 57, ill.); Sir Spencer LeMarchant; London (sale, Christie's, July 4, 1984, lot 128, ill.).

LITERATURE: Balis 1986, no. 6b, fig. 54, p. 128; Munich 1997–98, pp. 16–17.

EXHIBITIONS: London 1953, no. 276; London 1953–54, no. 525; London 1965, no. 30.

Rubens drew this man in a turban in preparation for the rider on a rearing horse at the extreme left in his *Lion Hunt,* one of four paintings with hunting scenes that Duke Maximilian of Bavaria (1573–1651) commissioned from Rubens, probably shortly after he had purchased Schleissheim castle, near Munich, from his father in 1616. The *Lion Hunt* therefore dates from 1616 at the earliest, and from April 1618 at the latest, as Rubens mentioned it in a letter of May 12, 1618, to the English diplomat and collector Sir Dudley Carleton.[1] The series was first recorded in an inventory at Schleissheim in 1637.[2] During the Napoleonic wars the hunts were taken to Paris. The *Lion Hunt* was later sent to the museum in Bordeaux, where it was lost in a fire in 1870. The composition, however, is still known, from a studio version in a Spanish private collection and from a copy in the Deutsches Jagdmuseum, Munich.[3] A drawing after Rubens's lost painting, attributed to Pieter Claesz. Soutman (ca. 1580–1657) and today in the National Gallery of Art, Washington, D.C., is the design for Soutman's reproductive etching of the painting in reverse.[4]

The rider on the present sheet was not included in a slightly earlier, sketchier compositional study in pen (British Museum, London), in which Rubens laid out the general arrangement of hunters on horseback battling lions.[5] Rubens added this turbaned rider only when he was working on the final painting and decided to close the composition at the left with a powerful figure, mounted on a rearing horse, striking directly at a lion and trying to kill the beast. He therefore prepared this separate study in black chalk, perhaps to use as a guideline in the painting, where the rider was, however, slightly modified (with chin touching arm, the figure was bent more noticeably toward the lion below). In the drawing Rubens concentrated on the gesture of the figure; the figure itself is sketched in quick contour lines, and the modeling is hastily indicated through broadly applied shading. The turban identifies the hunter as a non-European, possibly a Tartar from the Caucasus; he has also been referred to as an Oriental. In his letter of May 12, 1618, to Sir Dudley Carleton, Rubens referred to the *Lion Hunt* painting as "alla moresca e turcesca molto bizarra" ([a hunt with] Moorish and Turkish riders, very exotic), thus placing it in North Africa or Asia Minor.[6] In the painting the turbaned huntsman wears a red cape and a yellow tunic with blue stripes, with a strap running over his right shoulder.

The Italian inscription, "del medesimo" (by the same [artist]), at the lower right of the sheet is an indication that this study was likely once in an Italian collection in which there was at least one other Rubens drawing. In the twentieth century the drawing belonged to Michael Jaffé (1923–1997), the former director of the Fitzwilliam Museum, Cambridge, and an eminent Rubens scholar.[7]

1. Magurn 1955, p. 61, letter 29. A *Tiger Hunt* that was part of the series is reproduced in a painting by Jan Brueghel the Elder, dated 1617, which supports the dating of the commission to 1616. See Balis 1986, no. 6.
2. Balis 1986, p. 125. In 1657, when Joachim von Sandrart mentioned this *Lion Hunt* in his *Teutsche Academie,* it was still hanging in the castle (Sandrart 1925, p. 159).
3. Balis 1986, pp. 123–24, under no. 6, copy 1, fig. 51, and copy 5. The Munich version is reproduced in Munich 1980, p. 22, fig. 21a.
4. It bears an old annotation, "A.v.Dyck." Balis 1986, p. 124, under no. 6, copy 6, fig. 55.
5. Held 1986, no. 101, pl. 90, ca. 1615–16.
6. Magurn 1955, pp. 61–63, letter 29.
7. The other Rubens drawing in the exhibition that was formerly in the collection of Michael Jaffé is the *Study for a Halberdier* (cat. no. 15).

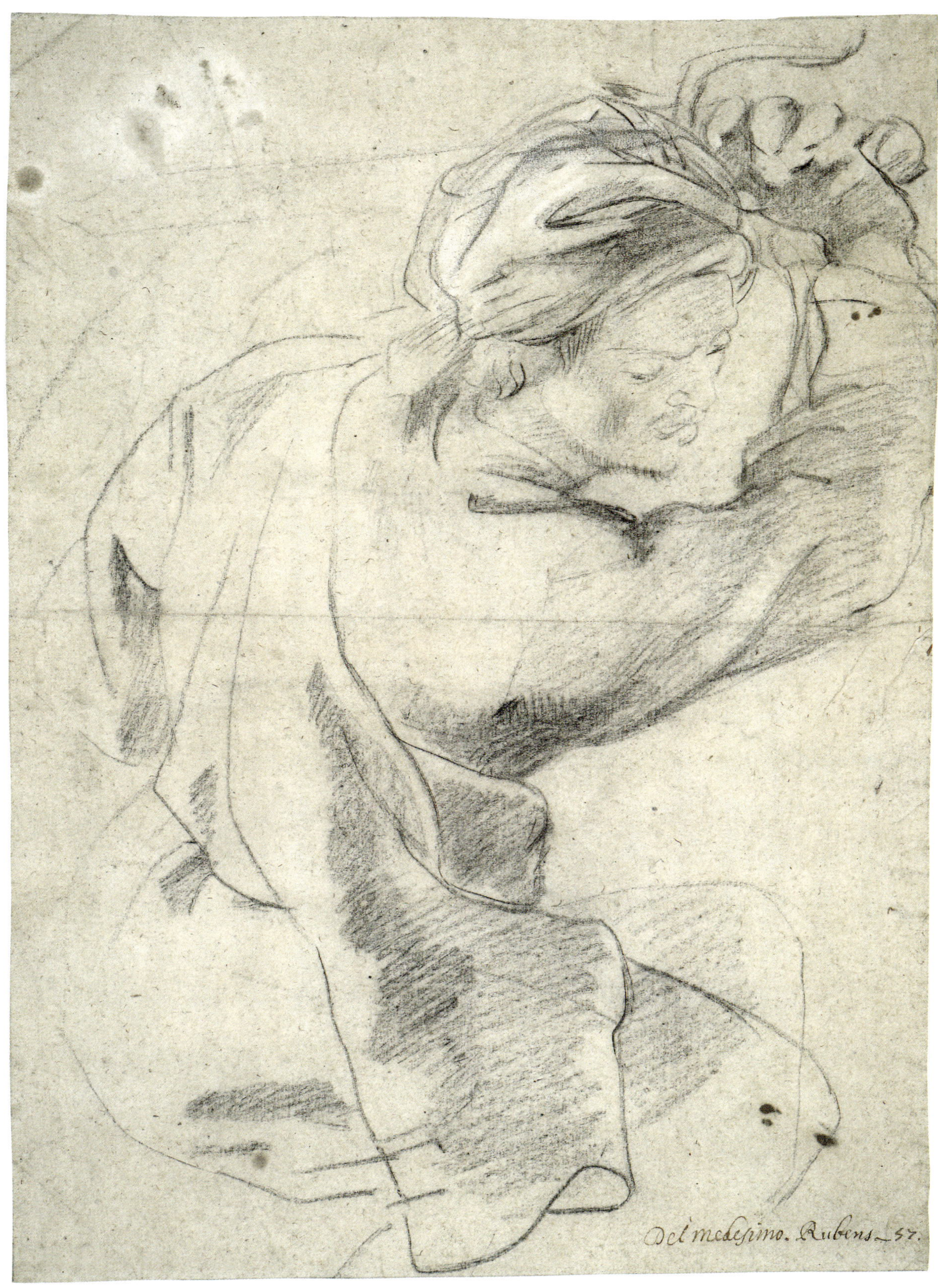

Cat. 61

62. *Woman Kneeling, Turned to the Left,* ca. 1617

Oily black chalk, heightened with white chalk, on light gray paper, 421 x 295 mm (16 9/16 x 11 5/8 in.)

Albertina, Vienna (8294)

PROVENANCE: Duke Albert of Sachsen-Teschen (1738–1822), Vienna (Lugt 174).

LITERATURE: R., vol. 5, no. 1431; Glück and Haberditzl 1928, no. 111, pl. 111; Held 1959, under no. 90; Held 1986, under no. 134; Brown in London 1996–97, p. 47, fig. 40.

EXHIBITIONS: Vienna 1977b, no. 23, ill.; New York and other cities 1997–99, no. 35, ill.; Lille 2004, no. 129, ill.

This rendering of a woman with artfully braided hair prepared the old peasant woman kneeling at the crib of the newborn Christ Child in Rubens's *Adoration of the Shepherds* of about 1617 (fig. 107).[1] Her hands folded on her chest express a deep devotion. (Rubens made a separate drawing each for the figure of Saint Joseph and for the young woman carrying a pitcher on her head.)[2] The *Adoration* is one of the three predella paintings that formerly belonged to the *Saint John* triptych in Mechelen. Rubens received the commission for the altarpiece on December 27, 1616;[3] the central panel, with the *Adoration of the Magi,* was installed on March 27, 1619.[4] However, the two wings with scenes from the life of Saint John the Baptist (on the left) and Saint John the Evangelist (on the right), together with the three predella paintings, had been delivered earlier, in 1617; the present study for the peasant woman adoring the Christ Child dates from about that year.

Rubens made use of the drawing once more, in a very different scene, in the *Farm at Laeken* (fig. 149).[5] In this painting the kneeling peasant woman appears prominently in the foreground. Instead of adoring the Christ Child, however, she pours from a pitcher.

1. K.d.K., ed. Oldenbourg 1921, no. 166; M. Jaffé 1989, no. 482F.
2. The study of Saint Joseph is in the Albertina, Vienna (Vienna 1977b, no. 24, ill.), and the study of the young woman is in the Kupferstichkabinett, Berlin (Berlin 1977, no. 26).
3. R., vol. 1, nos. 162–69.
4. In 1796 French troops took the altarpiece to Paris, where it remained until 1815, when it was restituted. However, two of the predella paintings—the *Adoration of the Shepherds* and the *Resurrection of Christ* (M. Jaffé 1989, no. 482H)—were shipped to Marseilles, where they have remained. The central predella, with *Christ Crucified,* is lost.
5. K.d.K., ed. Oldenbourg 1921, no. 186; M. Jaffé 1989, no. 515, 1618–19.

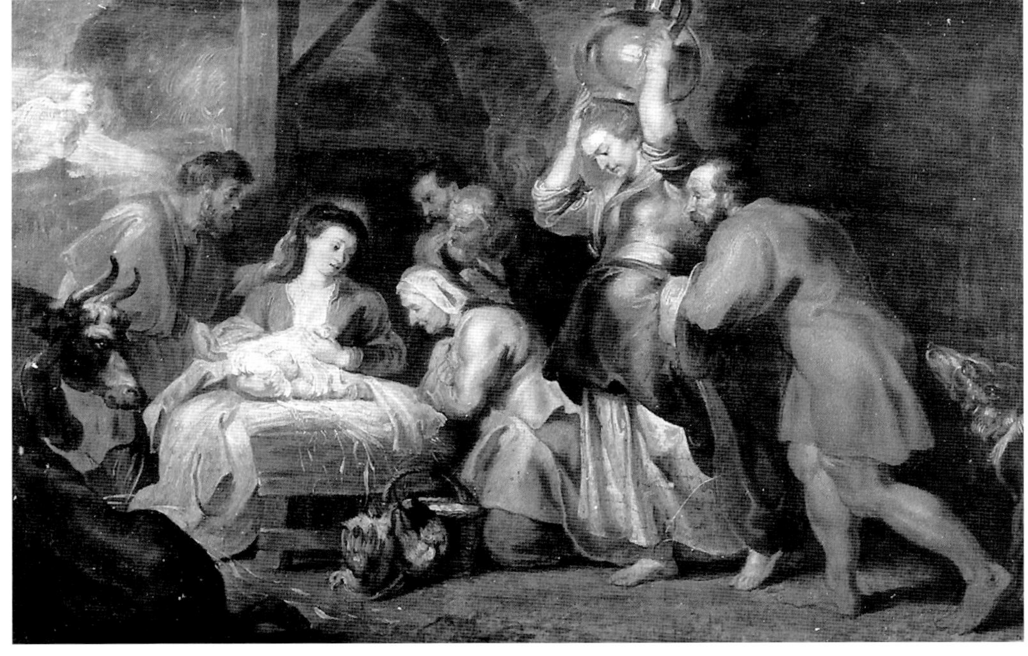

Fig. 107. Peter Paul Rubens, *The Adoration of the Shepherds,* ca. 1617. Oil on panel, 68 x 100 cm (26 3/4 x 39 3/8 in.). Musée des Beaux-Arts, Marseille (102)

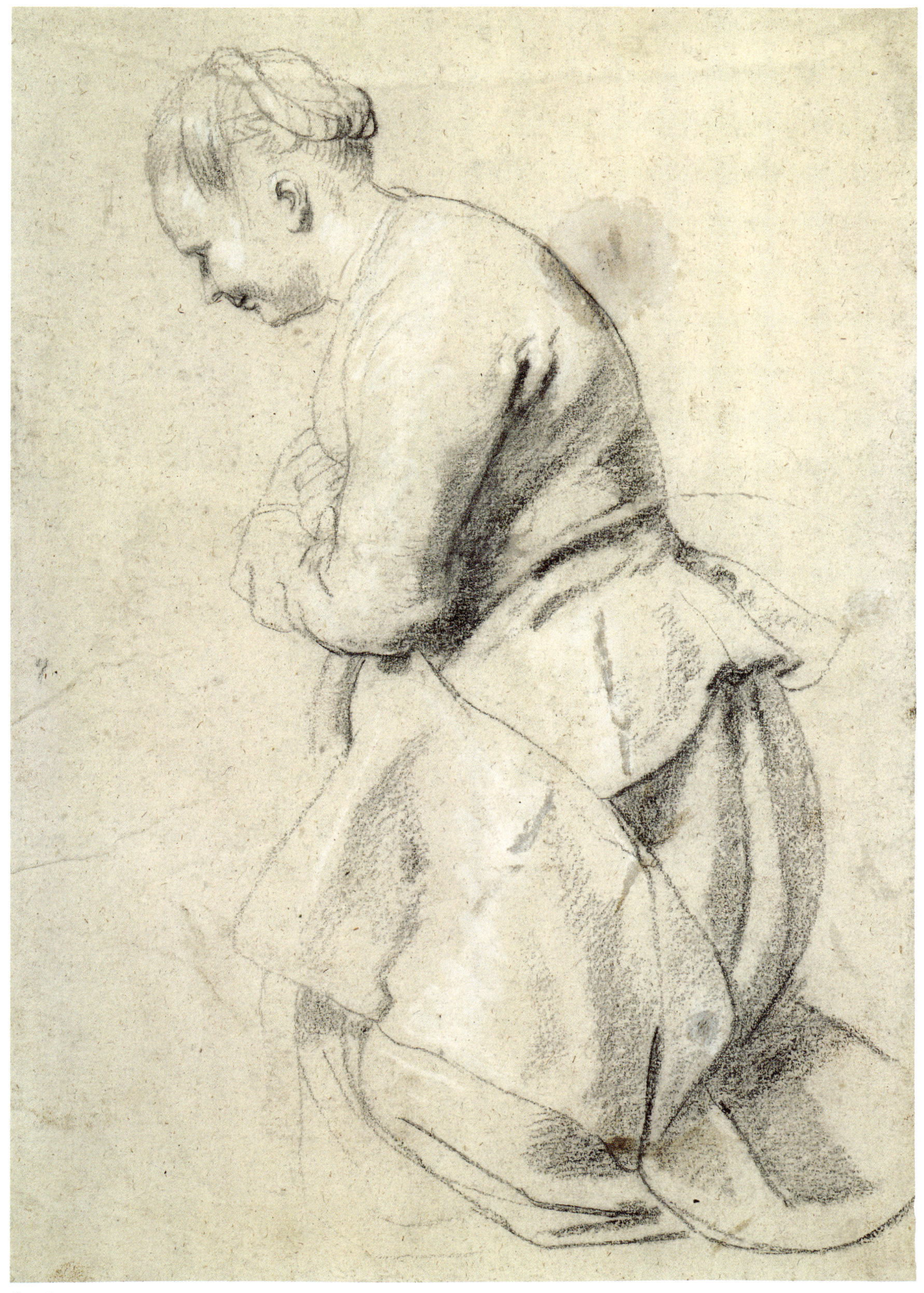

Cat. 62

63. *Young Woman Crouching, Turned to the Right,* ca. 1617–18

Black chalk, heightened with white chalk, silhouetted from the upper right to lower left along the head and back of the figure, on brownish paper, 376 x 269 mm ($14\frac{3}{4}$ x $10\frac{9}{16}$ in.)

Albertina, Vienna (8295)

PROVENANCE: Duke Albert of Sachsen-Teschen (1738–1822), Vienna (Lugt 174).

LITERATURE: R., vol. 5, no. 1430, pl. 407; Glück and Haberditzl 1928, no. 108, pl. 108; Held 1959, no. 90, pl. 99, pp. 6, 29, 73, 128, under no. 75, 132, under no. 88; Burchard and d'Hulst 1963, no. 99, pl. 99; Kuznetsov 1974, pl. 76; Held 1986, no. 134, pl. 129; M. Jaffé 1989, no. 370.

EXHIBITION: Vienna 1977b, no. 26, ill.

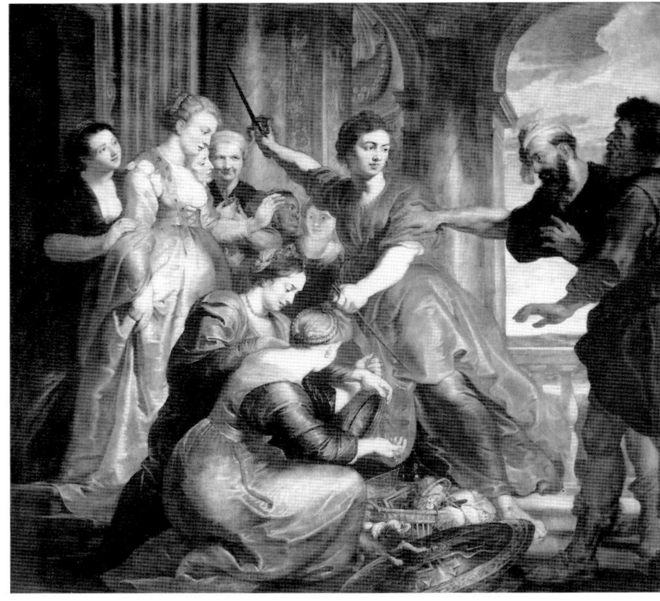

Fig. 108. Peter Paul Rubens and Anthony van Dyck, *Achilles among the Daughters of Lycomedes,* ca. 1616–18. Oil on canvas, 246 x 267 cm ($96\frac{7}{8}$ x $105\frac{1}{8}$ in.). Prado, Madrid (1661)

Rubens prepared this study for the daughter in the foreground of his painting *Achilles among the Daughters of Lycomedes,* dated ca. 1616–18 (fig. 108).[1] In the drawing a young woman in everyday dress and with beautifully braided hair crouches to admire a pearl necklace that she holds with her left hand and lets fall into her right. Rubens drew the figure with flowing outlines in black chalk that needed few corrections. The sheet was originally larger and at the left may have included another figure or a detail of the arm and hand that rest on the woman's shoulder in the painting. This section, however, was trimmed away along the woman's head and shoulder down to her lower back.

Achilles among the Daughters of Lycomedes must have been finished by April 28, 1618, when Rubens wrote to the English collector and diplomat Sir Dudley Carleton, offering it for sale.[2] As the artist explained in his letter, the painting was largely executed by "meglior mio discepolo." This "best disciple" has traditionally been identified as Anthony van Dyck (1599–1641). Van Dyck was Rubens's assistant and collaborator on a number of projects even before he registered as a master on February 11, 1618.[3] In the present case Rubens may have prepared such a careful study so that his assistant could easily understand it and transfer it to the painting. It seems, therefore, that the drawing dates close to the time when Rubens and his studio worked on the *Achilles* painting, especially since the young woman in the drawing is used in the painting with virtually no changes.[4]

Rubens returned to the drawing for a peasant girl in his *Polder Landscape with Eleven Cows* of about 1618 (fig. 150).[5] This was hardly the only time that Rubens reused a detailed figure study in a new context. He probably remembered the sketch and retrieved it from his study material, which was most likely arranged according to subject matter, as one can deduce from the Copenhagen *cantoor* drawings. Such repeated use of a single study occurred most frequently in the second half of the 1610s, when Rubens's studio was brimming with activity and students based figures in paintings on original chalk studies provided by the master and followed them carefully.

1. K.d.K., ed. Oldenbourg 1921, no. 130; M. Jaffé 1989, no. 370, ca. 1616.
2. Rooses and Ruelens 1887–1909, vol. 2, p. 137.
3. For Van Dyck's collaboration with Rubens, see Katlijne van der Stighelen, "Van Dyck's First Antwerp Period: Prologue to a Baroque Life Story," in Antwerp–London 1999b, pp. 39–42.
4. Held (1980, no. 228, pl. 237) thought this chalk study might have preceded the related oil sketch of ca. 1617 in the Fitzwilliam Museum, Cambridge; he also noted that this working sequence would have been exceptional.
5. K.d.K., ed. Oldenbourg 1921, no. 187, ca. 1620; M. Jaffé 1989, no. 521, 1618–19; Renger and Denk 2002, p. 460, no. 322, ca. 1618.

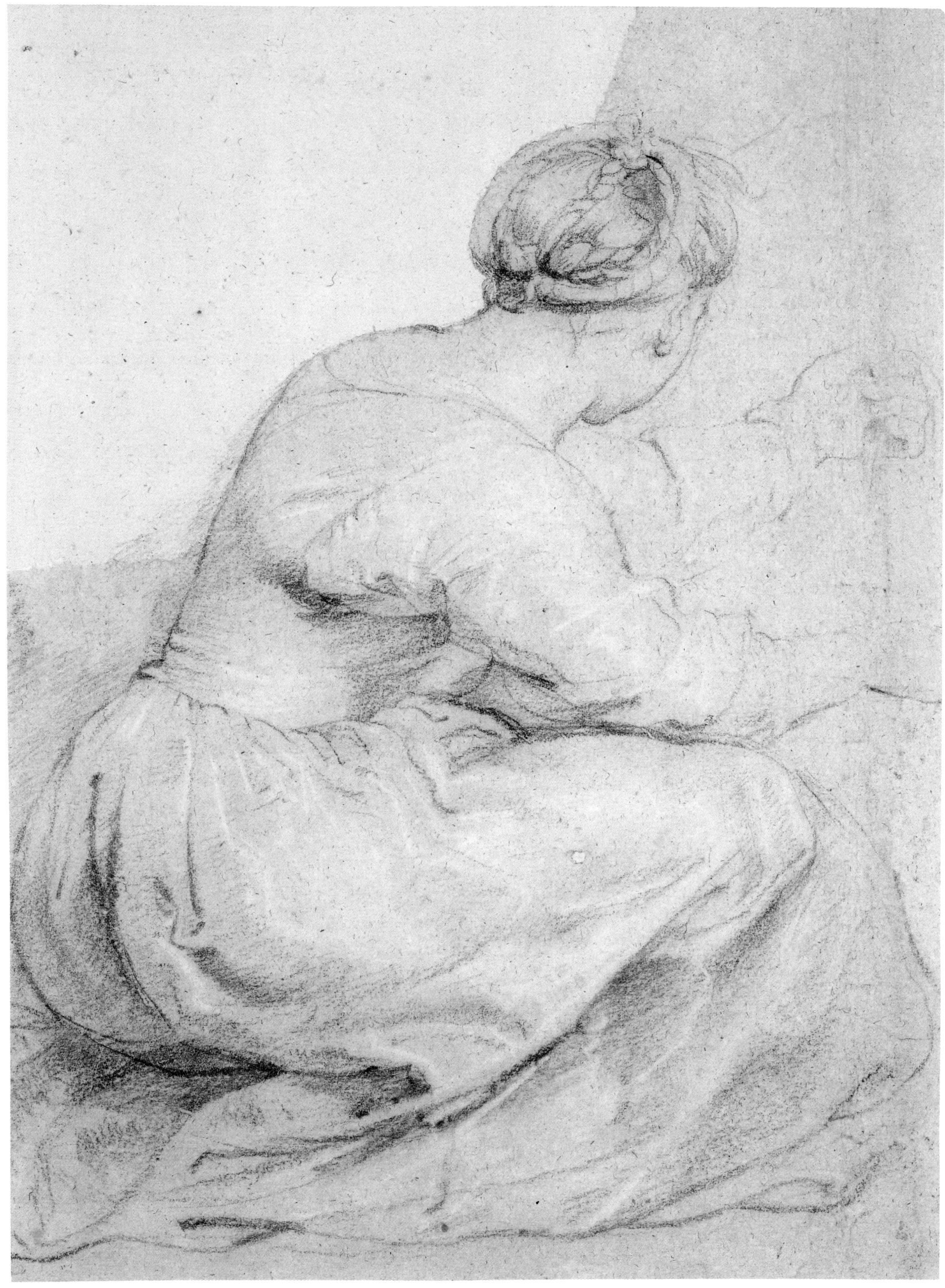

Cat. 63

64. *Blind Man with Outstretched Arms: Study for the "Miracles of Saint Francis Xavier,"* ca. 1617–18

Black chalk, heightened with white chalk, on brownish paper, 281 x 420 mm (11 1/16 x 16 1/2 in.)

Albertina, Vienna (17 641)

PROVENANCE: Hofbibliothek, Vienna; in 1796 acquired through exchange by Duke Albert of Sachsen-Teschen (1738–1822), Vienna (Lugt 174).

LITERATURE: R., vol. 5, no. 1381; Glück and Haberditzl 1928, no. 120, pl. 120; Held 1959, no. 100, pl. 109; Vlieghe 1973, no. 104d, fig. 13; Kuznetsov 1974, pl. 79; Held 1986, no. 128, pl. 139.

EXHIBITIONS: Antwerp 1977, no. 148, ill.; Vienna 1977b, no. 17, ill.; New York and other cities 1997–99, no. 33, ill.

This is one of four known black-chalk studies of individual figures that Rubens drew in preparation for his painting of the *Miracles of Saint Francis Xavier* (fig. 118), commissioned by the Jesuits in Antwerp for the high altar of their new church (today Saint Charles Borromeo).[1] It is likely that Rubens began to prepare the altarpiece before April 13, 1617, since the account book of the Jesuit church (now in the Rubenshuis, Antwerp) records that on that date Rubens was owed three thousand guilders, the exact amount that he was to receive for the *Saint Francis Xavier* altarpiece and for a *Miracles of Saint Ignatius Loyola* altarpiece commissioned for the same church.[2] (Rubens's two paintings were among the pictures displayed in turn, according to the Church calendar, on the high altar.) Both altarpieces are now in Vienna and probably date from about 1617–18.

As was his custom, Rubens first prepared a small oil sketch of the composition to submit to the Jesuit fathers for approval. (The two preliminary *modelli* are today in Vienna.)[3] Only then did he proceed to draw preliminary studies in black chalk for individual figures.

The present study prepares the man who gropes his way at the right of the *Saint Francis Xavier* altarpiece. As has been observed repeatedly, the man was inspired by the blind Elymas in Raphael's cartoon and tapestry of the *Conversion of the Proconsul (The Blinding of Elymas).* Rubens had seen Raphael's tapestry cartoons in Genoa and was instrumental in their acquisition by Charles I (today they are in the Victoria and Albert Museum, London). In Rubens's oil sketch the nearsighted man clutches a cane to help him find his way (fig. 109). In the drawing and the final altarpiece (fig. 118) he is blind and seems more pitiful as he moves forward only with outstretched arms. In this study Rubens clearly visualized the man's greater helplessness and dependence on others. The man's diminished state, however, only heightens the soon-to-come miracle of Saint Francis Xavier's restoration of the man's eyesight. Rubens probably executed the drawing close to the time the final altarpiece was begun, in order to provide a precise rendering for the assistants who collaborated with him.[4]

1. K.d.K., ed. Oldenbourg 1921, no. 205; M. Jaffé 1989, no. 481, 1618–19.
2. J. R. Martin 1968, pp. 30, 220; Vlieghe 1973, no. 104, fig. 6; Baudouin 1977, pp. 157–71; M. Jaffé 1989, no. 480, 1618–19.
3. Baudouin 1977, p. 157, pls. 36, 37; Held 1980, no. 408, pl. 397, before April 13, 1617, and no. 410, pl. 398; M. Jaffé 1989, nos. 478, 479, 1617–18.
4. Haberditzl (1912, p. 2) was the first to recognize that studies such as this one had to follow the oil sketches rather than vice versa. This observation was important to our understanding of Rubens's working procedure.

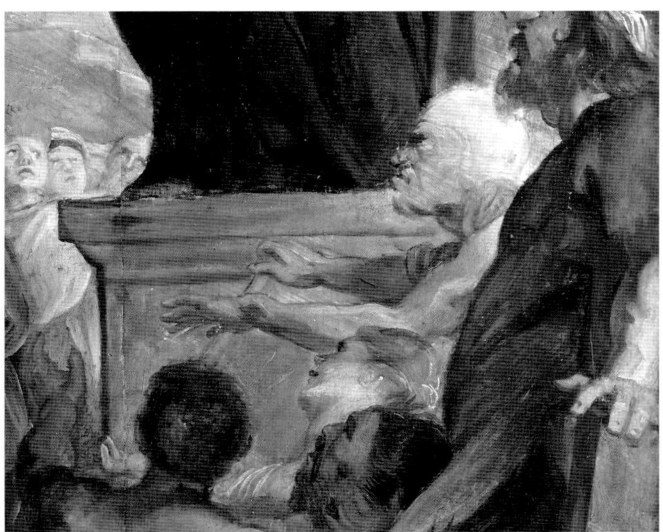

Fig. 109. Peter Paul Rubens, Detail of the *Miracles of Saint Francis Xavier*, ca. 1617–18. Oil on panel, 104.5 x 72.5 cm (41 1/8 x 28 9/16 in.). Kunsthistorisches Museum, Vienna (GG 528)

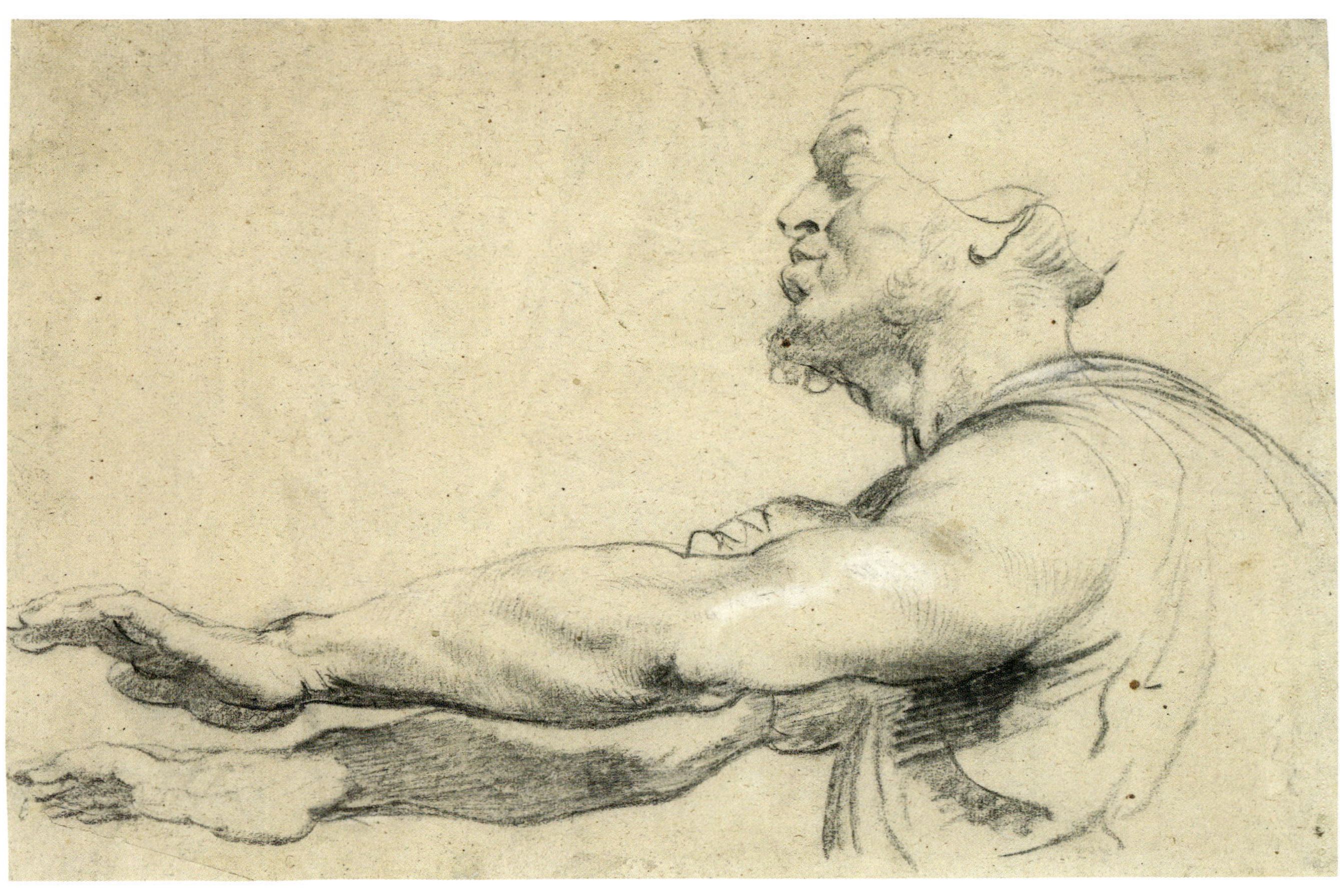

Cat. 64

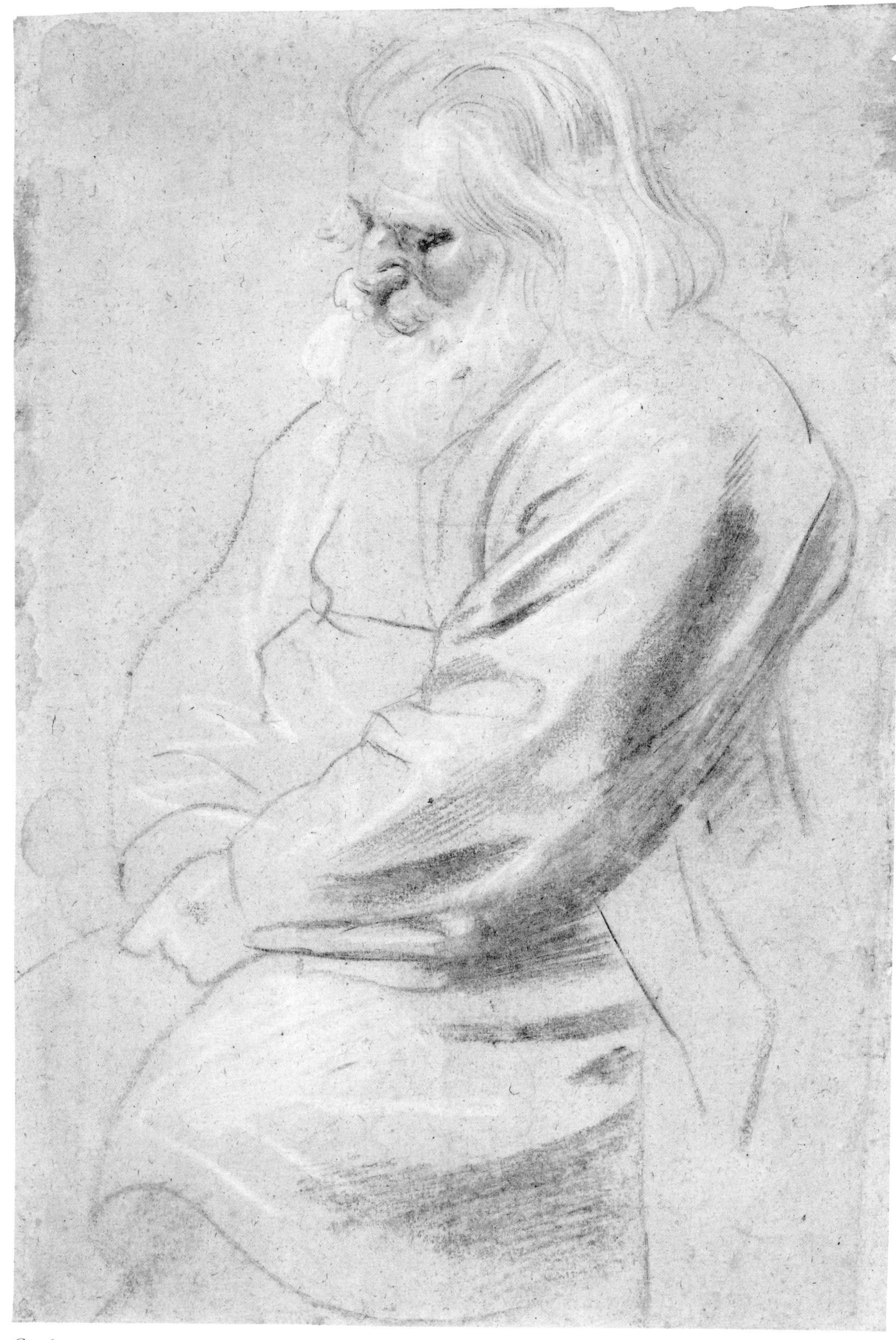

Cat. 65

65. *Seated Old Man,* ca. 1618–20

Black chalk, heightened with white chalk, on brownish paper, 419 x 271 mm (16½ x 10^{11}/16 in.)

Albertina, Vienna (8296)

PROVENANCE: Hofbibliothek, Vienna; in 1796 acquired through exchange by Duke Albert of Sachsen-Teschen (1738–1822), Vienna (Lugt 174).

LITERATURE: Glück and Haberditzl 1928, no. 109, pl. 109.

EXHIBITION: Vienna 1977b, no. 28, ill.

The bearded old man, apparently lost in thought, is sketched rather summarily, and the modeling is achieved with long parallel strokes that merge into dense areas of black, with bold lines in white chalk for highlights. At times the white and black chalk mix and turn gray. Only a general resemblance exists between this study and the heads of old men in several of Rubens's paintings, including the head of an old man leaning over a balustrade in the *Adoration of the Magi* of about 1618–20 now in Brussels.[1] A related head, in reverse, is found in one of the plates by Paulus Pontius (1603–1658) after designs by Rubens in the so-called *Drawing Book*. This sheet may have been one of many studies from life that Rubens kept in his studio to use in paintings as the need arose; his inventory listed a "parcell of Faces made after the life, vppon bord and Cloth as well by sr Peter Rubens as van dyke."[2]

1. K.d.K., ed. Oldenbourg 1921, no. 192; M. Jaffé 1989, no. 526, ca. 1619.
2. Muller 1989, p. 145.

66. *Young Man Carrying a Ladder,* ca. 1619–20

Greasy black chalk, heightened with white chalk, on brownish paper, irregularly cut at the left, 343 x 272 mm (13½ x 10¾ in.)

Albertina, Vienna (8298)

PROVENANCE: Hofbibliothek, Vienna; in 1796 acquired through exchange by Duke Albert of Sachsen-Teschen (1738–1822), Vienna (Lugt 174).

LITERATURE: Held 1959, no. 99, pl. 102, p. 73; Burchard and d'Hulst 1963, no. 120, pl. 120, p. 188, under no. 118; Kuznetsov 1974, pl. 84; Held 1986, no. 141, pl. 141; Judson 2000, no. 37b, fig. 114.

EXHIBITIONS: Antwerp 1977, no. 151, ill.; Vienna 1977b, no. 22, ill.; Vienna–Amsterdam 1989–90, no. 49, ill.

The man in this drawing carries his ladder in a rather unusual way, wrapping his arms around it and propping it against his shoulders so that his head sticks through the rungs. Julius Held was the first to spot a figure similar to this one in Rubens's small oil sketch, now in London, of the *Crucifixion (Coup de Lance)* (fig. 110).[1] The man is difficult to make out in the rather summary grisaille, painted in preparation for Rubens's large *Crucifixion of Christ with Thieves* altarpiece of 1620, generally known as the *Coup de Lance* (fig. 111).[2] (In the painting the Roman centurion Longinus, on horseback, pierces Christ's right side with a lance to verify that He is dead [John 19:32–34].) The man carrying a ladder can be seen more clearly in a copy from the Rubens studio after the London grisaille (fig. 112).[3] In the end Rubens did not include the man with the ladder in his altarpiece. In order to clarify the composition and give prominence to Longinus's deed, the artist brought the centurion's horse closer to the Cross, thus eliminating the space for the man and his ladder.

Such rethinking of figures is entirely in keeping with Rubens's creative process, especially in the case of an altarpiece as important, and with as many figures, as the *Coup de Lance.* The techniques involved at various stages are those that the artist employed in similar circumstances at this time. In the opinion of some scholars, however, the London grisaille is not by Rubens but by his pupil Anthony van Dyck; this debate goes back to the 1930s.[4] Recently, it has been suggested that the present drawing, too, is a work by Van Dyck.[5] We can understand

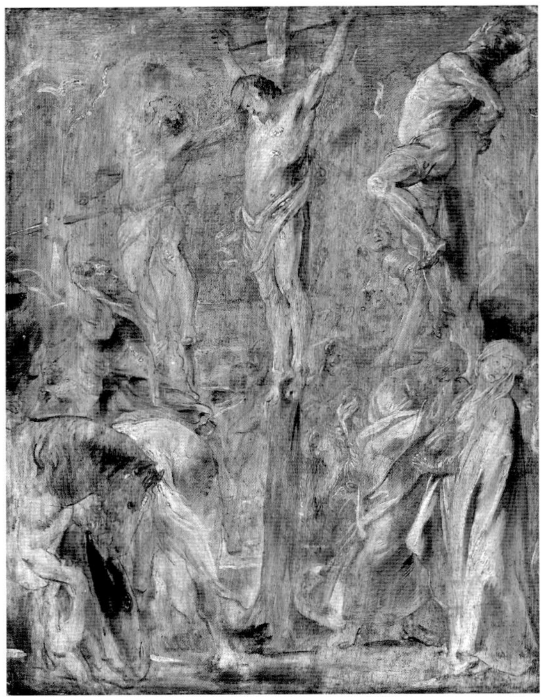

Fig. 110. Peter Paul Rubens, *The Crucifixion (Coup de Lance)*, ca. 1619–20. Oil on panel, 64.8 x 50 cm (25½ x 19¹¹⁄₁₆ in.). National Gallery, London (NG 1865)

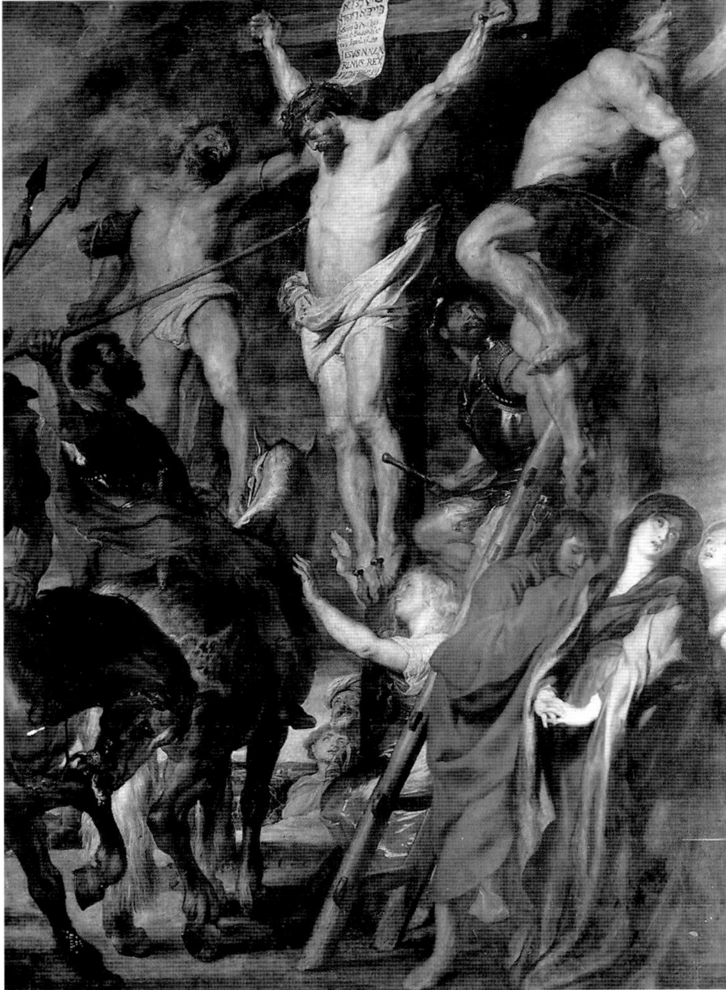

Fig. 111. Peter Paul Rubens, *Coup de Lance*, 1620. Oil on panel, 429 x 311 cm (168⅞ x 122⁷⁄₁₆ in.). Koninklijk Museum voor Schone Kunsten, Antwerp (297)

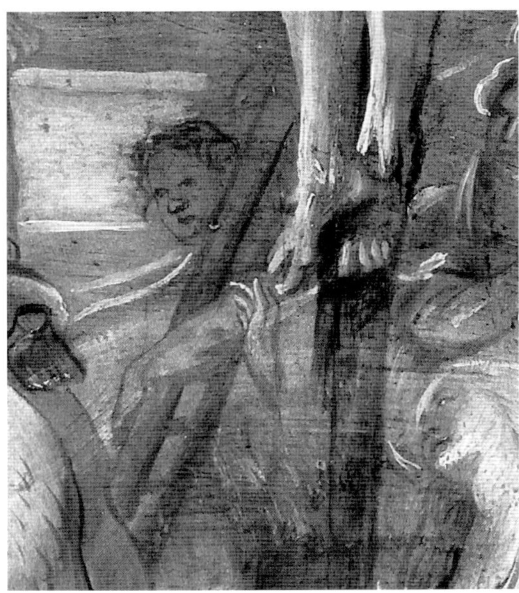

Fig. 112. Copy after Peter Paul Rubens, Detail of *Coup de Lance*, ca. 1620. Oil on panel, 65 x 50 cm (25⁹⁄₁₆ x 19¹¹⁄₁₆ in.). Suermondt-Ludwig-Museum, Aachen (6K442)

the mistaken attribution to Van Dyck of the London grisaille, but not of the Albertina drawing.

In our opinion both the grisaille and the drawing are by Rubens. The London grisaille should be compared with the unquestionably authentic grisailles, such as those now in Oxford and London,[6] that were made in preparation for Rubens's 1620 ceiling decorations for the Jesuit church in Antwerp. These grisailles, or exploratory *bozzetti*, were followed by more finished, colored *modelli;* Rubens apparently did not follow up the London grisaille with a colored oil sketch (or it has not survived), but in all likelihood his working procedure in both cases

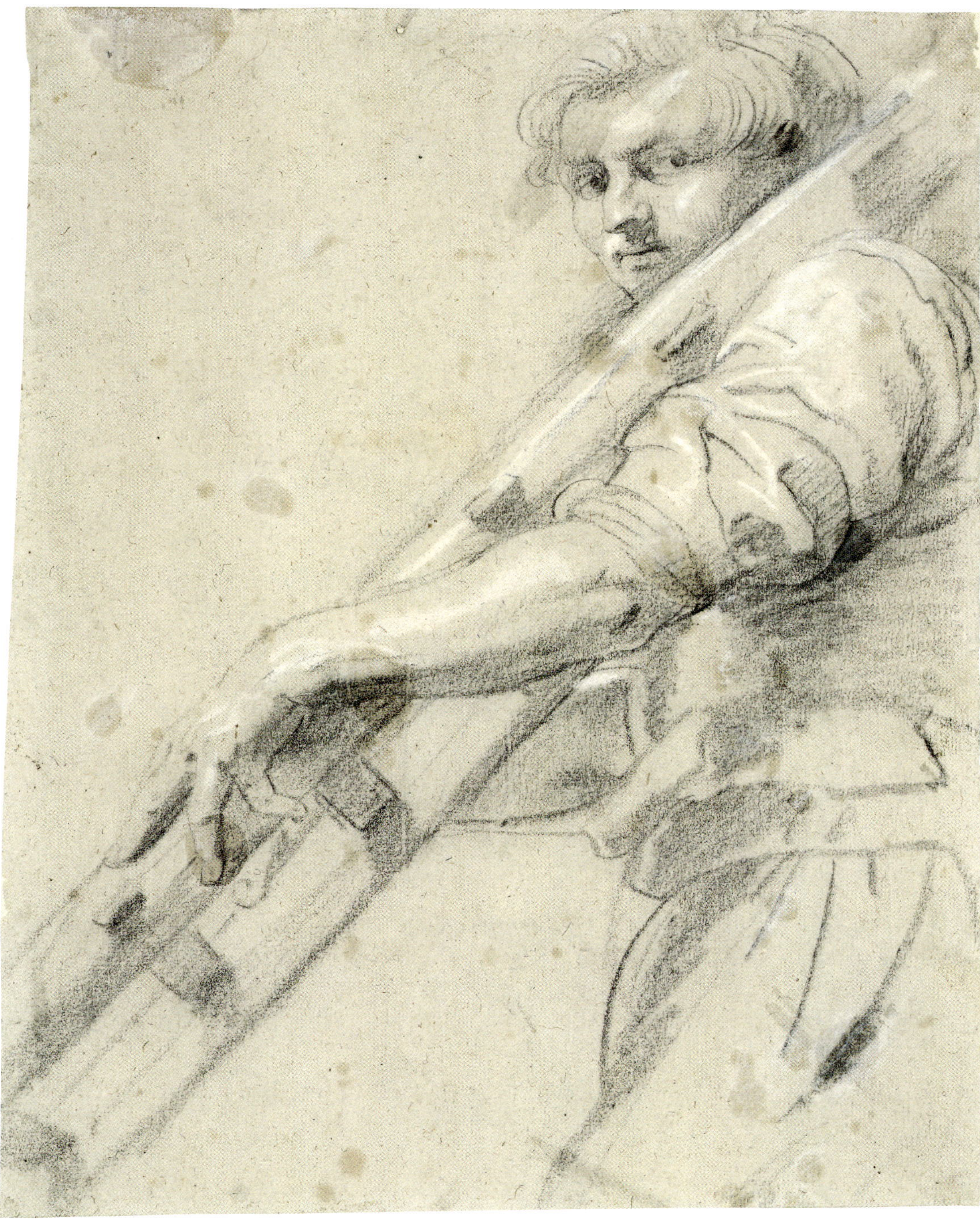

Cat. 66

was the same. Rubens's experimentation with grisailles about 1620—the time when Van Dyck was in closest personal contact with him—must have stimulated the younger artist's interest in this technique.[7]

We consider the Albertina drawing a characteristic work by Rubens, without any obvious connections to Van Dyck's drawn oeuvre. The execution is refined and the modeling is soft, exactly as in Rubens's other black-chalk figure studies from the same time, such as those for the *Raising of the Cross* (cat. nos. 37–39) and the *Descent from the Cross* (cat. no. 44). Despite this refined execution, the drawing exudes a power that we do not find easily in Van Dyck's black-chalk figure studies, which are usually drawn with more speed, but show less volume and corporeality. Finally, one might add that a depiction of a man carrying a ladder with his head through the rungs is the sort of everyday scene one expects sooner of Rubens than of Van Dyck.

1. Held 1980, no. 352, pl. 347, ca. 1619–20; M. Jaffé 1989, no. 543, 1619–20. Rubens had prepared the oil sketch with a quick sketch in pen and brown ink, now in Rotterdam (Rotterdam 2001, no. 19, ill.).
2. K.d.K., ed. Oldenbourg 1921, no. 216; M. Jaffé 1989, no. 545, 1619–20; Judson 2000, no. 37, fig. 110.
3. Reproduced in full in Held 1959, fig. 51, and in detail in Vienna 1977b, p. 54.
4. K.d.K., Van Dyck 1931, p. 519. Horst Vey (1956, p. 174) questioned the attribution of the grisaille to Van Dyck. Held (1980, p. 484, under no. 352) convincingly refuted Ludwig Burchard's idea that the grisaille was Van Dyck's *modello* after Rubens's *Coup de Lance* painting for Bolswert's engraving (Burchard and d'Hulst 1963, p. 190, under no. 120). Recently, Nico van Hout again supported attributing the grisaille to Van Dyck (at the Rubens meeting in Madrid, January 19, 2004), an opinion with which Konrad Renger and Gregory Martin strongly disagree. Nora de Poorter also believes that the grisaille is by Rubens. Taking the London grisaille away from Rubens and giving it to Van Dyck means, in our opinion, assigning Van Dyck the invention of the *Coup de Lance* as well. However, there are several sound historical reasons why at least the invention must be credited to Rubens; Held (1959, no. 99) sums them up. There is general agreement that the *Coup de Lance* painting was largely executed by Van Dyck.
5. Nico van Hout at the Rubens meeting in Madrid, January 19, 2004.
6. Held 1980, nos. 7, pl. 8, 11, pl. 12, 17, pl. 17, 22, pl. 24, 24, pl. 26.
7. Held suggested this influence in ibid., p. 484, under no. 352.

ANTHONY VAN DYCK

67. *A Young Woman with Her Left Arm Extended,* ca. 1620

Black chalk, heightened with white, 458 x 285 mm (18 x 11¼ in.)
Annotated in pen and brown ink at upper right: *AVD* (in monogram); at center right: *A V Dyck;* at bottom right: *42* (crossed out); 1788

Nationalmuseum, Stockholm (1981/1863)

PROVENANCE: Pierre Crozat (1665–1740), Paris; Count Carl Gustav Tessin (1695–1770), Stockholm (Lugt 2985); Royal Museum (1788).

LITERATURE: Vey 1962, no. 49, fig. 67; Washington 1990–91, p. 117, under no. 15, p. 118, fig. 3; Antwerp–Amsterdam 1999–2000, pp. 48–49, fig. 12.

EXHIBITIONS: Stockholm 1953, no. 99 [Rubens]; Antwerp–Rotterdam 1960, no. 27, fig. 14.

At first glance the woman in this black-chalk study seems to be performing some everyday job like washing or rolling out dough. If one looks carefully, however, one detects a snake in the woman's hands, in the lower left corner. Van Dyck drew this study in preparation for a figure in his youthful painting, dated 1620–21, of *Moses and the Brazen Serpent* (fig. 113).[1] The story of the brazen serpent comes from the Old Testament (Numbers 21:5–9). When the Jews crossing the desert complained about the hardships of their journey, God punished them by sending snakes to bite them. After many were killed, the people repented, and God instructed Moses to erect a brazen serpent: anyone who was bitten by a snake would be saved when he beheld the brazen serpent.

Van Dyck collaborated with Rubens most closely in the years between 1617 and 1620. He quickly evolved into a valued assistant and colleague, absorbing Rubens's style so well that at times it is very difficult to distinguish their work. This is especially true for drawings (see also cat. nos. 66, 100, 101). This sheet is included in the exhibition because it is a case where Van Dyck as a draftsman comes exceedingly close to Rubens.

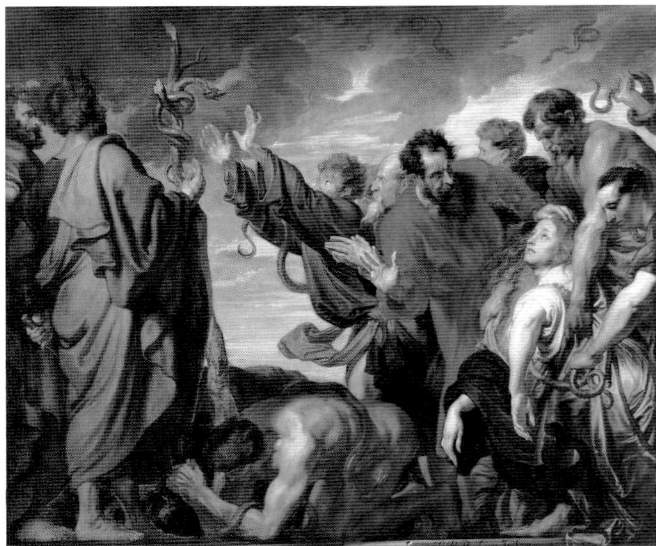

Fig. 113. Anthony van Dyck, *Moses and the Brazen Serpent*, 1620–21. Oil on canvas, 205 x 235 cm (80 11/16 x 92½ in.). Prado, Madrid (1637)

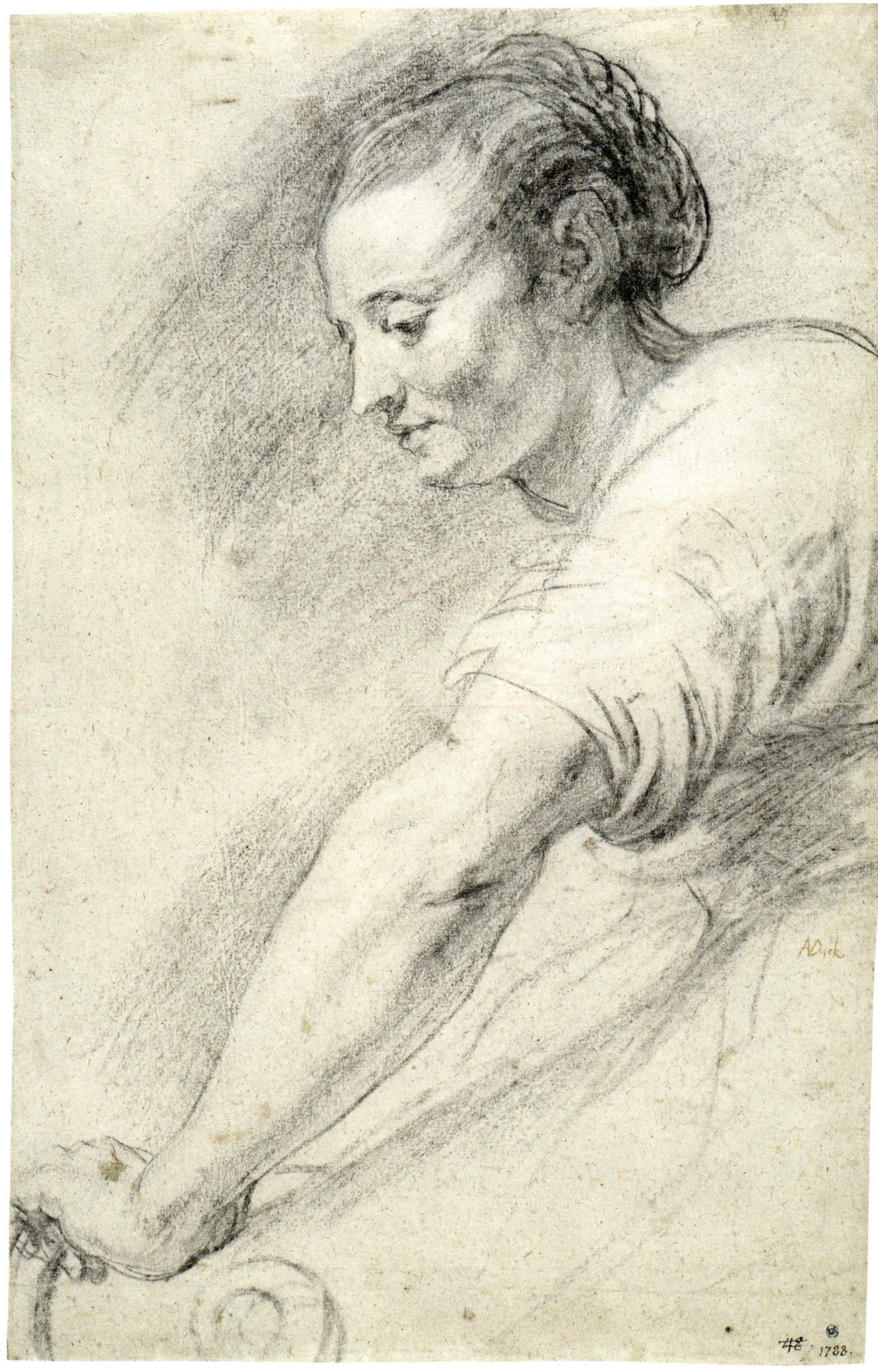

Cat. 67

Although Van Dyck excelled in absorbing Rubens's style and technique, there were areas where he clearly followed his own working method. For instance, Van Dyck's practice was to produce a series of related, individual compositional studies in pen and ink, enhanced with wash, before he started on a painting; he did not follow Rubens's habit of preparing an oil sketch of the composition. Nor, generally, did Van Dyck draw studies from life in the final preparation for the most important figures in a painting. In the present study, however, he did.[2] Like Rubens when he prepared a close-up drawing for a specific figure, Van Dyck used chalk rather than pen and ink. Van Dyck's chalk lines are less rounded than Rubens's, and his hatching is drier. The contours of the arm and face are less defined than they would be in a drawing by Rubens, and the shoulder is barely indicated. Nevertheless—and despite two apparently old annotations on the sheet referring to Van Dyck—the study was considered far into the twentieth century to be a work by Rubens. Only in 1960 was the drawing finally accepted as a work by Van Dyck.[3]

1. Washington 1990–91, no. 15, ill.
2. The woman on this sheet is absent from all Van Dyck's preliminary drawings for the painting, so that one wonders if the artist used Rubens's method here because only one figure needed definition.
3. Antwerp–Rotterdam 1960, no. 27, fig. 14.

68. *Young Woman Looking Down (Study for the Head of Saint Apollonia),* early 1628

Black and red chalk, heightened with white; eyes, eyelashes, and left eyebrow retouched with pen and brown ink, 414 x 287 mm ($16\frac{5}{16}$ x $11\frac{1}{4}$ in.)

Gabinetto Disegni e Stampe degli Uffizi, Florence (1043 E)

PROVENANCE: Cardinal Leopoldo de' Medici (1617–1675), Florence (Lugt 2712); museum mark at bottom right (Lugt 930).

LITERATURE: Glück and Haberditzl 1928, no. 173, pl. 173; Held 1959, no. 113, pl. 122, p. 78; Burchard and d'Hulst 1963, no. 148, pl. 148, p. 226, under no. 145; Kuznetsov 1974, pl. 122; Held 1986, no. 170, pl. 168; Kloek 1976, no. 526; Petrioli Tofani 1986–, vol. 1, pt. 2, p. 440, no. 1043E, ill.

EXHIBITION: Florence 1964, no. 63, fig. 63.

This magnificent drawing, one of Rubens's most sensitive studies, prepares the figure of Saint Apollonia in his monumental 1628 altarpiece for the church of the Augustinian Fathers in Antwerp, the *Virgin and Child Adored by Saints* (fig. 77).[1] In the painting she stands at the left, midway up the steps, next to Saint Agnes. Saint Apollonia was a virgin martyr who lived in Alexandria at the time of emperor Decius (r. 249–251). During an uprising against the Christians she threw herself in the fire rather than be tortured to death.

In this drawing Rubens focused on the young woman's head. (It is interesting to note, nonetheless, that she wears fashionable, contemporary dress.) His red-chalk strokes to render her face are applied in a painterly way; they merge with the black chalk and become more diffuse in the hair. In size and in its depiction of a woman of quiet dignity who appears lost in thought, the drawing prefigures Rubens's large-scale studies of the early 1630s, in black and red chalk, for the *Garden of Love* (cat. nos. 90–92) and the Ildefonso altarpiece (cat. nos. 70–72), as well as his portrait of Helena Fourment now in London (fig. 10).

Before starting on the final painting of the *Virgin and Child Adored by Saints,* Rubens prepared the work in a number of oil sketches, including two of the entire composition, in Frankfurt (fig. 78)[2] and in Berlin (fig. 79).[3] In the inclination of Saint Apollonia's head and the position of her right hand, this drawing closely corresponds to Rubens's last sketch (that in Berlin) and to the final altarpiece, which was installed in June 1628. Therefore, a date for the present drawing in the first part of 1628 is logical.

The drawing is much more finished than Rubens's usual preliminary figure studies, and no equally beautiful study for any of the other saints included in the Augustinians' altarpiece is known. It is possible, therefore, that the drawing is a portrait that Rubens drew for its own sake rather than a study from a model that he made specifically for the *Virgin and Child Adored by Saints.*[4] As the sheet bears a certain resemblance to the portrait drawing of Helena Fourment now in London (fig. 10), in the past it has been identified as a portrait of Helena. (We have seen examples where the artist used portrait drawings of family members in his religious paintings [see cat. nos. 59, 81].) This idea should be discarded, however, since in 1628 Helena was only fourteen. The present drawing may nevertheless still be connected to the Fourment family, as Helena had older sisters who might have sat for Rubens.

1. K.d.K., ed. Oldenbourg 1921, no. 305; M. Jaffé 1989, no. 902, 1628.
2. Held 1980, no. 384, pl. 375, ca. 1627–28; M. Jaffé 1989, no. 900, 1627–28.
3. Held 1980, no. 385, pl. 376, ca. 1627–28; M. Jaffé 1989, no. 901, 1627–28.
4. Rubens reintroduced the woman, in about 1635, in the *Rape of the Sabines* (National Gallery, London), where she appears in the background at the left (M. Jaffé 1989, no. 1181, 1635–37). An old copy of *Saint Apollonia,* without her hand, is in the Galleria di Palazzo Bianco, Genoa (Rooses 1903, p. 46, ill.); another copy, drawn predominantly in red chalk, with some black chalk, was sold at Christie's, London, June 30, 1950, lot 96, as Helena Fourment.

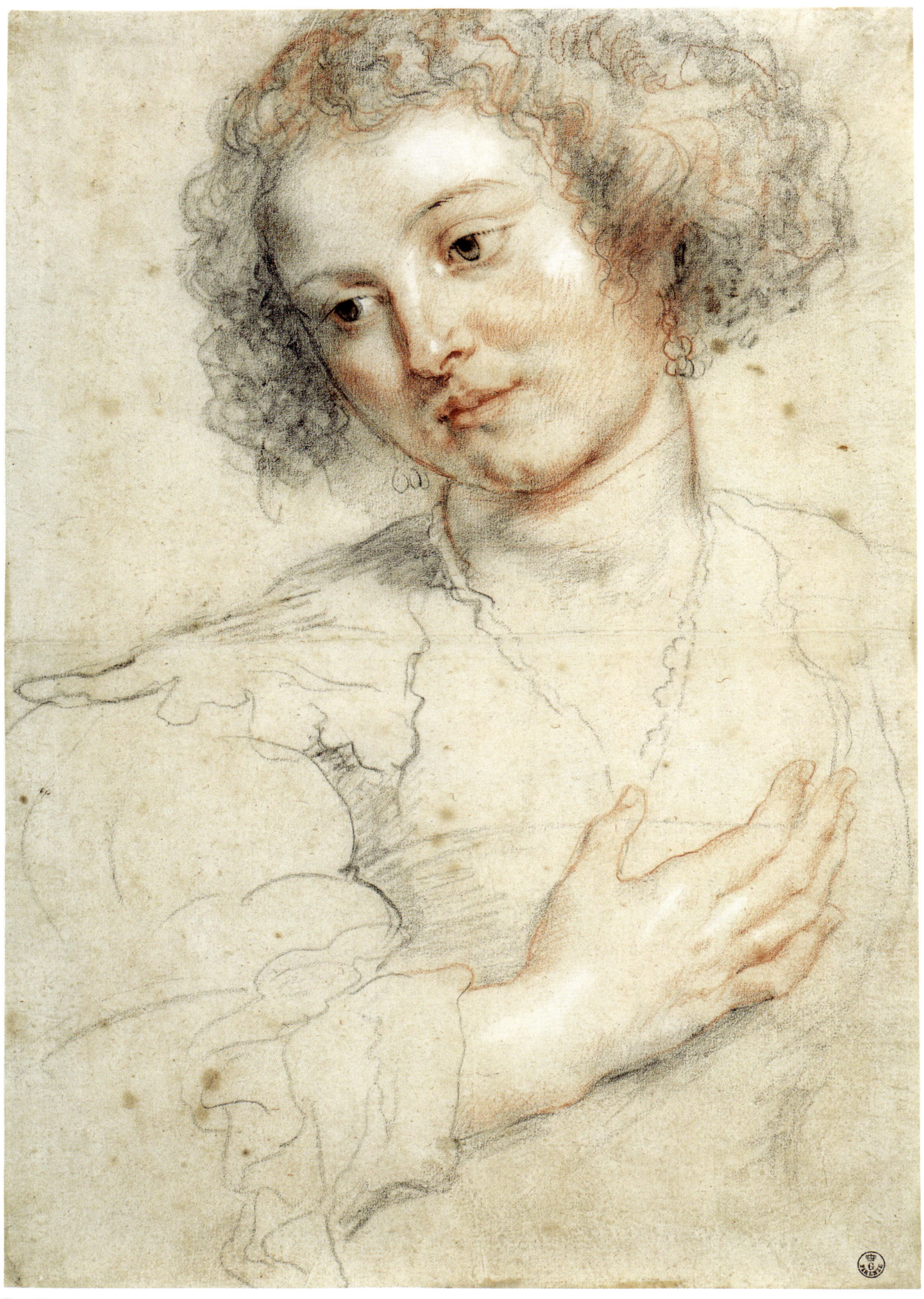

Cat. 68

69. *Woman Bending Forward, with a Laurel Wreath,* October–November 1628

Black chalk, heightened with white chalk, 319 x 236 mm (12 5/16 x 9 3/16 in.)

Albertina, Vienna (8301)

PROVENANCE: Hofbibliothek, Vienna; in 1796 acquired through exchange by Duke Albert of Sachsen-Teschen (1738–1822), Vienna (Lugt 174).

LITERATURE: R., vol. 5, no. 1567; Glück and Haberditzl 1928, no. 63, pl. 63; Burchard and d'Hulst 1963, no. 157, pl. 157; Kuznetsov 1974, pl. 116; Huemer 1977, no. 30a, fig. 87.

EXHIBITION: Vienna 1977b, no. 45, ill.

Between September 1628 and the end of April 1629, during his sojourn in Spain, Rubens found time during peace negotiations between England and Spain to paint no fewer than five portraits of King Philip IV (1605–1665), if we are to believe the artist Francisco Pacheco (1564–1644), who gave this account in his treatise on painting.[1] Of those paintings, a large equestrian portrait was the most significant commission the artist received from the monarch. In a letter of December 2, 1628, from Madrid, to his friend the French scholar Nicolas-Claude Fabri de Peiresc (1580–1637), Rubens wrote: "Here I keep to painting, as I do everywhere, and already I have done the equestrian portrait of His Majesty, to his great pleasure and satisfaction. He really takes an extreme delight in painting. . . . I know him already by personal contact, for since I have rooms in the palace, he comes to see me almost every day. I have also done the heads of all the royal family, accurately and with great convenience, in their presence, for the service of my Most Serene Infanta, my patroness."[2] An informal portrait drawing of Philip IV in half-length, preserved in Bayonne, gives the impression that the king was at ease with Rubens.[3]

Rubens's equestrian portrait of Philip IV hung in the prestigious Salón Nuevo of the Alcázar, the royal palace in Madrid. The painting was most likely destroyed in the fire of 1734 at the Alcázar, since it does not figure in the royal inventories after that date. The portrait is known today from a copy (fig. 114)[4] that is attributed to Juan Bautista Martínez del Mazo (ca. 1612–1667); Velázquez (1599–1660) is supposed to have painted the head of Philip IV in the copy, although the king he depicted was forty by that time, rather than in his twenties, as he had been when Rubens had painted him.[5] The painting shows the king performing the levade, with a native of the Americas carrying his helmet; two putti hold a globe behind his head—an allusion to Philip IV as the defender of the True Faith. Above the king hover the personifications of Divine Justice, who hurls a thunderbolt against the infidels, and of Faith. It was for this rather voluptuous personification of Faith that Rubens drew the present detailed black-chalk study, in order to define her gesture: with her right hand she presents a laurel wreath to Philip IV. In the painting Faith holds a crucifix in her left hand; with it she points to Spain on a globe.[6]

Were it not for the drawing's close association with this lost equestrian portrait of Philip IV, a painting that is securely dated to 1628, one would probably place the study earlier, in the later 1610s, when chalk studies abound among Rubens's drawings. No other preliminary study for the equestrian portrait of Philip IV is known. The sheet was probably cut at the bottom and perhaps also at the right.

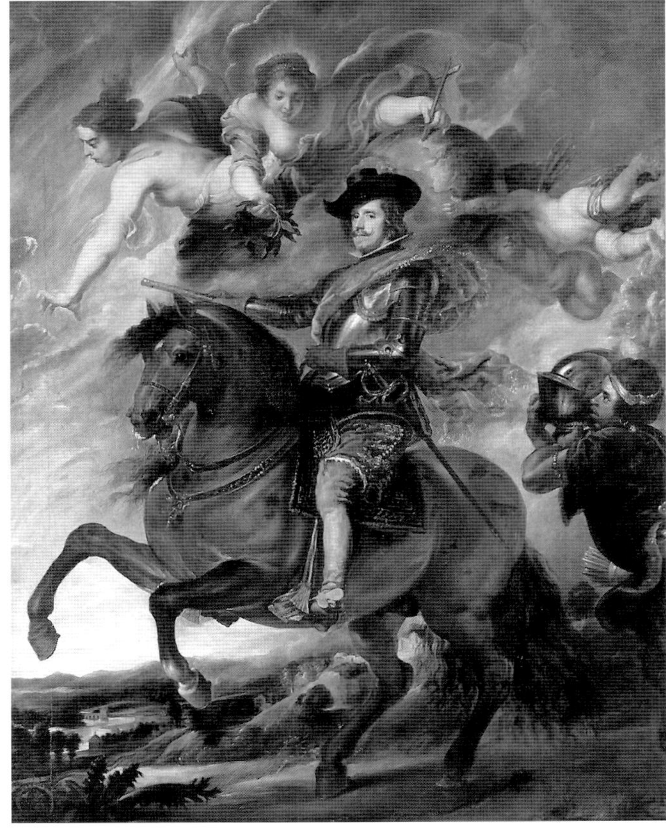

Fig. 114. Copy after Peter Paul Rubens, attributed to Juan Bautista Martínez del Mazo and Diego Rodríguez da Silva Velázquez, *Philip IV, King of Spain, on Horseback,* ca. 1644. Oil on canvas, approx. 339 x 267 cm (133 7/16 x 105 1/8 in.). Galleria degli Uffizi, Florence (792)

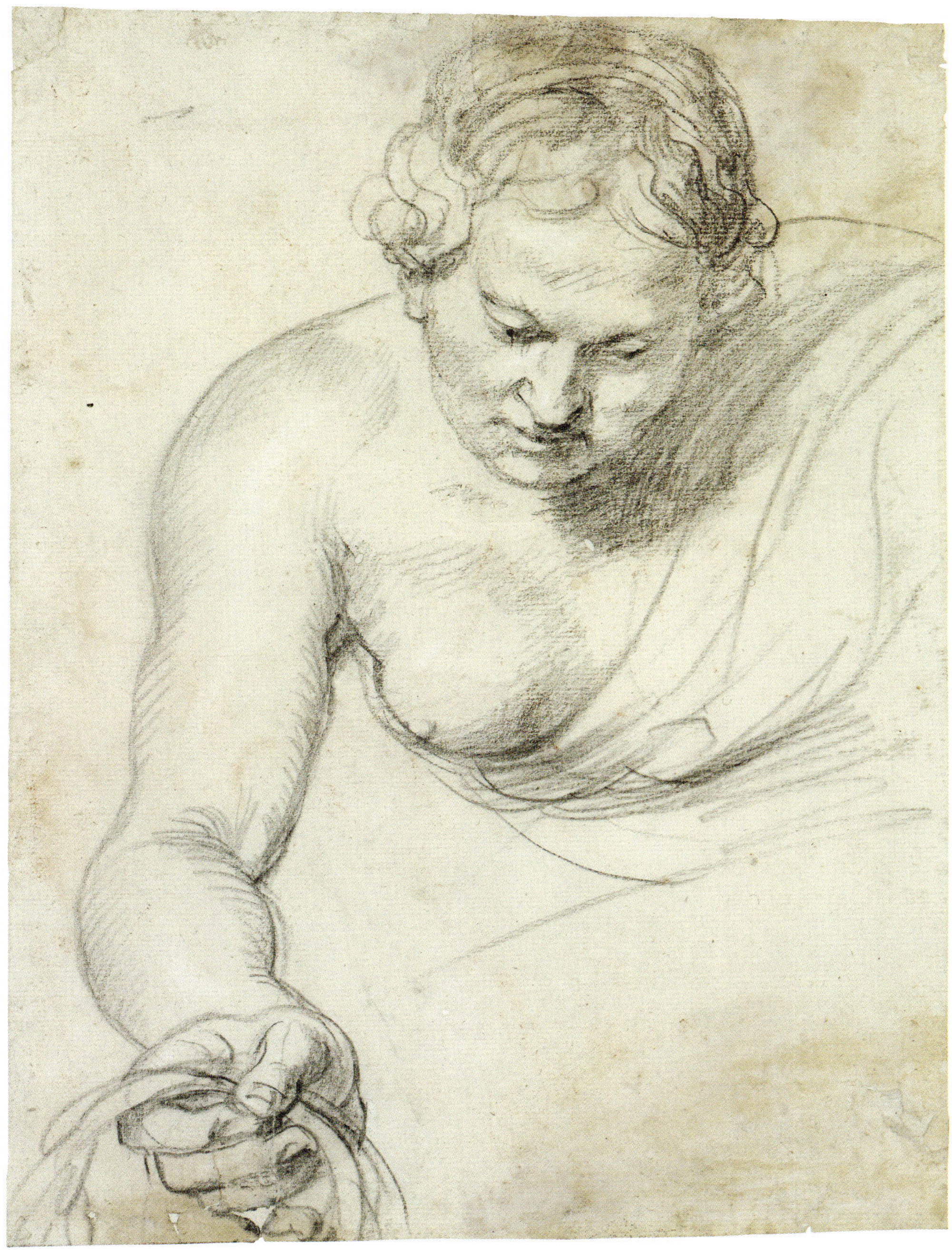

Cat. 69

1. Pacheco 1638 (1956 ed.), vol. 1, p. 153. Pacheco was the father-in-law of Velázquez.
2. Magurn 1955, p. 292, letter 180.
3. Held 1986, no. 173, pl. 173, (October–November?) 1628. See also Alejandro Vergara, "Rubens: Pintor de la monarquía española," in Madrid 2001–2, pp. 17–20 (in English, pp. 51–53).
4. Huemer 1977, no. 30, copy 1, fig. 91. See also Vergara 1999, pp. 72, 74–76, 109–10.
5. Velázquez's name was first mentioned in the 1636 inventory of the royal collection. See López Rey 1959, pp. 35–44. López Rey dates the copy to ca. 1644, close to Velázquez's portrait of Philip IV today in the Frick Collection, New York. Mazo was the son-in-law of Velázquez and his successor as court painter from 1661 to 1667.
6. According to Vosters (2001, p. 189), her not crowning the king means that victory is not yet at hand.

70. *Head of a Young Woman Looking Downward,* ca. 1630–31

Black and red chalk, touches of pen and brown ink in the left and right eyes, heightened and corrected (mouth) with white, 192 x 165 mm (7⁹⁄₁₆ x 6½ in.)
Annotated in pen and brown ink at bottom right: *P P Rubbens*

Albertina, Vienna (8272)

Provenance: Duke Albert of Sachsen-Teschen (1738–1822), Vienna (Lugt 174).

Literature: R., vol. 5, no. 1433, pl. 408; Glück and Haberditzl 1928, no. 194, pl. 194; Held 1959, pp. 30, 78, 139, under no. 110; Held 1986, p. 144, under nos. 190, 191.

Exhibitions: Vienna 1977b, no. 49, ill.; New York and other cities 1997–99, no. 37, ill.

71. *Head of a Young Woman Turned to the Left,* ca. 1630–31

Black and red chalk, stumped, nostrils and mouth strengthened with tip of the brush and red ink, heightened and corrected with white chalk, 250 x 165 mm (9¹³⁄₁₆ x 6½ in.)
Annotated in pen and brown ink at bottom right: *P P Rubbens*

Albertina, Vienna (8271)

Provenance: Hofbibliothek, Vienna; in 1796 acquired through exchange by Duke Albert of Sachsen-Teschen (1738–1822), Vienna (Lugt 174).

Literature: R., vol. 5, no. 1571; Glück and Haberditzl 1928, no. 195, pl. 195; Burchard and d'Hulst 1963, no. 175, pl. 175, pp. 290–91, under no. 187; Vlieghe 1973, no. 117d, fig. 54, p. 83, under no. 117; Kuznetsov 1974, pl. 123; Held 1980, p. 570, under no. 412; Held 1986, p. 144 under nos. 190, 191.

Exhibition: Vienna 1977b, no. 50, ill.

72. *Head of a Young Woman Turned to the Right,* ca. 1630–31

Black and red chalk, 247 x 158 mm (9⅝ x 6³⁄₁₆ in.)

Albertina, Vienna (8270)

Provenance: Hofbibliothek, Vienna; in 1796 acquired through exchange by Duke Albert of Sachsen-Teschen (1738–1822), Vienna (Lugt 174).

Literature: R., vol. 5, no. 1572; Glück and Haberditzl 1928, no. 196, pl. 196; Held 1959, pp. 78, 139, under no. 110; Burchard and d'Hulst 1963, no. 187, pl. 187, pp. 269, under no. 174, 270, under no. 175, 315, under no. 196; Vlieghe 1973, no. 117 c, fig. 55; Held 1986, under nos. 190, 191.

Exhibition: Vienna 1977b, no. 51, ill.

Shortly after his return to Antwerp in April 1630, after traveling for nearly two years in England and Spain on diplomatic missions on behalf of the Infanta Isabella, Rubens received a commission for an altar painting for the chapel of the Brotherhood of Saint Ildefonso in the church of Saint James on the Coudenberg (Sint Jacob op de Coudenberg) in Brussels, the parish church of the Brussels court. Archduke Albert had founded the confraternity in Lisbon in 1588, when he was governor of Portugal; in 1603, when he became governor of the Spanish Netherlands, he established a similar brotherhood in Brussels.

The Ildefonso altarpiece is today in the Kunsthistorisches Museum Vienna (fig. 115).[1] On the central panel of the triptych Rubens depicted the apparition of the Virgin to Saint Ildefonso,

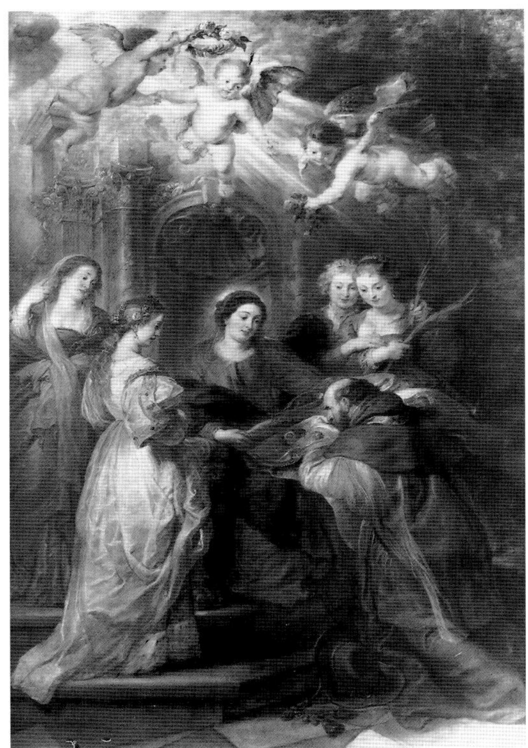

Fig. 115. Peter Paul Rubens, *Saint Ildefonso Receiving the Chasuble from the Virgin,* central panel of the Ildefonso altarpiece, 1630–31. Oil on panel, 352 x 236 cm (138⁹⁄₁₆ x 92¹⁵⁄₁₆ in.). Kunsthistorisches Museum, Vienna (GG 678)

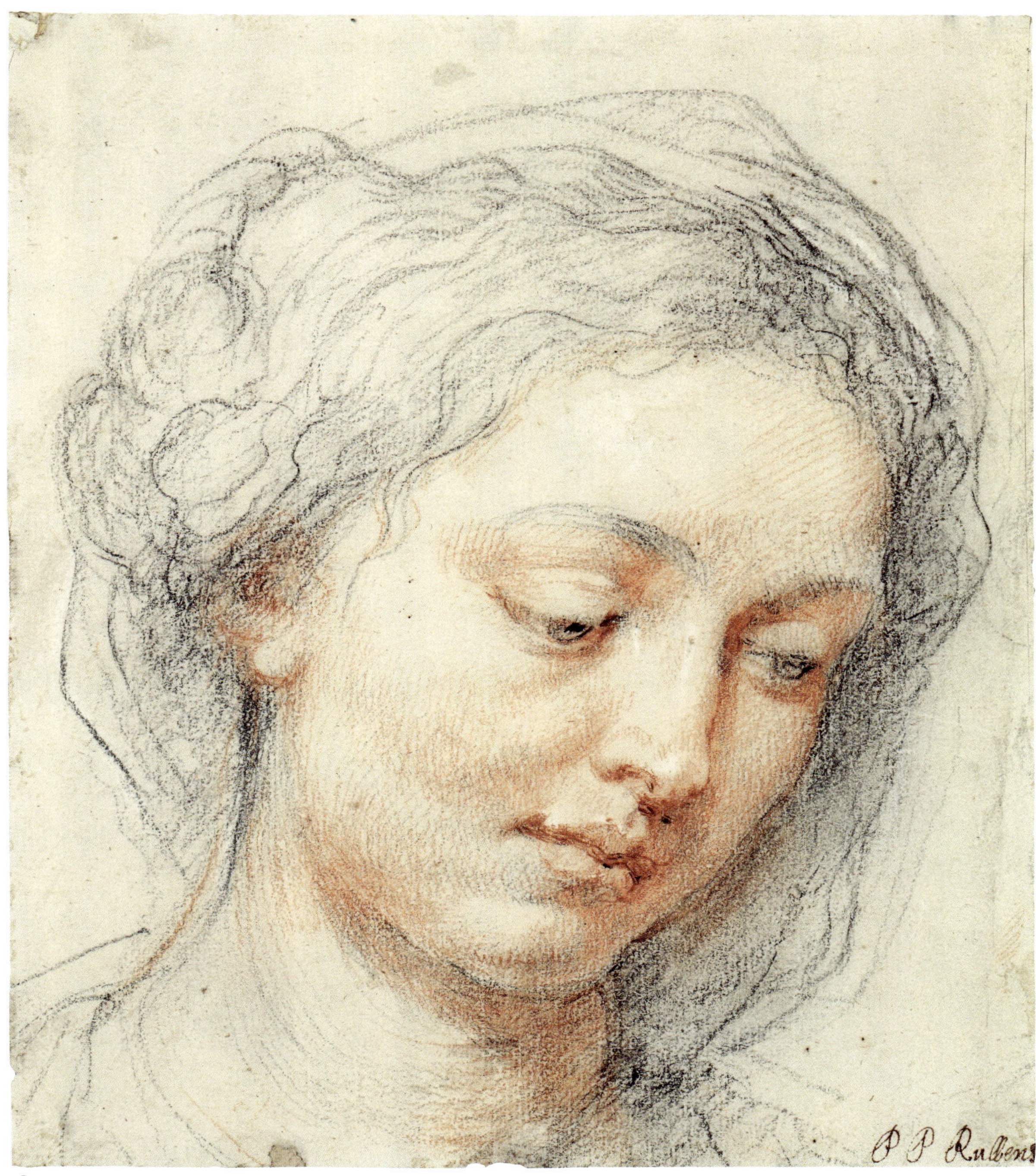

Cat. 70

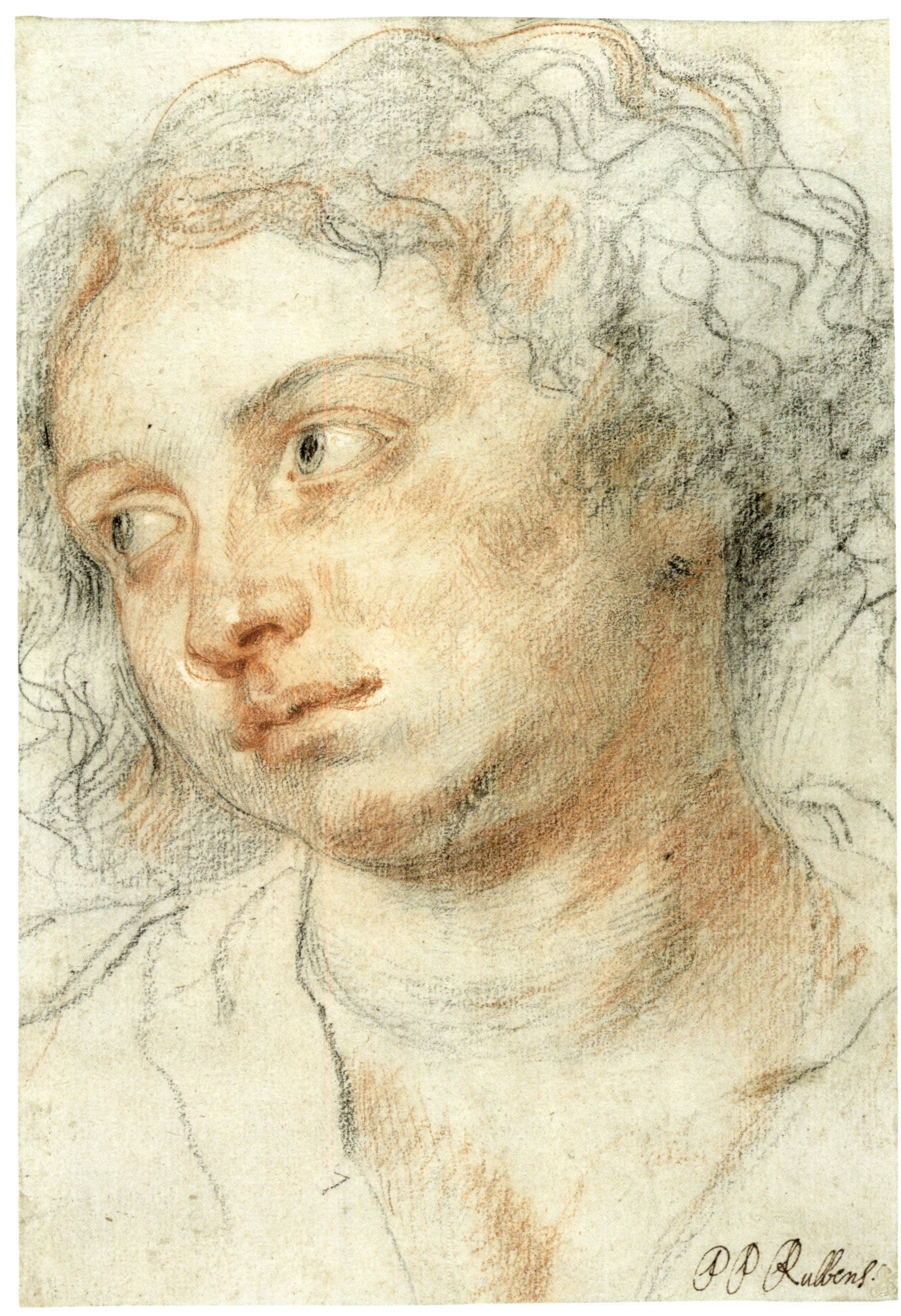

Cat. 71

a seventh-century archbishop of Toledo and the patron saint of the brotherhood. In the saint's vision, according to a seventeenth-century biography of Ildefonso, the Virgin had descended from heaven and was sitting in Ildefonso's chair in the cathedral, surrounded by female saints. When the saint approached her, uttering the Ave Maria, she presented him with a beautiful chasuble in gratitude for his *Libellus de virginitate S. Mariae contra tres infidels,* a defense of the Immaculate Conception.[2] In Rubens's preliminary oil sketch (fig. 116) he showed the Archduke Albert and Archduchess Isabella with their patron saints to the left and the right, partaking in the miracle;[3] in the final altar he painted them on the inner wings.[4] The altarpiece was unveiled in 1632, probably on January 23, the day honoring Ildefonso.[5]

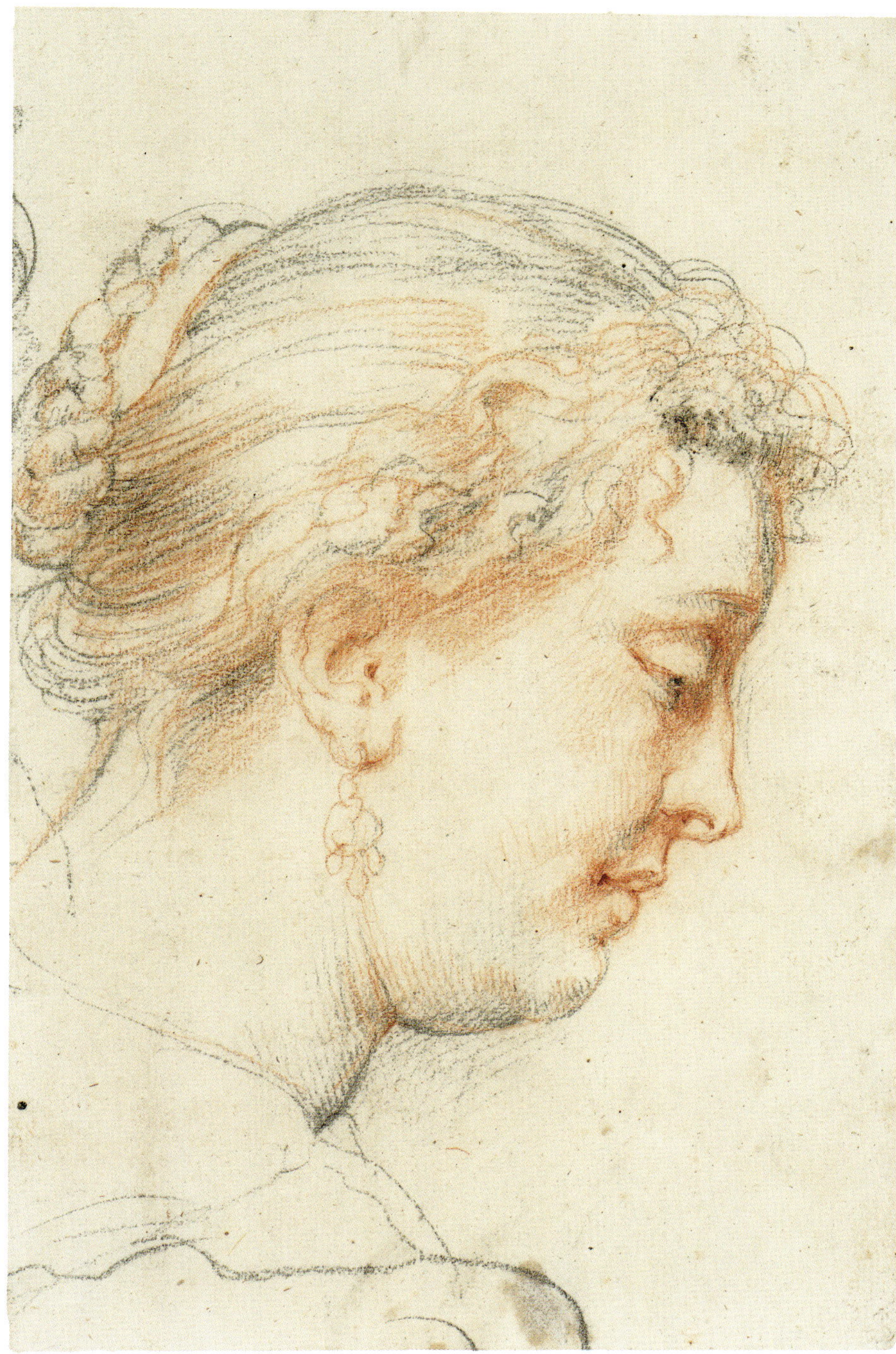

Cat. 72

The three drawings shown here are studies that Rubens drew for the head of the Virgin (cat. no. 70) and for the heads of two female saints (cat. nos. 71, 72) standing beside her in the central panel of the Ildefonso altarpiece. They are close to the final triptych and must have followed the oil sketch. For all three Rubens chose black chalk, enhanced with red chalk for the faces.

Rubens's study for the Virgin (cat. no. 70) shows her head bent forward so that she can observe Saint Ildefonso, who kneels before her and kisses the chasuble. In the painting the faintly indicated light veil covering her head becomes a heavenly light emanating behind her. In the tenderness of the Virgin's expression and the inclination of her head, the drawing relates closely to Rubens's magnificent large rendering of a seated woman with folded hands (Museum Boijmans Van Beuningen, Rotterdam).[6]

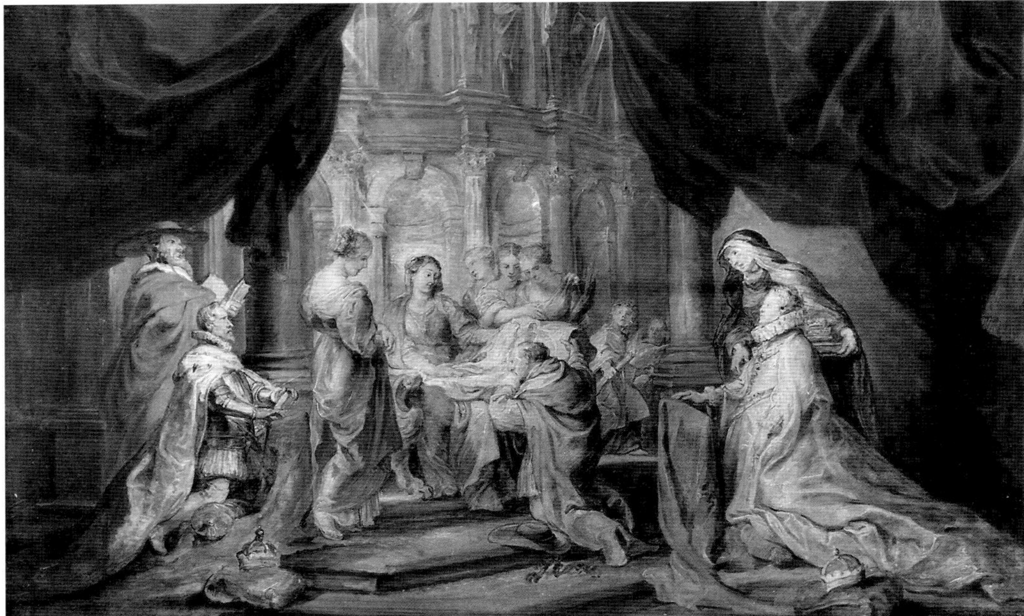

Fig. 116. Peter Paul Rubens, *The Vision of Saint Ildefonso*, ca. 1630–31. Oil on canvas transferred from wood, 52 x 83 cm (20½ x 32$^{11}/_{16}$ in.). The State Hermitage Museum, Saint Petersburg (678)

Rubens drew the female head turned to the left (cat. no. 71) for a saint standing in the right background and looking toward the Virgin. In its tilt, the head is closer to the final altarpiece than to the oil sketch. However, in the end Rubens painted the figure out in the altarpiece, choosing instead to continue the column that frames a niche. Climbing vines now obscure the pentimento of the head.[7]

The suggestion that catalogue number 71 was cut from a larger sheet that included the *Head of a Young Woman Turned to the Right* (cat. no. 72) seems correct.[8] Some strands of the young woman's hair in catalogue number 71 and part of her collar continue on catalogue number 72. The size of the original drawing, therefore, was likely about 275 x 326 mm (10$^{13}/_{16}$ x 12⅞ in.).

Two of the three head studies (cat. nos. 70, 71) bear the inscription "P P Rubbens," added by a later hand and found on a number of Rubens drawings that are today in the collection of the Albertina.

1. K.d.K., ed. Oldenbourg 1921, no. 325; M. Jaffé 1989, no. 998A, 1630–31. According to Balis, the entire triptych is by Rubens (Arnout Balis, "'Fatto da un mio discepolo': Rubens's Studio Practices Reviewed," in Tokyo 1993, p. 122, n. 54). Although Ferdinand d'Andelot, a member of the brotherhood, may have initiated the project, Archduchess Isabella paid for the triptych in honor of her late husband.
2. Held 1980, p. 569, under no. 412, and Portocarrero 1616, where the story varies slightly.
3. Held 1980, no. 412, pl. 401; M. Jaffé 1989, no. 996, 1630–31.
4. Rubens's preliminary drawing in pen and ink for Archduke Albert with his patron saint, Albert of Louvain, is in the Philadelphia Museum of Art (Held 1986, no. 190, pl. 182); the corresponding drawing for the Infanta Isabella is in the Amsterdams Historisch Museum (Schapelhouman 1979, no. 68, ill.; Held 1986, no. 191, pl. 183).
5. The Brotherhood of Saint Ildefonso was dissolved in 1657. Rubens's altar painting remained in the church until 1777, when Empress Maria Theresa acquired it.
6. For the Rotterdam drawing, see Held 1986, no. 192, pl. 180.
7. Reproduced in Vlieghe 1973, fig. 53, and in Vienna 1977b, p. 118.
8. This proposal was made first by Burchard and d'Hulst (1963, pp. 290–91, under no. 187).

PORTRAITS

73. *Portrait of Nicolas Trigault in Chinese Costume,* January 17, 1617

Black chalk, touches of red chalk in the face, blue-green chalk in the collar facings and bands of the sleeves and along the bottom of the robe, pen and brown ink, traces of heightening with white; profile sketch in pen and brown ink, 446 x 248 mm (17⁹⁄₁₆ x 9¾ in.)
Inscribed by the artist in pen and brown ink at top right: *nota quod color pullus non est / peculiaris Sinensium litteratis sed / Patribus S Iesù exceptis tamen fascijs / ceruleis quae (omnibus* [crossed out]) *ceteris [que] communes sunt / Sinenses porro vestis colore non uno / sed quovis colore promiscue utantur. / Si unum reserves flavum scilicet / qui proprius est Regis;* at bottom left: *Tricau . . . Soc. Jesu / delineatum / die 17 Januaris*
Annotated in pen and brown ink at bottom right: *A van Dyck fecit;* on the mount: *The Siamese Ambassador, an Armenian, sketched from life by Van Dyck*

The Metropolitan Museum of Art, New York; Purchase, Carl Selden Trust, several members of The Chairman's Council, Gail and Parker Gilbert, and Lila Acheson Wallace Gifts, 1999 (1999.222)

Provenance: Hendrik van Eyl Sluyter (1739–1814), Amsterdam (his sale, Amsterdam, Van der Schley . . . De Vries, September 26, 1814, album L, no. 7 ["Pater Trigautius"]); 3 florins, to Christiaan Josi (1768–1828); Abraham de Haas (1767–1823), Amsterdam (his sale, Amsterdam, De Vries . . . Roos, November 8, 1824, album R, no. 13 [Van Dyck]; 5 florins, to Hudson (not Thomas Hudson [1701–1779]); Marianne Scott (d. 1842), daughter and heiress of William, 1st Lord Stowell, and second wife of Addington, 1st Viscount Sidmouth (Lady Sidmouth); Eliza Hobhouse, granddaughter of Lady Sidmouth (according to an inscription, "Lady Sidmouth–/ Presented to Eliza Hobhouse 1842," on the mount, verso [1842]); Henry Hobhouse, Eliza's brother; Sir Arthur Hobhouse (d. 1967); Alan Rofe (1971); Agnew's, London; Robert Smith, Washington, D.C.; Christie's, London, January 28, 1999, lot 92; Kunsthandel Bellinger, Munich.

Literature: Wortley 1934–35, pp. 40–47, no. IV, pl. 44; Bernard 1953, pp. 308–13; Held 1959, p. 137, under no. 105; Burchard and d'Hulst 1963, no. 147, pl. 147; Kuznetsov 1974, pl. 100; Logan and Haverkamp-Begemann 1978, p. 97, fig. 16 [Van Dyck]; Held 1986, p. 120, under no. 131; Vlieghe 1987, no. 154b, fig. 227; Stampfle 1991, pp. 145–49, under no. 310; Held 1993, p. 288; Plomp 2001–2, pp. 235–36; Logan and Brockey 2003, pp. 157–60, fig. 1, colorpl. 4.

Exhibitions: Antwerp 1977, no. 156, ill.; Wellesley–Cleveland 1993–94, no. 48, ill.

74. *Portrait of Nicolas Trigault in Chinese Costume,* ca. 1617

Black chalk, heightened with white, touches of yellowish ocher and red chalk in the face and turquoise and blue-green chalk in the collar, on gray paper, 410 x 254 mm (16⅛ x 10 in.)
Annotated in pen and brown ink at lower right: *1775; 3*

Nationalmuseum, Stockholm (NMH 1968/1863)

Provenance: Pierre Crozat (1665–1740), Paris; Count Carl Gustav Tessin (1695–1770), Stockholm (Lugt 2985); Royal Library (Lugt 1638); transferred to the Nationalmuseum in 1866.

Literature: Wortley 1934–35, pp. 40–47, no. III, pl. 43; Bernard 1953, pp. 308–9, pl. 1; Held 1959, p. 137, under no. 105; Burchard and d'Hulst 1963, pp. 231–32, under no. 147; Logan and Haverkamp-Begemann 1978, p. 97; Held 1986, p. 120, under no. 131; Vlieghe 1987, pp. 191–95, and no. 154a, fig. 231; Goldner 1988, p. 212, under no. 93; Stampfle 1991, pp. 145–49, under no. 310; Held 1993, p. 288; Dunne 2001, p. 3839.

Exhibition: Washington–Fort Worth–San Francisco 1985–86, no. 78, ill.

75. *Korean Man,* 1617

Black chalk, touches of red chalk in the face, 384 x 235 mm (15⅛ x 9¼ in.)

The J. Paul Getty Museum, Los Angeles (83.GB.384)

Provenance: Jonathan Richardson Sr. (1665–1745), London (Lugt 2184; sale, London, Cock, January 29, 1747, lot 41); Jonathan Richardson Jr. (1694–1771), London (Lugt 2170); R. Willett, London; Baron Adalbert von Lanna (1836–1909), Prague (Lugt 2773, verso; sale, Stuttgart, Gutekunst, May 7, 1910, lot 476); Obach; Christopher Head (purchased from Obach in 1910); inherited by his widow, later Lady Du Cane, and by descent (sale, London, Christie's, November 29, 1983, lot 135).

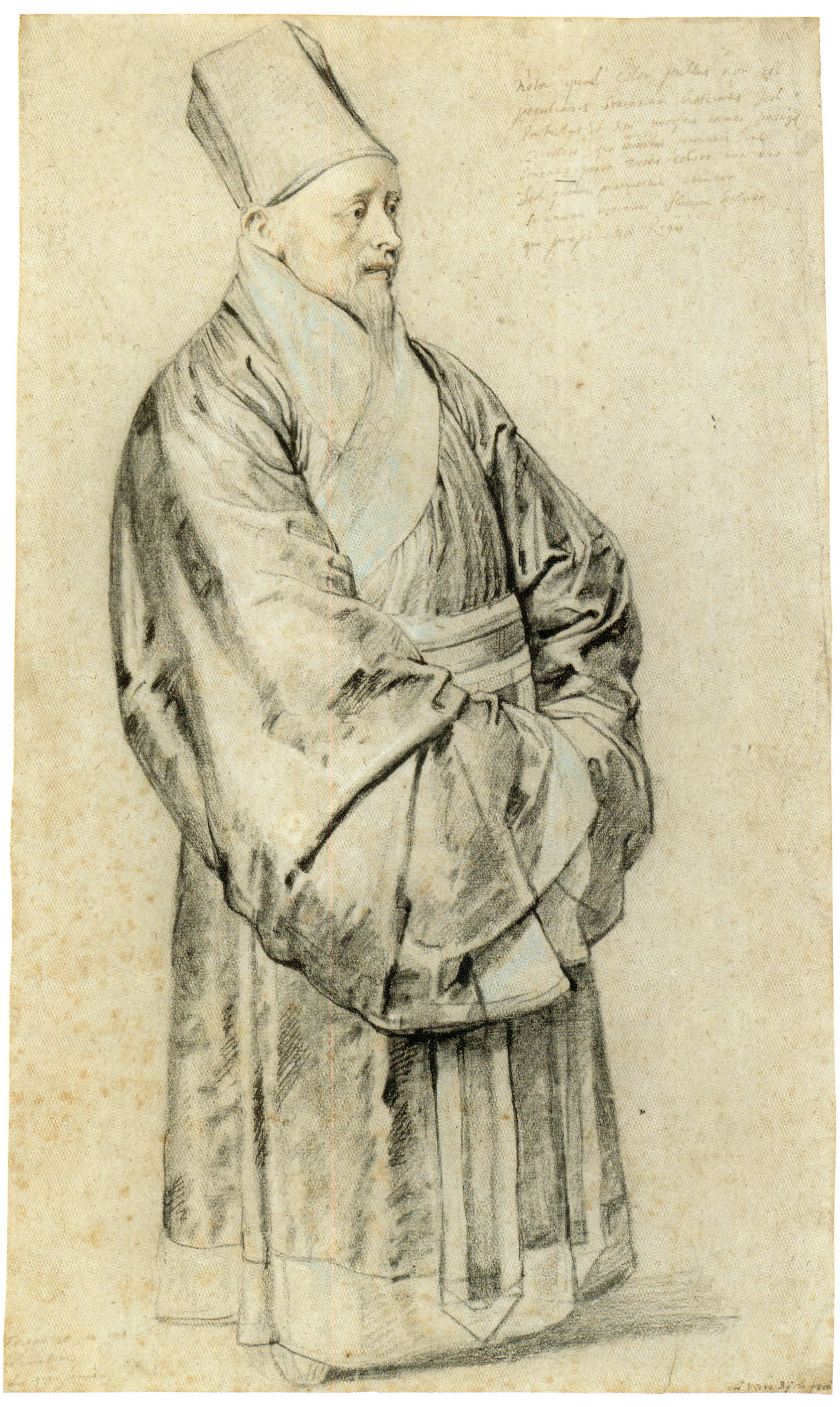

Cat. 73

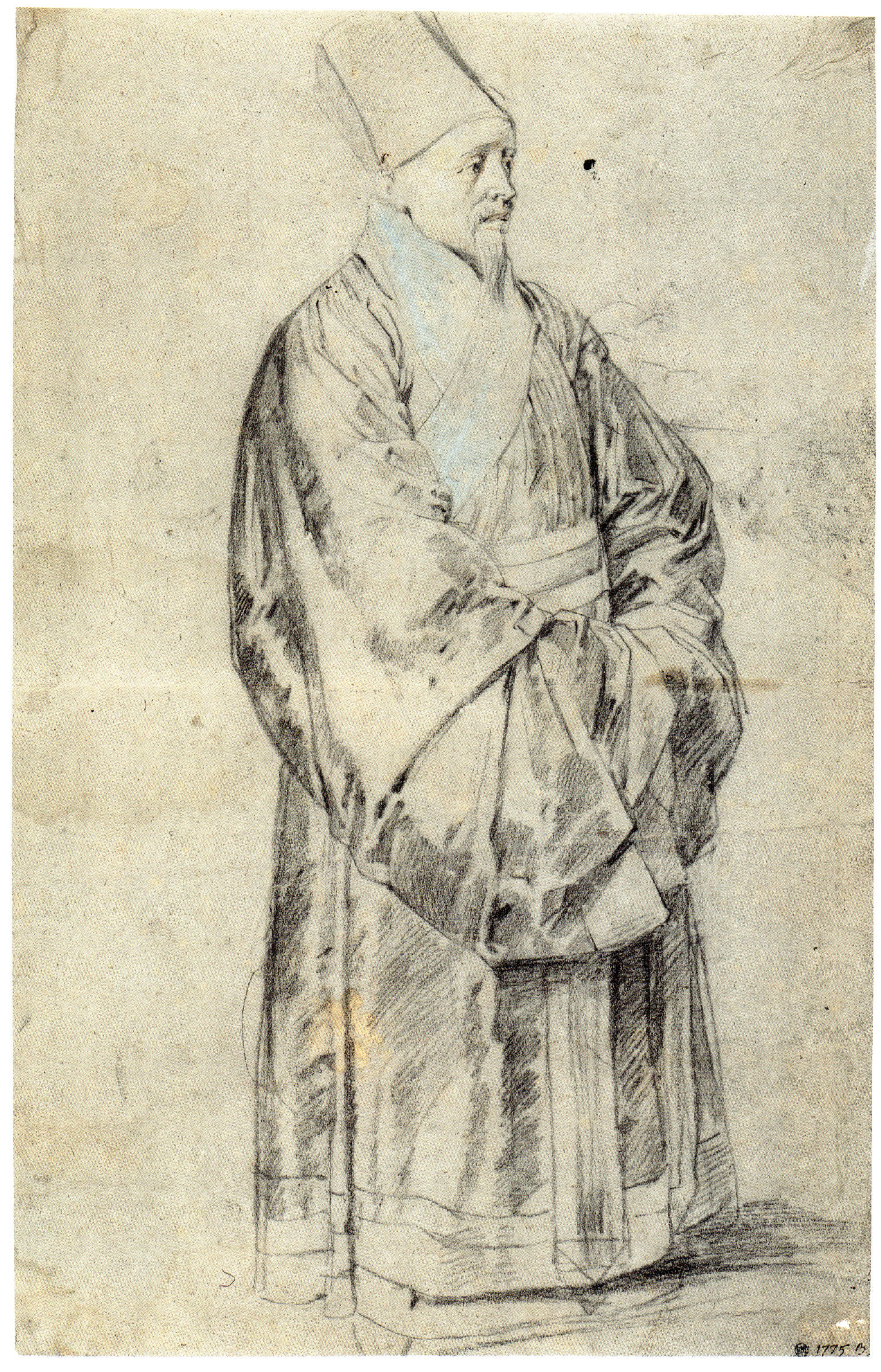

Cat. 74

Literature: Baillie 1792; R., vol. 5, no. 1531; Wortley 1934–35, pp. 40–47 no. I, pl. 41; Bernard 1953, p. 313; Held 1959, p. 137, under no. 105; Burchard and d'Hulst 1963, pp. 181, under no. 114, 183, under no. 115, 230–31, under no. 147; Vlieghe 1973, p. 31, under no. 104b; Held 1980, p. 561, under no. 408; Belkin 1980, p. 51; "Korean Model for Rubens" 1983, p. 25; Held 1986, no. 130, pl. 133; Vlieghe 1987, pp. 193–94, under no. 154; Goldner 1988, no. 93, pl. 11.

Exhibitions: London 1953, no. 281; London 1953–54, no. 522.

The impressive drawing in The Metropolitan Museum of Art shown in catalogue number 73 belongs to a group of five similar large studies of Jesuit missionaries.[1] It is the only one in the group that bears a long Latin inscription by Rubens. Until relatively recently, the identity of this missionary was unknown to art historians, although in 1953 the French Jesuit Henri Bernard tentatively suggested that the subject was Nicolas Trigault (1577–1628).[2] In 1987 Hans Vlieghe incorporated Bernard's article into the Rubens literature and added further information.[3] The Musée de la Chartreuse in Douai preserves a portrait of Trigault, attributed to the Rubens workshop. In this painting, an inscription on a tablet at the lower left identifies the sitter as "Nicolas Trigault, Jesuit with the Chinese mission, who returned to Flanders in 1616, was painted in 1617, and died in 1627 *[sic]*" (fig. 117).[4] There indeed exists a similarity between Rubens's drawn portrait and the painting in Douai. In both we see the same rather slight man with a triangular face and a pointed goatee wearing nearly identical Chinese robes. Finally, Rubens's faded inscription at the lower left of the drawing includes the partial name "Tricau."

Nicolas Trigault, born in 1577 in Douai—then part of the Southern Netherlands—left for China in 1610 to join some eighteen fellow Jesuit missionaries. Four years later, he returned for an extended visit to raise funds for his China mission and to recruit new missionaries. His travels are fairly well documented through letters, and he must have met Rubens when he passed through Antwerp or Brussels between November 20, 1616, and February 1617.[5] Based on Rubens's inscription on the drawing, Trigault sat for his portrait on January 17, 1617. Rubens drew the likeness in black chalk with some red chalk used for the face, and blue-green chalk for the silk bands and sashes. At the upper left in pen and brown ink, he lightly sketched a separate profile of Trigault's head. Father Trigault died in Hangzhou, in southern China, on November 14, 1628.

The opulent silk robe that Trigault wears in the drawing reflects the sartorial advice of the Italian Jesuit missionary Matteo Ricci (1552–1610), who had arrived in Beijing in 1601. Ricci shrewdly recognized that the usual unassuming garb of the European Jesuits was not suitable for the China mission. He suggested that by donning the robes of learned Chinese scholars, they might gain easier access to the imperial court.[6] Rubens's drawing records the special robe Father Ricci described in a letter: "[a dress] of purple silk, and the hem of the robe and the collar and the edges are bordered with a band of blue silk a little less than a palm wide; the same decoration is on the edges of the sleeves which hang open, rather in the style common in Venice. There is a side sash of the purple silk trimmed in blue which is fastened round the same robe and lets the robe hang comfortably open."[7] In his Latin inscription at the upper right of the drawing, Rubens explained the significance of the colors of the garment. It reads in translation: "Note that the dark color is not peculiar to Chinese scholars but to the Fathers of the Society of Jesus, except for the blue facings, which are common to all. The Chinese, furthermore, do not use one color only in their clothing, but any color they like, except yellow, which is reserved for the king [emperor]." His color notes correspond with the Douai portrait of Trigault (fig. 117).

In essence, this is a costume study, and it shows the same interest in foreign dress that Rubens demonstrated earlier when he recorded exotic clothing in his so-called *Costume Book* (British Museum, London; see cat. no. 5). No doubt the artist wanted to familiarize himself with the costumes of Jesuit missionaries in Asia in order to execute forthcoming commissions from the Antwerp Jesuits: two altarpieces for their new church (today Saint Charles Borromeo) dedicated to the founding fathers of their order, Ignatius Loyola (canonized in 1622) and Francis Xavier (beatified in 1619; for a Rubens drawing associated with this altar, see cat. no. 64). Rubens knew the mathematician François Aguilon (Franciscus Aguilonius; 1567–1617), the rector of the Jesuit college, who probably informed him of Trigault's journey; this contact likely resulted in the January sitting recorded in the New York drawing.

In the first half of the nineteenth century, the drawing was attributed to Anthony van Dyck (1599–1641) rather than Rubens, as we can see from the annotation at the lower right, "A van Dyck fecit." The inscription on the mount, "The Siamese Ambassador, an Armenian, sketched from life by Van Dyck," follows this erroneous attribution. The ambivalence regarding the authorship of this sheet dates at least from 1814, when it was in the Van Eyl Sluyter collection in Amsterdam. The drawing was sold in that year for three florins to Christiaan Josi as an original by Rubens. Ten years later, a Mr. Hudson acquired the drawing for five florins at the De Haas auction as a study by Anthony van Dyck.[8]

The relationship between the New York drawing (cat. no. 73) and the almost identical version in Stockholm (cat. no. 74) has puzzled many authors, who have proposed various interpretations. The two drawings are close in size and execution,

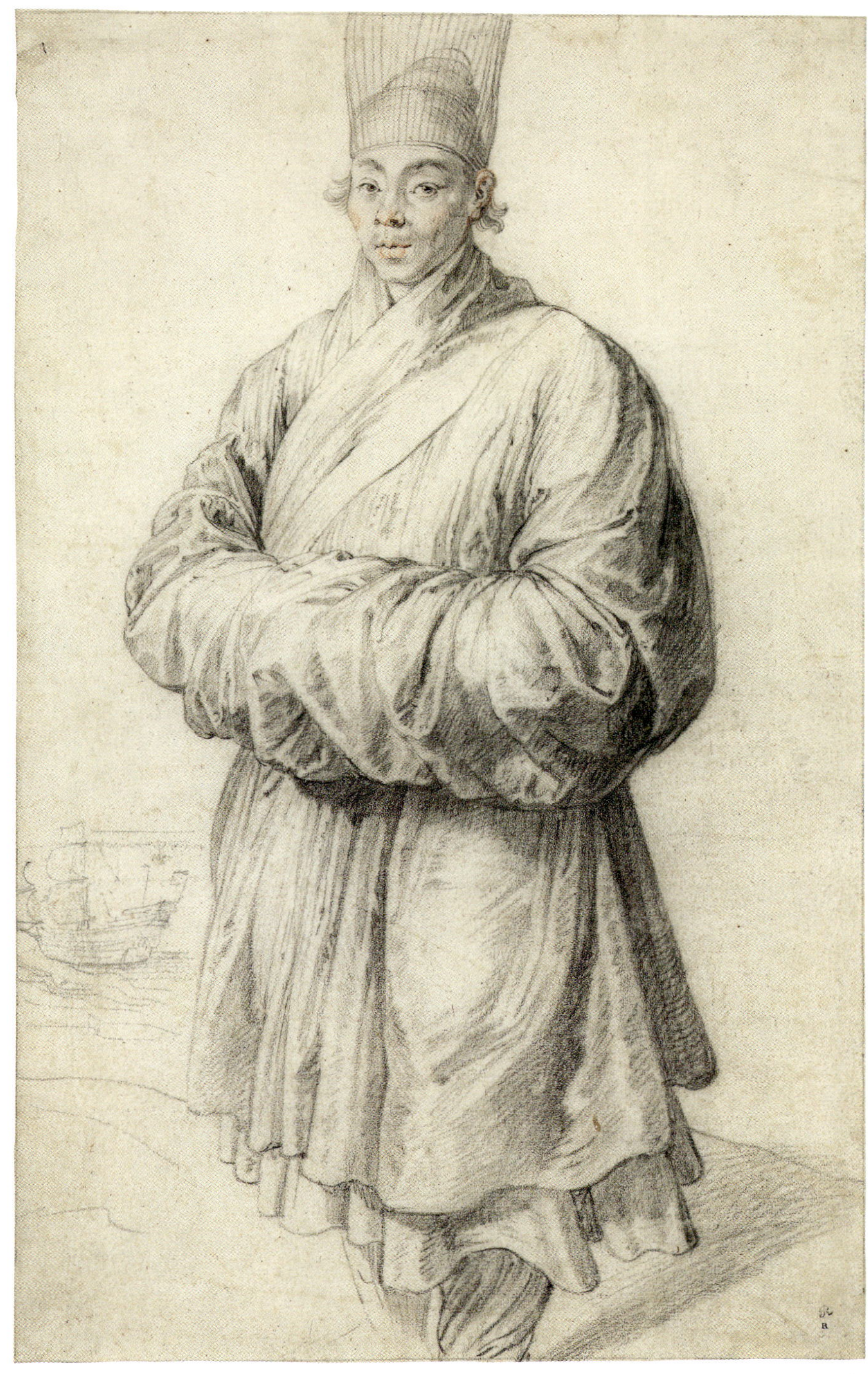

Cat. 75

even to the touches of blue-green chalk in the collar. Most often, the New York sheet has been interpreted as a second version, by Rubens, after the work in Stockholm.[9]

The Stockholm version appears to have been drawn more quickly but also more sloppily, since the hem of the robe extended too far and had to be revised. In particular, the parallel hatching modeling the garment was applied more mechanically than in the example in New York. The careful and controlled handling of the latter has led to the assumption that it followed the Stockholm version, since, as a rule, copies are more laborious, while drawings done on the spot tend to be more freely executed. However, small, but telling differences—for example, the lower end of the sash at the right, partially hidden in a fold, and the awkward rendering of the hem—

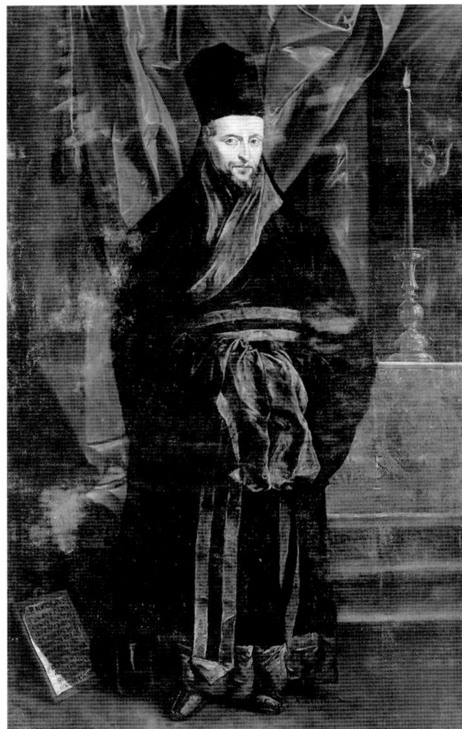

Fig. 117. Workshop of Rubens, *Nicolas Trigault*, 1617. Oil on canvas, 220 x 136 cm (86⅝ x 53 9/16 in.). Musée de la Chartreuse, Douai (27)

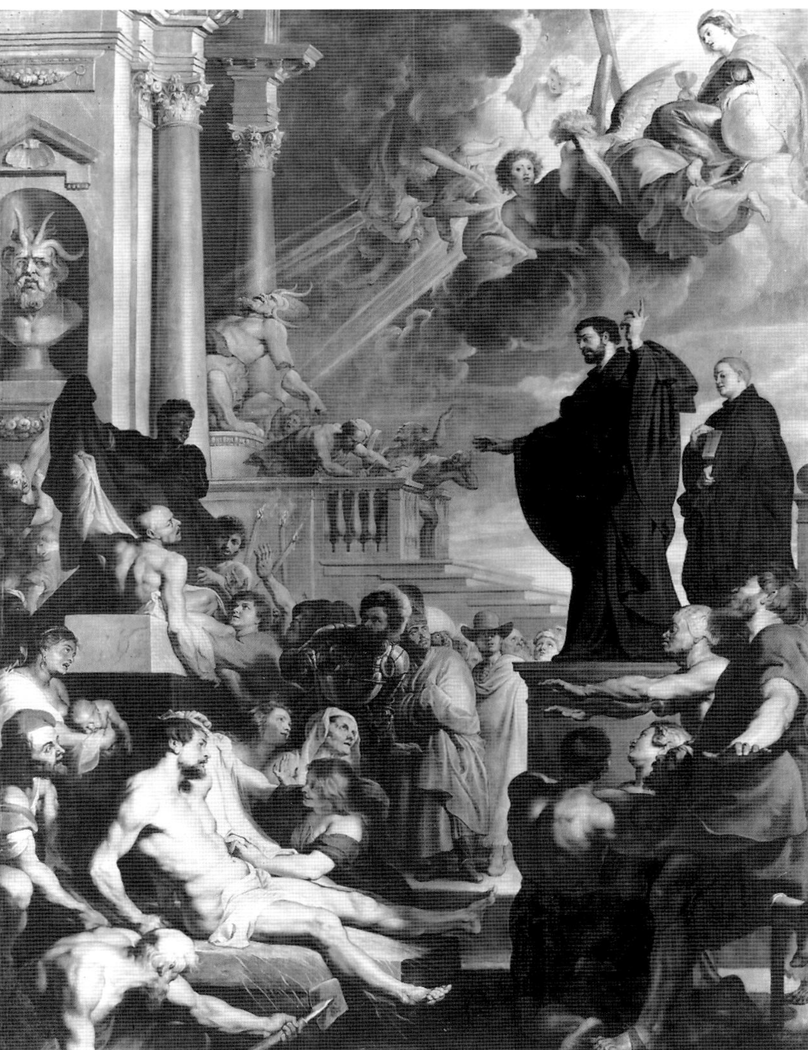

Fig. 118. Peter Paul Rubens, *The Miracles of Saint Francis Xavier*, ca. 1617–18. Oil on canvas, 535 x 395 cm (210⅝ x 155½ in.). Kunsthistorisches Museum, Vienna (GG 519)

seem to suggest that the draftsman of the Stockholm drawing was not always entirely clear about what he was sketching. Therefore the sequence of the two drawings could well be reversed, with the drawing in New York preceding that in Stockholm.[10]

The Stockholm drawing has a stellar provenance that begins with the late-seventeenth-century French collector Pierre Crozat (1665–1740), who owned numerous Rubens drawings. The well-known Swedish collector and connoisseur Count Carl Gustav Tessin (1695–1770) apparently purchased the sheet from Crozat's sale. (The drawings Tessin collected form the nucleus of the print room in the Nationalmuseum, Stockholm.) The New York drawing can be traced back to the eighteenth century, to the collection of Hendrik van Eyl Sluyter (1739–1814) in Amsterdam. As stated above, only that sheet bears an inscription by Rubens. Whether the master was also responsible for the Stockholm version is difficult to say, but this seems less likely.

The large portrait *Korean Man* (cat. no. 75), now in the J. Paul Getty Museum, is the only drawing among the five Rubens studies of Jesuit missionaries that portrays an Asian.[11] The subject wears a formal Korean dress with the characteristic transparent horsehair cap, or *got.* Yi Dynasty commoners may have worn this type of hat at formal functions.[12] The sketch of a ship at the left seems to indicate that the missionary traveled by sea from afar. This is the only example in the group that places the figure in a landscape setting. The man in the drawing remains to be identified with certainty, although one late-sixteenth-century Korean missionary is recorded living in Italy, where he was named accordingly, Antonio Corea.[13] A similar figure is found in the center of Rubens's *Miracles of Saint Francis Xavier,* originally painted for the high altar of the Jesuit church in Antwerp and now in the Kunsthistorisches Museum, Vienna (fig. 118).[14] It is interesting that in the oil sketch for the altarpiece[15] this figure wears a turban and looks up at the saint rather than at the viewer, as in the Getty drawing. Thus the latter cannot be considered a preliminary study. The likely explanation is that Rubens met this Jesuit missionary after he had begun the painting, drew his likeness, and adopted the Korean costume with the intriguing horsehair cap.[16] Rubens received the commission for the *Miracles of Saint Francis Xavier* prior to April 13, 1617, and the altarpiece was finished in 1617–18.

When catalogue number 75 was in the collection of R. Willett in London later in the eighteenth century, Captain William Baillie made an engraving after it and added the following text: "The Siamese Ambassador Who attended The Court of K Charles the 1st. Rubens made the above describ'd Drawing just before he left England anno 1636. W. Baillie f June 17, 1774."[17] The text has proven to be inaccurate, since Rubens left England in 1630 and most likely drew the study much earlier, in 1617.

1. The group, including the *Korean Man* (cat. no. 75), was attributed to Van Dyck until Clare Stuart Wortley published the drawings in 1934 as by Rubens, an attribution that has been generally accepted. According to her, the missionaries were drawn in Antwerp during the celebration of the canonization of Saint Ignatius Loyola and Saint Francis Xavier, held between July 23 and 25, 1622 (Wortley 1934–35, pp. 40–48).
2. Bernard 1953, pp. 308–13.
3. Marc Vandenven brought the article to Vlieghe's attention. See Vlieghe 1987, p. 194, under no. 154.
4. "R.P.NICOLAVS/TRIGAVLT DVA/CENSIS, SOCIETATIS/IESV SACERDOS,/ E CHINENSI MIS/SIONE, IN BELGIO/REVERSVS, A^{O}/1616, HOC IN HA/BITV A MVLTIS/A^{O} 1617, DVACIVI/SVS. OBIIT A^{O}/1627 IN CHINA." A later inscription specified "A^{O} AETATIS 40/1617." The painting came from the former Jesuit college in Douai, together with a pendant, a portrait of Petrus de Spira (Pierre van Spiere, born 1584, in Douai), a fellow missionary to China who joined Trigault there in 1611. W. Scheelen found documents that indicate the paintings were actually delivered in 1616. See Vlieghe 1987, nos. 154, 155, figs. 224, 225.
5. Lamalle 1940, p. 62, and passim.
6. In 1614 Trigault brought Ricci's diaries, written in Italian, to Rome, where he prepared a Latin translation that was published, in 1615, under the title *De Christiana Expeditione apud Sinas* (The Christian Expedition to China).
7. Stampfle 1991, p. 146; Stampfle quotes from Jonathan D. Spence, *The Memory Palace of Matteo Ricci* (New York, 1984), p. 115.
8. Plomp 2001–2, pp. 235–36.
9. See, for example, Bjurström in Washington–Fort Worth–San Francisco 1985–86, no. 78; Burchard and d'Hulst 1963, p. 231, under no. 147; and Held 1959, p. 137, under no. 105. In his 1986 revised edition of *Rubens: Selected Drawings,* Held (p. 120, under no. 131) added a question mark after "by Rubens's own hand" for the version now in New York. In 1978 Logan and Haverkamp-Begemann (p. 97) suggested that the New York version was by Van Dyck, who copied the Stockholm drawing that they accepted as Rubens's original, an opinion that was revised in 1991 and reiterated in 1993–94. See Logan in Stampfle 1991, p. 147, and Logan in Wellesley–Cleveland 1993–94, under no. 48.
10. The draftsman of the Stockholm sheet did not copy two pentimenti in the New York drawing, one in the lower fold of the front sleeve, the other above the sash. This is another indication that the Stockholm version followed the example in New York.
11. There is a copy after the head of the Korean man among the so-called *cantoor* group of drawings in the Statens Museum for Kunst, Copenhagen. See Copenhagen 1988, no. 145, pl. 147.
12. "Korean Model for Rubens" 1983, p. 25; see also Goldner 1988, p. 212, n. 1, under no. 93. The sheet was possibly even larger, since it appears to have been trimmed at the top and bottom (the cap is cropped and the figure's feet are missing). Kwak Cha-seop, professor of history at Pusan National University, asserts that the drawing represents a Chosun man of the Yi Dynasty, which ruled unified Korea from 1392 until the early twentieth century. Professor Kwak believes that Rubens met the missionary during his years in Italy, between 1600 and 1608 (e-mail communication from Lee Hendrix, February 5, 2004).
13. Corea was taken to Italy by an Italian merchant some time after the Japanese feudal lord Toyotomi Hideyoshi's invasions of Korea (1592, 1597), according to Father Choi Seok-woo of the Research Institute of Korean Church History (see "Korean Model for Rubens" 1983, p. 25; Goldner 1988, p. 212, n. 2, under no. 93).
14. M. Jaffé 1989, no. 481, 1618–19.
15. The oil sketches for the *Miracles of Saint Francis* and its pendant, the *Miracles of Saint Ignatius Loyola,* are, like the altarpieces, preserved in the Kunsthistorisches Museum, Vienna. See Vlieghe 1973, nos. 115, 115a, figs. 40, 41, and nos. 104, 104a, figs. 6, 7.
16. Bernard (1953, p. 313) stated that as far as is known, no Korean accompanied Trigault to Europe.
17. Schneevoogt 1873, s.v. "Portraits," p. 278.

76. *Marie de Médicis,* ca. 1622

Black chalk and touches of red chalk (in hair, neck, and face), wet red chalk (mouth and nose), and greasy black chalk (eye), heightened with white, 332 x 245 mm (13⅜ x 9¾ in.)
Annotated by Padre Sebastiano Resta in pen and brown ink at bottom center: *l..306*; at bottom left: *Monsù Bernardo discep.º di Rambrand dubitò che fusse / David Bex Suedese d.º il Gondonlene (?) p[er] Christina Regina di Suetia* (Monsù Bernardo, pupil of Rembrandt, doubted that [the portrait] was by David Beck, a painter in the service of Queen Christina of Sweden); at bottom right by another hand (?): *Monsù Malville lo chiamò (?) / di Rubbens & Maria de Medici / in Parigi* (Mr. Malville identified it as [a drawing] by Rubens of Marie de Médicis)[1]

Victoria and Albert Museum, London (D.906-1900)

PROVENANCE: Padre Sebastiano Resta (1635–1714), Milan (Lugt 2992); John, Lord Somers (1650–1715); Emily Frances Dalton (her bequest to the Victoria and Albert Museum, 1900).

LITERATURE: Glück and Haberditzl 1928, no. 151, pl. 151; Burchard and d'Hulst 1963, no. 130, pl. 130; Thuillier and Foucart 1970, pp. 50–51, 65, 90, fig. 42; M. Jaffé 1989, under no. 746.

EXHIBITIONS: London 1977a, no. 153, ill.; Paris 1991, no. 37.

Rubens drew this portrait of Marie de Médicis (1573–1642) in preparation for the most important commission he received in France: the so-called Medici cycle, a series of twenty-one lifesize paintings chronicling Marie's life from her girlhood to her coronation to advanced age and exile.[2] Rubens's canvases were to decorate the Grande Galerie in the queen's newly finished Luxembourg Palace in Paris. The cycle was completed by May 11, 1625, the day Marie's daughter, Marie-Henriette (or Henrietta Maria, as she became known), was married by proxy to King Charles I of England. Today the Luxembourg Palace houses the French senate and the Medici cycle is installed in the Louvre, Paris.[3]

This portrait is drawn in black chalk with touches of red chalk and white highlights. It is Rubens's preliminary study for the likeness of Marie de Médicis in the *Majority of Louis XIII,* the sixteenth painting of the cycle (fig. 119). There, the queen mother looks at her son and points toward the rudder that will guide the ship of state. In the finished canvas, just as in the preparatory oil sketch (fig. 120),[4] she meekly tilts her head to show deference to her heir and king. In the drawing,

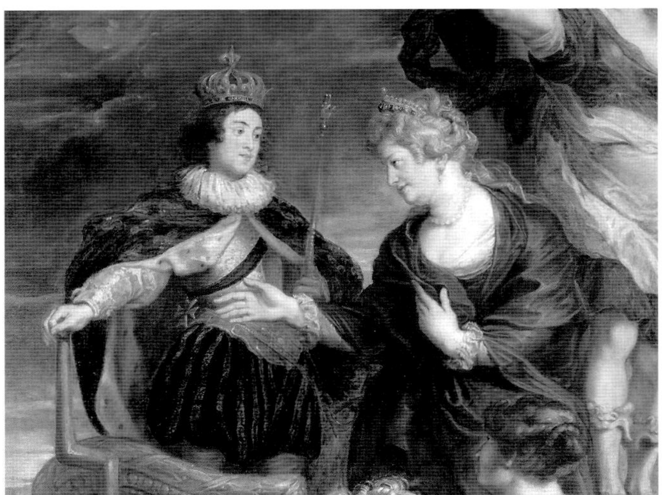

Fig. 119. Peter Paul Rubens, Detail of the *Majority of Louis XIII,* ca. 1625. Oil on canvas, 394 x 295 cm (155⅛ x 116⅛ in.). Département des Peintures du Musée du Louvre, Paris (1784)

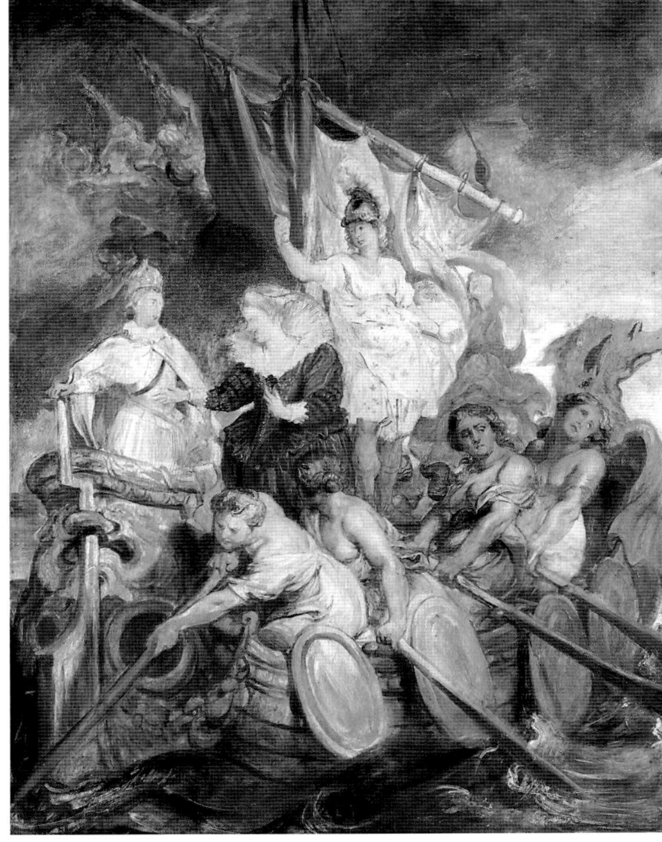

Fig. 120. Peter Paul Rubens, *The Majority of Louis XIII,* 1622. Oil on panel, 64.9 x 50.1 cm (25 9/16 x 19¾ in.). Bayerische Staatsgemäldesammlungen, Alte Pinakothek, Munich (104)

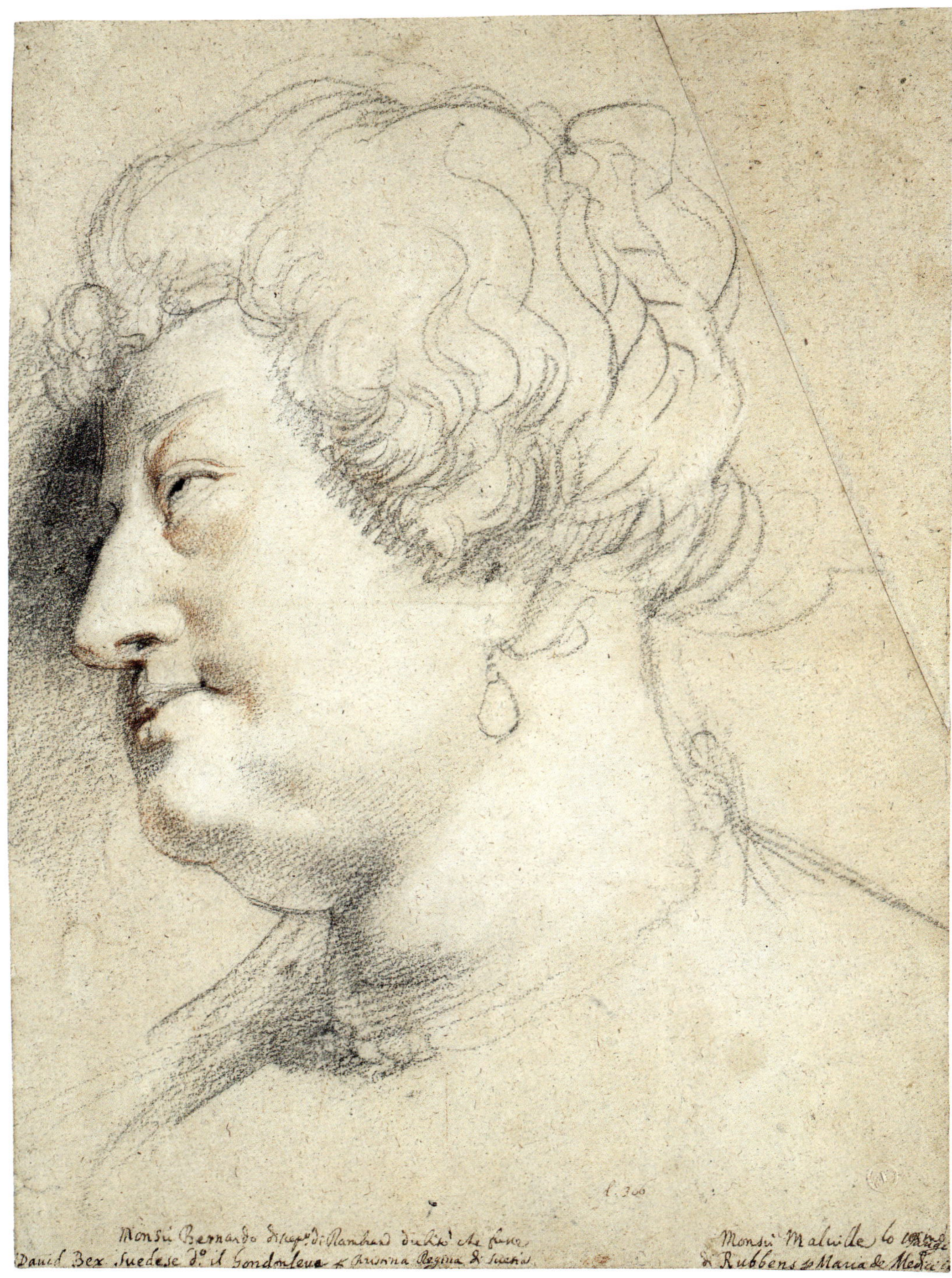

Cat. 76

however, she appears slightly less submissive, with her head more upright.

It is possible that the portrait drawing was done from life.[5] Roger de Piles, Rubens's early biographer, recounted that the queen, who was fond of painting and drew well herself, asked Rubens to paint two pictures for the Medici cycle in her presence so that she could observe him at work, and the surviving portrait drawings of Marie de Médicis may date from one of these sessions.[6] In 1622, the same time that he was working on the *Majority of Louis XIII,* Rubens also painted the portrait now in the Prado, Madrid. (King Philip IV of Spain acquired this from the artist's estate sometime after 1640.)[7]

Padre Sebastiano Resta, the Oratorian father and early drawings collector who inscribed catalogue number 76 along the bottom edge, wrote elsewhere that he had purchased some of his sheets from a Fleming who had traveled to Rome, and who in turn had obtained them from Rubens's studio.[8] This chalk portrait of Marie de Médicis may have been among these drawings.

1. Bernhard Keil, better known as Monsù Bernardo (1624–1687), was a pupil of Rembrandt's in 1642 and left for Rome in 1651. David Beck (1621–1656) was appointed court painter to Queen Christina of Sweden in 1647 and worked in Rome in 1653. Resta may have recorded these opinions about the drawing at a gathering of drawings connoisseurs, as noted by Genevieve Warwick (2000, p. 85).
2. From a recently discovered letter written from Antwerp on September 9, 1621, we learn that Rubens was first approached about decorating the "Gabinet" of Her Majesty as early as late August or early September 1621. See Merle du Bourg 2000, pp. 70–72.
3. K.d.K., ed. Oldenbourg 1921, nos. 243–65; M. Jaffé 1989, nos. 709–55, 1622–25.
4. Held 1980, no. 75, pl. 76, 1622; M. Jaffé 1989, no. 746, 1622; Renger and Denk 2002, pp. 431, 433–34, no. 104, color ill.
5. In 1622 Rubens asked for a sculpted bust of the queen as an aid for his portraits; a cast from a small bronze portrait by Barthélemy Prieur (ca. 1540–1611) was promised, but had still not arrived by February 9, 1623. Rubens therefore likely drew her from life.
6. Piles 1677, p. 28. For other portrait drawings by Rubens of Marie de Médicis, in Vienna and Paris, see London 1977a, under no. 153.
7. Díaz Padrón 1995, vol. 2, p. 968, no. 1685; Huemer 1977, no. 27, fig. 83; M. Jaffé 1989, no. 697, January–February 1622.
8. Wood 1990, pp. 7, 9, and app. I, II.

77. *George Villiers, 1st Duke of Buckingham,* March–June 1625

Black, red, and touches of white chalk; pupils strengthened with pen and dark brown ink, 385 x 267 mm (15 1/16 x 10 1/2 in.)
Annotated in red chalk at top: *hertoeg van bochengem P. P. Rubbens. F*[1]

Albertina, Vienna (8256)

PROVENANCE: Hofbibliothek, Vienna; in 1796 acquired through exchange by Duke Albert of Sachsen-Teschen (1738–1822), Vienna (Lugt 174).

LITERATURE: R., vol. 5, no. 1501, pl. 419; Glück 1921, no. 7, ill.; Glück and Haberditzl 1928, no. 156, pl. 156; Held 1959, no. 107, pl. 119, pp. 77, 138, under no. 106; Kuznetsov 1974, pl. 106; Held 1986, no. 165, pl. 160; Vlieghe 1987, no. 80a, fig. 52.

EXHIBITIONS: Vienna 1977b, no. 39, ill.; London 1995–96, no. 115, ill.

George Villiers (1592–1628), named 1st Duke of Buckingham and Lord High Admiral in 1623, was the favorite of Kings James I and Charles I of England. Thanks to his power, he assembled a fortune that enabled him to form one of the most important art collections in England. Buckingham and Rubens must have first met between May 14 and June 2, 1625, when both were at the French court. Rubens was in Paris to deliver the series of paintings (now in the Louvre) commissioned by Marie de Médicis (1573–1642) for the new Luxembourg Palace, which was inaugurated during the festivities on May 11 to celebrate the marriage between King Charles I and Henrietta Maria, daughter of Marie de Médicis. Buckingham was on hand to escort the new queen back to England. During this Parisian visit, the duke probably commissioned two paintings from Rubens: a half-length, official portrait known from a version now in the Palazzo Pitti, Florence (fig. 121),[2] and an equestrian portrait that was lost in the fire at Osterley Park in 1949.[3] This portrait study in the Albertina, Vienna, served directly for the former, in which the duke wears the same flat, starched lace collar. The artist caught the look of self-assurance of the Englishman, who faces slightly to the left and gazes steadily at the viewer. In a letter written in December 1625, Rubens commented on his "caprice" and "arrogance."[4]

Rubens also used the Vienna study for the duke's equestrian portrait, which is known today through the preliminary oil sketch now in the Kimbell Museum, Fort Worth (fig. 122).[5] Here, the Duke of Buckingham is portrayed as commander of the navy, a title bestowed on him that very year, 1625. Atop a bay horse in a levade pose, he is dressed in armor, while warships are anchored in the background. Rubens probably completed the painting by September 18, 1627.[6] The equestrian portrait may also allude to the duke's position as master of the horse to Charles I.

During the same sojourn in Paris, perhaps during the drawing session, Buckingham initiated negotiations for the purchase of Rubens's renowned collection of art and antique marbles, gems, and medals that the artist had acquired from Sir Dudley Carleton. Two years later, the works of art and antiquity, sold for 100,000 florins, were indeed shipped to England. Buckingham further commissioned Rubens to paint an allegorical ceiling for York House, the duke's residence on the Strand; this represented the duke borne to the Temple of Virtue in the sky,

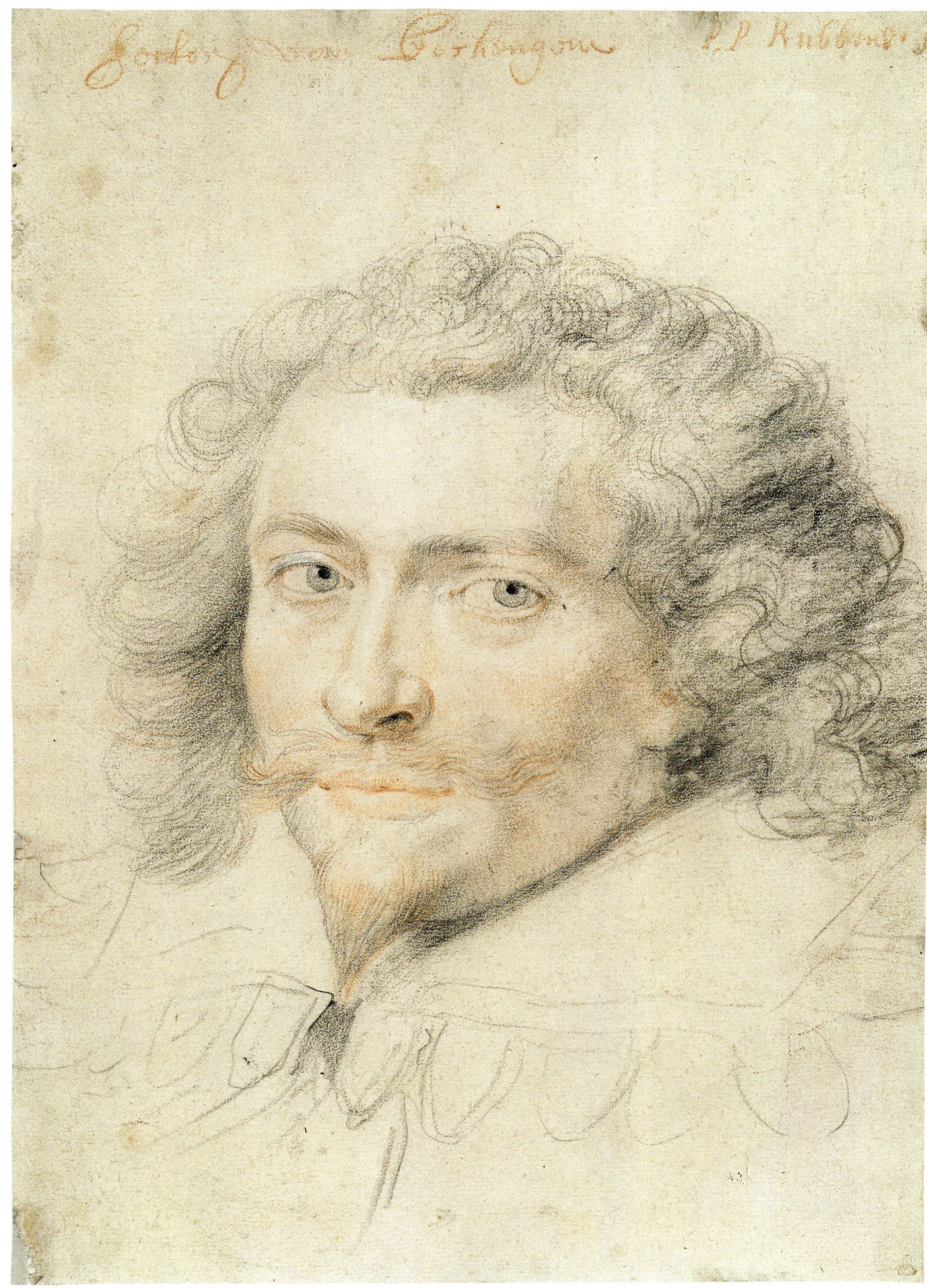

Cat. 77

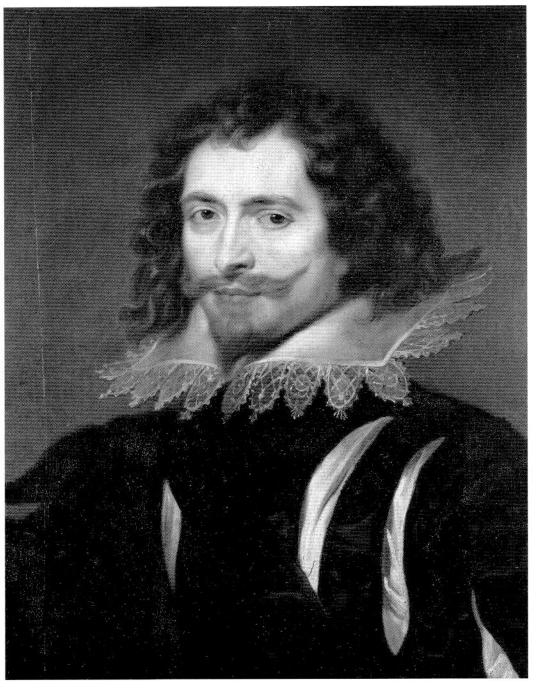

Fig. 121. Workshop of Rubens, *George Villiers, 1st Duke of Buckingham*, ca. 1625. Oil on panel, 63 x 48 cm (24 13/16 x 18 7/8 in.). Palazzo Pitti, Florence

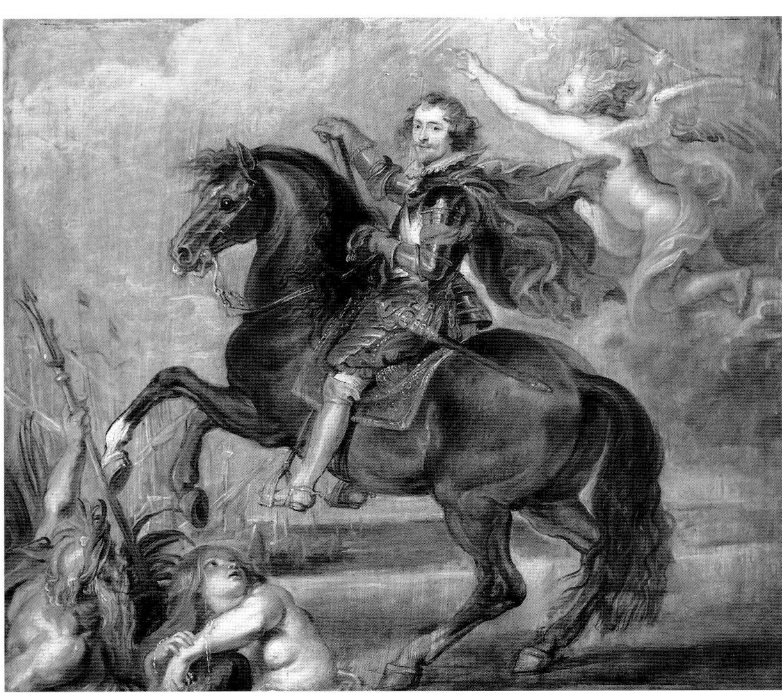

Fig. 122. Peter Paul Rubens, *Study for the Equestrian Portrait of the 1st Duke of Buckingham*, 1625. Oil on panel, 466 x 517 cm (183/16 x 203 9/16 in.). Kimbell Art Museum, Fort Worth (AP 1876.08)

assisted by Minerva and Mercury and accompanied by Fame.[7] As if that was not enough, the duke acquired over the years at least thirty other works by the Flemish master, the largest number of Rubens paintings in an English collection.[8]

1. The same anonymous hand that correctly identified the sitter in an annotation in red chalk is also found on other figure drawings in the Albertina (see Vienna 1977b, nos. 21, 37–40, 43, 44, ill.). These identifications may have been added about 1643 (since Marie de Médicis is referred to as "reyne mere"), that is, shortly after Rubens's death, by someone familiar with the traditional names of the sitters. Grossmann (1957, p. 126) and Held (1959, p. 138, under no. 106; 1986, p. 133, under no. 162) suggested Erasmus II Quellinus (1607–1678) as a candidate.
2. The Florence portrait is considered a studio replica after the lost original listed in Rubens's estate (K.d.K., ed. Rosenberg 1905, no. 257; Vlieghe 1987, pp. 62–63, under no. 80, fig. 51; M. Jaffé 1989, nos. 789, 789a [copy], ca. 1625). Rubens also drew the likeness of Catherine Manners, Duchess of Buckingham, which is in the Albertina as well and served for the portrait at the Dulwich Art Gallery, London (M. Jaffé 1989, no. 790, ca. 1625). Since she did not accompany her husband to Paris, Rubens may have drawn her portrait from a miniature.
3. K.d.K., ed. Oldenbourg 1921, no. 267; M. Jaffé 1989, no. 792, 1625.
4. Magurn 1955, p. 123, letter 72. In the same year Rubens was paid five hundred pounds for the equestrian portrait (Sainsbury 1859, p. 68, n. 107a).
5. Held 1980, no. 292, pl. 294, colorpl. 11; M. Jaffé 1989, no. 791, ca. 1625.
6. See note 3 above and Vlieghe 1987, p. 65.
7. Listed in the 1635 inventory of York House. This work, too, perished in the fire of 1949 (M. Jaffé 1989, no. 795, ca. 1625).
8. See Fairfax 1758 and Binyon 1910, pp. 277–78.

78. *Don Diego Messía (Mexía), Marquis of Leganés,* September–December 1627

Black and red chalk, traces of white chalk; pupils reinforced with brush and black ink at a later date; vertical squaring lines through center of face and horizontal lines through mouth and eyes, top of nose, and top of head, 384 x 276 mm (15 x 10 13/16 in.)
Annotated in red chalk at top left: *P P Rubbens;* at bottom left: *Marquis de la genesse*

Albertina, Vienna (8258)

PROVENANCE: Hofbibliothek, Vienna; in 1796 acquired through exchange by Duke Albert of Sachsen-Teschen (1738–1822), Vienna (Lugt 174).

LITERATURE: R., vol. 5, no. 1510, pl. 41; Glück and Haberditzl 1928, no. 164, pl. 164; Held 1959, pp. 77, 138, under no. 106; Kuznetsov 1974, pl. 107; Held 1986, pp. 58, 133, under no. 162; Vlieghe 1987, no. 115a, fig. 137.

EXHIBITIONS: Vienna 1977b, no. 44, ill.; New York and other cities 1997–99, no. 38 (New York), ill., no. 19 (Bilbao), ill.

The annotation in red chalk at the lower left of this portrait drawing identifies the sitter as Diego Messía (Mexía) Felipe de Guzmán (1580?–1655), 1st Marquis of Leganés. Messía was a special envoy from King Philip IV of Spain to Archduchess Isabella. In June 1622 he was named to the council of war, and in 1625 he was appointed general field marshal of the king of Spain (Leganés commanded the Spanish artillery and cavalry in the Southern Netherlands).[1] He was elevated to Marquis of Leganés in 1627, at which time he also adopted the surname of Gaspar de Guzmán y Pimental, Spain's all-powerful Count Duke of Olivares. Rubens first referred to Leganés in a letter to the Infanta Isabella from Paris on March 15, 1625.[2] Three years later, on January 27, 1628, the artist wrote to Pierre Dupuy (1582–1651), a royal librarian in Paris and Rubens's regular correspondent, that he counted Leganés "among the greatest connoisseurs of . . . art in the world."[3]

Over a faint grid, Rubens first sketched the marquis's head in outline, then in more detail. The ruff collar framing the face is indicated only summarily. Despite this methodical approach, the portrait is lively and personal. The Vienna drawing served as a study for the three-quarter-length portrait of the Marquis de Leganés, now in a private collection (fig. 123).[4] Rubens followed it carefully, not just for the position of the head, but also for the gaze of the eyes, the ruff collar, and even the curls of the hair.

Rubens most likely encountered the Marquis de Leganés when the latter stayed in Brussels from September 9, 1627, until January 3, 1628.[5] As a special envoy of the Spanish king, the marquis came to inform the Archduchess Isabella that Philip IV had just signed a treaty between Spain and France against England, which was contrary to Rubens's fervent hopes for peace between Spain and England.[6] Due to this turn of events, the artist made repeated trips to the Brussels court to assist in negotiations during Leganés's stay. As Don Diego Messía became 1st Marquis of Leganés in 1627, he may have commissioned his portrait from Rubens to commemorate this honor; at about the same time, he was also to marry the daughter of Ambrogio Spinola, the victor in the Battle of Breda. The dating of the painting to September–October 1627 suggested by Michael Jaffé[7] is likely for the drawing as well, although one might extend this to December to include all the months of negotiations in Brussels in which Rubens also participated.

According to the painter Francisco Pacheco (1564–1644), the father-in-law of Velázquez, Don Diego was a great admirer of Rubens ("grande aficionado suyo") and responsible for one

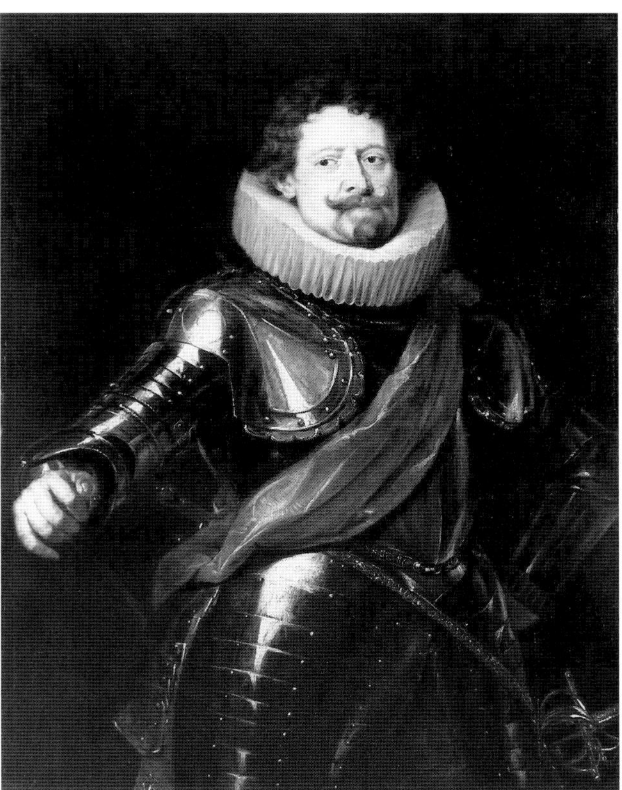

Fig. 123. Peter Paul Rubens, *Don Diego Messía, Marquis of Leganés,* 1627. Oil on canvas, 117 x 89 cm (46 1/16 x 35 1/16 in.). Private collection (423)

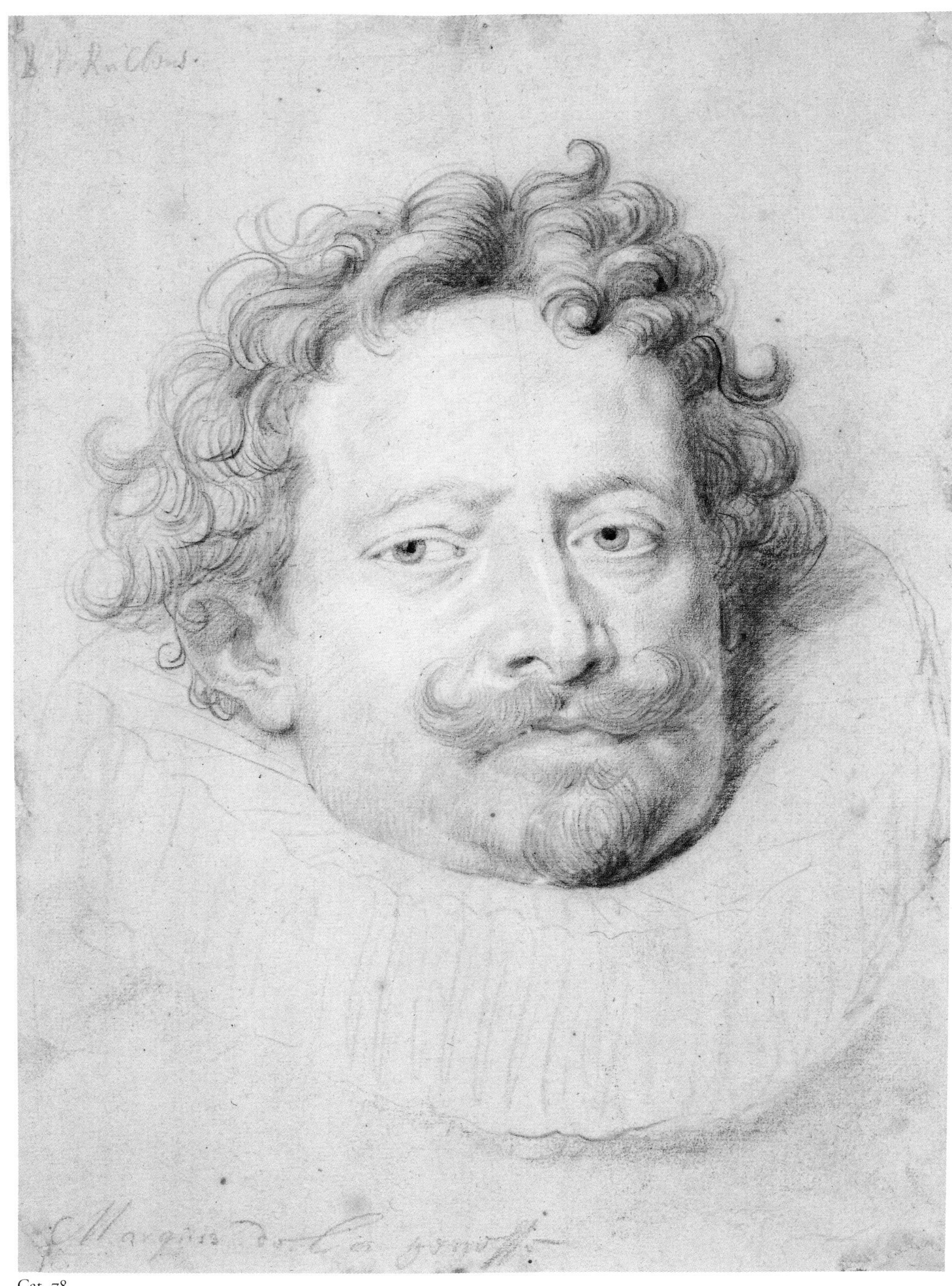

Cat. 78

of the few non-portrait commissions that Rubens received in Spain, namely, an *Immaculate Conception* today in the Prado, Madrid.[8] When Messía died in 1655, his inventory listed 1,333 paintings, with many works by Flemish artists, including at least 30 by Rubens.[9]

1. Rubens mentioned this appointment in his letter of December 12, 1625. Magurn 1955, p. 120, letter 71. See also Vergara 1999, pp. 93–94.
2. Magurn 1955, p. 107, letter 61.
3. Magurn 1955, p. 234, letter 145. According to Rubens, Spinola did not go to see the Medici cycle, since he had "no taste for painting," in contrast to his son-in-law, Leganés, who did.
4. Vlieghe 1987, no. 115, figs. 135, 136; M. Jaffé 1989, no. 891, September–October 1627; Hans Vlieghe in Münster 2003, p. 66, no. 35, color ill.
5. Hans Vlieghe (in Lille 2004, under no. 85) maintains that Leganés remained at the court in Brussels through March 1628. However, according to Rubens's letter of March 23, 1628, to Dupuy in Paris, Leganés was married to Polyxena Spinola in Madrid on February 28, 1628 (Magurn 1955, p. 247, letter 155).
6. Magurn 1955, p. 202, letter 125, September 18, 1627, to Balthasar Gerbier.
7. See note 4 above. Vlieghe dated Rubens's portrait to the early 1630s, when Leganés resided in Brussels.
8. M. Jaffé 1989, no. 945, 1628–29. The marquis must have presented it immediately to Philip IV, since it does not figure in the 1630 Leganés inventory but is listed in 1636 in the royal inventory as his gift. The painting hung in the king's oratory on the ground floor of his summer apartments (Pacheco 1638 [1956 ed.], vol. 1, pp. 153–54). Later in the century, Velázquez partly repainted the arched top when he altered the picture's format. Díaz Padrón 1995, vol. 2, pp. 860–63, no. 1627, color ill.
9. Summarized in Rooses 1900a, pp. 168–71. See López Navío 1962, pp. 289–90, and Volk 1980, pp. 256–68.

79. *Thomas Howard, 2nd Earl of Arundel,* 1629–30

Pen and brush and brown ink over black and red chalk, traces of heightening in white body color, 275 x 193 mm ($10\frac{13}{16}$ x $7\frac{5}{8}$ in.)

Ashmolean Museum, Oxford (WA 1994.27)

PROVENANCE: Count Duchastel-Dandelot, Brussels (1890); Maurice Delacre (1862–1932), Ghent (Lugt 747a); De la Croix family, France.

LITERATURE: R., vol. 5, no. 1497, pl. 418; Glück and Haberditzl 1928, no. 226, pl. 226; Held 1959, p. 32; Huemer 1977, no. 4a, fig. 49; Held 1986, p. 140, under no. 180; White 1995a, p. 68, ill.; White 1995b, pp. 316–19, fig. 36, ill. on cover.

EXHIBITIONS: Malibu 1995, pl. 5; Madrid 2002, no. 26, ill.; London 2003–4b, no. 173, ill.

80. *Thomas Howard, 2nd Earl of Arundel,* ca. 1629–30

Brush and brown ink, dark brown oil color (?), brown and gray wash, heightened with white, touches of red wash, 460 x 355 mm ($18\frac{1}{4}$ x 14 in.)

Sterling and Francine Clark Art Institute, Williamstown, Massachusetts (1955.991)

PROVENANCE: Unidentified 17th-century collector G. H. (perhaps Guillaume Hubert, first half 18th century); Jonathan Richardson Sr. (1665–1745), London (Lugt 2184; sale, London, Cock, January 22, 1747); Thomas Hudson (1701–1779), London (Lugt 2432; sale, London, Langford, March 15–16, 1779, lot 69); Lord Selsey (sale, London, Sotheby's, June 20–28, 1872, probably lot 2637); Robert P. Roupell (1798–1866), London (Lugt 2234; sale, London, Christie's, July 12–14, 1887, lot 1120); private collection, London; acquired by the Clark Art Institute in 1926.

LITERATURE: Glück and Haberditzl 1928, no. 178, pl. 178; Burchard and d'Hulst 1963, no. 170, pl. 170; Haverkamp-Begemann, Lawder, and Talbot 1964, vol. 1, no. 22; Huemer 1977, no. 5a, fig. 51; Held 1986, no. 180, colorpl. 4; Fehl 1988, pp. 7–23, fig. 9; White 1995b, p. 318.

EXHIBITIONS: Antwerp 1977, no. 161, ill.; London–New Haven 1987, no. 28, pl. 28; Wellesley–Cleveland 1993–94, no. 51, ill.

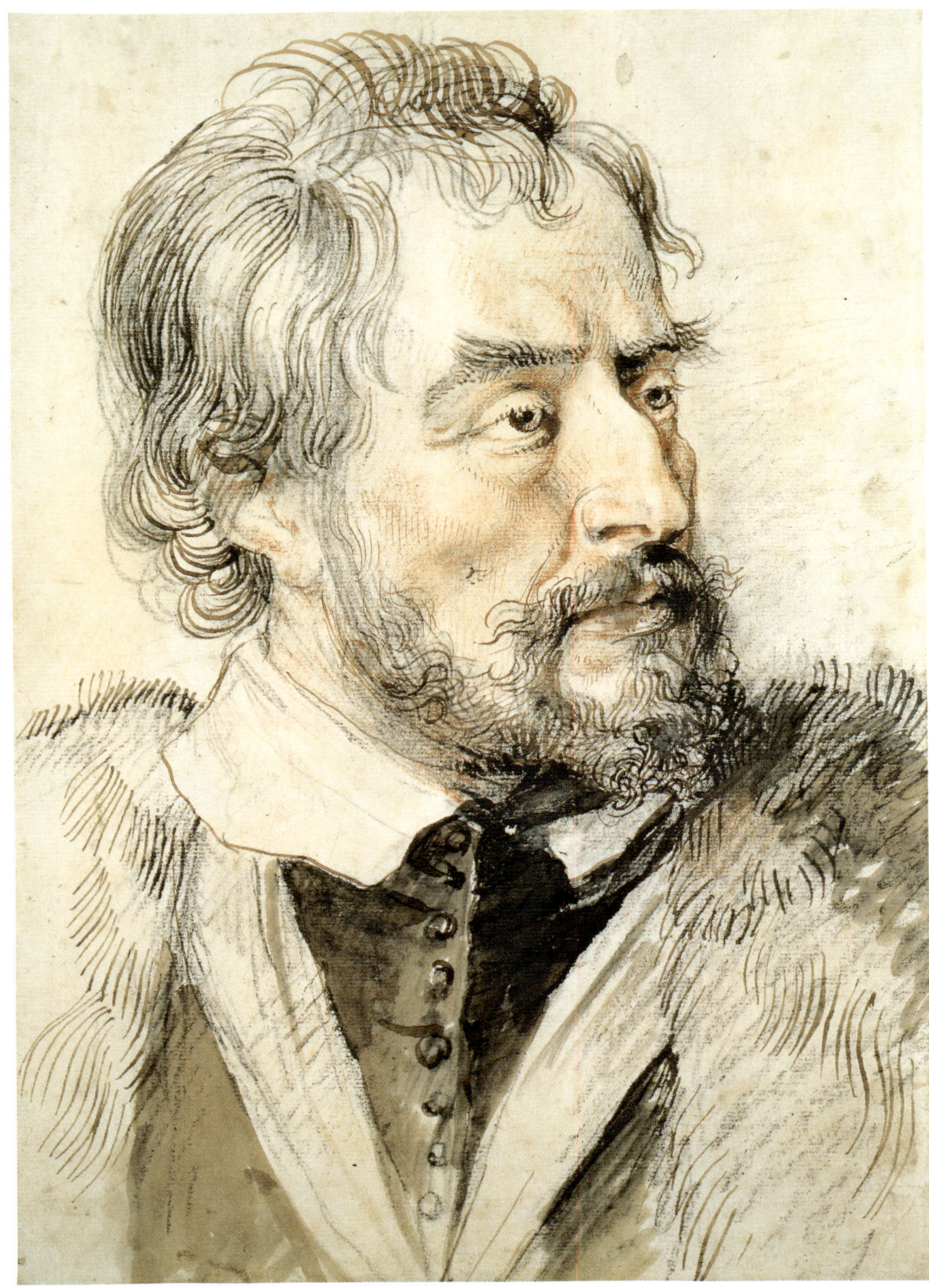

Cat. 79

From June 30, 1629, until March 23, 1630, Rubens was in London on a diplomatic mission on behalf of Archduchess Isabella to promote peace between England and Spain. One of the highlights of this stay in the English capital must have been his encounter with Thomas Howard, 2nd Earl of Arundel (1585–1646), whom Rubens called "one of the four Evangelists and the Supporter of our Art."[1] Arundel was the earliest and most important English collector at the Stuart court of Charles I (r. 1625–49). Initially, he collected antiquities, while later on he would become one of the first connoisseurs of old master drawings in England. Rubens must have been eager to make his acquaintance and visit his famous collection of "ancient statues and Greek and Latin inscriptions" at Arundel House. As Rubens praised Arundel's antiquities in a letter of August 9, 1629,

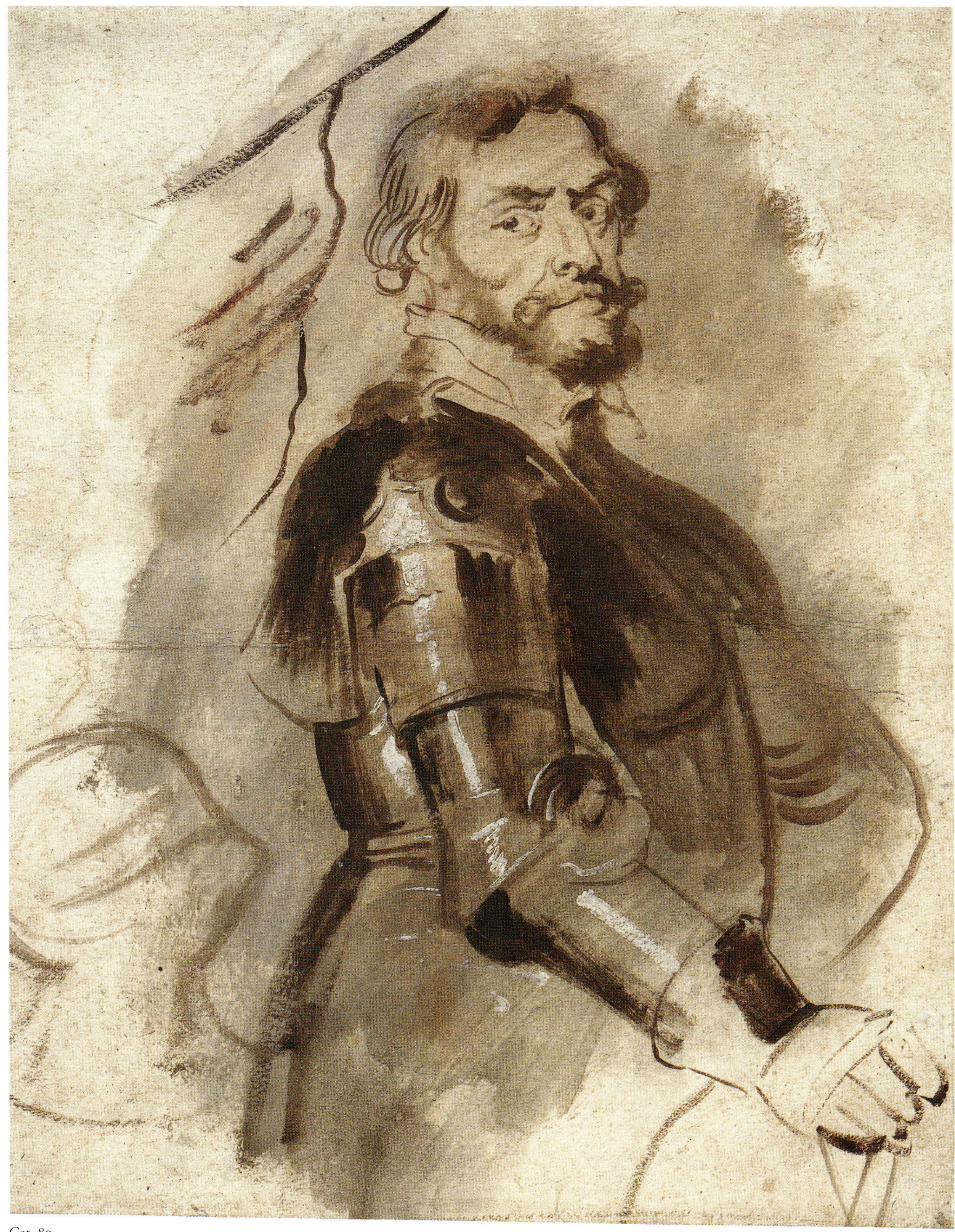

Cat. 80

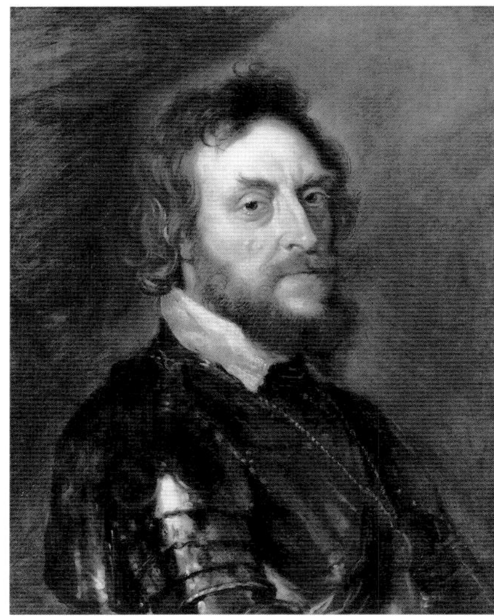

Fig. 124. Peter Paul Rubens, *Thomas Howard, 2nd Earl of Arundel*, 1629. Oil on canvas, 66.5 x 52 cm (26 3/16 x 20 1/2 in.). National Portrait Gallery, London (NPG 2391)

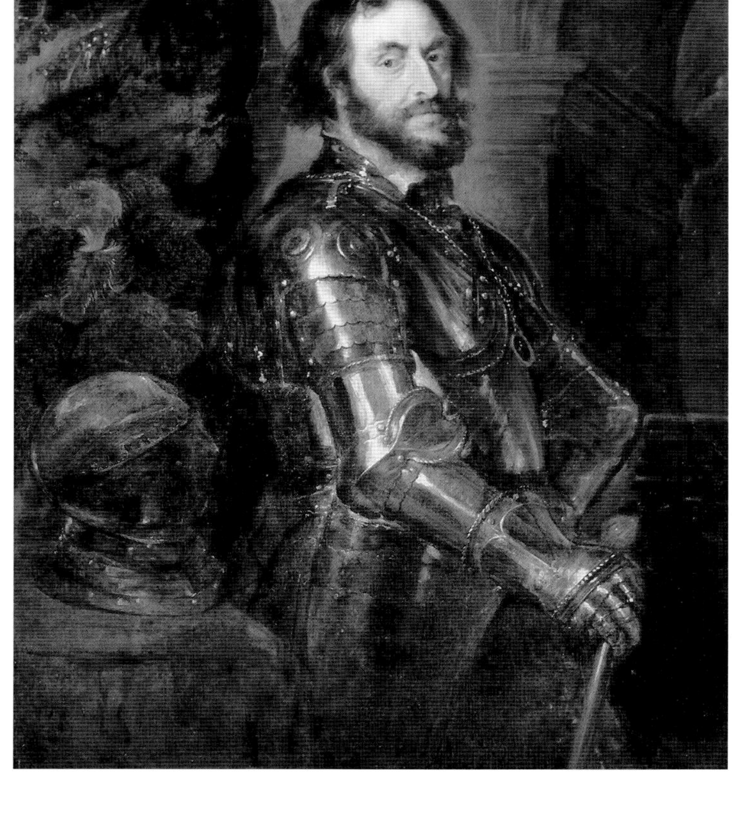

Fig. 125. Peter Paul Rubens, *Thomas Howard, 2nd Earl of Arundel*, ca. 1630. Oil on canvas, 122.2 x 102.1 cm (48 1/8 x 40 3/16 in.). The Isabella Stewart Gardner Museum, Boston (ISG 113857)

to the French scholar Nicolas-Claude Fabri de Peiresc, a meeting between the artist and the collector must have taken place before that date.[2]

It was probably during that visit or another in 1629–30—the two men with such similar interests in art surely met more than once—that Rubens drew these two portraits, now in Oxford (cat. no. 79)[3] and Williamstown (cat. no. 80). The drawings are very different in execution and show the wide range of Rubens's draftsmanship. The example in Oxford is drawn in several media, beginning with black chalk, to which the artist added red chalk for the flesh tones in the face. He used pen and brown ink to indicate the hair, beard, fur, and even the small mole on Arundel's cheek. Rubens completed the portrait by applying brown wash to the buttoned vest and the fur collar of the coat. The portrait in Williamstown is much closer to an oil sketch. Rubens drew it entirely with the brush and various shades of brown ink and brown wash. The two drawings also differ in the ways they represent the earl. Whereas the Oxford portrait conveys a certain informality, that in Williamstown, showing Arundel in full armor and with a stern demeanor, expresses an official formality.

The drawing in Williamstown (cat. no. 80) is Rubens's preliminary study for his lifesize portrait of the earl, now in the Isabella Stewart Gardner Museum, Boston (fig. 125).[4] Besides these two studies and the Boston picture, Rubens painted two different, half-length portraits, both in London, in the National Portrait Gallery (fig. 124)[5] and the National Gallery.[6] As the former shows the earl turned to the right, it resembles the drawing in Oxford. The Williamstown drawing relates more closely to the portrait now in the National Portrait Gallery, since there Arundel also wears armor and looks out at the viewer.

1. Hervey 1921, p. 174.
2. Magurn 1955, pp. 321–23, letter 196. Thomas Howard's wife, Aletheia, Countess of Arundel and Surrey, who was a collector in her own right, commissioned Rubens to paint her portrait in 1620, when she passed through Antwerp on her way to Venice; the painting is now in Munich. K.d.K., ed. Oldenbourg 1921, no. 200; Huemer 1977, fig. 35; M. Jaffé 1989, no. 652; Renger and Denk 2002, p. 272, no. 352.
3. The drawing resurfaced in Paris only in the summer of 1993. It was acquired the following year by the Ashmolean Museum, where it joined the many classical antiquities from the Arundel collection. As Arundel is wearing fur, the study probably dates from the winter months of 1629–30.
4. Huemer 1977, no. 5, fig. 52; M. Jaffé 1989, no. 975, ca. 1630.
5. Huemer 1977, no. 5b, fig. 53; M. Jaffé 1989, no. 971, 1629.
6. Huemer 1977, no. 4, fig. 48; M. Jaffé 1989, no. 972, winter 1629–30. The 1640 inventory of Rubens's estate lists, under no. 97: "The picture of the Earle of Arvndell uppon Cloth." Since all three extant portraits are painted on canvas, each has been considered the one listed. Muller 1989, p. 114, no. 97.

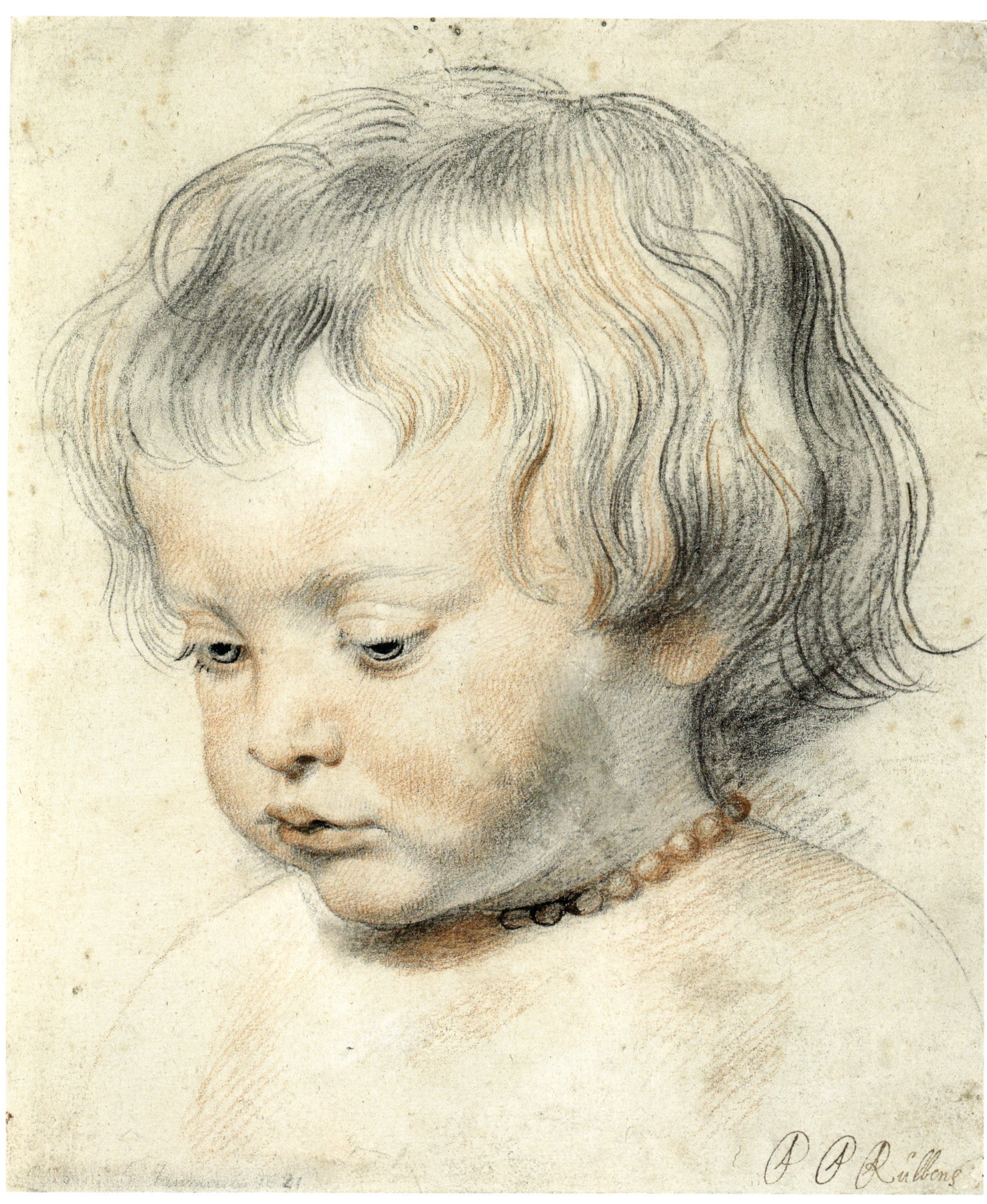

Cat. 81

81. *Nicolaas Rubens Wearing a Coral Necklace,* ca. 1619

Black and red chalk, heightened with white chalk, with the eyes, part of the necklace, and sections of the mouth strengthened with pen and dark brown ink, on brownish paper, 252 x 202 mm (9 15/16 x 7 15/16 in.) Annotated in pen and brown ink at bottom right: *P. P. Rubbens;* in black chalk at bottom left: *1621* (partly erased)

Albertina, Vienna (17650)

PROVENANCE: Duke Albert of Sachsen-Teschen (1738–1822), Vienna (Lugt 174).

LITERATURE: R., vol. 5, no. 1520, pl. 424; Haberditzl 1912, pp. 8–9; Glück and Haberditzl 1928, no. 116, pl. 116; Held 1959, no. 98, pl. 100, colorpl. opp. p. 16, p. 33; Burchard and d'Hulst 1963, no. 126, pl. 126, p. 215, under no. 138; Benesch 1967, no. 149, ill.; Kuznetsov 1974, pl. 97; Heiden 1982, p. 31, fig. 25; Held 1986, no. 144, pl. 156.

EXHIBITIONS: Antwerp 1977, no. 152, ill.; Vienna 1977b, no. 35, ill.; Vienna–Amsterdam 1989–90, no. 50, ill.

This is one of Rubens's most famous drawings, taken from life "con amore," to quote Max Rooses (1839–1914), the first scholar to undertake a catalogue raisonné of Rubens's oeuvre. The little boy is traditionally identified as Nicolaas Rubens, the younger of Rubens's two sons with his first wife, Isabella Brant. Judging from this and other drawings of his children, Rubens must have adored them and drawn them repeatedly, often while they were absorbed in other things, seemingly unaware of their father. He recorded them swiftly, sketching in black chalk with touches of red chalk for their faces. Eyes, nose, and mouth were often strengthened, as here, with pen and brown ink.

Much less is known about Nicolaas Rubens than about his elder brother, the learned Albert, Rubens's favorite. He received his Christian name in honor of the Genoese patrician, Niccolò Pallavicini, banker to the Gonzaga, who was his godfather. In 1640 Nicolaas married Constance Helman (1609–1678) and three years later purchased the castle of Rameyen (Hof van ter Rameyen) in Gestel (since 1964, called Berlaar), built in the fourteenth century. He also owned the Hof van Ursele in Ekeren, north of Antwerp, which his older brother ceded to him in 1646. He was the father of seven children and died in 1655.[1]

The coral beads strung on a cord around the child's neck are not just for decoration but also for protection from "fits and anxiety," according to the *Cruydt-Boeck* (Herbal) by Rembertus Dodonaeus (Antwerp, 1554).[2] Children were often depicted wearing double or even triple strings of coral beads on their wrists, as in the slightly later portrait by a fellow artist from Antwerp, Cornelis de Vos (1584–1651), who painted his daughter Susanna in 1627 (Städelsches Kunstinstitut, Frankfurt).[3]

Rubens used portraits of his children several times in paintings for the Christ Child or the young Saint John the Baptist. This study in Vienna, which probably dates from 1619 when Nicolaas was a little over one year old, was used for the head of the Christ Child in Rubens's painting of the *Virgin with Jesus and the Infant Saint John the Baptist,* now in Kassel (fig. 126).[4] Except for the tilt of the head, which is slightly more inclined toward one of the penitents genuflecting below him, Christ's face and expression are virtually the same. (For the body of the Christ Child, Rubens adapted a study he drew after his son Albert; see cat. no. 59.)

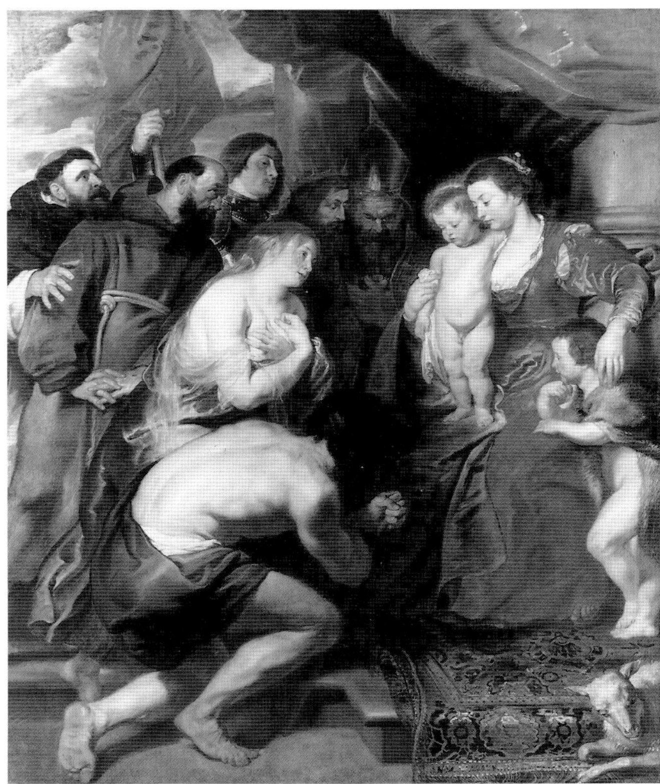

Fig. 126. Peter Paul Rubens, *The Virgin with Jesus and the Infant Saint John the Baptist,* 1619–20. Oil on canvas on oak, 258 x 204 cm (101 9/16 x 80 5/16 in.). Gemäldegalerie Alte Meister, Staatliche Museen Kassel (GK 119)

1. Douxchamps 1977, pp. 187–95.
2. Antwerp 2000, no. 8.
3. Ibid., no. 24. See also "Koralle," in *Handwörterbuch des deutschen Aberglaubens,* vol. 5 (Berlin and Leipzig, 1932–33), cols. 239–41.
4. K.d.K., ed. Oldenbourg 1921, no. 129, 1615–17; M. Jaffé 1989, no. 541, 1619–20.

82. *Isabella Brant,* recto, ca. 1621; *Rubens, Helena Fourment, and Their Son,* verso, ca. 1638

Black and red chalk, heightened with white, the eyes retouched in pen and black ink, the nose in brush and red body color, on light gray-brown paper, recto; black and red chalk, verso, 381 x 294 mm (15 x 11½ in.)

The British Museum, London (1893.7.31.21)

PROVENANCE: Prosper Henry Lankrink (1628?–1692), London (Lugt 2090); Sir John Thornhill (1675–1734); Jonathan Richardson Sr. (1665–1745), London (Lugt 2184; his annotation in pen and ink on a strip of paper, now lost, attached to the verso: "No 27 Given me by S^r^. Ja:Thornhill. Oct 1724. JR"[1]; Earl Spencer (1734–1783), Althorp (Lugt 1531); R. S. Holford (1808–1892), London (his sale, London, Christie's, July 11–14, 1893, lot 668); purchased for the British Museum on July 31, 1893.

LITERATURE: R., vol. 5, no. 1500; Hind 1923, p. 29, no. 92, pl. XI; Glück and Haberditzl 1928, no. 160, pl. 160; Held 1959, no. 103, pl. 115, pp. 33, 77; Burchard and d'Hulst 1963, no. 135, pl. 135; Kuznetsov 1974, pl. 103; Heiden 1982, p. 12, fig. 7; Vlieghe 1983, p. 106; Held 1986, no. 149, pl. 154; Liedtke 1984, vol. 1, pp. 181–82; Vlieghe 1987, no. 75a, fig. 38 (recto), no. 139a, fig. 190 (verso), p. 110, under no. 102a; White 1987, pp. 61, 65, pl. 84.

EXHIBITIONS: London 1977a, no. 154, ill.; London 1984, no. 87, ill.

The portraits of Rubens's first wife, Isabella Brant, and his second wife, Helena Fourment, and their children are among Rubens's most admired drawings, and rightly so. They reflect a deep personal affection for the sitters and a wonderful freshness of observation. The largest group of drawings rendering Rubens's immediate family members is today in the Albertina, Vienna.

This careful, intimate drawing of Isabella Brant (1591–1626) is highly finished, almost as if Rubens considered it an independent work. With a slight smile, she is observing her husband of many years sketching her portrait. Rubens beautifully captured her essential features, especially the large dimples in her cheeks, creating a vivid portrait full of life.[2] Isabella was the mother of their two sons, Albert (1614–1657) and Nicolaas Rubens (1618–1655), whose portraits Rubens drew repeatedly; three studies of Nicolaas in the Albertina, Vienna, are in the present exhibition (cat. nos. 81, 85, 86). Isabella died on June 20, 1626, probably from the plague that swept through Antwerp. How deeply Rubens mourned her loss is expressed in a letter he wrote to Pierre Dupuy in Paris on July 15, 1626: "Truly I have lost an excellent companion, whom one could love—indeed had to love, with good reason—as having none of the faults of her sex. She had no capricious moods, and no feminine weaknesses, but was all goodness and honesty."[3]

This is Rubens's only portrait drawing of Isabella known today. None of Rubens's paintings of her follows it closely enough to be considered a specific preliminary study. The portraits in the Cleveland Museum of Art[4] and the Uffizi, Florence (fig. 128),[5] come closest; in both, however, Isabella wears a lower-cut dress, and one or both hands are included. In the Cleveland example, she appears closer in age to the young woman in the London drawing and the hairstyle is similar, but her head is tilted more to the left. In the Uffizi portrait, dated about 1625–26, close to the time of her death, she looks heavier and older. This latter version—in which Isabella looks straight at the viewer as in the drawing but wears a jeweled barrette—remained with Rubens.

Closer than any work by Rubens to the London drawing is a portrait by Anthony van Dyck, in which Isabella wears her hair swept back in the same manner. Van Dyck may have seen this study by Rubens or a related one and used it for his own portrait of Isabella. In Van Dyck's painting, she is seated in front of the portico of her house in Antwerp (fig. 127). As he took her likeness before his departure for Italy in October 1621, it is thought that he presented the portrait to Rubens as a parting gift.[6] Because of this association, the London sheet is usually dated about 1621.

In 1964 the drawing of Isabella Brant was lifted from its mount and an extraordinary discovery was made. On the verso is a full-length portrait of Rubens with his second wife, Helena Fourment, and one of their children out for a stroll. It is sketched much more freely than the recto, again in black with some red chalk. Rubens probably drew this later study in connection with the lifesize family group portrait now in The Metropolitan Museum of Art, New York (fig. 135).[7] Opinions vary on the sex of the child, who must be either the couple's first-born, Clara Johanna (b. January 18, 1632), or their youngest son, Peter Paul (b. March 1, 1637). Accordingly, the painting is dated either about 1632–33 or about 1639. The later date is preferred here, since another self-portrait drawing of the artist, now at Windsor Castle (cat. no. 89), that relates to the New York painting must date from his last years.

It is also interesting to note that Rubens picked up an earlier portrait drawing of his first wife, Isabella Brant, to jot down a compositional idea for another family portrait with his second wife, Helena Fourment. These two examples indicate that Rubens kept drawings of family members together and apparently revisited them for future portraits. It is well known that the portraits he painted of his family were primarily for his own enjoyment and that he proudly displayed them in his house. In his testament written in 1640, he specified that these paintings should remain with his children rather than be sold after his death. For this reason, the family portraits are not listed in his estate inventory; thus we have no idea how many paintings there might once have been.

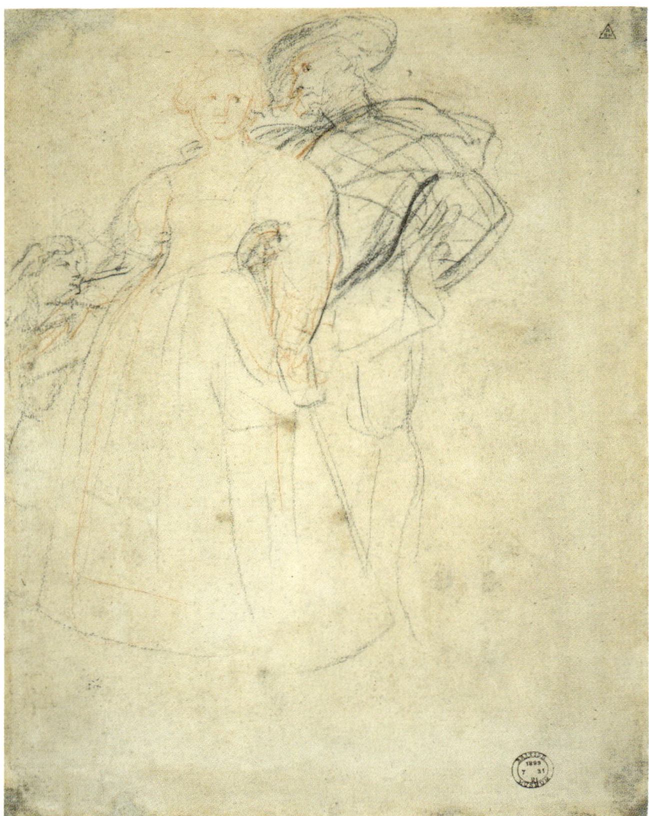

Cat. 82 verso

1. Jeremy Wood has pointed out that a misreading of Richardson's initials, "JR," as "JC" caused the misattribution of the drawing to the collection of John Clive. The Clive collection is omitted, therefore, from the provenance given here. (See Wood 1988, pp. 12–13, n. 26.)
2. Jonathan Richardson Sr., who owned catalogue number 82 in the eighteenth century, seems to have taken a different view of the drawing. He described a certain portrait drawing of Rubens's first wife—in all likelihood this one—as follows: "[her] face is one of the most disagreeable I have ever seen, and I am sure it is more so than was necessary for the likeness, however ugly she really was" (quoted from Wood 1988, p. 12).
3. Magurn 1955, pp. 135–36, letter 84.
4. Vlieghe 1987, no. 75, fig. 36, very early 1620s; M. Jaffé 1989, no. 786, 1624–25.
5. Vlieghe 1987, no. 76, figs. 40, 41, ca. 1626; M. Jaffé 1989, no. 875, 1626.
6. Félibien 1725, vol. 7, pp. 439–40. See also Muller 1989, p. 148, no. 6.
7. Vlieghe 1987, no. 141, figs. 195–97, ca. 1632–33; M. Jaffé 1989, no. 1401, ca. 1639. Vlieghe (1987, no. 139a) associated the drawing with the painting, today in Munich, of the artist walking in a garden with Helena Fourment and Nicolaas Rubens, a work now attributed to the studio of Rubens and dated ca. 1640 (Renger and Denk 2002, pp. 284–87, no. 313).

Fig. 127. Anthony van Dyck, *Isabella Brant,* ca. 1621. Oil on canvas, 153 x 120 cm ($60\frac{1}{4}$ x $47\frac{1}{4}$ in.). National Gallery of Art, Washington, D.C.; Andrew W. Mellon Collection (1937.1.47 [47])

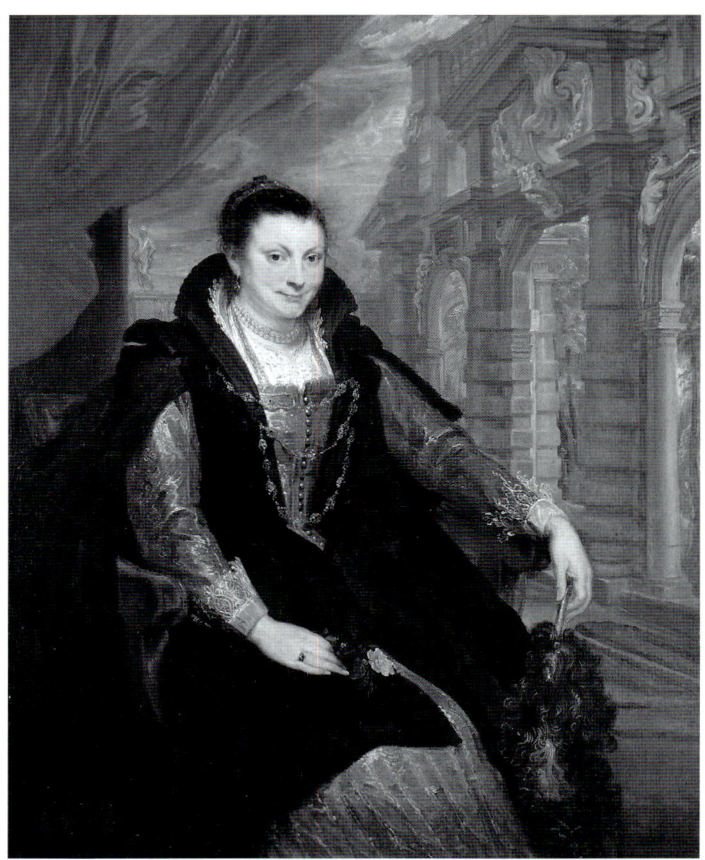

Fig. 128. Peter Paul Rubens, *Isabella Brant,* ca. 1625–26. Oil on panel, 86 x 62 cm ($33\frac{7}{8}$ x $24\frac{7}{16}$ in.). Galleria degli Uffizi, Florence (779)

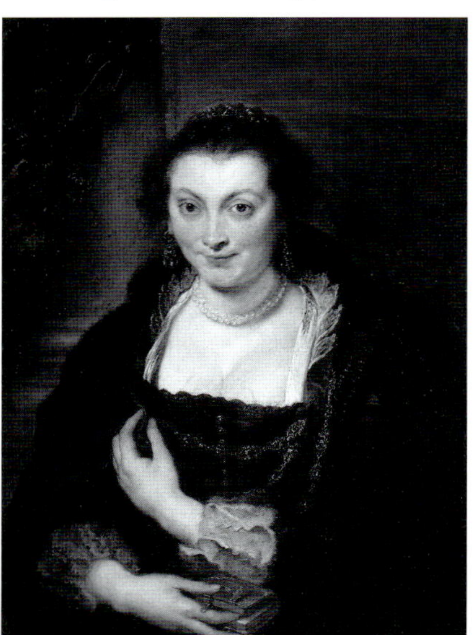

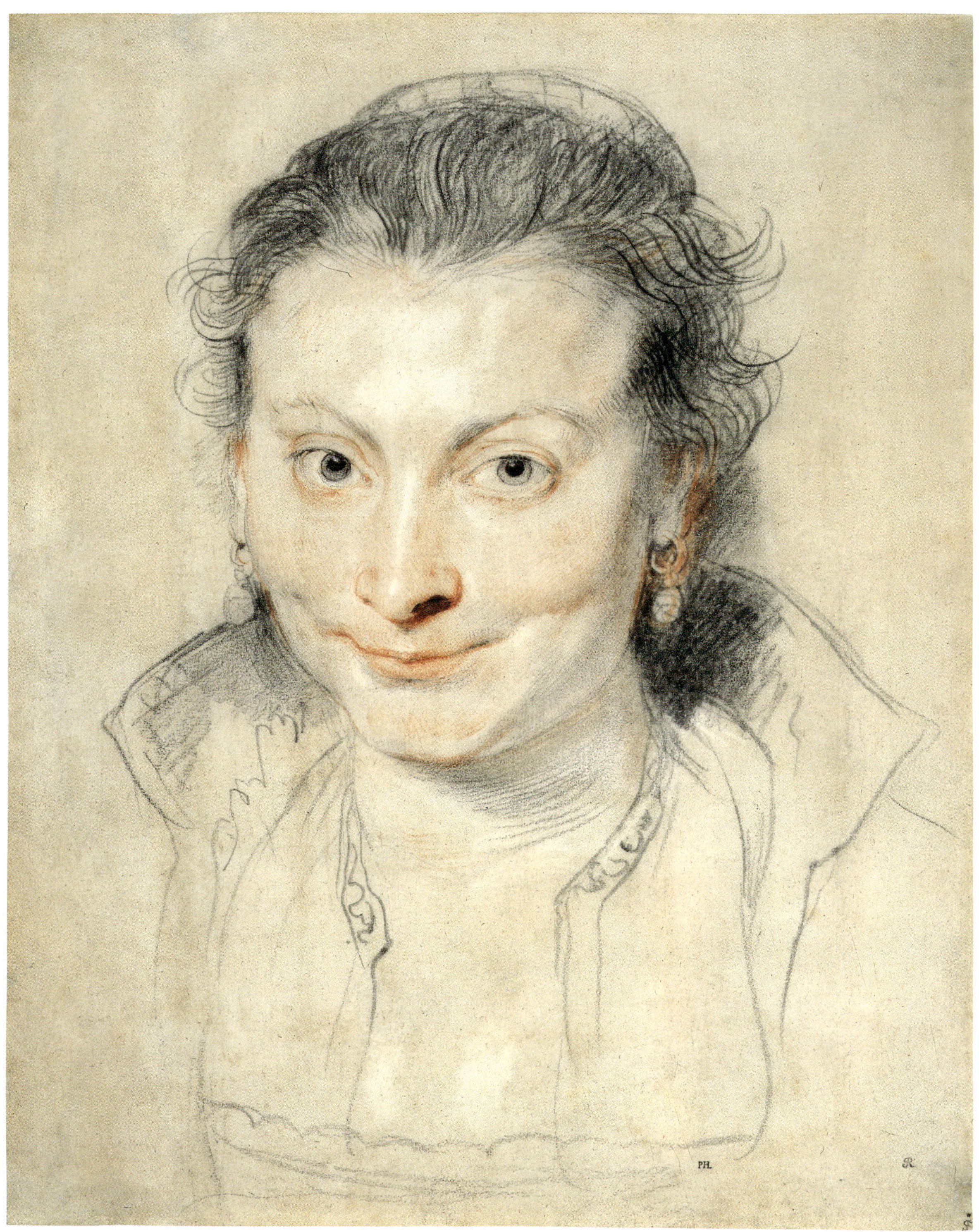

Cat. 82 recto

83. *Portrait of Susanna Fourment,* early 1620s

Black and red chalk, heightened with white chalk; pupils, eyebrows, and eyelashes strengthened with pen and dark brown ink, on brownish paper, 345 x 260 mm ($13\frac{3}{4}$ x $10\frac{1}{4}$ in.)
Annotated in red chalk at top left: *Suster van Heer Rubbens* (sister of Mr. Rubens); in pen and brown ink at bottom right: *P. P. Rubbens;* in pencil at bottom left: *No / 8*

Vienna, Albertina (17651)

PROVENANCE: Duke Albert of Sachsen-Teschen (1738–1822), Vienna (Lugt 174).

LITERATURE: R., vol. 5, no. 1506, pl. 420; Glück and Haberditzl 1928, no. 162, pl. 162; Kuznetsov 1974, pl. 117; Vlieghe 1987, no. 102a, fig. 113.

EXHIBITIONS: Vienna 1977b, no. 43, ill.; Washington–New York–Vienna 1984–86, no. 37, ill.; Sydney 2002, no. 53, ill.

This is one of sixteen portrait drawings by Rubens that are today in the collection of the Albertina, Vienna: all are executed in black and red chalk, heightened with white, and date from the 1620s. The young woman in this drawing appears not to have posed but, rather, to have observed the artist while he worked, not quite knowing what to expect. In its directness the study resembles the snapshots to which we are so accustomed today.

The study belongs to the well-known group of portraits that Rubens drew of his immediate family (see cat. nos. 81, 84–86). It is believed to represent Susanna Fourment (1599–1628) and serves as a reference for several of Rubens's portraits of her.[1] Susanna was an older sister of Helena Fourment, who became Rubens's second wife in 1630. The Fourment family and the Rubens family were linked through intermarriage in several ways. In 1617 Susanna married Raymond del Monte. In 1641 their only child, Clara del Monte, born in 1618, married Rubens's oldest son, Albert (1614–1657), from his first marriage, to Isabella Brant. (In 1620–21 Anthony van Dyck painted a sensitive portrait of Susanna Fourment and the young Clara del Monte [fig. 129].)[2] Susanna was also related to Rubens through Isabella Brant, Rubens's first wife: Susanna's eldest brother, Daniel Fourment (1592–1648), married Isabella's sister, Clara Brant.

The inscription in red chalk on the drawing, "Suster van Heer Rubbens," identifies the sitter as Rubens's sister. The inventory drawn up in 1822 after the death of the drawing's owner, Albert von Sachsen-Teschen, indicates the same.[3] However, the artist's sisters, Blandina (1564–1606) and Clara (1565–1580), died years before the drawing was made. The inscription has sometimes been interpreted, therefore, as a reference to Rubens's "sister-in-law" *(schoonzuster).*[4] However, Susanna, who died in 1628, would have become Rubens's sister-in-law only in 1630, after the artist's marriage to Helena Fourment.[5] When the inscription was added, after Rubens's death, Susanna could indeed be called his sister-in-law. Nonetheless, this matter remains puzzling.

Susanna Fourment was widowed in 1621, and in 1622 she married Arnold Lunden, a friend of Rubens's, whose estate contained many Rubens paintings, including four of Susanna. The present drawing is not close enough to any of the known painted portraits of Susanna to be considered a specific preliminary study. The study probably dates from the early 1620s, about the time of Susanna's marriage to Lunden.

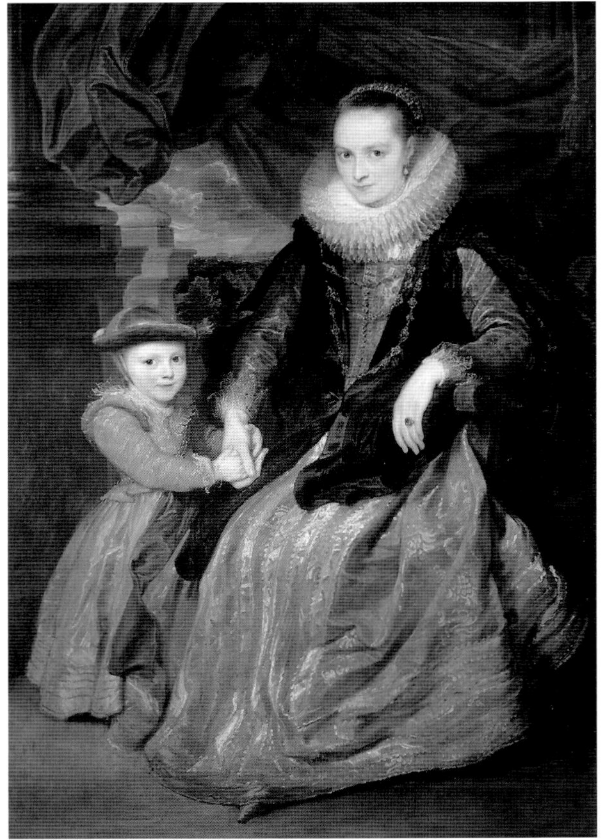

Fig. 129. Anthony van Dyck, *Susanna Fourment and Her Daughter,* 1620–21. Oil on canvas, 172.7 x 117.5 cm (68 x $46\frac{1}{4}$ in.). National Gallery of Art, Washington, D.C.; Andrew W. Mellon Collection (1937.1.48 [48])

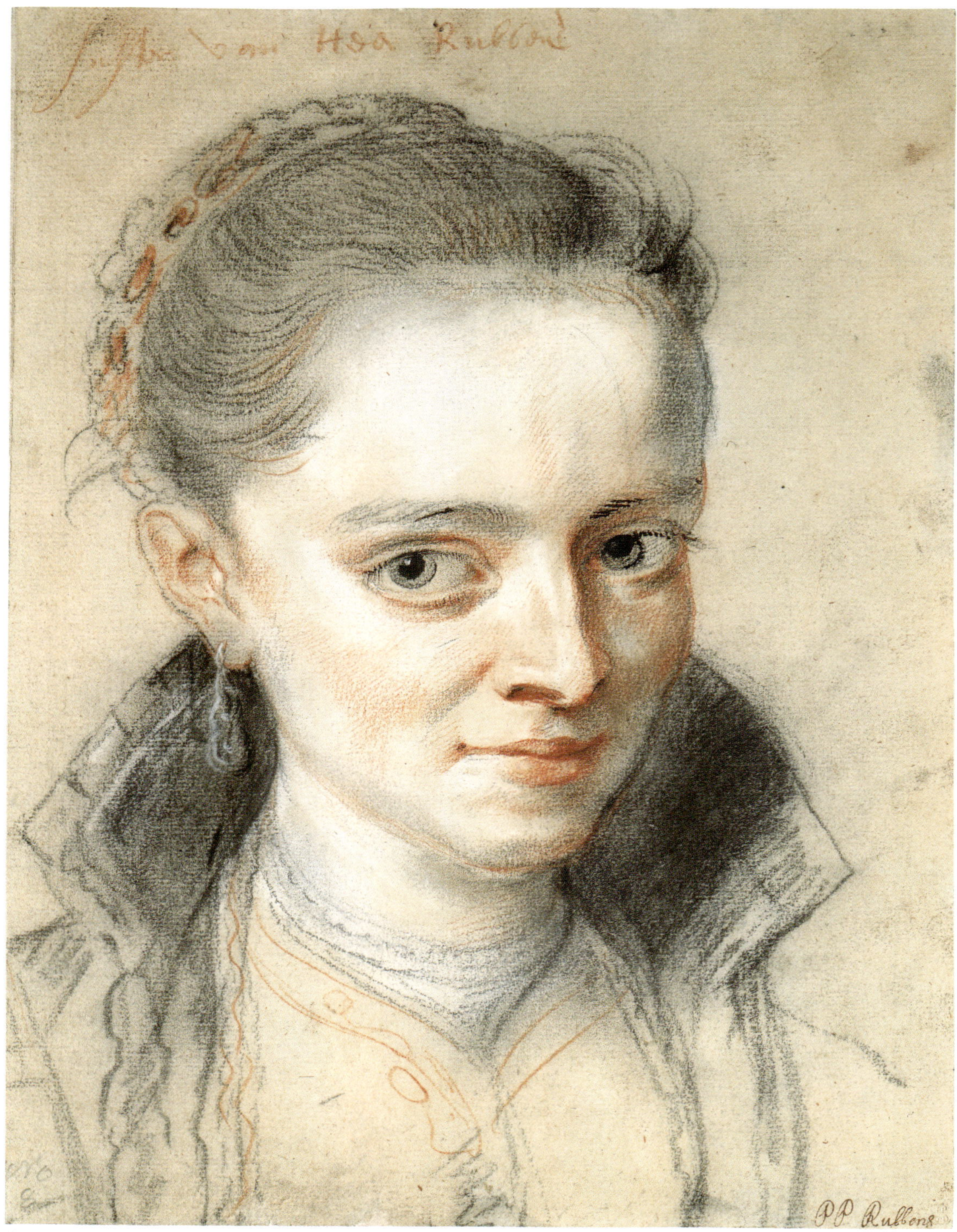

Cat. 83

1. For the date of Susanna's death, see Vlieghe 1983, p. 108.
2. Washington 1990–91, no. 21, ill.
3. The inventory listed "Seize Portraits parmi lesquels ceux du Duc de Buckingham et son Epouse, celui de la Reine Marie de Medicis, et celui de la Soeur de Rubens—tous aux deux Crayons." Mitsch in Vienna 1977b, pp. viii–ix.
4. Walter Liedtke (1984, vol. 1, pp. 173, 174, n. 4) pointed out that Susanna had earlier been the sister-in-law of Rubens's sister-in-law Clara Brant and that "the term 'sister' is, in any case, broadly employed."
5. An old annotation on the old mount of another Rubens drawing, now in the Museum Boijmans Van Beuningen, Rotterdam, refers to the sitter as "Mademoiselle forment soeur de la seconde femme de Rubens" (Miss Fourment, sister of Rubens's second wife). Today the woman in the drawing (Rotterdam 2001, no. 2, color ill.) is identified only as a member of the Fourment family. The sitter in the Rotterdam drawing and the sitter in the present sheet do not seem to be the same woman.

84. *Lady-In-Waiting to Infanta Isabella (Portrait of Clara Serena Rubens?)*, ca. 1623

Black chalk, some red chalk in the face, heightened and slightly corrected (top of hair) with white chalk; eyes, eyebrows, nostrils, and mouth strengthened with pen and dark brown ink, on brownish paper, 353 x 283 mm (13 3/4 x 11 1/8 in.)
Annotated in red chalk at top: *Staetdochter van de Infante tot Brussel;* in pen and brown ink at bottom right: *P P Rubbens;* at bottom left: *No / 4.*

Albertina, Vienna (8259)

PROVENANCE: Duke Albert of Sachsen-Teschen (1738–1822), Vienna (Lugt 174).

LITERATURE: R., vol. 5, no. 1541, pl. 426; Glück and Haberditzl 1928, no. 165, pl. 165; Held 1959, no. 106, pl. 116, colorpl. facing p. 32, pp. 33, 135, under no. 98; Burchard and d'Hulst 1963, no. 137, pl. 137; Kuznetsov 1974, pl. 104; Held 1986, no. 162, colorpl. 3.

EXHIBITION: Vienna 1977b, no. 38, ill.

This is a formal and rather serious portrait. As the inscription at the top of the sheet notes, the subject is a "staet dochter," or an unmarried young girl of noble origin who belonged to the entourage of a noble lady.[1] The noblewoman in this case, again according to the inscription, was the Infanta Isabella in Brussels. Nonetheless, it has been suggested time and time again that the girl represented in the drawing is Clara Serena (1611–1623), Rubens's oldest daughter from his first marriage, to Isabella Brant. Unfortunately, no portrait that can securely be said to depict Clara Serena seems to have survived.[2] As several scholars have noted, however, one can detect a family resemblance between the girl depicted here and Isabella Brant (see cat. no. 82).[3] Furthermore, the girl appears in several portraits by or after Rubens. In The Metropolitan Museum of Art, New York, there is a portrait from the Rubens school of very much the same young girl, though in a simple dress; it was probably done after a lost Rubens work in oil.[4] Indeed, the girl in the Metropolitan Museum's painting so resembles the girl in the present drawing that it has been suggested that the drawing was the prototype for Rubens's lost painting.[5] In addition, a portrait probably painted in the Rubens studio (fig. 130) is evidently based on the drawing. Finally, Rubens's vivacious

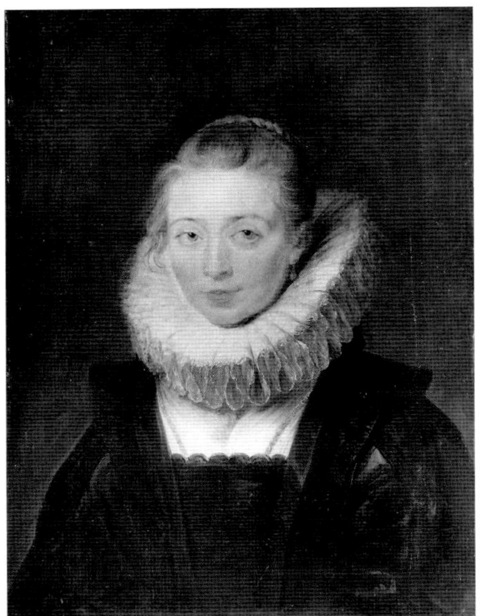

Fig. 130. Studio of Peter Paul Rubens, *Portrait of Lady-in-Waiting to the Infanta Isabella (Portrait of Clara Serena?)*, ca. 1623. Oil on panel, 64 x 48 cm (25 3/16 x 18 7/8 in.). The State Hermitage Museum, Saint Petersburg (478)

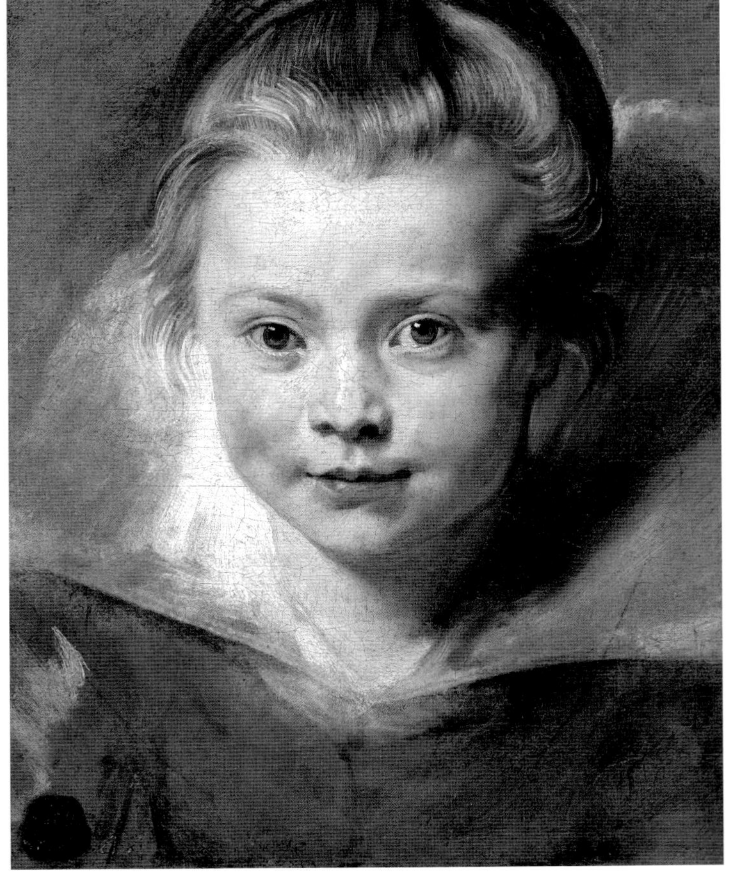

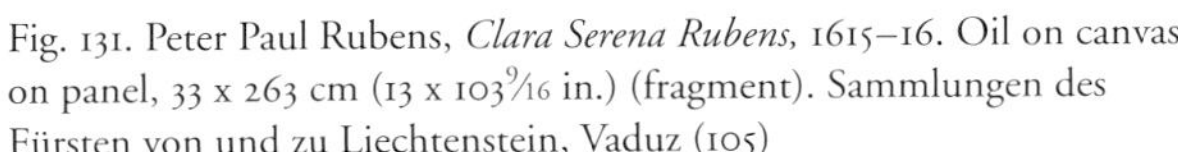

Fig. 131. Peter Paul Rubens, *Clara Serena Rubens,* 1615–16. Oil on canvas on panel, 33 x 263 cm (13 x 103 9/16 in.) (fragment). Sammlungen des Fürsten von und zu Liechtenstein, Vaduz (105)

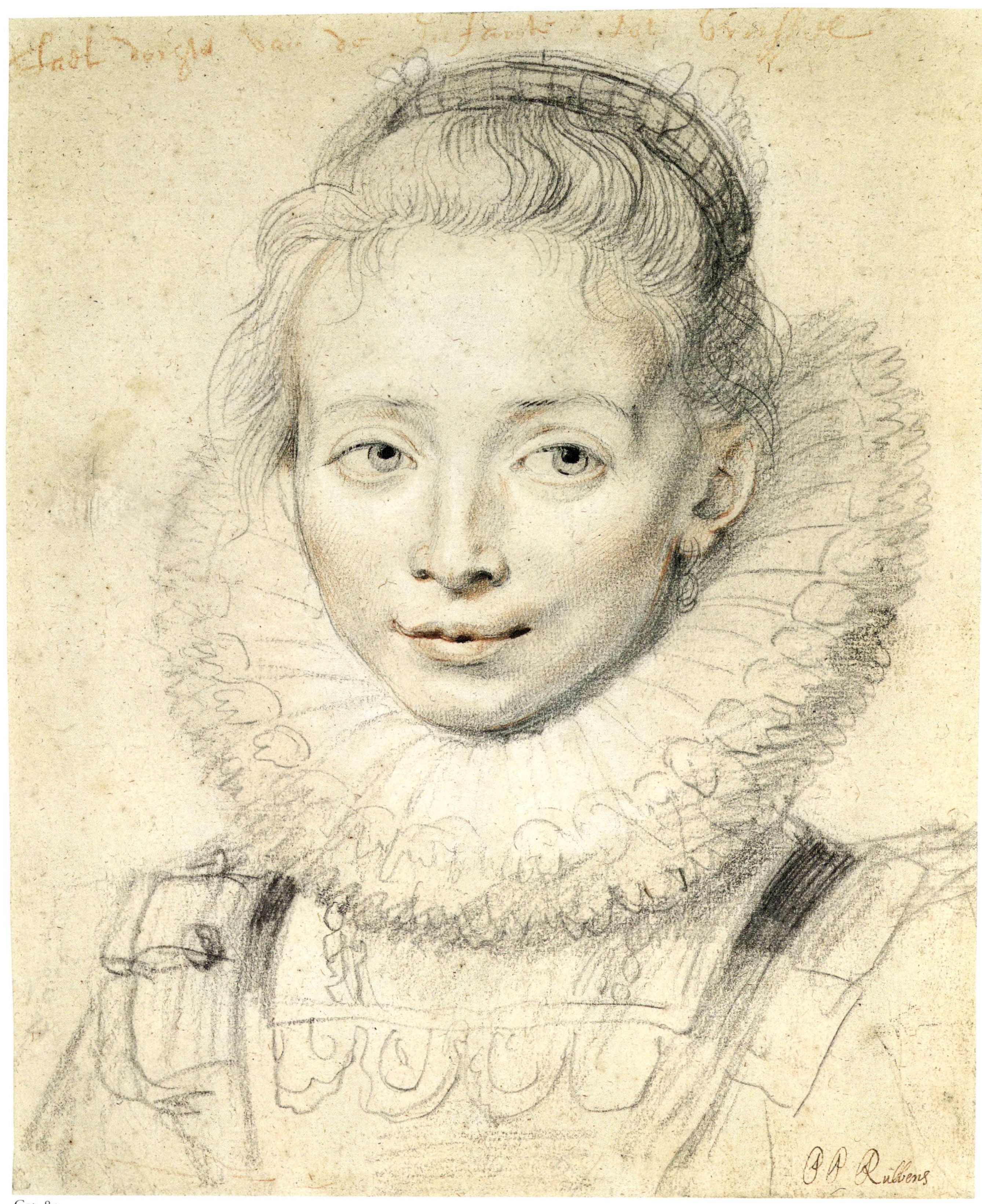

Cat. 84

portrait of a young girl now in the Liechtenstein Museum, Vienna (fig. 131), also seems to depict the same model, though at a younger age.[6] This repeated portrayal of apparently the same sitter suggests close personal contact between the artist and the model. Perhaps the infanta did Rubens a favor and accepted his daughter as a lady-in-waiting in her entourage in Brussels (the young Rubens himself had served as a page in the house of the Countess de Lalaing).[7]

The annotation in pen at the lower right of the sheet, "P P Rubbens," and the inclusion of the drawing among the group of intimate portraits of the artist and his family kept together after his death support the notion that the sitter was one of Rubens's family members or acquaintances.[8] It is not strange that the red-chalk annotation at the top of the sheet gives a general rather than a specific reference to the sitter. The author of the inscription (and of similar inscriptions on other sheets in the ensemble of family portraits) seems to have been a friend or close acquaintance of the family. Here, as with the portraits of Rubens's sons Nicolaas (cat. nos. 85, 86) and Albert, there was apparently no need to identify the sitter by name.[9] Her honored position as lady-in-waiting to the infanta was what mattered.

Stylistically, the present drawing is characteristic of Rubens's portrait drawings from the early to mid-1620s, such as the other portrait drawings in the Albertina (see cat. nos. 77, 81, 83) and the study of Isabella Brant now in London (cat. no. 82). This again corroborates—or at least does not contradict—the suggestion that Clara Serena is depicted on this sheet. However, all the evidence for the identification is circumstantial. For the moment, though, we keep open the possibility that in this drawing Rubens documented his daughter Clara Serena embarking on a new phase in her life as a "staet dochter."

1. The annotation has traditionally been read as "sael dochter van de infante tot brussel." For the term "staet dochter," see R. van der Meulen, J. A. N. Knuttel, and J. H. van Lessen, eds., *Woordenboek der Nederlandsche taal,* vol. 15 (The Hague and Leiden, 1940), p. 287.
2. As Held observed, a portrait of Clara Serena on panel was listed in 1639 in the estate of Jan Brant, Rubens's father-in-law and the girl's grandfather (see Held 1959, p. 138, under no. 106; see also Denucé 1932, p. 54).
3. See Liedtke 1984, vol. 1, pp. 231, 232, n. 8.
4. Ibid., pp. 231–33, vol. 2, pl. 88 *(Portrait of a Young Girl, possibly Clara Serena Rubens, the Artist's Daughter).* Liedtke also mentions an inferior copy of the painting, or another version, in the Musée Diocésain, Liège.
5. Held 1959, p. 138, under no. 106.
6. For the Saint Petersburg portrait, see Vienna 1977b, p. 92, ill. For the Liechtenstein portrait, see K.d.K., ed. Oldenbourg 1921, no. 135R; M. Jaffé 1989, no. 333, 1615–16.
7. Held 1959, p. 138, under no. 106.
8. See cat. nos. 70, 71, 81, 83, 84, 86, 87.
9. For red-chalk annotations, see cat. nos. 58, 77, 78, 83, 84, and Vienna 1997b, nos. 37, 40, ill.

85. *Nicolaas Rubens Wearing a Red Felt Cap,* 1625–27

Red and black chalk, stumped, heightened with white chalk on brownish paper, 292 x 232 mm (11½ x 9⅛ in.)

Albertina, Vienna (8266)

PROVENANCE: Duke Albert of Sachsen-Teschen (1738–1822), Vienna (Lugt 174).

LITERATURE: R., vol. 5, no. 1524; Glück and Haberditzl 1928, no. 163, pl. 163; Held 1959, no. 109, pl. 118; Burchard and d'Hulst 1963, p. 198, under no. 126; Held 1986, no. 164, pl. 163; Vlieghe 1987, no. 143, fig. 205.

EXHIBITIONS: Vienna 1977b, no. 41, ill.; Vienna–Amsterdam 1989–90, no. 51, ill.; New York and other cities 1997–99, no. 37, ill.; Pittsburgh–Louisville–Fresno 2002, no. 53, ill.

The boy portrayed on this sheet has traditionally been identified as Nicolaas Rubens (1618–1655), the younger of Rubens's sons with his first wife, Isabella Brant. This identification seems confirmed by the close resemblance of the boy in the drawing to the portrait of Nicolaas in Rubens's *Albert and Nicolaas Rubens* (fig. 132), painted shortly after Isabella died in June 1626.[1]

It appears that Rubens drew the study without a specific painting in mind. The drawing may have originated simply with a father quietly observing his son.[2] The collection of the Albertina is especially rich in highly personal portraits that Rubens drew of members of his family. In all likelihood the

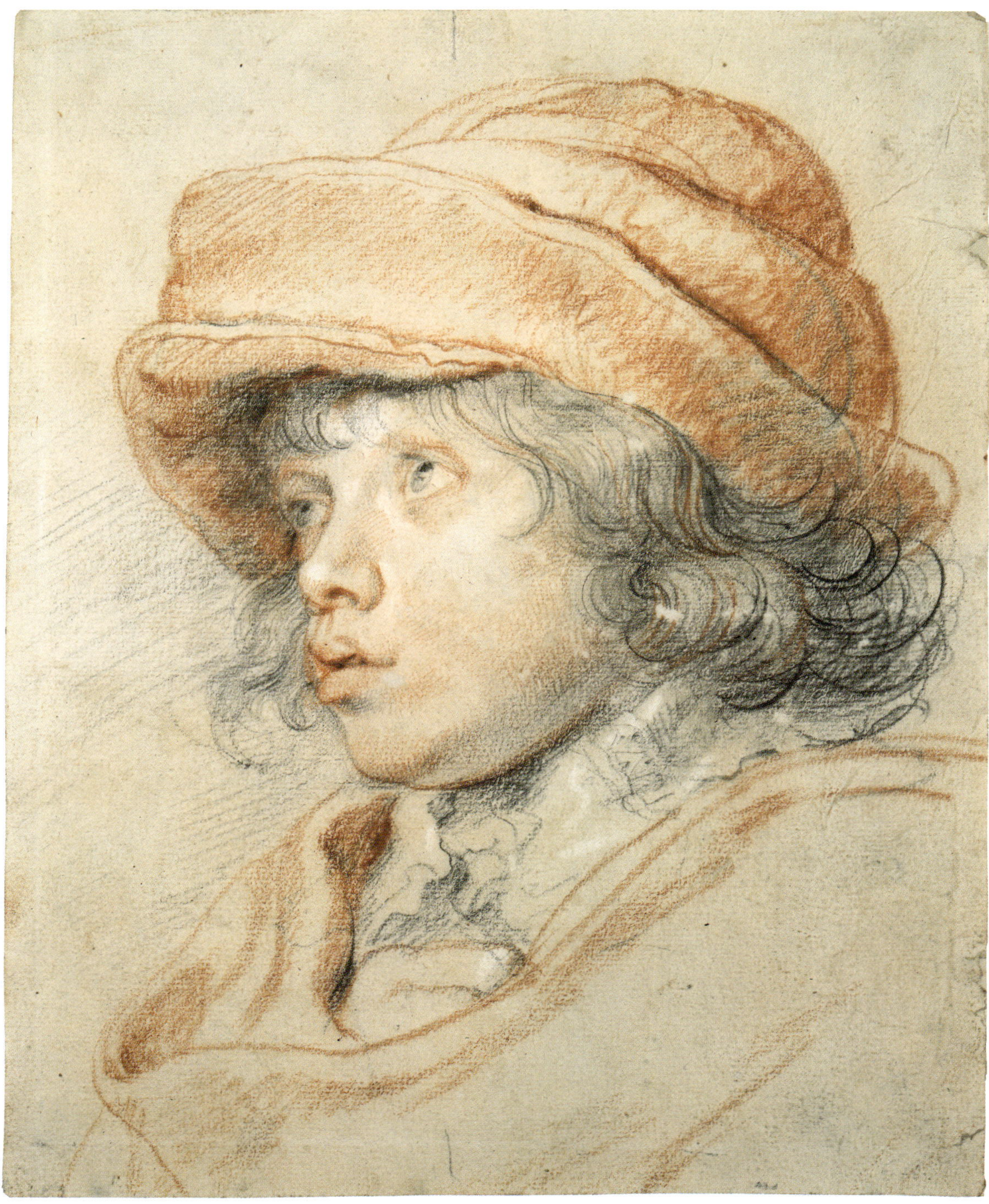

Cat. 85

artist kept these drawings together; after his death many of them remained together, and they entered the Albertina as a group. (For two other drawings of Nicolaas in the Albertina, see catalogue numbers 81 and 86.) The traditional dating of the study to 1625–27 is based on Nicolaas's age in the drawing, which appears to be between seven and nine.

1. K.d.K., ed. Oldenbourg 1921, no. 281; M. Jaffé 1989, no. 879, 1626–27. Today the painting is in the Liechtenstein Museum, Vienna.
2. A copy after the drawing, incorrectly attributed to Antoine Watteau (1684–1721), was last recorded with Stephen Mazoh, New York. See Rosenberg and Prat 1996, vol. 3, rejected drawings, no. R 428, ill., as 17th-century Flemish.

86. *Nicolaas Rubens*, ca. 1626–27

Black chalk, heightened with white chalk, on brownish paper, 228 x 181 mm (8 15/16 x 7 1/8 in.)
Annotated in pen and brown ink at bottom right: *P. P. Rubbens*

Albertina, Vienna (17648)

PROVENANCE: Duke Albert of Sachsen-Teschen (1738–1822), Vienna (Lugt 174).

LITERATURE: R., vol. 5, no. 1523; Glück and Haberditzl 1928, no. 159, pl. 159; Held 1959, no. 108, pl. 117, pp. 13–14, 29, 33, 77, 135, under no. 98, 139, under no. 109; Burchard and d'Hulst 1963, no. 138, p. 198, under 126; Kuznetsov 1974, pl. 125; Heiden 1982, p. 31, fig. 24; Held 1986, no. 163, pl. 162; Vlieghe 1987, no. 142b, fig. 204.

EXHIBITIONS: Vienna 1977b, no. 42, ill.; Sydney 2002, no. 52, ill.

This quick chalk study of Nicolaas Rubens (1618–1655), the artist's younger son from his first marriage, prepares the boy's portrait with his older brother in *Albert and Nicolaas Rubens* (fig. 132).[1] The painting of the two brothers did not appear in the inventory drawn up after the death of Rubens's first wife, Isabella Brant, on June 20, 1626.[2] Its absence indicates that Rubens painted the double portrait only after she passed away—most likely soon thereafter, in 1626–27. Rubens kept the painting all his life and bequeathed it to Albert, who died in 1657.

On the sheet Rubens drew Nicolaas in much the same pose as he later appeared in the painting, but not yet as focused. In the painting the boy, whose hair is a bit more tousled than in the drawing, watches and restrains a goldfinch fluttering in front of him, attached to a perch with bells, which he holds in his right hand. (Depictions of children playing with captive birds can be found in other Flemish paintings of the time.)[3] A similar study from life that Rubens drew of Albert in the pose required for the painting is lost but known from a copy last recorded in the collection of Count Duchastel-Dandelot, in Brussels.[4] In the final portrait Rubens contrasted the carefree playfulness of Nicolaas with the studiousness of Albert.

The drawing bears an annotation in pen and brown ink, "P. P. Rubbens," at the lower right, familiar from a number of drawings in the Albertina (see cat. nos. 70, 71, 81, 83, 84, 87; see also cat. no. 99).[5]

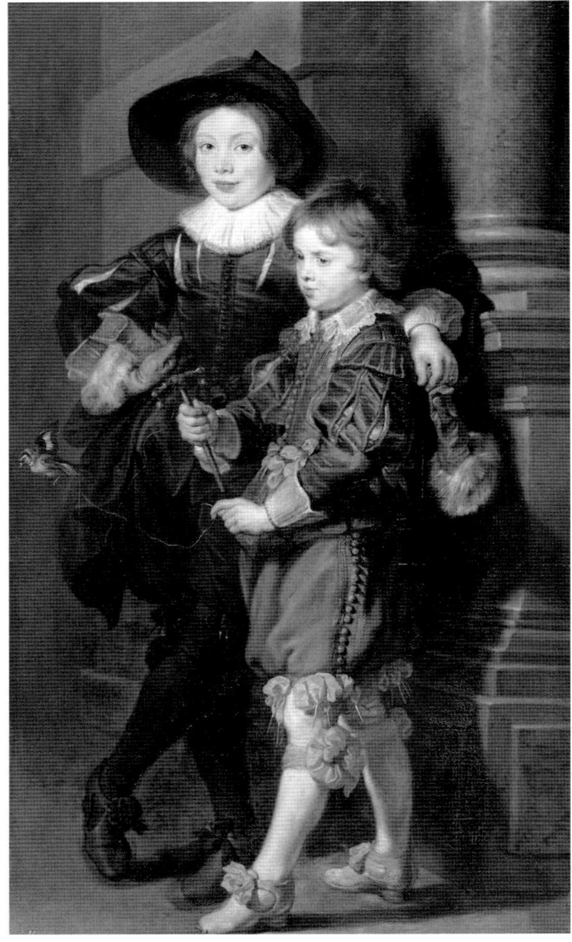

Fig. 132. Peter Paul Rubens, *Albert and Nicolaas Rubens,* ca. 1626. Oil on panel, 158 x 92 cm (62 3/16 x 36 1/4 in.). Sammlungen des Fürsten von und zu Liechtenstein, Vaduz (114)

1. K.d.K., ed. Oldenbourg 1921, no. 281, ca. 1625; M. Jaffé 1989, no. 879, 1626–27.
2. Rooses 1895, pp. 154–88.
3. For various interpretations of the game with the bird, see Vlieghe 1987, pp. 177, 178, n. 4, under no. 142.
4. Ibid., no. 142a, fig. 203.
5. Glück and Haberditzl (1928) thought that the "signature" was added when the drawings were still in Rubens's estate. However, some annotations of this type appear on drawings that have been cut, such as two of the studies for the Ildefonso altarpiece (cat. nos. 71, 72), which implies, as Held reasoned (1986, p. 124, under no. 144), that the annotations were added at a later time.

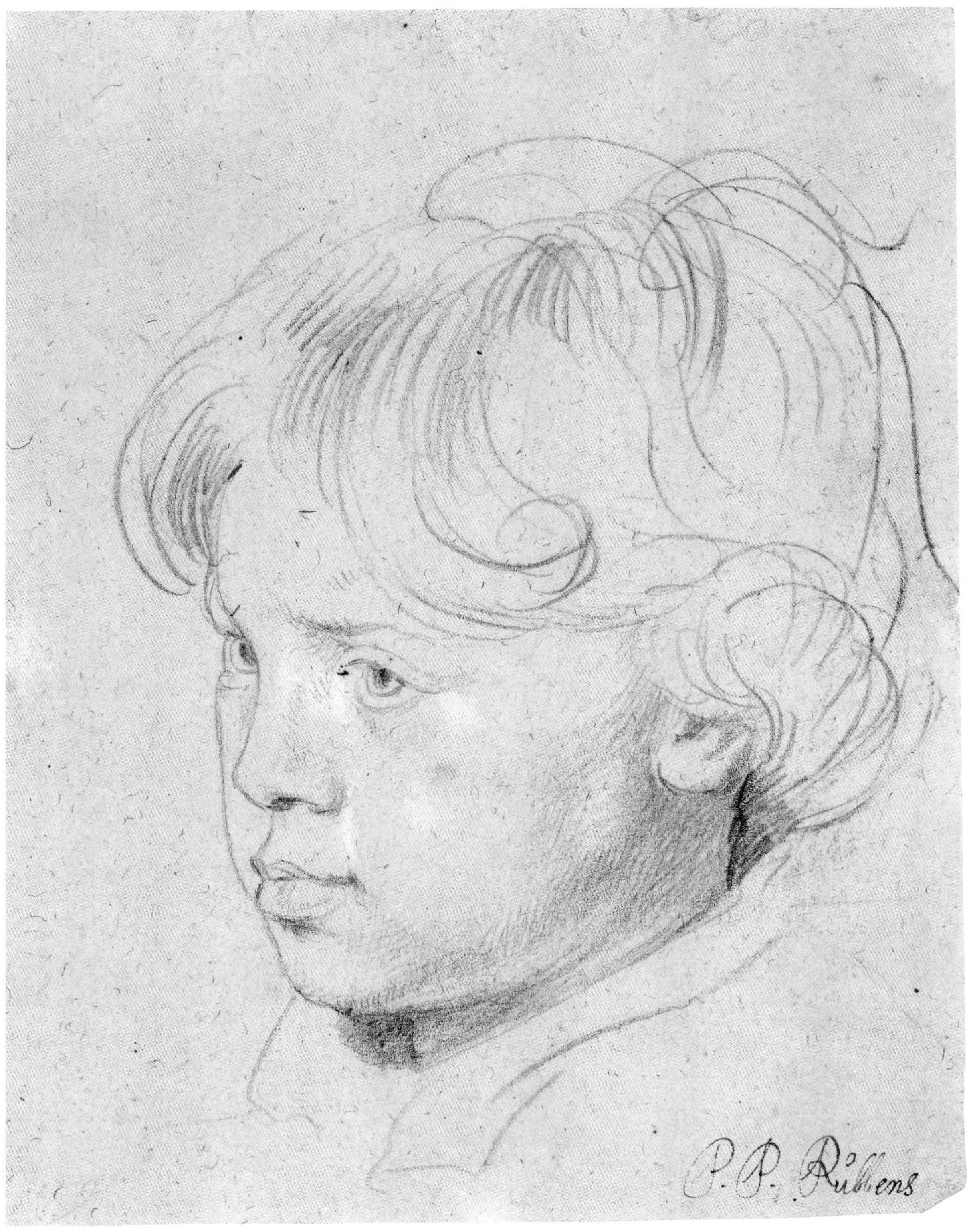

Cat. 86

87. *Portrait of George Gerbier, Son of Balthasar Gerbier,* 1629–30

Black and some red chalk, traces of heightening with white chalk, eyes, mouth, and nose strengthened with pen and dark brown ink, on brownish paper, 288 x 219 mm (11$\frac{5}{16}$ x 8$\frac{5}{8}$ in.)
Annotated in pen and brown ink at bottom right: *P P Rubbens*

Albertina, Vienna (8267)

PROVENANCE: Duke Albert of Sachsen-Teschen (1738–1822), Vienna (Lugt 174).

LITERATURE: R., vol. 5, no. 1574; Glück and Haberditzl 1928, no. 180, pl. 180; Burchard and d'Hulst 1963, pp. 229, under no. 146, 266–67, under no. 172; G. Martin 1970, pp. 119–21; Stechow 1973, p. 13, fig. 5; Held 1986, pp. 31, 124, under no. 144.

EXHIBITION: Vienna 1977b, no. 46, ill.

In 1629 Philip IV appointed Rubens secretary of his privy council in the Netherlands to negotiate the "cessation of armes" on his and the Archduchess Isabella's behalf. When the artist arrived in London in early June 1629 to continue peace negotiations with England, he stayed at York House in the Strand, the Duke of Buckingham's residence in London. Balthasar Gerbier (1592–1667) and his family resided there as well. Gerbier, a Flemish miniaturist, had come in England in 1616 and entered the service of the Duke of Buckingham. Rubens had first met him in 1625 in Paris, during the festivities for the wedding of Marie de Médicis's daughter to Charles I. In 1626 Gerbier had helped broker the sale of Rubens's collection of antique statues, gems, and coins to Buckingham.[1]

During his stay at York House Rubens of course saw the two works that the late Duke of Buckingham had commissioned from him: the equestrian portrait (see cat. no. 77 for the preliminary drawing) and the ceiling decoration representing the *Glorification of the Duke of Buckingham* (both destroyed in a fire in 1949). Rubens also found time to paint. The most impressive work that he created during his stay is the allegorical painting *Minerva Defending Peace from Mars (War and Peace),* which the artist presented to Charles I in 1630 (fig. 133).[2] The gift was less a personal gesture than an official statement from the painter-diplomat. On March 3, 1630, the king knighted Rubens for his services, at the palace of Whitehall, where the *Minerva* hung in the Bear Gallery.

In the center of the painting Minerva repels Mars, to prevent him from harming the seated woman, a personification of Peace. At the right Rubens included the torch-bearing Hymen, god of marriage. For that figure he used the present drawing, which is believed to be a portrait of George Gerbier, Balthasar's oldest son. Hymen holds a crown over the head of a young girl, probably a likeness of Elizabeth Gerbier, the oldest daughter.[3] The little girl holding grapes in the foreground has been identified as Susan, another of Gerbier's children. Rubens's preliminary study for the figure is in Weimar.[4]

Although Rubens made use of the drawings believed to represent Gerbier's children in the allegorical painting of *Minerva,*

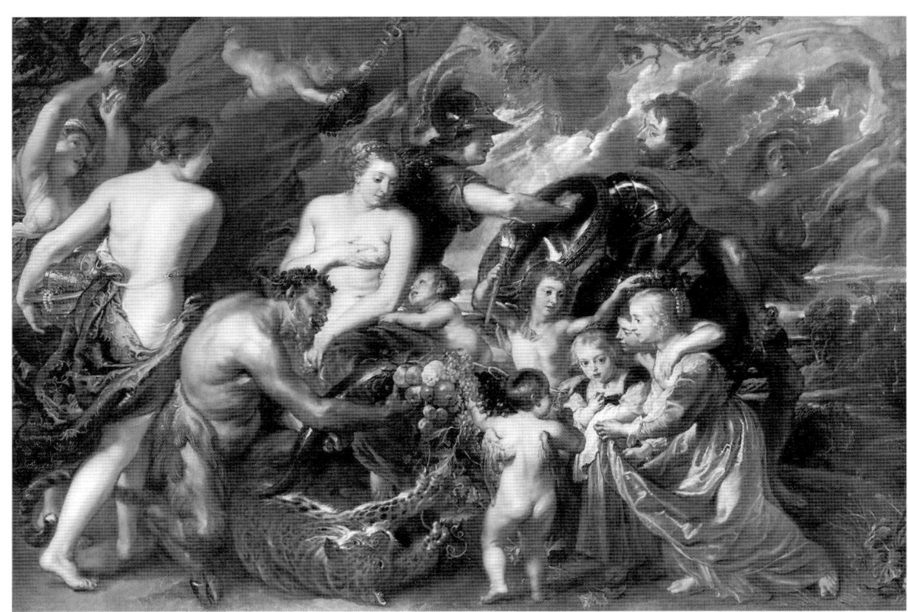

Fig. 133. Peter Paul Rubens, *Minerva Defending Peace from Mars (War and Peace),* 1629–30. Oil on panel, 203.5 x 298 cm (80$\frac{1}{8}$ x 117$\frac{5}{16}$ in.). National Gallery, London (NG 46)

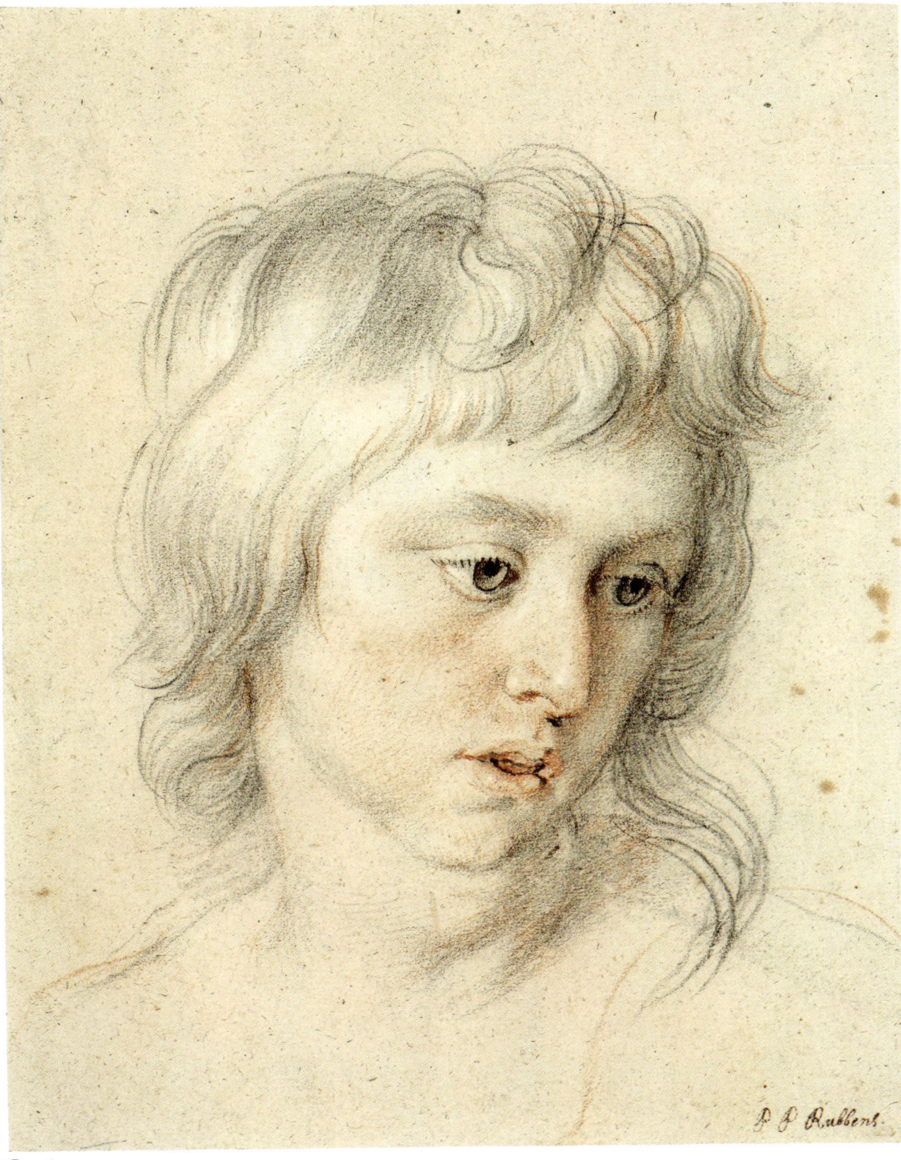

Cat. 87

he probably sketched them originally for a more personal reason. He may have prepared them initially for his family portrait of Deborah Kip, Gerbier's wife, with four of her children, now in the National Gallery of Art, Washington, D.C.[5] It has been suggested, rather plausibly, that Rubens presented the painting to Balthasar Gerbier in gratitude for his and his wife's hospitality.[6] Rubens worked on the Gerbier family portrait and the *Minerva* during the same months in London, and it would not have been exceptional for him to use his drawings of the Gerbier children in both contexts. (When required, Rubens did the same with drawings of his own children [see cat. nos. 59, 81].)

For the annotation "P P Rubbens" in pen and brown ink at the lower right, see catalogue number 86.

1. After Buckingham's assassination in 1628 Gerbier remained at York House as keeper of the duke's collection and entered the service of King Charles I as a secret diplomatic agent.
2. K.d.K., ed. Oldenbourg 1921, no. 312; M. Jaffé, 1989, no. 969, 1629–30. Two cursory chalk sketches of Hymen and the children and putto immediately surrounding him, drawn on the same sheet, are in Rotterdam (Rotterdam 2001, no. 23, ill.).
3. The painting is associated with a drawing in the Hermitage, Saint Petersburg, in which she looks slightly older (Held 1986, no. 178, pl. 175, ca. 1629–30). Gerbier had three sons and five daughters, but their dates of birth are unknown.
4. Glück and Haberditzl 1928, no. 179, pl. 179. According to Jeremy Wood (letter of August 6, 2001), the study was possibly worked up in the face and hair by Richard Cosway.
5. M. Jaffé 1989, no. 976, ca. 1630.
6. The painting was not listed in Rubens's estate in 1640. Gerbier returned to Flanders with his family in 1631 and stayed in contact with Rubens. Michael Jaffé (1981, p. 75) identified the older girl as Susan, the younger as Mary, and the baby as Charles.

88. *Study for the Portrait of Helena Fourment,* ca. 1631

Black and touches of red chalk, heightened with white, 488 x 320 mm (19¼ x 12⅝ in.)
Annotated in pencil at bottom left: *470 a*

Museum Boijmans Van Beuningen, Rotterdam (V45)

PROVENANCE: Gabriel Huquier (1695–1772), Paris (Lugt 1285); Count Moriz von Fries (1777–1826), Vienna (Lugt 2903); Sir Thomas Lawrence (1769–1830), London (Lugt 2445); H. Wellesley, Oxford (sale, London, Sotheby, June 25, 1866, no. 2392); J. P. Heseltine (b. 1843), London (Lugt 1507); Franz Koenigs (1881–1941), Haarlem (Lugt 1023a; acquired in 1927); D. G. van Beuningen (1877–1955), Rotterdam, acquired in 1940 and donated to the Boymans Museum Foundation in 1941.

LITERATURE: Glück and Haberditzl 1928, no. 193, pl. 193; Held 1959, no. 115, pl. 129; Heiden 1982, p. 22, fig. 12; Held 1986, no. 201, pl. 193; Vlieghe 1987, no. 96a, fig. 86; Goodman 1992, fig. 36.

EXHIBITIONS: New York–Fort Worth–Cleveland 1990–91, no. 25, ill.; Rotterdam 2001, no. 24, ill.

On December 6, 1630, Rubens, fifty-three years old and four years a widower, married Helena Fourment (1614–1673), then sixteen. (Helena was the same age as Rubens's first-born son, Albert.) She was the daughter of the well-to-do Antwerp tapestry and silk merchant Daniel Fourment. The Antwerp humanist Gaspar Gevaert (Gevartius) praised her in a poem in which he compared her to the beautiful Greek Helena whom Zeuxis had painted; he added that, thanks to Rubens's art, the beauty of the Antwerp Helena was far greater. Cardinal-Infante Ferdinand seconded this opinion; in 1639 he wrote to his brother, King Philip IV of Spain, that she was "without doubt the most beautiful woman to be found in Flanders."[1]

In this large drawing the artist rendered his young wife seated in a chair and apparently lost in thought. It is one of Rubens's earliest portraits of Helena, and she seems comfortable sitting for her husband. Her ease was important to Rubens, who wrote to his friend the French scholar Nicolas-Claude Fabri de Peiresc (1580–1637) in 1634, "I have taken a young wife of honest but middle-class family, although everyone tried to persuade me to make a Court marriage. But I feared pride, that inherent vice of nobility, particularly in that sex, and that is why I chose one who would not blush to see me take my brushes in hand."[2]

The study served as a preliminary drawing for Rubens's stately *Helena Fourment* (fig. 134),[3] in which, it has been said, the artist depicted his wife in her wedding dress. There is no evidence to support this interpretation; she merely wears an expensive dress of the kind that was fashionable in the early 1630s. The informality of the drawing was not transferred to the painting, which is reminiscent of a formal state portrait. Helena is seated in a large armchair before an opening to a terrace, separated from the room by a large curtain and a column. She is no longer lost in thought but gazes directly at the viewer. Her sumptuous dress is fuller and cut lower, and its richly patterned brocade bespeaks wealth. With a sprig of orange blossom in her hair—a symbol, variously, of chastity, love, or fertility—Helena appears full of life and ready to embrace her future.

An analysis of the panels Rubens used for this portrait has revealed that the painting originally was much smaller, a knee-length portrait. In the course of painting he must have decided to represent Helena in a full-length portrait instead. It appears, therefore, that Rubens prepared the drawing only after he had decided to greatly enlarge the painted portrait and represent his wife full-length. Pentimenti in the paint show that Rubens spontaneously introduced modifications, especially in the neckline of

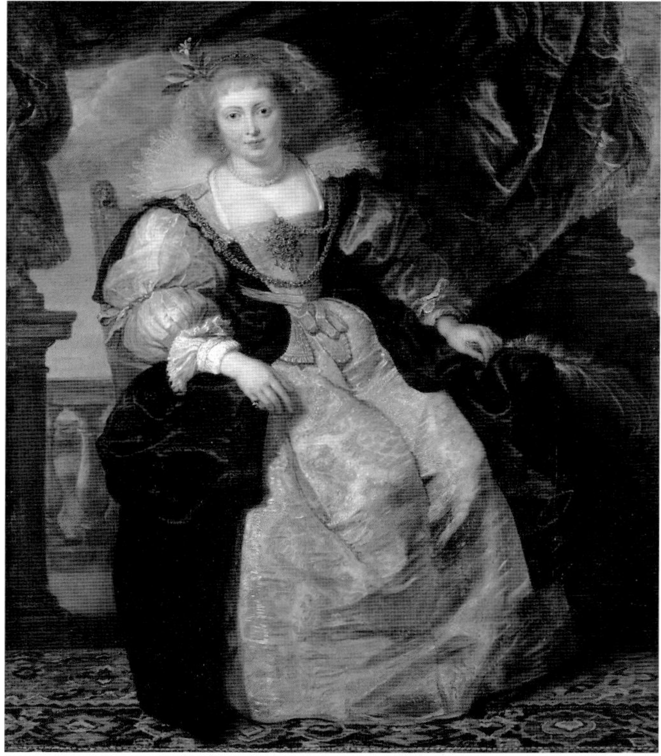

Fig. 134. Peter Paul Rubens, *Helena Fourment,* ca. 1631. Oil on panel, 163.5 x 137 cm (64⅜ x 53$^{15}/_{16}$ in.). Bayerische Staatsgemäldesammlungen, Alte Pinakothek, Munich (340)

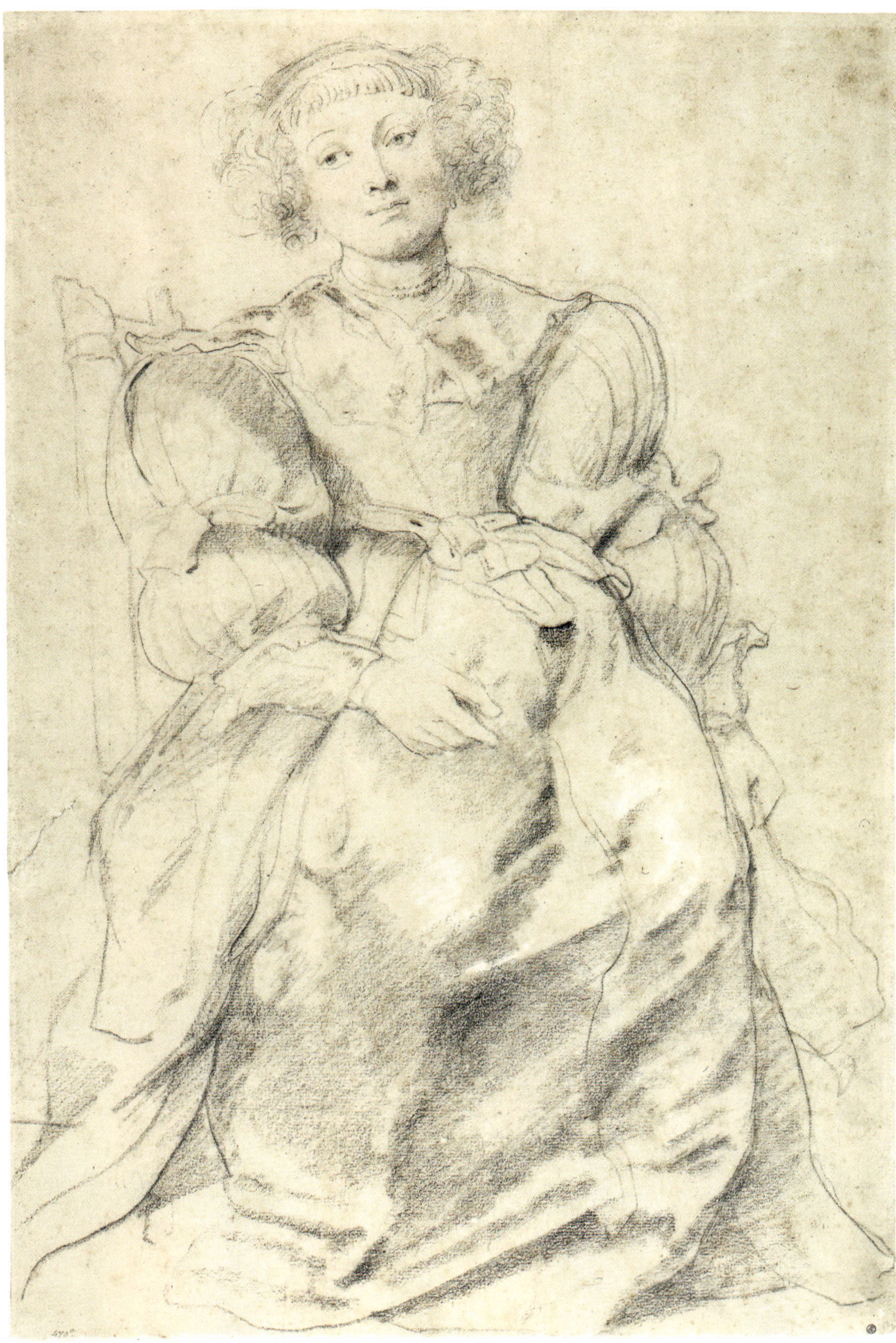

Cat. 88

Helena's dress, which at first closely resembled the soft collar in the drawing.[4] The change of proportions in the final portrait—the study shows a more vertical format—was probably also a matter that Rubens decided in the process of painting.

The masterful, loose application of the black chalk, combined with touches of red chalk and white highlights, as well as Helena's rich attire relate this sheet to Rubens's large studies for the *Garden of Love* painting (cat. nos. 90–92). For this reason, at one time the study was thought to be a preliminary drawing for one of the women in that composition.[5]

1. Rooses and Ruelens 1887–1909, vol. 6, pp. 228–29, no. 816.
2. Magurn 1955, p. 393, letter 235, December 18, 1634.
3. K.d.K., ed. Oldenbourg 1921, no. 328; M. Jaffé 1989, no. 994, ca. 1630–31; Renger and Denk 2002, pp. 258–63, no. 340.
4. See Poll-Frommel and Schmidt 2001, figs. 1a–c.
5. Max Rooses (1900b, p. 196) suggested this prior to associating the drawing with the portrait of Helena.

89. *Self-Portrait in Old Age,* recto, 1633–40; *A Man and a Woman Embracing,* verso, 1637–40

Black chalk, heightened with white, on oatmeal paper, pen and brown ink lines at top left and bottom right corners, recto; black chalk, verso, 200 x 160 mm ($7\frac{7}{8}$ x $6\frac{5}{16}$ in.)
Inscribed at lower center, probably by the artist: *29* (corrected to *27*); on the left by another hand: *Mr Pieter Bac . . .*

Lent by Her Majesty Queen Elizabeth II, Royal Library, Windsor Castle (6411)

PROVENANCE: George III of England (1738–1820).

LITERATURE: Held 1959, no. 126, pl. 139, pp. 34, 83, 143, under 123; Heiden 1982, p. 32, fig. 26; Liedtke 1984, vol. 1, pp. 178–81, fig. 39; Held 1986, no. 236, pl. 206; Vlieghe 1987, no. 137b, fig. 181; White and Crawley 1994, no. 437, ill.

EXHIBITIONS: Montreal–Raleigh–Indianapolis 1994–95, no. 24, ill.; London 1996–97, no. 49; Lille 2004, no. 72, ill.

In the self-portrait on the recto of this sheet Rubens gazes pensively at the viewer. It is quite a contrast to Rubens's only other known self-portrait, the large drawing in the Louvre (fig. 1), which is a formal, almost courtly portrait. Rubens began this drawing on a much larger sheet, as we can tell from the fragments in pen and ink at the top left (an arm?) and at the bottom right (drapery) that do not seem to belong to the

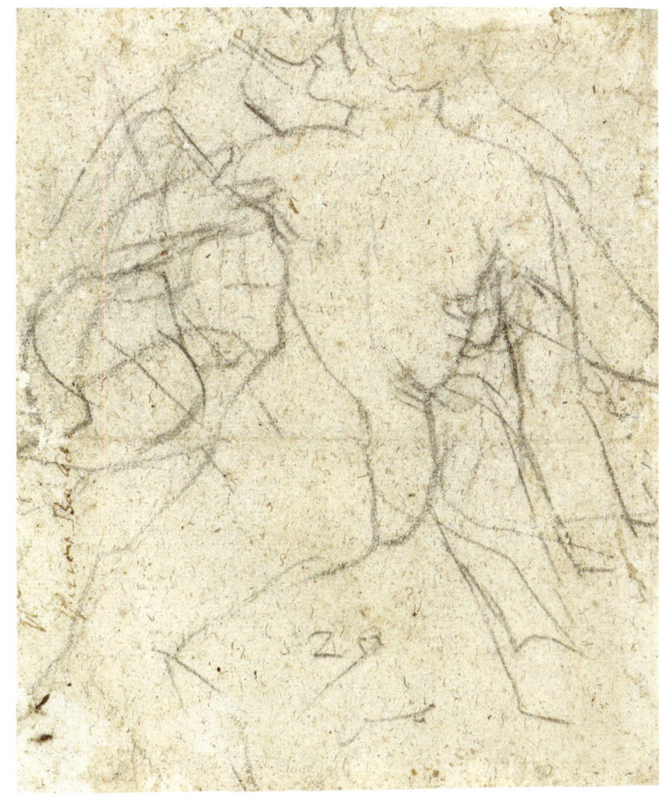

Cat. 89 verso

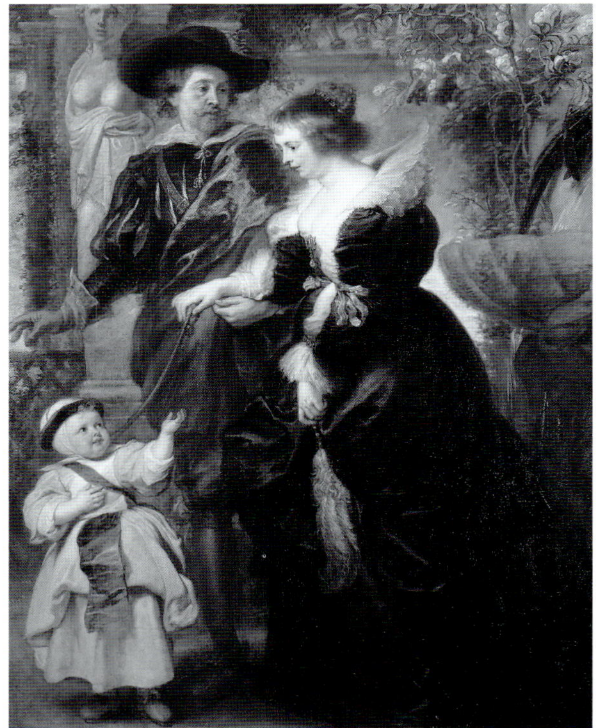

Fig. 135. Peter Paul Rubens, *Rubens, His Wife Helena Fourment, and Their Son Peter Paul,* ca. 1639. Oil on wood, 203.8 x 158.1 cm (80¼ x 62¼ in.). The Metropolitan Museum of Art, New York; Gift of Mr. and Mrs. Charles Wrightsman, in honor of Sir John Pope-Hennessy, 1981 (1981.238)

Fig. 136. X radiograph of detail of fig. 135.

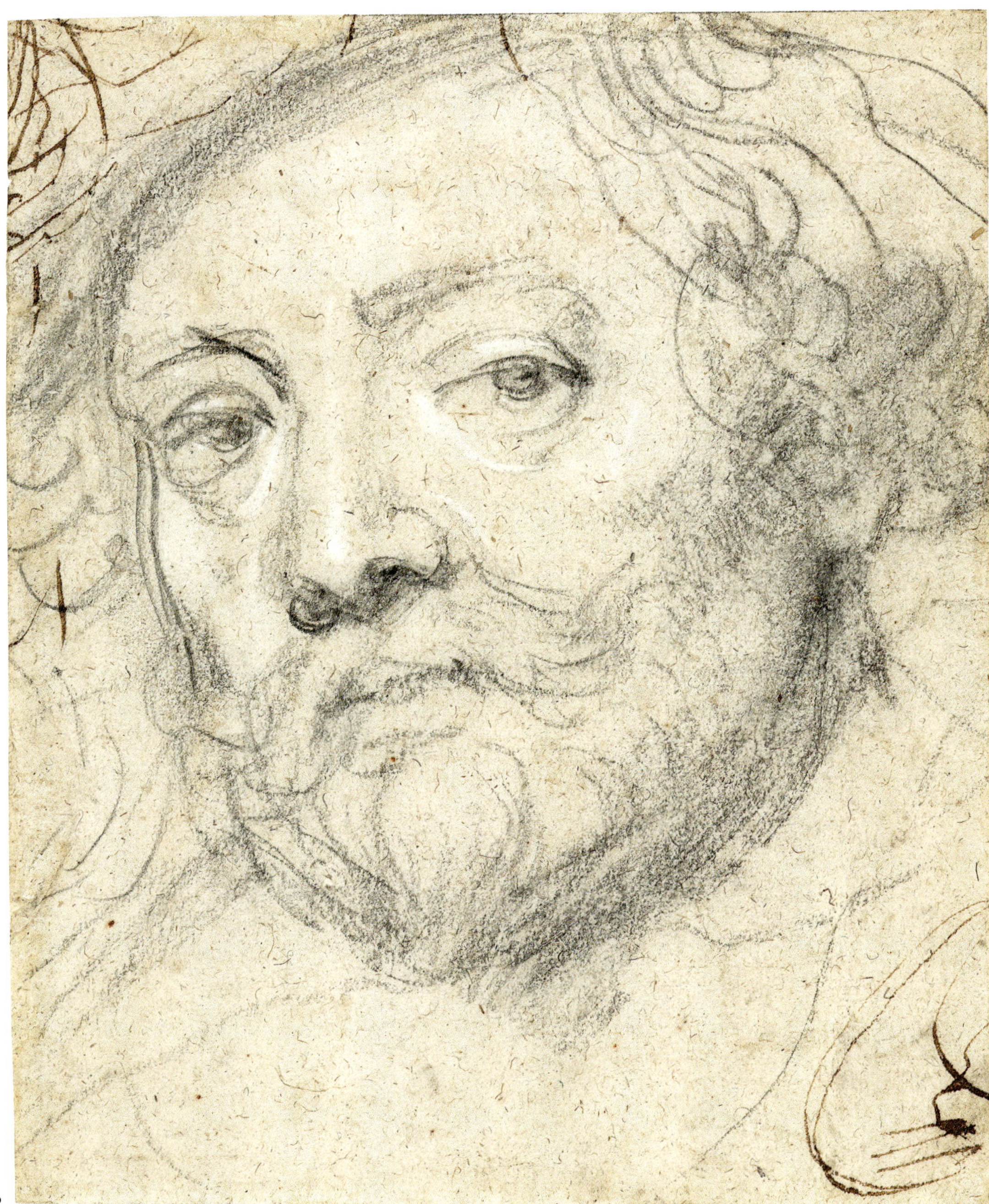

Cat. 89 recto

self-portrait in chalk. The eyes and the left contour of the face have been redrawn.

The drawing corresponds to an early state of Rubens's self-portrait in *Rubens, His Wife Helena Fourment, and Their Son Peter Paul* in The Metropolitan Museum of Art, New York (fig. 135).[1] An X radiograph of the artist's head in that painting shows that initially it was tilted exactly as in the drawing, with the artist glancing out at the viewer (fig. 136). The date of the New York painting and the identification of the child are intertwined. Walter Liedtke has argued, however, that given the Rubens children's ages, Netherlandish customs of dress (at that time in the Netherlands, very young boys, like girls, wore dresses), and a dating of the painting, on stylistic grounds, to about 1639, the child in the painting is "almost certainly" Rubens and Helena's third child, Peter Paul (b. 1637).[2] However, if, as Hans Vlieghe contended, Rubens depicted his and Helena's first child, Clara Johanna, born in early 1632, the painting and the present drawing would be close in date to the *Garden of Love* (fig. 137) of 1632–33.[3] Given the divergence of scholarly opinion, it may be best to date the drawing to a wide range of years, between 1633 and 1640. (It is also possible that Rubens originally drew the present self-portrait with a different painting in mind.)[4]

The drawing on the verso became visible only in 1977, when the sheet was lifted. It shows a summary sketch in black chalk of a seated couple embracing. The study has some relation to Rubens's late paintings of nymphs and satyrs in playful encounters.[5] The chalk is applied loosely, as in Rubens's compositional drawings from the later 1630s. It has been said that, after Rubens's death, Helena Fourment destroyed "nudities" in her husband's work.[6] As the figures on the verso appear to be naked, and as the drawing is obviously cut so as to save only Rubens's self-portrait, one wonders if there were once scenes on the verso that fell victim to Helena's suppression.

1. M. Jaffé 1989, no. 1401, ca. 1639.
2. Liedtke 1984, vol. 1, p. 177. The blue sash that the child wears, according to Liedtke, "would not be expected on a little girl." However, Vlieghe (1987, pp. 171, 173, n. 2) cited an example of a seventeenth-century portrait in which a girl wears a comparable sash.
3. Vlieghe (1987, p. 171, under no. 141) identified the child as Clara Johanna on the assumption that Rubens would not have omitted his sons Frans (b. 1633) and Peter Paul were they alive at the time. He also based his dating of the painting to 1632–33 on his opinion that the figure of Helena in the New York painting was a model for one of the female saints in the *Mystic Marriage of Saint Catherine,* now in Toledo, Ohio (see M. Jaffé 1989, no. 1092, 1633). For another possible dating for the latter painting, see cat. nos. 90–92.
4. According to Vlieghe, Rubens may have drawn the self-portrait in connection with his late painted self-portrait in Vienna (K.d.K., ed. Oldenbourg 1921, no. 427; M. Jaffé 1989, no. 1379, 1638–39).
5. His *Nymphs and Satyrs* in the Prado, Madrid (K.d.K., ed. Oldenbourg 1921, no. 381; M. Jaffé 1989, no. 1347), are one example.
6. Michel 1771, p. 269.

THE GARDEN OF LOVE

90. *Seated Young Woman with Raised Arms,* ca. 1631–32

Black and red chalk (face and hands), heightened with white, vertical fold through right of center, 423 x 500 mm ($16\frac{5}{8}$ x $19\frac{11}{16}$ in.)

Staatliche Museen zu Berlin, Kupferstichkabinett (KdZ 4003)

PROVENANCE: Jonathan Richardson Jr. (1694–1771), London (Lugt 2170); Earl of Aylesford (1786–1859), London (Lugt 58; sale, London, July 18, 1893, lot 271); acquired 1893.

LITERATURE: Glück and Haberditzl 1928, no. 200, pl. 200; Bock and Rosenberg 1930, vol. 1, p. 252, no. 4003, vol. 2, pl. 185; Burchard and d'Hulst 1963, no. 183, pl. 183, p. 282, under no. 181; Glang-Süberkrüb 1975, pp. 73–76; Díaz Padrón 1995, vol. 2, pp. 984–87, under no. 1690, ill.

EXHIBITIONS: Antwerp 1977, no. 165, ill.; Berlin 1977, no. 36, ill.; Berlin 1994, no. IV.44, ill.

91. *Young Man Embracing a Young Woman,* ca. 1631–32

Black and red chalk (in man's face and left hand), heightened with white on light brown paper, 322 x 300 mm ($12\frac{11}{16}$ x $11\frac{13}{16}$ in.)

Amsterdams Historisch Museum; Bequest of Carel Joseph Fodor (A 10 301)

PROVENANCE: Thomas Hudson (1701–1779), London (according to 1835 London exhibition); Sir Thomas Lawrence (1769–1830), London (Lugt 2445; one of the four drawings for the *Garden of Love* listed in the inventory in "case 6 and 7 drawer 2"); William II of the Netherlands (1792–1849), The Hague (his sale, The Hague, J. de Vries et al., August 12, 1850, probably no. 290); Carel Joseph Fodor (1801–1860).

LITERATURE: R., vol. 5, nos. 1482, 1486; Glück and Haberditzl 1928, no. 198, pl. 198; Held 1959, no. 120, pl. 131; Burchard and d'Hulst 1963, no. 181, pl. 181; Kuznetsov 1974, pl. 129; Glang-Süberkrüb 1975, pp. 73–76; Schapelhouman 1979, no. 64, ill.; Held 1986, no. 206, colorpl. 6; Díaz Padrón 1995, vol. 2, pp. 984–87, under no. 1690, ill.

EXHIBITIONS: Antwerp 1977, no. 164, ill.; Lyons 1980, no. 59, ill.

92. *Young Man Descending Stairs,* ca. 1631–32

Black and red chalk, heightened with white, on light brown paper, 561 x 405 mm ($22\frac{1}{8}$ x $15\frac{15}{16}$ in.)

Amsterdams Historisch Museum; Bequest of Carel Joseph Fodor (A 10 299)

PROVENANCE: Thomas Hudson (1701–1779), London (according to 1835 London exhibition); Sir Thomas Lawrence (1769–1830), London (Lugt 2445; one of the four drawings for the *Garden of Love* listed in the inventory in "case 6 and 7 drawer 2"); William II of the Netherlands (1792–1849), The Hague (his sale, The Hague, J. de Vries et al., August 12, 1850, probably no. 288); Carel Joseph Fodor (1801–1860; Lugt 1036).

LITERATURE: R., vol. 5, no. 1483, pl. 417, and no. 1487; Glück and Haberditzl 1928, no. 205, pl. 205; Held 1959, no. 119, pl. 134; Burchard and d'Hulst 1963, no. 181, pl. 181; Glang-Süberkrüb 1975, pp. 73–76;

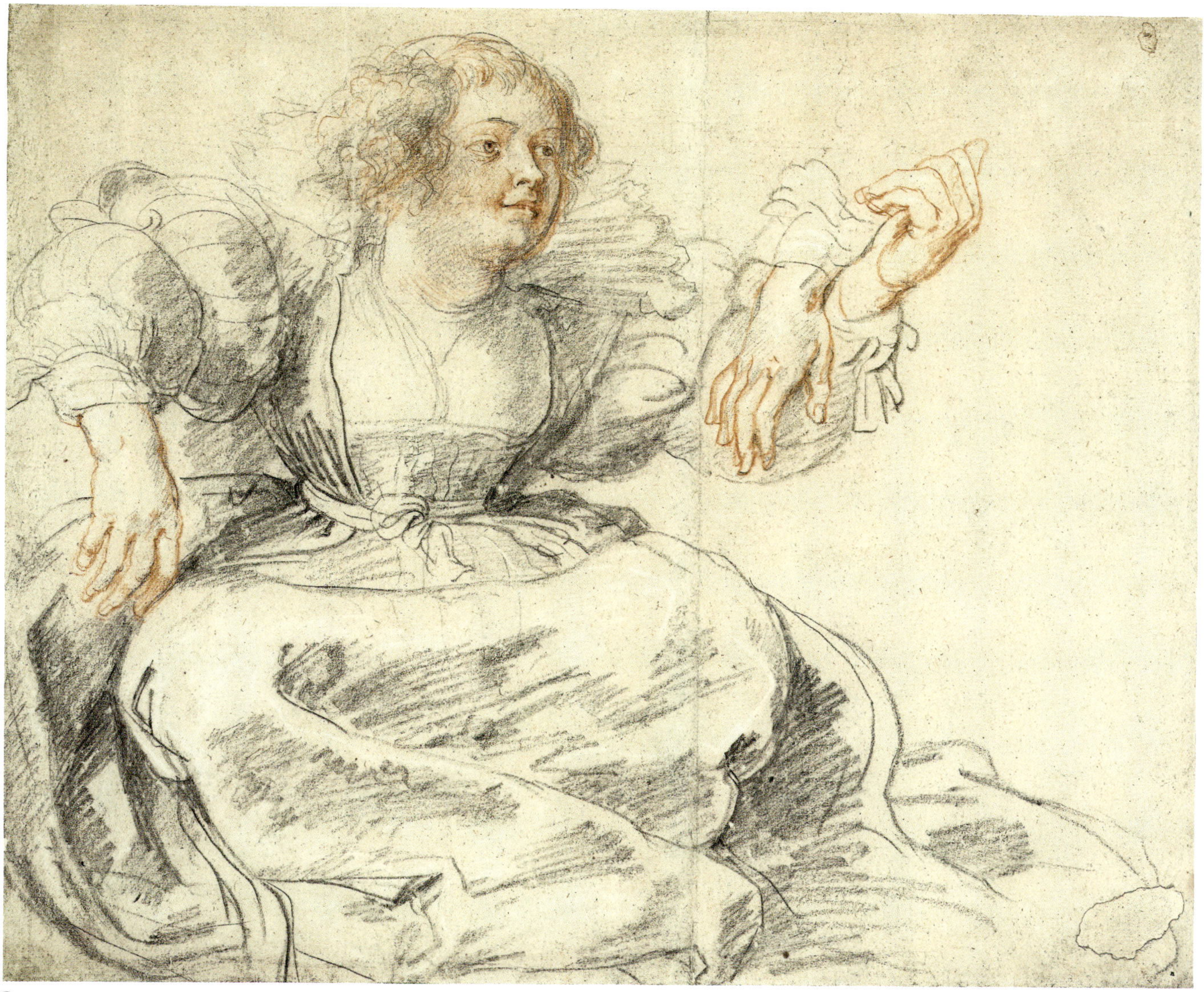

Cat. 90

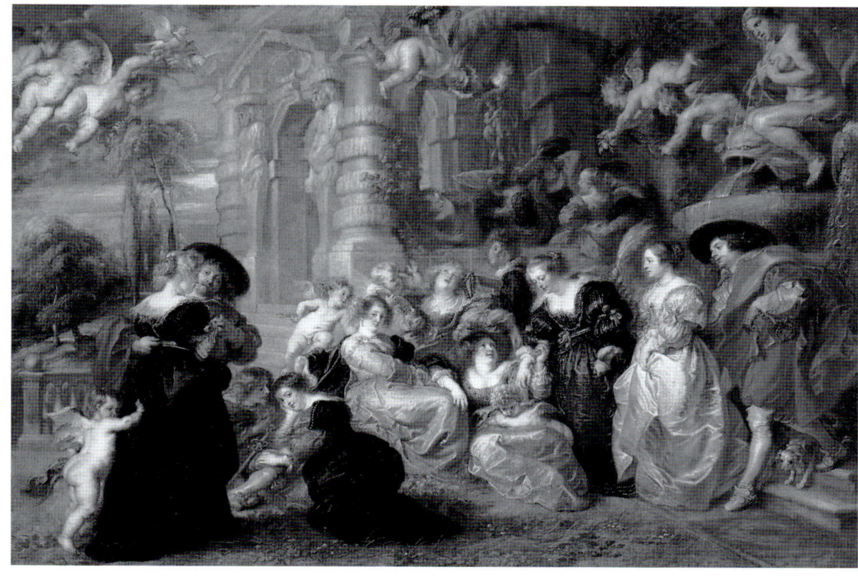

Fig. 137. Peter Paul Rubens, *The Garden of Love,* ca. 1632–33. Oil on canvas, 198 x 283 cm ($77\frac{15}{16}$ x $111\frac{7}{16}$ in.). Prado, Madrid (1690)

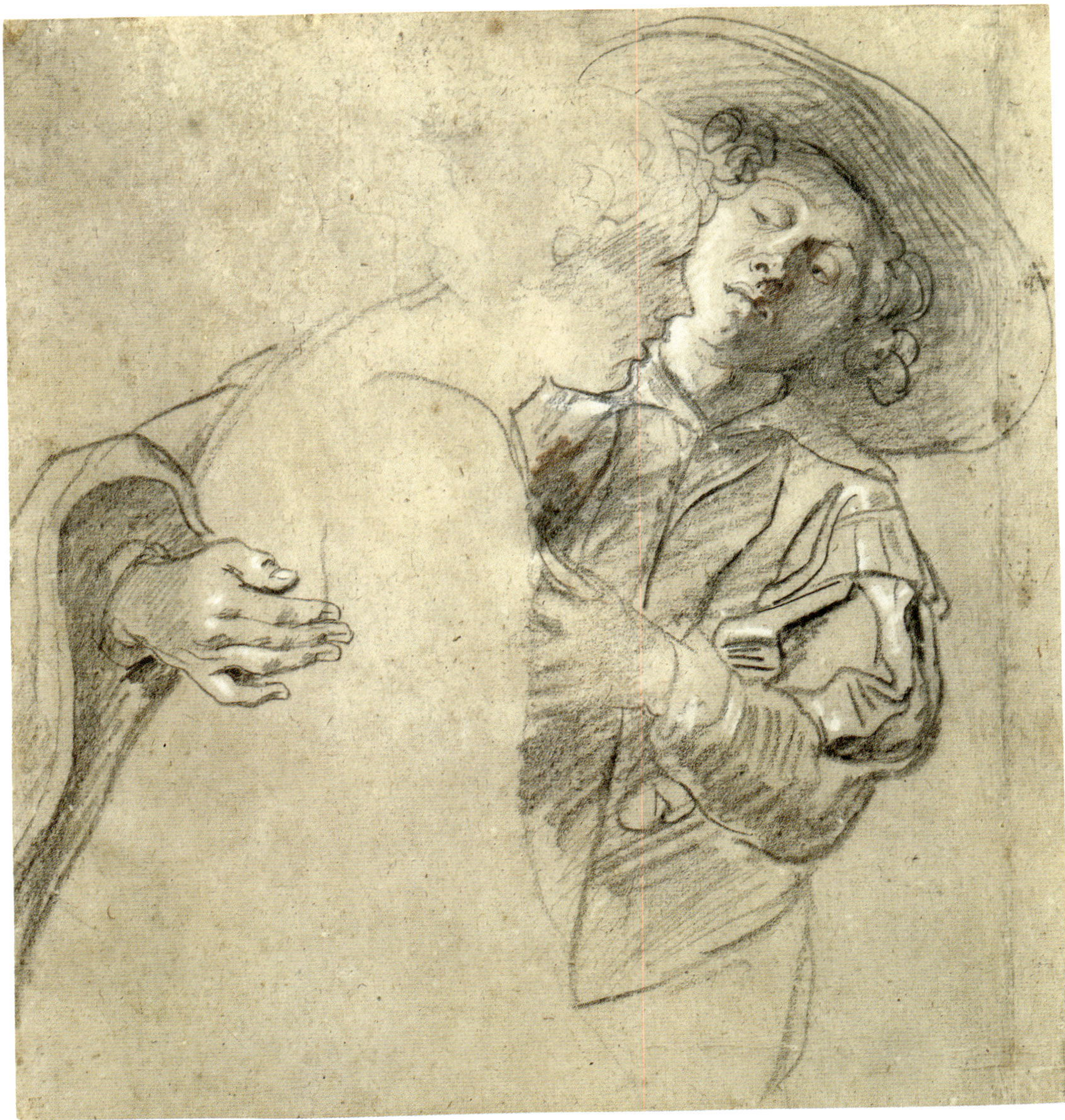

Cat. 91

Schapelhouman 1979, no. 67, ill.; Held 1986, no. 209, pl. 202; Díaz Padrón 1995, vol. 2, pp. 985–87, under no. 1690, ill.

Exhibitions: Antwerp 1977, no. 166, ill.; Lyons 1980, no. 62, ill.

Rubens's painting, from about 1632–33, of the *Garden of Love* (fig. 137) is one of his most admired and copied works.[1] The artist probably painted it for his own enjoyment and exhibited it in his home, where in all likelihood it remained until his death.[2] It is first recorded in the Spanish royal collection in 1666, referred to as a *sarao,* or festive gathering.[3]

In Rubens's time the painting was known as a "conversatie à la mode" (in the seventeenth century the term *conversatie,* to denote a conversation among young women, was often understood to mean a gathering of friends).[4] Some couples in the painting enjoy themselves playing games in a lavish garden setting in front of a large stone building, with a trick fountain spraying water. Others stroll or listen to a singer accompanied by a lutenist in the center of the composition.

Rubens prepared at least nine exceptionally large preliminary studies in black and red chalk, heightened with white, for almost all the major figures in the *Garden of Love;* only a study for the woman turned to the right and seated on a stool in the center is lacking. In no other instance in Rubens's oeuvre are so many preliminary studies for a painting known. The drawings show an exuberance and a freedom of movement of the chalk that are found primarily in Rubens's studies of the 1630s, and they have rightly been praised as his finest and most magnificent sheets. Earlier in Rubens's career he would probably have prepared an oil sketch of the entire composition in advance of the drawings, but none is recorded, possibly because the artist had only himself, and not a patron, to please.

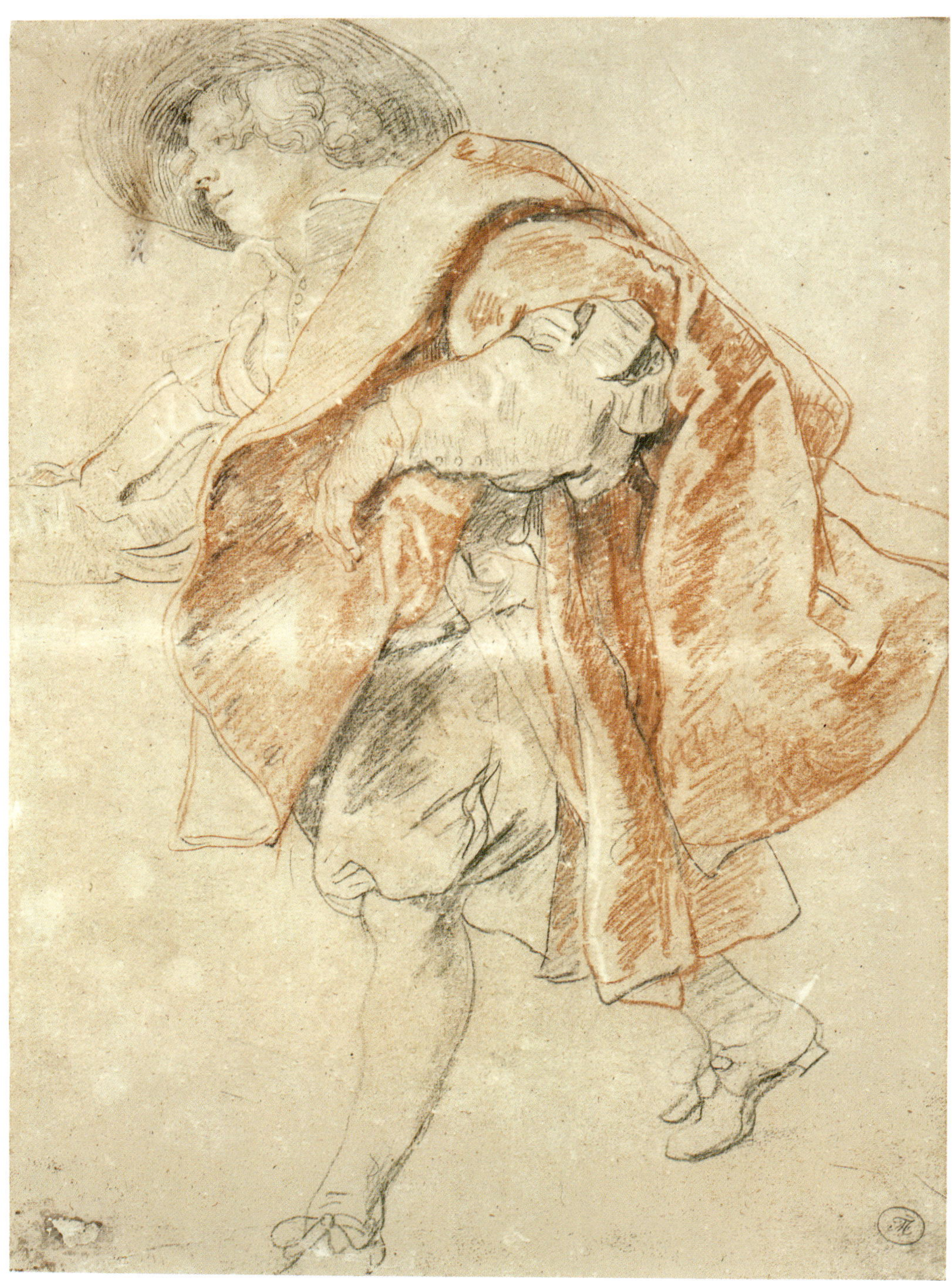

Cat. 92

Since Rubens followed these studies of individual figures closely in his painting, he must have prepared them after he had clearly established the composition on the canvas. The black-chalk study of a cavalier in a wide-brimmed hat who gently guides his companion forward (cat. no. 91) prepares the couple entering at the left of the painting, where the cavalier is bearded and the young woman is turned slightly more toward him. The *Seated Young Woman* (cat. no. 90) prepares the cheerful lady in the center of the painting. Rubens improved her looks in the picture by adorning her with a large plumed hat; he also added a putto reclining in her lap. She rests her right arm on the knee of a companion seated next to her and looks upward to converse with another sumptuously dressed young woman. The drawing helped to clarify not only the pose of the seated woman but also the interplay of her left hand with the right hand of the woman standing at her side. (A separate preliminary study for the standing woman—*Woman Looking Down,* formerly in the Koenigs collection, Rotterdam—is now in the Pushkin Museum, Moscow.)[5] The study of a *Young Man Descending Stairs* (cat. no. 92) must have been one of the last that Rubens prepared, since he corresponds to a figure that the artist painted on a strip that was added to the original canvas. The drawing prepares the spirited young cavalier in a red cloak who descends a set of stairs at the right of the painting. In the drawing Rubens did not need to complete the right arm, since in the painting it is obscured by the young woman whom he escorts. The youth has a mustache and carries gloves in the final work, and a small dog has been added between his legs.

The figures in the *Garden of Love* have often been associated with members of the artist's immediate family. Some of the women in these chalk studies indeed resemble Rubens's second wife, Helena Fourment, in the artist's sensitive portrait drawing (cat. no. 88) of about the same time. It is more likely, however, that she is reflected in Rubens's young women only as an ideal.

These large drawings of individual figures are generally dated to the years immediately following the artist's marriage to Helena Fourment, in early December 1630. Three of them—the study of a *Standing Woman* in Frankfurt, the *Woman Kneeling* in Paris, and the *Woman Looking Down* in Moscow—were also used in a religious context, as female saints in Rubens's *Mystic Marriage of Saint Catherine* in Toledo, Ohio.[6] If Rubens indeed received payment for the *Mystic Marriage of Saint Catherine* painting in 1631, as an eighteenth-century source states,[7] rather than in 1633, as was traditionally believed, then these three studies were prepared for the *Mystic Marriage of Saint Catherine,* which the Augustinians had commissioned for their church in Mechelen in about 1631, rather than for the *Garden of Love.* The artist may have worked on the two paintings more or less simultaneously.

1. K.d.K., ed. Oldenbourg 1921, no. 348; M. Jaffé 1989, no. 1808, ca. 1632–33.
2. The account of the sales from Rubens's estate that his heirs submitted to the city of Antwerp on November 17, 1645, mentions a *Conversatie à la mode op panneel* (a "conversatie à la mode" on panel), whereas the Prado painting is on canvas (Duverger 1984–, vol. 5, p. 272). The painting is not listed in the Spanish royal collection before 1666. Díaz Padrón 1995, vol. 2, pp. 982–86, no. 1690; Vergara 1999, p. 158.
3. The *Garden of Love* hung in the king's bedroom between works by Raphael and Andrea del Sarto. See Vergara 1999, p. 163.
4. See Goodman 1992. Wieseman in Boston–Toledo 1993–94, pp. 183–93.
5. See Elen 1989, no. 521, ill.
6. K.d.K., ed. Oldenbourg 1921, no. 343; M. Jaffé 1989, no. 1092, 1633. Rubens also adapted some of the *Garden of Love* studies for his two large *modelli* for Christoffel Jegher's woodcuts (cat. nos. 93, 94).
7. In a manuscript of 1776, J. F. Mols refers to a document in the registers of the Augustinians in Mechelen, asserting that Rubens received 620 florins for the work delivered to their church in 1631; see L. W. Nichols in Boston–Toledo 1993–94, no. 32.

PETER PAUL RUBENS AND CHRISTOFFEL JEGHER

93. *The Garden of Love* (left half), ca. 1633–35

Black chalk, pen and brown ink, probably brush and gray-green wash and dark brown ink, 463 x 705 mm (18¼ x 27¾ in.); strip at left folded under 25 mm, strip 65 mm wide added at right
Annotated in pen and brown ink at bottom: *Petrus Pauwlo Rubbens;* so-called Crozat number added by Mariette: *27;* at bottom center of mount: *133*

The Metropolitan Museum of Art, New York; Fletcher Fund, 1958 (1958.96.1)

94. *The Garden of Love* (right half), ca. 1633–35

Black chalk, pen and brown ink, brush and grayish white and greenish gouache, accented with brush and dark brown ink and wash, 476 x 706 mm (18¾ x 27 13/16 in.).
Annotated in pen and brown ink at bottom left: *Pietro Paolo Rubbens;* at bottom center of mount: *134*

The Metropolitan Museum of Art, New York; Fletcher Fund, 1958 (1958.96.2)

Provenance: Probably Johannes Philippus Happaert (d. 1686), Antwerp, (both drawings; his inventory of February 27, 1686, in Antwerp,

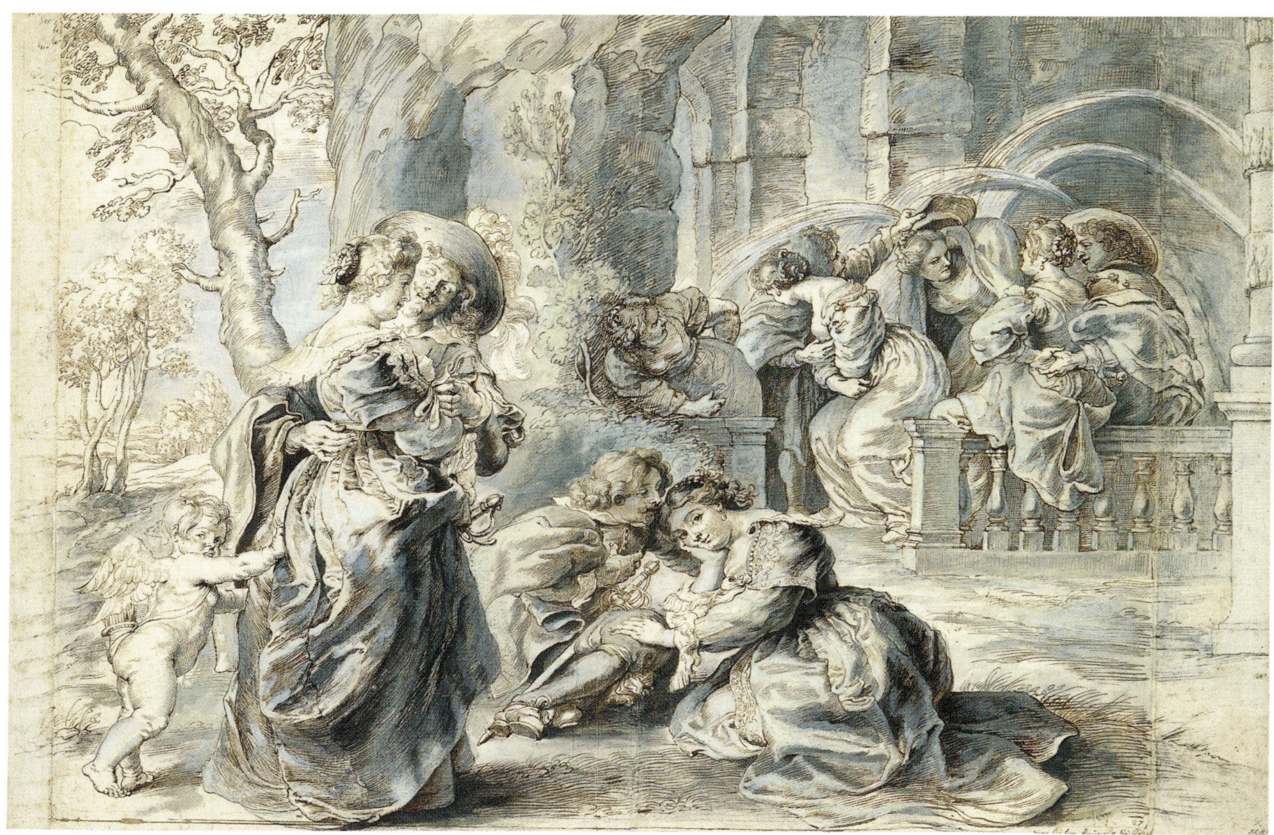
Cat. 93

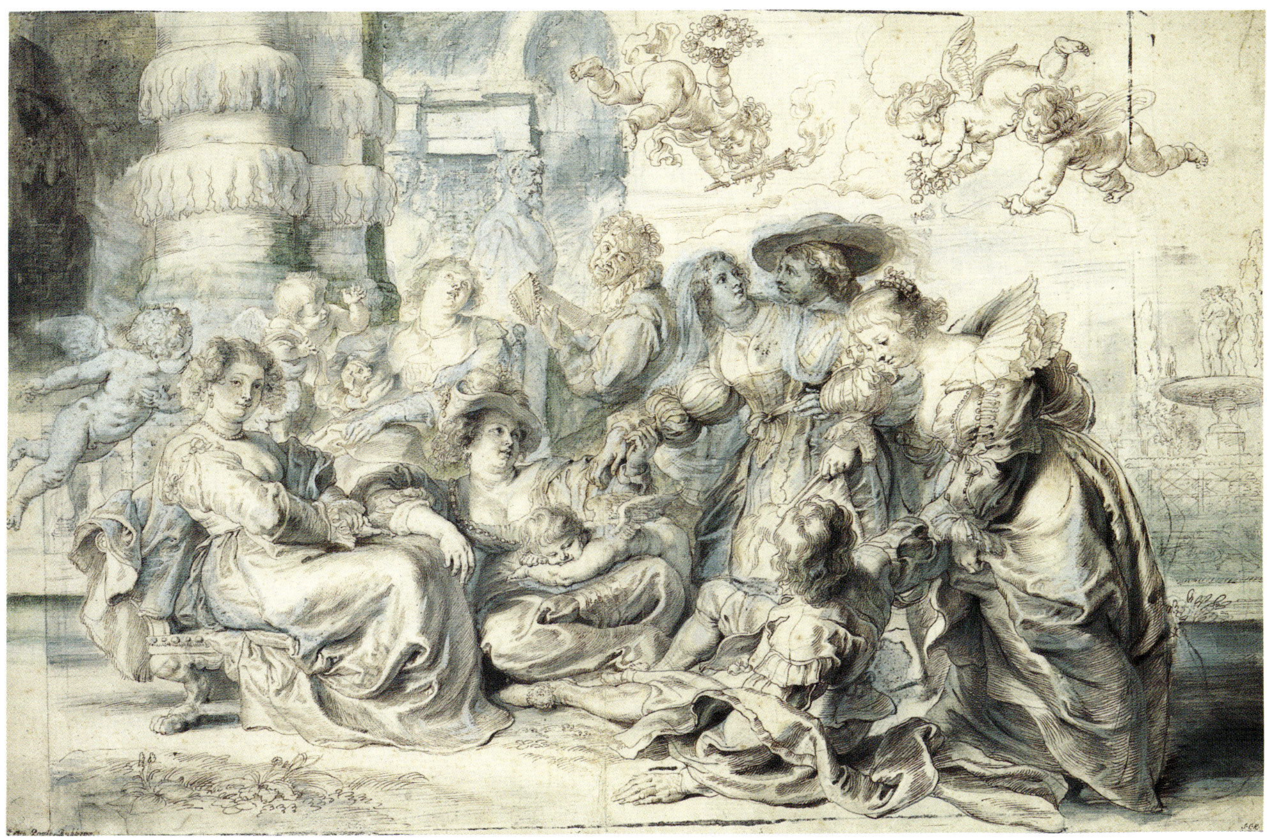
Cat. 94

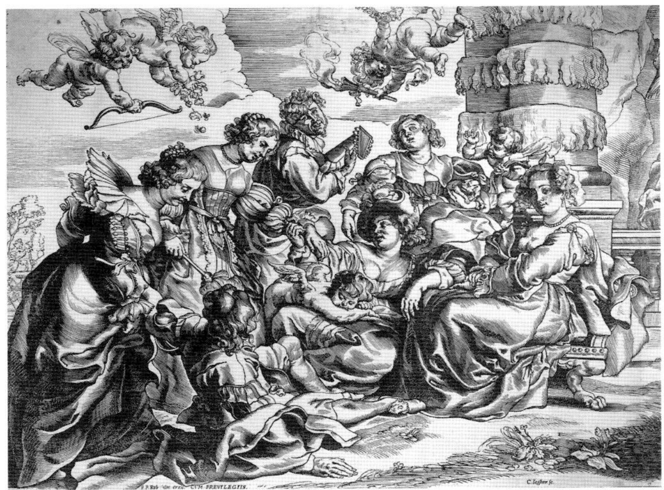

Fig. 138. Christoffel Jegher, *The Garden of Love* (left half), ca. 1633–34. Woodcut, 464 x 603 mm (18¼ x 23¾ in.). The Metropolitan Museum of Art, New York; Harris Brisbane Dick Fund, 1930 (30.53.17a)

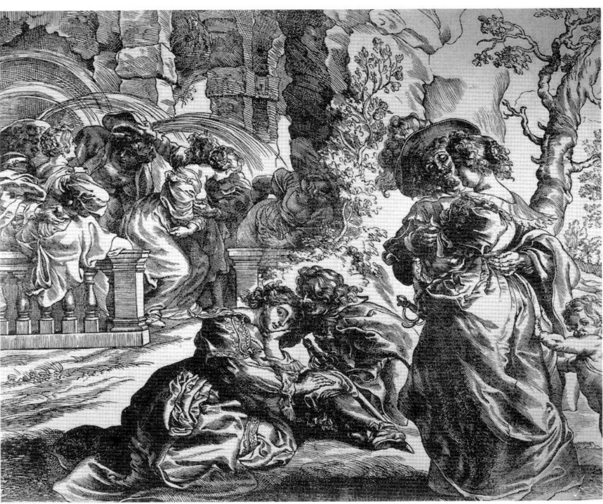

Fig. 139. Christoffel Jegher, *The Garden of Love* (right half), ca. 1633–34. Woodcut, 460 x 535 mm (18⅛ x 21$\frac{1}{16}$ in.); clipped impression. The Metropolitan Museum of Art, New York; Harris Brisbane Dick Fund, 1930 (30.53.17b)

nos. 221–23: "eene teeckeninge van Rubbens bestaende in twee stucken" [a drawing by Rubens in two parts]);[1] Pierre Crozat (1665–1740), Paris (Lugt 2951; drawing of left half only with Crozat number 27 added by Mariette; his sale, Paris, Pierre-Jean Mariette, April 10–May 13, 1741, part of no. 828); bought by Pierre-Jean Mariette (who received as a gift the drawing of the right half from Crozat's nephew, Louis Antoine Crozat, Baron de Thiers [1699–1770], Paris); Pierre-Jean Mariette (1694–1774), Paris (Lugt 1852; both drawings; his sale, Paris, November 15, 1774–January 30, 1775, part of no. 994); bought by Basan; brought to Holland by the dealer Pieter Fouquet, Amsterdam; Jan Gildemeester Jansz. (1744–1799), Amsterdam (his sale, Amsterdam, Van der Schley . . . Pruyssenaar, November 24, 1800, and following days, album B, no. 1); bought by J. Vinkeles, Amsterdam; Hendrik van Eyl Sluyter (1739–1814), Amsterdam (his sale, Amsterdam, Van der Schley . . . De Vries, September 26, 1814, and following days, portfolio N, no. 1); bought by Christiaan Josi, London and Amsterdam; Heneage Finch, 5th Earl of Aylesford (1786–1859), London and Packington Hall, Warwickshire (Lugt 58; sale, London, Christie's, July 17–18, 1893, no. 272); Sir John Charles Robinson (1824–1913), London (Lugt 1433; sale, London, Christie's, May 12–14, 1902, no. 334); to Agnew's, London; William Hesketh, 1st Viscount Leverhulme, Thornton Manor, Thornton Hough, Wirral, Cheshire; Lady Lever Art Gallery, Port Sunlight, Cheshire; Thomas Agnew and Sons, London; acquired by the Metropolitan Museum in 1958.

Literature: R., vol. 4, pp. 69–70, no. 1322, pl. 269; Held 1959, no. 152, pls. 162, 163, pp. 21, 37–38, 81, 107, under no. 31, 141, under no. 115, 142, under no. 119; Bean 1962, pp. 166–67, ill.; Burchard and d'Hulst 1963, no. 180, pl. 180, p. 278, under no. 179; Bean 1964, no. 81, ill. (right half); Myers 1966, pp. 16–17, figs. 21, 22; Kuznetsov 1974, pls. 134, 135; Glang-Süberkrüb 1975, pp. 49–53, 73–76; Renger 1975, pp. 181–89, figs. 12 a,b; Heiden 1982, p. 25, fig. 17; Held 1986, nos. 210, pl. 203, 211, pl. 204; Goodman 1992, pp. 73–83; Díaz Padrón 1995, vol. 2, pp. 985–87, under no. 1690, ill. (right half).

Exhibitions: London 1977a, nos. 172a–b, ill.; Haarlem–Paris 2001–2, no. 68, ill. (right half); Valenciennes 2004, nos. 17, 18.

These two impressive drawings are based on Rubens's famous painting, from 1632–33, of the *Garden of Love* (fig. 137)[2] and served as designs, or *modelli,* for two woodcuts (in reverse from the drawings; figs. 138, 139) by Christoffel Jegher (1596–1652/53). The woodcut, which had seen its heyday in the sixteenth century, was a new medium for Rubens, and his interest spurred its revival. Jegher's *Garden of Love* woodcuts count as his masterpieces and are among the finest examples produced in the seventeenth century. Rubens himself published the nine woodcuts Jegher made after his designs; they carry his signature and privilege, "P. P. Rub. delin. et ex. cum Privilegiis" (Rubens drew and published it with the privileges), followed by Jegher's signature ("C Iegher sc.").

Each of the two *Garden of Love* drawings is a self-contained composition. For the drawing based on the left half of the Madrid painting (cat. no. 93), Rubens combined the cavalier guiding a lady into the garden, the couple seated on the ground, and the grottolike garden architecture in the background, where figures amuse themselves around a water fountain. For the drawing corresponding to the right half of the painting (cat. no. 94), Rubens selected the closely knit group of figures gathered around the lutenist and the seated ladies in front. He omitted the prominent fountain with a statue of Venus seated on a dolphin, spouting water from her breasts, and the peacock perched next to her on the basin. In its stead Rubens added—with a few quick strokes—a fountain with the Three Graces that appears in the center background of the painting. He also left out the cavalier at the right, draped in a cloak, and the lady he escorts. To round out the group Rubens added a new figure:

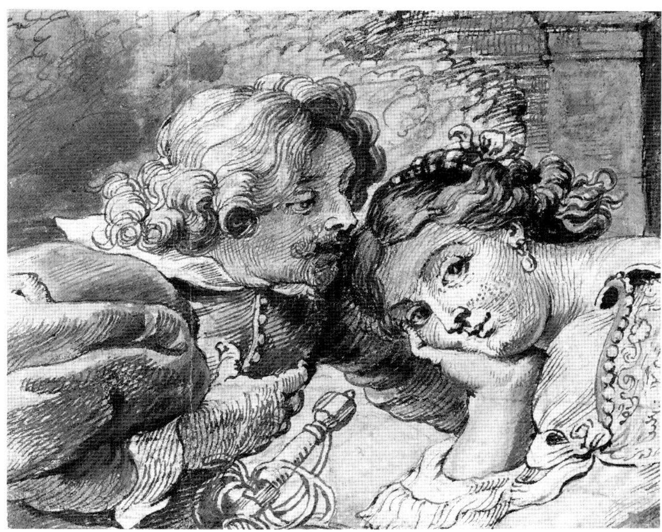

Fig. 140. Peter Paul Rubens and Christoffel Jegher, Detail of cat. 93

a seated cavalier, in the foreground, who engages a young lady in conversation. The putti hovering above the couple are taken directly from the painting.

Rubens probably began these two compositional drawings only upon completion of the *Garden of Love* painting—that is, about 1632–33—as some of the figures in the drawings are based on the painting rather than on the preliminary studies of individual figures for the painting (see cat. nos. 90–92). For example, in the left half of the compositional drawing, the couple approaching the garden are clearly based on the canvas rather than on the preliminary drawing (cat. no. 91), in which the cavalier is clean-shaven; the lady with a plumed hat, seated in the center of the other drawing, is bareheaded in the preparatory study (cat. no. 90).

Rubens made these two large drawings specifically for Jegher, with whom he collaborated closely from about 1633 until 1635.[3] For Rubens, this was a new experience, because heretofore he had dealt mainly with engravers in order to reproduce his paintings. (Engravings entailed a different working method; see cat. nos. 53, 56.) From his work with engravers, Rubens was accustomed to preparing *modelli* on paper, and he did so again in this case, even though in the woodcut technique the preliminary drawing was made directly on the block. We are lucky that he did so, because any drawing on the woodblock would have been destroyed during the cutting and carving.

A close examination of the two *modelli* reveals that they were created in three distinct phases. Initially, a black-chalk drawing of the entire composition was spread over the two large sheets. Here and there these initial black-chalk lines can still be seen where the pen lines did not follow carefully—for example, in the tree branches and foliage at the upper left of catalogue number 93. This work in black chalk is in all likelihood Rubens's initial design for Jegher's woodcut and is acknowledged in the print's inscription "P.P. Rub. delin." (Rubens drew it).[4] In a second phase, the two sheets were gone over meticulously with pen and brown ink, to clarify the chalk drawing. This additional pen work, which includes even parallel hatching (see fig. 140), prefigures the woodcut lines in Christoffel Jegher's print. In our opinion it was Jegher who added the methodical pen work, possibly to indicate to Rubens how the woodcut would look, since Rubens's initial drawing in black chalk is very free (see fig. 141).[5] These two elaborate drawings (without the extensions on the right in catalogue number 93) closely correspond to Jegher's woodcuts in reverse (figs. 138, 139).[6]

There are indications that Rubens may have intended to add a tone block to the *Garden of Love* woodcuts. That he was experimenting with adding color blocks is corroborated by the woodcut of the *Rest on the Flight into Egypt,* of which there is a proof impression in orange-brown with white highlights (see cat. no. 95). Rubens seems to have worked on the drawings for woodcuts of the *Garden of Love* and the *Rest on the Flight into Egypt* at the same time.[7] The greenish wash applied to catalogue number 93 may indicate a trial before proceeding to the color block.[8] An impression of the *Garden of Love* in a private collection that was colored (probably by Jegher) with brown-gray wash and white body color in imitation of a chiaroscuro tone block also suggests that Rubens

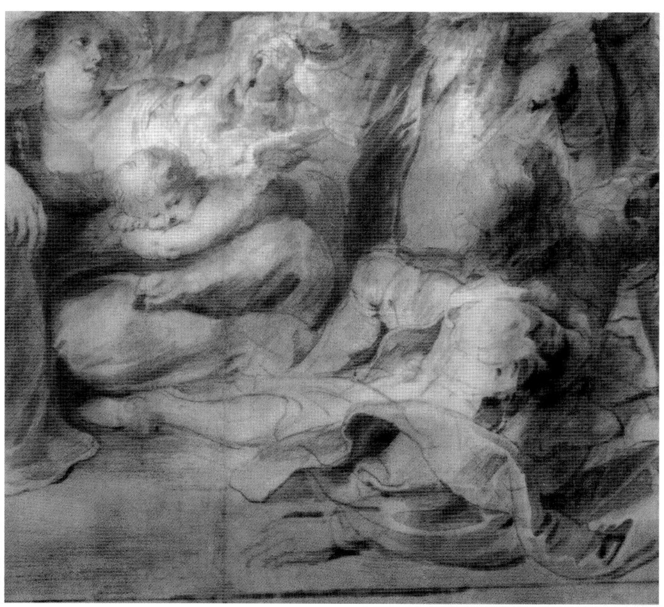

Fig. 141. Infrared reflectogram of detail of cat. 94

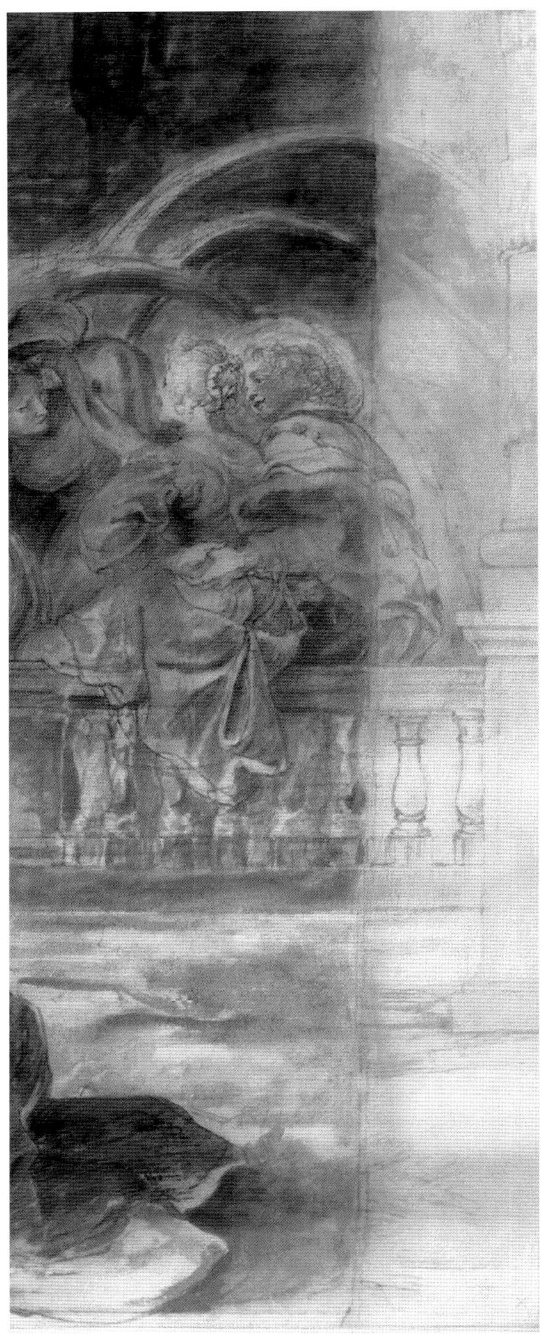

Fig. 142. Infrared reflectogram of detail of cat. 93

and Jegher experimented with a color tone block for the *Garden of Love* woodcuts.[9]

During a third phase Rubens introduced changes in one of the drawings (cat. no. 94), but only after it had served Jegher for the woodcut. The most notable additions and changes are found in the putto hovering near the seated lady at the left,[10] in the arched passageway in the background supported by caryatids, and in the figure of the young man with a plumed hat at the right, who approaches a lady turning around in surprise. All these changes were made with brush and brown ink and greenish white gouache. Here, Rubens intervened in one of his own drawings very much in the manner that he retouched other artists' drawings throughout his life. We do not know why Rubens introduced these changes, however.

Catalogue number 93 was modified during the eighteenth century. Recently, the number 27, added in the lower right corner before a strip of paper was attached, was recognized as a so-called Crozat number. The number was inscribed by Pierre-Jean Mariette (1694–1774), the most important drawings collector in France in the second half of the eighteenth century, at the time he prepared the catalogue of the collection of Pierre Crozat (1665–1740) for auction in Paris in the spring of 1741. Catalogue number 93 originally ended right after the number 27. This was the drawing's size at the time Crozat owned it and before Mariette acquired it for his own collection. When Mariette received the other drawing (cat. no. 94) as a gift from Crozat's nephew, Mariette himself must have added the 65-mm-wide strip of paper at the right, in order to make both *Garden of Love* drawings the same size; he most likely did the enlargement himself.[11] The continuation of the drawing into the added strip of paper ends with a column drawn over a strict grid in pencil and includes the backs of the revelers and sprays of water.[12] Infrared reflectography brings this out even more clearly (fig. 142). A 25-mm vertical strip at the left seems to have been folded under when the drawing was framed after it left Rubens's collection. With this section brought back and with the strip added at the right, the left half of the *Garden of Love* drawing is now more or less the same size as the right half. Mariette apparently liked the drawings in his collection to be close in size.

1. Duverger 1984–, vol. 11, p. 379.
2. K.d.K., ed. Oldenbourg 1921, no. 348; M. Jaffé 1989, no. 1080, ca. 1632–33.
3. The earliest documented collaboration between Rubens and Jegher dates from July 1633. They must have worked very closely together, for in November 1635 Rubens was named godfather to Jegher's ninth child, christened Peter Paul (Bouchery and Van den Wijngaert 1941, p. 101, n. 1).
4. Glück suggested this in 1933 (pp. 115, 118), but his opinion was not universally accepted.
5. Ludwig Burchard, Julius Held, and Konrad Renger, among others, accepted both the black-chalk drawing and the pen work over it as entirely Rubens's work. An examination of both sheets by infrared reflectography, performed in 2003 by Alison Gilchrest of the Sherman Fairchild Center for Works on Paper and Photograph Conservation at The Metropolitan Museum of Art, clearly revealed a rather complete underdrawing in black chalk (see fig. 141); the free-flowing lines resemble those known from Rubens's large studies for individual figures. Rubens's preliminary drawing for the seated cavalier in

the foreground is loosely sketched, with little evidence of modeling besides areas to which wash was added to indicate shading. The putto resting on the lap of the young woman seated in the center, with his head nestled on his arms, is especially clear; the head of the lutenist behind them, on the contrary, is quite indistinct and needed to be rendered in more detail in the pen overlay. We are grateful to Alison Gilchrest for undertaking this lengthy task and for her excellent infrared composites of the two halves.

6. The drawings themselves are not traced for transfer, and the dimensions of the drawings and prints differ: the original sheet of the left portion is 463 x 617 mm; the drawing of the right portion is 476 x 706 mm; and the complete woodcuts after each portion are basically 460 x 600 mm.

7. Recently, a faint sketch in black chalk was found on the verso of the *Rest on the Flight into Egypt* drawing in Poznań (cat. no. 95); the figures correspond almost exactly to the couple entering the garden in catalogue number 93. We thank Grażyna Hałasa, curator of prints and drawings in Poznań, for sending a tracing of the verso of the drawing in Poland.

8. In the opinion of Nadine M. Orenstein, curator in the Department of Drawings and Prints at The Metropolitan Museum of Art, the green wash was most likely added by Jegher, to indicate light and shade.

9. According to Michael Jaffé, Jegher added the brown-gray wash; see Cambridge 1990, no. 37, color ill. of detail on cover.

10. This putto is reproduced in the version of the *Garden of Love* on panel in the Rothschild collection at Waddesdon Manor, Aylesbury, Buckinghamshire—a strong reason to consider that painting later than the Madrid *Garden of Love* and these two New York drawings. Michael Jaffé (1989) and Peter C. Sutton (in Boston–Toledo 1993–94) associated the two drawings with the Waddesdon Manor *Garden of Love,* thus following the opinion of Ludwig Burchard. Burchard believed that the Waddesdon Manor picture was Rubens's earliest representation of the *Garden of Love,* followed by the two New York drawings and the painting in the Prado. This sequence, however, was rejected by, among others, Held (1959, no. 152) and Glang-Süberkrüb (1975, pp. 66, 93–94, as Theodoor van Thulden). The Waddeson Manor *Garden of Love* must be a version by a member of the Rubens studio who based it on the Madrid painting and these two large drawings.

11. Kristel Smentek identified the number 27 as a "Crozat number." She is familiar with Mariette's way of cutting and remounting drawings in order to have them fit his regular mounts; the way the paper strip was attached conforms, in her opinion, to Mariette's practice as she has observed it. We thank Ms. Smentek for sharing these observations.

12. Held (1959, no. 152) cautioned, rightly, that the addition at the right of catalogue number 93 was too weak to be by Rubens.

PETER PAUL RUBENS AND CHRISTOFFEL JEGHER

95. *Rest on the Flight into Egypt,* recto; *Studies for the "Garden of Love,"* verso, ca. 1633–35

Pen and brown ink, retouched by Rubens with brush and black ink, heightened with white and grayish white body color, over preliminary drawing in black chalk, some corrections with black chalk, on cream-colored paper, recto; black chalk, verso, 465 x 605 mm (18⅝ x 23$^{13}/_{16}$ in.)
Annotated in pen and brown ink at bottom right: *Rubens*

Fundacja im. Raczyńskich, Muzeum Narodowe, Poznań (Fr. 396)

PROVENANCE: Pierre-Jean Mariette (1694–1774), Paris (Lugt 1852); Stanisław II Augustus Poniatowski of Poland (1732–1798), Warsaw; Count Atanazy Raczyński, 1810; on deposit at the Muzeum Narodowe since 1903.

LITERATURE: Mańkowski 1932, p. 477, no. 11; Burchard and d'Hulst 1963, no. 179, pl. 179; Mrozińska and Sawicka 1976, no. 57; Mrozińska and Sawicka 1980, no. 57; Rościszewska 1993, pp. 78–83, figs. 1, 5, 6, 14–16; Díaz Padrón 1995, vol. 2, p. 872, under no. 1640, ill.; Van Hout 2004, pp. 100–103, ill. fig. 63 [artist unknown, retouched by Rubens].

EXHIBITIONS: Antwerp 1977, no. 168, ill.; London and other cities 1980, no. 79, fig. 62; Kansas City and other cities 1993–94, no. 77, ill.; Poznań 1995, no. 21, ill.

The drawing on the recto of this sheet is Rubens's design, or *modello,* for a woodcut by Christoffel Jegher (1596–1652/53; fig. 144). We attribute the careful drawing in pen and ink to Jegher, who executed it over Rubens's initial design in black chalk. Rubens's black-chalk study is a modification of his painting of the *Madonna and Child in a Landscape with Saint George and Other Saints* (fig. 143).[1] In the drawing Rubens omitted Saints George, Margaret, and Catherine, who appear in the painting, and focused more closely on the Virgin and Child and the small children playing with a sheep in the foreground at the right; Joseph is barely noticeable in the background, asleep against a tree. By leaving out the three saints Rubens emphasized the landscape, a genre that interested him at the end of his life (see cat. nos. 104, 105).

Upon Jegher's completion of his work in pen and brown ink, Rubens selectively retouched the design with white and grayish white body color; this is most obvious in the Virgin and Child and the tree she rests against. In execution the drawing closely resembles the two designs for Jegher's woodcuts after the *Garden of Love* (cat. nos. 93, 94). In this drawing we see the

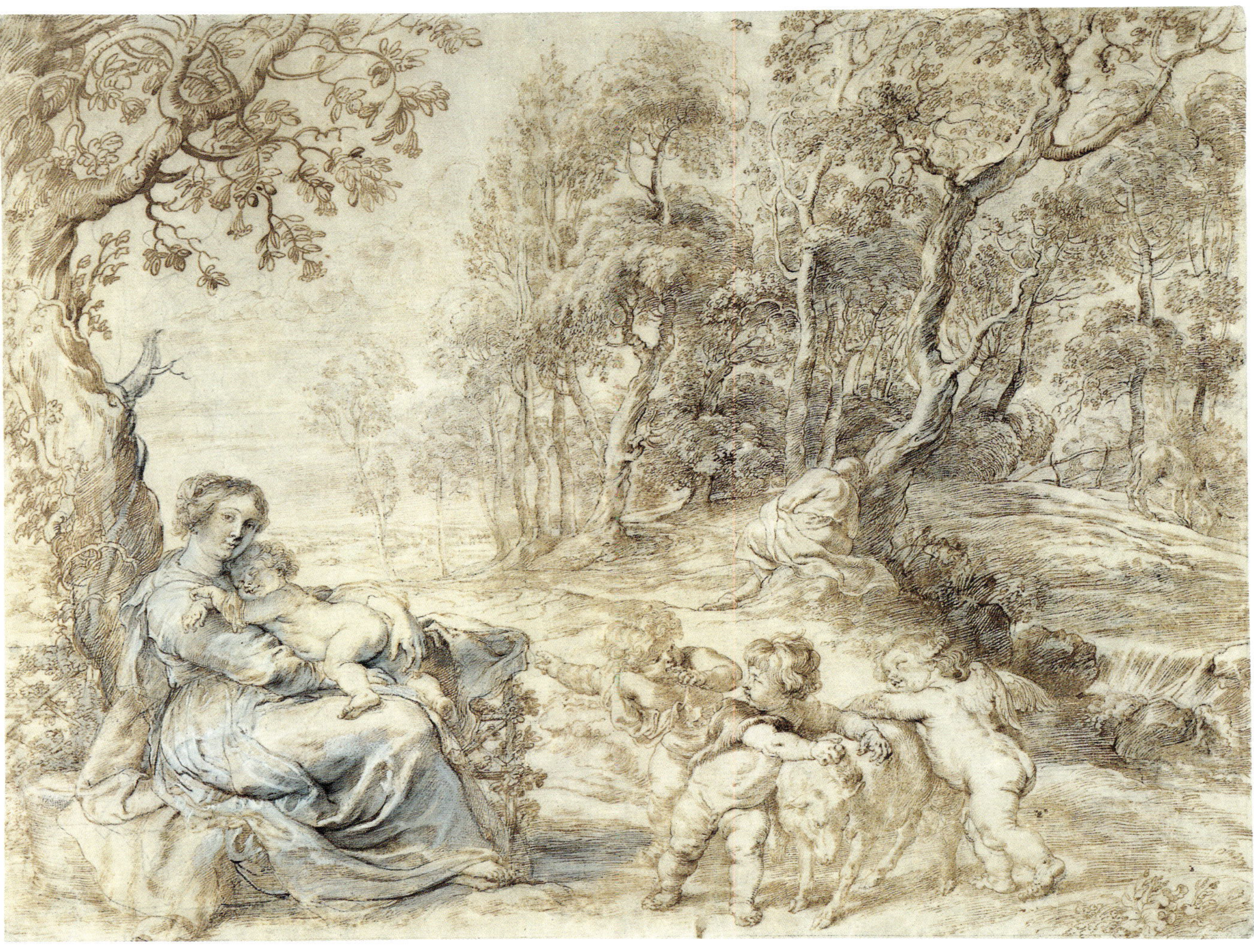

Cat. 95 recto

same division of labor between the two artists, with Rubens furnishing the initial design in black chalk and Jegher completing it in pen and brown ink before transferring the design to the woodblock to be cut. Rubens probably worked on the three *modelli* in close succession, possibly beginning with this work, which, because of its religious subject, would be the more popular.

Jegher's woodcut of the *Rest on the Flight into Egypt* exists in no fewer than six different proof impressions. Rubens retouched many of them, in brush and ocher and white or greenish body color, indicating, for example, areas to be lightened or otherwise altered, such as the sky in the distance at the right. In its first state, known in three impressions, one of them a counterproof in the Bibliothèque Nationale, Paris, Jegher's woodcut reproduces the present drawing almost exactly. Rubens retouched the unique counterproof of the second state, again in Paris, which shows that he was as involved in supervising Jegher's prints as he had been with the earlier reproductive engravings of his paintings. In the third state Rubens experimented with an orange-brown tone block with white highlights to which the black block outlining the composition was added; the result was a chiaroscuro woodcut as the fourth and last state.[2] These various retouched proofs are testimony to the artist's great interest in this—for him—new method of reproducing his paintings.

Recently, the sheet was lifted from its old backing and a light sketch in soft black chalk was revealed on the verso: it shows a young lady pushed along by a putto and a seated cavalier and lady. These figures appear in the left half of Rubens's *Garden of Love* drawing in New York (cat. no. 93).[3] Indeed, when a tracing of the woman and putto was overlaid on the New York drawing, there was an extremely close correspondence.[4] This suggests that Rubens worked on the *Garden of Love* drawings and the *Rest on the Flight into Egypt* at the same time.

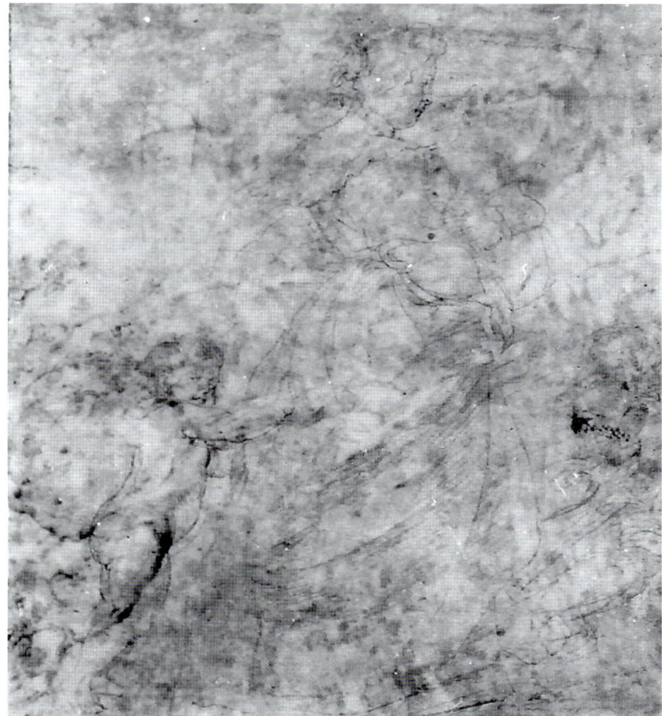

Cat. 95 verso, detail

Fig. 143. Peter Paul Rubens, *Madonna and Child in a Landscape with Saint George and Other Saints,* 1632–33. Oil on canvas, 87 x 125 cm (34¼ x 49$^{3}/_{16}$ in.). Prado, Madrid (1640)

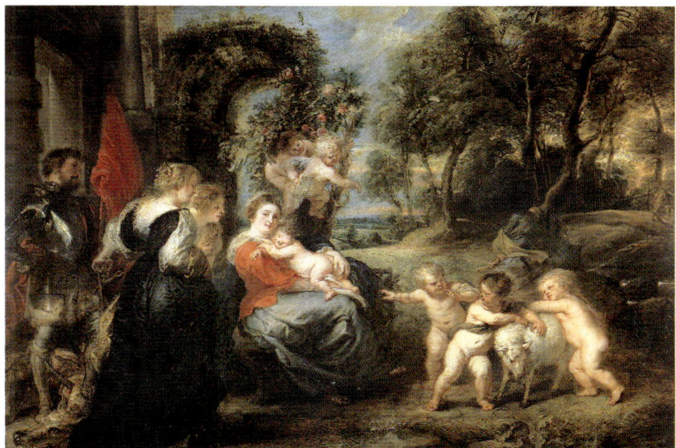

1. K.d.K., ed. Oldenbourg 1921, no. 345; M. Jaffé 1989, no. 1086, ca. 1632–35. The painting was still in Rubens's collection at the time of his death. King Philip IV of Spain acquired it from the artist's estate (Muller 1989, p. 111, 1, no. 84, pl. 33).
2. Hollstein 1949–, vol. 9, pp. 181–92, nos. 1, 4, 5, 6, 10, 15, 16, 17a,b, 20.
3. See Myers 1966, pp. 10–13; Renger 1975, pp. 189–96; Van Hout 2004, pp. 92–107.
4. Reproduced in Rościszewska 1993, pp. 78, 82, figs. 5, 6, 14–16. We thank Grażyna Hałasa, curator of prints and drawings at the Muzeum Narodowe, for creating this overlay.

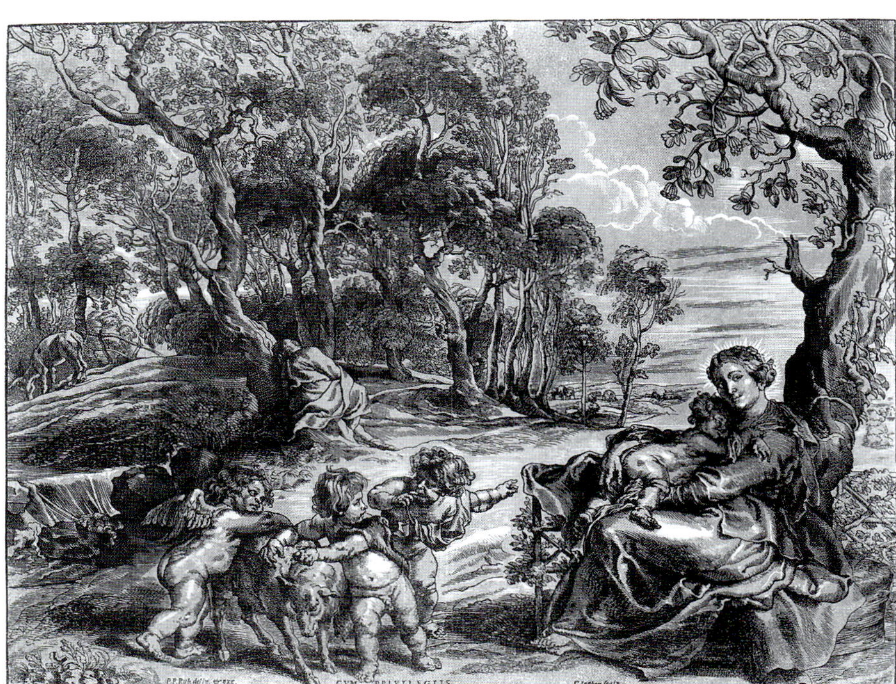

Fig. 144. Christoffel Jegher, *Rest on the Flight into Egypt,* ca. 1633–34. Chiaroscuro woodcut; one line block and one tone block, 462 x 599 mm (18$^{3}/_{16}$ x 23$^{9}/_{16}$ in.). The Metropolitan Museum of Art, New York; The Elisha Whittelsey Collection, The Elisha Whittelsey Fund, 1951 (51.501.7332)

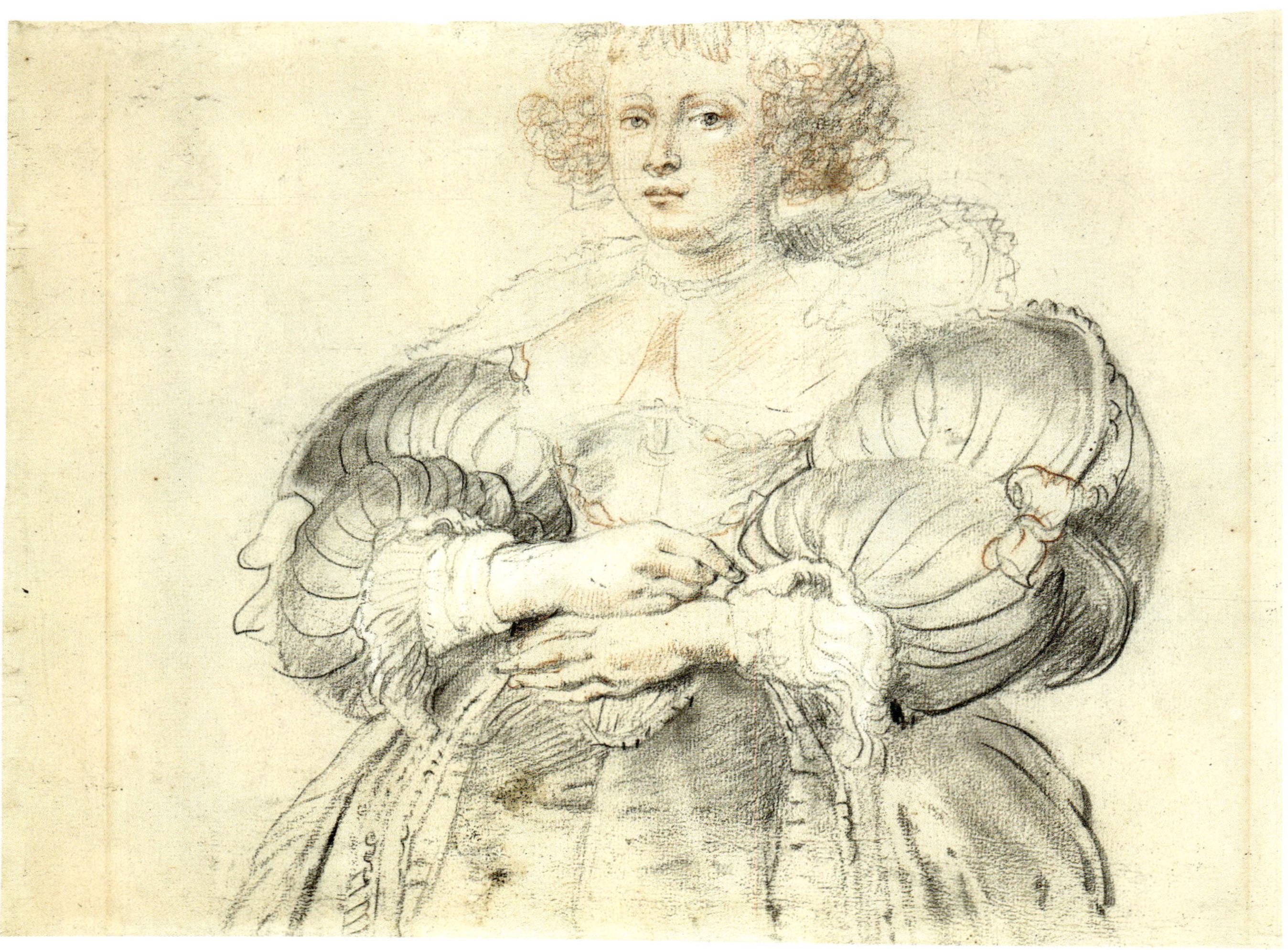

Cat. 96 recto

96. *Study of a Young Woman (Helena Fourment?),* recto, early 1630s; *Study of Drapery,* verso, ca. 1638–39

Black chalk (charcoal?) and some red chalk (in face, breast, hands, ribbon), heightened with white chalk, recto; black and some red chalk (right hand), traces of heightening with white chalk, verso, 320 x 405 mm (12⅝ x 16⅛ in.)

Albertina, Vienna (8255)

PROVENANCE: Hofbibliothek, Vienna; in 1796 acquired through exchange by Duke Albert of Sachsen-Teschen (1738–1822), Vienna (Lugt 174).

LITERATURE: R., vol. 5, no. 1540 (recto and verso); Glück and Haberditzl 1928, no. 232, pl. 232 (recto), no. 233, pl. 233 (verso); Vlieghe 1987, no. 100b, fig. 106 (recto), no. 100c, fig. 107 (verso).

EXHIBITIONS: Vienna 1977b, nos. 52, 53, ill.; Vienna–Amsterdam 1989–90, no. 52, ill.; New York and other cities 1997–99, no. 40, ill; Toronto–New York 2000, pl. 31, ill. (verso).

The lady in a fashionable dress seen in three-quarter length on the recto of this sheet resembles the woman wearing a plumed hat and holding an ostrich feather in her right hand in Rubens's full-length portrait *Susanna Fourment* (called), now in the Calouste Gulbenkian Museum, Lisbon (fig. 145).[1] The similarity is most apparent in the posture of the figures and in the way they hold their hands; in dress and facial features, the women vary. The Lisbon portrait is dated to the early 1630s, a date that also seems reasonable for the recto drawing. Stylistically, the study is close to Rubens's large chalk drawings for individual figures in his *Garden of Love* painting (see cat. nos. 90–92).

The women represented in the drawing and in the portrait

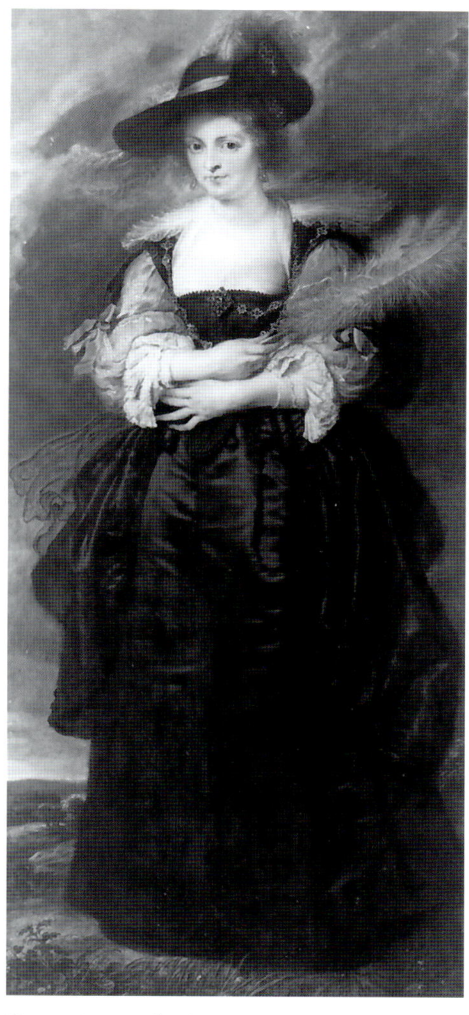

Fig. 145. Peter Paul Rubens, *Susanna Fourment* (called), early 1630s. Oil on panel, 187 x 86 cm (73⅝ x 33⅞ in.). Calouste Gulbenkian Museum, Lisbon (959)

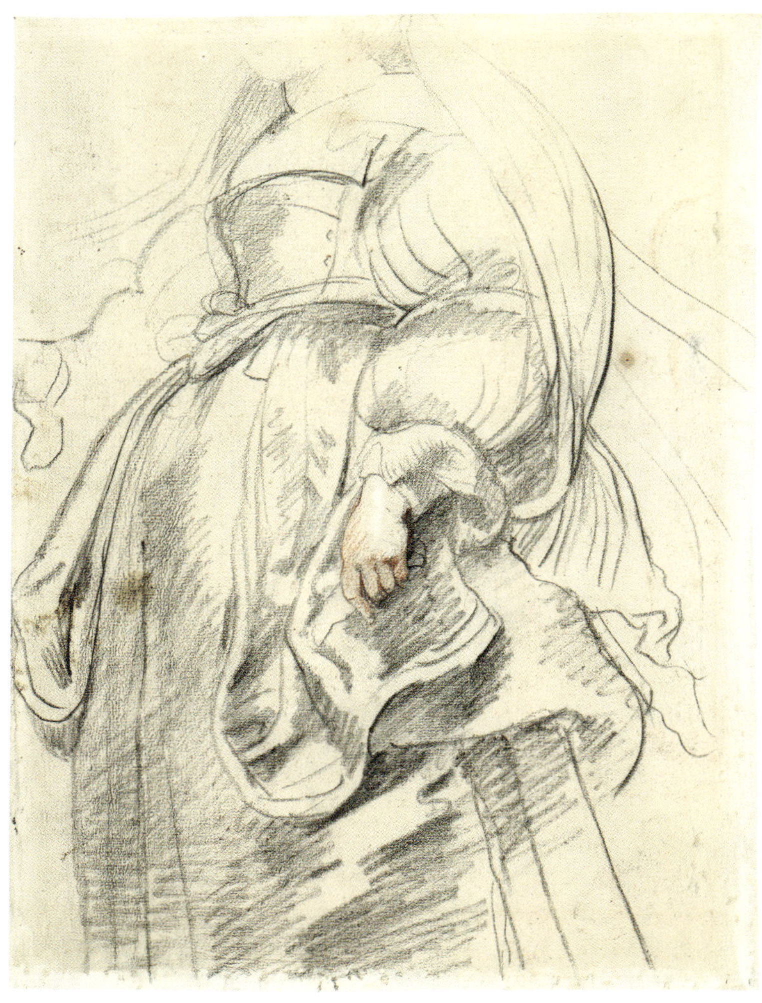

Cat. 96 verso

in Lisbon have previously been identified either as Helena Fourment (1614–1673), Rubens's second wife, or as Susanna Fourment (1599–1628), Helena's older sister, who died two years before Helena's marriage to the artist.[2] Today, scholars consider the identity of the women portrayed uncertain, although they favor Helena. A general likeness with the Fourment sisters may mean that both the drawing and the painting represent another woman in the family—Helena had five older sisters besides Susanna.

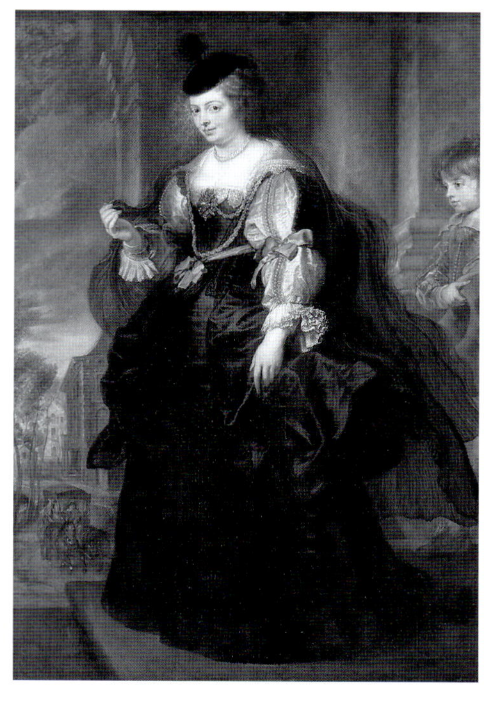

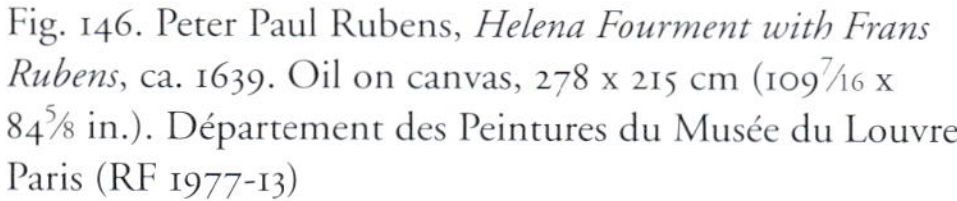

Fig. 146. Peter Paul Rubens, *Helena Fourment with Frans Rubens*, ca. 1639. Oil on canvas, 278 x 215 cm (109 7/16 x 84⅝ in.). Département des Peintures du Musée du Louvre, Paris (RF 1977-13)

The drapery study on the verso of the sheet is also connected with a Rubens painting: his late (about 1639) full-length portrait of Helena leaving the family's residence with Rubens's and her son Frans (fig. 146).[3] The overall arrangement of the dress, falling in heavy folds, is similar to that in the painting, and the sketch may be one that Rubens made while he was working on the painting, which began, like the drawing, as a half- or three-quarter-length portrait.[4] The drawing's association with the painting makes plausible a date of about 1638–39 for the drapery study.

Both the recto and the verso were tampered with at a later date; the most obvious intervention is the addition of red chalk. Some of the outlines of the drapery study have been strengthened, and the clumsy hatching at the lower left is not by Rubens. This sheet is also one of several in the Albertina that were cut after they left Rubens's studio (see also cat. nos. 41, 58, 63). Here, part of the woman's head on the recto was trimmed away, but in order to make the drawing more appealing, it was later "restored" by the addition of a strip 12 mm wide. The strip was recently removed.

1. K.d.K., ed. Oldenbourg 1921, no. 329; M. Jaffé 1989, no. 1002, ca. 1631.
2. Susanna died on July 31, 1628, and therefore cannot be the sitter in the Lisbon portrait. See Vlieghe 1983, p. 108.
3. K.d.K., ed. Oldenbourg 1921, no. 425; M. Jaffé 1989, no. 1400, ca. 1639.
4. As Evers (1942, p. 448) realized, the painting consists of several panels that were pieced together. Besides panels along the sides, a larger panel 70 cm wide was added at the bottom of the central section (which measured 106 x 60 cm). See Foucart 1977, p. 353, n. 39.

FARM LIFE AND LANDSCAPES

97. *A Saddled Horse and Detail of Tucked Front Legs,* ca. 1615–18

Black and red chalk, heightened with white chalk (?), 413 x 428 mm (15¾ x 16¾ in.)
Annotated in pen and brown ink at bottom left: *P P R*; in black chalk at bottom center: *bra* (?)

Albertina, Vienna (8252)

PROVENANCE: Duke Albert of Sachsen-Teschen (1738–1822), Vienna (Lugt 174).

LITERATURE: R., vol. 5, no. 1582, pl. 428; Glück and Haberditzl 1928, no. 139, pl. 139; Held 1959, no. 87, pl. 105; Kuznetsov 1974, pl. 73; Held 1986, no. 109, pl. 108.

EXHIBITIONS: Vienna 1977b, no. 18, ill.; Vienna–Amsterdam 1989–90, no. 48, ill.

This impressive study of a horse[1] is found among the sizable group of Rubens's portrait drawings in the Albertina. Indeed, in execution the drawing is not unlike Rubens's portrait studies in black and red chalk. Furthermore, it does not seem to have been made in preparation for a painting. One wonders, therefore, if the horse was a special one to Rubens, perhaps a favorite riding horse. Rubens was an excellent horseman, which must have been known to Duke Vincenzo Gonzaga of Mantua, who in 1603 entrusted the artist with escorting seven exceptionally beautiful horses to Spain as gifts for King Philip III. Rubens's nephew Philip recalled that—health permitting—his uncle enjoyed relaxing by riding a Spanish horse.[2] However, the horse Rubens drew here is an ordinary riding horse.[3] The horse is saddled up, with the right hind leg relaxed, waiting for the rider; the tucked legs in the detail at the left, with the chest far forward, show the position of a horse when it jumps over low hedges or walls.

Rubens most likely drew the animal from life in black chalk and finished the study in the studio, adding the dark red chalk (which approximates a brown coat). The date of 1615–18 that Held suggested for the drawing places it in the years when Rubens was working on the *Decius Mus* paintings cycle and the various *Hunts,* all subjects in which horses play a prominent role. A closely related copy, of the horse's head only, is preserved among the *cantoor* drawings in Copenhagen,[4] along with several other studies of horses, including a horse with an overlay of measurements for the right proportions. Rubens's student Willem Panneels (ca. 1600–1634), who made a copy after the Rubens original, annotated his version as follows: "This horse I have also taken from the *cantoor,* and it is the

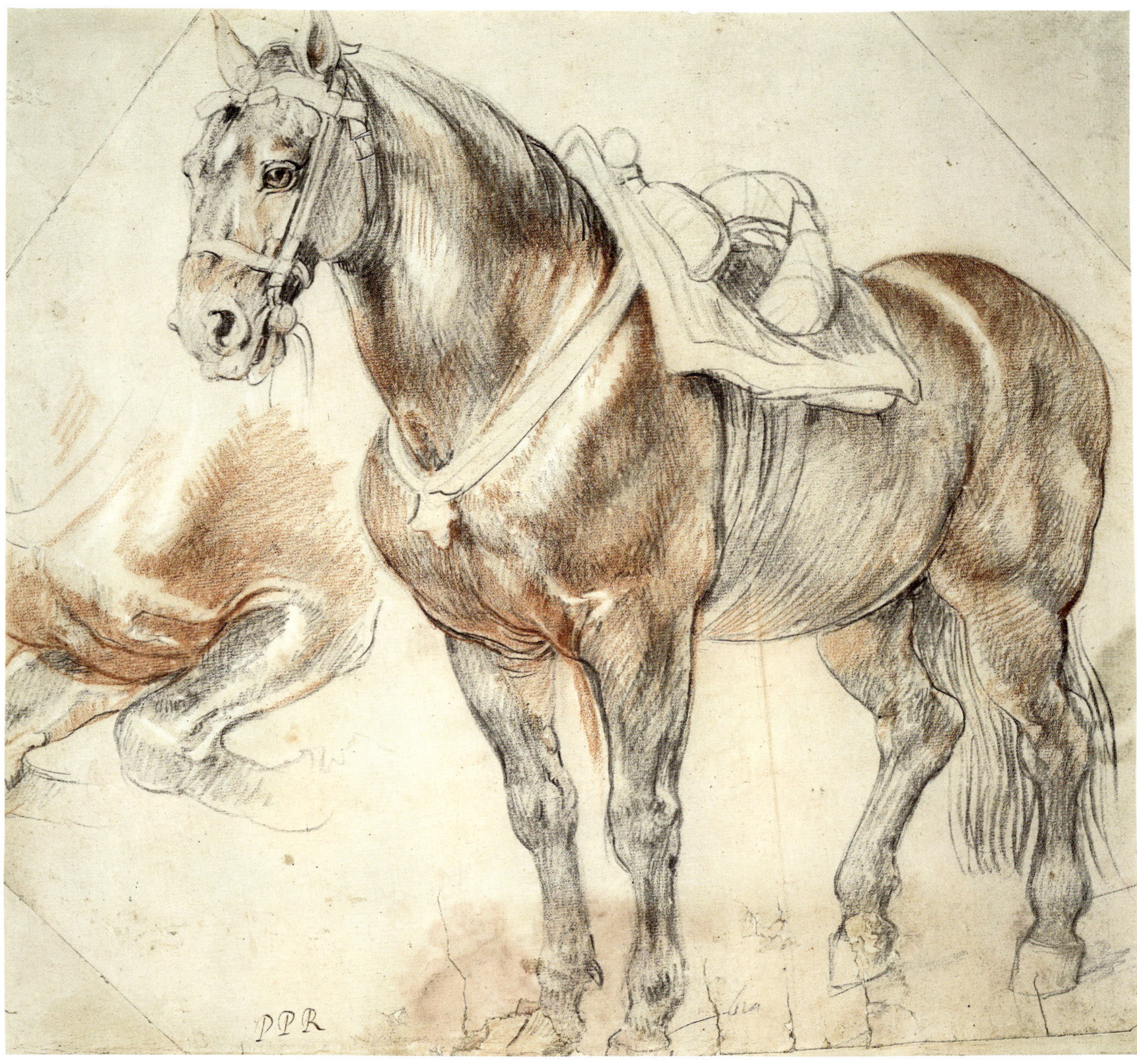

Cat. 97

right proportion for horses, and it is like an 'anatomy.'"[5]

The initials "P P R," inscribed on the sheet in pen and ink, were probably added by an early owner of the drawing, in the seventeenth or eighteenth century. The same inscription is found, also in pen and ink, on another study in the Albertina, *An Ox* (cat. no. 99), and, in chalk and slightly different handwriting, on Rubens's *Copy after the "Belvedere Torso"* in The Metropolitan Museum of Art (cat. no. 34 verso). The shared inscription may indicate that these sheets were once together in the same collection.

1. We believe that Lugt (1949, nos. 1269, 1270) was correct to attribute to a Rubens follower the drawings of horses today in the Louvre. Held, who saw Rubens's hand in those drawings, added two more sheets to the group (Held 1959, no. 87, pl. 105; Held 1986, no. 109, pl. 108). However, they are no more likely than the others to be by Rubens.
2. Based on his correspondence with Philip, Roger de Piles (1635–1709) recounted that Rubens frequently finished his day with a ride at five in the afternoon outside Antwerp or on the ramparts, to enjoy the fresh air. Memorandum to de Piles for his life of Rubens, in Ruelens 1883, p. 165.
3. We thank Walter Liedtke, curator in the Department of European Paintings at The Metropolitan Museum of Art, for this information.
4. Inv. VI, 79; red over black chalk, heightened with white, 196 x 131 mm.
5. Copenhagen 1988, no. 161, ill.: "ditpaerdekenhebbeick oockvantcantoorgehaelt / endedit isdrechtermate vandepaerdendit / is gelijck eenannotomie."

98. *A Man Threshing beside a Wagon, Farm Buildings Behind,* ca. 1617–18

Black and some red, blue-green, yellow, and green chalk, pen and dark brown ink, on pale gray paper, 252 x 414 mm (10 x 16¼ in.)

The J. Paul Getty Museum, Los Angeles (84.GG.693)

PROVENANCE: William, 2nd Duke of Devonshire (1673–1729), Chatsworth; by descent to the 11th Duke of Devonshire (1920–2004), Chatsworth (sale, London, Christie's, July 3, 1984, lot 52, ill.).

LITERATURE: Glück and Haberditzl 1928, no. 94, pl. 94; Burchard and d'Hulst 1963, no. 101, pl. 101; Kuznetsov 1974, pl. 61; Adler 1982, no. 26a, fig. 76, pp. 82, under no. 20, 100, under no. 26; Held 1986, no. 113, pl. 115; Goldner 1988, no. 92, pl. 10; M. Jaffé 2002, no. 1155, ill.

EXHIBITION: London 1977a, no. 202, ill.

On this sheet Rubens recorded a typical harvest-time scene: a man threshing (corn?) with a wooden flail, next to an empty wagon parked beside a barn. There are a number of pentimenti, most noticeably in the position of the flail and in the farmer's right hand, which was originally placed higher up on the implement. Rubens rendered the empty wagon at the right with few corrections or changes, but accentuated several parts with the pen in order to clarify its structure. The inclusion of colored chalks—yellow, green, blue-green, and red—is unusual for Rubens. However, the same blue-green chalk is found in Rubens's drawings of the Jesuit missionary Nicolas Trigault (cat. nos. 73, 74) and in the study of another missionary, perhaps Johann Schreck, in the Pierpont Morgan Library, New York.[1]

Rubens's painstaking drawing of the wagon betrays an early interest in farm life. The same wagon, or an almost identical one, reappears in three paintings by Rubens and in one drawing. The farmer, by contrast, is not found in any of Rubens's paintings of country life. From Rubens's closely related drawing of *Two Wagons* (fig. 147),[2] we gather that one of the wagon's uses was to transport sheaves of corn. This type of wagon was used frequently in Antwerp's environs, especially in the so-called Waasland, west of the river Scheldt.[3]

Although the wagon was characteristic of the Antwerp region, Rubens had no difficulty depicting it, in *Landscape with a Mired Cart* (Hermitage, Saint Petersburg),[4] in an imaginary mountainous landscape that is more reminiscent of the Ardennes than of the lowland around the river Scheldt. In the painting the wagon is shown, as it is in the drawing, from the rear; the perspective, however, is slightly different. A wagon seen from exactly the same angle as in the drawing, even with the same background, is found in Rubens's *Prodigal Son,* painted about 1618 (fig. 148).[5] (Rubens may have made the present drawing specifically for this painting.) The third time this wagon appears is in *Winter,* now at Windsor Castle,[6] in which it is again presented from the same angle as in the drawing. The view is partially blocked, however, by a wooden pillar. As all three paintings are generally dated in the second half of the 1610s, the same date is logical for the present drawing.

1. Stampfle 1991, no. 310, ill.
2. Held 1986, no. 118, pl. 118.
3. Theuwissen 1977, p. 362.
4. K.d.K., ed. Oldenbourg 1921, no. 185; M. Jaffé 1989, no. 402, ca. 1616.
5. K.d.K., ed. Oldenbourg 1921, no. 182, ca. 1618; M. Jaffé 1989, no. 502, 1618–19.
6. K.d.K., ed. Oldenbourg 1921, no. 238, ca. 1618; Adler 1982, no. 26, ca. 1619; M. Jaffé 1989, no. 669, 1620–25.

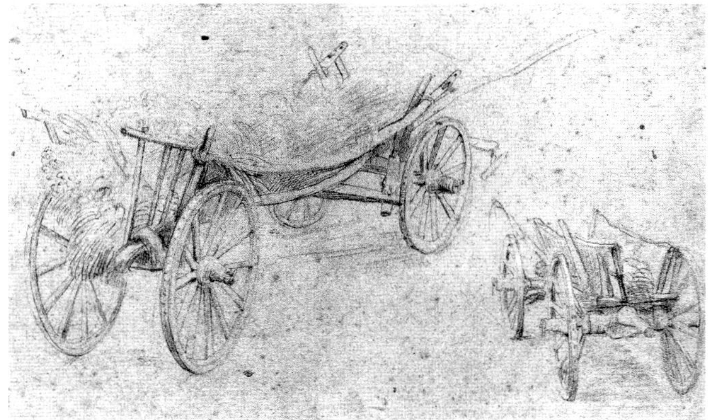

Fig. 147. Peter Paul Rubens, *Two Wagons,* ca. 1617–18. Black chalk, pen and brown ink, traces of red, yellow and green chalk, heightened with white, on brownish paper, 22.4 x 37.5 cm (8¹³⁄₁₆ x 14¾ in.). Staatliche Museen zu Berlin–Preussischer Kulturbesitz, Kupferstichkabinett, Berlin (KdZ 3237)

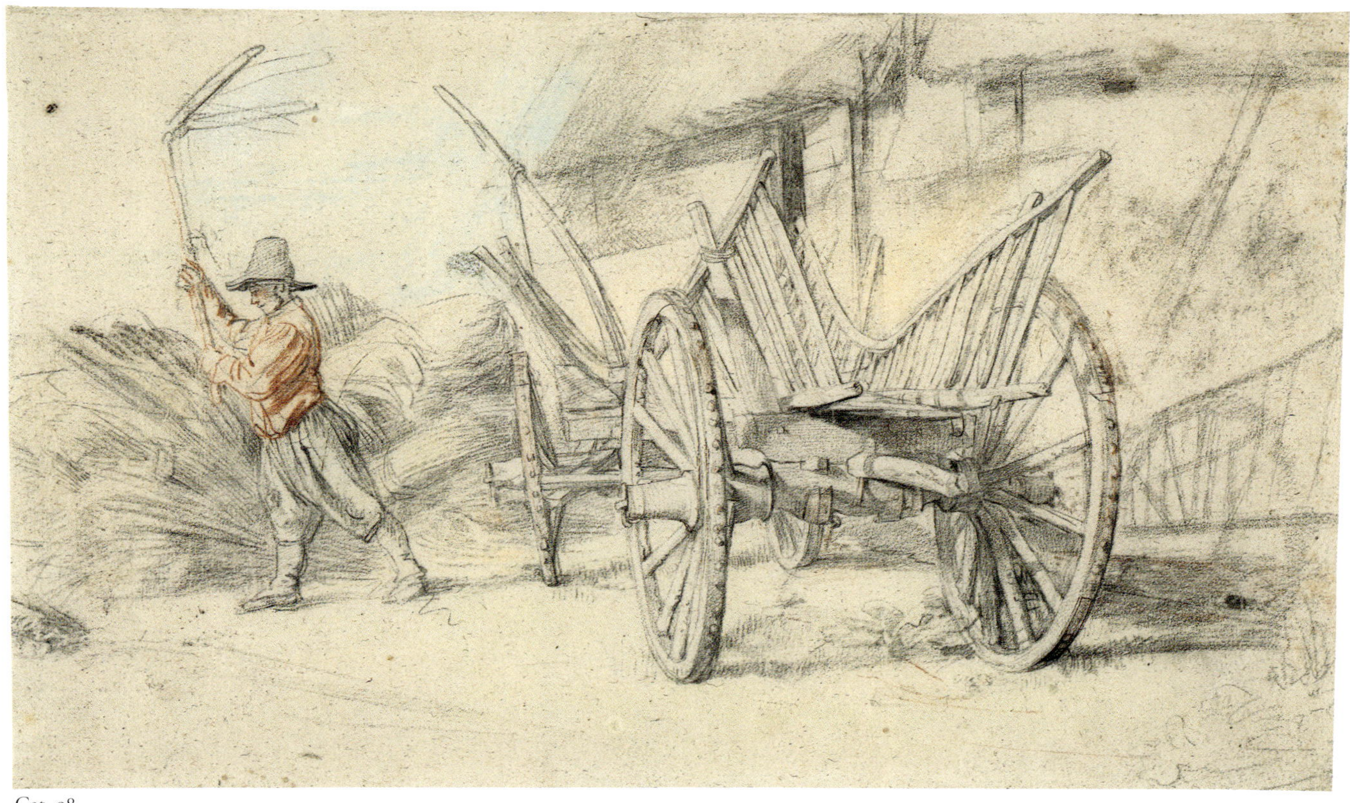

Cat. 98

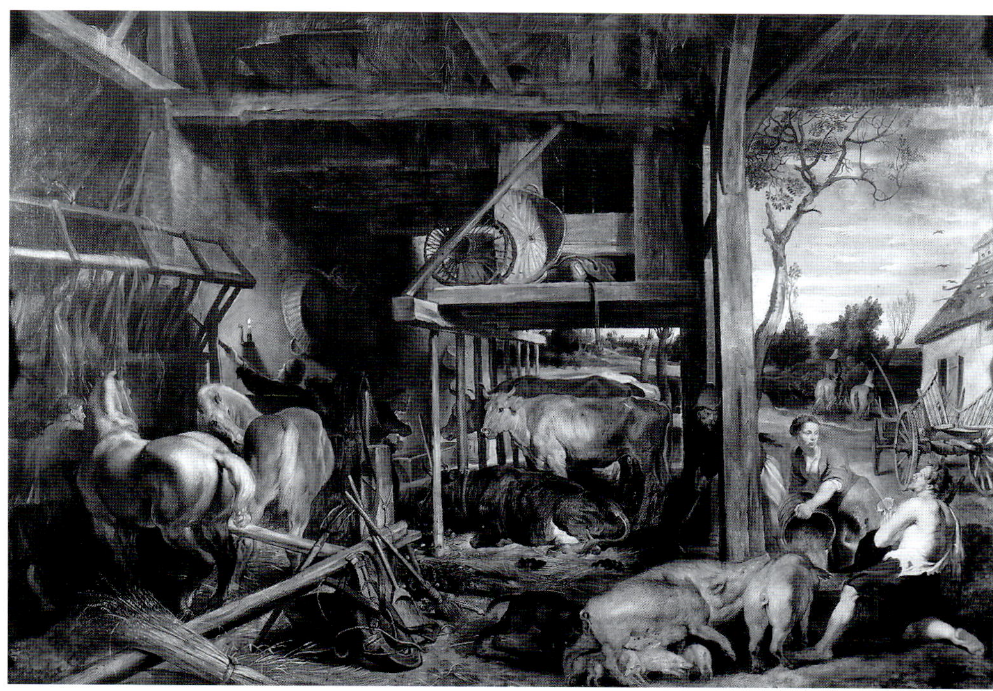

Fig. 148. Peter Paul Rubens, *The Prodigal Son,* ca. 1618. Oil on panel, 107 x 155 cm (42⅛ x 61 in.). Koninklijk Museum voor Schone Kunsten, Antwerp (781)

99. *An Ox*, ca. 1618

Black and red chalk, traces of heightening with white, brush and brown and some gray ink, 286 x 440 mm (11 x 13⅝ in.)
Annotated in pen and brown ink at bottom center: *P P R*

Albertina, Vienna (8253)

PROVENANCE: Duke Albert of Sachsen-Teschen (1738–1822), Vienna (Lugt 174).

LITERATURE: R., vol. 5, no. 1583; Glück and Haberditzl 1928, no. 138, pl. 138; Held 1959, no. 91, pl. 106; Kuznetsov 1974, pl. 72; Adler 1982, no. 20a, fig. 64 [Rubens?], p. 82, under no. 20, copy 2; Held 1986, no. 110, pl. 109; Brown in London 1996–97, p. 47, fig. 34.

EXHIBITIONS: Vienna 1977b, no. 30, ill.; New York and other cities 1997–99, no. 36 (New York), ill.; Sydney 2002, no. 51, ill.

Together with Rubens's depiction of a horse (cat. no. 97), this close-up study of an ox is one of the artist's most impressive surviving drawings of domestic animals. The artist likely sketched the animal from life, in black-chalk outlines, and later finished the study in the studio, adding the dark red chalk. The elaborate technique used sets this drawing (and the study of a horse) apart from Rubens's usual preliminary studies. Rubens presents the ox gazing out at the viewer, and in such detail, that it seems like a portrait. Perhaps the ox was a prize animal kept on one of the farms outside Antwerp that Rubens inherited after the death of his mother, Maria Pypelincx, in 1608, and after his brother Philip passed away in 1611. There is a tradition in Netherlandish art of representing prize animals, alone, in very much the way Rubens represented the ox in this drawing.[1]

Although the "portrait" of the ox was in all likelihood not made with a specific purpose in mind, Rubens did not hesitate to turn to it for use in his paintings. A similar, slightly more compact ox stands in the center of Rubens's *Farm at Laeken* (fig. 149), dated about 1618–19.[2] The same ox appears in the much later *Landscape with Duck Hunters*, in the right foreground.[3]

The annotation in pen and brown ink at the bottom of the sheet, "P P R," was probably inscribed by an early collector and is also found on Rubens's *Saddled Horse* (cat. no. 97). One can discern the same annotation, possibly in the same handwriting, on a study of Rubens's son Albert (Hermitage, Saint Petersburg),[4] in a drawing of a tree that has at times been attributed to Rubens,[5] and in Rubens's early *Copy after the "Belvedere Torso"* (cat. no. 34 verso). In the seventeenth and eighteenth centuries it was not unusual for collectors to write on drawings. (See, for example, the inscriptions by Padre Sebastiano Resta on Rubens's portrait of Marie de Médicis [cat. no. 76] and on Rubens's copy after the so-called Dying Seneca [cat. no. 23].) Seventeenth-century collectors added Rubens's "signature"—"P P Rubbens" or "Rubbens"—to several of the artist's most beautiful drawings.[6]

1. See Dordrecht–Leeuwarden 1988–89.
2. K.d.K., ed. Oldenbourg 1921, no. 186; M. Jaffé 1989, no. 515, 1618–19.
3. M. Jaffé 1989, no. 1219, 1635–38.
4. Dobroklonskii 1940, no. 11, pl. 13; Vienna 1977b, under no. 18.
5. As observed by Held (1959, under no. 87). For the drawing of a tree, see Glück and Haberditzl 1928, no. 184. In this case, however, the initials are followed by the full name, as noted by Mitsch (Vienna 1977b, under no. 18).
6. See cat. nos. 11, 59 ("Rubbens"), and 70, 71, 81, 83, 84, 86, 87 ("P P Rubbens").

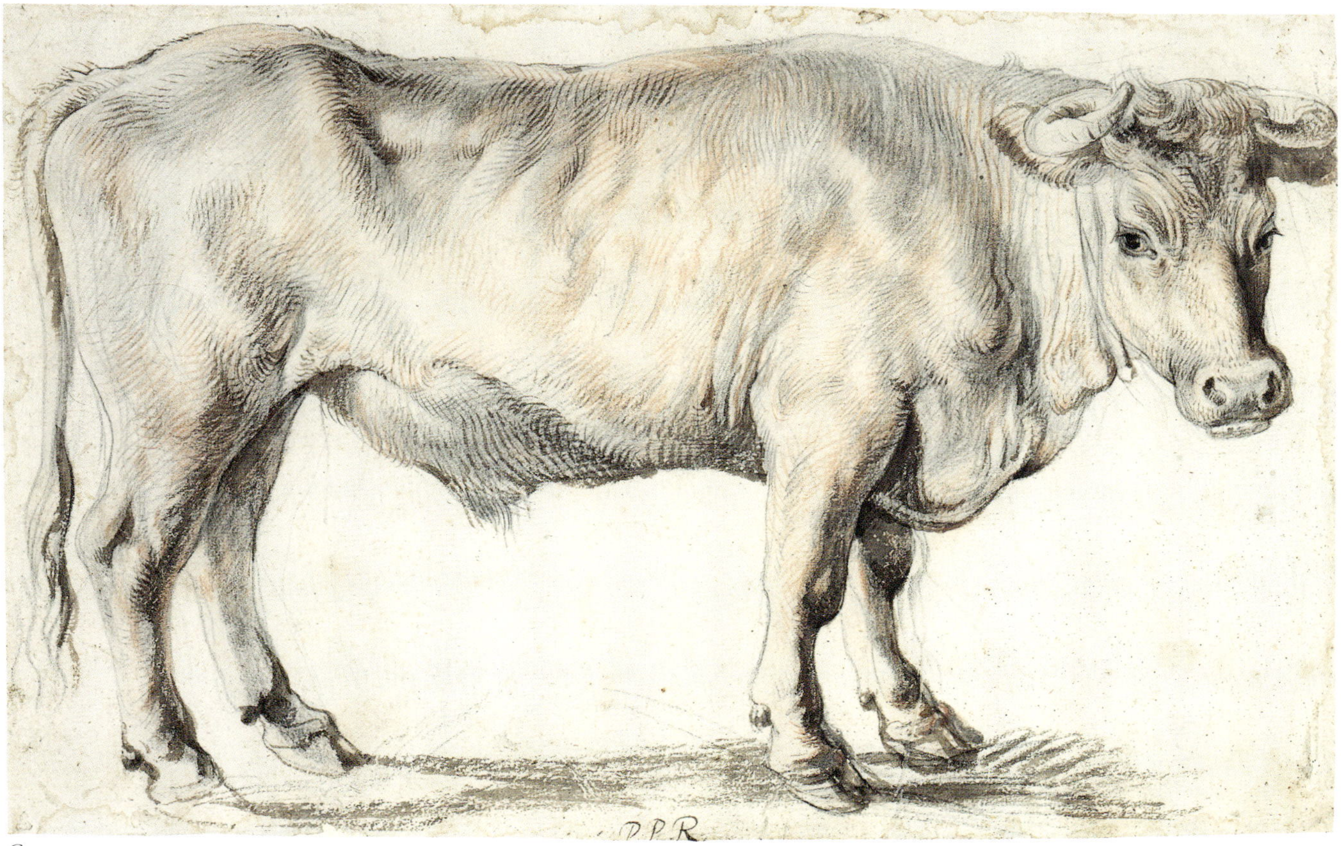

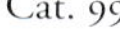

Cat. 99

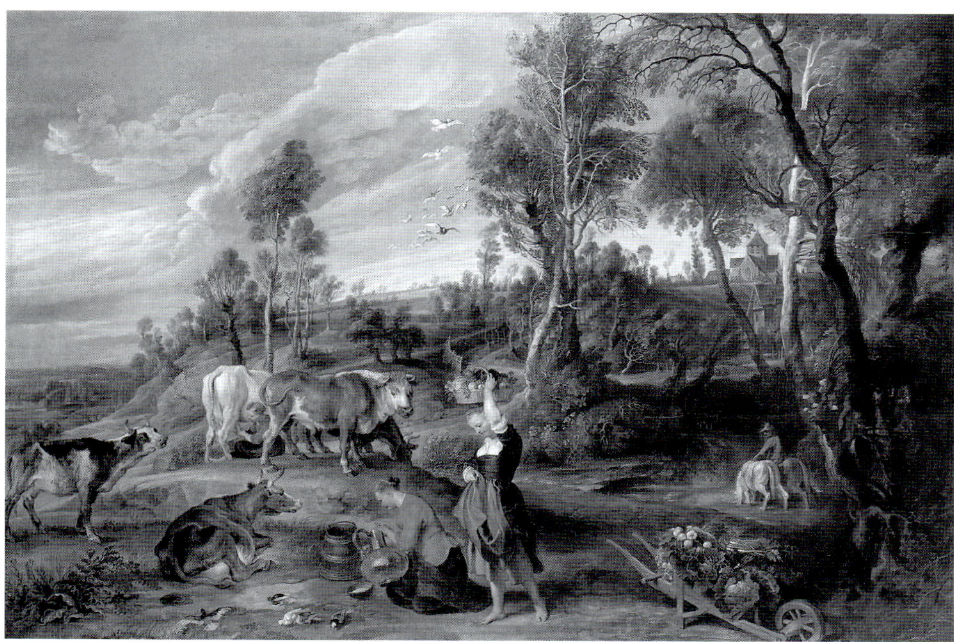

Fig. 149. Peter Paul Rubens, *The Farm at Laeken*, ca. 1618–19. Oil on panel, 84.5 x 125.5 cm ($33\frac{1}{4}$ x $49\frac{7}{16}$ in.). Collection of Her Majesty the Queen, Buckingham Palace, London (RCIN 405333)

ANTHONY VAN DYCK

100. *Cattle in Pasture,* ca. 1618–20

Pen and brown ink and some brown wash, 318 x 515 mm (12½ x 20¼ in.)
Annotated (in a 17th- or 18th-century hand?) in pen and brown ink at bottom center: *Ant. van Dyck*

The Duke of Devonshire and the Chatsworth Settlement Trustees, Chatsworth (964)

PROVENANCE: Nicolaes A. Flinck (1646–1723), Rotterdam (Lugt 959); presumably acquired by William, 2nd Duke of Devonshire (1673–1729), in 1723.

LITERATURE: R., vol. 5, no. 1584 [Rubens]; Hind 1923, p. 36, under no. 118; Glück and Haberditzl 1928, p. 47, under no. 136 [Rubens]; Held 1959, pp. 12, 133, under no. 88, p. 133, fig. 21 [Rubens?]; Adler 1982, pp. 104–6, under no. 27b, copy 1, fig. 81; Held 1986, p. 14, fig. 2; Brown in New York–Fort Worth 1991, p. 27, n. 8 [more likely Rubens]; M. Jaffé 2002, no. 973, ill.

EXHIBITIONS: London 1977a, no. 200; Richmond and other cities 1979–80, no. 86; London 1993–94, no. 161, ill.

PETER PAUL RUBENS (?)

101. *Cattle in Pasture,* ca. 1618–20

Pen and brown ink and touches of gray wash, 340 x 522 mm (13⅜ x 20½ in.)
Annotated in pen and brown ink at bottom right: *P. P. Rubbens*

The British Museum, London (1895.9.15.1046)

PROVENANCE: Dirk Versteegh (1751–1822), Amsterdam (his sale, Amsterdam, De Vries . . . Roos, November 3, 1823, portfolio 2, lot 41 or 42; Sir Thomas Lawrence (1769–1830), London (Lugt 2445); Samuel Woodburn (his sale, London, Christie's, June 7, 1860, lot 794); William II of the Netherlands (1792–1849), The Hague (his sale, The Hague, August 12, 1850, lot 300); Gerard Leembruggen Jzn (1801–1865), Hillegom (Lugt 2988; sale, Amsterdam, March 5, 1866, and following days); J. C. Robinson (1824–1913), London (Lugt 1433; sale, Paris, May 7–8, 1868, lot 587); John Malcolm (1805–1893), London (Lugt 1780); purchased by the British Museum in 1895.

LITERATURE: Hind 1923, p. 36, no. 118, pl. XVII [Rubens]; Glück and Haberditzl 1928, no. 136, pl. 136 [Rubens]; Held 1959, p. 12; Adler 1982, pp. 104–6, under no. 27b, copy 2, fig. 82; Held 1986, pp. 13–14 [Rubens?]; Royalton-Kisch in Antwerp–London 1999a, p. 17, fig. 7 [Rubens? After Van Dyck]; M. Jaffé 2002, under no. 973.

EXHIBITION: London 1977a, no. 201, ill. [Rubens studio].

PAULUS PONTIUS

102. *Cows,* 1640–58

Engraving, 222 x 327 mm (8¾ x 12⅞ in.)

Albertina, Vienna (DG2003/2599)

In the past, copying was a major occupation of the artist. It was an essential learning device for the apprentice, of course, but accomplished artists copied, too, emulating the works of both their predecessors and, to stay current, their contemporaries. Among the many students in Rubens's active

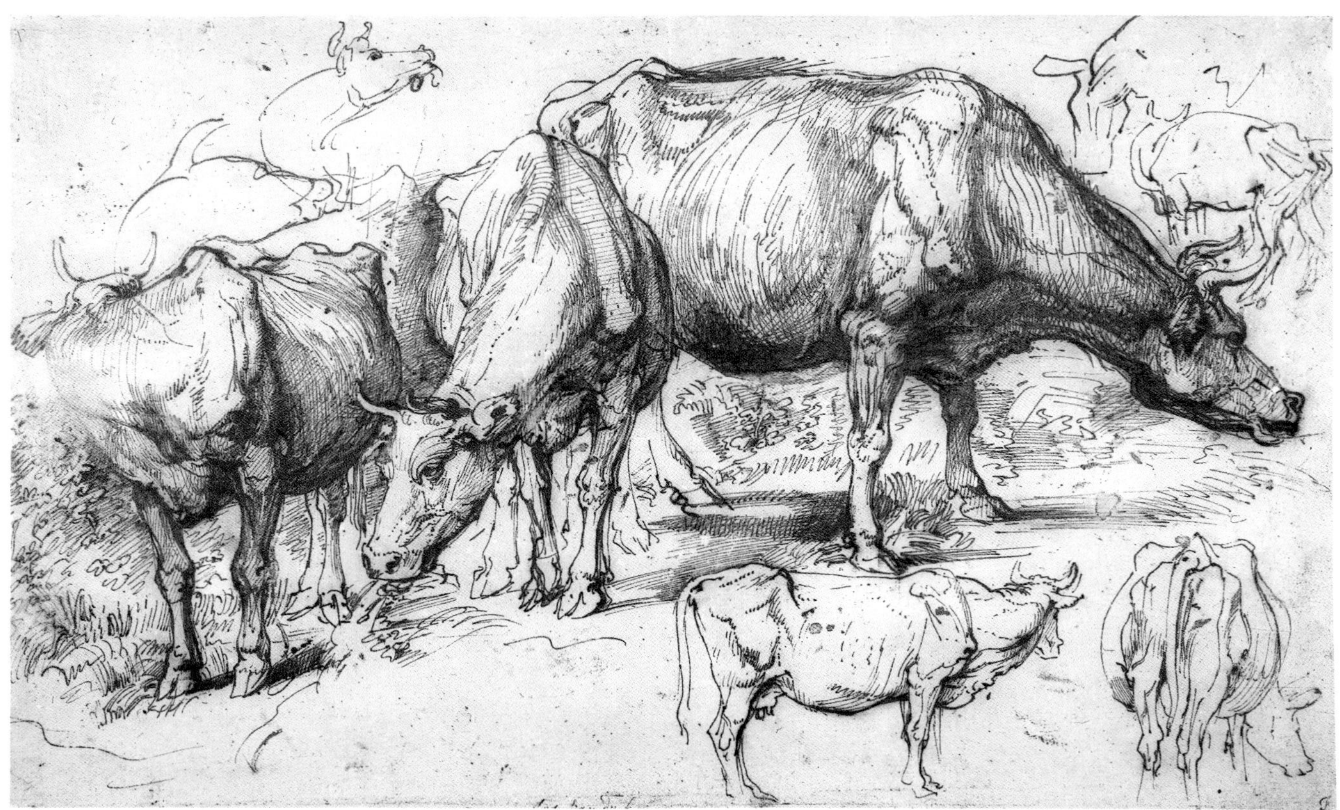

Cat. 100

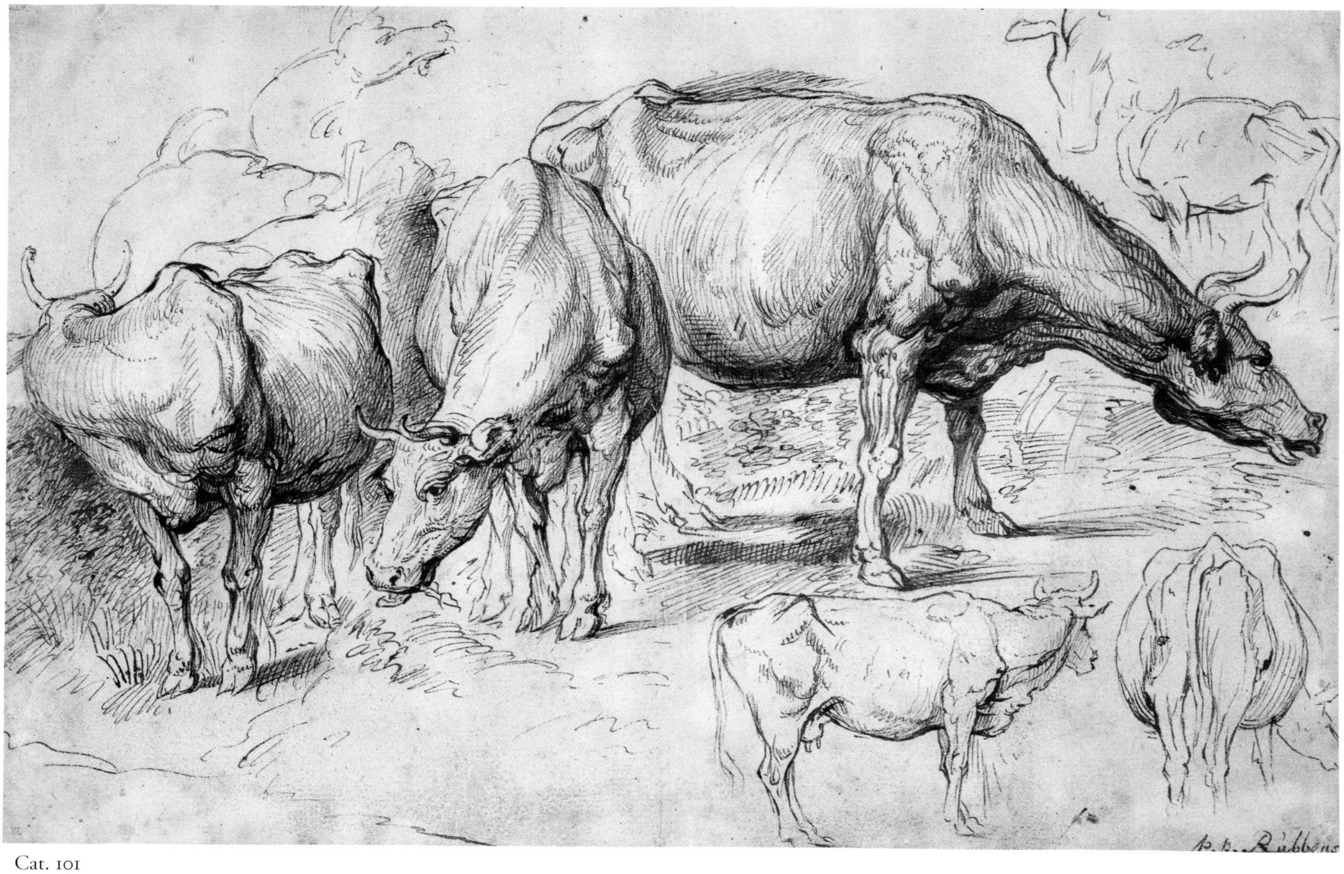

Cat. 101

studio, copying must have been a frequent task. An important group of copies from Rubens's studio has remained together to this day, in the so-called Rubens *cantoor* in Copenhagen; they are for the most part the work of Willem Panneels (ca. 1600–1634; see cat. no. 21). It is not always simple, however, to detect which among multiple versions of a drawing is the original. The drawing *Cattle in Pasture* is a famous and difficult case of distinguishing who copied whom, involving Rubens and his most brilliant collaborator, Anthony van Dyck (1599–1641).

The *Cattle in Pasture* is known through four versions of almost equal size, all executed in pen and ink (of various sorts): two examples are in the British Museum, London (cat. no. 101 is the superior of the two), one is at Chatsworth (cat. no. 100), and one was formerly in an English private collection.[1] In addition, Paulus Pontius (1603–1658) engraved the composition in reverse and included it in the so-called *Drawing Book* (published in Antwerp after Rubens's death) as plate 16 (cat. no. 102), indicating that the print was after a Rubens drawing. Rubens's name, added by later owners, is found on both versions of the drawing in London. On the Chatsworth version, however, one finds the name of Anthony van Dyck, written, it has been suggested, in his own hand.

The Chatsworth sheet (cat. no. 100) and one of the London drawings (cat. no. 101) are of obviously greater quality than the other two, and the version at Chatsworth seems to have been the example for the two lesser drawings. However, Pontius appears to have taken the inferior of the two London drawings as the model for his etching, which is perhaps an indication that at the time originality was not the important issue that it is today.

A close comparison of the Chatsworth *Cattle in Pasture* (cat. no. 100) and the superior of the drawings in London (cat. no. 101) indicates that the Chatsworth sheet is drawn with more vigor and less hesitation. There, the cow grazing in the foreground is also more realistic. In one detail—the contour of the rump of the cow in the center facing to the right—the London drawing follows a corrected contour in the Chatsworth example, which seems to indicate that it is based on the latter. The small dots found in some of the lines in the Chatsworth drawing are traditionally associated with Van Dyck, however, not with Rubens. Moreover, the younger artist also preferred the darker brown ink of the drawing at Chatsworth, while Rubens generally used the lighter brown bistre ink.

Unfortunately, there is little in Van Dyck's oeuvre with which to compare the Chatsworth drawing in support of its attribution to him; one beautiful drawing of horses is included in his Italian sketchbook, but the sketch is looser, with many pentimenti.[2] No painting by Rubens or Van Dyck, and no oil sketch by Rubens, includes the same closely knit group of grazing cattle. Similar cattle do appear in Rubens's *Polder Landscape*

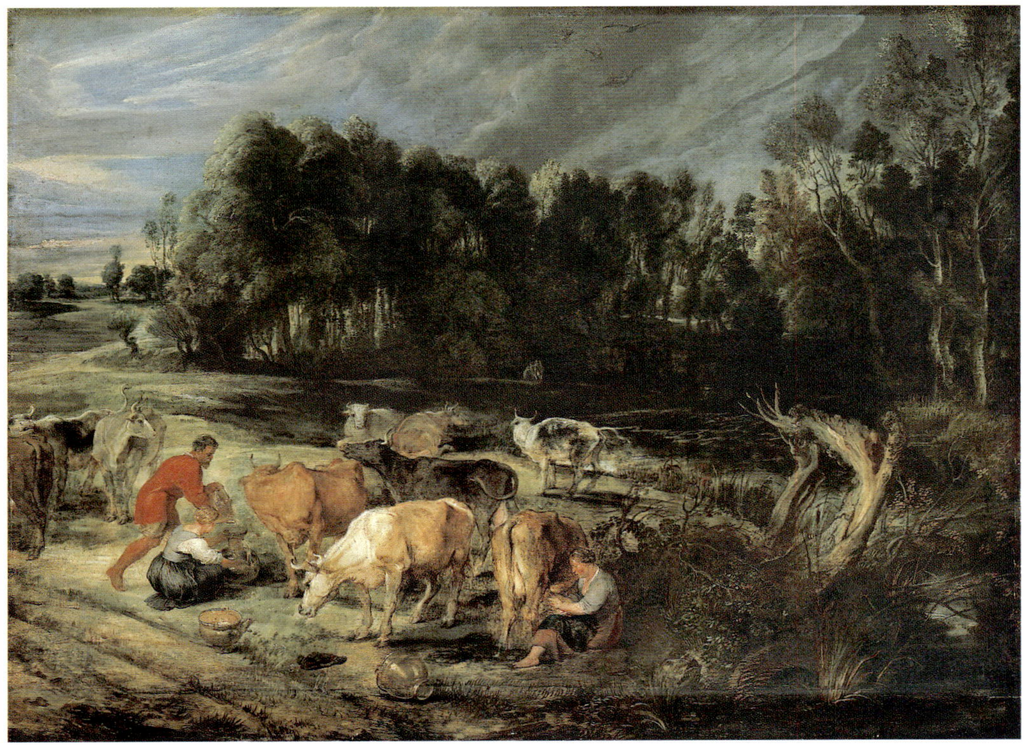

Fig. 150. Peter Paul Rubens, *Polder Landscape with Eleven Cows,* ca. 1618. Oil on panel, 81 x 106.5 cm (31⅞ x 41$^{15}/_{16}$ in.). Bayerische Staatsgemäldesammlungen, Alte Pinakothek, Munich (322)

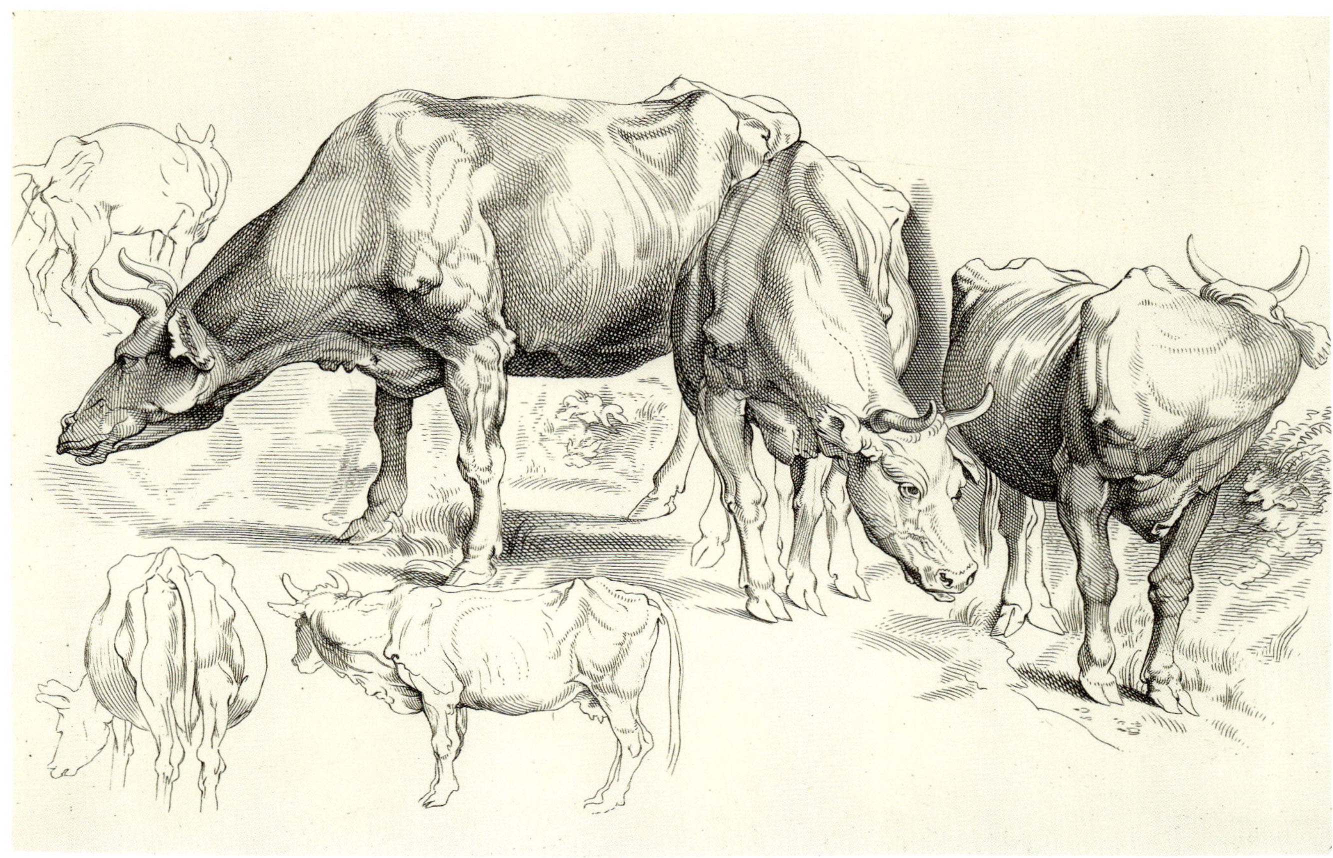

Cat. 102

with Eleven Cows (fig. 150), a painting dated to about 1618, a time when Van Dyck was collaborating with Rubens,[3] and in the late *Landscape with Cows and Sportsmen* in Berlin.[4] Since the drawings are so closely associated with Rubens and Van Dyck, the Chatsworth drawing and the superior of the versions in London probably date from about 1618–20, when the two artists collaborated.[5]

If the Chatsworth version is indeed an original by Van Dyck, an attribution that we support, it is difficult to imagine that the London version, an apparent copy, could be by Rubens. It would be the only known instance of the older, established artist copying a drawing by his younger collaborator. Julius Held's thought that the "real" original may be lost has much to recommend it.[6]

1. For the second example, of lesser quality, in the British Museum, see Hind 1923, pp. 45–46, no. 122. This version of the composition shows squaring, which is underneath the pen drawing and must have served to transfer the design. The drawing lacks the cows at the upper left and a cow's head at the upper right, and thus has the same grouping as in Pontius's engraving in reverse. Hind suggested in 1923 that it had served as the preliminary design for the engraving, although the drawing is larger than the print and not traced. A fourth version of *Cattle in Pasture* was last recorded in 1920, in the Northwick collection (sale cat., London, Sotheby, Wilkinson and Hodge, November 1–4, 1920, no. 200, as after Rubens; pen and brown ink, 300 x 510 mm). According to Hind (1923, p. 36, under no. 118), it is probably a copy after the example in Chatsworth.
2. Brown in New York–Fort Worth 1991, p. 43, figs. 1, 2. We have not seen the study of a *Horse* in the Uffizi, Florence, that Martin Royalton-Kisch (in Antwerp–London 1999a, p. 14, fig. 4) attributed to Van Dyck.
3. M. Jaffé 1989, no. 521, 1618–19; Renger and Denk 2002, p. 460, no. 322, ca. 1618.
4. M. Jaffé 1989, no. 1219, ca. 1635–38.
5. Glück and Haberditzl (1928) accepted the better of the two versions in the British Museum as Rubens's original drawing. Hind (1923) recognized Rubens's hand in both the Chatsworth and the more accomplished version in London. Wolfgang Adler (1982), following the opinion of Ludwig Burchard, catalogued all four versions as copies after a lost Rubens drawing. Held (1986, p. 14) left the attribution open, although he considered the Chatsworth drawing "more spirited," with "a certain intensity and excitement in its lines which is absent from the more placid forms of the London page."
6. Held 1986, p. 13.

103. *Seventeen Studies of Dancing Peasants for a Kermis,* recto; *Various Studies of Revelers for a Kermis,* verso, ca. 1630–36

Black chalk and pen and brown ink and a few traces of red chalk, recto; pen and dark brown ink over preliminary drawing in black chalk, verso, 595 x 512 mm (22 15/16 x 20 3/16 in.)
Inscribed by the artist in pen and dark brown ink on verso at bottom center: *Hier ghebreken Bedelaer(s) ende rozens /vruchten mans [mand?] ende kinderen* (Here lack beggars and roses / fruit men [basket] and children); above the head of man at upper right: *vrolyck . . .* (gay); twice, in black and in red chalk, in coat of standing woman: *root* (red); in pen and brown ink at upper right: *root* and *blauw* (blue); in black chalk: *geel* (yellow) and *viol* (purple); on recto in black chalk at top left: *Oct 16*
Annotated in pen and dark brown ink on recto at bottom left: *P. P. Rubens* and *487*; on verso: *No 23*

The British Museum, London (1885.5.9.50)

PROVENANCE: Jonathan Richardson Sr. (1665–1745), London (Lugt 2184); Sir Thomas Lawrence (1769–1830), London (Lugt 2445); Samuel Woodburn (1786–1853), London (Lugt 2584; sale, London, Christie's, June 8, 1860, lot 799); Alphonse Wyatt Thibaudeau (ca. 1840–ca. 1892), Paris; William Russell.

LITERATURE: R., vol. 5, no. 1488; Hind 1923, p. 16, no. 33, pl. V (recto and verso); Held 1959, no. 57, pls. 70, 71 (recto), 67–69 (verso), pp. 21, 23, 30, 78, 80, 118, under no. 55, 123, under no. 64; Burchard and d'Hulst 1963, no. 150, pl. 150, p. 236, under no. 149, p. 238, under no. 151; Kuznetsov 1974, pls. 111, 112; Held 1986, nos. 193, 194, pls. 184, 185, frontis.

EXHIBITION: London 1977a, no. 178, ill.

On the recto of this large sheet Rubens sketched seventeen couples dancing, and on the verso, groups of peasants sitting and conversing, drinking, or slumbering. The sketches represent initial ideas for his painting *Flemish Kermis* or *Village Wedding* (fig. 151),[1] which records the aftermath of a village wedding. Rubens borrowed some of the motifs from his predecessors, primarily Pieter Bruegel the Elder (ca. 1525/30?–1569), and from one contemporary, Adriaen Brouwer (1605/6?–1638). (Rubens owned at least a dozen paintings by Bruegel the Elder and seventeen by Brouwer).

As late as 1684 the painting was still referred to as *Noce de Village* (Village Wedding).[2] A 1636 inventory of the Spanish royal collection listed two "Flemish weddings by Rubens," one of which might be the *Kermis.* If this is so, the painting, and consequently the drawing, would date from the early to mid-1630s (the paintings Rubens sent to Spain tended to be ones that had been recently completed).[3]

In the eighteenth century, when the drawing was in the collection of Jonathan Richardson Sr. (1665–1745), the earliest recorded owner of the study, the side that today is considered the verso was the recto, where Richardson always put his collector's mark.[4] Although it is less dynamic than today's recto, with many sketches of dancing couples, it seems to be the side on which Rubens began his studies for the *Kermis.* Rubens filled the entire sheet, possibly starting at the upper right and

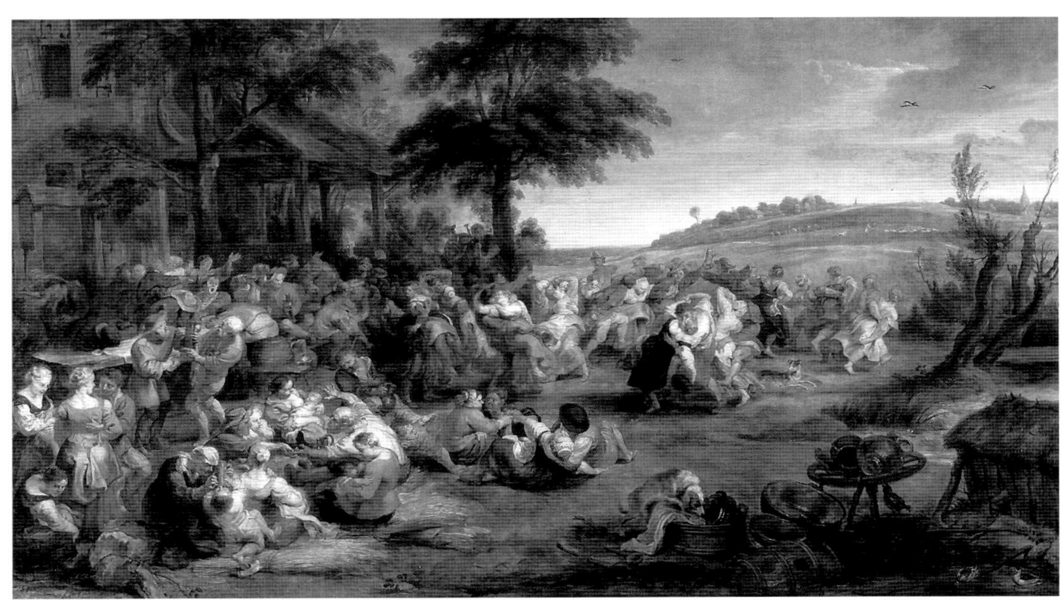

Fig. 151. Peter Paul Rubens, *Flemish Kermis* or *Village Wedding,* 1635–38. Oil on panel, 149 x 261 cm (58 11/16 x 102 3/4 in.). Département des Peintures du Musée du Louvre, Paris (1797)

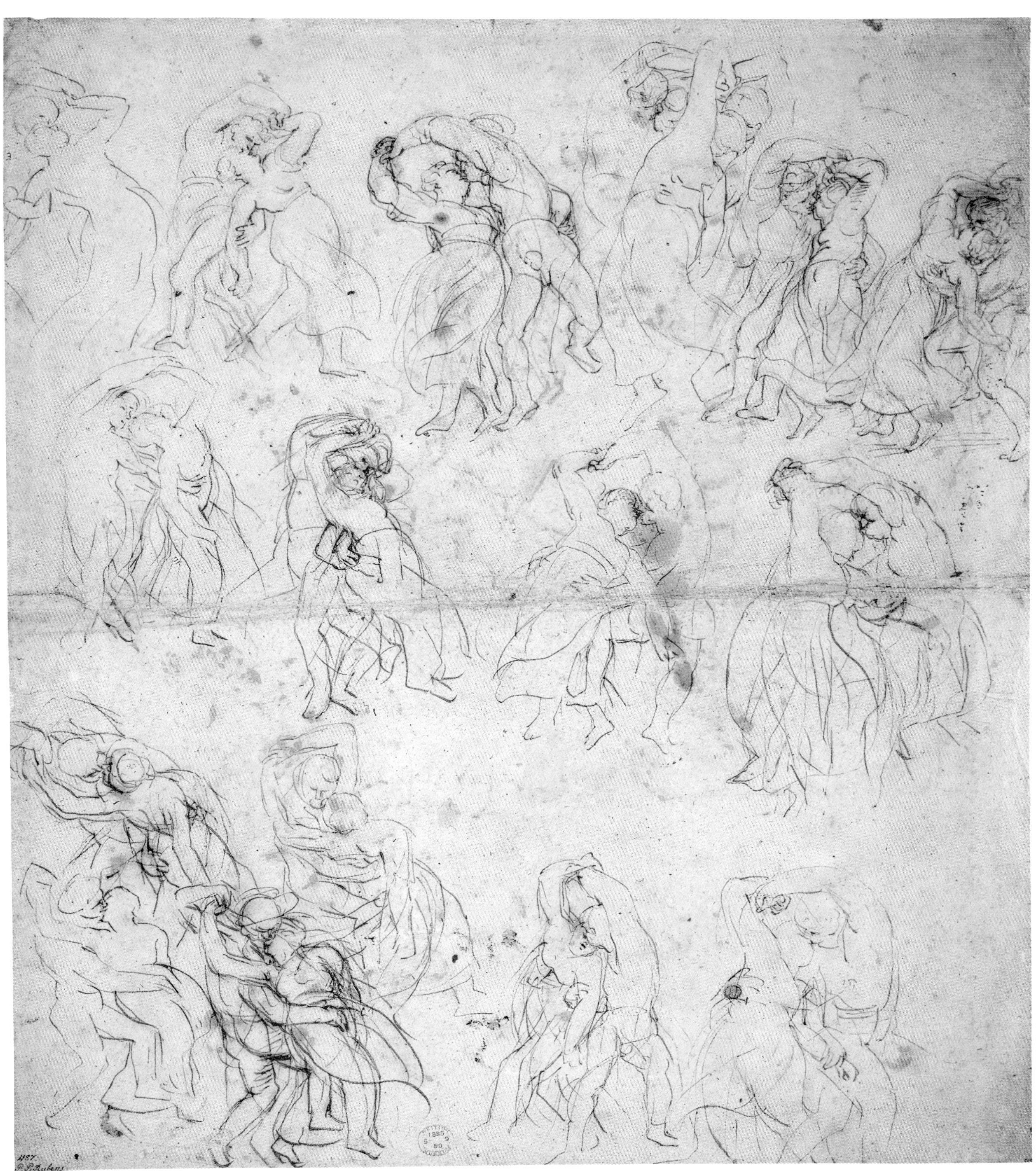

Cat. 103 recto

working toward the lower left. The figures are so realistic that one wonders if they were drawn from groups of people Rubens observed at a party (his inscription on the sheet seems to point in this direction; see below). Rubens also filled the obverse (today's recto) from top to bottom. On this side Rubens drew more freely, perhaps not from life but inspired by the exuberant dancers he may have witnessed.

In his painting Rubens used and rearranged many clusters of figures from both the recto and the verso. (For many figures in the painting, however, there are no known preliminary sketches.)[5] Rubens's inscription, in Flemish, on the verso states that beggars, roses, men, and children are missing from the sketches. The meaning of this inscription is not clear, as there are many men in the drawing; perhaps when Rubens wrote *mans* (men), he meant *mand* (basket). In any case, Rubens's inscription seems to be a reminder to himself that he left out important elements of the scene. Nonetheless, in the final painting he did not include beggars, children, or roses, either. He focused on the carefree, exuberant, almost wild mood of the peasants.

Rubens drew first in black chalk, and then he redrew with the pen those figures he wanted to develop further, not slavishly following the earlier formulation in black chalk, but often redefining it. He sketched some ideas twice or three times, with minor variations, sometimes next to each other (as is the case with the two dancing couples sketched twice in the bottom left corner of the verso), sometimes in different areas of the sheet (the sprawling man, for example, at the upper left and toward the center at the right of the verso). Occasionally, after having sketched a motif in black chalk and pen, Rubens quickly drew it once more with the pen only, modifying it in some details. In appearance the drawing may qualify as a *crabbelinge*, or so-called scribble, but in execution it is more defined and worked up.

1. K.d.K., ed. Oldenbourg 1921, no. 406, ca. 1635–38; M. Jaffé 1989, no. 1213, 1635–38.
2. R., vol. 4, p. 71.
3. Ibid., vol. 1, p. 131. For the 1636 inventory, see Vergara 1999, p. 29.
4. Two drawings of a "dance of Boors" are listed in the Richardson sale, London, Cock, January 22, 1747, and days following, p. 26, lot 20, and p. 40, lot 42.
5. In all likelihood Rubens made additional drawings for the painting. For example, the portion of the inventory of Rubens's collaborator Erasmus II Quellinus (1607–1678) drawn up on March 22, 1679, listed a quick sketch of peasants by Rubens: "Boeren ende Boerinne, crabbelinge, Rubens." See Duverger 1984–, vol. 10, p. 285.

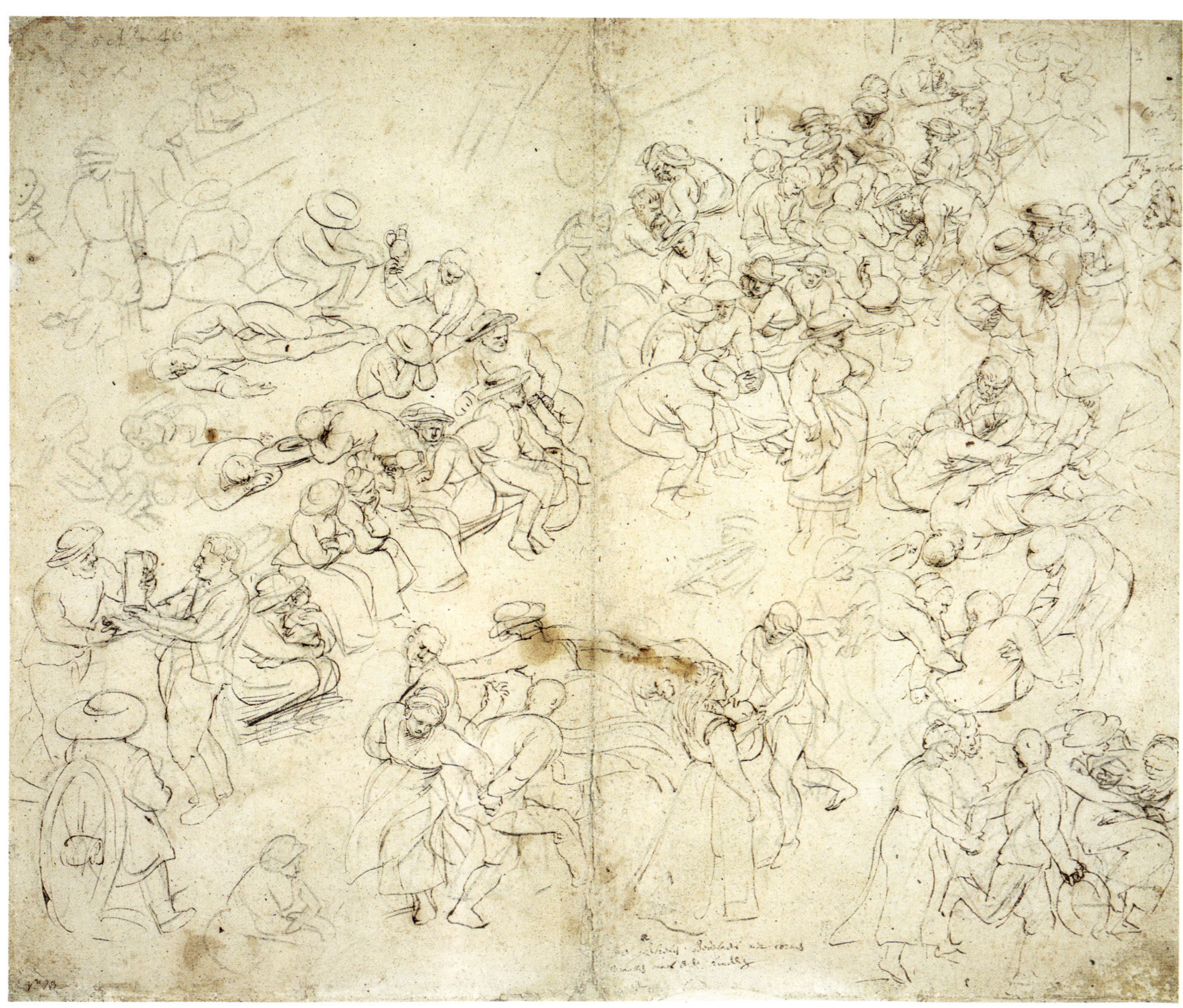

Cat. 103 verso

104. *Trees Reflected in Water at Sunset,* ca. 1635–38

Black, orange-red, and red chalk, heightened with white, on buff paper, 276 x 454 mm (10¾ x 17⅞ in.)
Inscribed by the artist in pen and brown ink at lower right: *de boomen wederschyn [en] In het Waeter bruynder / ende veel perfecter In het Waeter als de boomen selvde*
Annotated below artist's inscription: *Thee Shadow of a Tree is greatter in ye watter / and more parfect then ye treess themselves, and / darker*[1]

The British Museum, London (Gg.2.229)

PROVENANCE: Jonathan Richardson Sr. (1665–1745), London (Lugt 2184); Rev. Clayton Mordaunt Cracherode (1730–1799), London (Lugt 606); bequeathed to the British Museum in 1799.

LITERATURE: Hind 1923, pp. 33–34, no. 108, pl. XV; Glück and Haberditzl 1928, no. 171, pl. 171; Held 1959, no. 135, colorpl. facing p. 80, pp. 45–46, 82; Adler 1982, no. 77, fig. 165; Held 1986, no. 226, colorpl. 7.

EXHIBITIONS: London 1977a, no. 195, ill. p. 102; London 1996–97, no. 32, pl. 90.

After Rubens purchased his country estate of Het Steen, near Mechelen, in 1635, his interest in nature greatly increased, as is obvious from the many landscapes he produced at this time. In 1681 Roger de Piles wrote in his biography of Rubens (based on correspondence with the artist's nephew Philip) that the artist enjoyed living in solitude and painting the mountains and surrounding valleys, at sunrise and sunset.[2] The artist may indeed have sketched small landscapes outdoors—"au naturel," as de Piles wrote.[3] Rubens's known drawings and paintings seem to corroborate de Piles's account. Many landscape paintings were in his house at his death, including such major works as the pendants *Landscape with a View of Het Steen* (National Gallery, London) and *Landscape with a Rainbow* (Wallace Collection, London).[4]

This beautiful, atmospheric drawing of a setting sun on the horizon stands out among Rubens's landscape drawings because it is the only one that depicts a particular effect of light. (In his landscape paintings and oil sketches—more of which seem to have survived—one encounters all sorts of effects of light, from moonlit nights and rainbows to sunsets and sunrises.) In his Flemish inscription on the drawing Rubens indicated that he tried to catch the moment, which occurs only at sunset, when "the reflection of the trees in the water is browner and more perfect in the water than the trees themselves." Julius Held showed that the first part of the inscription may be connected to a passage in book five of Franciscus Aguilonius's *Opticorum Libri Sex* (Optics) that deals with shadows.[5] Rubens knew Aguilonius (1567–1617), and the book was familiar to him, since he designed a title page and six vignettes for it when it was published in Antwerp in 1613 by the Plantin Press. Aguilonius wrote that "the closer the shadow to an opaque body, the darker it is; and it appears to be even darker than the thing itself."[6]

Rubens probably had in mind that moment when the viewer, the trees on the far side of the water, and the light behind the trees are located in a straight line, and when, therefore, the shadows and the images reflected in the water coincide—just as they do in this drawing. Rubens stressed the evening glow through the addition of red and orange-red chalk in the sky.

1. The annotation was previously thought to have been added by Jonathan Richardson Sr., but according to Carol Gibson-Wood (see Wood 2003, p. 95, n. 66), Richardson did not write on the drawings in his collection.
2. Rubens's nephew Philip wrote to Roger de Piles that "[Rubens] y prenoit grand plaisir de vivre dans la solitude, pour tant plus vivement pouvoir dépeindre au naturel les montagnes, plaines, vallées et prairies d'alentour, au lever et coucher du soleil, avec leurs orizons." Published in Ruelens 1883, p. 167.
3. Brown 2000, pp. 267–78.
4. M. Jaffé 1989, no. 1226, ca. 1636 (Wallace Collection), no. 1227, ca. 1636 (National Gallery).
5. Held 1979a, pp. 257–64.
6. Judson and Van de Velde 1978, vol. 1, nos. 10–16, vol. 2, figs. 55, 56, 60–63, 65–68; see also Judith C. Weiss in Williamstown 1977, pp. 51–53, no. 2, and Held 1979a, p. 261.

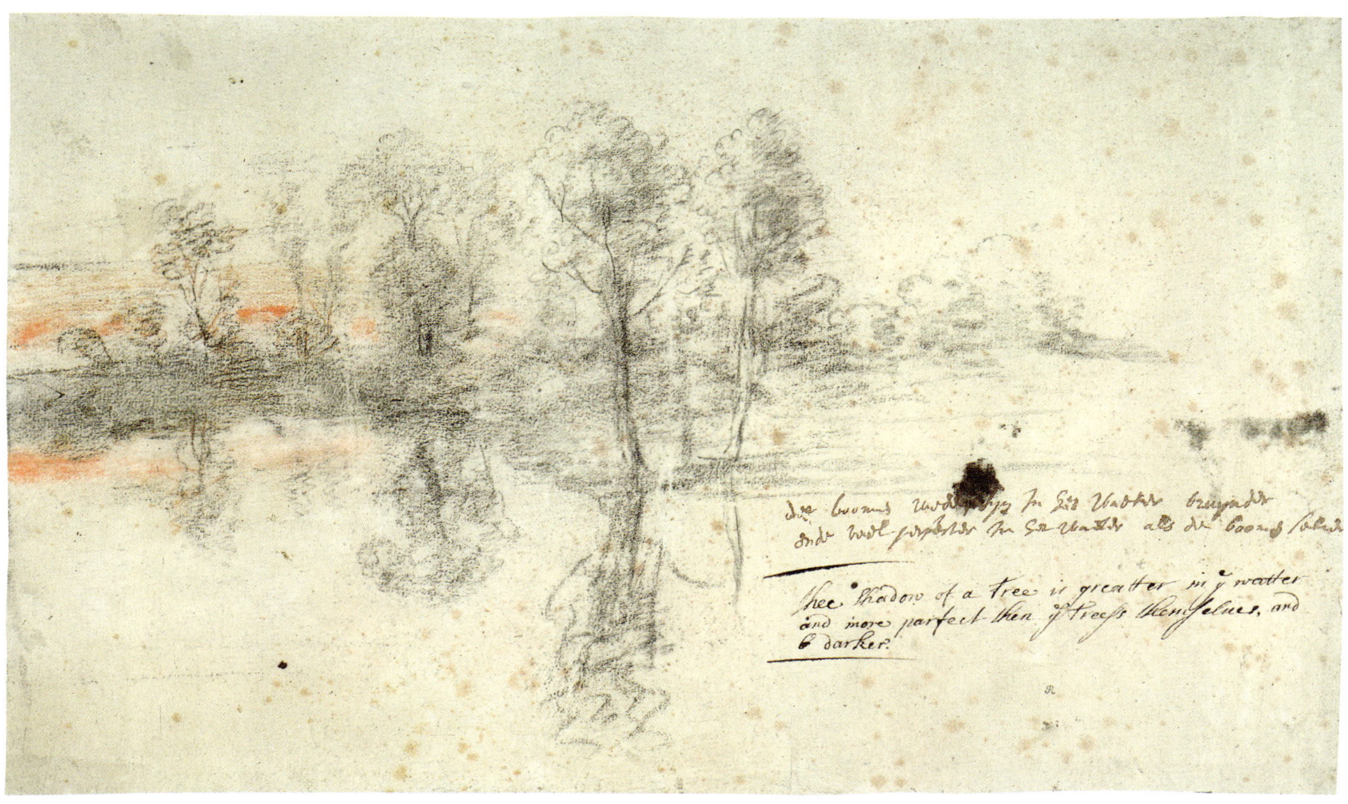
thee shadow of a tree is greater in ye watter
and more parfect then ye treess themselues, and
be darker.

Cat. 104

105. *Woodland Scene*, ca. 1635–38

Black chalk, touched with red and white chalks, and white body color on stone-colored paper, 383 x 499 mm (15⅛ x 19¾ in.)

The Ashmolean Museum, Oxford (WA 1855.122)

PROVENANCE: Prosper Henry Lankrink (1628?–1692), London (Lugt 2090); Chambers Hall (1786–1855), Southampton and London (Lugt 551), who bequeathed it to Oxford University in 1855.

LITERATURE: Glück and Haberditzl 1928, no. 170, pl. 170; Held 1959, no. 137, pl. 146, pp. 58, 146, under nos. 132, 136; Burchard and d'Hulst 1963, no. 207, pl. 207; Kuznetsov 1974, pl. 146; Adler 1982, no. 74, fig. 160; Held 1986, no. 228, pl. 200; Wadum 1996, pp. 393–95; Brown in London 1996–97, p. 90.

EXHIBITIONS: Antwerp 1977, no. 171, ill.; Oxford–London 1988, no. 10, ill.; London 1996–97, no. 30, pl. 88.

This drawing probably dates from the years when the artist spent a great deal of time at his country estate near the village of Elewijt, about half a day's journey on horseback from Antwerp. The little bridge leading over a stream bordered by pollard willows and slender deciduous trees with transparent foliage makes for a peaceful scene. The white body color, spread densely between the trees along the horizon and more thinly in the sky, adds an illusion of airiness and depth. Perhaps Rubens was trying to capture a special effect of light that he had witnessed (see cat. no. 104). The sheet is folded horizontally and vertically, probably to provide Rubens with rough guidelines for the horizon and the placement of the wooden fence in the foreground. Landscapes such as this one were in all likelihood an end in themselves for Rubens. He probably made them for his own enjoyment, referring to them only in a general way in paintings such as *Pastoral Landscape with a Rainbow* (Hermitage, Saint Petersburg).[1]

Relatively few landscape drawings by Rubens have been preserved. More definitely once existed. Johannes Philippus Happaert (d. 1686), the Antwerp canon and art dealer who acquired almost all of the drawings in Rubens's estate at auction in 1657, probably sold most of them before his death. The inventory of his estate undoubtedly lists only a small portion of the drawings he once owned; still, in it one encounters six landscape drawings by Rubens.[2] In the inventory of the Antwerp painter Erasmus II Quellinus (1607–1678), who collaborated with Rubens in the 1630s on book designs and on designs for the triumphal entry of Cardinal-Infante Ferdinand into Antwerp (1635), as well as on the Torre de la Parada commissions, we encounter some "crabbelinge lantschap Rubens" (sketches landscape [by] Rubens).[3] Such—in all likelihood—cursory landscape drawings (possibly done outdoors) seem not to have survived at all. Later collectors did not appreciate these summary pen studies and made no effort to preserve them.

1. Adler 1982, no. 39, fig. 113.
2. Duverger 1984–, vol. 11, no. 3754, p. 379; inventory of February 27, 1686.
3. Ibid., vol. 10, no. 3333, p. 365; inventory of November 7, 1678.

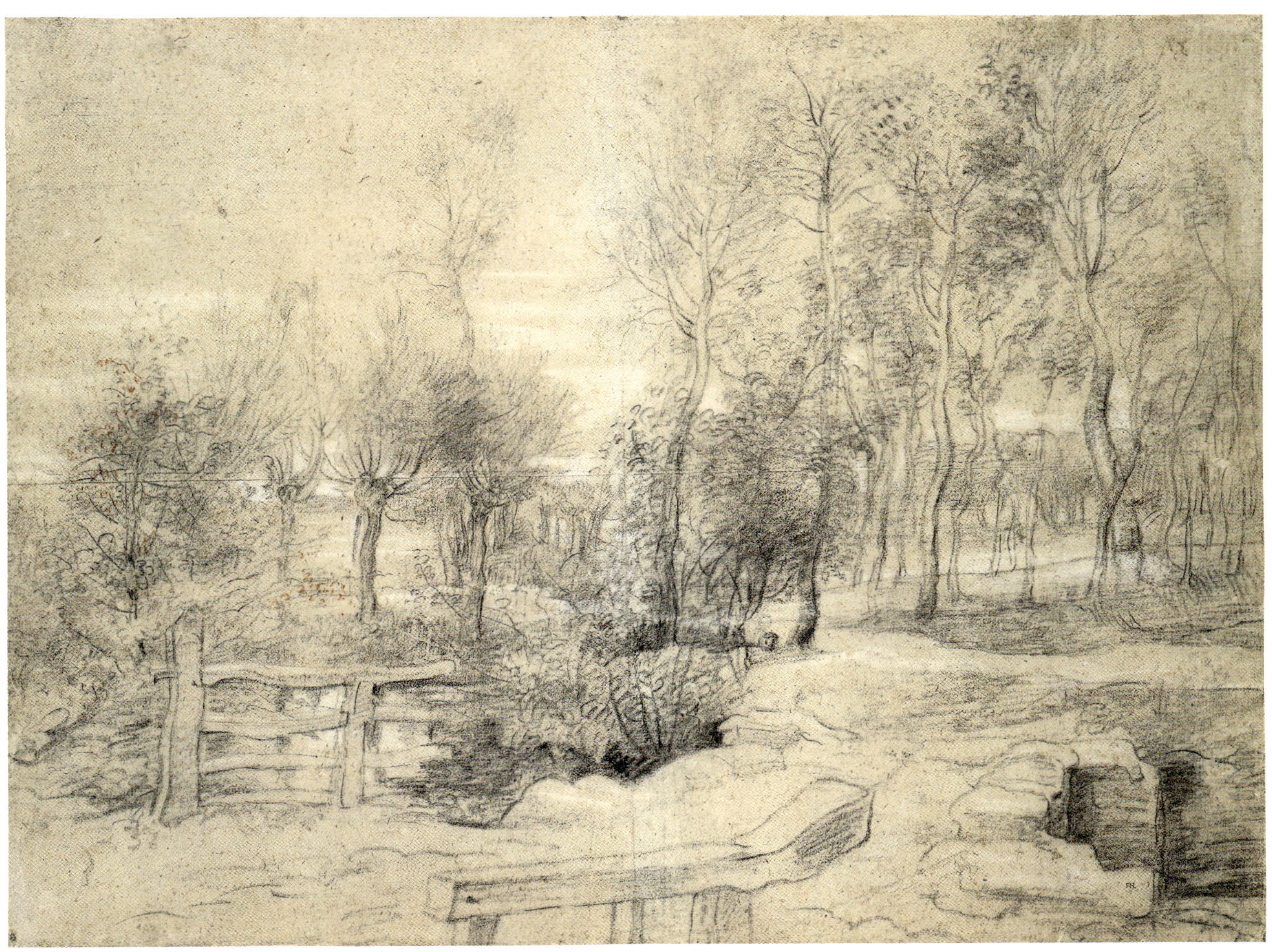

Cat. 105

LATE DRAWINGS, 1632–40

106. *Hercules and Minerva Fighting Mars,* ca. 1632–35

Gouache and brush and brown ink over preliminary drawing in black chalk, on light brown paper, 370 x 539 mm (14⁹⁄₁₆ x 21³⁄₁₆ in.)

Département des Arts Graphiques du Musée du Louvre, Paris (20.183)

PROVENANCE: Everhard Jabach (1618–1695), Cologne and Paris (Lugt 2961); entered the French royal collection in 1671; Robert de Cotte (1656–1735), Paris (Lugt 1964); museum mark (Lugt 1899 and 2207).

LITERATURE: Reiset 1866, no. 552; R., vol. 5, no. 1475, pl. 1415; Glück and Haberditzl 1928, no. 182, pl. 182; Lugt 1949, no. 1014, pl. XVI; Held 1959, no. 66, pl. 74, ill. opp. p. 64, pp. 7, 155, under no. 154; Burchard and d'Hulst 1963, no. 169, pl. 169; Kuznetsov 1974, pl. 140; Held 1986, no. 229, colorpl. 8.

EXHIBITIONS: Paris 1977–78, no. 146, ill.; Paris 1978, no. 28, ill.

The subject of war and peace was foremost in Rubens's mind during his diplomatic missions to Madrid and London between 1628 and 1630, where he assisted in the negotiations to bring peace between Spain and England and to contain France. In 1630 the artist presented a much admired painting with this theme, *Minerva Defending Peace from Mars* (also known as *War and Peace*; fig. 133), to King Charles I of England, who hung it in the Bear Gallery at Whitehall.[1]

On this sheet Minerva, protector of peace, attempts to restrain Mars, god of war. Dead bodies are spread across the foreground, and a city in flames is visible in the distance. Mars drags a young woman by her hair, while her child tries to hold on to her; Hercules swings his club at the left, trying to assist Minerva; and the eagle of Jupiter with a thunderbolt in his claws hovers over the scene. The drawing stands out in Rubens's oeuvre as one of the few known examples executed with the brush and colored gouache, very much in the manner of an oil sketch. (The portrait drawing of the 2nd Earl of Arundel [cat. no. 80], although more monochromatic, is another example; see also cat. no. 107.) Over a rough outline in black chalk he sketched the initial composition with the brush in a light brown ink and then added color before going over the entire composition once more, placing accents and strengthening contours with dark brown ink. The drawing is essentially a colored oil sketch on paper. Oil sketches on panel and drawings in gouache on paper were more or less interchangeable in Rubens's time and each was often referred to simply as a "drawing" (*dessein* or *teekening*). The 1620 contract for the ceiling decoration of the Jesuit church in Antwerp stipulated, for example, that Rubens prepare "drawings" (*teekeninge*), which are actually small sketches in oil on panel.[2] The present drawing shows clearly how similar Rubens's approach to drawing with the brush and gouache on paper was to his method of painting with the brush and oil on panel.

Rubens painted a closely related version of this sheet in oil on panel (Koninklijk Museum voor Schone Kunsten, Antwerp).[3] The oil sketch is almost the same size as the drawing, but its composition is simpler, and it is therefore generally assumed that the oil sketch predates the drawing. Rubens may have prepared both the drawing and the oil sketch for a painting that is now lost but known from a copy on copper in a private collection in Seville.[4] Two additional close variations on the theme of Minerva restraining Mars appear in oil sketches by Rubens now in Rotterdam[5] and Paris.[6]

The violent struggle between Minerva and Mars depicted on this sheet recalls in particular Rubens's oil sketch of *Wisdom (Minerva) Keeping Armed Rebellion (Mars) from the Throne of King James* (Musées Royaux des Beaux-Arts, Brussels), painted about 1632–33 for the Whitehall ceiling.[7] There, too, Rubens showed the two protagonists in a fierce fight. This similarity suggests that the drawing dates from the same time.[8]

1. K. d. K., ed. Oldenbourg 1921, no. 312; Brown 1979, n. p.; M. Jaffé 1989, no. 969, ca. 1629–30.
2. J. R. Martin 1968, app., p. 214. As Jeffrey Muller (1975, pp. 371–77) established, the *desseins* after Venetian artists listed in Rubens's inventory were oil sketches, not drawings.
3. Held 1980, no. 244, pl. 254, ca. 1630–35; M. Jaffé 1989, no. 1114, ca. 1635.
4. Seville 1978, ill. In 1925 another painted copy was with Asscher and Welker in London and supposedly sold to F. Koenigs, Haarlem (Foto Cooper 21 254).
5. Held 1980, no. 253, pl. 235, ca. 1635; M. Jaffé 1989, no. 1113, ca. 1635.
6. Held 1980, no. 268, pl. 266, 1634–36; M. Jaffé 1989, no. 1172, ca. 1634–36.
7. K.d.K., ed. Oldenbourg 1921, no. 337; Held 1980, no. 132, pl. 137, ca. 1632–33; M. Jaffé 1989, no. 1009, ca. 1632–33. The similarity was noted by Frans Baudouin in Elewijt 1962, p. 170, no. 152.
8. Held (1986, no. 229) suggested that the drawing is associated with Rubens's late *Horrors of War,* painted ca. 1637–38 (Pitti Palace, Florence; K.d.K., ed. Oldenbourg 1921, no. 428; M. Jaffé 1989, no. 1353, 1637–38). This is less likely than its association with the Whitehall ceiling painting.

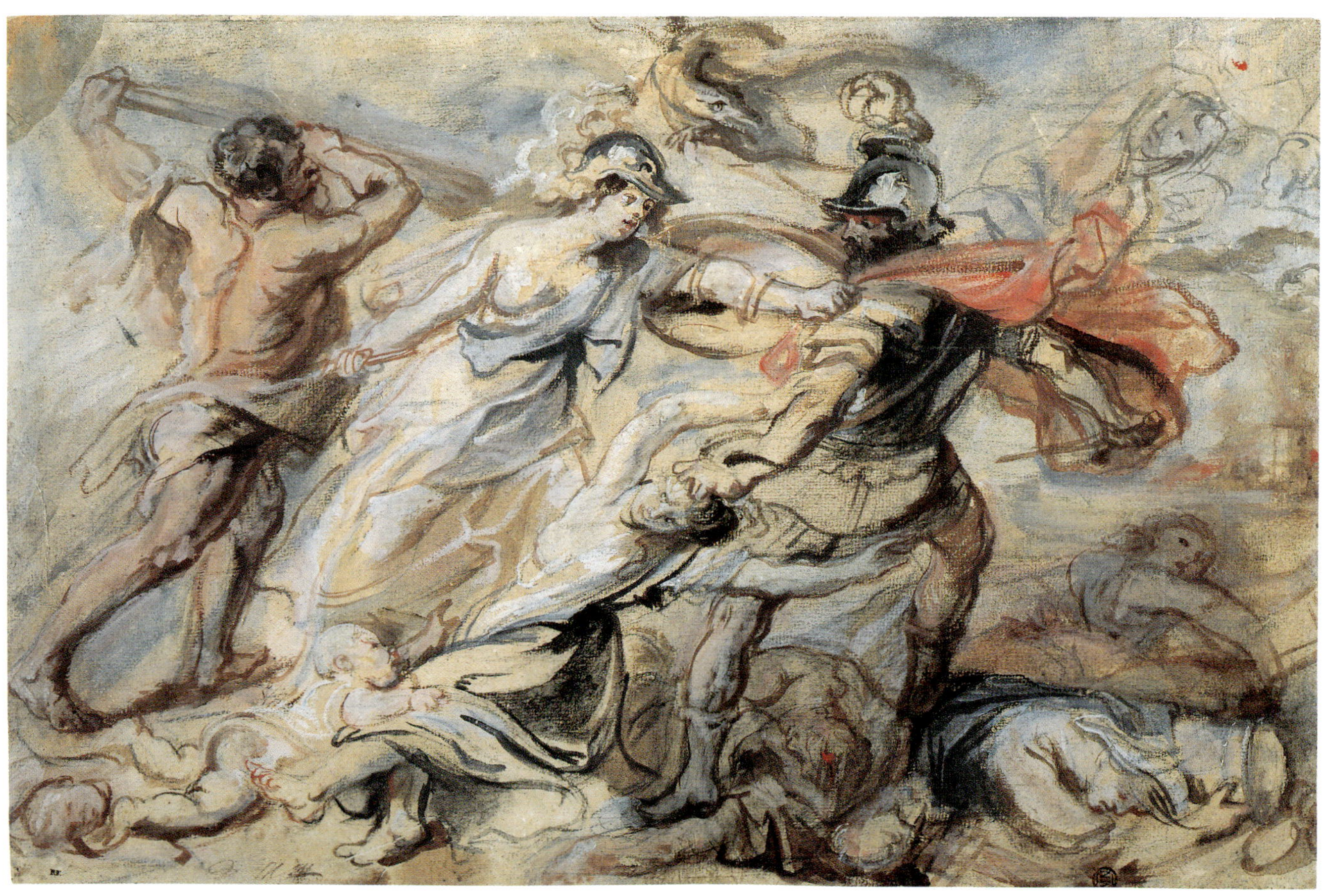

Cat. 106

107. *A Sermon in a Village Church*, ca. 1633–35

Black chalk, brush and brown-red ink, watercolor, and gouache, 422 x 573 mm (16⅝ x 22⁹⁄₁₆ in.)

The Metropolitan Museum of Art, New York; Harris Brisbane Dick Fund, 2000 (2000.483)

PROVENANCE: Pierre Crozat (1655–1740), Paris (Lugt 2985; his sale, Paris, Mariette, 1741, under lot 856, among one of six drawings by Jacob Jordaens); Count Carl Gustav Tessin (1695–1770), Stockholm (Lugt 2985); Queen Louisa Ulrica of Sweden; Princess Sophia Albertina; Count Stenbock; Count Nils Barck (1820–1896), Paris and Madrid (Lugt 1959); Count Narcisse-Adolphe Thibaudeau (1795–1856), Paris (his sale, Paris, April 20, 1857); Sir John Charles Robinson (1824–1913), London; Hans M. Calmann (1899–1982), London; Katrin Bellinger Kunsthandel, Munich, 2000.

LITERATURE: R., vol. 5, no. 1441; Held 1986, no. 181, pl. 177; Logan 1987, pp. 75–76; *MMAB* 2001, p. 30, ill.

EXHIBITIONS: London 1977a, no. 203; London 2001, no. 16, ill.

Several features of this drawing cause it to stand out in Rubens's oeuvre. First, the *Sermon* is drawn with watercolor and gouache on paper.[1] The watercolor was applied rather thinly over a free-flowing preliminary sketch in black chalk; the dogs in the foreground were added with brush and dark brown ink. The only comparable colored drawing by Rubens is *Hercules and Minerva Fighting Mars* (cat. no. 106), but the brushwork on that sheet has a spontaneity and liveliness that one associates with an exploratory sketch and that are absent here. Second, a religious service in what appears to be a simple rustic church is a new subject for Rubens. The congregation is segregated by sex; the men, with their hats removed, stand and sit at the left, and the women are seated at the right. All listen to a sermon given by a Catholic priest standing in the pulpit at the right.[2] The church has heavy columns at the right and ends in a barnlike space toward the back. Since the congregation consists of farmers, in this drawing Rubens most likely rendered a religious service in the neighborhood of his estate, Castle Steen, near Elewijt. The present drawing is highly finished, and it does not give the impression of being a preliminary study that led to another work; it appears, rather, to be a record of a special event. One wonders if the drawing was made in special circumstances, since the subject matter, although religious, seems to be very personal, perhaps family-oriented. The sermon possibly had a special meaning for Rubens or his family. It may be a romantic fiction, but the elegant lady in a wide-brimmed hat seated in the second row at the right, looking out at the viewer, reminds one of Rubens's young second wife, Helena Fourment. But even if the figure is she, the drawing's subject matter remains puzzling.

Only toward the end of his life, after he purchased his country estate in 1635, did Rubens turn in earnest to subjects taken from farm and country life, reflected in his many landscapes and scenes from Flemish rural life. The people in the congregation very much resemble the farmers whom Rubens drew and painted at this time. The *Sermon in a Village Church* drawing probably dates from the mid-1630s, when Rubens spent a great deal of time at his country estate, away from Antwerp.[3]

At least four copies—three paintings and one watercolor—after the *Sermon* sheet are known.[4] One of them was recently on the London art market (fig. 152). At the right all the copies show a cluster of people sitting on the floor around the ladder leading to the pulpit. This section of the composition is missing from the present drawing and in all likelihood was cut off, at an unknown time.

1. The watercolor may have led Pierre Crozat (and probably Mariette as well) to believe that the sheet was by Jacob Jordaens (1593–1678). See Mariette 1741, p. 99, under lot 856: "Six desseins colorés, des plus beaux que ce Maître ait produit, dont un représente un Sermon qui se fait dans une Eglise de Village."
2. We thank Guus van den Hout, director of the Museum Catherijneconvent, Utrecht, for verifying this.
3. Held (1986, no. 181) suggested that Rubens drew the *Sermon* during his brief stay in 1629–30 in England, where the Dutch artist Pieter Angillis (1685–1734) copied it (see note 4 below). The painted copy of the drawing in the possession of the dukes of Newcastle (recently on the art market; fig. 152) may explain the English connection. Gustav Waagen spotted it at the ducal estate at Cumberland Park, which he visited between 1854 and 1856 (Waagen 1857, p. 510: "Rubens.—3. A Jesuit preaching to a country audience. Very animated, but too highly hung to admit of a closer inspection"). During the mid-1650s William Cavendish, Duke of Newcastle (1592–1676), had rented Rubens's house in Antwerp from Helena Fourment and may have had a copy made from the present drawing.
4. Closest in size is the painted version in the Musée Francisque Mandet, Riom, France, attributed to David Teniers the Elder (1582–1649); see Logan 1987, p. 76, fig. 6. A copy in watercolor, with a spurious Teniers signature, is in a private collection in Belgium. A second painted copy (fig. 152) was in the Cavendish collection; sold on eBay through Sotheby's on October 11, 2002, lot OMS1, as Circle of Adriaen Rombouts. The largest version, painted by Pieter Angillis, shows a vaulted ceiling and a mixed congregation of men and women; it was formerly in the collection of P. O. Kristeller, New York (Held 1986, p. 140, fig. 17).

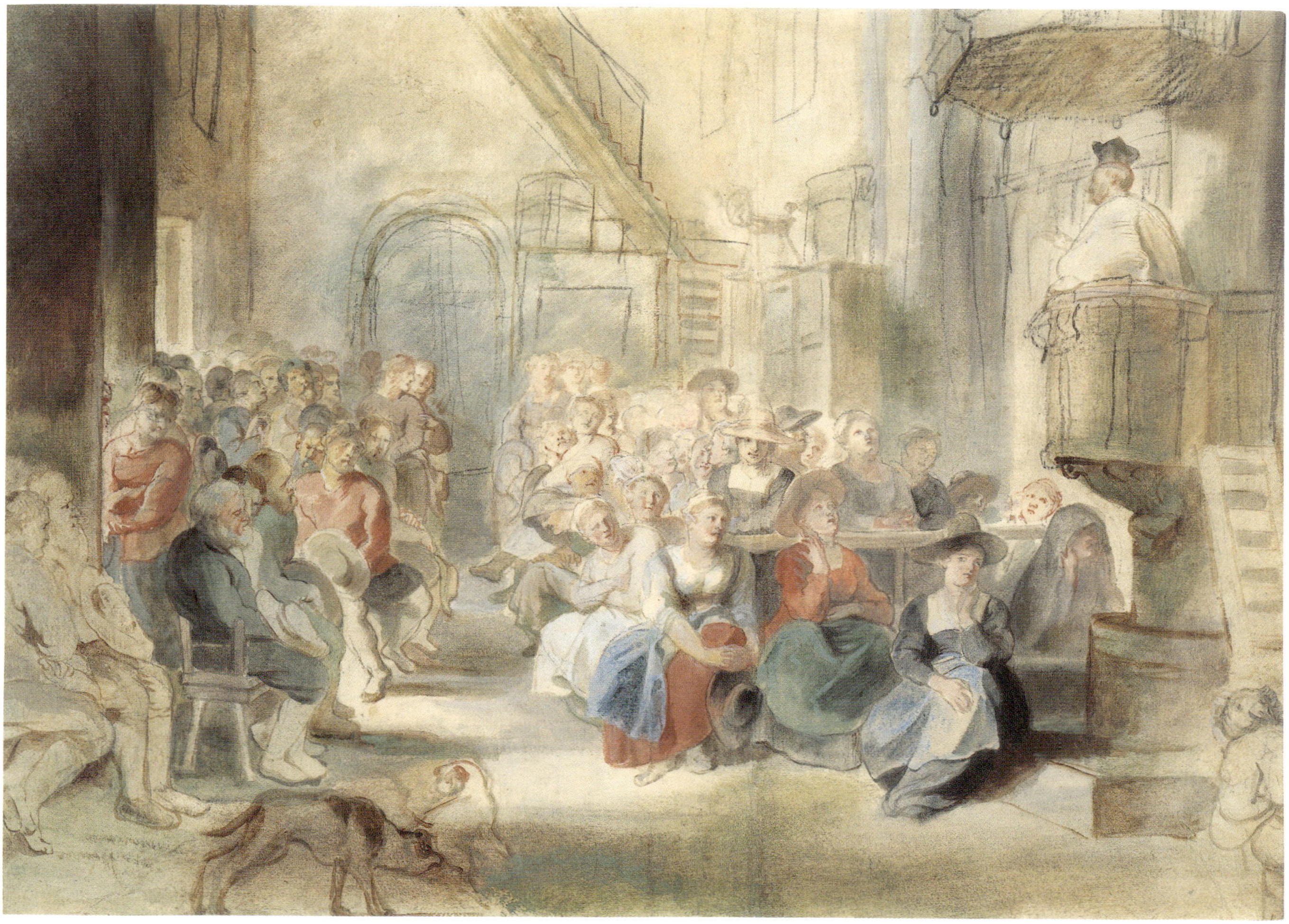

Cat. 107

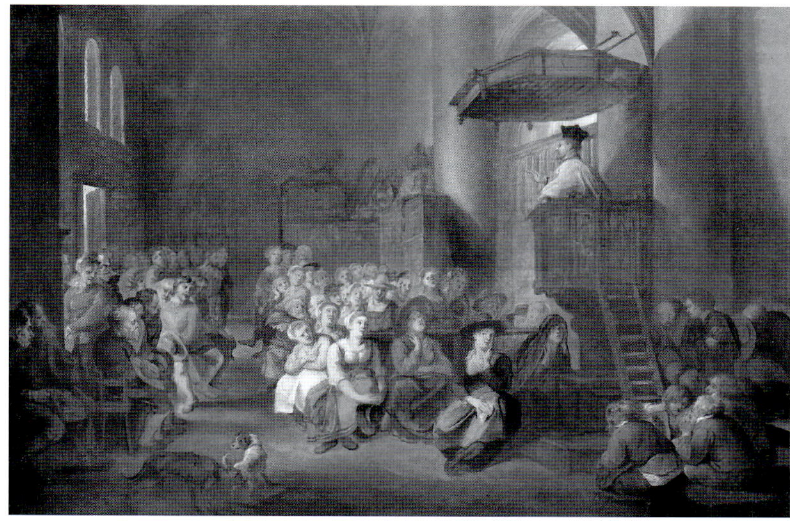

Fig. 152. After Peter Paul Rubens, *A Sermon in a Village Church,* ca. 1640. Oil on paper (?) laid down on panel, 50.8 x 74.9 cm (20 x 29½ in.). Photograph courtesy of Sotheby's, Inc. © 1981

108. *Venus Admonishing the Fettered Cupid,* recto; *Satyr and Nymph,* verso, ca. 1633–35

Black chalk, heightened with white, redefined and amplified with broad pen and brown ink, recto; black and some red chalk, heightened with white, redefined and amplified with pen and brown ink, 277 x 161 mm (10⅞ x 6⅜ in.)
Inscribed by the artist in pen and brown ink on recto at upper right: *Cupido Captivus*

Staatliche Museen zu Berlin, Kupferstichkabinett (KdZ 12 222)

PROVENANCE: Chambers Hall (1786–1855), Southampton and London (Lugt 551); Charles Scarisbrick (?) (1801–1860; Lugt 522).

LITERATURE: Glück and Haberditzl 1928, no. 222, pl. 222 (recto), no. 223, pl. 223 (verso); Bock and Rosenberg 1930, vol. 1, p. 250, no. 12 222, vol. 2, pl. 180; Held 1959, no. 65, pl. 76 (recto), pl. 75 (verso), pp. 44, 81, 154–55, under no. 154; Burchard and d'Hulst 1963, no. 198, pl. 198; Kuznetsov 1974, pl. 137; Held 1986, no. 219, pl. 217.

EXHIBITION: Berlin 1977, no. 39, ill.

In the drawing on the recto of this double-sided sheet Venus, seated in her chariot, points her finger at the fettered Cupid, reprimanding him. Cupid stands in front of her with his hands tied behind his back, to prevent him from committing more mischief. Rubens quickly outlined the two figures in black chalk and heightened them with white before jotting down Venus twice more, at the upper left in pen and ink (now partly cut off and continued on the fragment in Chantilly; see below) and at the upper right in black chalk, with a second hand added in red chalk (there, part of Cupid's face, now cut off, is also visible). For the figure of Cupid, Rubens used a drawing after an antique (?) sculpture that he made during his stay in Rome; the drawing is now lost but known from a copy by Rubens's student Willem Panneels (ca. 1600–1634) in the Copenhagen *cantoor*.[1] As if Rubens had not depicted the subject clearly enough, he added the Latin inscription "Cupido Captivus" (captive, or tamed, Cupid) at the upper right.

On the verso of the sheet Rubens drew a satyr lustfully grabbing a nymph, who tries to fend him off. The artist again began with a brief outline in black chalk, heightened with white, before reinforcing some of the contours with pen and brown ink. Both sides of the sheet are drawn in a very similar manner and therefore likely date from the same time. They are among the rare late Rubens drawings that seem to show the artist exploring a theme for a painting, though no corresponding painting is known. The mixture of media and the looseness of the line indicate that the drawings belongs to the early to mid-1630s. In execution the studies relate to Rubens's drawings of revelers at a Flemish kermis (cat. no. 103); there, too, Rubens made initial quick sketches in black chalk before defining the figures more clearly with pen and brown ink.

The present format of the sheet is not its original one. It is a fragment, once part of the drawing with the *Drunken Hercules* (recto) and *Nymphs and Satyrs* (verso), today in the Musée Condé, Chantilly,[2] which was cut apart after it left Rubens's studio. Until the early 1960s, when it was recognized that the present sheet and the Chantilly sheet were fragments of a single drawing,[3] the section in Chantilly was attributed to Jacob Jordaens (1593–1678). The scene of the drunken Hercules, supported by two satyrs, continues the representation of Venus admonishing the fettered Cupid on the recto; they form a self-contained composition (fig. 153). (The drunken Hercules has at times been interpreted as the drunken Silenus.) The nymphs and satyrs on the verso are hastily, indistinctly drawn and do not rival the recto. The original size of the sheet must have been approximately 277 x 461 millimeters. Initially, the drawing probably extended still farther at the right, since both the figure of Venus at the top right of the recto of the present sheet and the head of Cupid, whose profile is barely visible along the right edge, end abruptly, as do the wings of the standing Cupid at the lower right.

1. See Copenhagen 1988, nos. 253, 254, pls. 256, 257.
2. Held 1986, no. 212, fig. 218, ca. 1633–35.
3. Müller Hofstede (1965c, p. 175, figs. 14a,b and 16a,b) established that the Berlin and Chantilly sheets belong together.

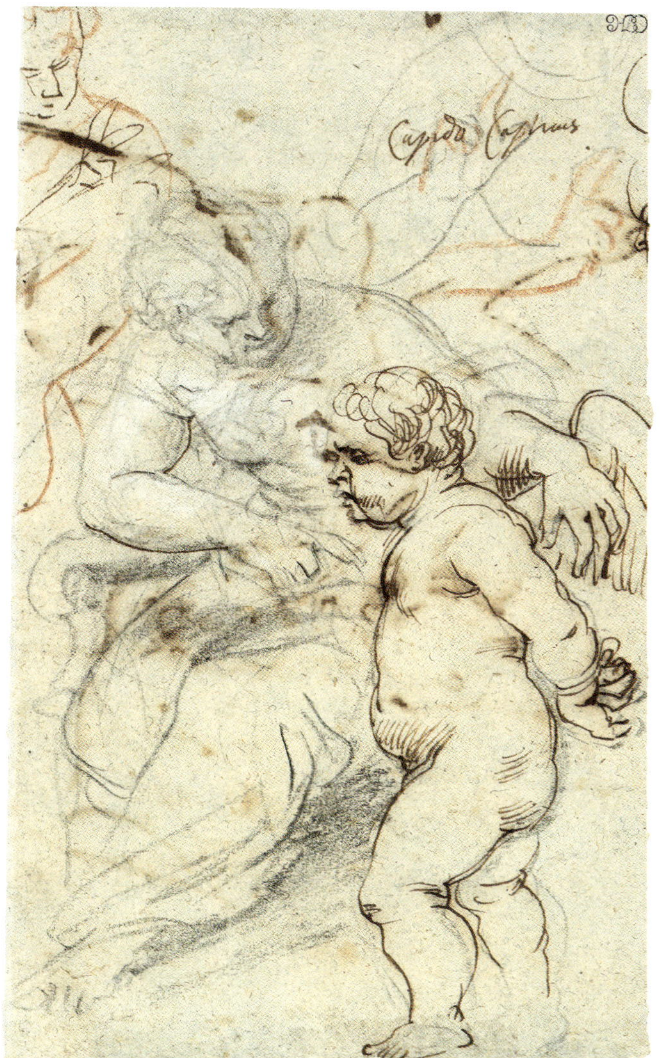

Cat. 108 recto

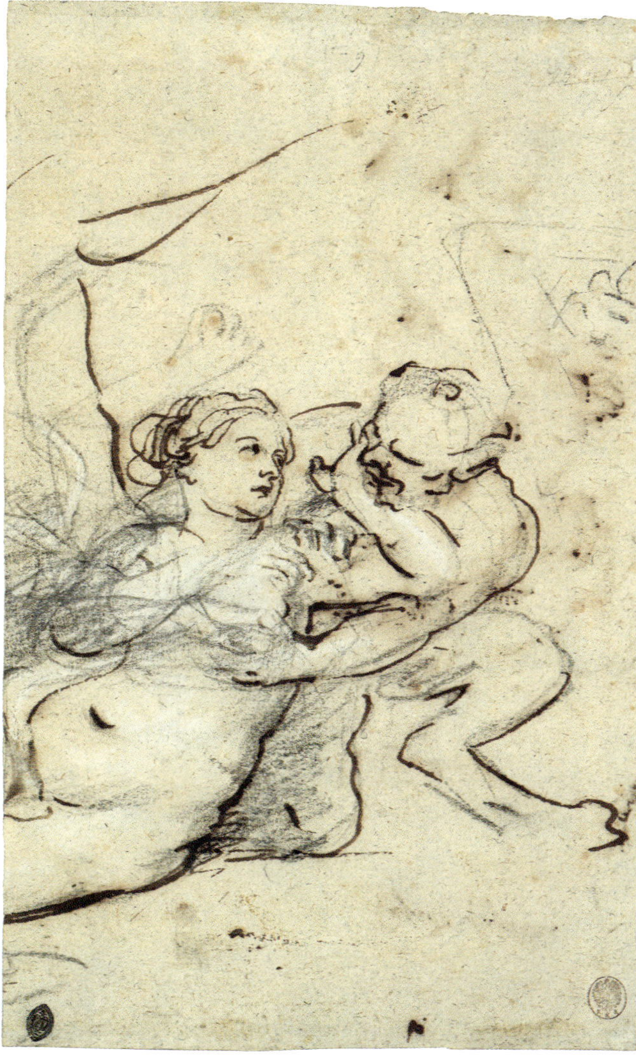

Cat. 108 verso

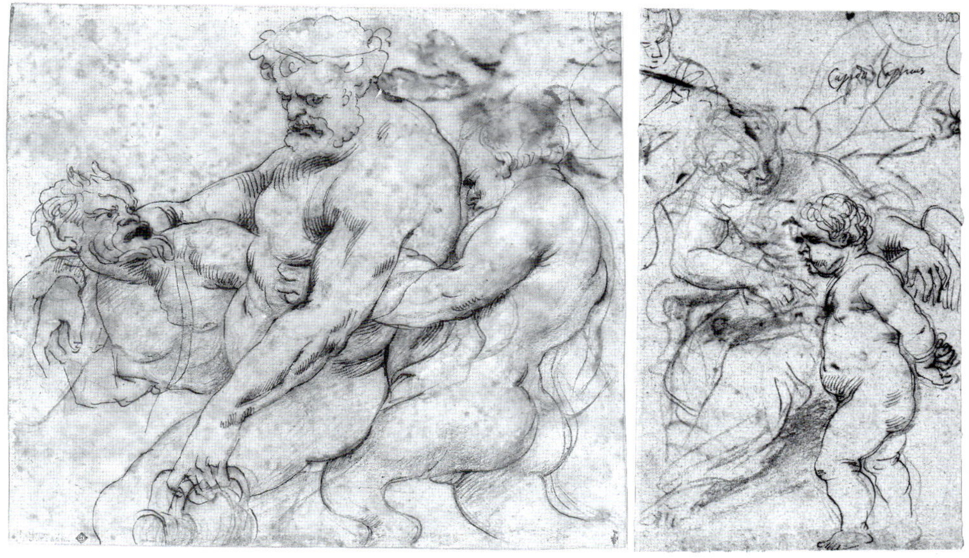

Fig. 153. Reconstruction of drawing by Peter Paul Rubens, ca. 1633–35. Right: cat. 108 recto. Left: *Drunken Hercules.* Black and red chalk, heightened with white chalk, pen and brown ink, 270 x 300 mm ($10\frac{5}{8}$ x $11\frac{13}{16}$ in.). Musée Condé, Chateau de Chantilly (911 recto)

109. *Study of a Seated Woman, Turned to the Right,* ca. 1633–35

Red and black chalk, heightened with white body color and traces of brush and brown ink in the hair, 463 x 283 mm (18¼ x 11⅛ in.)

Département des Arts Graphiques du Musée du Louvre, Paris (20.345)

PROVENANCE: Former French royal collection; museum mark (Lugt 1886).

LITERATURE: Evers 1942, pp. 454, 457; Lugt 1949, no. 1032, pl. XXX; Held 1959, pp. 28, 79, n. 1, 180; Vienna 1977b, p. 134, under no. 57; Held 1986, pp. 31, 61, n. 10; Díaz Padrón 1995, vol. 2, p. 928, under no. 1671.

EXHIBITIONS: Antwerp 1977, no. 163, ill.; Paris 1978, no. 17, ill.

Although Rubens's place in the popular imagination is as "the artist who painted all those female nudes," he hardly ever drew one; certainly, very few have survived. This sheet and his study for Psyche (cat. no. 36) are two of his better-known drawings of female nudes. While the figure of Psyche was most likely drawn from a male model, Rubens did draw from female models. The 1679 inventory of the Antwerp painter Erasmus II Quellinus (1607–1678), with whom Rubens collaborated in the 1630s, mentions studies of women, including "naked seated women by Rubens" ("naeckte sittende vrouwkens crabbelinge Rubbens") and "half-dressed women drawn from life by Rubens" ("half ontcleede vrouwkens naer't leven Rubbens").[1]

Since the 1940s the present drawing has been recognized as an original study by Rubens, yet it has appeared only rarely in the Rubens literature. This may have to do with the medium Rubens used: red chalk, which in the 1630s the artist employed frequently for compositional drawings, such as the *Studies for the Exploits of Hercules* (British Museum, London) of about 1630–35,[2] *Hercules Strangling the Nemean Lion* (cat. no. 110), and the *Adoration of the Magi* (Musée des Beaux-Arts, Besançon) of ca. 1633,[3] but rarely for figure drawings. In this case Rubens probably chose red chalk because the woman was naked. He often used red chalk for faces and hands in his portrait drawings, to indicate flesh tones; for figure drawings, however, he seems to have preferred black chalk. Here, Rubens introduced black chalk only in a second reworking, and very selectively, in the hair, for the garment falling over the woman's left shoulder, for the soft pillow on which she sits, and for the fine drapery that extends over her thigh. A later hand added the touches of brush and brown wash in the mouth, nose, eyes, and hair and may also have strengthened some of the contours.

The intimacy of the image—the woman seems to have just awakened and taken off her nightshirt—suggests that Rubens's model for the drawing was someone whom he knew very well. She may have been his second wife, Helena Fourment.[4] This suggestion is supported by the strong relation between the drawing and Rubens's famous late painting of Helena Fourment, known as the *Little Fur* or *Het Pelsken* (fig. 154).[5] The painting was a personal one, which the artist kept for himself and willed to his wife, who never disposed of it. Although Helena, possibly represented as Venus at the Bath, stands in the painting, her face and her right arm held across her upper body are positioned as in the drawing; again like the woman in the drawing, she wears a headband. The study relates equally, however, to several late Rubens paintings representing Diana at her bath, attended by her nymphs. Rubens used a closely related seated female figure in *Pan Seducing Diana with Wool* (formerly in Berlin)[6] and in *Diana and Callisto* (Prado, Madrid).[7] These are late Rubens paintings, and thus the present study likely dates from the early to mid-1630s as well.

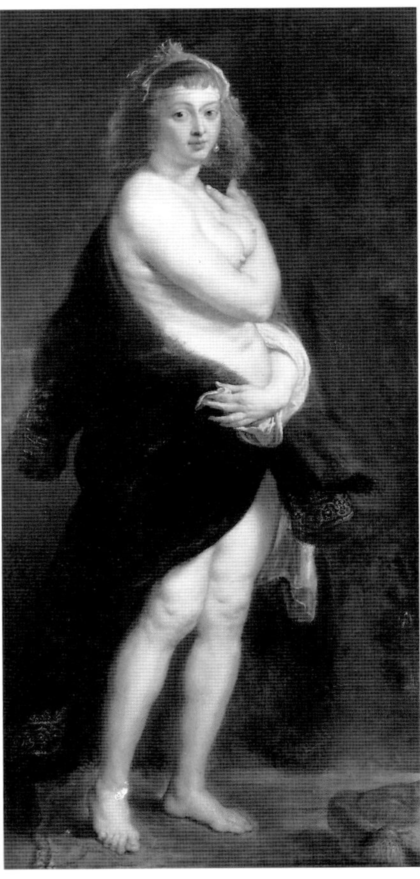

Fig. 154. Peter Paul Rubens, *The Little Fur,* ca. 1638. Oil on panel, 176 x 83 cm (69 5/16 x 32 11/16 in.). Kunsthistorisches Museum, Vienna (GG 688)

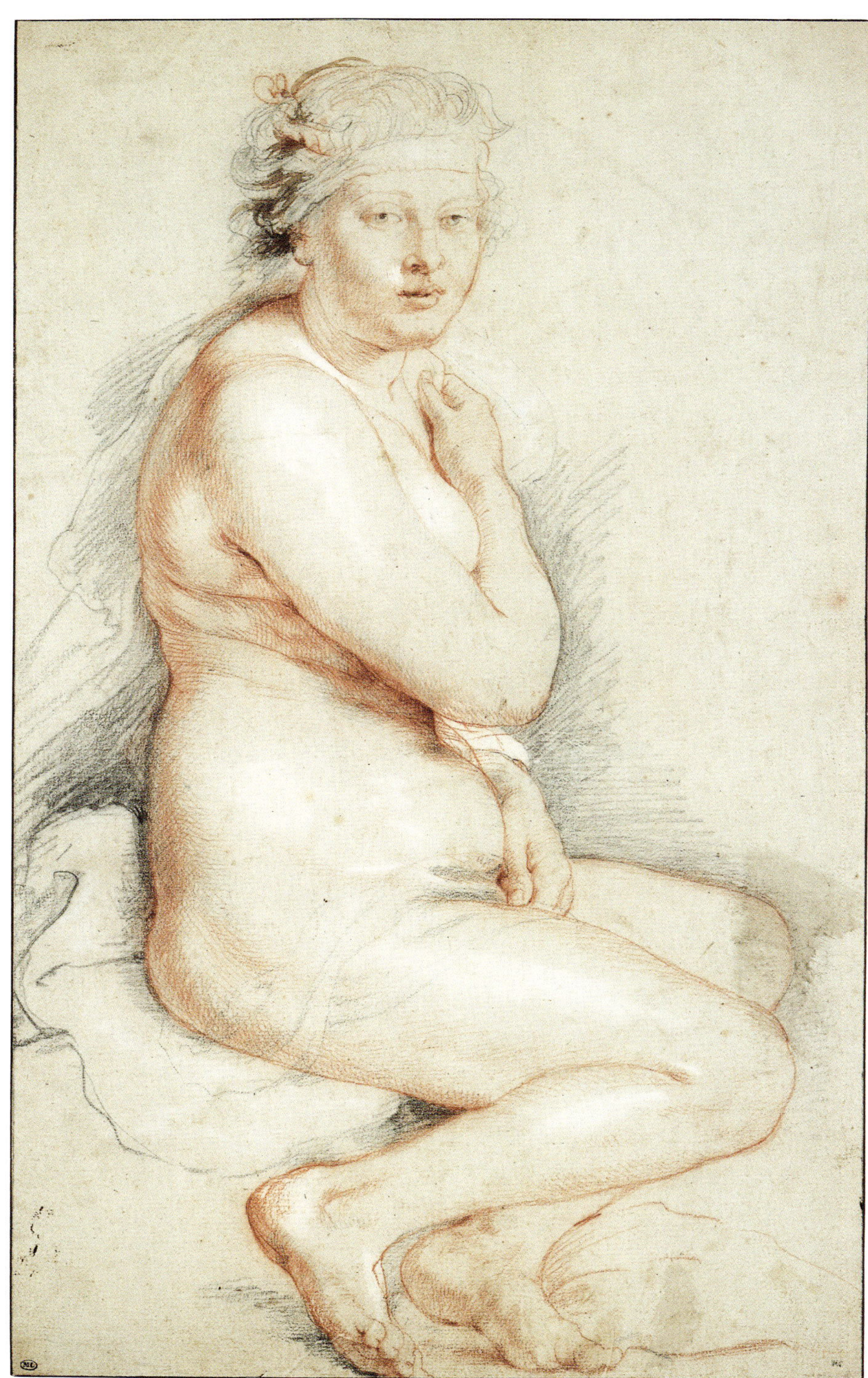

Cat. 109

1. Duverger 1984–, vol. 10, no. 3333, pp. 359–62, 364; Denucé 1932, p. 286.
2. Held 1986, no. 217, pl. 216.
3. Ibid., no. 221, pl. 211.
4. Volker Manuth, "'As stark naked as one could possibly be painted . . .': The Reputation of the Nude Female Model in the Age of Rembrandt," in Edinburgh–London 2001, pp. 47–53, and Thøfner 2004.
5. M. Jaffé 1989, no. 1364, ca. 1638; Muller 1989, p. 148, no. 7. The association was made first by Evers (1942), who also defended Rubens's authorship of the drawing, and it was supported by Lugt (1949).
6. McGrath 1983a, pp. 52–69; M. Jaffé 1989, no. 1200, ca. 1635–38.
7. M. Jaffé 1989, no. 1352, 1637–38.

110. *Hercules Strangling the Nemean Lion,* 1635–38

Red and some black chalk, 363 x 498 mm (14¼ x 19⅝ in.)
Annotated in pen and brown ink at bottom center: *II 18*

Museum Plantin-Moretus / Stedelijk Prentenkabinet, Antwerp (A XIV.7)

PROVENANCE: Anonymous collector (sale, Antwerp, Van der Straelen, Moons, Van Lerius, May 20, 1886, cat. 7, no. 268); Clement van Cauwenberghs, Antwerp.

LITERATURE: Held 1959, no. 34, pl. 32, p. 22; Burchard and d'Hulst 1963, no. 192, pl. 192, pp. 298–99, under no. 190; Held 1986, no. 97, pl. 89.

EXHIBITIONS: Düsseldorf–Cologne 1979, no. 5, ill.; Tokyo 1982, no. 64, ill.; Florence 1986–87, no. 28, ill.; Retretti 1991, pp. 40–41, ill.

The Greek hero Hercules, the personification of physical strength and courage, was an immensely popular subject among Baroque artists. Of the twelve labors that he carried out for King Eurystheus of Tiryns, as penance for slaying his own wife and children in a fit of madness, the first labor, his strangling of the Nemean lion, was the one most often depicted. Rubens rendered Hercules and the Nemean lion many times, in drawings, oil sketches, and paintings. At least four drawings of the subject by Rubens are known. In them Hercules invariably clamps his arm around the Nemean lion's head, trying to choke it to death. On all four sheets Rubens used red chalk, a medium he did not use that frequently. Some of the sheets have additional work in black chalk; Rubens partially reinforced one of them with pen and brown ink. The present large study in red and black chalk is the most dramatic.[1]

The drawing shows Rubens searching for the most effective stance for Hercules in his struggle with the powerful lion. The artist began the composition in red chalk and drew another rough sketch at the upper right, now only faintly visible. With another quick sketch in black chalk at the upper left, Rubens introduced several changes in the position of the legs. He drew Hercules' right leg three times, and his left leg twice. Through these modifications Rubens changed Hercules' action from strangling the lion to wrestling down the powerful animal. The painted composition most closely related to the drawing is the *Hercules and the Nemean Lion* (private collection, Brussels),[2] dated to about 1615, in which man and beast form the same closely knit half circle as in the drawing. The drawing cannot be a preliminary study for the painting, however, because in the painting Hercules is depicted in a more upright position, and his stance is different.

A wide range of dates has been suggested for the Antwerp drawing, from 1600–1602 (early in Rubens's stay in Italy) to the 1630s, and with several possibilities in between.[3] In our opinion, the sheet should be dated in the mid-1630s. The loose chalk strokes, the focus on the action rather than anatomy, and the heavy paper that Rubens used with greater frequency later in his career are characteristics that point to such a date.[4]

1. The drawings are in the Louvre, Paris (Lugt 1949, no. 1012, pl. XV; Paris 1978, no. 13, ill.); the Sterling and Francine Clark Art Institute, Williamstown (Haverkamp Begemann, Lawder, and Talbot 1964, no. 20, pls. 23, 24); and the British Museum, London (Hind 1923, pp. 13–14, no. 23, pl. III; Held 1986, no. 217, pl. 216). The Louvre sheet dates to 1600–1605, the example in Williamstown to ca. 1605–10, and the British Museum sheet to ca. 1630–35.
2. M. Jaffé 1989, no. 290, ca. 1615.
3. Delen (1932–33) dated it to early in Rubens's stay in Mantua, 1600–1602; Lugt (1949, p. 13, under no. 1012) placed it in Rubens's Italian period, 1600–1608; Held (1959, no. 34; 1986, no. 97) dated it to ca. 1613–16; and Burchard and d'Hulst (1963, no. 192) considered it a late drawing, from the 1630s.
4. The same features can be observed in the Hercules drawing in the British Museum (see note 1 above), which Held (1986, no. 217) dated ca. 1630–35.

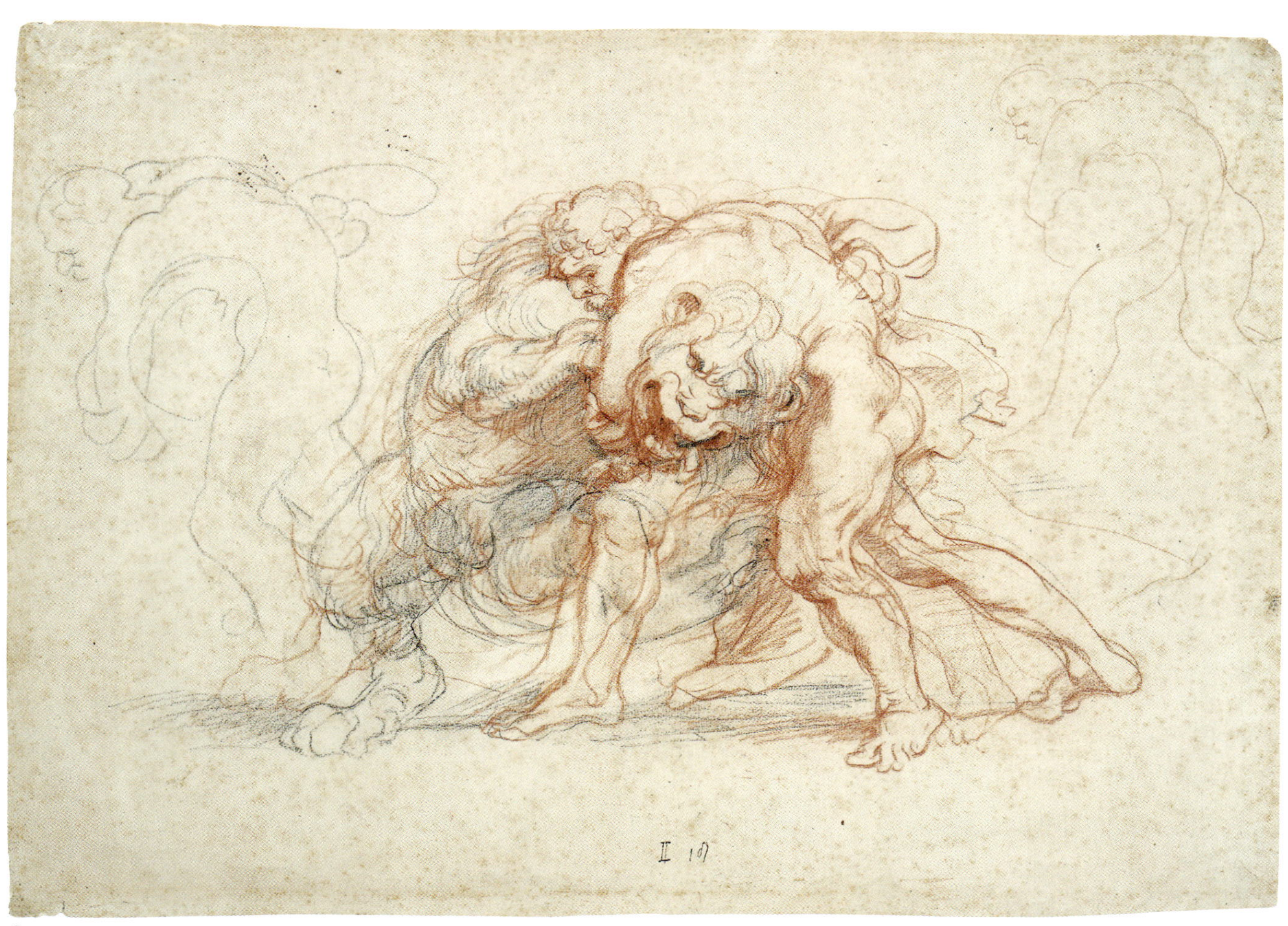

Cat. 110

111. *Boar Hunt*, ca. 1635–38

Pen and brown ink over preliminary drawing in black chalk, 414 x 569 mm (16¼ x 22 5/16 in.)
Annotated in black chalk at bottom right: *Rubens*

Albertina, Vienna (15 097)

PROVENANCE: Johann Gottfried Schumann (1761–1810), Dresden (Lugt 2344); Duke Albert of Sachsen-Teschen (1738–1822), Vienna (Lugt 174).

LITERATURE: Held 1959, p. 145, under no. 131 [Rubens pupil; Soutman?]; Evers 1961, pp. 95–97, 140, fig. 5; Winner 1981, pp. 163–64, fig. 32 [pen by another hand]; Adler 1982, no. 18b, fig. 61 [not Rubens]; Balis 1986, p. 118, n. 20, under no. 4; Held 1986, p. 114, under no. 115 [Rubens pupil; Soutman?]; Royalton-Kisch in Antwerp–London 1999a, p. 64, under no. 1 [probably Van Dyck].

EXHIBITION: Vienna 1977b, no. 71, ill. [Rubens?].

In this depiction of a boar hunt, two horsemen at the right tower above the boar, while in the center several peasants climb over a fallen tree and attack the boar with spears and hayforks. The composition is essentially the same as in Rubens's painting of a *Boar Hunt,* generally dated 1615–20 (fig. 155).[1] In the painting there is more space on all sides of the figures, allowing more of the landscape to be shown. There are other differences as well, some more subtle than others: the youth restraining the hounds at the left is placed on a lower level than in the drawing; the riders approaching at the right do not appear in the drawing at all, nor do the lower branch of the uprooted tree and the three dogs. A peasant in the background has his stick behind him in the painting, but in front of him in the drawing (the pentimento is still visible). The pollard tree branch at the left of the drawing is not in the painting.

Several generations of art historians have commented on the relationship between the drawing and the painting; almost all possible opinions have been expressed, and the drawing has been called everything from an "expressionless" copy by an unknown artist to a "superb" preliminary study by Rubens.[2] It seems obvious, however, that the sheet is no straightforward copy—not only are there too many differences between it and the painting, as noted above, but its combination of a rough chalk underdrawing and a loose pen sketch over it point in another direction. It also appears clear that the drawing, in the power of almost every line and in its rough but effective simplicity, is a work by Rubens. Yet it does not seem logical that Rubens made the drawing as a study for the painting. Its assertive, almost crude pen lines place the sheet with drawings like the *Feast of Herod* (cat. no. 112 recto) and the *Lansquenets Carousing* (cat. no. 113 recto), all dated in the mid-1630s.[3] The painting, by contrast, exhibits all the characteristics of a Rubens work from the mid-1610s. Furthermore, it is documented that Rubens sold the painting to the Duke of Buckingham in 1627.

Here, we may be confronted with a rare example of Rubens's modified repetition of his own work. Where he made the drawing, and why, are intriguing questions. As the painting had left for England in 1627, it is unlikely that he drew in front of the original painting; or was he able to do so during his last trip to England, in 1629–30? The drawing shows so many changes with respect to the painting that perhaps it was made on the basis of studio material, such as *crabbelingen* (scribbles) and individual figure studies, that is no longer known today. A record of the composition had to be available in Rubens's studio, because as late as 1642 Pieter Claesz. Soutman (ca. 1580–1657) published an etching after it.[4] Even if Rubens did return to his painting from 1615–20 on this sheet from the mid-1630s, we have no evidence why he would have done so. Obviously, the last word on this fascinating drawing has not been said.

1. K.d.K., ed. Oldenbourg 1921, no. 184; M. Jaffé 1989, no. 401, ca. 1616.
2. In a handwritten annotation on the mount of the drawing, Joseph Meder ascribed the sheet to Anthony van Dyck, while Lugt (1925, pp. 194–96), Evers (1961, pp. 95–97), and Müller Hofstede (handwritten inscription on the mount) attributed the drawing to Rubens. Burchard and d'Hulst (1963, p. 169, under no. 104) and Michael Jaffé (1969, p. 436, n. 5: "superb drawing for the composition of men and animals for the Dresden painting") also favored an attribution to Rubens. Held (1959, p. 145, under no. 131) attributed the sheet to Pieter Soutman, while Adler (1982, p. 78, under no. 18b) was against an attribution to Rubens, calling the drawing "flabby and expressionless in line and texture." Balis (1986, p. 118, n. 20) doubted that Rubens would have repeated an earlier composition so closely without adapting the style of the figures.
3. The bold underdrawing in black chalk on the sheet, which establishes only the broadest outlines of the composition, is reminiscent of the summary chalk lines in several of Rubens's late oil sketches, made visible in infrared photography. These include the figure of Hispania on the front of his *Arch of the Mint* of late 1634, painted for the triumphal entry of Cardinal-Infante Ferdinand, governor of the Netherlands, into Antwerp on April 17, 1635 (oil on panel, 104 x 73 cm, Koninklijk Museum voor Schone Kunsten, Antwerp; Held 1980, no. 163, pl. 164; M. Jaffé 1989, no. 1160).
4. For Soutman's etching in two plates, see Hollstein 1949–, vol. 27, p. 232, no. 20. It is possible that Rubens or a pupil made a painted copy after the *Boar Hunt* painting before it was sold to Buckingham. In the inventory of Rubens's estate, we encounter "Een verkensjacht op panneel" (A boar hunt on panel), which could very well be a copy after the painting (see Adler 1982, p. 72, under no. 18, copy 1). For many seventeenth-century copies after the *Boar Hunt* painting, see Adler 1982, under no. 18, pp. 72–73 and Balis 1986, pp. 113–14, under no. 4.

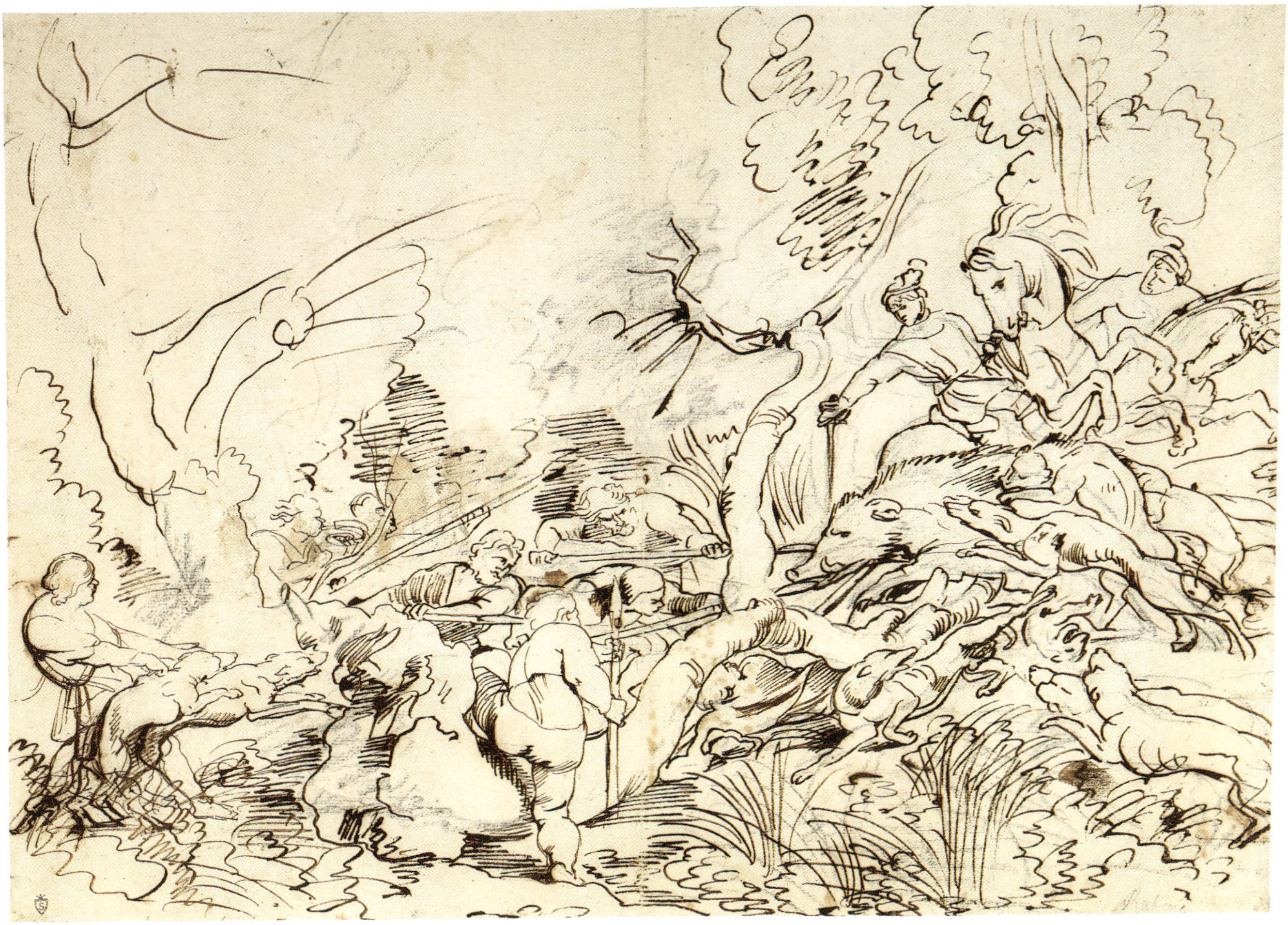

Cat. 111

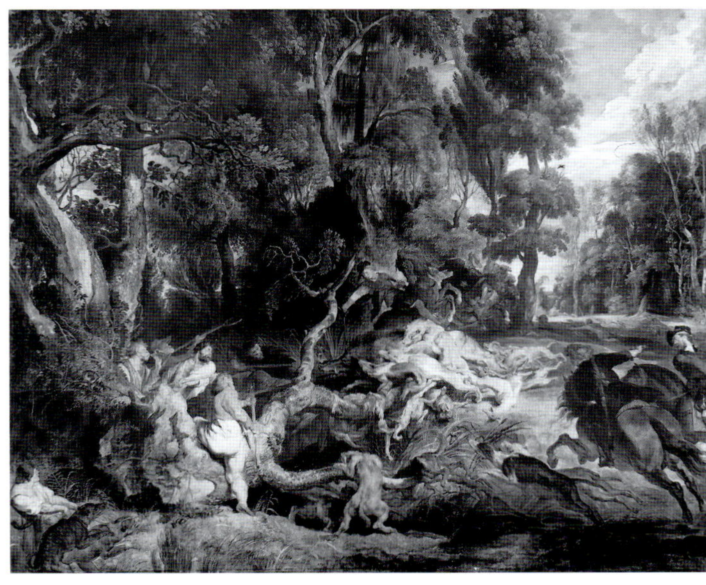

Fig. 155. Peter Paul Rubens, *Boar Hunt,* 1615–20. Oil on panel, 137 x 168.5 cm (53 15/16 x 66 5/16 in.). Gemäldegalerie Alte Meister, Staatliche Kunstsammlungen Dresden (962)

112. *The Feast of Herod,* recto; *Queen Tomyris with the Head of Cyrus,* verso, ca. 1637–38

Black chalk, pen and brown ink on coarse paper; red chalk (two figures at top left), touch of white body color (Herod's turban), recto; pen and brown ink, traces of black and red chalk, verso, 272 x 472 mm (10 11/16 x 18 9/16 in.); cut vertically through the center and pasted together
Inscribed by the artist in pen and brown ink on recto at top center: *de Herodias wat hooger;* at bottom right: *den [*or *deze] stoel te [cort?];* on verso: *plus spatij*

The Cleveland Museum of Art; Delia E. Holden and L. E. Holden Funds (1954.2a-b)

PROVENANCE: Unidentified collector (Lugt 622; probably Austrian collection, ca. 1800); English private collection; purchased by the Cleveland Museum in 1954.

LITERATURE: Held 1959, no. 67, pl. 77 (recto), pp. 45, 81, under no. 65, 124, 155, under no. 154; Burchard and d'Hulst 1963, no. 196, pl. 196; Kuznetsov 1974, pl. 148; Held 1986, no. 230, pl. 205; McGrath 1997, vol. 2, no. 5, vol. 1, fig. 17 (verso).

EXHIBITIONS: Cambridge, Mass.–New York 1956, no. 26, pl. 16; Wellesley–Cleveland 1993–94, no. 58, ill.; Sabine M. Kretschmar in Cleveland–New York 2000–2001, pp. 174–75, ill.

This is the last of three known Rubens drawings rendering either the Feast of Herod or Tomyris with the Head of Cyrus, and the only one where the two subjects are combined on the recto and verso of the same sheet; the other two examples, the *Feast of Herod* (cat. no. 57) and *Queen Tomyris with the Head of Cyrus* (cat. no. 55), are both *modelli* for engravings.[1] Of the two compositional sketches on this sheet, the *Feast of Herod* is much more definite and more forcefully drawn with a broad quill pen that held a large amount of ink that bled partly through even this coarse paper, the type that Rubens preferred in the 1630s.[2] (The thicker quill pen and the forceful pen lines are characteristic of Rubens's late drawings, such as his *Lansquenets Carousing* [cat. no. 113 recto].) It is difficult to establish if Rubens intended the two subjects as pendants or combined them as separate but related events, each of which depicts a reversal of fortune at the hands of a vengeful woman. He may have experimented with the two subjects in order to submit them as ideas for paintings to Gaspar Roomer (d. 1674), a Flemish collector living in Naples who apparently was fond of such horrific scenes. Indeed, the compositional drawing on the recto of this sheet reflects Rubens's initial ideas for the *Feast of Herod* painting (fig. 156)[3] that Roomer purchased and that in all likelihood arrived in Naples about 1640, soon after Rubens died.[4]

In the drawing Salome, standing in front of the table, presents the severed head of Saint John the Baptist on a salver to King Herod, who recoils in horror (for the biblical story of the beheading of the Baptist, see cat. no. 57). His wife, Herodias, sitting next to him at the table, gleefully points with a fork at the tongue of Saint John that had spoken against her marriage to Herod. (Rubens's rendering of Herodias pointing her fork at the saint's tongue is based on a passage in book 3 of Saint Jerome's *Apologia adversus libros Rufini.*[5] Jerome compares Herodias's treatment of John the Baptist's severed head with the action of Fulvia, the wife of Mark Antony, who pierced the tongue of Cicero's severed head with a pin that she removed from her hair.) In his inscription on the sheet Rubens identified the figure of Salome incorrectly as Herodias; he added an arrow and the words "wat hooger" to remind himself to paint her "somewhat taller." At the left a servant carries a cup on a tray; in the center, above the pen sketches, Rubens inserted another study of Herodias and Herod, this one in black chalk. A young woman seen in profile in red chalk at the top left resembles the figure of Salome; at the top right Rubens summarily indicated part of a canopy. His inscription at the lower right, "den stoel te cort," or the "chair is too short," may refer to Herod's throne, which he thought he should enlarge in the painting. The faces in pen at the upper right have bled through from Rubens's drawing of *Queen Tomyris with the Head of Cyrus* on the verso. The final painting includes thirteen figures, the drawing only six. The canvas, probably unfinished at the time of Rubens's death in late May 1640, was greatly enlarged before it was com-

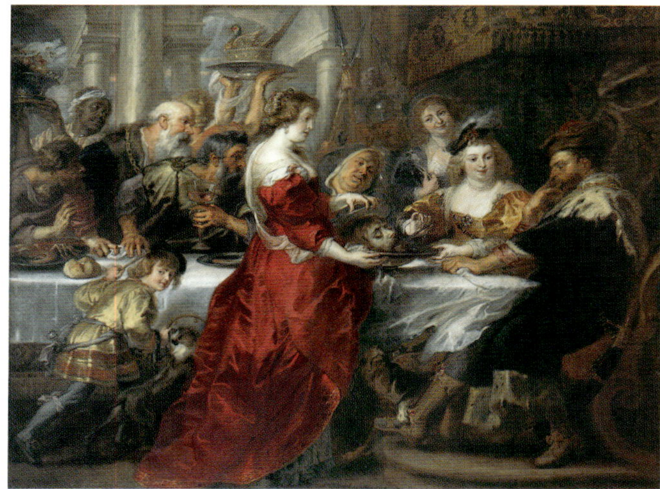

Fig. 156. Peter Paul Rubens, *The Feast of Herod,* ca. 1638. Oil on canvas, 203 x 318 cm (79 15/16 x 125 3/16 in.). National Gallery of Scotland, Edinburgh (NG 2193)

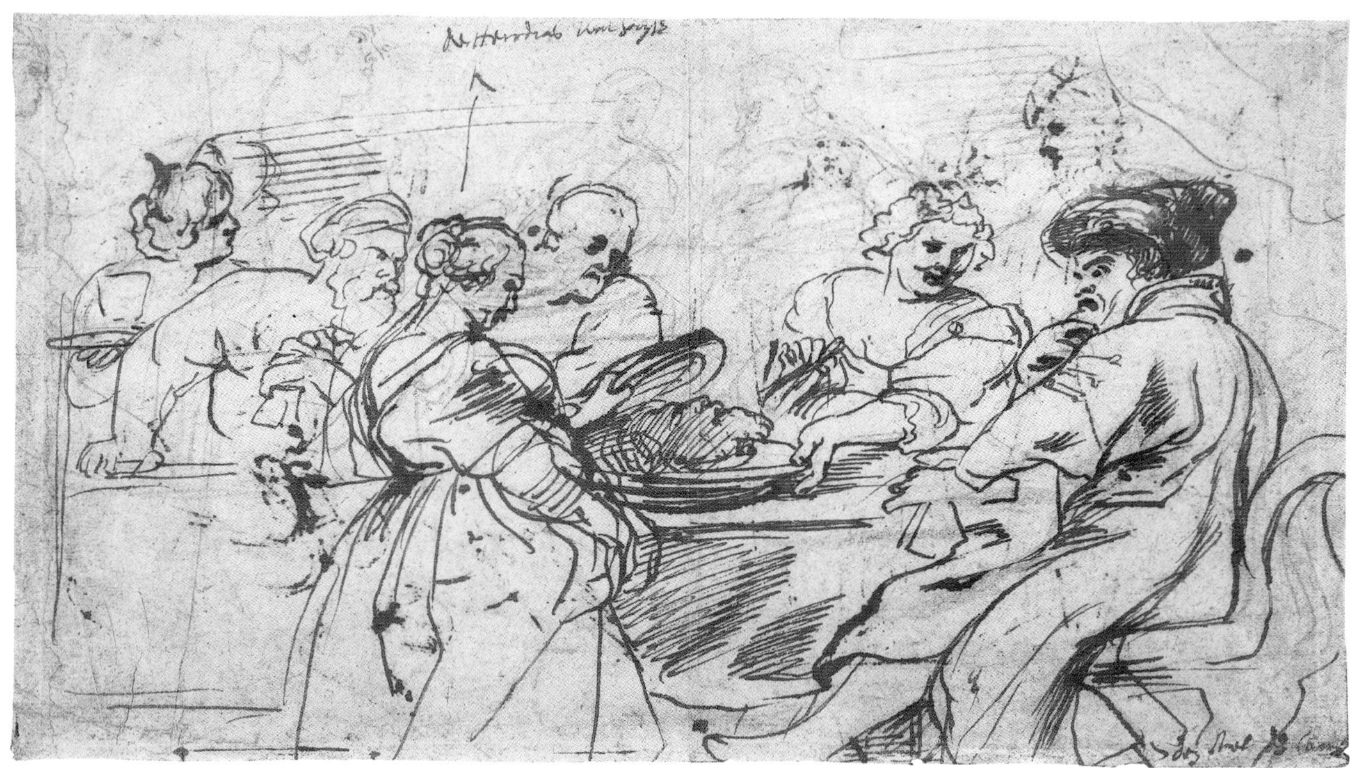

Cat. 112 recto

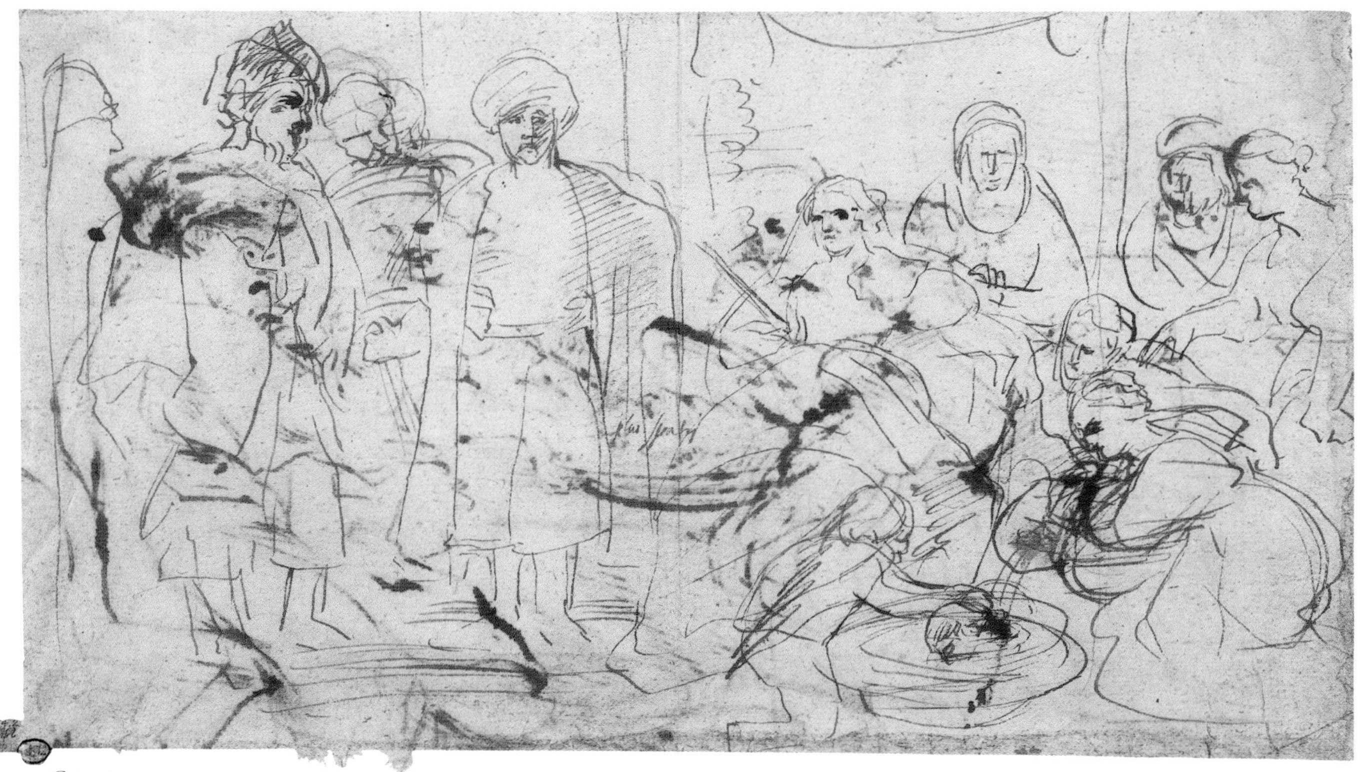

Cat. 112 verso

pleted, shortly thereafter, and this is at least one reason for the discrepancy. Originally, the painting ended at the left very much as the drawing does, at the spot where Rubens drew two vertical lines.[6] The drawing may therefore record the state of the painting before it was enlarged.

Some of the figures from the *Feast of Herod* show through in the sketch, drawn with a fine pen, on the verso and render the composition difficult to follow. Rubens represented Queen Tomyris seated under a canopy at the right and holding a scepter as she witnesses the immersion of the severed head of Cyrus in a vessel filled with his blood (for the story of Queen Tomyris and Cyrus, see cat. no. 55). The artist had employed a similar arrangement earlier, in about 1625, in a painting in a vertical format that is now in the Louvre, Paris.[7] The horizontal layout of this late drawing and the inclusion of a heavy-set figure in Eastern dress relate the sheet more closely to Rubens's large *Queen Tomyris and Cyrus* painting in the Museum of Fine Arts, Boston, dated most recently to 1622–23.[8] Two women kneeling in the foreground and three standing farther back observe the event, as does a group of four men at the left. Rubens's inscription in the center, "plus spatij" (more space), was probably a reminder to himself to add space between the two main groups of figures.[9] For all the detail of the drawing, no painting by Rubens based on it is known.

1. Elizabeth McGrath discusses two additional drawings of Tomyris and Cyrus, one in the Hermitage, Saint Petersburg (1997, vol. 2, p. 25, under no. 2a, copy 1 [Rubens?], vol. 1, fig. 9), the other in the Fitzwilliam Museum, Cambridge (1997, vol. 2, p. 26, under no. 2a, copy 2 [Jacob Jordaens?], vol. 1, fig. 15). In her opinion, both may reflect a lost Rubens drawing or oil sketch (1997, vol. 2, p. 26, under no. 2a).
2. As Held (1959, under no. 67) observed, an old, weak copy of the *Feast of Herod* is in the Rijksprentenkabinet, Amsterdam (inv. 40:633).
3. M. Jaffé 1989, no. 1187, ca. 1635.
4. According to Michael Jaffé (ibid.), the painting was in Roomer's collection before Rubens died. This is doubtful, since the painting seems to have been substantially enlarged by another hand (Thompson and Brigstocke 1970, pp. 84–85)—something that one can hardly imagine happening while Rubens was alive. For Roomer, see Meijer 1985–86, p. 72.
5. Burchard 1953, p. 384, n. 2.
6. See Thompson and Brigstocke 1970, pp. 84–85.
7. K.d.K., ed. Oldenbourg 1921, no. 237; M. Jaffé 1989, no. 666, 1620–25.
8. K.d.K., ed. Oldenbourg 1921, no. 175; M. Jaffé 1989, no. 510, 1618–19; McGrath 1997, vol. 2, no. 2, vol. 1, figs. 7, 11.
9. Elizabeth McGrath (1997, vol. 2, no. 5) suggested that Rubens intended to move the group of men farther into the background in order to make the queen more prominent.

113. *Lansquenets Carousing,* recto, ca. 1638; *Studies for Figures in "Pastoral Landscape with Shepherds and Rainbow,"* verso, ca. 1632–35

Pen and brown ink over black chalk, 272 x 355 mm (10¾ x 14 in.)
Inscribed by the artist in black chalk on verso at top left: *met een groot slecht lantschap* (with a large flat landscape)
Annotated in pen and brown ink at top right: *B.H.B no 16*

Collection Frits Lugt, Institut Néerlandais, Paris (I 2335)

PROVENANCE: Canon Johannes Philippus Happaert (d. 1686), Antwerp;[1] Prosper Henry Lankrink (1628?–1692), London; Jonathan Richardson Sr. (1665–1745), London; possibly Gerard Hoet (1698–1760), Utrecht and The Hague (his sale, The Hague, August 25–28, 1760, p. 24, album H, lot 451);[2] Sir Joshua Reynolds (1723–1792), London; E. Wauters (sale, Amsterdam, F. Muller and Co., April 15, 1926, lot 174; to Frits Lugt).

LITERATURE: Glück and Haberditzl 1928, no. 219, pl. 219 (recto), no. 218, pl. 218 (verso); Lugt 1943, pp. 107–8, figs. 6, 7; Held 1959, no. 68, pl. 79, pp. 21, 45, 58, 82, 124, under no. 65, 154–55, under no. 154; Kuznetsov 1974, pl. 150; Fishman 1982, pp. 45–61, fig. 24; Adler 1982, no. 39b, fig. 112, p. 133, under no. 39; Held 1986, no. 232, pl. 208; Brown in London 1996–97, p. 79, fig. 75 (verso).

EXHIBITIONS: London–Paris–Bern–Brussels 1972, no. 85, pls. 44, 45; Leningrad–Moscow–Kiev 1974, no. 113, ill.; Paris 1974, no. 105, pls. 86, 87.

With a heavy quill pen and few pentimenti, Rubens drew the group of lansquenets on the recto of this sheet in preparation of a painting, traditionally known as *Lansquenets Carousing* or *Marauding Soldiers,*[3] that is lost but known from several copies and from an etching in reverse by Frans van den Wyngaerde (1614–1679) that identifies Rubens as the painter (fig. 157).[4] The lost painting most likely dated from the artist's last years.[5] It is associated with the entry in the inventory of Rubens's estate drawn up in 1640 that records "A troop of Swiss who force peasants to give them money and set the table, on canvas."[6] At some time between 1640 and 1645 the Spanish king Philip IV purchased the painting from Rubens's estate, for 880 florins, but the work seems never to have reached Spain.[7]

To properly read the composition, one must turn to the various copies,[8] for the present drawing is mutilated: about one-third of the composition was cut away at the left, with part of a woman's left arm and hand left behind. In the center foreground of the composition is the seated lansquenet who raises a glass of wine in one hand and steadies a large sword with the

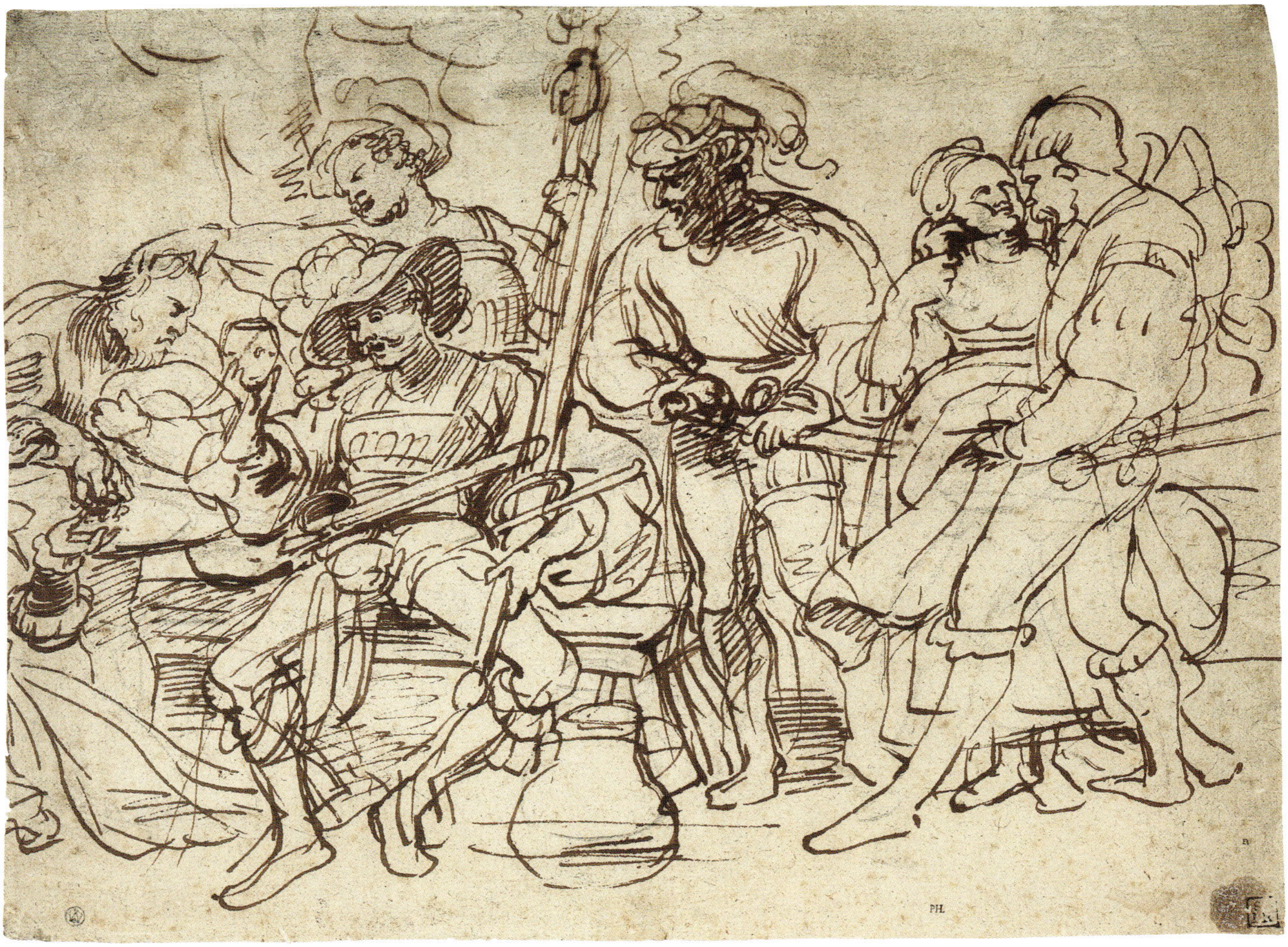

Cat. 113 recto

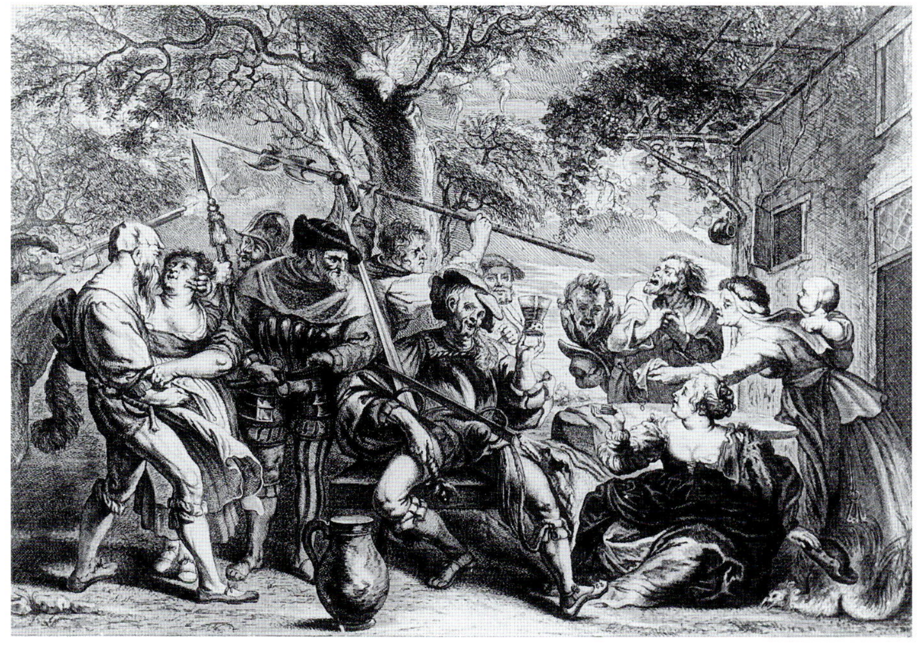

Fig. 157. Frans van den Wyngaerde, *Soldiers and Peasants Sitting and Fighting near a Table,* ca. 1640. Etching, 250 x 355 mm ($9\frac{13}{16}$ x 14 in.). Teylers Stichting, Haarlem

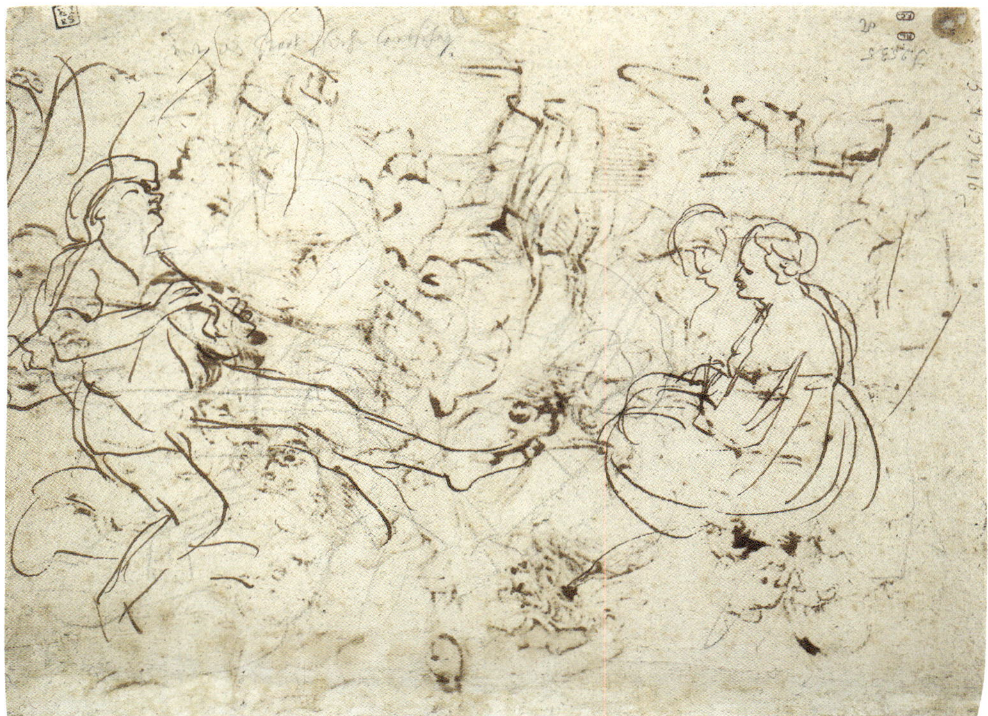

Cat. 113 verso

other; because of the trimming of the sheet, he is now off center, to the left. In the drawing his eyes are downcast, but in the painting he toasts the viewer. Since he and the lansquenets standing next to and behind him, as well as the amorous soldier at the right, are wearing sixteenth-century garb, Rubens may have thought of the composition as a historicizing scene. At the left (now missing from the drawing) a seated young woman extends her hand to receive coins from a peasant, who is forced to this action by a soldier standing behind him and rudely grasping his head. The well-dressed woman, as we see her in the painted copies and Van den Wyngaerde's print, resembles the elegant ladies found in Rubens's *Garden of Love* (fig. 137) dating from the early 1630s. Scholars do not agree on Rubens's reason for including this figure or on her identity: is she a victim or an accomplice of the soldiers, a mourning allegorical figure or a prostitute?

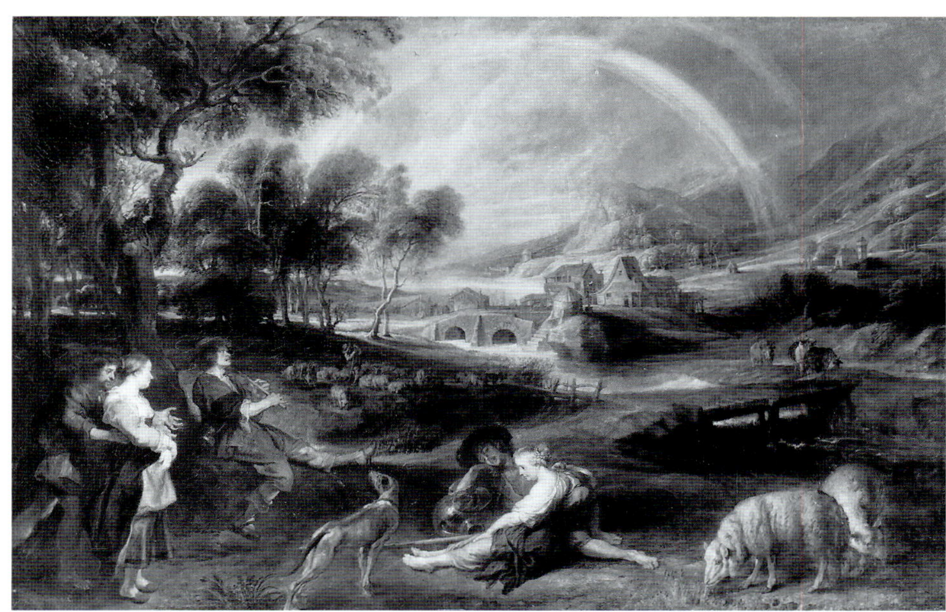

Fig. 158. Peter Paul Rubens, *Pastoral Landscape with Shepherds and Rainbow,* ca. 1636. Oil on canvas, 86 x 130 cm ($33\frac{7}{8}$ x $51\frac{3}{16}$ in.). The State Hermitage Museum, Saint Petersburg (482)

During the Middle Ages the word "Swiss" and as of the sixteenth century the word "lansquenet" were used to refer to foot soldiers hired for pay. They terrorized the countryside and victimized the peasants. Rubens's drawing—and more so, his painting—illustrates the arbitrary violence that the soldiers inflicted on the country folk.[9] In Rubens's letters from this time, we read about his increasing disillusionment at the fighting and lawlessness around him—which gave him a motive, perhaps, for drawing and painting this subject.

The few quick pen sketches on the verso of the sheet are early ideas for the principal figures in Rubens's painting *Pastoral Landscape with Shepherds and Rainbow* (fig. 158).[10] The figures are grouped as they are in the painting. At one point, Rubens apparently thought of adding one or two figures behind the shepherd; eventually he decided on a couple strolling in from the lower left instead. The landscape is barely indicated by the tree at the left, but it was obviously planned, as can be gleaned from the notes that Rubens made on the drawing: "with a large, simple—or flat—landscape." Some of the landscape may have been lost when the sheet was later trimmed. The verso probably has to be dated earlier than the recto, since the painting of the *Landscape with Shepherds* in all likelihood dates from about 1636, whereas the painting of the marauding soldiers is more likely a late work, of about 1638.

1. As Held (1959, no. 68) observed, cat. no. 113 may be identical with a "Plunderinkexken von Rubens" (plundering by Rubens) mentioned in Happaert's 1686 inventory; Denucé 1932, p. 337: Duverger 1984–, vol. 10, no. 3754, p. 380, no. 262.
2. Described as "Een ryke Ordinantie, met O.I. Ink en Roet, fraai van Licht en Bruin: Bekend door de Print, inzonderheid by den Brabanderen, onder den Naam van 'Schelme Leeven'" (A rich composition with black and brown ink, beautiful in light and shade: known through the print—especially in Brabant—under the name of "roguery").
3. M. Jaffé 1989, no. 1210, lost, ca. 1635–38?. Klessmann (1995, pp. 137–42, fig. 4) suggested a different reading of Rubens's composition. He identified the central lansquenet with Don Quixote, the eponymous hero of Cervantes's novel, published in Madrid in 1605 and 1615.
4. Schneevoogt 1873, p. 152, no. 128; Hollstein 1949–, vol. 55, p. 176, no. 16, ill.
5. Held (1986, p. 160, under no. 232) suggested, plausibly, that Rubens worked on the painting at his country estate outside Antwerp in the early fall of 1638. In a letter of August 17, 1638, Rubens asked Lucas Faid'herbe in Antwerp to send him a panel with three heads of soldiers, one angry and wearing a black cap, one crying, and one laughing; these heads seem to correspond with figures in the *Marauding Soldiers*. For Rubens's letter, see Rooses and Ruelens 1887–1909, vol. 6, pp. 222–23; Magurn 1955, p. 410, letter 244.
6. Muller 1989, p. 113, no. 90: "Vne troupe des Suisses qui contraignent les paysans de leur donner de l'argent & couurir la table, sur toile," or "A Switzer where the Boores bringe him money and Cover a table."
7. Vergara 1999, p. 149.
8. According to Klessmann (1995, p. 137), the copy in Munich by Simon de Vos (?), is the best. For a drawing by Jean-Honoré Fragonard (1732–1806) based on a version formerly in the Palazzo Colonna, Rome, see Saint-Non 2000, p. 356, no. 86, ill. We thank Konrad Renger for these references. A painting that reflects Rubens's lost work is included in the painting *Cabinet of Rubens* in the Palazzo Pitti, Florence, attributed to Cornelis de Baeilleur (1607–1671) and dated about 1640 (Florence 1977, no. 1, ill.).
9. Fishman 1982, pp. 45–61, and Larry Silver in Rotterdam–New York 2001, pp. 75–80.
10. K.d.K., ed. Oldenbourg 1921, no. 356; M. Jaffé 1989, no. 1218, 1635–38.

RETOUCHED DRAWINGS

ANONYMOUS 16TH-CENTURY DRAFTSMAN AFTER RAPHAEL, RETOUCHED BY PETER PAUL RUBENS

114. *The Prophets David and Daniel,* ca. 1601–2

Red chalk, some pouncing, heightened with white, retouched by Rubens with brush and dark red ink and greenish yellow body color; canted corners at top, 341 x 286 mm (13 7/16 x 11 1/4 in.)
Annotated by Jonathan Richardson Sr. in pen and brown ink on mount at bottom center: *Rubens from Raffaële;* on verso at top: *In the Madonna della Pace at Rome; 'tis a part of the famous Work of Raffaele there. Y. 18 / N. 10 Y. J. Richardson;* his shelf marks: *15/N 10 Y*

The Metropolitan Museum of Art, New York; Purchase, Harris Brisbane Dick Fund and Mr. and Mrs. Christopher Rupp Gift, 1995 (1995.401)

PROVENANCE: Jonathan Richardson Sr. (1665–1745), London (Lugt 2184); private collection, Rome; sale, London, Christie's, July 4, 1995, lot 127, ill.; Hazlitt, Gooden and Fox Ltd., London.

LITERATURE: M. Jaffé 1996, p. 462, no. G, fig. 8.

The drawing reproduces the prophets David and Daniel from the fresco in the two-storied Chigi chapel in the church of Santa Maria della Pace, Rome, that Agostino Chigi commissioned from Raphael (1483–1520) before February 21, 1511.[1] Raphael and his school decorated the lower story, above the niche for the altar, with four sibyls, and the upper story with depictions of the prophets Hosea, Jonah, David, and Daniel. David and Daniel are frescoed in the lunette to the right of the chapel's window and are seen in slight foreshortening. David, the older prophet, holds a tablet on which are inscribed prophecies pertaining to the Resurrection of Christ; Daniel copies from the tablet. The drawing has been known as *Jeremiah Dictating the Word of God to Baruch,* which was derived from an earlier title, *Baruch Copying from the Tablet of Jeremiah,* that in 1933 was given to a related version—executed in almost the same technique and with almost the same dimensions—in a private collection.[2]

The present drawing was discovered in a private collection in Rome in 1994.[3] It shows accents placed with the tip of the brush and red ink and white body color on top of a study in red chalk, which suggests that Rubens worked over a design by another hand. The sheet therefore belongs to the rather large group of drawings by other artists—very often sixteenth-century Italian—that Rubens retouched and reworked in his own style (see also cat. nos. 116, 117). As was customary for the artist, he applied his retouchings with a pointed brush and red wash to enhance faces, hands, and feet and to increase the corporeality of figures and garments. These alterations are not easily separated from the underlying red-chalk drawing. Scholars differ, therefore, and not everyone accepts the alterations as retouches.[4]

Two artists appear to have been involved in creating the present drawing, one who provided the initial copy and Rubens who "improved" it. Rubens's interventions are most visible in the wavy lines in David's beard and Daniel's hair, in the strengthening of Daniel's right arm, and in the enlargement and redefinition of much of the lower part of David's garment at the left. The shading with parallel strokes of the brush along the left edge to add depth are also additions by Rubens, as are the squiggly lines applied in red wash at the lower right. White highlights, drawn in a big swirl to indicate the angel's wings, must be Rubens's as well. These sensitive interventions, which introduce accents rather than notable changes, are more likely to date from Rubens's first visit to Rome, in 1601–2, when he began collecting compositions after Raphael and Michelangelo that caught his eye, than from his later stay in that city, in 1605–8.

The version in a private collection, mentioned above, is slightly larger. In general it is close to the New York drawing, although the parallel hatching in the background is heavier and less differentiated, and the angel is placed slightly lower. In several areas, such as the facial expressions of the angel and of Daniel, the angel's arms, and Daniel's hair, it also appears stiffer and less accomplished. Furthermore, the white highlights are less pronounced. These differences support our contention that the example in a private collection depends on the Metropolitan Museum's drawing. Rubens's hand is present in the Metropolitan Museum's drawing, and the study in a private collection is in all likelihood the work of a member of Rubens's studio.

There are at least two other instances in which a drawing retouched by Rubens has survived in other versions: there are two examples, one in the Louvre, Paris,[5] and another on the art market,[6] of the *Parable of the Laborers in the Vineyard,* based on Andrea del Sarto's lost fresco, painted about 1511–12, for the garden of Santissima Annunziata in Florence; there are three known versions—one each in Angers,[7] in Haarlem,[8] and in Vienna[9]—of the drawing of *Two Bound Prisoners,* after Francesco Salviati's fresco in the Palazzo Farnese, Rome. These secondary versions after Rubens's retouched drawings may have originated in Rubens's studio.

1. Oberhuber 1999, pp. 136–39.
2. Exhibited in Amsterdam 1933, no. 69 (*Baruch Copying from the Tablet of Jeremiah* by Rubens, ca. 1601–2, after Raphael); Cologne 1977, no. 69, ill. (*The Prophets David and Daniel with an Angel,* copied by Rubens during second Roman sojourn, 1605–8). Last discussed in M. Jaffé 1996, p. 462, under no. G (as the prophets David and Daniel; copied by Rubens in Rome, 1605–8; example for drawing now in New York).
3. Gregory Martin (quoted in M. Jaffé 1996, p. 463, n. 22) recognized it as a copy by Rubens, an opinion seconded by Michael Jaffé (ibid., p. 462). According to Jaffé, the version in a private collection was drawn by Rubens in the Chigi chapel, during his second visit to Rome, in 1605–8, and the Metropolitan Museum's drawing is a copy of that drawing made by Rubens in Antwerp in the late 1620s.
4. Michael Jaffé (1996, p. 462) and Gregory Martin (quoted in ibid., p. 463, n. 22), for example, consider the drawing the work of a single artist, Rubens.
5. Inv. 20.269. Paris 1978, no. 104, ill.
6. New York 1996, no. 11, ill.
7. M. Jaffé 1977, p. 50, pl. 125.
8. Teylers Museum, Haarlem; Scholten 1904, p. 69, O 29.
9. Albertina, Vienna; Vienna 1977b, no. 105, ill. Michael Jaffé (in Ottawa 1968–69, p. 16, fig. II) suggested Jacob Jordaens (1593–1678) as the author of this version, an attribution d'Hulst (1974, D24, fig. 617) rejected.

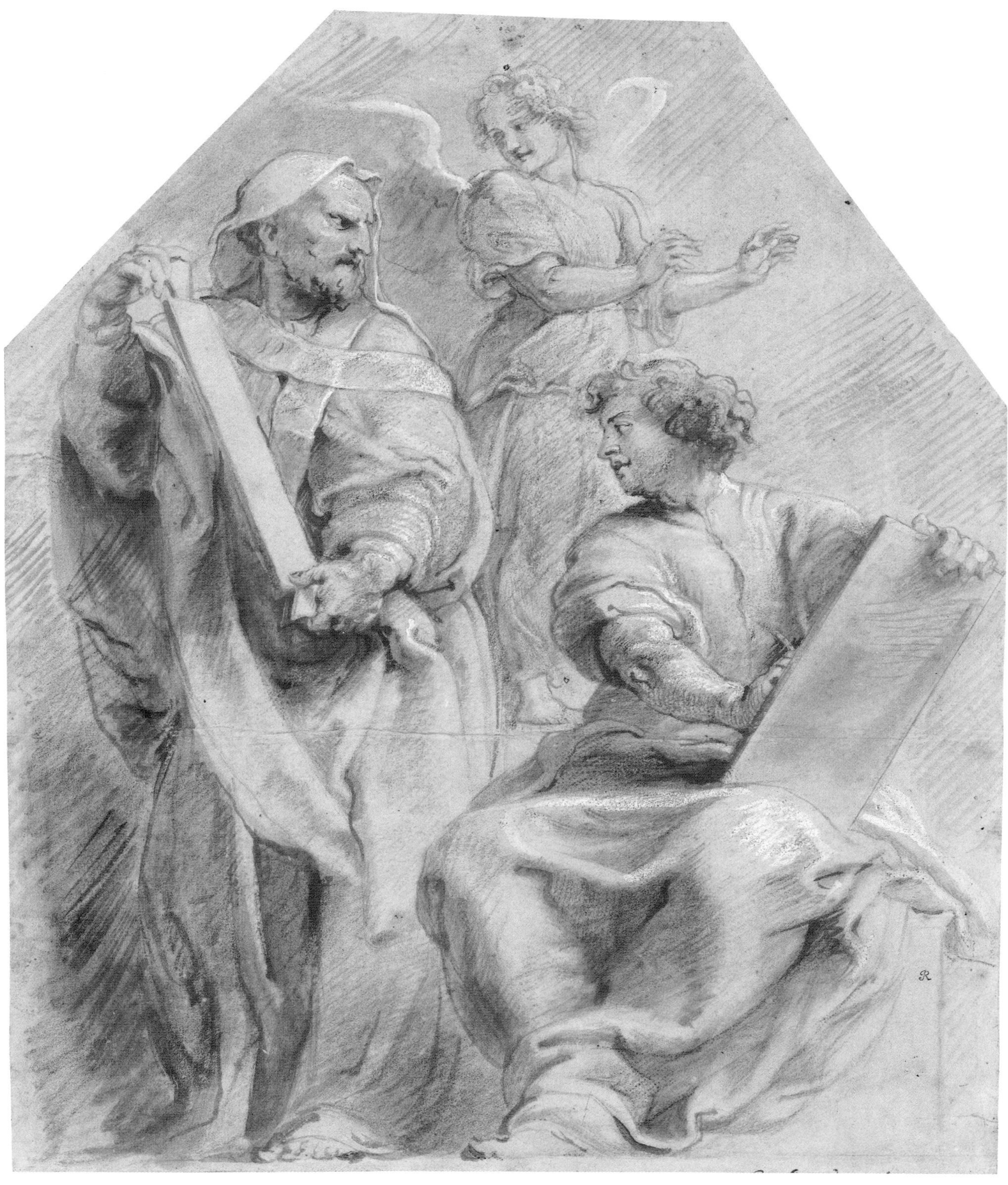

Cat. 114

115. *God the Father Surrounded by Angels,* 1601–2

Red chalk, gone over with tip of the brush and red ink and yellowish white body color, 255 x 286 mm (10 1/16 x 11 1/4 in.); irregularly cut out and made up in lower left corner

National Museums, Liverpool (The Walker) (WAG 1995.83)

PROVENANCE: Jonathan Richardson Sr. (1665–1745), London (Lugt 2184; sold February 11, 1746/47 as part of lot 54); bt. Trevor; William Roscoe (1753–1831), Liverpool (his sale, Liverpool, Winstanley, September 1816, lot 476); bt. Slater; Charles Robert Blundell of Ince (1761–1837), near Liverpool; Colonel Joseph Weld of Lulworth Manor, Dorset; acquired by the Walker Art Gallery from his executors through Christie's by private sale in 1995.

LITERATURE: Guarino 1990, pp. 10–29, fig. 8.

EXHIBITIONS: London 1998, no. 90, ill. Liverpool–London 1998–99, no. 77, ill.; Edinburgh–Nottingham 2002, no. 11.

The drawing records Michelangelo's famous representation of *God the Father,* painted between the fall of 1510 and 1512 in the center of his ceiling fresco in the Sistine Chapel at the Vatican. Rubens was deeply impressed by Michelangelo's fresco and copied several figures from it: he made at least eight large copies in black and red chalk after six prophets and two sibyls, as well as a copy after an *ignudo,* or nude male youth, in red chalk alone, with a few accents added with the tip of the brush and red ink (fig. 11). (For Rubens's drawing after Michelangelo's Libyan Sibyl, see cat. no. 4.)

This sheet is in all likelihood a copy by Rubens in red chalk that he retouched with the tip of the brush and red ink and some yellowish white body color.[1] The additions with the tip of the brush are typical of the artist. Rubens's sharp accents on this sheet are found in the faces and the hair of the figures, in the feet of God the Father, the knee, thighs, and buttock of the angel supporting him, and in the swirling cloth in the background—the sort of areas in which he commonly intervened.

In execution the sheet resembles Rubens's *Nude Youth Turning to the Right* (fig. 11), his copy after one of Michelangelo's *ignudi.* The latter is somewhat more delicate in the modeling of human anatomy, however. Rubens used very fine parallel hatching for the modeling of the legs, for example, which is not the case on the sheet with *God the Father Surrounded by Angels.* A closer examination of the initial underlying drawing in red chalk reveals a certain dryness and evenness in the delineation of the figures and especially of the limbs.

The sheet has been dated to 1606, at the beginning of Rubens's second stay in Rome (1605–8), since the application of the red chalk is more refined than in Rubens's copies after the prophets and sibyls in the Sistine ceiling.[2] However, we prefer a date to Rubens's first Roman sojourn, in 1601–2, since the retouchings are slight and involve accents rather than changes. During his second Roman sojourn Rubens appears to have been preoccupied with studying antique sculpture and working on the commission for an altarpiece for the church of Santa Maria in Vallicella.

Rubens's *God the Father Surrounded by Angels* must have enjoyed some popularity, to judge by two drawn copies and one lithograph after it. The Národní Galerie in Prague owns one of the drawings,[3] and the second is at the Clark Art Institute in Williamstown (on loan from the late Julius Held).[4] The latter was once attributed to the young Antoine Watteau (1684–1721), but was recently considered more likely to be Flemish.[5] It is not known if J. C. Lödel's lithograph was made after the present drawing, the one in Prague, or the one in Williamstown.[6]

1. See Brooke in Liverpool–London 1998–99, no. 77.
2. See Wood in Edinburgh–Nottingham 2002, no. 11.
3. Red chalk, rose accents with tip of the brush, and wash in red-brown and brown, heightened with buff color and white, 233 x 300 mm. Annotated in pencil on verso: "P. P. Rubbens"; inv. K54511. See Rollová 1997–98, pp. 124–27, fig. 3.
4. Binghamton and other cities 1970, no. 75, ill.
5. Jacques Mathey (see ibid.) ascribed it to the young Watteau, copying after Rubens. Rosenberg and Prat (1996, vol. 3, rejected drawings, under no. R 143) rejected the Watteau attribution; they saw the drawing as a "typical Flemish" one.
6. Schneevoogt 1873, p. 71, no. 54 bis.

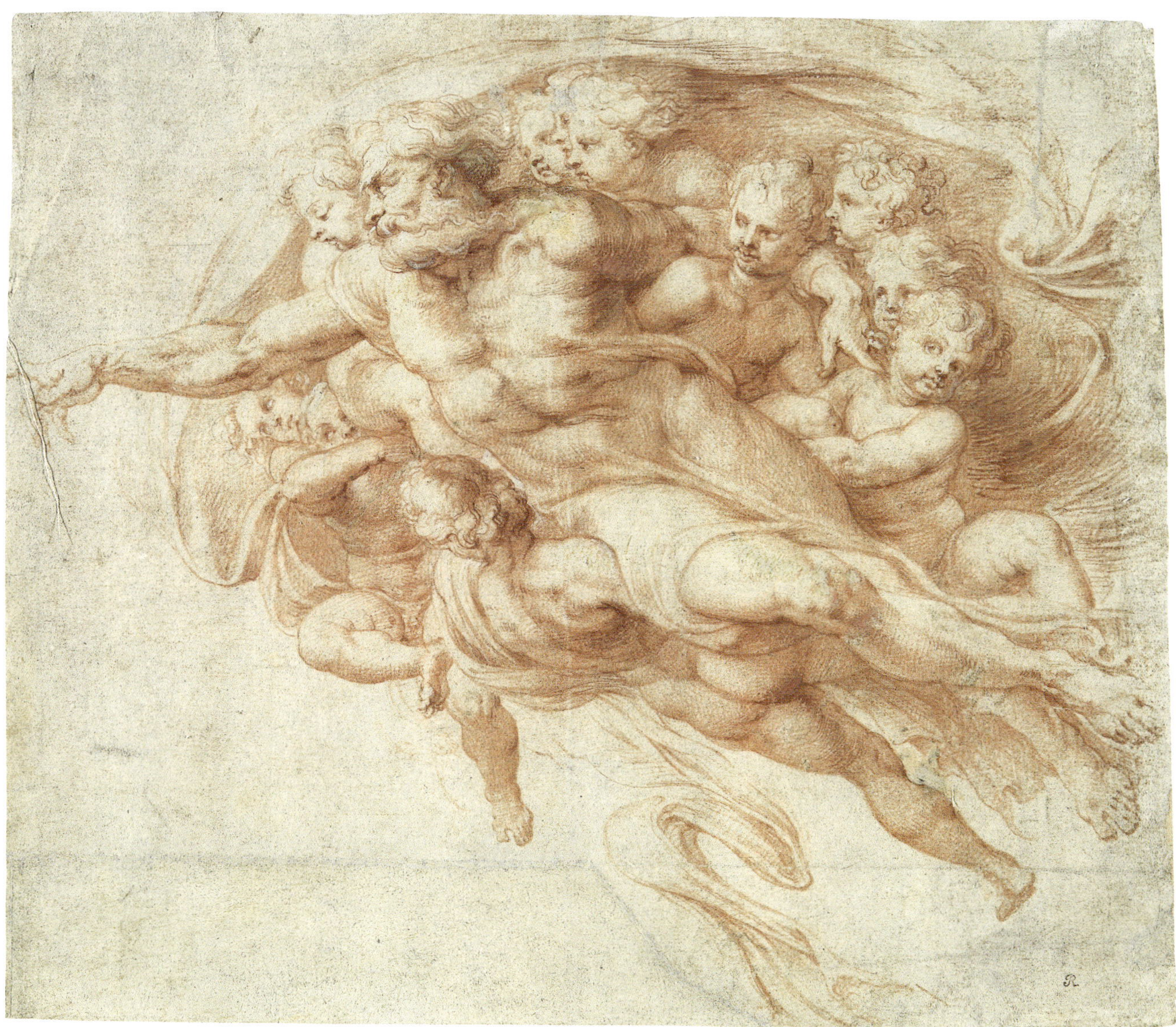

Cat. 115

16TH-CENTURY ITALIAN ARTIST, FORMERLY ATTRIBUTED TO TADDEO ZUCCARO, RETOUCHED BY PETER PAUL RUBENS

116. *God the Father*, ca. 1625–28

Black chalk, heightened with white, squared in black chalk for transfer (ca. 40 x 40 mm), reworked and retouched by Rubens with brush and dark brown ink and white and grayish white body color, 410 x 368 mm (16⅛ x 14½ in.); bottom and top corners cut; arched top section added (75 mm); two irregular pieces of paper inserted on each side

Annotated in pen and brown ink at bottom left: *Taddeus Zuccarus;*[1] and at bottom right: *514*

Victoria and Albert Museum, London; Dyce Bequest (514)

PROVENANCE: Valerius Röver (1686–1739), Delft (listed in his inventory, album 39, p. 194);[2] Charles Rogers (1711–1784), London (Lugt 624); Reverend Alexander Dyce (1798–1869), London (Lugt 711 bis).

LITERATURE: Held 1959, no. 170, pl. 177; Burchard and d'Hulst 1963, no. 140, pl. 140; Held 1986, no. 174, pl. 172.

EXHIBITIONS: London 1977a, no. 183, ill.; Edinburgh–Nottingham 2002, no. 68, ill.

In the early eighteenth century this drawing was owned by the renowned Delft collector Valerius Röver (1686–1739), who ascribed it to a "Zuccaro," without specifying which of the artist-brothers he had in mind. Röver may have based his attribution on a comparable figure of God the Father in a drawing by Federico Zuccaro (1540/42–1609) that was then in his collection: the *Annunciation* reproducing Federico's fresco of the *Annunciation Surrounded by Prophets* of 1566 (formerly in the Jesuit church of Santa Maria Annunziata, Rome; taken down in 1626). The drawing served for the engraving by Raphael Sadeler I (1561–ca. 1628), dated 1580, as Röver dutifully noted in his inventory.[3] Röver's drawing does not seem to have survived, but a similar sheet by Federico is now in the Louvre.[4] In the end Röver's attribution cannot be supported. Indeed, the careful squaring of the initial black-chalk drawing on the sheet that lies underneath Rubens's retouchings indicates that it was a study for another work of art, which has not been identified.

Röver saw correctly, however, that Rubens had retouched the composition. (He even coined a special term—"Rubenisato"—for the drawings that Rubens retouched, or "Rubenized.")[5] Rubens reworked the drawing with brush and dark brown ink and grayish white body color, to add volume and depth, especially in the billowing cloak of God the Father at the left, which now covers the underlying drawing completely. He also indicated clearly that the light fell on the figure from the right, casting the left side in shadow. He added strong highlights with white body color to enliven the garments' folds. With the tip of the brush, finally, he accented some of the contours and introduced more strands in the hair and beard.

More than one set of dates has been suggested for Rubens's reworking of the drawing: between about 1615 and 1628 (since Rubens painted similar figures of God the Father in oil sketches during this period)[6] or about 1628–29 (by association with Rubens's oil sketch of the *Incarnation as Fulfillment of All the Prophecies* in the Barnes Foundation, Merion, Pennsylvania).[7] The volume that Rubens introduced in the folds of the cloak may indeed support dating the sheet to the later 1620s. Rubens's changes in this drawing are not unlike those he introduced in the *Fashionable Young Woman Holding a Shield* (cat. no. 117), in which he moved the coat of arms from the front to the back, and in the process enhanced the woman's voluminous skirt.

1. According to Wood (in Edinburgh–London 2002, no. 68), Rubens perhaps wrote "Zuccarus," and an early hand was responsible for "Taddeus." However, one would expect Rubens to have used the Italian spelling of the artist's surname. It is doubtful, moreover, that the handwriting is Rubens's.
2. "Zittend oúde MansBeeld rústende met de eene hand op de Waereldskloot, en met de Rechterhand opgeheeven om den zegen te geeven, zijnde een Stúdie Beeld voor de Dio Padre van Raphael, door Zúccaro eerst met swart krijt geteekent, en in t' graaúw met het pinceel door Rúbbens geretoùcheerd, daar is een groot vùùr en deftigheid in de Actitúde van dit Beeld, ook een úijtmùntend schoon licht en brúijn. ziet Richardson tom.1. pag. 61" (Seated old Man, resting his one hand on the globe and his right hand raised to give a blessing; this is a study for God the Father by Raphael, first drawn by Zuccaro with black chalk, and retouched by Rubens with brush and gray wash. There is a great ardor and stateliness in the pose of this figure, also strikingly beautiful light and shadow. See Richardson, vol. 1, p. 61). Valerius Röver, handwritten inventory of his art collection (now in the Universiteitsbibliotheek van Amsterdam [inv. II A 18]).
3. Valerius Röver, inventory (see note 2 above), album 36, p. 179: "'Een Grootsche en zinnebeeldige Ordinantie van Fred. Zuccaro, verbeeldende de bootschap van den Engel aan Maria, boven en Hemel vol Engelen en

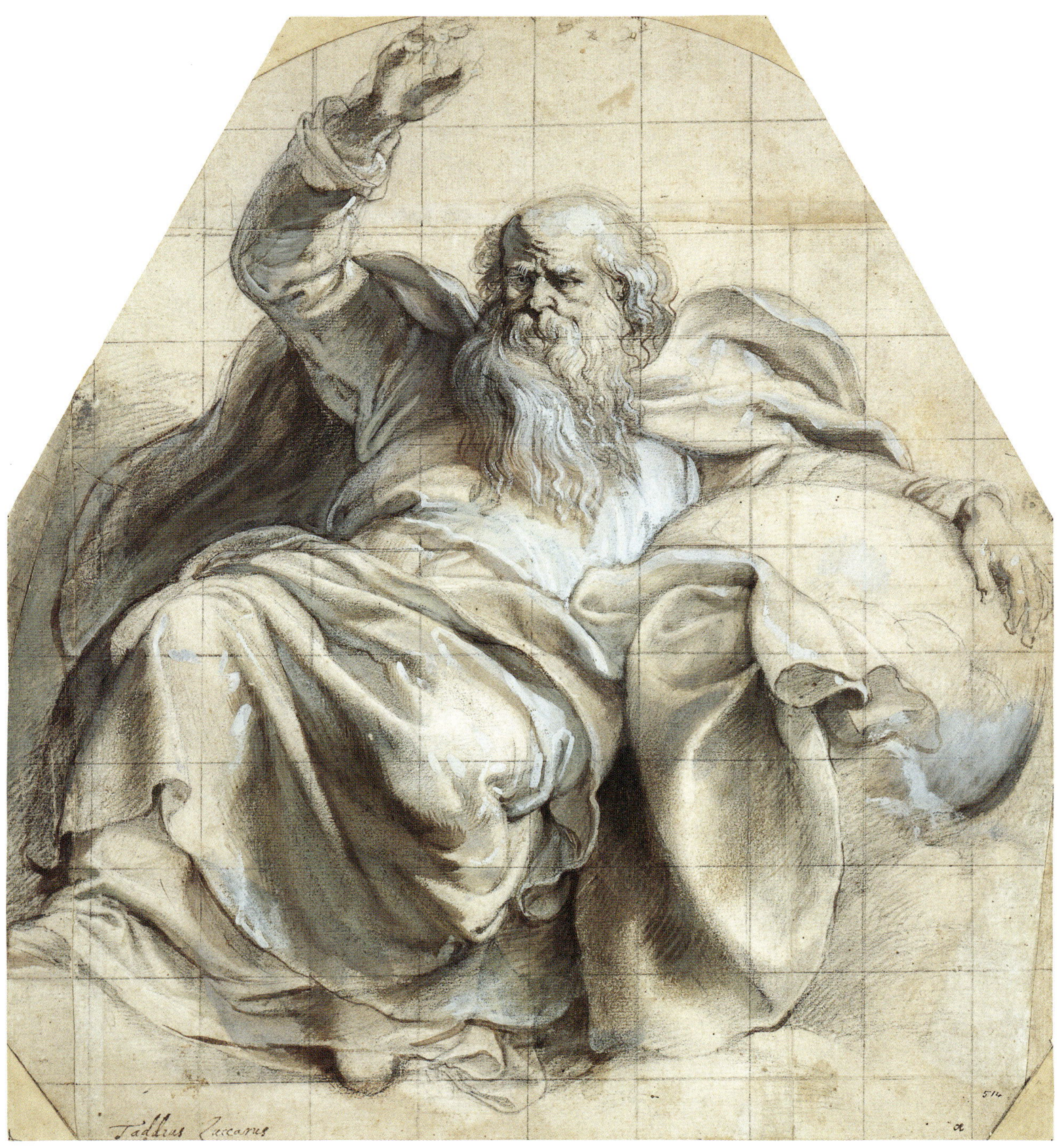

Cat. 116

beneden diverse profeten als Moses / David etc. met de pen, en roetkleur gewassen, door R: Sadeler in print gebragt. / uit de Collectie van Bergestein, deze tekening beschrijft Richardson, Essai sur la theorie de la peintures, pag: 205. . . . f. 15.' " For Sadeler's print, see Hollstein 1949–, vol. 21, p. 216, no. 12, vol. 22, p. 185, ill.

4. Paris 1969, no. 51.

5. Valerius Röver, handwritten inventory (see note 2 above), album 39, p. 194; Plomp 2001–2, pp. 136–37. The late John Gere, who published widely on the brothers Taddeo and Federico Zuccaro, did not accept Röver's attribution to the Zuccari; he judged the drawing to be entirely by Rubens (letter of March 5, 1987). James Mundy also doubted the attribution and suggested Girolamo Siciolante da Sermoneta (1521–1575) as a more likely author of the initial drawing in black chalk (oral communication, July 2003).

6. Wood in Edinburgh-Nottingham 2002, no. 68.

7. Held 1980, no. 319, pl. 316, ca. 1628–29; M. Jaffé 1989, no. 947, 1628–29.

117. *Fashionable Young Woman Holding a Shield: Design for Glass*, retouched ca. 1630–35

Pen and gray ink and gray wash, heightened with white, retouched and reworked by Rubens in brush and brown ink and brown wash, heightened with white and ocher body color and some green wash, 261 x 210 mm (10¼ x 8¼ in.)

The Duke of Devonshire and the Chatsworth Settlement Trustees, Chatsworth (838)

PROVENANCE: Nicolaes A. Flinck (1646–1723), Rotterdam (Lugt 959); acquired in 1723–24 by William, 2nd Duke of Devonshire (1673–1729).

LITERATURE: Thöne 1940, p. 64, fig. 1; Held 1959, no. 168, pl. 178, fig. 44, p. 59; Held 1986, no. 233, pl. 224; M. Jaffé 2002, no. 1581, ill.

EXHIBITIONS: Washington and other cities 1969–70, no. 104, ill.; London 1973–74, no. 104; London 1993–94, no. 185, ill.

This drawing is one of the clearest and most interesting examples of an old master drawing retouched by Rubens. Thanks to an infrared photograph of the drawing first published by Julius Held (fig. 159), we have an idea of the sheet's original appearance, of the extent of Rubens' retouches, and of how, in Held's words, the drawing was "brilliantly brought to life by Rubens' magic."[1] The initial drawing is by an anonymous sixteenth-century Swiss artist, probably a designer of stained glass working under the influence of Hans Holbein the Younger (1497/98–1543). What is still visible from this early state is the architecture (except for the highlights on the pilaster at the left), the plumes of the woman's hat, her right sleeve, and the pattern of her undergarment, all neatly drawn in pen and black ink. Originally, the woman stood behind and held the armorial shield, which was depicted in full and bore two pitchers and a house mark, presumably of some Swiss family. Rubens reworked this area to such an extent that little is left of the underlying drawing. He changed the contour of the shield to form an integral part of the woman's skirt by merging it at the left into the heavy folds. Now this fashionably dressed young woman, positioned in front of the shield, appears to lift her skirt. Rubens also softened her face, puffed up her left sleeve, and rearranged her hair spilling out from under her hat. The artist reshaped her left hand, which now steadies the shield, and he ended the top of the shield, at the right, with a "horn" and "curl," probably in order to enliven that part of the drawing, possibly to give the sheet a more "authentic" sixteenth-century look.[2] Rubens also added highlights with white oil color in the folds, to increase the volume.

This heavy retouching and considerable rethinking of the young woman's action place Rubens's intervention on this sheet with certainty in his later years. Scholars have generally dated Rubens's reworking of this sheet to about 1625–35.[3] However, a narrower time span of about 1630–35 may be preferable, for the primarily greenish and ocher body color that Rubens used for his retouches on this sheet recall the grayish white and greenish gouache with which he reworked the design for the right half of the *Garden of Love* drawing (cat. no. 94), which is datable to the early 1630s.

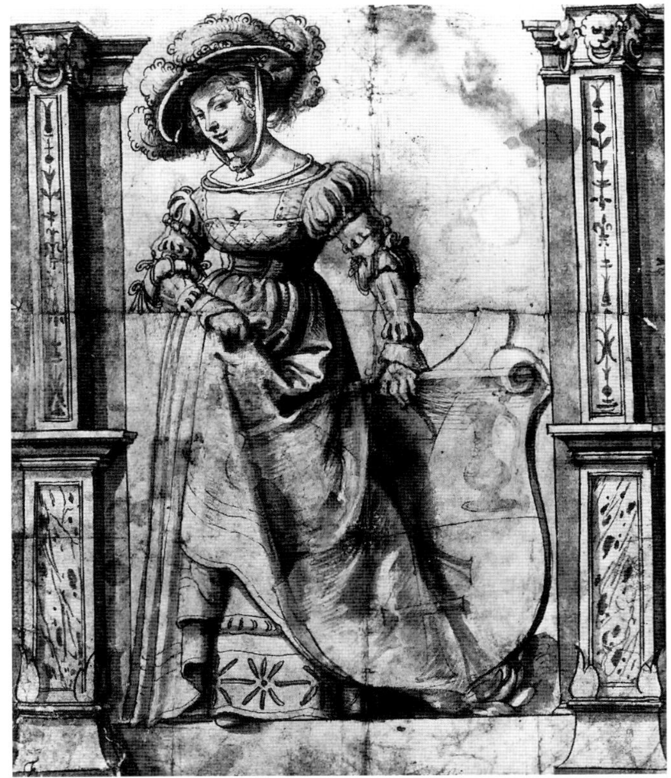

Fig. 159. Infrared photograph of cat. 117. Research Library, The Getty Research Institute, Los Angeles; Julius Held Papers (990056)

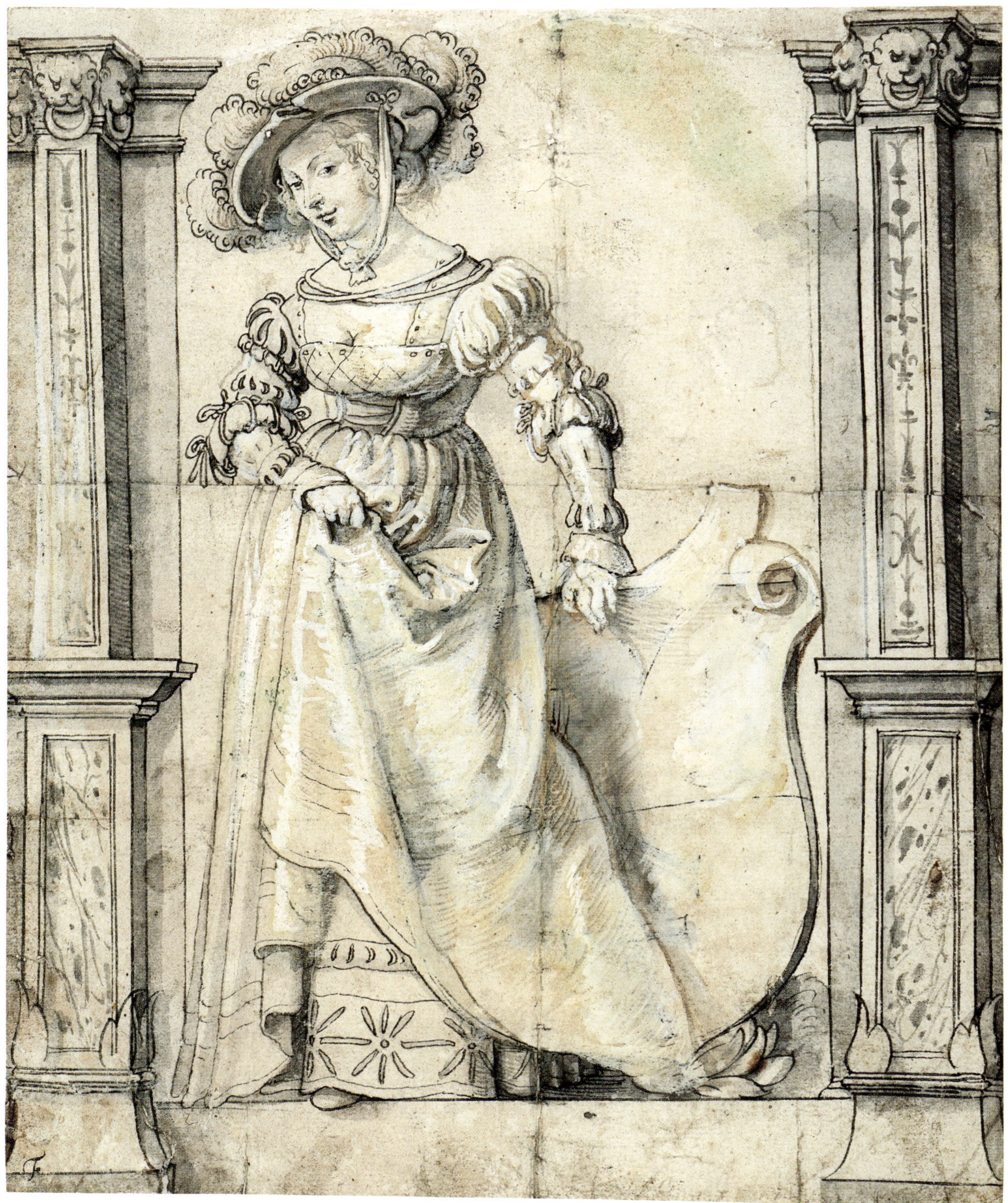

Cat. 117

1. Held 1959, p. 59 and fig. 44. Thöne (1940) was the first to suggest that Rubens might have reworked an older drawing.
2. M. Jaffé 2002, no. 1581.
3. Held (1959, no. 168; 1986, no. 233) suggested ca. 1625–35, a date that Michael Jaffé (2002, no. 1581) accepted.

BIBLIOGRAPHY

Adler 1982
Adler, Wolfgang. *Landscapes.* Corpus Rubenianum Ludwig Burchard 18, vol. 1. London, 1982.

Aerts and Nieuwenhuizen 1992
Aerts, Willem, and Jos Van Den Nieuwenhuizen. "L'histoire de l'érection de la croix après la Révolution Française." In d'Hulst et al. 1992, pp. 99–124.

Alpers 1971
Alpers, Svetlana. *The Decoration of the Torre de la Parada.* Corpus Rubenianum Ludwig Burchard 9. London and New York, 1971.

Alpers 1995
Alpers, Svetlana. *The Making of Rubens.* New Haven, 1995.

Amsterdam 1933
Catalogus der Rubens-tentoonstelling. Exh. cat. Amsterdam, J. Goudstikker; 1933. Amsterdam, 1933.

Amsterdam 1995
Putti en cherubijntjes: Het religieuze werk van Jacob de Wit (1695–1754). Exh. cat. ed. Guus van den Hout and Robert Schillemans. Amsterdam, Museum Amstelkring; 1995. Haarlem, 1995.

Amsterdam 2001
Drawn to Warmth: Seventeenth-Century Dutch Artists in Italy. Exh. cat. by Peter Schatborn, with an essay by Judith Verberne. Amsterdam, Rijksmuseum; 2001. Zwolle and Amsterdam, 2001.

Amsterdam 2003
Jacob de Wit (1695–1754): Een bedrieger in het paleis/Master of Deception. Exh. cat. by Eymert-Jan Goossens. Amsterdam, Royal Palace; 2003. Amsterdam, 2003.

Amsterdam–Ghent 1982–83
Met Huygens op reis: Tekeningen en dagboeknotities van Constantijn Huygens Jr. (1628–1697), secretaris van stadhouder-koning Willem III. Exh. cat. by J. F. Heijbroek et al. Amsterdam, Rijksprentenkabinet, Rijksmuseum, and Ghent, Museum voor Schone Kunsten; 1982–83. Zutphen, 1982.

Amsterdam–New York 2003
Willem van Tetrode, Sculptor (c. 1525–1580): Guglielmo Fiammingo scultore. Exh. cat. by Frits Scholten et al. Amsterdam, Rijksmuseum, and New York, The Frick Collection; 2003. Amsterdam, New York, and Zwolle, 2003.

Amsterdam–New York–Toledo 2003–4
Hendrick Goltzius (1558–1617): Drawings, Prints and Paintings. Exh. cat. by Huigen Leeflang et al. Amsterdam, Rijksmuseum; New York, The Metropolitan Museum of Art; and Toledo Museum of Art; 2003–4. Zwolle, 2003.

Andreae 1991
Andreae, Bernard. *Laokoon und die Kunst des Pergamon: Die Hybris der Giganten.* Frankfurt, 1991.

Andrews 1985
Andrews, Keith. *Catalogue of Netherlandish Drawings in the National Gallery of Scotland.* 2 vols. Edinburgh, 1985.

Antwerp 1971
Rubens en zijn tijd: Tekeningen uit Belgische verzamelingen. Exh. cat. by Frans Baudouin and Roger-A. d'Hulst. Antwerp, Rubenshuis; 1971. Antwerp, 1971.

Antwerp 1977
P. P. Rubens: Schilderijen, olieverfschetsen, tekeningen. Exh. cat. Antwerp, Koninklijk Museum voor Schone Kunsten; 1977. English ed., *P. P. Rubens: Paintings—Oilsketches—Drawings.* Antwerp, 1977.

Antwerp 1991
David Teniers de Jonge: Schilderijen, tekeningen. Exh. cat. by Margret Klinge. Antwerp, Koninklijk Museum voor Schone Kunsten; 1991. Ghent, 1991.

Antwerp 1993
Rubens Cantoor: Een verzameling tekeningen ontstaan in Rubens' atelier. Exh. cat. Antwerp, Rubenshuis; 1993. Ghent, 1993.

Antwerp 1996–97
The Illustration of Books Published by the Moretuses. Exh. cat. by Karen L. Bowen et al. Ed. D. Imhof. Antwerp, Plantin-Moretus Museum; 1996–97. Antwerp, 1996.

Antwerp 2000
Images of Death: Rubens Copies Holbein. Exh. cat. by Kristin Lohse Belkin and Carl Depauw, with contributions by Michael Kwakkelstein and Volker Manuth. Antwerp, Rubenshuis; 2000. Antwerp, 2000.

Antwerp 2004a
Een hart voor boeken: Rubens en zijn bibliotheek. Exh. cat. ed. Marcus De Schepper. Antwerp, Plantin-Moretus Museum; 2004. Schoten, 2004.

Antwerp 2004b
A House of Art: Rubens as Collector. Exh. cat. by Kristin Lohse Belkin, Fiona Healy, and Gregory Martin, with an introductory essay by Jeffrey M. Muller. Antwerp, Rubenshuis; 2004. Schoten, 2004.

Antwerp 2004c
Rubens et l'art de la gravure. Exh. cat. ed. Nico van Hout. Antwerp, Koninklijk Museum voor Schone Kunsten; 2004. Antwerp, 2004.

Antwerp–Amsterdam 1999–2000
Anthony van Dyck as a Printmaker. Exh. cat. by Carl Depauw and Ger Luijten, with contributions by Erik Duverger et al. Antwerp, Plantin-Moretus Museum and Stedelijk Prentenkabinet, and Amsterdam, Rijksprentenkabinet, Rijksmuseum; 1999–2000. Antwerp and Amsterdam, 1999.

Antwerp–London 1999a
The Light of Nature: Landscape Drawings and Watercolours by Van Dyck and His Contemporaries. Exh. cat. by Martin Royalton-Kisch. Antwerp, Rubenshuis, and London, British Museum; 1999. London, 1999.

Antwerp–London 1999b
Van Dyck, 1599–1641. Exh. cat. by Christopher Brown and Hans Vlieghe, with contributions by Frans Baudouin et al. Antwerp, Koninklijk Museum voor Schone Kunsten, and London, Royal Academy of Arts; 1999. London and Antwerp, 1999.

Antwerp–Münster 1990
Jan Boeckhorst, 1604–1668: Maler der Rubenszeit. Exh. cat. Antwerp, Rubenshuis, and Münster, Westfälisches Landesmuseum für Kunst und Kulturgeschichte; 1990. Freren, 1990.

Antwerp–Rotterdam 1960
Antoon van Dyck: Tekeningen en olieverfschetsen. Exh. cat. by Roger-A. d'Hulst and Horst Vey. Antwerp, Rubenshuis, and Rotterdam, Museum Boymans-van Beuningen; 1960. Antwerp, 1960.

Arents 2001
Arents, Prosper. *De bibliotheek van Pieter Pauwel Rubens: Een reconstructie.* Ed. Alfons K. L. Thijs. Antwerp, 2001.

Babelon 1897
Babelon, Ernest. *Catalogue des camées antiques et modernes de la Bibliothèque Nationale.* 2 vols. Paris, 1897.

Baillie 1792
Baillie, William. *Catalogue of Prints Engraved by Captain William Baillie after Pictures and Drawings in Various Collections.* London, 1792.

Baker, Elam, and Warwick 2003
Baker, Christopher, Caroline Elam, and Genevieve Warwick, eds. *Collecting Prints and Drawings in Europe, c. 1500–1750.* Aldershot and Burlington, Vt., 2003.

Balis 1986
Balis, Arnout. *Rubens Hunting Scenes.* Corpus Rubenianum Ludwig Burchard 18, vol. 2. London and Oxford, 1986.

Balis 2000
Balis, Arnout. "Working It Out: Design Tools and Procedures in Sixteenth- and Seventeenth-Century Flemish Art." In Vlieghe, Balis, and Van de Velde 2000, pp. 129–51.

Balis 2001
Balis, Arnout. "Rubens und Inventio: Der Beitrag seines *Theoretischen Studienbuches.*" In Heinen and Thielemann 2001, pp. 11–40.

Bambach 1997
Bambach, Carmen C. Review of Perrig 1991. *Master Drawings* 35 (Spring 1997), pp. 67–72.

Basel 1984
Spätrenaissance am Oberrhein: Tobias Stimmer, 1539–1584. Exh. cat. ed. Dieter Koepplin and Paul Tanner. Basel, Kunstmuseum; 1984. Basel, 1984.

Baudouin 1972
Baudouin, Frans. "Altars and Altarpieces before 1620." In *Rubens before 1620,* ed. John Rupert Martin, pp. 45–91. Princeton, 1972.

Baudouin 1977
Baudouin, Frans. *Pietro Pauolo Rubens.* Trans. Elsie Callander. New York, 1977.

Baudouin 1992
Baudouin, Frans. "L'Érection de la Croix de Pierre Paul Rubens." In d'Hulst et al. 1992, pp. 45–96.

Baudouin 2000
Baudouin, Frans. "Concept, Design and Execution: The Intervention of the Patron." In Vlieghe, Balis, and Van de Velde 2000, pp. 1–26.

Bauer and Bauer 1999
Bauer, Linda [Freeman], and George Bauer. "Artists' Inventories and the Language of the Oil Sketch." *Burlington Magazine* 141 (September 1999), pp. 520–30.

L. Bauer 1992
Bauer, Linda Freeman. "Rubens Oil Sketches for Architecture." In *An Architectural Progress in the Renaissance and Baroque—Sojurns in and out of Italy: Essays in Architectural History Presented to Hellmut Hager on His Sixty-Sixth Birthday,* ed. Henry A. Millon and Susan Scott Munshower, pp. 224–43. Papers in Art History from the Pennsylvania State University 8, pts. 1 and 2. University Park, Pa., 1992.

Bazzotti 1992
Bazzotti, Ugo. "Precisiazioni sulla Pala della Trinità di Mantova." In Limentani Virdis and Bottacin 1992, pp. 39–48.

Bean 1962
Bean, Jacob. "The Drawings Collection." *The Metropolitan Museum of Art Bulletin* 20 (January 1962), pp. 157–75.

Bean 1964
Bean, Jacob. *One Hundred European Drawings in The Metropolitan Museum of Art.* New York, 1964.

Bean 1979
Bean, Jacob. *Seventeenth-Century Italian Drawings in The Metropolitan Museum of Art.* New York, 1979.

Bean 1982
Bean, Jacob, with Lawrence Turčić. *Fifteenth and Sixteenth Century Italian Drawings in The Metropolitan Museum of Art.* New York, 1982.

Belkin 1980
Belkin, Kristin Lohse. *The Costume Book.* Corpus Rubenianum Ludwig Burchard 24. Brussels, 1980.

Belkin 1989
Belkin, Kristin Lohse. "Rubens's Latin Inscriptions on His Copies after Holbein's *Dance of Death.*" *Journal of the Warburg and Courtauld Institutes* 52 (1989), pp. 245–50.

Belkin 1994
Belkin, Kristin Lohse. "The Classification of Rubens's Drawings Collection." *Wallraf-Richartz-Jahrbuch* 55 (1994), pp. 105–14.

Belkin 1998
Belkin, Kristin Lohse. *Rubens.* London, 1998.

Belkin 2000
Belkin, Kristin Lohse. "Rubens's Copies after German and Netherlandish Prints." In Antwerp 2000, pp. 63–111.

Belkin 2004
Belkin, Kristin Lohse. "Rubens as Collector of Drawings." In Antwerp 2004b, pp. 310–13.

Bellori 1672
Bellori, Giovanni Pietro. *Le vite de' pittori, scultori et architetti moderni.* Rome, 1672. 1968 ed.: Ed. Elena Caciagli. Quaderni dell'Istituto di Storia dell'Arte della Università di Genova 4. Genoa, [1968?]. 1976 ed.: Ed. E. Borea. I milenni. Turin, 1976.

Benesch 1943
Benesch, Otto. *Artistic and Intellectual Trends from Rubens to Daumier as Shown in Book Illustration.* Cambridge, Mass., 1943.

Benesch 1957
Benesch, Otto. "Die grossen flaämischen Maler als Zeichner." *Jahrbuch der kunsthistorischen Sammlungen in Wien,* n.s., 17 (1957), pp. 9–32.

Benesch 1959
Benesch, Otto. "Zum zeichnerischen Oeuvre des jungen Van Dyck." In *Festschrift Karl M. Swoboda zum 28. Januar 1959,* ed. Otto Benesch et al., pp. 35–37. Vienna, 1959.

Benesch 1967
Benesch, Otto, with Eva Benesch. *Master Drawings in the Albertina: European Drawings from the Fifteenth to the Eighteenth Century.* Greenwich, Conn., [1967].

Benevento 1964
Fortuna di Michelangelo nell'incisione. Exh. cat. Benevento, Museo del Sannio; 1964. Benevento, 1964.

Berlin 1977
Peter Paul Rubens: Kritischer Katalog der Zeichnungen—Originale, Umkreis, Kopien. Exh. cat. by Hans Mielke and Matthias Winner. Berlin, Kupferstichkabinett, Staatliche Museen zu Berlin; 1977. Zeichnungen alter Meister im Berliner Kupferstichkabinett. Berlin, 1977.

Berlin 1994
Das Berliner Kupferstichkabinett: Ein Handbuch zur Sammlung. Exh. cat. ed. Alexander Dückers. Berlin, Kupferstichkabinett, Staatliche Museen zu Berlin; 1994. Berlin, 1994.

Berlin 2002–3
Kunstsinn der Gründerzeit: Meisterzeichnungen der Sammlung Adolf von Beckerath. Exh. cat. by Hein-Th. Schulze Altcappenberg et al. Berlin, Kupferstichkabinett, Staatliche Museen zu Berlin; 2002–3. Berlin, 2002.

Berlin and other cities 1999–2000
Linie, Licht und Schatten: Meisterzeichnungen und Skulpturen der Sammlung Jan und Marie-Anne Krugier-Poniatowski. Exh. cat. ed. Alexander Dückers, with contributions by Sigrid Achenbach et al. Berlin, Kupferstichkabinett, Staatliche Museen zu Berlin; Venice, Peggy Guggenheim Collection; Madrid, Museo Thyssen-Bornemisza; and Geneva, Musée d'Art et d'Histoire; 1999–2000. Berlin, 1999. English ed.: *The Timeless Eye: Master Drawings from the Jan and Marie-Anne Krugier-Poniatowski Collection.* Berlin, 1999.

Bernard 1953
Bernard, Henri. "Un portrait de Nicolas Trigault dessiné par Rubens?" *Archivum Historicum Societatis Jesu* 22 (1953), pp. 308–13.

Białostocki 1964
Białostocki, Jan. "The Descent from the Cross in Works by Peter Paul Rubens and His Studio." *Art Bulletin* 46 (December 1964), pp. 511–24.

Bieneck 1992
Bieneck, Dorothea. *Gerard Seghers, 1591–1651: Leben und Werk des Antwerpener Historienmalers.* Flämische Maler im Umkreis der grossen Meister 6. Lingen, 1992.

Binghamton and other cities 1970
Selections from the Drawing Collection of Mr. and Mrs. Julius S. Held. University Art Gallery, State University of New York at Binghamton, and other cities; 1970. Exh. cat. Binghamton, 1970.

Binyon 1910
Binyon, Laurence. "Catalogue du duc de Buckingham (1635)." *Bulletin-Rubens* 5, pt. 4 (1910), pp. 277–78.

Birke and Kertész 1992–
Birke, Veronika, and Janine Kertész. *Die italienischen Zeichnungen der Albertina: Generalverzeichnis.* 4 vols. Vienna, 1992–.

Birmingham 1978
Rubens and Humanism. Exh. cat. comp. John David Farmer. Birmingham, Alabama, Birmingham Museum of Art; 1978. Birmingham, 1978.

Bleyerveld 2000–2001
Bleyerveld, Yvonne. "Chaste, Obedient and Devout: Biblical Women as Patterns of Female Virtue in Netherlandish and German Graphic Art, ca. 1500–1750." *Simiolus* 28 (2000–2001), pp. 219–50.

Bock and Rosenberg 1930
Bock, Elfried, and Jakob Rosenberg. *Die niederländischen Meister: Beschreibendes Verzeichnis sämtlicher Zeichnungen.* 2 vols. Staatliche Museen zu Berlin. Berlin, 1930.

Bolten 1985
Bolten, Jaap. *Method and Practice: Dutch and Flemish Drawing Books, 1600–1750.* Landau, 1985.

Boon 1966
Boon, K. G. "Een blad met schetsen voor een Diana en haar Nimfen door Rubens." *Bulletin van het Rijksmuseum* 14 (1966), pp. 150–57.

Boorsch and Spike 1986
Boorsch, Suzanne, and John T. Spike, eds. *Italian Artists of the Sixteenth Century.* Vol. 31 of *The Illustrated Bartsch.* New York, 1986.

Boston–Toledo 1993–94
The Age of Rubens. Exh. cat. by Peter C. Sutton, with Marjorie E. Wieseman et al. Boston, Museum of Fine Arts, and Toledo Museum of Art; 1993–94. Boston, 1993.

Bouchery and Van den Wijngaert 1941
Bouchery, Herman F., and Frank van den Wijngaert. *P. P. Rubens en het Plantijnsche Huis: Petrus Paulus Rubens en Balthasar I Moretus.* Maerlantbibliotheek 4. Antwerp, 1941.

Braunschweig 2004
Peter Paul Rubens: Barocke Leidenschaften. Exh. cat. by Nils Büttner and Ulrich Heinen, with Birgit Franke et al. Braunschweig, Herzog Anton Ulrich-Museum; 2004. Munich, 2004.

Broos 1981
Broos, Ben. *Oude tekeningen in het bezit van de Gemeentemusea van Amsterdam waaronder de collectie Fodor.* Vol. 3, *Rembrandt en tekenaars uit zijn omgeving.* Amsterdam, 1981.

Broos 1989
Broos, Ben. "Improving and Finishing Old Master Drawings: An Art in Itself." *Hoogsteder Naumann Mercury* 8 (1989), pp. 34–55.

Broos and Wadum 1993
Broos, Ben, and Jørgen Wadum. "Vier panelen uit één boom." *Mauritshuis in Focus* 6, no. 1 (1993), pp. 13–16.

Brown 1979
Brown, Christopher. *"Peace and War": Minerva Protects Pax from Mars.* Painting in Focus. London, 1979.

Brown 2000
Brown, Christopher. "The Construction and Development of Rubens's Landscapes: Reflections on the London Exhibition." In Vlieghe, Balis, and Van de Velde 2000, pp. 267–78.

Brunswick, Me., and other cities 1985–86
Old Master Drawings at Bowdoin College. Exh. cat. by David P. Becker. Brunswick, Maine, Bowdoin College Museum of Art; Williamstown, Massachusetts, Sterling and Francine Clark Art Institute; Lawrence, Kansas, Helen Foresman Spencer Museum of Art, University of Kansas; and Toronto, Art Gallery of Ontario; 1985–86. Brunswick, Me., 1985.

Brussels 1969
Vijftien jaar aanwinsten: Sedert de eerste steenlegging tot de plechtige inwijding van de Bibliotheek. Exh. cat. Brussels, Bibliothèque Royale Albert Ier; 1969. Brussels, 1969.

Brussels–Rome 1995
Fiamminghi a Roma, 1508–1608: Artistes des Pays-Bas et de la principauté de Liège à Rome à la Renaissance. Brussels, Palais des Beaux-Arts, and Rome, Palazzo delle Esposizioni; 1995. Milan, 1995.

Brussels–Rotterdam–Paris 1972–73
Dessins flamands et hollandais du dix-septième siècle: Collections de l'Ermitage, Leningrad et du Musée Pouchkine, Moscou. Exh. cat. Brussels, Bibliothèque Royale Albert Ier; Rotterdam, Museum Boymans-van Beuningen; and Paris, Institut Néerlandais; 1972–73. [Brussels, 1972.]

Buffa 1982
Buffa, Sebastian, ed. *Italian Artists of the Sixteenth Century.* Vol. 34 of *The Illustrated Bartsch.* New York, 1982.
Burchard 1953
Burchard, Ludwig. "Rubens' 'Feast of Herod' at Port Sunlight." *Burlington Magazine* 95 (September 1953), pp. 383–87.
Burchard and d'Hulst 1963
Burchard, Ludwig, and Roger-A. d'Hulst. *Rubens Drawings.* 2 vols. Nationaal Centrum voor de Plastische Kunsten van de XVIde en XVIIde Eeuw, Monographien, 2. Brussels, 1963.
Burroughs 1925
Burroughs, Bryson. "Drawings by Michelangelo for the Libyan Sibyl." *Bulletin of The Metropolitan Museum of Art* 20 (January 1925), pp. 6–14.
Cambridge 1981–82
Drawings from the Collection of Louis C. G. Clarke, 1881–1960. Exh. cat. Fitzwilliam Museum, University of Cambridge; 1981–82. Cambridge, 1981.
Cambridge 1990
Rubens and Printmaking. Exh. cat. Cambridge, Fitzwilliam Museum; 1990. Cambridge, 1990.
Cambridge, Mass. 1980
Drawings for Book Illustrations: The Hofer Collection. Exh. cat. by David P. Becker. Cambridge, Massachusetts, Houghton Library, Harvard University; 1980. Cambridge, Mass., 1980.
Cambridge, Mass.–New York 1956
Drawings and Oil Sketches by P. P. Rubens, from American Collections. Exh. cat. Cambridge, Massachusetts, Fogg Art Museum, Harvard University, and New York, The Pierpont Morgan Library; 1956. Cambridge, Mass., 1956.
Canberra 1988
Rubens' Self-Portrait in Focus. Exh. cat. by David Jaffé. Canberra, Australian National Gallery; 1988. Canberra, 1988.
Van Claerbergen 2003–4
Van Claerbergen, Ernst Vegelin. "'Everything Connected with Rubens Interests Me': Collecting Rubens' Oil Sketches. The Case of Count Antoine Seilern." In London 2003–4a, pp. 23–30.
Cleveland–New York 2000–2001
Master Drawings from the Cleveland Museum of Art. Exh. cat. ed. Diane De Grazia and Carter E. Foster. Cleveland Museum of Art and New York, The Pierpont Morgan Library; 2000–2001. Cleveland, 2000.
Cologne 1977
Peter Paul Rubens, 1577–1640. Vol. 1, *Rubens in Italien: Gemälde, Ölskizzen, Zeichnungen.* Exh. cat. Cologne, Wallraf-Richartz-Museum; 1977. Triumph der Eucharistie, Wandteppiche aus dem Kölner Dom. Cologne, 1977.
Cologne–Antwerp–Vienna 1992
Von Bruegel bis Rubens: Das goldene Jahrhundert der flämischen Malerei. Exh. cat. ed. Ekkehard Mai and Hans Vlieghe. Cologne, Wallraf-Richartz-Museum; Antwerp, Koninklijk Museum voor Schone Kunsten; and Vienna, Kunsthistorisches Museum; 1992. Cologne, 1992.
Comblen-Sonkes and Van den Bergen-Pantens 1977
Comblen-Sonkes, Micheline, and Christiana Van den Bergen-Pantens. *Les mémoriaux d'Antoine de Succa.* 2 vols. Brussels, 1977.
Copenhagen 1988
Rubens Cantoor: The Drawings of Willem Panneels. A Critical Catalogue. Exh. cat. by Jan Garff and Eva de la Fuente Pedersen. 2 vols. Copenhagen, Kongelige Kobberstiksamling; 1988. Copenhagen, 1988.
Danesi Squarzina 1990
Danesi Squarzina, Silvia. "Rubens e Caravaggio." In *Studi sul Seicento fiammingo e olandese,* pp. 7–38. Rome, 1990.
Daugherty 1976
Daugherty, Frances Perry. *The Self-Portraits of Peter Paul Rubens.* Ann Arbor, 1976.
Denucé 1932
Denucé, Jean. *De Antwerpsche "Konstkamers": Inventarissen van kunstverzamelingen te Antwerpen in de 16e en 17e eeuwen.* Bronnen voor de geschiedenis van de Vlaamsche kunst 2. Antwerp, 1932. English ed.: *The Antwerp Art-Galleries: Inventories of the Art-Collections in Antwerp in the Sixteenth and Seventeenth Centuries.* Historical Sources for the Study of Flemish Art 2. The Hague, 1932.
Dethloff 1992
Dethloff, Diana. "Patterns of Drawing Collecting in Late Seventeenth- and Early Eighteenth-Century England." In *Drawings* 1992, pp. 197–207.
Dethloff 2003
Dethloff, Diana. "Sir Peter Lely's Collection of Prints and Drawings." In Baker, Elam, and Warwick 2003, pp. 123–39.
De Tolnay 1943–
De Tolnay, Charles. *Michelangelo.* 5 vols. Princeton, 1943–.
De Tolnay 1975–80
De Tolnay, Charles. *Corpus dei disegni di Michelangelo.* 4 vols. Novara, 1975–80.
Detroit Institute of Arts 1992
Detroit Institute of Arts. *Italian, French, English, and Spanish Drawings and Watercolors: Sixteenth through Eighteenth Centuries.* Introduction by Ellen Sharp; essays by Victor Carlson et al. New York and Detroit, 1992.
Dezallier d'Argenville 1745–52
Dezallier d'Argenville, A.-J. *Abrégé de la vie des plus fameux peintres.* 3 vols. Paris, 1745–52.
Dezallier d'Argenville 1762
Dezallier d'Argenville, A.-J. *Abrégé de la vie des plus fameux peintres.* 3 vols. Paris, 1762. Reprint, Geneva, 1972.
Díaz Padrón 1995
Díaz Padrón, Matías, with Aída Padrón Mérida. *El siglo de Rubens en el Museo del Prado: Catálogo razonado de pintura flamenca del siglo XVII.* 3 vols. Barcelona and Madrid, 1995.
Dittrich 1987
Dittrich, Christian. "Die Zeichnungssammlung Gottfried Wagner: Eine barocke Privatsammlung im Kupferstich-Kabinett Dresden und der Versuch ihrer Rekonstruktion." *Jahrbuch* [Staatliche Kunstsammlungen Dresden] 19 (1987), pp. 7–38.
Dobroklonskii 1940
Dobroklonskii, Mikhail Vasilevich. *Risunki Rubensa.* Katalogi sobranii Ermitazha 3. Moscow, 1940.
Dordrecht–Leeuwarden 1988–89
Meesterlijk vee: Nederlandse veeschilders, 1600–1900. Exh. cat. ed. C. Boschma et al. Dordrechts Museum and Leeuwarden, Fries Museum; 1988–89. Zwolle and The Hague, 1988.
Douxchamps 1977
Douxchamps, Hervé. "Rubens et ses descendants." *Le Parchemin (Recueil généalogique et héraldique)* 25 (1977), pp. 187–95.
Downes 1980
Downes, Kerry. *Rubens.* London, 1980.
***Drawings* 1992**
Drawings—Masters and Methods, Raphael to Redon: Papers Presented to the Ian Woodner Master Drawings Symposium at the Royal Academy of Arts, London. Ed. Diana Dethloff. London, 1992.
Dresden–Vienna 1997–98
Van Eyck, Bruegel, Rembrandt: Niederländische Zeichnungen des 15. bis 17. Jahrhunderts aus dem Kupferstich-Kabinett Dresden. Exh. cat. by Christian Dittrich. Dresden, Albertinum, and Vienna, Kunstforum; 1997–98. Eurasburg, 1997.
Dunne 2001
Dunne, G. "Trigault, Nicolas." In *Diccionario histórico de la Compañía de Jesús,* ed. Charles E. O'Neill and Joaquín María Domínguez, vol. 4, pp. 3838–39. Rome and Madrid, 2001.
Düsseldorf–Cologne 1979
P. P. Rubens & J. Jordaens: Handzeichnungen aus öffentlichen belgischen Sammlungen. Exh. cat. Düsseldorf, Kunstmuseum, and Cologne, Wallraf-Richartz-Museum and Museum Ludwig; 1979. Düsseldorf, 1979.
Dussler 1959
Dussler, Luitpold. *Die Zeichnungen des Michelangelo: Kritischer Katalog.* Berlin, 1959.
Duverger 1984–
Duverger, Erik. *Antwerpse kunstinventarissen uit de zeventiende eeuw.* 12 vols. Fontes Historiae Artis Neerlandicae. Brussels, 1984–.
Edinburgh–London 2001
Rembrandt's Women. Exh. cat. by Julia Lloyd Williams, with contributions by S. A. C. Dudok van Heel et al. Edinburgh, National Gallery of Scotland, and London, Royal Academy of Arts; 2001. Edinburgh, 2001.
Edinburgh–Nottingham 2002
Rubens Drawing on Italy. Exh. cat. by Jeremy Wood. Edinburgh, National Gallery of Scotland, and Nottingham, Djanogly Art Gallery; 2002. Edinburgh, 2002.
Eidelberg 1997
Eidelberg, Martin. "An Album of Drawings from Rubens' Studio." *Master Drawings* 35 (Fall 1997), pp. 234–66.
Elen 1989
Elen, Albert J. *Missing Old Master Drawings from the Franz Koenigs Collection Claimed by the State of the Netherlands.* The Hague, 1989.
Elewijt 1962
Rubens diplomate. Exh. cat. Elewijt, Rubenskasteel; 1962. [Elewijt?], 1962.
Essen 2003
Die flämische Landschaft, 1520–1700: Eine Ausstellung der Kulturstiftung Ruhr Essen und des Kunsthistorischen Museums Wien. Exh. cat. by Hanna Benesz et al. Kulturstiftung Ruhr Essen, Villa Hügel; 2003. Lingen, 2003.
Evers 1942
Evers, Hans Gerhard. *Peter Paul Rubens.* Munich, 1942.
Evers 1943
Evers, Hans Gerhard. *Rubens und sein Werk.* New ed. Brussels, 1943.
Evers 1961
Evers, Hans Gerhard. "Zu einem Blatt mit Zeichnungen von Rubens im Berliner Kupferstichkabinett." *Pantheon* 19 (March–April, May–June 1961), pp. 93–97, 136–40.
Fairfax 1758
Fairfax, Brian. *A Catalogue of the Curious Collection of Pictures of George Villiers, Duke of Buckingham, in Which Is Included the Valuable Collection of Sir Peter Paul Rubens: With the Life of George Villiers, Duke of Buckingham, the Celebrated Poet.* London, 1758.
Falk 1992
Falk, Tilman. "An Unknown Collection of Drawings in the Eighteenth Century." In *Drawings* 1992, pp. 177–96.
Fehl 1988
Fehl, Philipp P. "The Ghost of Homer: Observations

on Rubens's *Portrait of the Earl of Arundel.*" *Fenway Court 1987* (pub. 1988), pp. 7–23.

Félibien 1725

Félibien, André. *Entretiens sur les vies et sur les ouvrages des plus excellens peintres anciens et modernes.* Rev. ed. 6 vols. Paris, 1725.

Finsten 1993

Finsten, Jill. "A Self-Portrait Drawing by Jonathan Richardson." *J. Paul Getty Museum Journal* 21 (1993), pp. 43–54.

Fishman 1982

Fishman, Jane Susannah. *Boerenverdriet: Violence between Peasants and Soldiers in Early Modern Netherlands Art.* Studies in the Fine Arts, Iconography, 5. Ann Arbor, 1982.

Florence 1964

Mostra di disegni fiamminghi e olandesi. Exh. cat. ed. Emil K. J. Reznicek. Florence, Gabinetto Disegni e Stampe degli Uffizi; 1964. Florence, 1964.

Florence 1977

Rubens e la pittura fiamminga del Seicento nelle collezioni pubbliche fiorentine/Rubens et la peinture flamande du XVIIème siècle dans les collections publiques florentines. Exh. cat. ed. Didier Bodart. Florence, Palazzo Pitti; 1977. Florence, 1977.

Florence 1986–87

Il tempo di Rubens: Disegni e stampe dal Seicento fiammingo. Exh. cat. Florence, Palazzo Medici Riccardi; 1986–87. Milan, 1986.

Florence 2003–4

Daniele da Volterra: Amico di Michelangelo. Exh. cat. ed. Vittoria Romani. Florence, Casa Buonarroti; 2003–4. Florence, 2003.

Florence–Philadelphia 1996–97

Rodin and Michelangelo: A Study in Artistic Inspiration. Exh. cat. by Flavio Fergonzi et al. Florence, Casa Buonarroti, and Philadelphia Museum of Art; 1996–97. Philadelphia, 1997. Italian ed.: *Michelangelo nell'Ottocento: Rodin e Michelangelo.* Exh. cat. by Flavio Fergonzi, Maria Mimita Lamberti, and Christopher Riopelle. Milan, 1996.

Foucart 1977

Foucart, Jacques. "Un nouveau Rubens au Louvre." *La revue du Louvre et des musées de France* 27 (1977), pp. 343–53.

Foucart 1985

Foucart, Jacques. "Quelques inédits d'Otho Vaenius." In *Rubens and His World: Bijdragen/Études/Studies/Beiträge,* ed. Roger-A. d'Hulst, pp. 97–108. Antwerp, 1985.

Frankfurt 2000

Nach dem Leben und aus der Phantasie: Niederländische Zeichnungen vom 15. bis 18. Jahrhundert aus dem Städelschen Kunstinstitut. Exh. cat. by Annette Strech, with Jutta Schütt, Martin Sonnabend, and Margret Stuffmann. Frankfurt, Städelsches Kunstinstitut und Städtische Galerie, Graphische Sammlung; 2000. Frankfurt, 2000.

Freedberg 1978

Freedberg, David. "L'année Rubens: Manifestations et publications en 1977." *Revue de l'art,* no. 39 (1978), pp. 82–91.

Freedberg 1984

Freedberg, David. *Rubens: The Life of Christ after the Passion.* Corpus Rubenianum Ludwig Burchard 7. London and New York, 1984.

Van Gelder 1965

Van Gelder, Jan Gerrit. "The Triumph of Scipio by Rubens: P. Crozat Sale (1741), Lot 814." *Duits Quarterly,* no. 8 (Autumn 1965), pp. 5–20.

Van Gelder 1978

Van Gelder, Jan Gerrit. "Rubens Marginalia I." *Burlington Magazine* 120 (July 1978), pp. 455–57.

Van Gelder and Jost 1985

Van Gelder, Jan Gerrit, and Ingrid Jost. *Jan de Bisschop and His Icones and Paradigmata: Classical Antiquities and Italian Drawings for Artistic Instruction in Seventeenth-Century Holland.* Ed. Keith Andrews. 2 vols. Doornspijk, 1985.

Génard 1865

Génard, P. "De nalatenschap van Peter Paul Rubens." *Antwerpsch archievenblad* 2 (1865), pp. 69–179.

Génard 1895

Génard, P. "Het laatste testament van P. P. Rubens." *Bulletin-Rubens* 4, pt. 3 (1895), pp. 125–41.

Génard 1896

Génard, P. "Het laatste testament van Aalbrecht Rubens." *Bulletin-Rubens* 4, pt. 4 (1896), pp. 253–59.

Genoa 1977–78

Rubens e Genova. Exh. cat. ed. Giuliana Biavati et al. Genoa, Palazzo Ducale; 1977–78. Genoa, 1977.

Genoa 1997

Van Dyck a Genova: Grande pittura e collezionismo. Exh. cat. ed. Susan J. Barnes et al. Genoa, Palazzo Ducale; 1997. Milan, 1997.

Genoa 2004

L'età di Rubens: Dimore, committenti e collezionisti genovesi. Exh. cat. ed. Piero Boccardo, with Clario Di Fabio, Anna Orlando, and Farida Simonetti. Genoa, Palazzo Ducale, Galleria di Palazzo Rosso, and Galleria Nazionale di Palazzo Spinola; 2004. Milan, 2004.

Gibson-Wood 2003

Gibson-Wood, Carol. "'A Judiciously Disposed Collection': Jonathan Richardson Senior's Cabinet of Drawings." In Baker, Elam, and Warwick 2003, pp. 155–71.

Glang-Süberkrüb 1975

Glang-Süberkrüb, Annegret. *P. P. Rubens: Der Liebesgarten: Eine Untersuchung über die Bedeutung der Konfiguration für das Bildthema im Spätwerk des Peter Paul Rubens.* Kieler kunsthistorische Studien 6. Bern and Frankfurt, 1975.

Glen 1977

Glen, Thomas L. *Rubens and the Counter Reformation: Studies in His Religious Paintings between 1609 and 1620.* Outstanding Dissertations in the Fine Arts. New York, 1977.

Glück 1921

Glück, Gustav. *Rubens Zeichnungen der Wiener Albertina in zwölf Faksimiledrucken.* Munich, 1921.

Glück 1933

Glück, Gustav. *Rubens, Van Dyck und ihr Kreis.* Vienna, 1933.

Glück 1940

Glück, Gustav. "Rubens as a Portrait Painter." *Burlington Magazine* 76 (June 1940), pp. 173–83.

Glück and Haberditzl 1928

Glück, Gustav, and Franz Martin Haberditzl, eds. *Die Handzeichnungen von Peter Paul Rubens.* Berlin, 1928.

Goldner 1988

Goldner, George R., with Lee Hendrix and Gloria Williams. *European Drawings, 1: Catalogue of the Collections.* The J. Paul Getty Museum. Malibu, 1988.

Goldner and Hendrix 1992

Goldner, George R., and Lee Hendrix, with Kelly Pask. *European Drawings, 2: Catalogue of the Collections.* The J. Paul Getty Museum. Malibu, 1992.

Goodman 1992

Goodman, Elise. *Rubens: The Garden of Love as "Conversatie à la mode" and the Tradition of the Love Garden.* Oculi Studies in the Arts of the Low Countries 4. Amsterdam and Philadelphia, 1992.

Göttler 1997

Göttler, Christine. "Nomen mirificum: Rubens's *Beschneidung Jesu* für den Hochaltar der Jesuitenkirche in Genua." In *Aspekte der Gegenreformation,* ed. Victoria von Flemming, pp. 796–844. Zeitsprünge 1, nos. 3 and 4. Frankfurt, 1997.

Göttler 1999

Göttler, Christine. "'Actio' in Peter Paul Rubens' Hochaltarbildern für die Jesuitenkirche in Antwerpen." In *Barocke Inszenierung,* ed. Joseph Imorde, Fritz Neumeyer, and Tristan Weddingen, pp. 10–31. Emsdetten and Zürich, 1999.

Grossmann 1957

Grossmann, F. "Flemish Paintings at Bruges." *Burlington Magazine* 99 (April 1957), pp. 125–26.

Guarino 1990

Guarino, Sergio. "Rubens a Roma: I lavori per S. Croce in Gerusalemme e S. Maria in Valicella." In Rome 1990, pp. 10–29.

Haarlem–Antwerp 2000–2001

Pride and Joy: Children's Portraits in the Netherlands, 1500–1700. Exh. cat. ed. Jan Baptist Bedaux and Rudi Ekkart. Haarlem, Frans Halsmuseum, and Antwerp, Koninklijk Museum voor Schone Kunsten; 2000–2001. Ghent, 2000.

Haarlem–Paris 2001–2

Collectionner, passionnément. Exh. cat. [Vol. 1]: see Plomp 2001–2. [Vol. 2], *Les plus beaux dessins dans les collections hollandaises du XVIIIe siècle* by Mària van Berge-Gerbaud et al. Haarlem, Teylers Museum, and Paris, Institut Néerlandais; 2001–2. Paris, 2001. Dutch ed.: *Hartstochtelijk verzameld: Beroemde tekeningen in 18de-eeuwse Hollandse collecties.* Paris and Bussum, 2001.

Haberditzl 1912

Haberditzl, Franz Martin. "Über einige Handzeichnungen von Rubens in der Albertina." *Die graphischen Künste* 35 (1912), pp. 1–14.

Hamilton–New York–Amsterdam 1985–86

The Fodor Collection: Nineteenth-Century French Drawings and Watercolors from the Amsterdams Historisch Museum. Exh. cat. by Wiepke Loos. Hamilton, New York, Picker Art Gallery, Colgate University; New York, Baruch College Art Gallery; and Amsterdams Historisch Museum; 1985–86. Hamilton, N.Y., and Amsterdam, 1985.

Härting 1989

Härting, Ursula. *Frans Francken der Jüngere (1581–1642): Die Gemälde mit kritischem Oeuvrekatalog.* Flämische Maler im Umkreis der grossen Meister 2. Freren, 1989.

Hartt 1958

Hartt, Frederick. *Giulio Romano.* 2 vols. New Haven, 1958.

Hartt 1970

Hartt, Frederick. *Michelangelo Drawings.* New York, 1970.

Haskell and Penny 1981

Haskell, Francis, and Nicholas Penny. *Taste and the Antique: The Lure of Classical Sculpture, 1500–1900.* New Haven, 1981.

Hattori 1997

Hattori, Cordélia. "À la recherche des dessins de Pierre Crozat." *Bulletin de la Société de l'Histoire de l'Art Français,* 1997 (pub. 1998), pp. 179–208.

Hattori 2003

Hattori, Cordélia. "The Drawings Collection of Pierre Crozat (1665–1740)." In Baker, Elam, and Warwick 2003, pp. 173–81.

Haverkamp-Begemann 1969

Haverkamp-Begemann, Egbert. Review of the exhibition "Jacob Jordaens, 1593–1678" at the National Gallery of Canada. *Master Drawings* 7 (Summer 1969), pp. 173–78.

Haverkamp-Begemann 1975
Haverkamp-Begemann, Egbert. *The Achilles Series.* Corpus Rubenianum Ludwig Burchard 10. London, 1975.
Haverkamp-Begemann, Lawder, and Talbot 1964
Haverkamp-Begemann, Egbert, Standish D. Lawder, and Charles W. Talbot Jr. *Drawings from the Clark Art Institute.* 2 vols. New Haven, 1964.
Haverkamp-Begemann and Logan 1970
Haverkamp-Begemann, Egbert, and Anne-Marie Logan. *European Drawings and Watercolors in the Yale University Art Gallery, 1500–1900.* 2 vols. New Haven, 1970.
Healy 1997
Healy, Fiona. *Rubens and the Judgement of Paris: A Question of Choice.* Pictura Nova 3. [Turnhout?], 1997.
Healy 2004
Healy, Fiona. "Rubens as Collector of Antiquities." In Antwerp 2004b, pp. 260–63.
Heiden 1982
Heiden, Rüdiger an der. *Peter Paul Rubens und die Bildnisse seiner Familie in der Alten Pinakothek.* Künstler und Werke 4. Munich, 1982.
Heiland 1969
Heiland, Susanne. "Two Rubens Paintings Rehabilitated." *Burlington Magazine* 111 (July 1969), pp. 421–27.
Heinen and Thielemann 2001
Heinen, Ulrich, and Andreas Thielemann, eds. *Rubens passioni: Kultur der Leidenschaften im Barock.* Rekonstruktion der Künste 3. Göttingen, 2001.
Held 1951
Held, Julius S. "Rubens' Pen Drawings." *Magazine of Art* 44 (November 1951), pp. 286–91.
Held 1954
Held, Julius S. "Rubens's 'Feast of Herod.'" *Burlington Magazine* 96 (January 1954), p. 122.
Held 1956
Held, Julius S. "Drawings and Oil Sketches by Rubens from American Collections." *Burlington Magazine* 98 (April 1956), pp. 123–24.
Held 1959
Held, Julius S. *Rubens: Selected Drawings.* 2 vols. London, 1959.
Held 1960
Held, Julius S. "Rubens' Designs for Sepulchral Monuments." *Art Quarterly* 23 (Autumn 1960), pp. 247–70.
Held 1963a
Held, Julius S. "The Early Appreciation of Drawings." In *Studies in Western Art: Acts of the Twentieth International Congress of the History of Art,* vol. 3, pp. 72–95. Princeton, 1963.
Held 1963b
Held, Julius S. "Prometheus Bound." *Bulletin* [Philadelphia Museum of Art] 59 (1963), pp. 17–32.
Held 1967
Held, Julius S. "Het Pelsken." In *Essays in the History of Art Presented to Rudolf Wittkower,* ed. Douglas Fraser, Howard Hibbard, and Milton J. Lewine, pp. 183–93. London, 1967.
Held 1976
Held, Julius S. "Zwei Rubensprobleme." *Zeitschrift für Kunstgeschichte* 39 (1976), pp. 34–46.
Held 1979a
Held, Julius S. "Rubens and Aguilonius: New Points of Contact." *Art Bulletin* 61 (June 1979), pp. 257–64.
Held 1979b
Held, Julius S. "Rubens and the Book." *Harvard Library Bulletin* 27, no. 1 (1979), pp. 114–53.
Held 1980
Held, Julius S. *The Oil Sketches of Peter Paul Rubens: A Critical Catalogue.* 2 vols. Kress European Studies in the History of European Art 7. Princeton, 1980.
Held 1981
Held, Julius S. Review of the exhibition "European Drawings, 1375–1825" at the Pierpont Morgan Library. *Master Drawings* 19 (Summer 1981), pp. 172–77.
Held 1982a
Held, Julius S. *Rubens and His Circle: Studies.* Ed. Anne W. Lowenthal, David Rosand, and John Walsh Jr. Princeton, 1982.
Held 1982b
Held, Julius S. "Rubens and Titian." In *Titian: His World and His Legacy,* ed. David Rosand, pp. 283–339. Bampton Lectures in America 21. New York, 1982.
Held 1983
Held, Julius S. "Thoughts on Rubens' Beginnings." *Ringling Museum of Art Journal,* 1983, pp. 14–35.
Held 1985
Held, Julius S. "Nachträge zum Werk des Johann Bockhorst (alias Jan Boeckhorst)." *Westfalen* 63 (1985), pp. 14–37.
Held 1986
Held, Julius S. *Rubens: Selected Drawings.* 2nd ed. New York, 1986.
Held 1991
Held, Julius S. Review of Copenhagen 1988. *Master Drawings* 29 (Winter 1991), pp. 416–30.
Held 1993
Held, Julius S. Review of Stampfle 1991. *Master Drawings* 31 (Autumn 1993), pp. 285–99.
Held and Fubini 1964
Held, Julius S., and Giorgio Fubini. "Padre Resta's Rubens Drawings after Ancient Sculpture." *Master Drawings* 2 (1964), pp. 123–41.
Helsinki 1952–53
P. P. Rubens: Esquisses, dessins, gravures. Exh. cat. Helsinki, Ateneumin Taidemuseo; 1952–53. Helsinki, 1952.
's-Hertogenbosch–Rome 1992–93
Da Van Heemskerck a Van Wittel: Disegni fiamminghi e olandesi del XVI–XVII secolo dalle collezioni del Gabinetto dei Disegni e delle Stampe. Exh. cat. by J. C. N. Bruintjes and N. Köhler. 's-Hertogenbosch, Noordbrabants Museum, and Rome, Gabinetto dei Designi e delle Stampe, Istituto Nazionale per la Grafica; 1992–93. Rome, 1992.
Hervey 1921
Hervey, Mary F. S. *The Life, Correspondence and Collections of Thomas Howard, Earl of Arundel.* Cambridge, 1921.
Hind 1923
Hind, Arthur M. *Catalogue of Drawings by Dutch and Flemish Artists Preserved in the Department of Prints and Drawings in the British Museum.* Vol. 2, *Drawings by Rubens, Van Dyck and Other Artists of the Flemish School of the XVII Century.* London, 1923.
Hinterding and Horsch 1989
Hinterding, Erik, and Femy Horsch. "'A Small but Choice Collection': The Art Gallery of King Willem II of the Netherlands (1792–1849)." *Simiolus* 19 (1989), pp. 5–122.
Hirschmann 1921
Hirschmann, Otto. *Verzeichnis des graphischen Werkes von Hendrick Goltzius.* Leipzig, 1921.
Hirst 1988
Hirst, Michael. *Michelangelo and His Drawings.* New Haven, 1988.
Hollstein 1949–
Hollstein, F. W. H. *Dutch and Flemish Etchings, Engravings, and Woodcuts, ca. 1450–1700.* Amsterdam, 1949–.
Hollstein 1986
Hollstein, F. W. H. *German Engravings, Etchings, and Woodcuts, ca. 1400–1700.* Vol. 24, *Israhel van Meckenem.* Ed. Fritz Koreny and Tilman Falk. Ghent, 1986.
Hollstein 1993–
Hollstein, F. W. H. *The New Hollstein: Dutch and Flemish Etchings, Engravings, and Woodcuts, 1450–1700.* Roosendaal, 1993–.
Van Hout 2004
Van Hout, Nico. "Less Is More: Rubens et la gravure sur bois." In Antwerp 2004c, pp. 92–107.
Howarth 1985
Howarth, David. *Lord Arundel and His Circle.* New York and London, 1985.
Hubala 1978
Hubala, Erich. "Triumph der Weibermacht: Bemerkungen zu einer Komposition von Rubens." In *Festschrift Herbert Siebenhüner,* ed. Erich Hubala and Gunter Schweikhart, pp. 143–64. Würzburg, 1978.
Huemer 1977
Huemer, Frances. *Portraits.* Corpus Rubenianum Ludwig Burchard 19, vol. 1. Brussels and New York, 1977.
Huemer 1996
Huemer, Frances. *Rubens and the Roman Circle: Studies of the First Decade.* New York, 1996.
Hughes 1980
Hughes, Anthony. "Naming the Unnameable: An Iconographical Problem in Rubens's 'Peace and War.'" *Burlington Magazine* 122 (March 1980), pp. 157–65.
d'Hulst 1974
d'Hulst, Roger-A. *Jordaens Drawings.* 4 vols. Nationaal Centrum voor de Plastische Kunsten van de XVIde en XVIIde Eeuw, Monographien, 5. London and New York, 1974.
d'Hulst and Vandenven 1989
d' Hulst, Roger-A., and M. Vandenven. *Rubens: The Old Testament.* Trans. P. S. Falla. Corpus Rubenianum Ludwig Burchard 3. London and New York, 1989.
d'Hulst et al. 1992
d'Hulst, Roger-A., et al. *L'Érection de la Croix: Pierre Paul Rubens.* Collection Histoire d'un tableau. Brussels, 1992.
Huvenne 1993
Huvenne, Paul. "Over Rubens' Cantoor, Panneels en de Kopenhaagse Cantoor-tekeningen/On Rubens' Cantoor, Panneels and the Copenhagen Cantoor Drawings." In Antwerp 1993, pp. 16–37.
Huygens 1881
Huygens, Constantijn. *Journaal van Constantijn Huygens, den zoon, gedurende de veldtochten der jaren 1673, 1675, 1676, 1677 en 1678.* Historisch Genootschap [Utrecht], Werken, n.s., 32. Utrecht, 1881.
Incisa della Rocchetta 1962
Incisa della Rocchetta, Giovanni. "Documenti editi e inediti sui quadri del Rubens nella Chiesa Nuova." *Rendiconti* [Pontificia Accademia Romana di Archeologia], ser. 3, 35 (1962–63), pp. 161–83.
D. Jaffé 1997
Jaffé, David. "Reproducing and Reading Gems in Rubens's Circle." In *Engraved Gems: Survivals and Revivals,* ed. Clifford Malcolm Brown, pp. 181–93. Studies in the History of Art 54; Studies in the History of Art, Symposium Papers, 32. Washington, D.C., 1997.
D. Jaffé 2000
Jaffé, David. "Rubens Front and Back: The Case of the National Gallery *Samson and Delilah.*" *Apollo* 152 (August 2000), pp. 21–25.

D. Jaffé and Bradley 2003
Jaffé, David, and Amanda Bradley. *Rubens's Massacre of the Innocents.* London, 2003.
M. Jaffé 1953
Jaffé, Michael. "Two Rubens Drawings Rediscovered." *Art Quarterly* 16 (Summer 1953), pp. 131–36.
M. Jaffé 1955
Jaffé, Michael. "Rubens en de leeuwenkuil." *Bulletin van het Rijksmuseum* 3 (1955), pp. 59–67.
M. Jaffé 1956a
Jaffé, Michael. "Some Drawings by Annibale and by Agostino Carracci." *Paragone,* no. 837 (1956), pp. 12–16.
M. Jaffé 1956b
Jaffé, Michael. "Rubens' Drawings at Antwerp." *Burlington Magazine* 98 (September 1956), pp. 314–21.
M. Jaffé 1958a
Jaffé, Michael. "Un chef-d'oeuvre mieux connu." *L'oeil* 43–44 (July–August 1958), pp. 15–20, 80.
M. Jaffé 1958b
Jaffé, Michael. "Rubens in Italy: Rediscovered Works." *Burlington Magazine* 100 (December 1958), pp. 411–22.
M. Jaffé 1963
Jaffé, Michael. "Peter Paul Rubens and the Oratorian Fathers." *Proporzioni* 4 (1963), pp. 209–41.
M. Jaffé 1964–66
Jaffé, Michael. "Rubens as a Collector of Drawings." *Master Drawings* 2 (1964), pp. 383–97; 3 (1965), pp. 21–35; 4 (1966), pp. 127–48.
M. Jaffé 1965
Jaffé, Michael. "Rubens as a Draughtsman." *Burlington Magazine* 107 (July 1965), pp. 372–81.
M. Jaffé 1966
Jaffé, Michael. *Van Dyck's Antwerp Sketchbook.* 2 vols. London, 1966.
M. Jaffé 1967
Jaffé, Michael. "Rubens and Raphael." In *Studies in Renaissance and Baroque Art Presented to Anthony Blunt on His Sixtieth Birthday,* pp. 98–107. London, 1967.
M. Jaffé 1969
Jaffé, Michael. "Rediscovered Oil Sketches by Rubens: I." *Burlington Magazine* 111 (July 1969), pp. 435–44.
M. Jaffé 1970a
Jaffé, Michael. "A Sheet of Drawings from Rubens' Italian Period." *Master Drawings* 8 (1970), pp. 42–51.
M. Jaffé 1970b
Jaffé, Michael. "Some Recent Acquisitions of Seventeenth-Century Flemish Painting." In *Report and Studies in the History of Art, 1969* [National Gallery of Art, Washington, D.C.] (pub. 1970), pp. 7–33.
M. Jaffé 1971
Jaffé, Michael. "Figure Drawings Attributed to Rubens, Jordaens, and Cossiers in the Hamburg Kunsthalle." *Jahrbuch der Hamburger Kunstsammlungen* 16 (1971), pp. 39–50.
M. Jaffé 1972
Jaffé, Michael. "Rubens's *Le Christ à la Paille* Reconsidered." *Apollo* 95 (February 1972), pp. 107–14.
M. Jaffé 1977
Jaffé, Michael. *Rubens and Italy.* Oxford, 1977.
M. Jaffé 1981
Jaffé, Michael. "Rubens's *Madame Gerbier and Her Children."* In *A Dealer's Record: Agnew's, 1967–81,* pp. 72–77. London, 1981.
M. Jaffé 1987
Jaffé, Michael. "Rubens's Anatomy Book." In Christie, Manson and Woods, London, *Old Master Drawings from Chatsworth,* sale cat., July 6, 1987, pp. 58–83.
M. Jaffé 1988
Jaffé, Michael. "Rubens and Nicolò Pallavicino." *Burlington Magazine* 130 (July 1988), pp. 523–27.
M. Jaffé 1989
Jaffé, Michael. *Rubens: Catalogo completo.* Trans. Germano Mulazzani. Milan, 1989.
M. Jaffé 1992
Jaffé, Michael. "Rubens before 1620, with Particular Reference to Aspects of His Commissions for the Company of Jesus." In Limentani Virdis and Bottacin 1992, pp. 13–20.
M. Jaffé 1996
Jaffé, Michael. "Seven Unpublished Drawings by Rubens." In *Ars Naturam Adiuvans: Festschrift für Matthias Winner, zum 11. März 1996,* ed. Victoria von Flemming and Sebastian Schütze, pp. 453–63. Mainz, 1996.
M. Jaffé 2002
Jaffé, Michael. *The Devonshire Collection of Northern European Drawings.* 5 vols. Turin, London, and Venice, 2002.
Joannides 1988
Joannides, Paul. "Leonardo da Vinci, Peter-Paul Rubens, Pierre-Nolasque Bergeret and the 'Fight for the Standard.'" *Achademia Leonardi Vinci* 1 (1988), pp. 76–86.
Joannides 2003
Joannides, Paul. *Michel-Ange élèves et copistes.* Musée du Louvre, Département des Arts Graphiques, Inventaire général des dessins italiens, 6. Paris, 2003.
Josi 1821
Josi, Christiaan. *Collection d'imitations de dessins d'après les principaux maîtres hollandais et flamands, commencée par Ploos van Amstel.* 2 vols. London, 1821.
Judson 1984
Judson, J. Richard. "Observations on Rubens's Representations of Christ on the Cross." In *Liber Amicorum Herman Liebaers,* pp. 471–83. Brussels, 1984.
Judson 2000
Judson, J. Richard. *Rubens: The Passion of Christ.* Corpus Rubenianum Ludwig Burchard 6. Turnhout, 2000.
Judson and Van de Velde 1978
Judson, J. Richard, and Carl Van de Velde. *Book Illustrations and Title-Pages.* 2 vols. Corpus Rubenianum Ludwig Burchard 21. London and Philadelphia, 1978.
Kansas City and other cities 1993–94
Master European Drawings from Polish Collections. Exh. cat. ed. Anna Kozak and Maciej Monkiewicz, with Teresa Sulerzyska. Kansas City, Nelson-Atkins Museum of Art; Milwaukee Art Museum; Montreal, Museum of Fine Arts; and Hartford, Wadsworth Atheneum; 1993–94. Washington, D.C., 1993.
Kassel–Frankfurt 2004
Pan & Syrinx—eine erotische Jagd: Peter Paul Rubens, Jan Brueghel und ihre Zeitgenossen. Exh. cat. by Justus Lange et al. Kassel, Staatliche Museen, and Frankfurt, Städelsches Kunstinstitut; 2004. Kataloge der Staatlichen Museen Kassel 31. Kassel, 2004.
K.d.K., ed. Oldenbourg 1921
Oldenbourg, Rudolf, ed. *P. P. Rubens: Des Meisters Gemälde in 538 Abbildungen.* 4th ed. Klassiker der Kunst in Gesamtausgaben 5. Stuttgart, 1921.
K.d.K., ed. Rosenberg 1905
Rosenberg, Adolf, ed. *P. P. Rubens: Des Meisters Gemälde in 551 Abbildungen.* Klassiker der Kunst in Gesamtausgaben 5. Stuttgart and Leipzig, 1905. This edition is cited only when the painting does not appear in the Oldenbourg edition (see K.d.K., ed. Oldenbourg 1921).
K.d.K., Van Dyck 1931
Glück, Gustav, ed. *Van Dyck: Des Meisters Gemälde.* 2nd ed. Klassiker der Kunst in Gesamtausgaben 13. Stuttgart, 1931.
Klemm 1986
Klemm, Christian. *Joachim von Sandrart: Kunst-Werke und Lebens-Lauf.* Berlin, 1986.
Klessmann 1995
Klessmann, Rüdiger. "A Lost Painting by Rubens and Its Meaning." In *Shop Talk: Studies in Honor of Seymour Slive, Presented on His Seventy-Fifth Birthday,* ed. Cynthia P. Schneider, William W. Robinson, and Alice I. Davies, pp. 137–42. Cambridge, Mass., 1995.
Kloek 1976
Kloek, Wouter. *Beknopte catalogus van de Nederlandse tekeningen in het prentenkabinet van de Uffizi te Florence.* Utrecht, 1976.
Konow 1940
Konow, Helga. "Eine Zeichnungssammlung aus dem Besitz Matthäus Merians des Jüngeren: Ein Beitrag zur Geschichte des Berliner Kupferstichkabinetts." *Berliner Museen* 61 (1940), pp. 58–63.
"Korean Model for Rubens" 1983
"Who Was Korean Model for Rubens?" *Korean News Review,* December 10, 1983, p. 25.
Koschatzky, Oberhuber, and Knab 1971
Koschatzky, Walter, Konrad Oberhuber, and Eckhart Knab, eds. *Italian Drawings in the Albertina.* Greenwich, Conn., 1971.
Kuznetsov 1974
Kuznetsov, Yuri. *Risunki Rubensa.* Leningrad, 1974.
Kuznetsov 1984
Kuznetsov, Yuri. *Peter Paul Rubens: Zeichnungen.* Leipzig, 1984.
Kwakkelstein 2000
Kwakkelstein, Michael. "Copying Prints as an Aspect of Artistic Training in the Renaissance." In Antwerp 2000, pp. 35–62.
Labbé and Bicart-Sée 1996
Labbé, Jacqueline, and Lise Bicart-Sée. *La collection de dessins d'Antoine-Joseph Dezallier d'Argenville, reconstituée d'après son "Abrégé de la vie des plus fameux peintres," édition de 1762.* Notes et documents des musées de France 27. Paris, 1996.
Lamalle 1940
Lamalle, Edmond. "La propagande du P. Nicolas Trigault en faveur des missions de Chine." *Archivum Historicum Societatis Jesu* 9 (1940), pp. 49–120.
Lanciani 1902–12
Lanciani, R. *Storia degli scavi di Roma, e notizia intorno le collezioni romane di antichità.* Rome, 1902–12.
Laneyrie-Dagen 2003
Laneyrie-Dagen, Nadeije, ed. *Théorie de la figure humaine/Peter Paul Rubens.* Paris, 2003.
"Lankrink's Collection" 1945
"P. H. Lankrink's Collection." *Burlington Magazine* 86 (1945), pp. 29–35.
Lassalle 1972
Lassalle, Hélène. "Douze grisailles d'Otto Voenius." *La revue du Louvre et des musées de France* 22 (1972), pp. 280–82.
Lawrence 1999
Lawrence, Cynthia. "Before *The Raising of the Cross:* The Origins of Rubens's Earliest Antwerp Altarpieces." *Art Bulletin* 81 (June 1999), pp. 267–96.
Leningrad–Moscow–Kiev 1974
Risunki flamandskikh i gollandskikh masterov XVII veka: Iz muzeev Belgii, Gollandii i Niderlandskogo insti-

tuta v Parizhe. Exh. cat. by A. V. F. M. Mei and Jeroen Giltaij et al. Leningrad, State Hermitage Museum; Moscow, Pushkin Museum; and Kiev; 1974. Moscow, 1974.

Liedtke 1984
Liedtke, Walter A. *Flemish Paintings in The Metropolitan Museum of Art.* 2 vols. New York, 1984.

Lille 2000
Lille au XVIIe siècle: Des Pays-Bas espagnols au Roi-Soleil. Exh. cat. Lille, Palais des Beaux-Arts and Musée de l'Hospice Comtesse; 2000. Paris, 2000.

Lille 2004
Rubens. Exh. cat. Lille, Palais des Beaux-Arts; 2004. Ghent and Lille, 2004.

Limentani Virdis and Bottacin 1992
Limentani Virdis, Caterina, and Francesca Bottacin, eds. *Rubens dall' Italia all'Europa: Atti del Convegno Internazionale di Studi, Padova, 24–27 maggio 1990.* Vicenza, 1992.

Lind 1946
Lind, L. R. "The Latin Life of Peter Paul Rubens by His Nephew Philip: A Translation." *Art Quarterly* 9 (Winter 1946), pp. 37–44.

Liverpool–London 1998–99
Mantegna to Rubens: The Weld-Blundell Drawings Collection. Exh. cat. by Xanthe Brooke. Liverpool, Walker Art Gallery, and London, British Museum; 1998–99. London, 1998.

Logan 1977
Logan, Anne-Marie. "Rubens Exhibitions, 1977." *Master Drawings* 15 (Winter 1977), pp. 403–17.

Logan 1987
Logan, Anne-Marie. Review of Held 1986. *Master Drawings* 25 (Spring 1987), pp. 63–82.

Logan 1999
Logan, Anne-Marie. "Rubens' Design for Pontius' Engraving of the 'Assumption of the Virgin.'" *Master Drawings* 37 (Fall 1999), pp. 231–37.

Logan and Brockey 2003
Logan, Anne-Marie, and Liam M. Brockey. "Nicolas Trigault, SJ: A Portrait by Peter Paul Rubens." *Metropolitan Museum Journal* 38 (2003), pp. 157–67.

Logan and Haverkamp-Begemann 1978
Logan, Anne-Marie, and Egbert Haverkamp-Begemann. "Dessins de Rubens." *Revue de l'art,* no. 42 (1978), pp. 89–99.

London 1835
A Catalogue of One Hundred Original Drawings by Sir P. P. Rubens, Collected by Sir Thomas Lawrence, Late President of the Royal Academy. Exh. cat. by S. and A. Woodburn. London, Lawrence Gallery, Royal Academy of Arts; 1835. London, 1835.

London 1953
Drawings by Old Masters. Exh. cat. by Karl Theodore Parker and James Byam Shaw. London, Royal Academy of Arts; 1953. London, 1953.

London 1953–54
Flemish Art, 1300–1700. Exh. cat. London, Royal Academy of Arts; 1953–54. London, 1953.

London 1965
Art Historians and Critics as Collectors. Exh. cat. London, Agnew; 1965. London, 1965.

London 1977a
Rubens: Drawings and Sketches. Exh. cat. by John Rowlands. London, British Museum; 1977. London, 1977.

London 1977b
Rubens and His Engravers. Exh. cat. London, P & D Colnaghi; 1977. London, 1977.

London 1978
Gainsborough and Reynolds in the British Museum: The Drawings of Gainsborough and Reynolds with a Survey of Mezzotints after Their Paintings and a Study of Reynolds' Collection of Old Master Drawings. Exh. cat. by Timothy Clifford, Antony Griffiths, and Martin Royalton-Kisch. London, British Museum; 1978. London, 1978.

London 1979
Thomas Hudson, 1701–1779, Portrait Painter and Collector: A Bicentenary Exhibition. Exh. cat. by Ellen G. Miles. Kenwood, London; 1979. London, 1979.

London 1981–82
Splendours of the Gonzaga. Exh. cat. ed. David Chambers and Jane Martineau. London, Victoria and Albert Museum; 1981–82. London, 1981.

London 1984
Master Drawings and Watercolours in the British Museum. Exh. cat. ed. John Rowlands. London, British Museum; 1984. London, 1984.

London 1986
Master Drawings in the Royal Collection: From Leonardo da Vinci to the Present Day. Exh. cat. by Jane Roberts. London, The Queen's Gallery, Buckingham Palace; 1986. London, 1986.

London 1988–89
Rubens: Paintings, Drawings, Prints in the Princes Gate Collection. Exh. cat. by Helen Braham. London, Courtauld Institute Galleries, University of London; 1988–89. London, 1988.

London 1993–94
Old Master Drawings from Chatsworth. Exh. cat. by Michael Jaffé. London, British Museum; 1993–94. London, 1993.

London 1995–96
Dynasties: Painting in Tudor and Jacobean England, 1530–1630. Exh. cat. ed. Karen Hearn. London, Tate Gallery; 1995–96. London, 1995.

London 1996
Old Master Drawings from the Malcolm Collection. Exh. cat. by Martin Royalton-Kisch, Hugo Chapman, and Stephen Coppel. London, British Museum; 1996. London, 1996.

London 1996–97
Rubens's Landscapes: Making and Meaning. Exh. cat. by Christopher Brown. London, National Gallery; 1996–97. London, 1996.

London 1997
"Treasures for Everyone: Saved by the National Art Collections Fund." London, Christie's; 1997.

London 1998
Art Treasures of England: The Regional Collections. Exh. cat. by G. Waterfield et al. London, Royal Academy of Arts; 1998. London, 1998.

London 2001
Master Drawings. Exh. cat. London; 2001. Katrin Bellinger Kunsthandel. Munich, 2001.

London 2002–3
Royal Treasures: A Golden Jubilee Celebration. Exh. cat. ed. Jane Roberts. London, The Queen's Gallery, Buckingham Palace; 2002. London, 2002.

London 2003–4a
Peter Paul Rubens: A Touch of Brilliance—Oil Sketches and Related Works from the State Hermitage Museum and the Courtauld Institute Gallery. Exh. cat. London, Courtauld Institute of Art; 2003–4. Munich, 2003.

London 2003–4b
Saved! One Hundred Years of the National Art Collections Fund. Exh. cat. by Richard Verdi, with Martin Bailey et al. London, Hayward Gallery; 2003–4. London, 2003.

London and other cities 1980
One Hundred of the Finest Drawings from Polish Collections. Exh. cat. London, Heim Gallery; Birmingham, City Museum and Art Gallery; Dublin, National Gallery of Ireland; Cambridge, Fitzwilliam Museum; and Cardiff, National Museum of Wales; 1980. London, 1980.

London–New Haven 1987
Drawing in England from Hilliard to Hogarth. Exh. cat. by Lindsay Stainton and Christopher White. London, British Museum, and New Haven, Yale Center for British Art; 1987. London, 1987.

London–Paris–Bern–Brussels 1972
Flemish Drawings of the Seventeenth Century from the Collection of Frits Lugt, Institut Néerlandais, Paris. Exh. cat. London, Victoria and Albert Museum; Paris, Institut Néerlandais; Bern, Kunstmuseum; and Brussels, Royal Library of Belgium; 1972. Paris, 1972.

López Navío 1962
López Navío, José. "La gran colección de pinturas del Marqués de Leganés." *Analecta Calasanctiana* 7–8 (1962), pp. 259–330

López Rey 1959
López Rey, José. "A Head of Philip IV by Velázquez in a Rubens Allegorical Composition." *Gazette des beaux-arts,* 6th ser., 53 (1959), pp. 35–44.

Lugt
Lugt, Frits. *Les marques de collections de dessins & d'estampes.* Amsterdam, 1921. *Supplément.* The Hague, 1956.

Lugt 1925
Lugt, Frits. "Notes sur Rubens." *Gazette des beaux-arts,* 5th ser., 12 (1925), pp. 179–202.

Lugt 1943
Lugt, Frits. "Rubens and Stimmer." *Art Quarterly* 6 (Spring 1943), pp. 99–115.

Lugt 1949
Lugt, Frits. *Inventaire général des dessins des écoles du nord, publié sous les auspices du Cabinet des Dessins. École flamande.* 2 vols. Paris, 1949.

Lusheck 2000
Lusheck, Catherine H. "Content in Form: Rubens's *Kneeling Man* and the Graphic Reformation of the Ideal, Robust Male Nude." *Jaarboek van het Koninklijk Museum voor Schone Kunsten Antwerpen,* 2000, pp. 127–63.

Lyons 1980
Dessins de maîtres des Pays-Bas méridionaux et septentrionaux nés avant 1600. Lyons, Musée des Beaux-Arts; 1980. Lyons, 1980.

McGrath 1983a
McGrath, Elizabeth. "Pan and the Wool." *Ringling Museum of Art Journal,* 1983, pp. 52–69.

McGrath 1983b
McGrath, Elizabeth. "'The Drunken Alcibiades': Rubens's Picture of Plato's *Symposium.*" *Journal of the Warburg and Courtauld Institutes* 46 (1983), pp. 228–35.

McGrath 1984
McGrath, Elizabeth. "Rubens's 'Susanna and the Elders' and Moralizing Inscriptions on Prints." In *Wort und Bild in der niederländischen Kunst und Literatur des 16. und 17. Jahrhunderts,* ed. Herman Vekeman and Justus Müller Hofstede, pp. 73–90. Erftstadt, 1984.

McGrath 1991
McGrath, Elizabeth. Review of Munich 1990–91. *Burlington Magazine* 133 (October 1991), pp. 717–19.

McGrath 1997
McGrath, Elizabeth. *Rubens: Subjects from History.* 2 vols. Corpus Rubenianum Ludwig Burchard 13. London, 1997.

Madrid 2001–2
Rubens: Dibujos para el retrato ecuestre del duque de Lerma. Exh. cat. by Sarah Schroth, Alejandro Vergara, and Thea Vignau-Wilberg. Madrid, Museo del Prado; 2001–2. Madrid, 2001.

Madrid 2002
La almoneda del siglo: Relaciones artísticas entre España

y Gran Bretaña, 1604–1655. Exh. cat. by Jonathan Brown and John Elliott. Madrid, Museo del Prado; 2002. Madrid, 2002.

Maeyer 1953

Maeyer, M. de. "Rubens en de altaarstukken in het hospitaal te Grasse." *Gentse bijdragen tot de kunstgeschiedenis* 14 (1953), pp. 75–86.

Magnusson 1977

Magnusson, Börje. "Rubens som tecknare." In Stockholm 1977, pp. 86–130.

Magurn 1955

Magurn, Ruth Saunders, trans. and ed. *The Letters of Peter Paul Rubens.* Cambridge, Mass., 1955. Reprint, Evanston, 1991.

Malibu 1995

The Earl and Countess of Arundel: Renaissance Collectors. Exh. cat. by David Jaffé et al. Malibu, The J. Paul Getty Museum; 1995. London, 1995.

Mańkowski 1932

Mańkowski, Tadeusz. *Galerja Stansilawa Augusta.* Lwów, 1932.

Mariette 1741

Mariette, Pierre-Jean. *Description sommaire des desseins des grands maistres d'Italie, des Pays-Bas et de France, du cabinet de feu M. Crozat.* Paris, 1741. Reprint, Geneva, 1973.

Mariette 1851–60

Mariette, Pierre-Jean. *Abecedario de P. J. Mariette et autres notes inédites de cet amateur sur les arts et les artistes: Ouvrage publié d'après les manuscripts autographes, conservés au Cabinet des Estampes de la Bibliothèque Imperiale.* Ed. Philippe de Chennevières and Anatole de Montaiglon. 6 vols. Paris, 1851–60. Reprint, Archives de l'art français, 2, 4, 6, 8, 10. Paris, 1966.

G. Martin 1970

Martin, Gregory. *The Flemish School, circa 1600–circa 1900.* National Gallery Catalogues. London, 1970.

J. R. Martin 1968

Martin, John Rupert. *The Ceiling Paintings for the Jesuit Church in Antwerp.* Corpus Rubenianum Ludwig Burchard 1. London and New York, 1968.

J. R. Martin 1972

Martin, John Rupert. *The Decorations for the Pompa Introitus Ferdinandi.* Corpus Rubenianum Ludwig Burchard 16. London and New York, 1972.

Martinelli 1644

Martinelli, Fioravante. *Roma ricercata nel suo sito.* Rome, 1644.

Megow 1987

Megow, Wolf-Rüdiger. *Kameen von Augustus bis Alexander Severus.* Antike Münzen und geschnittene Steine 11. Berlin, 1987.

Meijer 1985–86

Meijer, Bert W. "Collezioni e collezionisti fiamminghi e olandesi in Italia." *Incontri,* n.s., 1985–86, pp. 72–76.

Meijer 1992

Meijer, Bert W. "Rubens, Van Dyck e la Continenza di Scipione." In Limentani Virdis and Bottacin 1992, pp. 131–44.

Memphis and other cities 2003–5

The Devonshire Inheritance: Five Centuries of Collecting at Chatsworth. Exh. cat. by Nicolas Barker. Memphis, Dixon Gallery and Gardens; New York, Bard Graduate Center for Studies in the Decorative Arts, Design, and Culture; Salem, Massachusetts, Peabody Essex Museum; Palm Beach, Society of the Four Arts; Mobile, Alabama, Mobile Museum of Art; and Tyler, Texas, Tyler Museum of Art; 2003–5. Circulated by Art Services International, Alexandria, Virginia. Alexandria, Va., 2003.

Mena Marqués 1982

Mena Marqués, Manuela B. "La procedencia del dibujo de la Sibila Libica de Miguel Angel en el Metropolitan Museum de Nueva York." In *Miscelánea de arte,* pp. 90–92. Madrid, 1982.

Mendes da Costa 1902

Mendes da Costa, M. B. *Catalogus der handschriften.* Vol. 2, *De handschriften der Stedelijke Bibliotheek met de latere aanwinsten.* 2 vols. Bibliotheek, Universiteit van Amsterdam. Amsterdam, 1902.

Merle du Bourg 2000

Merle du Bourg, Alexis. "La genèse de la galerie Médicis de Rubens: Un document retrouvé." *Revue de l'art,* no. 127 (2000), pp. 70–72.

Van der Meulen 1975

Van der Meulen, Marjon. *Petrus Pavlus Rubens Antiquarius: Collector and Copyist of Antique Gems.* Alphen aan den Rijn, 1975.

Van der Meulen 1994

Van der Meulen, Marjon. *Rubens Copies after the Antique.* Ed. Arnout Balis. 3 vols. Corpus Rubenianum Ludwig Burchard 23. London, 1994.

Michel 1771

Michel, J. F. M. *Histoire de la vie de Rubens, chevalier & seigneur de Steen.* Brussels, 1771.

Mitsch 1977

Mitsch, Erwin. "Zum 400. Geburtstag von Peter Paul Rubens: Zeichnungen der Albertina, Wien." *Die Weltkunst* 47 (June 1977), pp. 1176–78.

***MMAB* 1998**

The Metropolitan Museum of Art Bulletin 56, no. 2 (Fall 1998).

***MMAB* 2001**

The Metropolitan Museum of Art Bulletin 59, no. 2 (Fall 2001).

Monballieu 1965

Monballieu, A. "P. P. Rubens en het 'Nachtmael' voor St.-Winoksbergen (1611): Een niet uitgevoerd schilderij van de meester." *Jaarboek van het Koninklijk Museum voor Schone Kunsten Antwerpen,* 1965, pp. 183–205.

Monbeig Goguel 1988

Monbeig Goguel, Catherine. "Taste and Trade: The Retouched Drawings in the Everhard Jabach Collection in the Louvre." *Burlington Magazine* 130 (November 1988), pp. 821–35.

Mongan and Sachs 1940

Mongan, Agnes, and Paul Sachs. *Drawings in the Fogg Museum of Art.* 2 vols. Cambridge, Mass., 1940.

Montpellier 1997

Petits et grands maîtres du Musée Atger, II: Dessins italiens et nordiques des XVIe, XVIIe et XVIIIe siècles. Exh. cat. by Christiane Nicq and Pierre Nicq, with a foreword by Claude Solassol and Huguette Brelaz. Bibliothèque Interuniversitaire de Montpellier; 1997. Montpellier, 1997.

Montreal–Raleigh–Indianapolis 1994–95

Dutch and Flemish Drawings from the Royal Library, Windsor Castle. Exh. cat. by Christopher White. Montreal, Museum of Fine Arts; Raleigh, North Carolina Museum of Art; and Indianapolis Museum of Art; 1994–95. Raleigh, 1994.

Morel d'Arleux

Manuscript inventory of the drawings in the Louvre, circa 1802, by Louis-Marie-Joseph Morel d'Arleux, curator of the Cabinet des Dessins du Louvre from 1797 to 1827. 9 albums. Département des Arts Graphiques, Musée du Louvre, Paris.

Morford 1991

Morford, Mark. *Stoics and Neostoics: Rubens and the Circle of Lipsius.* Princeton, 1991.

Morford 1998

Morford, Mark. "Towards an Intellectual Biography of Justus Lipsius: Pieter Paul Rubens." *Bulletin de l'Institut Historique Belge de Rome/Bulletin van het Belgisch Historisch Instituut te Rome* 68 (1998), pp. 387–403.

Mrozińska and Sawicka 1976

Mrozińska, Maria, and Stanisława Sawicka. *Rysunki szkól obcych w zbiorach polskich.* Warsaw, 1976.

Mrozińska and Sawicka 1980

Mrozińska, Maria, and Stanisława Sawicka. *Polskie kolekcjonerstwo grafiki i rysunku.* Polskie zbiory graficzne. Warsaw, 1980.

Von zur Mühlen 1990

Von zur Mühlen, Ilse. "Nachtridentinische Bildauffassungen: Cesare Baronio und Rubens' Gemälde für S. Maria in Vallicella in Rom." *Münchner Jahrbuch der bildenden Kunst* 41 (1990), pp. 23–60.

Von zur Mühlen 1996

Von zur Mühlen, Ilse. "S. Maria in Vallicella: Zur Geschichte des Hauptaltars." *Römisches Jahrbuch der Bibliotheca Hertziana* 31 (1996), pp. 247–72.

Von zur Mühlen 1998

Von zur Mühlen, Ilse. *Bild und Vision: Peter Paul Rubens und der "Pinsel Gottes."* Europäische Hochschulschriften, ser. 28, Kunstgeschichte 334. Frankfurt, 1998.

Von zur Mühlen 2001

Von zur Mühlen, Ilse. "Rubens, Restorer or: Rubens' Paintings for Sta. Croce in Gerusalemme in Rome—the Vagaries of Place and Their Consequences." *Jaarboek van het Koninklijk Museum voor Schone Kunsten Antwerpen,* 2001, pp. 105–35.

Muller 1975

Muller, Jeffrey M. "Oil-Sketches in Rubens's Collection." *Burlington Magazine* 117 (June 1975), pp. 371–77.

Muller 1989

Muller, Jeffrey M. *Rubens: The Artist as Collector.* Princeton, 1989.

Müller Hofstede 1962

Müller Hofstede, Justus. Review of Held 1959. *Kunstchronik* 15 (April, May 1962), pp. 93–107, 129–37.

Müller Hofstede 1964

Müller Hofstede, Justus. "Some Early Drawings by Rubens." *Master Drawings* 2 (1964), pp. 3–17.

Müller Hofstede 1965a

Müller Hofstede, Justus. "Beiträge zum zeichnerischen Werk von Rubens." *Wallraf-Richartz-Jahrbuch* 27 (1965), pp. 259–356.

Müller Hofstede 1965b

Müller Hofstede, Justus. "Rubens' St. Georg und seine frühen Reiterbildnisse." *Zeitschrift für Kunstgeschichte* 28 (1965), pp. 69–112.

Müller Hofstede 1965c

Müller Hofstede, Justus. "Zeichnungen des späten Rubens." *Pantheon* 23 (May–June 1965), pp. 163–80.

Müller Hofstede 1965d

Müller Hofstede, Justus. "Bildnisse aus Rubens' Italienjahren." *Jahrbuch der Staatlichen Kunstsammlungen in Baden-Württemberg* 2 (1965), pp. 89–154.

Müller Hofstede 1966a

Müller Hofstede, Justus. Review of Burchard and d'Hulst 1963. *Master Drawings* 4 (1966), pp. 435–54.

Müller Hofstede 1966b

Müller Hofstede, Justus. "Zu Rubens' zweitem Altarwerk für Sta. Maria in Vallicella." *Nederlands kunsthistorisch jaarboek* 17 (1966), pp. 1–78.

Müller Hofstede 1968a

Müller Hofstede, Justus. "Zur Kopfstudie im Werk von Rubens." *Wallraf-Richartz-Jahrbuch* 30 (1968), pp. 223–52.

Müller Hofstede 1968b
Müller Hofstede, Justus. "Rubens und Jan Brueghel: Diana und ihre Nymphen." *Jahrbuch der Berliner Museen,* n.s., 10 (1968), pp. 200–232.
Müller Hofstede 1970
Müller Hofstede, Justus. "Rubens in Rom, 1601–1602: Die Altargemälde für S. Croce in Gerusalemme." *Jahrbuch der Berliner Museen,* n.s., 12 (1970), pp. 61–110.
Müller Hofstede 1988
Müller Hofstede, Justus. "Neue Beiträge zum Oeuvre Anton van Dycks." *Wallraf-Richartz-Jahrbuch* 48–49 (1987–88), pp. 123–86.
Munich 1980
Wittelsbacher Jagd. Exh. cat. by Bernd E. Ergert and Werner Loibl. Munich, Deutsches Jagdmuseum; 1980. Munich, 1980.
Munich 1990–91
Peter Paul Rubens: Altäre für Bayern. Exh. cat. by Konrad Renger. Munich, Alte Pinakothek; 1990–91. Munich, 1990.
Munich 1995–97
Zehn Meisterzeichnungen: Neuzugänge der Graphischen Sammlung. Exh. cat. by Tilman Falk and Thea Vignau-Wilberg. Munich, Neue Pinakothek; 1995–97. Munich, 1996.
Munich 1997–98
Die Pranke des Löwen: Rubens-Skizzen aus St. Petersburg und München. Exh. cat. by Konrad Renger. Munich, Neue Pinakothek; 1997–98. Munich, 1997.
Münster 2003
Sammlerlust: Europäische Kunst aus fünf Jahrhunderten. Gemälde, Zeichnungen, und Kunsthandwerk aus einer westfälischen Privatsammlung. Exh. cat. ed. Monika Bachtler. Münster, Westfälisches Landesmuseum für Kunst und Kulturgeschichte; 2003. Munich and New York, 2003.
Musée des Beaux-Arts, Lille 1999–
Musée des Beaux-Arts, Lille. *Catalogue sommaire illustré des peintures.* Paris, 1999–.
Museo Nazionale Romano 1979–
Museo Nazionale Romano. *Le sculture.* Ed. Antonio Giuliano. Rome, 1979–.
Myers 1966
Myers, Mary L. "Rubens and the Woodcuts of Christoffel Jegher." *The Metropolitan Museum of Art Bulletin* 25 (Summer 1966), pp. 7–23.
New York 1965–66
The Italian Renaissance. Exh. cat. by Jacob Bean and Felice Stampfle. New York, The Metropolitan Museum of Art; 1965–66. Drawings from New York Collections 1. New York, 1965.
New York 1979–80
William and Mary and Their House. New York, The Pierpont Morgan Library; 1979–80. New York, 1979.
New York 1981
European Drawings, 1375–1825. Exh. cat. by Cara D. Denison and Helen B. Mules, with Jane V. Shoaf. New York, The Pierpont Morgan Library; 1981. New York, 1981.
New York 1988
Creative Copies: Interpretative Drawings from Michelangelo to Picasso. Exh. cat. by Egbert Haverkamp-Begemann, with Carolyn Logan. New York, Drawing Center; 1988, New York, 1988.
New York 1996
Selected Drawings. Exh. cat. New York, C. G. Boerner; 1996. New York, 1996.
New York 1998
Master Drawings, 1500–1900. Exh. cat. New York, W. M. Brady and Company; 1998. Thomas Le Claire Kunsthandel ll. New York, 1998.
New York 1998–99
Master Drawings from the Hermitage and Pushkin Museums. Exh. cat. by Marina Bessonova et al. New York, The Pierpont Morgan Library; 1998–99. New York, 1998.
New York 1999
Old Master Paintings. Exh. cat. New York, Otto Naumann Ltd.; 1999. New York, 1999.
New York 2003
Leonardo da Vinci: Master Draftsman. Exh. cat. ed. Carmen C. Bambach. New York, The Metropolitan Museum of Art; 2003. New York, 2003.
New York and other cities 1997–99
A Quintessence of Drawing: Masterworks from the Albertina. Exh. cat. New York, Solomon R. Guggenheim Museum; Berlin, Deutsche Guggenheim; Bilbao, Guggenheim Museum; and Vienna, Graphische Sammlung Albertina; 1997–99. Milan, 1997. Spanish ed.: *De Durero a Rauschenberg: La quintaesencia del dibujo. Obras maestras de las colecciones Albertina y Guggenheim.* Bilbao, 1999. German ed.: *Von Dürer bis Rauschenberg: Eine Quintessenz der Zeichnung. Meisterwerke aus der Albertina und dem Guggenheim.* Vienna, 1999.
New York–Fort Worth 1991
The Drawings of Anthony van Dyck. Exh. cat. by Christopher Brown. New York, The Pierpont Morgan Library, and Fort Worth, Kimbell Art Museum; 1991. New York, 1991.
New York–Fort Worth–Cleveland 1990–91
Pisanello to Cézanne: Master Drawings from the Museum Boymans-van Beuningen, Rotterdam. Exh. cat. by Ger Luijten and A. W. F. M. Meij. New York, The Pierpont Morgan Library; Fort Worth, Kimbell Art Museum; Cleveland Museum of Art; 1990–91. Rotterdam and Alexandria, Va., 1990.
New York–London 2000
An Exhibition of Master Drawings. Exh. cat. by Stephen Ongpin. New York, Adam Williams Fine Art, and London, P & D Colnaghi; 2000. London, 2000.
Nicolson 1967
Nicolson, Ben. "Current and Forthcoming Exhibitions." *Burlington Magazine* 109 (1967), pp. 372–75, 377.
Nicq 1996
Nicq, Christiane. *Bibliothèque Interuniversitaire de Montpellier: Inventaire des dessins du Musée Atger.* Montpellier, 1996.
Nieuwenhuizen 1962
Nieuwenhuizen, J. van den. "La Descente de Croix de Rubens: Histoire matérielle." *Bulletin* [Institut Royal du Patrimoine Artistique] 5 (1962), pp. 27–85.
Norgate 1997
Norgate, Edward. *Miniatura, or, The Art of Limning.* Ed. Jeffrey M. Muller and Jim Murrell. New Haven, 1997.
Oberhuber 1978
Oberhuber, Konrad. *The Works of Marcantonio Raimondi and of His School.* 2 vols. Vols. 26 and 27 of *The Illustrated Bartsch.* New York, 1978.
Oberhuber 1999
Oberhuber, Konrad. *Raphael: The Paintings.* New York, 1999.
Ottawa 1968–69
Jacob Jordaens, 1593–1678. Exh. cat. by Michael Jaffé. Ottawa, National Gallery of Canada; 1968–69. Ottawa, 1968.
Otterlo, Rijksmuseum Kröller-Müller 1959
Rijksmuseum Kröller-Müller, Otterlo. *Catalogus van schilderijen uit de XVe tot en met de XVIIIe eeuw: Benevens een keuze uit de tekeningen van die periode.* 2nd ed. Otterlo, 1959.
Oud and Van Oosterzee 1999
Oud, I., and L. van Oosterzee. *Oude tekeningen in het bezit van het Amsterdams Historisch Museum, waaronder de collectie Fodor.* Vol. 5, *Nederlandse tekenaars geboren tussen 1660 en 1745.* Amsterdam and Zwolle, 1999.
Oudinet 1736
Oudinet, Antoine. "Sur deux autres Agathes du mesmes Cabinet du Roy." In *Histoire de l'Académie Royale des Inscriptions et Belles Lettres,* vol. 1. Paris, 1736.
Oxford–London 1988
Rubens in Oxford: An Exhibition of Drawings from Christ Church and the Ashmolean Museum. Exh. cat. by Brigid Cleaver, Christopher White, and Jeremy Wood. Ed. Catherine Whistler and Jeremy Wood. Oxford, The Picture Gallery, Christ Church, and London, P & D Colnaghi; 1988. London and New York, 1988.
Pacheco 1638 (1956 ed.)
Pacheco, Francisco. *Arte de la pintura. Ed. del manuscrito original, acadabro el 24 de enero de 1638.* Ed. F. J. Sánchez Cantón. 2 vols. Madrid, 1956.
Pacheco 1649
Pacheco, Francisco. *Arte de la pintura.* Seville, 1649.
Padua–Rome–Milan 1990
Rubens: Pietro Paolo Rubens (1577–1640). Exh. cat. by Didier Bodart et al. Padua, Palazzo della Ragione; Rome, Palazzo delle Esposizioni; and Milan, Società per le Belle Arte ed Esposizione Permanente; 1990. Rome, 1990.
Panofsky 1933
Panofsky, Erwin. "Der gefesselte Eros." *Oud Holland* 50 (1933), pp. 193–217.
Panofsky 1939
Panofsky, Erwin. *Studies in Iconology.* New York, 1939.
Paris 1965
Exposition le décor de la vie privée en Hollande au XVIIe siècle. Exh. cat. Paris, Institut Néerlandais; 1965. Paris, 1965.
Paris 1967
Le cabinet d'un grand amateur, P.-J. Mariette, 1694–1774: Dessins du XVe siècle au XVIIIe siècle. Exh. cat. by Roseline Bacou, Françoise Viatte, and Sylviane d'Origny. Paris, Musée du Louvre; 1967. Paris, 1967.
Paris 1969
Dessins de Taddeo et Federico Zuccaro. Exh. cat. Paris, Cabinet des Dessins, Musée du Louvre; 1969. Paris, 1969.
Paris 1974
Dessins flamands et hollandais du dix-septième siècle: Collections Musées de Belgique, Musée Boymans-Van Beuningen, Rotterdam, Institut Néerlandais, Paris. Exh. cat. ed. A. W. F. M. Meij et al. Paris, Institut Néerlandais; 1974. Paris, 1974.
Paris 1977–78
Collections de Louis XIV: Dessins, albums, manuscrits. Exh. cat. ed. Jean Adhémar et al. Paris, Orangerie des Tuileries; 1977–78. Paris, 1977.
Paris 1978
Rubens, ses maîtres, ses élèves: Dessins du Musée du Louvre. Exh. cat. by Arlette Sérullaz. Paris, Cabinet des Dessins, Musée du Louvre; 1978. Paris, 1978.
Paris 1987
La collection Saint-Morys au Cabinet des Dessins du Musée du Louvre. Exh. cat. by Jacqueline Labbé, with Lise Bicart-Sée. Vol. 2, *Répertoire des dessins.* Paris, Musée du Louvre; 1987. Paris, 1987.
Paris 1991
Marie de Médicis et le Palais du Luxembourg. Exh. cat. by Marie-Noëlle Baudouin-Matuszek et al. Paris, Musée du Luxembourg; 1991. Paris, 1991.

Paris–Antwerp–London–New York 1979–80
Rubens and Rembrandt in Their Century: Flemish and Dutch Drawings of the Seventeenth Century from the Pierpont Morgan Library. Exh. cat. by Felice Stampfle. Paris, Institut Néerlandais; Antwerp, Koninklijk Museum voor Schone Kunsten; London, British Museum; and New York, The Pierpont Morgan Library; 1979–80. New York, 1979. French ed.: *Le siècle de Rubens et de Rembrandt: Dessins flamands et hollandais du XVIIe siècle de la Pierpont Morgan Library de New York.* New York, 1979.

Parker 1929–30
Parker, K. T. "Unpublished Drawings by Rubens in the Victoria and Albert Museum." *Old Master Drawings* 4 (1929–30), pp. 17–20.

Perrig 1976
Perrig, Alexander. *Michelangelo Studien.* Vol. 1, *Michelangelo und die Zeichnungswissenschaft: Ein methodologischer Versuch.* Kunstwissenschaftliche Studien 1. Frankfurt, 1976.

Perrig 1991
Perrig, Alexander. *Michelangelo's Drawings: The Science of Attribution.* Trans. Michael Joyce. New Haven, 1991.

Petrioli Tofani 1986–
Petrioli Tofani, Annamaria, ed. *Inventario: Gabinetto Disegni e Stampe degli Uffizi.* Florence, 1986–.

Piles 1677
Piles, Roger de. *Conversations sur la connoissance de la peinture, et sur le jugement qu'on doit faire des tableaux, où par occasion il est parlé de la vie de Rubens, et de quelques-uns de ses beaux ouvrages.* Paris, 1677.

Piles 1699
Piles, Roger de. *Abrégé de la vie des peintres, avec des reflexions sur leurs ouvrage et un traité du peintre parfait, de la connoissance des desseins, de l'utilité des estampes.* Paris, 1699.

Piles 1715
Piles, Roger de. *Abrégé de la vie des peintres, avec des reflexions sur leurs ouvrage, et un traité du peintre parfait; de la connoissance des desseins; de l'utilité des estampes.* 2nd ed. Paris, 1715.

Piles 1743
Piles, Roger de. *The Principles of Painting . . . in Which Is Contained an Account of the Athenian, Roman, Venetian, and Flemish Schools. . . .* London, 1743. Translation of *Cours de peinture par principes.* Paris, 1708.

Pittsburgh–Louisville–Fresno 2002
Masterworks from the Albertina. Exh. cat. by Klaus Albrecht Schröder and Maria Luise Sternath. Pittsburgh, Frick Art and Historical Center; Louisville, Speed Art Museum; and Fresno, Metropolitan Museum of Art, History and Science; 2002. Wolfratshausen, 2001.

Plomp 2001–2
Plomp, Michiel C. *Collectionner, passionnément: Les collectionneurs hollandais de dessins au XVIIIe siècle.* Paris, 2001. [Vol. 1] of Haarlem–Paris 2001–2. Dutch ed.: *Hartstochtelijk verzameld: 18de-eeuwse Hollandse verzamelaars van tekeningen en hun collecties.* Paris and Bussum, 2001.

Plomp 2002
Plomp, Michiel C. "'Een voortreffelyke Liefhebberye': Het verzamelen van tekeningen door voorname liefhebbers in de Republiek en later het Koninkrijk der Nederlanden, 1732–1833." Ph.D. diss., Rijksuniversiteit Groningen, 2002.

Plomp forthcoming
Plomp, Michiel C. "Acquisitions for the English Royal Collection from the 1759 Abraham van Broyel Sale." *Oud Holland.* Forthcoming.

Poll-Frommel and Schmidt 2001
Poll-Frommel, Veronika, and Jan Schmidt. "Anstückungen bei Tafelgemälden von Peter Paul Rubens." *Restauro* 107 (2001), pp. 432–37.

De Poorter 1978
De Poorter, Nora. *The Eucharist Series.* 2 vols. Corpus Rubenianum Ludwig Burchard 2. London and Philadelphia, 1978.

Popham 1935–36
Popham, A. E. "Drawings by Rubens and Van Dyck from the National Gallery." *British Museum Quarterly* 10 (1935–36), pp. 10–18.

Popham and Wilde 1949
Popham, A. E., and Johannes Wilde. *The Italian Drawings of the XV and XVI Centuries in the Collection of Her Majesty the Queen at Windsor Castle.* London, 1949. Reprint, New York, 1982.

Portocarrero 1616
Portocarrero, Francisco. *Libro de la Descencion de Nuestra Señora a la Santa Yglesia de Toledo, y vida de San Ilefonso Arçobispo.* Madrid, 1616.

Poznań 1995
Miedzy renesansem a klasycyzmem: Rysunki mistrzów europejskich w zbiorach Muzeum Narodowego w Pozananiu/Between Renaissance and Classicism: European Master's Drawings from the Collection of the National Museum in Poznań. Exh. cat. ed. Tadeusz Żuchowski. Poznań, Muzeum Narodowe; 1995. Poznań, 1995.

Van Puyvelde 1942
Van Puyvelde, Leo. *The Flemish Drawings in the Collection of His Majesty the King at Windsor Castle.* London, 1942.

Py 2001
Py, Bernadette. *Everhard Jabach, collectionneur (1618–1695): Les dessins de l'inventaire de 1695.* Notes et documents des musées de France 36. Paris, 2001.

R.
Rooses, Max. *L'oeuvre de P. P. Rubens: Histoire et description de ses tableaux et dessins.* 5 vols. Antwerp, 1886–92.

Van Regteren Altena 1972
Van Regteren Altena, J. Q. "Het vroegste werk van Rubens." *Mededelingen* [Koninklijke Academie voor Wetenschappen, Letteren en Schone Kunsten van België, Klasse der Schone Kunsten] 34 (1972), pp. 3–23.

Van Regteren Altena 1977
Van Regteren Altena, J. Q. *Peter Paul Rubens: Tekeningen naar Hans Holbeins Dodendans.* Amsterdam, 1977.

Reiset 1866
Reiset, Frédéric. *Notice des dessins, cartons, pastels, miniatures et émaux exposés dans les salles du 1er [et du 2e] étage au Musée Impérial du Louvre.* Vol. 1, *Écoles d'Italie, écoles allemande, flamande et hollandaise.* Paris, 1866.

Renger 1973
Renger, Konrad. "Rubens Dedit Dedicavit." *Mitteilungen der Gesellschaft für Vergleichende Kunstforschung in Wien* 26 (1973), pp. 6–8.

Renger 1974a
Renger, Konrad. "Rubens Dedit Dedicavitque: Rubens' Beschäftigung mit der Reproduktionsgrafik. I. Der Kupferstich." *Jahrbuch der Berliner Museen,* n.s., 16 (1974), pp. 122–75.

Renger 1974b
Renger, Konrad. "Planänderungen in Rubensstichen." *Zeitschrift für Kunstgeschichte* 37 (1974), pp. 1–30.

Renger 1975
Renger, Konrad. "Rubens Dedit Dedicavitque: Rubens' Beschäftigung mit der Reproduktionsgrafik. II. Radierung und Holzschnitt—die Widmungen." *Jahrbuch der Berliner Museen,* n.s., 17 (1975), pp. 166–213.

Renger 1978
Renger, Konrad. Review of the exhibitions "Rubens, Drawings and Sketches," British Museum, London, and "Peter Paul Rubens," Wallraf-Richartz-Museum, Cologne. *Kunstchronik* 31 (1978), pp. 133–47.

Renger and Denk 2002
Renger, Konrad, and Claudia Denk. *Flämische Malerei des Barock in der Alten Pinakothek.* Cologne, 2002.

Rennes 1980–81
Le Brun 80. Exh. cat. by Sylvie Blottière. Rennes, Musée des Beaux-Arts; 1980–81. Rennes, 1980.

Retretti 1991
Rubens. Exh. cat. ed. Katriina Salmela-Hasan and Ilkka Karttunen. Retretti, Finland, Taidekeskus Retretti; 1991. Retretti, 1991.

Reznicek 1961
Reznicek, Emil K. J. *Die Zeichnungen von Hendrick Goltzius.* Orbis Atrium; Utrechtse kunsthistorische Studiën 6. Utrecht, 1961.

Reznicek 1992
Reznicek, Emil K. J. "Rapporti tra Goltzio e Rubens." In Limentani Virdis and Bottacin 1992, pp. 121–29.

Richardson 1719
Richardson, Jonathan. *Two Discourses: I. An Essay on the Whole Art of Criticism as It Relates to Painting . . . II. An Argument in Behalf of the Science of a Connoisseur.* London, 1719.

Richardson 1722
Richardson, Jonathan. *An Account of the Statues, Bas-Reliefs, Drawings and Pictures in Italy, &c. with Remarks by Mr. Richardson Sen. and Jun.* London, 1722.

Richardson 1725
Richardson, Jonathan. *An Essay on the Theory of Painting.* London, 1725.

Richardson 1728
Richardson, Jonathan. *Traité de la peinture et de la sculpture.* 3 vols. Amsterdam, 1728.

Richardson 1754
Richardson, Jonathan. *An Account of the Statues, Bas-Reliefs, Drawings and Pictures in Italy, France, etc. with Remarks.* 2nd ed. London, 1754.

Richmond and other cities 1979–80
Treasures from Chatsworth: The Devonshire Inheritance. Exh. cat. Richmond, Virginia Museum of Fine Arts, and other cities; 1979–80. Organized by the International Exhibitions Foundation. Washington, D.C., 1979.

G. Richter 1956
Richter, Gisela M. A. *Catalogue of Engraved Gems: Greek, Etruscan, and Roman.* The Metropolitan Museum of Art, New York. Rome, 1956.

J. P. Richter 1939
Richter, Jean Paul, comp. and ed. *The Literary Works of Leonardo da Vinci, Compiled and Edited from the Original Manuscripts.* 2nd ed. 2 vols. London, 1939.

J. P. Richter 1977
Richter, Jean Paul, comp. and ed. *The Literary Works of Leonardo da Vinci, Compiled and Edited from the Original Manuscripts.* Commentary by Carlo Pedretti. 2 vols. National Gallery of Art Kress Foundation Studies in the History of European Art 5. Berkeley, 1977.

Te Rijdt 2001
Te Rijdt, Robert-Jan. "Jacob Jordaens (1593–1678) en Jacob de Wit (1695–1754)." *Delineavit et Sculpsit,* no. 23 (July 2001), pp. 34–37.

Rogers 1778
Rogers, Charles. *Collection of Prints in Imitation of Drawings.* London, 1778.

Rollová 1997–98
Rollová, Anna. "Loedel after Rubens?" *Bulletin Národní Galerie v Praze* 7–8 (1997–98; pub. 1999), pp. 124–27.

Rome 1990
Rubens e Roma. Exh. cat. Rome, Palazzo delle Esposizioni; 1990. Rome, 1990.

Rome 1991
La Sistina riprodotta: Gli affreschi di Michelangelo dalle stampe del Cinquecento alle campagne fotografiche Anderson. Exh. cat. ed. Alida Moltedo. Rome, Calcografia; 1991. Rome, 1991.

Rome 1995
La regola e la fama: San Filippo Neri e l'arte. Exh. cat. Rome, Museo Nazionale del Palazzo di Venezia; 1995. Milan, 1995.

Rooses 1886–92. See **R.**

Rooses 1895
Rooses, Max. "Staat van goederen in het sterfhuis van Isabella Brant." *Bulletin-Rubens* 4, pt. 3 (1895), pp. 154–88.

Rooses 1897
Rooses, Max. "Staet ende inventaris van den sterffhuyse van Mynheer Albertus Rubens ende vrouwe Clara Del Monte." *Bulletin-Rubens* 5, pts. 1 and 2 (1897), pp. 11–59.

Rooses 1900a
Rooses, Max. "La galerie du Marquis de Léganès." *Bulletin-Rubens* 5, pt. 3 (1900), pp. 164–71.

Rooses 1900b
Rooses, Max. "Oeuvre de Rubens: Addenda et corrigenda." *Bulletin-Rubens* 5, pt. 3 (1900), pp. 172–204.

Rooses 1903
Rooses, Max. "De teekeningen der Vlaamse meesters: Rubens (1577–1640)." *Onze kunst* 2 (1903), pp. 1–9, 44–50.

Rooses 1905
Rooses, Max. "The Portrait of Isabella Brant in the Hermitage." *Burlington Magazine* 6 (1905), pp. 496–97.

Rooses 1910
Rooses, Max. "De vreemde reizigers Rubens of zijn huis bezoekende." *Bulletin-Rubens* 5, pt. 4 (1910), pp. 221–29.

Rooses and Ruelens 1887–1909
Rooses, Max, and Charles Ruelens, eds. and trans. *Correspondance de Rubens et documents épistolaires concernant sa vie et ses oeuvres.* 6 vols. Antwerp, 1887–1909.

Rośсiszewska 1993
Rościszewska, Danuta. "A Contribution to the Study on the Dating of the 'Garden of Love' by P. P. Rubens in Reference to Discovery of a Sketch on the Backside of Drawing 'A Rest on the Flight to Egypt.'" *Studia muzealne* [Muzeum Narodowe, Poznań] 17 (1993), pp. 78–83.

Rosenberg and Prat 1996
Rosenberg, Pierre, and Louis-Antoine Prat. *Antoine Watteau, 1684–1721: Catalogue raisonné des dessins.* 3 vols. Milan, 1996.

Rott 2002
Rott, Herbert W. *Rubens: Palazzi di Genova—Architectural Drawings and Engravings.* Corpus Rubenianum Ludwig Burchard 22; Architecture and Sculpture 1. London, 2002.

Rotterdam 2001
Rubens, Jordaens, Van Dyck and Their Circle: Flemish Master Drawings from the Museum Boijmans Van Beuningen. Exh. cat. by A. W. F. M. Meij, with Maartje de Haan. Rotterdam, Museum Boijmans Van Beuningen; 2001. Rotterdam and New York, 2001.

Rotterdam–Madrid 2003–4
Peter Paul Rubens: The Life of Achilles. Exh. cat. by Friso Lammertse and Alejandro Vergara, with contributions by Annetje Boersma, Guy Delmarcel, and Fiona Healy. Rotterdam, Museum Boijmans Van Beuningen, and Madrid, Museo del Prado; 2003–4. Rotterdam and Madrid, 2003.

Rotterdam–New York 2001
Pieter Bruegel the Elder: Drawings and Prints. Exh. cat. ed. Nadine M. Orenstein. Rotterdam, Museum Boijmans Van Beuningen, and New York, The Metropolitan Museum of Art; 2001. New York, 2001.

Ruelens 1883
Ruelens, Charles. "La vie de Rubens par Roger de Piles." *Bulletin-Rubens* 2 (1883), pp. 157–75.

Rutgers 1999
Rutgers, Jaco. "Vierhonderd jaar Van Dyck." *Desipientia* 6 (December 1999), pp. 56–61.

Sainsbury 1859
Sainsbury, William Noel. *Original Unpublished Papers Illustrative of the Life of Sir Peter Paul Rubens as an Artist and a Diplomatist.* London, 1859.

Saint Non 2000
Saint Non, Jean Claude Richard de. *Panopticon italiano: Un diario di viaggio ritrovato, 1759–1761.* Rev. ed. Ed. Pierre Rosenberg, with Barbara Brejon de Lavergnée. Rome, 2000.

Sandrart 1925
Sandrart, Joachim von. *Joachim von Sandrarts Academie der Bau, Bild und mahlerey Künste von 1675.* Ed. A. R. Peltzer. Munich, 1925.

Schapelhouman 1979
Schapelhouman, Marijn. *Oude tekeningen in het bezit van de Gemeentemusea van Amsterdam waaronder de collectie Fodor.* Vol. 2, *Tekeningen van Noord- en Zuidnederlandse kunstenaars geboren voor 1600.* Amsterdam, 1979.

Schatborn 1981
Schatborn, Peter. "Van Rembrandt tot Crozat: Vroege verzamelingen met tekeningen van Rembrandt." *Nederlands kunsthistorisch jaarboek* 32 (1981), pp. 1–54.

Schneevoogt 1873
Schneevoogt, C. G. Voorhelm. *Catalogue des estampes gravées d'après P. P. Rubens, avec l'indication des collections où se trouvent les tableaux et les gravures.* Haarlem, 1873.

Scholten 1904
Scholten, H. J. *Catalogue raisonné des dessins des écoles française et hollandaise.* Teylers Museum. Haarlem, 1904.

Schönbrunner and Meder 1896–1908
Schönbrunner, Josef, and Joseph Meder, eds. *Handzeichnungen alter Meister aus der Albertina und anderen Sammlungen.* 12 vols. Vienna, 1896–1908.

Schroth 1990
Schroth, Sarah. "The Private Picture Collection of the Duke of Lerma." Ph.D. diss., Institute of Fine Arts, New York University, 1990.

Schwarz 1990
Schwarz, Michael Viktor. "Der Kupferstich 'Le Christ au Coup de Poing': Rubens antwortet Michelangelo." *Wiener Jahrbuch für Kunstgeschichte* 43 (1990), pp. 112–28.

Schwinn 1973
Schwinn, Christa. *Die Bedeutung des Torso vom Belvedere für Theorie und Praxis der bildenden Kunst vom 16. Jahrhunderts bis Winckelman.* Europäische Hochschulschriften, ser. 28, Kunstgeschichte 1. Bern and Frankfurt, 1973.

Scoppola 1987
Scoppola, Francesco, ed. *Palazzo Altemps: Indagini per il restauro della fabbrica Riario, Soderini, Altemps.* Rome, 1987.

Seilern 1955
Seilern, Antoine. *Flemish Paintings and Drawings at 56 Princes Gate, London SW7.* London, 1955.

Seitz and Lidel 1983
Seitz, Reinhard H., and Albert Lidel. *Die Hofkirche Unserer Lieben Frau zu Neuburg Neubergan der Donau: Ein Kirchenbau zwischen Reformation und Gegenreformation.* Kunst in Bayern und Schwaben 4. Weissenhorn, 1983.

Seville 1978
La pintura flamenca en la época de Rubens. Exh. cat. Seville, Reales Alcázares; 1978. Seville, 1978.

Sonkes 1969
Sonkes, Micheline. *Dessins du XVe siècle: Groupe Van der Weyden.* Les primitifs flamands 3; Contributions à l'étude des primitifs flamands 5. Brussels, 1969.

De Staelen 2004
De Staelen, Carolien. "Rubens's 'Samson and Delilah' in the National Gallery: New Facts Relating to Its Provenance." *Burlington Magazine* 146 (July 2004), pp. 467–69.

Stampfle 1991
Stampfle, Felice, with Ruth S. Kraemer and Jane Shoaf Turner. *Netherlandish Drawings of the Fifteenth and Sixteenth Centuries in the Pierpont Morgan Library.* New York and Princeton, 1991.

Starcky 1988
Starcky, Emmanuel. *Inventaire général des dessins des écoles du nord: Écoles allemande, des Anciens Pays-Bas, flamande, hollandaise et suisse du XVe–XVIIIe siècles. Suppléments aux inventaires publiés par Frits Lugt et Louis Demonts.* Paris, 1988.

Staring 1958
Staring, Adolph. *Jacob de Wit, 1695–1754.* Amsterdam, 1958.

Stechow 1968
Stechow, Wolfgang. *Rubens and the Classical Tradition.* Martin Classical Lectures 22. Cambridge, Mass., 1968.

Stechow 1973
Stechow, Wolfgang. "Peter Paul Rubens's *Deborah Kip, Wife of Sir Balthasar Gerbier, and Her Children.*" In *Studies in the History of Art* [National Gallery of Art, Washington, D.C.], 1973, pp. 6–22.

Stix and Fröhlich-Bum 1932
Stix, Alfred, and Lili Fröhlich-Bum. *Die Zeichnungen der toskanischen, umbrischen und römischen Schulen.* Beschreibender Katalog der Handzeichnungen in der Graphischen Sammlung Albertina 3. Vienna, 1932.

Stockholm 1953
Dutch and Flemish Drawings in the Nationalmuseum and Other Swedish Collections. Exh. cat. Stockholm, Nationalmuseum; 1953. Stockholm, 1953.

Stockholm 1977
Rubens i Sverige. Exh. cat. Stockholm, Nationalmuseum; 1977. Stockholm, 1977.

Suter 1937
Suter, Karl Friedrich. *Das Rätsel von Leonardos Schlachtenbild.* Zur Kunstgeschichte des Auslands 137. Strassburg, 1937.

Sutton 1983
Sutton, Peter C. "'Tutti finiti con amore': Rubens' 'Prometheus Bound.'" In *Essays in Northern European Art Presented to Egbert Haverkamp-Begemann on His Sixtieth Birthday,* pp. 270–75. Doornspijk, 1983.

Sutton 1990
Sutton, Peter C. *Northern European Paintings in the Philadelphia Museum of Art from the Sixteenth through the Nineteenth Century.* Philadelphia, 1990.

Sydney 2000
Drawing the Figure: From Leonardo da Vinci to Lucien Freud. Exh. cat. Sydney, Art Gallery of New South Wales; 2000. Sydney, 2000.
Sydney 2002
Albertina: Old Master Drawings from Vienna. Exh. cat. by Peter Raissis and Anna Hayes. Sydney, Art Gallery of New South Wales; 2002. Sydney, 2002.
Teyssèdre 1965
Teyssèdre, Bernard. *Roger de Piles et les débats sur le coloris au siècle de Louis XIV.* La bibliothèque des arts 13. Paris, 1965.
Theuwissen 1977
Theuwissen, J. "De wereld van de boer zoals Rubens die zag." *Spiegel historiael* 12 (June 1977), pp. 356–62.
Thode 1908–13
Thode, Henry. *Michelangelo: Kritische Untersuchungen über seine Werke.* 3 vols. Berlin, 1908–13.
Thøfner 2004
Thøfner, Margit. "Helena Fourment's *Het Pelsken.*" *Art History* 27 (February 2004), pp. 1–33.
Thompson and Brigstocke 1970
Thompson, Colin, and Hugh Brigstocke. *Shorter Catalogue: National Gallery of Scotland.* Edinburgh, 1970.
Thöne 1940
Thöne, Friedrich. "Eine Zeichnungssammlung aus dem Besitz Matthäus Merian des Jüngeren." *Berliner Museen* 61 (1940), pp. 58–67.
Thuillier and Foucart 1970
Thuillier, Jacques, and Jacques Foucart. *Rubens' Life of Marie de' Medici.* New York, 1970.
Tokyo 1982
Rūbensu to sono jidai/Rubens en zijn tijd. Exh. cat. [Captions in Japanese and English.] Tokyo, Seibu Museum of Art; 1982. Tokyo, 1982.
Tokyo 1993
Rubens and His Workshop: The Flight of Lot and His Family from Sodom. Exh. cat. ed. Toshiharu Nakamura. Tokyo, National Museum of Western Art; 1993. Tokyo, 1994.
De Tolnay
Listed under the letter D.
Toronto 2001
Rubens and His Age: Treasures from the Hermitage Museum, Russia. Exh. cat. ed. Christina Corsiglia. Toronto, Art Gallery of Ontario; 2001. London and Toronto, 2001.
Toronto–New York 2000
Albertina: The History of the Collection and Its Masterpieces. Exh. cat. by Barbara Dossi. Trans. Joan Clough-Laub. Toronto, Art Gallery of Ontario, and New York, The Frick Collection; 2000. Munich and New York, 1999.
Turner 1994
Turner, Nicholas. "John Bouverie as a Collector of Drawings." *Burlington Magazine* 136 (February 1994), pp. 90–99.
Van Tuyll van Serooskerken 2000
Van Tuyll van Serooskerken, Carel. *The Italian Drawings of the Fifteenth and Sixteenth Centuries in the Teyler Museum.* Haarlem, Ghent, and Doornspijk, 2000.
Valenciennes 2004
Watteau et la fête galante. Exh. cat. Valenciennes, Musée des Beaux-Arts; 2004. Paris, 2004.
Vasari 1568 (1906 ed.)
Vasari, Giorgio. *Le vite de' piu eccellenti pittori, scultori ed architettori.* Florence, 1568. 1906 ed.: Ed. Gaetano Milanesi. 9 vols. Florence, 1906.
Vasari 1907
Vasari, Giorgio. *Vasari on Technique: Being the Introduction to the Three Arts of Design, Architecture, Sculpture, and Painting, Prefixed to the Lives of the Most Excellent Painters, Sculptors and Architects.* Trans. Louisa S. Maclehose. Ed. G. Baldwin Brown. New York and London, 1907.
Vasari 1962
Vasari, Giorgio. *La vita di Michelangelo, nelle redazioni del 1550 e del 1568.* Ed. Paola Barocchi. 5 vols. Milan, 1962.
Vekeman and Müller Hofstede 1984
Vekeman, Herman, and Justus Müller Hofstede, eds. *Wort und Bild in der niederländischen Kunst und Literatur des 16. und 17. Jahrhunderts.* Erftstadt, 1984.
Van de Velde 1975
Van de Velde, Carl. "Rubens' Hemelvaart van Maria in de Kathedraal te Antwerpen." *Jaarboek van het Koninklijk Museum voor Schone Kunsten Antwerpen,* 1975, pp. 245–77.
Vergara 1999
Vergara, Alexander. *Rubens and His Spanish Patrons.* Cambridge, 1999.
Vergara 2004
Vergara, Alexander, ed. *The Adoration of the Magi in the Prado, Madrid.* Madrid, 2004.
Vey 1956
Vey, Horst. "Anton van Dycks Ölskizzen." *Bulletin* [Musées Royaux des Beaux-Arts], September–December 1956, pp. 167–208.
Vey 1962
Vey, Horst. *Die Zeichnungen Anton van Dycks.* 2 vols. Nationaal Centrum voor de Plastische Kunsten van de XVIde en XVIIde Eeuw, Monographien, 1. Brussels, 1962.
Vienna 1977a
Peter Paul Rubens, 1577–1640. Exh. cat. by Klaus Demus et al. Vienna, Kunsthistorisches Museum; 1977. Vienna, 1977.
Vienna 1977b
Die Rubenszeichnungen der Albertina: Zum 400. Geburtstag. Exh. cat. by Erwin Mitsch. Vienna, Graphische Sammlung Albertina; 1977. Vienna, 1977.
Vienna 1978
Die Albertina und das Dresdner Kupferstich-Kabinett und die Albertina: Meisterzeichnungen aus zwei Sammlungen. Exh. cat. ed. V. Birke et al. Vienna, Graphische Sammlung Albertina; 1978. Vienna, 1978.
Vienna–Amsterdam 1989–90
Begegnungen: Meisterwerke der Zeichnung und Druckgraphik aus dem Rijksprentenkabinet in Amsterdam und der Albertina in Wien/Ontmoetingen: Meesterwerken van teken- en prentkunst uit de Albertina in Wenen en het Rijksprentenkabinet in Amsterdam. Exh. cat. ed. Marian Bisanz-Prakken. Vienna, Graphische Sammlung Albertina, and Amsterdam, Rijksprentenkabinet, Rijksmuseum; 1989–90. The Hague, 1989.
Vignau-Wilberg 1998
Vignau-Wilberg, Thea. "Rubens' Study in Munich for 'The Duke of Lerma on Horseback.'" *Master Drawings* 36 (1998), pp. 275–87.
Vignau-Wilberg 1999
Vignau-Wilberg, Thea. *Peter Paul Rubens: Studie zum Reiterbildnis des Herzogs von Lerma.* Staatliche Graphische Sammlung, Munich. Munich, 1999.
Vlieghe 1972
Vlieghe, Hans. *Saints.* Corpus Rubenianum Ludwig Burchard 8, vol. 1. Trans. P. S. Falla. London and New York, 1972.
Vlieghe 1973
Vlieghe, Hans. *Saints.* Corpus Rubenianum Ludwig Burchard 8, vol. 2. Trans. P. S. Falla. London and New York, 1973.
Vlieghe 1977
Vlieghe, Hans. "Une grande collection anversoise du dix-septième siècle: Le cabinet d'Arnold Lunden, beau-frère de Rubens." *Jahrbuch der Berliner Museen,* n.s., 19 (1977), pp. 172–204.
Vlieghe 1983
Vlieghe, Hans. "Some Remarks on the Identification of Sitters in Rubens' Portraits." *Ringling Museum of Art Journal,* 1983, pp. 106–15.
Vlieghe 1986
Vlieghe, Hans. Review of Liedtke 1984. *Oud Holland* 100 (1986), pp. 200–204.
Vlieghe 1987
Vlieghe, Hans. *Rubens Portraits of Identified Sitters Painted in Antwerp.* Corpus Rubenianum Ludwig Burchard 19, vol. 2. Brussels, 1987.
Vlieghe 2001
Vlieghe, Hans, ed. *Van Dyck, 1599–1999: Conjectures and Refutations.* Turnhout, 2001.
Vlieghe, Balis, and Van de Velde 2000
Vlieghe, Hans, Arnout Balis, and Carl Van de Velde, eds. *Concept, Design and Execution in Flemish Painting (1550–1700).* Turnhout, 2000.
Volk 1980
Volk, Mary Crawford. "New Light on a Seventeenth-Century Collector: The Marquis of Leganés." *Art Bulletin* 62 (June 1980), pp. 256–68.
De Vos 1999
De Vos, Dirk. *Rogier van der Weyden: The Complete Works.* Antwerp, 1999.
Vosters 2001
Vosters, Simon A. "Das *Reiterbild Philipps IV.* von Spanien als Allegorie der höfischen Affekt-regulierung." In Heinen and Thielemann 2001, pp. 180–91.
Vynckier 1992
Vynckier, Jozef. "Examen dendochronologique des volets." In d'Hulst et al. 1992, pp. 156–79.
Waagen 1857
Waagen, Gustav. *Galleries and Cabinets of Art in Great Britain: Being an Account of More Than Forty Collections of Paintings, Drawings, Sculptures, Mss., &c. &c . . . Forming a Supplemental Volume to the Treasures of Art in Great Britain.* London, 1857.
Wadum 1996
Wadum, Jørgen. "A Preliminary Attempt to Identify Rubens's Studio Practice." In ICOM Committee for Conservation, *Eleventh Triennial Meeting, Edinburgh, Scotland, 1–6 September 1996: Preprints,* vol. 1, pp. 393–95. London, 1996.
Wadum 2002
Wadum, Jørgen. "Latest News from Paradise: A Preliminary Attempt to Identify Rubens's Studio Practice. Part II." In ICOM Committee for Conservation, *Thirteenth Triennial Meeting, Rio de Janeiro, 22–27 September 2002: Preprints,* vol. 1, ed. Roy Vontobel, pp. 473–78. London, 2002.
Warwick 2000
Warwick, Genevieve. *The Arts of Collecting: Padre Sebastiano Resta and the Market for Drawings in Early Modern Europe.* Cambridge, 2000.
Washington 1978
Master Drawings from the Collection of the National Gallery of Art and Promised Gifts. Exh. cat. Washington, D.C., National Gallery of Art; 1978. Washington, D.C., 1978.
Washington 1988
Michelangelo: Draftsman. Exh. cat. by Michael Hirst. Washington, D.C., National Gallery of Art; 1988. Milan, 1988.
Washington 1990–91
Anthony van Dyck. Exh. cat. by Arthur K. Wheelock Jr. et al. Washington, D.C., National Gallery of Art; 1990–91. New York, 1990.

Washington 1998
A Collector's Cabinet. Exh. cat. by Arthur K. Wheelock Jr. Washington, D.C., National Gallery of Art; 1998. Washington, D.C., 1998.

Washington and other cities 1969–70
Old Master Drawings from Chatsworth. Exh. cat. by J. Byam Shaw. Washington, D.C., National Gallery of Art; New York, The Pierpont Morgan Library; Toronto, Art Gallery of Ontario; Art Institute of Chicago; Los Angeles County Museum of Art; San Francisco, M. H. de Young Memorial Museum; Kansas City, William Rockhill Nelson Gallery of Art; and Providence, Rhode Island School of Design; 1969–70. Washington, D.C., 1969.

Washington–Fort Worth–San Francisco 1985–86
Dürer to Delacroix: Great Master Drawings from Stockholm. Exh. cat. by Per Bjurström, with Ulf Cederlöf and Börje Magnusson. Washington, D.C., National Gallery of Art; Fort Worth, Kimbell Art Museum; and Fine Arts Museums of San Francisco; 1985–86. Fort Worth, 1985.

Washington–London 1982
Painting in Naples from Caravaggio to Giordano. Exh. cat. ed. Clovis Whitfield and Jane Martineau. Washington, D.C., National Gallery of Art, and London, Royal Academy of Arts; 1982. Washington, D.C., 1982.

Washington–New York–Vienna 1984–86
Zeichnungen alter Meister aus der Albertina. Exh. cat. Washington, D.C., National Gallery of Art; New York, The Pierpont Morgan Library; and Vienna, Graphische Sammlung Albertina; 1984–86. Washington, D.C., 1984. English ed.: *Old Master Drawings from the Albertina.* New York, 1984.

Wegner 1966
Wegner, Max. *Die Musensarkophage.* Die antiken Sarkophagreliefs 5, pt. 3. Berlin, 1966.

Wellesley–Cleveland 1993–94
Flemish Drawings in the Age of Rubens: Selected Works from American Collections. Exh. cat. by Anne-Marie Logan. Wellesley, Massachusetts, Davis Museum and Cultural Center, Wellesley College, and Cleveland Museum of Art; 1993–94. Wellesley, Mass., 1993.

Westfehling 2001
Westfehling, Uwe. "Drei verschollene Zeichnungen von Peter Paul Rubens." *Wallraf-Richartz-Jahrbuch* 62 (2001), pp. 171–222.

Wethey 1969–75
Wethey, Harold E. *The Paintings of Titian: Complete Edition.* 3 vols. London, 1969–75.

Weyerman 1729–69
Weyerman, Jacob Campo. *De levens-beschrijvingen der Nederlandsche konst-schilders en konst-schilderessen.* 4 vols. The Hague, 1729–69.

White 1977–78
White, Christopher. "Rubens and Old Age." *Allen Memorial Art Museum Bulletin* 35 (1977–78), pp. 40–56.

White 1987
White, Christopher. *Peter Paul Rubens: Man and Artist.* New Haven, 1987.

White 1995a
White, Christopher. *Anthony van Dyck: Thomas Howard, the Earl of Arundel.* Malibu, 1995.

White 1995b
White, Christopher. "Rubens's Portrait of Thomas Howard, Second Earl of Arundel." *Burlington Magazine* 137 (May 1995), pp. 316–19.

White and Crawley 1994
White, Christopher, and Charlotte Crawley. *The Dutch and Flemish Drawings of the Fifteenth to the Early Nineteenth Centuries in the Collection of Her Majesty the Queen at Windsor Castle.* Cambridge, 1994.

Wickhoff 1892
Wickhoff, Franz. "Die italienischen Handzeichnungen der Albertina." Part 2, "Die römische Schule." *Jahrbuch der kunsthistorischen Sammlungen des Allerhöchsten Kaiserhauses* 13 (1892), pp. CLXXV–CCCLXXXIII.

Williamstown 1977
Rubens and the Book: Title Pages by Peter Paul Rubens. Exh. cat. ed. Julius S. Held. Williamstown, Massachusetts, Chapin Library, Stetson Hall; 1977. Williamstown, Mass., 1977.

Winner 1981
Winner, Matthias. "Zu Rubens' 'Eberjagd' in Dresden (Landschaft oder Historienbild)." In *Peter Paul Rubens: Werk und Nachruhm,* pp. 157–85. Munich, 1981.

Winther 1973
Winther, Annemarie. "Die Zeichnungen des Jacob de Wit in der Kunsthalle Bremen." *Niederdeutsche Beiträge zur Kunstgeschichte* 12 (1973), pp. 27–46.

Wood 1980
Wood, Jeremy. Review of the exhibition "The Century of Rubens and Rembrandt: Seventeenth Century Dutch and Flemish Drawings from the Pierpont Morgan Library." *Pantheon* 38 (January–March 1980), pp. 19–20.

Wood 1988
Wood, Jeremy. "Some Early Collectors of Rubens Drawings in England." In Oxford–London 1988, pp. 8–18.

Wood 1990
Wood, Jeremy. "Padre Resta's Flemish Drawings: Van Diepenbeeck, Van Thulden, Rubens, and the School of Fontainebleau." *Master Drawings* 28 (Spring 1990), pp. 3–53.

Wood 1994
Wood, Jeremy. "Rubens's Collection of Drawings: His Attributions and Inscriptions." *Wallraf-Richartz-Jahrbuch* 55 (1994), pp. 333–51.

Wood 2003
Wood, Jeremy. "Nicholas Lanier (1588–1666) and the Origins of Drawings Collecting in Stuart England." In Baker, Elam, and Warwick 2003, pp. 85–121.

Wortley 1934–35
Wortley, Clare Stuart. "Rubens's Drawings of Chinese Costumes." *Old Master Drawings* 9 (1934–35), pp. 40–47.

INDEX

Note: Page numbers in *italics* refer to illustrations; captions are indexed as text.

PHOTOGRAPH CREDITS

© ACL: fig. 148
Albertina, Vienna: cat. nos. 11, 18, 40, 41, 43, 44, 50, 58, 59, 60, 62, 63, 64, 65, 66, 69, 70, 71, 72, 77, 78, 81, 83, 84, 85, 86, 87, 96, 97, 99, 102, 111; figs. 30, 31
Alinari/Art Resource, New York: figs. 56, 81, 114
Amsterdams Historisch Museum: cat. nos. 26, 91, 92
The Art Institute of Chicago: cat. no. 19
Artic Photodesign, The Hague: cat. no. 38
The Ashmolean Museum, Oxford: cat. nos. 79, 105; figs. 15, 23
Jean Luc Baroni, London: cat. no. 57
Nicolo Orsi Battaglini/Art Resource, New York: fig. 45
Bayerische Staatsgemäldesammlungen, Alte Pinakothek, Munich: figs. 46, 62, 70, 106, 120, 134, 150
Bibliothèque Nationale de France, Paris: fig. 63
Bibliothèque Royale Albert Ier, Bruxelles (Cabinet des Estampes): cat. no. 15
BIU Montpellier Service Photo: cat. no. 29
W. M. Brady and Co., New York: fig. 53
© The British Museum, London: cat. nos. 12, 47, 48, 82, 101, 103, 104; figs. 11, 25, 28, 29
© Calouste Gulbenkian Museum, Lisbon: fig. 145
© Centre des Monuments Nationaux (CNMHS), Paris: fig. 105
Chromatics PhotoImaging, Nashville: cat. no. 52
Cincinnati Art Museum, Mr. and Mrs. Harry S. Lehman Endowment/photograph by Tony Walsh 9/1999: fig. 68
© The Cleveland Museum of Art, 2003; Delia E. Holden and L.E. Holden Funds: cat. no. 112
Collection Frits Lugt, Institut Néerlandais, Paris: cat. no. 113
The Samuel Courtauld Trust, Courtauld Institute of Art Gallery, London: figs. 4, 10, 16, 20, 27, 72, 94
Denkmalpflege, Munich: fig. 98
Department of Printing and Graphic Arts, Houghton Library, Harvard College Library: cat. no. 51
Devonshire Collection, Chatsworth. Reproduced by permission of the Duke of Devonshire and the Chatsworth Settlement Trustees: cat. nos. 100, 117; figs. 19, 43
Reproduction by Permission of the Syndics of the Fitzwilliam Museum, Cambridge: cat. no. 61; figs. 22, 32
Fundacja im. Raczyńskich, Muzeum Narodowe, Poznań: cat. no. 95
© Gemäldegalerie Alte Meister, Staatliche Kunstsammlungen Dresden: fig. 155
© Gemäldegalerie der Akademie der Bildenden Künste, Vienna: figs. 55, 58
Gemäldegalerie, Staatliche Museen zu Berlin–Preussischer Kulturbesitz/photograph by Jörg P. Anders: fig. 79
© The J. Paul Getty Museum, Los Angeles: cat. nos. 7, 8, 53, 75, 98
Groninger Museum, The Netherlands; Collection C. Hofstede de Groot/photograph by John Stoel: fig. 84
Herzog Anton Ulrich-Museum Braunschweig, Kunstmuseum des Landes Niedersachsen/photograph by Michael Lindner: cat. no. 5
© IRPA-KIK, Brussels: figs. 7, 8, 50, 77, 87, 92, 93, 111
Isabella Stewart Gardner Museum, Boston, Massachusetts, USA/Bridgeman Art Library: fig. 125
© 2003 by Kimbell Art Museum: fig. 122
Kunsthistorisches Museum, Vienna: figs. 89, 109, 115, 118, 154
Kupferstichkabinett, Staatliche Museen zu Berlin–Preussischer Kulturbesitz/photograph by Jörg P. Anders: cat. nos. 6, 24, 33, 90, 108; fig. 147
Library of Congress, Prints and Photographs Division, Washington, D.C.: fig. 97
Musée de la Chartreuse, Douai/photograph by Claude Theriez: fig. 117
Musée des Beaux-Arts, Marseille: fig. 107
© 2003 Museum of Fine Arts, Boston: fig. 101
Museum Plantin-Moretus, Antwerp/© photograph by Peter Maes: cat. nos. 54, 110
Museum Plantin-Moretus and Stedelijk Prentenkabinet, Antwerp: figs. 3, 96
Image © 2003 Board of Trustees, National Gallery of Art, Washington, D.C.: cat. no. 46
Image © 2004 Board of Trustees, National Gallery of Art, Washington, D.C./photograph by Dean Beasom: cat. no. 42
Image © National Gallery of Art, Washington, D.C.: figs. 40, 127, 129; photograph by Lyle Peterzell: fig. 95
© The National Gallery, London: figs. 69, 110, 133
© The National Gallery of Scotland, Edinburgh: figs. 41, 156; photograph by Antonia Reeve: cat. no. 10
The National Museum of Fine Arts, Stockholm: cat. nos. 67, 74; figs. 9, 17, 80
National Museums Liverpool (The Walker): cat. nos. 17, 115
Otto Naumann Ltd., New York: fig. 66
The Photograph Studio, The Metropolitan Museum of Art, New York (Barbara Bridgers, Mark Morosse, Kathy Dahab, Eugenia Tinsley-Burnett, Rachel Mustalish, Alison Gilchrest): cat. nos. 3, 16, 25, 30, 34, 73, 93, 94, 107, 114; figs. 2, 16, 33, 34, 35, 36, 38, 39, 53, 54, 64, 67, 72, 99, 102, 135, 136, 138, 139, 140, 141, 142, 144
Photographic Services © 2003 President and Fellows of Harvard College: cat. no. 37
Picture Library, National Portrait Gallery, London: fig. 124
© The Pierpont Morgan Library 2002/photograph by Schecter Lee: cat. no. 45; photograph by Joseph Zehavi: cat. nos. 1, 49
© The Pierpont Morgan Library 2003: fig. 24
Prado, Madrid: figs. 42, 48, 83, 108, 113, 137, 143
Private collections: cat. no. 55; figs. 76, 123
Research Library, The Getty Research Institute, Los Angeles/photograph by John Freeman, London: fig. 159
Rheinisches Bildarchiv Köln: cat. no. 20
Rijksmuseum, Amsterdam: cat. nos. 28, 32
RMN/Art Resource, New York/photograph by Michele Bellot: cat. no. 14; figs. 1, 13; photograph by J. G. Berizzi: cat. no. 109; figs. 18, 21, 47; photograph by Gerard Blot: cat. no. 106; fig. 5; photograph by Chuzeville: fig. 61; photograph by C. Jean: cat. no. 4; photograph by H. Lewandowski: figs. 59, 88, 146; photograph by R-G Ojéda: figs. 6, 16, 75, 86, 103, 153; photograph by Ojéda/Le Mage: fig. 119; photograph by Jean Schorman: fig. 151
Royal Cabinet of Paintings, Mauritshuis, The Hague: fig. 74
The Royal Collection © 2003, Her Majesty Queen Elizabeth II: cat. nos. 31, 36, 89
The Royal Collection © Her Majesty Queen Elizabeth II: figs. 91, 149
Royal Collections (Koninklijk Huisarchief), The Hague: cat. no. 39
Sammlungen des Fürsten von und zu Liechtenstein, Vaduz/photograph by Fotostudio Heinz Preute, Vaduz: figs. 73, 131, 132
© Scala/Art Resource, New York: figs. 37, 51, 57, 65, 121, 128
Soprintendenza Speciale per il Polo Museale Fiorentino/photograph by Paolo Tosi: cat. no. 68
Photograph Courtesy of Sotheby's, Inc. © 1981: fig. 26; © 2002: figs. 85, 152
Staatliche Graphische Sammlung Munich/photograph by Engelbert Seehuber: cat. no. 13
© Staatliche Museen Kassel, Gemäldegalerie Alte Meister: fig. 126
Städelsches Kunstinstitut, Frankfurt am Main/photograph by Gabriele Busch-Hauck: fig. 78; © photograph by Ursula Edelmann, Frankfurt am Main: cat. nos. 2, 27
The State Hermitage Museum, Saint Petersburg: cat. nos. 9, 22; figs. 71, 90, 116, 130, 158
© The State Pushkin Museum of Fine Arts, Moscow: cat. no. 21
Statens Museum for Kunst, Copenhagen/SMK Foto: figs. 52, 60, 82
© Sterling and Francine Clark Art Institute, Williamstown, Massachusetts: cat. no. 80
Stichting Museum Boijmans Van Beuningen, Rotterdam: cat. nos. 35, 56, 88; figs. 12, 14
Suermondt-Ludwig-Museum, Aachen/© Anne Gold: fig. 112
Teylers Stichting, Haarlem: fig.157
Toledo Centro Fotografico: fig. 49
Trustees of The Wallace Collection, London: fig. 104